Tempora cinxisset Foliorum densior umbra:
Debetur Genio laurea Sylva tuo.
Tempora et Illa Tibi mollis redimisset Oliva;
Scilicet excludis Versibus Arma tuis.
Admisces Antiqua Novis, Jucunda Severis:
Hinc Juvenis discat, Fœmina, Virgo, Senex.
Ut solo minor es Phœbo, sic major es Unus
Omnibus, Ingenio, Mente, Lepore, Stylo.
W. Marshall Fecit.
scripsit I.H.C.W.M.

ROBERT HERRICK

THE POETICAL WORKS OF

Robert Herrick

EDITED BY

L. C. MARTIN

OXFORD
AT THE CLARENDON PRESS
1956

Oxford University Press, Amen House, London E.C. 4
GLASGOW NEW YORK TORONTO MELBOURNE WELLINGTON
BOMBAY CALCUTTA MADRAS KARACHI CAPE TOWN IBADAN
Geoffrey Cumberlege, Publisher to the University

PRINTED IN GREAT BRITAIN

PREFACE

THE first object of this volume is to provide a reliable text of all Herrick's ascertained writings and of all such other writings as can reasonably be attributed to him. Most of the material comes from his own collection, *Hesperides* (with *His Noble Numbers*), first published in 1648 and not again until the nineteenth century. That volume contains over fourteen hundred poems and for a very large proportion of these it is the sole authority. It also seems to give revised versions of the relatively few poems which had already been printed or copied into manuscript commonplace-books; and no later revisions are known to have been made. It is therefore the indispensable basis of any modern text and is closely followed in the present edition. Variant readings, which often seem to preserve the unrevised text, are supplied from specified sources. A number of poems not previously ascribed to Herrick are included. An appendix contains the letters which Herrick addressed while at Cambridge to his uncle, Sir William Herrick.

An outline of his life is given in the Introduction, with a brief survey of his reputation in the seventeenth century and after; there too some considerations are offered on the Herrick canon, on his apparent revisions of his work, and on the chronology of the poems.

Herrick's poetry has never been very fully annotated and Moorman's edition of 1915 had no commentary. That which is now supplied owes a considerable debt to earlier editions and studies and to such works of reference as *The Oxford Dictionary of English Proverbs* and M. P. Tilley's *The Proverbs in England in the Sixteenth and Seventeenth Centuries*. But the greatest help has come from a scholar, no longer living, whose work has never been duly appreciated because it has never been generally accessible. This was the Rev. Charles Percival Phinn (d. 1906), who seems to have devoted the leisure of many years to the study of Herrick's poetry, and whose copious and learned notes are inscribed in a copy of Grosart's three-volume *Herrick* now in the British Museum. At Phinn's own suggestion a number of these notes were utilized by A. W. Pollard in his second edition (1898) of Herrick's *Poems* in the Muses' Library, though Pollard was not allowed to name his collaborator.

Some time after Phinn's death the volumes were bought by Pollard, and presented to the British Museum; and as this was done expressly[1] for the advantage of future editors, the opportunity has been taken to incorporate in the present Commentary all such items as are likely to be of most interest to students of English poetry, chiefly classical, Biblical, and patristic analogues, and a number of parallels from Elizabethan literature.[2] Phinn left a good deal for later scholars to discover, as in the matter of Herrick's acquaintance with Burton's *Anatomy*, which needed much fuller illustration; and it is fair to observe that even if Phinn's notes had been lost, much would still be known about the poet's certain or possible indebtedness to various Roman or Renaissance poets, thanks to the independent work of such investigators as Kathryn A. McEuen, who devotes many pages to Herrick in her book, *Classical Influence on the Tribe of Ben* (1939), and F. Delattre, whose chapter on 'L'Imitation' in his study of *Robert Herrick* (1912, pp. 391–443) is invaluable. It remains true that Phinn was considerably better informed than anyone else has yet appeared to be on the subject of Herrick's literary and intellectual affiliations.

The footnotes to *Hesperides* and *His Noble Numbers* show (*a*) where the present text differs from that of 1648, and (*b*) where copies of the 1648 text differ from one another. The variants found in other printed works or in manuscripts of the seventeenth century, together with modern readings of any importance, are recorded in notes at the end of the volume, as they were in the edition of 1915 now revised. In this way it has been possible to preserve the 1915 pagination in respect of pp. 1–419, and thus to facilitate the continued use of M. MacLeod's *Concordance to the Poems of Robert Herrick* (New York: O.U.P., 1936), wherein the

1 In a note prefixed to vol. i.

2 The notes are written very small and close, crowded into the marginal and other spaces round the printed text. They are not always easy to make out and the task of perusal, selection, and verification has been done with some care on the supposition that few will wish to repeat it. The microfilm used for this edition has been placed in the University Library, Liverpool.

page-references are to the 1915 edition.[1] MacLeod also numbers the poems, as some editors have done, and gives number-references as well; but as nearly all Herrick's poems are short they can usually be found easily enough by means of page-references alone, and this has the merit of avoiding a number in the text before or after each title—a procedure not much in keeping with the spirit (at best a 'wild civility') which seems to have governed the arrangement or disarrangement of the poems in the original edition. In order, however, to save the large amount of space which would be taken up by referring to each poem always by its title, and in order also to assist identification, references in the Introduction and Commentary are usually given by a page-number followed by a second number which is that of the poem on that page. A third number, where necessary, indicates the line. Thus '126. 3. 1' means page 126, poem 3, line 1, the poem being 'A New-yeares gift sent to Sir Simeon Steward'. '1' after the page-number always applies to the first poem to *begin* on that page, not to the continuation of a poem begun on a preceding page; such continuations are referred to by page and line-numbers only, e.g. '91, l. 25'.

I wish to thank all those who have helped me while this revised edition has been in hand, especially Colonel C. H. Wilkinson and Mr. L. W. Hanson for their generous and valuable advice. Other help from individual scholars is acknowledged at the relevant places. The work as a whole could not have been done without the co-operation of many librarians, particularly those in the American libraries mentioned on pp. xxii–xxiii who answered over two hundred queries about readings in the copies of *Hesperides*, 1648, under their care. I am greatly indebted also to the officials of the Bodleian Library, the British Museum, and the Victoria and Albert Museum (Dyce Collection); the University Libraries of Birmingham, Edinburgh, and Liverpool; the Libraries of St. John's College, Cambridge, the Fitzwilliam Museum, Christ Church, Oxford, and the Royal College of Music; the Manuscripts Repository in the House of Lords, the Public Record Office, the Search Room at Somerset House, the Society of Genealogists, and the Department of Archives in the County

[1] Keeping the pagination of 1915 has entailed the placing of some new footnotes at the end of the volume (p. 462).

Offices at Leicester, under the direction of Dr. L. A. Parker. The Rev. C. B. Underwood, Vicar of Dean Prior, kindly allowed me access to the parish registers.

Special thanks are due to the Shakespeare Institute at Stratford-upon-Avon for the award to me of the Foyle Research Fellowship in the years 1953–1955, and for obtaining microfilms of manuscript commonplace-books in the Folger Shakespeare Library, the Library of Harvard University, and the Huntington Library, San Marino, California; and I am obliged to these libraries for permission to cite the manuscripts in question, as also, for similar favours, to the New York Public Library, the Rosenbach Foundation Library, and the residuary legatees of Miss E. K. Church (permission to cite the Henry Lawes autograph manuscript, now on loan to the British Museum). Mr. Edwin Wolf 2nd, of Philadelphia, gave me information about the Folger and the Rosenbach manuscript collections. Mr. J. P. Cutts drew my attention to the occurrence of poems by Herrick in the John Gamble manuscript song-book (New York Public Library). Mr. Arthur A. Houghton, of New York, sent me a photostat of the letter by Herrick in his possession (XII A, p. 452 below).

I am grateful also to the Clarendon Press for suggesting that I should undertake this work, and for the care with which they have improved and produced it.

The largest personal debt is to my wife, for her unfailing interest, for her help in verification, and for the numerous benefits which have come from her own researches. The responsibility for all errors and omissions remains with me.

L. C. M.

The Shakespeare Institute
Stratford-upon-Avon

CONTENTS

INTRODUCTION

I. BIOGRAPHICAL

I. Outline of Life

ROBERT HERRICK had many forebears and relations in Leicestershire, where the family is known to have been established since about 1300.[1] The name had been variously spelt and was not aspirated in writing until towards the end of the sixteenth century. Tradition associated it with Scandinavia, and Swift referred to this tradition in the account he wrote of his own family, his father having married 'Mrs. Abigail Erick, of Leicestershire'.[2]

It is unnecessary here to go farther back than the middle of the sixteenth century, to the family of John and Mary Eyrick, the poet's grandparents, among whose twelve children were Robert the eldest son, Nicholas the second, and William the fifth. Nicholas was the poet's father and the first of John Eyrick's several children to migrate to London. He went there in 1556 as a goldsmith's apprentice. After establishing himself as goldsmith and banker he married in 1582 Juliana or Julian, daughter of William Stone, mercer, of London, and they seem to have had eight children, of whom the youngest was posthumous. The baptisms of the other seven are recorded in the Register of St. Vedast, Foster Lane (Harl. Soc. 1902–3): William, 1585; Martha, Jan. 1586; Mercie, Dec. 1586; Thomas, 1588; Nicholas, 1589; Anne, 1590; Robert, 1591, 'the xxiiiith day of Auguste'. Nicholas, their father, died in 1592, when Robert was fourteen months old.

1 Standard sources of information about the Herricks of Leicestershire are *The History and Antiquities of the County of Leicester*, II. ii and III. i (1798, 1800), by John Nichols; *The History of Market Harborough* (1875), by J. H. Hill; and *The Records of the Borough of Leicester* (1899–1905), ed. Mary Bateson. Other authorities are cited in the biographies of Robert Herrick by F. W. Moorman (1910), F. Delattre (1912), and Emily Easton (1934). Delattre's is the most scholarly and reliable account.

2 Swift says that the Ericks 'derive their lineage from Erick the forester, a great commander, who raised an army to oppose the invasion of William the Conqueror, by whom he was vanquished, but afterward employed to command that prince's forces; and in his old age retired to his house in Leicestershire, where his family hath continued ever since, but declining every age, and are now in the condition of very private gentlemen' (fragment of Autobiography, *Works*, ed. Temple Scott, 1907, xi, p. 375).

He had made his will on 7 November.[1] His death occurred about two days later, when he fell from a window of his house in Goldsmiths' Row. He was buried at St. Vedast's on the 10th. Suicide was suspected and an inquiry at once initiated by the Bishop of Bristol, who was at the time High Almoner and through whom, as such, the property of 'persons felons of themselves' was legally forfeit to the Crown. The report on this inquiry[2] is dated 29 November, and shows that, although the question of suicide had not yet been cleared up, the Bishop, 'being moved wth charity and for dyvers other good causes and consideracons', had decided to grant the estate to Julian Herrick and her children as provided in the will, viz. one-third to Julian and two-thirds to be divided equally between *six* children.

One of the seven children listed above must therefore have died; and the will of Nicholas Herrick supports the statement of Nichols that this was William, the eldest; for the next two boys, Thomas and Nicholas, are named as executors, not William. Years afterwards Robert Herrick wrote a poem 'To his dying Brother, Master William Herrick' (73. 1), doubtless the youngest brother, posthumously born in 1593. William was still alive in 1629, when Julian Herrick's will[3] was proved. Nichols (op. cit. II. ii, p. 631) records a tradition that Julian's youngest child was born at Hampton-on-Thames at the house of Harry Campion, her brother-in-law; and Robert's biographers have sometimes concluded from this that Julian lived for some time at Hampton and brought Robert up there. But there are no solid grounds for this and it is impossible to say where Robert spent his infancy or where he went to school.

References by Herrick to his near relations are so far as possible explained in the Commentary, but can be summarized as follows. He alludes to one sister, Mercy (269.5), who married John Wingfield (210. 3); and, apart from William, two brothers, Thomas (see note to 34. 3) and Nicholas (330. 4), who became prosperous in London. The Elizabeth Herrick referred to in 145. 2 was apparently the daughter of William; Susanna (193. 1), Bridget (203. 2), and Thomas (305. 3) were probably the children of

[1] The will is printed by Grosart in his edition of Herrick (1876), i, p. xl.

[2] *Miscellanea Genealogica et Heraldica*, ed. J. J. Howard, Second Series, 1886, i, pp. 41–42. Quoted in full by Delattre, pp. 511–13. Other documents concerning the estate of Nicholas Herrick which were formerly at Beaumanor, near Leicester, are now in the archives in the County Offices.

[3] Printed by Grosart, op. cit. i, pp. lxxxiv–lxxxvi.

Nicholas. Their mother is addressed in 304. 2. Herrick also writes a poem 'Upon [the death of] his Sister-in-Law, Mistresse Elizab: Herrick' (23. 4), widow of either Thomas or William. Herrick's sisters, Martha and Anne, find no place in his poems. His mother, Julian, is referred to once (316, l. 16); his father also once (27. 1).

The estate of the poet's father, Nicholas Herrick, estimated in his will at £3,000, turned out to be £5,068 (Nichols, II. ii, p. 631); and the third part of it left to Julian was renounced by her, so that the six children would inherit about £800 each.

When Nicholas made his will in November 1592 he named two of his brothers, Robert and William, as 'overseers', or advisers to the executors, and Letters of Administration were granted, in the minority of the two executors, to Robert on 13 February 1592/3 (P.C.C., Book Nevell, f. 95; Grosart, i, p. xl). Robert was a wealthy iron-merchant of Leicester, where he was thrice Mayor, and he was the poet's godfather.[1] William, his brother, afterwards Sir William, had gone to London about 1574 as apprentice to Nicholas, and had thereafter set up in business as a goldsmith for himself, so successfully that he was able to rent the estate of Beaumanor, in Leicestershire, in 1594–5. He was knighted in 1605. (Nichols, op. cit. III. i, pp. 150–1.)

It was to this uncle, Sir William Herrick, that Robert, aged 16, was apprenticed on 25 September 1607.[2] The apprenticeship was to last ten years, but by 1613 it had been decided that Robert should go to Cambridge, and he entered St. John's as a fellow commoner in that year (*Alumni Cantabrigienses*). Of the same college were John Weekes (132. 3, &c.), Fellow 1613, and Clipseby Crew (112. 3, &c.), student. From Cambridge Herrick wrote the letters to his uncle (pp. 445–53) asking for advances of the money which Sir William was holding on his account. Towards the end of his undergraduate career he moved to Trinity Hall (see p. 452) and graduated B.A. therefrom in 1617. He took the degree of M.A. in 1620 and, with John Weekes, was ordained in 1623 (Peterborough), deacon on 24 April, and priest the next day. His ordination was thus considerably earlier than had been supposed until these particulars were given in *Alumni Cantabrigienses* in 1922.

Very little else is known about his life during the twelve years between his first graduation and his appointment in 1629 to the living of Dean Prior in Devonshire. Wood's belief that he

[1] Howard, loc. cit., p. 65. [2] Moorman, *Life*, p. 26.

was 'elected fellow of Alls. coll.' in 1628 was mistaken. It has commonly been assumed that he was living in London and he may well have been there for at least part of the time, forming or developing his acquaintance with Endymion Porter (41. 2, &c.), Mildmay Fane (40. 1 and 172. 3), Jonson (150. 1, &c.), Selden (142. 5), William Lawes, 'the rare Musitian' (288. 3), Henry Lawes, 'the excellent Composer of his Lyricks' (276. 4), and other persons of the city or the court who are celebrated in *Hesperides.* He was well known as a poet by 1625.[1] Whether he had any specific office has yet to be discovered.

In 1627 he went on the expedition to the Isle of Rhé as a chaplain to its leader, the Duke of Buckingham. No details about this appointment have come to light and the fact is known only from Herrick's own statement in 1630 (see next paragraph). After the expedition had failed and been followed by Buckingham's assassination in 1628 Herrick was nominated to the vicarage of Dean Prior, made vacant by the promotion (15 March 1628–9) of his predecessor, Barnaby Potter (q.v. *D.N.B.*), to the bishopric of Carlisle.

Apparently he did not take over the duties at Dean Prior at once, as Potter was granted tenure 'in Commendam' until Michaelmas 1630. There was then written

To the Kinges most excellent Majesty

The humble peticion of Robert Hericke Chaplayne to
the late Duke of Buckingham in the Isle of Reis.

Whereas yt was your Majesty's especiall fauour to bestowe on the peticioner the vicaridge of Deane, by the remoouall of Doctor Potter to the Bishopprick of Carlisle. It may now please your most sacred Majesty (the Comendation granted to him by your Majesty being expired this present Michaelmas) that your soueraigne comand may goe forth to the signature, for the dispatch of the peticioner, who shall euer pray for your Majesty's longe and happie raigne.

—— caetera mando Deo.[2]

About his life in Devonshire Herrick himself is the best authority. His occasional pieces throw light on his relations with the wealthier of his parishioners, such as the Giles, Lowman, Northleigh, and Yard families, and are in keeping with Wood's observation that he 'became much beloved by the Gentry in those parts for his florid and witty Discourse'.[3] That he was often

[1] See below, p. xvii.

[2] *S.P.Dom.*, Sept. 1630, vol. clxxiii, No. 93. Manuscript contractions expanded here and on pp. xvi–xvii. [3] *Athenae Oxon.*, 1721, ii, col. 122.

happy is the easier to believe because he records not only 'His content in the Country' but his 'Discontents in Devon'. He was certainly in a position to illustrate the words of Burton on '*nimia solitudo*':

> this enforced solitarinesse . . . produceth his effect soonest in such as have spent their time jovially, peradventure in all honest recreations, in good company, in some great family or populous City, and are upon a sudden confined to a desart countrey Cottage farre off, restrained of their liberty, and barred from their ordinary associates; solitarinesse is very irkesome to such, most tedious . . . .

It might nevertheless give new zest to the pleasures of the imagination and the practice of poetry; and it appears to have done this with Herrick, who says (19. 3) that he had never before invented such 'Ennobled numbers for the Press', meaning probably not the specifically Christian poems alone but any that could seem to be of a higher strain than he had yet risen to. We may include among them, if we wish, those which are most highly valued today. None of these has been precisely dated; but, as suggested below (p. xxxix), there is reason to think that at least some of them were written in Devonshire during the 1630's.

The first of his acknowledged poems to be published was the elegy (145. 2) 'Upon his kinswoman Mistris Elizabeth Herrick', printed in 1633 in Stow's *Survey of London* from a memorial tablet in St. Margaret's, Westminster. Soon after this a version of 'Oberon's Feast' (see p. 454) appeared in a small miscellaneous collection containing in all five poems, four of them certainly or probably not by Herrick. Several years later his poetry was to be seen in more distinguished company. This was in 1640, when 'The Apparition of his Mistress calling him to Elysium' (205. 5), 'The Primrose' (208. 1), and 'Am I despis'd' (63. 1) were included with one contribution each by Jonson and Francis Beaumont as 'An Addition of some Excellent Poems, to those precedent, of Renowned *Shakespeare*, By other Gentlemen' (see below, p. xxiv). In this earlier form of 'The Apparition' Herrick mentions Shakespeare as well as Jonson and Beaumont. In *Hesperides* Shakespeare and Beaumont have become Beaumont and Fletcher.

An entry in the Stationers' Register, 29 April 1640 (application by Andrew Crooke), shows that a whole volume of Herrick's poetry was then intended:

> Entred for his Copie vnder the hands of Master Hansley and Master Bourne warden, *The seuerall Poems* written by Master Robert Herrick. vj^d

—but apparently no such volume is extant and it is most likely that *Hesperides*, &c., 1648, represents Herrick's single independent appearance in print during his lifetime.

That he was in London for some time in or near 1640 would appear from a private note by Archbishop Laud's secretary, William Dell, which is conjecturally attributed to that year though not dated when it was written.[1] This alleges that Herrick, without leave of absence from Devonshire, had been lodging in Westminster, and points to him as the father of an illegitimate child by Thomasine Parsons (see note to 304. 4). No corroboration of this report is recorded and no steps are known to have been taken in connexion with it; so that it is impossible to confirm or deny it. Herrick's assertions in verse to the effect that although his Muse was jocund his life was chaste (p. 355, &c.) need not be the less trustworthy because they echo Ovid and Martial. And whether his verses about 'The suspition upon his over-much familiarity with a Gentlewoman' (48. 3) have a bearing on Dell's report is another question that has to be left unanswered.

Herrick's sister-in-law Elizabeth Herrick, who for some time kept house for him (13. 4), died in 1643 (23. 4) and was buried at Dean Prior (Parish Register). If she was the widow of Thomas Herrick she had long before been commended in Robert's early poem, 'A Country life' (34. 3), but more probably she was the widow of William.[2]

Other poems besides 23. 4 certainly attributable to the 1640's are concerned with friends and relations, with incidents of the Civil War and with its depressing effects (see, for instance, 84. 3, 'On the untuneable Times'). Herrick, having remained loyal, was ejected from Dean Prior in 1647, and did not return to his post until 1660. In that year he presented the following petition:[3]

To the right honourable the Lords in Parlyament Assembled.

The humble peticion of Robert Herricke [Clerke *erased*] Vicar of

[1] *C.S.P. Dom.* [1640 ?], vol. ccccl xxiv, No. 77.

[2] Herrick's apparent self-revelations in his poems are often questionable. Many of them probably reveal no more than his liking for make-believe and the strength of his creative fancy. His numerous 'mistresses', for example, may well have had as little factual reality as the 'supposed Wife' to whom he addressed parting-verses when he travelled (174. 1). It is unlikely that Herrick would have put direct self-revelation very high among motives for writing poetry.

[3] *Hist. MSS. Com.*, *Seventh Report*, p. 106*b* (Calendar of House of Lords Manuscripts).

Deane prior in the County of Devon Sheweth That the Vicaridge aforesayd hath bin for Divers yeares sequestred from your Peticioner for the affection that he bore to his late Majesty of blessed Memory. Your Peticioner humbly prayes That the Tythes, Glebes, and all other profitts belonging to the [Rectory afores *erased*] Vicaridge aforesayd may be secured & sequestred in the hands of the Churchwardens or Overseers of the poore of the parish aforesayd untill your peticioner doe prove his Tytle by Lawe.

And your peticioner shall ever pray &c
Robert Herrick

John Walker, *Sufferings of the Clergy*, 1714, p. 263, notes that 'after his *Ejectment* he retired to *London* [see 242. 1], and having no Fifths paid him, was subsisted by Charity, until the Restoration'; but it need not be concluded that the charity was meagre, having regard to the social standing of his relations. Wood states that he lived for a time in the parish of St. Anne's, Westminster.

After the appearance of *Hesperides* in 1648 Herrick is not known to have written any verses except those on the death of the young Lord Hastings (416. 1, published 1649); he may also have written during this later period the epitaph on the Gileses (419. 1) for the monument, itself of uncertain date, in Dean Prior Church.

The parish register at Dean Prior records that 'Robert Herrick Vicker was buried ye 15th day of October—1674'. There is nothing to show where he lies and no monument was raised in the church until some two hundred years later.

II. Reputation

Of the references to Herrick printed in the seventeenth century the earliest is the most impressive, since it takes his abilities for proven and puts him, at the age of thirty-four, on a footing with two of the most distinguished of Elizabethan veterans. This was in 1625, when Richard James in *The Muses Dirge* (on the death of James I) tries to explain why the King had not been duly praised while he lived by some really well-known poet:

Some *Johnson*, *Drayton*, or some *Herick*.

This single line, the most flattering public compliment that Herrick is known to have received, is also part of the evidence that his contemporary reputation never stood higher than in the 1620's, before he went into Devonshire.

The publication of his collected poems in 1648 seems to have brought him little fresh renown; and when after that any of his pieces appeared in other volumes, such as *Witt's Recreations* or the song-books, it was generally without their author's name. The poet himself is very seldom mentioned. His friend John Harmar (301. 5), who ushered in *Hesperides* with the kind of praise that convinces no one, making Herrick second only to Apollo, tempered that praise a year later in favour of Lovelace:

Herrico *succede meo: dedit ille priora*
Carmina, carminibus non meliora Tuis.

'Yong Herric' (now 64) is mentioned in *Musarum Deliciae*,[1] 1655, p. 2 ('To Parson WEEKS'), as having written verses about Sack (45. 1 or 77. 2), and there is a broken-backed compliment in *Naps upon Parnassus*, 1658, f. A3^{v}, in verses on the Roman poets:

And then *Flaccus Horace*,
He was but a sowr-ass,
And good for nothing but *Lyricks*:
There 's but One to be found
In all English ground
Writes as well; who is hight *Robert Herick.*

Poole, in *The English Parnassus*, 1657, cites Herrick but does not mention him. And apparently the edition of 1648 had not been sold out some twenty years after, when Peter Parker advertised *Hesperides* in a list[2] of 'Books Printed and Sould' by him (under 'Books of Divinity').

The neglect is not surprising. Herrick was 57 when his poems were published and many of them belonged to an earlier taste as well as to an earlier time. Their directness and apparent ease would be generally much less attractive in 1648 than the ingenuities and 'strong lines' of the metaphysical poets, whom Herrick had not greatly cared to imitate.[3] And when the mid-century modes faded out or were absorbed in the Augustan order, the change brought him no advantage. It was too late to accept his poetry without question and too soon to realize that some of it is timeless. A few of his lyrics continued to be sung, but it does not appear that he was often remembered as the

[1] Compiled by Herrick's friends, Sir John Mennes (194. 2) and James Smith (see note to 136, ll. 131–2, p. 529).

[2] A copy of this list (10 leaves) is bound up with the copy of *Hesperides* in the Ashley Collection in the British Museum. It includes items referring to incidents of 1665 and 1668.

[3] A few of the *Noble Numbers* (notably 346. 4, 357. 4, and 369. 3) seem indebted to the example of George Herbert.

author of the words. Perhaps in his old age he still found his own lines consoling:

> I make no haste to have my Numbers read.
> *Seldome comes Glorie till a man be dead.*

A year after he died he was mentioned, ingloriously, by Edward Phillips in *Theatrum Poetarum*, 1675: 'That which is chiefly pleasant in these Poems is now and then a pretty Floury and Pastoral gale of Fancy, a vernal prospect of some Hill, Cave, Rock, or Fountain; which but for the interruption of other trivial passages might have made up none of the worst Poetic Landskips', an account echoed by Winstanley in the *Lives*, 1687. Wood, who was apparently at fault in putting Herrick into *Athenae Oxonienses* (1721, ii, cols. 122–3), may not have been better informed in saying that his poems 'made him much admired in the time when they were published, especially by the generous and boon loyalists'. About fifty years later there was a brief account of him, derived from Phillips and Wood, in Granger's *Biographical History of England* (1769–74), ii, p. 309; and after about twenty years more (in 1790) three of Herrick's pieces found a place in Ellis's *Specimens of the Early English Poets*. He had no attention from Headley, or Anderson, or even from Chalmers, as late as 1810, and very little from anyone during the greater part of the eighteenth century.[1] Barron Field, visiting Devonshire in 1809, found that some of Herrick's verses had been preserved there by oral tradition.[2] By that time, however, the foundations of his future fame were being securely laid. Inquiry in the *Gentleman's Magazine* (May 1796) had elicited some fresh information about him and in 1804 three appreciative articles were printed in the third edition of Nathan Drake's *Literary Hours*.[3]

The first volume to be devoted to Herrick's poetry since 1648 appeared at Bristol in [1810]: *Select Poems from the Hesperides*, ed. J. N[ott]. This gave 284 of the poems; 'to republish all were unnecessary; many are better withdrawn from the publick eye'. A similar reflection on Herrick's vein of coarseness was made by Campbell, who included him in *Specimens of the British Poets*, 1819; and the combination of grossness and delicacy in Herrick's work was to exercise the minds of many later critics, of whom

1 See N. Ault, 'Herrick and the Song Books', *T.L.S.*, 20 April 1933.

2 *Quarterly Review*, August 1810.

3 'I hesitate not to consider him in the same degree superior to Carew, as Carew assuredly is to Waller, whose versification has embalmed his memory' (p. 49).

some, like Southey, were merely scandalized, while others (notably Morley and Delattre) tried to explain how such delightful roses and such offensive thorns could grow from the same plant.[1]

Southey's attack is in *Attempts in Verse by J. Jones, with an Introductory Essay on our Uneducated Poets*, 1831 (pp. 85–86), and it deplores the recent republication of Herrick's work in its entirety. This had occurred in 1823, when Thomas Maitland (Lord Dundrennan) produced in Edinburgh *The Works of Robert Herrick, Edited with a Biographical Notice*, which with Nott's selection of 1810 inaugurated the spate of modern reprints. Herrick's popularity in the nineteenth century was assisted by the growing respect for lyrical poetry and 'nature poetry', and already in 1822 he was acclaimed in the *Retrospective Review* 'the very best of English Lyric Poets'. Elizabeth Barrett Browning, in *The Greek Christian Poets and the English Poets*, 1863, transforms him into 'the Ariel of poets, sucking "where the bee sucks" from the rose-heart of nature, and reproducing the fragrance idealized'; and enthusiasm for Herrick's genius culminates, since it could go no farther, in Swinburne's eulogy of him as 'the greatest song-writer—as surely as Shakespeare is the greatest dramatist—ever born of English race' (*Studies in Prose and Poetry*, 1894, p. 45).

In the twentieth century Herrick has been appreciated with less rapture and more discrimination, but his standing remains high. Better knowledge of Jacobean and Caroline poetry has revealed more clearly what he had in common with other writers and what he contributed of his own. The seriousness expressed or implied in much that he wrote has been brought more fully into light, and it is an advantage also that his work as a whole can now be seen to share in the complexity which belongs generally to Renaissance humanism, with its roots in classical literature, Christian doctrine, and medieval philosophy, symbolism, and superstition; for this composite inheritance, with its stimulating variety and contrasts, probably did more than the example of any single poet, Horace, Martial, or even Jonson, to make Herrick's poetry what it was.[2]

[1] Herrick's own explanation would probably have been on the lines of his epigram on love:

> Love 's of it self, too sweet; the best of all
> Is, when loves hony has a dash of gall—

and the apparent disorder of the poems in *Hesperides* may well have been calculated, so that each poem might be a foil to its immediate neighbours.

[2] See S. Musgrove, *The Universe of Robert Herrick*, Auckland Univ. Coll., 1950.

But whatever his work may owe to traditions and influences it is above all his artistry, not his thought, that has hitherto made him seem eminent among the poets of his time. None of them excelled him in care at once for design and detail, in the spirited management of words and rhythms, in command of the transfiguring phrase, in regard for 'the rule of not too much'. He attempted many kinds of poetry with varying success; but his best work continues to justify his own opinion that it would bring him lasting renown:

> Live by thy Muse thou shalt; when others die
> Leaving no Fame to long Posterity:
> When Monarchies trans-shifted are, and gone;
> Here shall endure thy vast Dominion.

II. TEXT AND CANON

I. *HESPERIDES* AND *HIS NOBLE NUMBERS*

This is the only source for the great majority of the poems.

Titles: reproduced pp. 1 and 337. Variant imprint in some copies (e.g. British Museum G. 11495 and Yale University) as follows (after 'Eglesfield'): and are to be sold by Tho. Hunt, Bookseller in Exon. 1648.

Collation: [A]^4 B^8 C^8 (±C7) D–L^8 M^8(± M8) N^8 O^8 (±O8) P–2C^8; ^{2}2A–2E^8. \$1–4 signed. B4 not signed. P4 mis-signed Y4.

Pages: [8], 1–27, 29, 28, 30–153, 54, 155–161, 166, 167, 164, 165, 162, 163, 168, 169, 174, 175, 172, 173, 170, 171, 276, 177–303, 302, 305–387, 288, 389–395, 693, 397, 398; [2]^2 1–79 [80]. In some copies (e.g. the two in the Dyce Collection, South Kensington, Harvard University, and Worcester College, Oxford) the inner forme of X is misnumbered 274, 275, 278, 279, 282, 283, 286, 287 for 306, 307, 310, 311, 314, 315, 318, 319.

Contents: [A]1^r blank, [A]1^v portrait, [A]2^r title-page, [A]2^v blank, [A]3 dedication, [A]4^r errata, [A]4^v blank. B1^r–2C7^v text of *Hesperides*, 2C8^r title-page of *His Noble Numbers*, 2C8^v blank, ^{2}2A1^r–2E8^r, text of *His Noble Numbers*, 2E8^v blank, sometimes followed by errata leaf.

No running titles.

Catchwords and original page-numbers are not given in the

present edition. Of the differences between catchwords and their sequents most are caused by ordinary misprints, variant spellings, or omission of stanza-numbers. The following, however, may deserve more attention.

	Original page-number	Place in present edn.	Catchword	Sequent
(*a*)	45	after 43. 1. 24	You	5. Yet
(*b*)	111	„ 99. 3	*His*	*To*
(*c*)	155	„ 135, l. 112	Then	15. Thus
(*d*)	159	„ 138. 4	*Ver-*	*A Hymne*
(*e*)	176 ('276')	„ 153. 1	*Selfe*	*Liberty.*
(*f*)	177	„ 153. 6	She	*Upon*
(*g*)	307	„ 261. 2. 3	When	Next
(*h*)	second 23	„ 358, l. 10	*His*	*Gods*

Of these (*e*) and (*f*) seem the most interesting. They could have arisen if a poem of two or three lines with such a title as '*Selfe Love*' had been excised after a first set-up. Had such a poem been there it could have caused the page to end after 153. 6. 4, when 'She' would be the first word on the next page and so the correct catchword for the original page 177.

As usual in this period some of the formes were corrected and some were not. The corrections include the three cancels mentioned in the collation above (C7, M8, O8).[1] The cancellanda occur fairly often. Out of twenty-one copies taken as a specimen set, four contain the original C7 and the same four the original O8; and eight (including three of the same four again) contain the original M8. Thus nine copies have one or more of the cancellanda and twelve have none. Three of the nine have all the cancellanda. The following is a list of the copies examined or reported on for this purpose. The uncancelled leaves present in these copies are indicated by their signatures.

- A   Ashley Library, British Museum. (M8.)
- B   Boston Public Library.
- C   Clark Memorial Library, University of California, Los Angeles. (M8.)
- D   Douce H. 311, Bodleian Library. (M8.)
- E   E. 1090, British Museum.
- F   Fitzwilliam Museum, Cambridge (formerly owned by G. C. Macaulay).

[1] In the present edition 28.3.7–29.2.12 corresponds to $C7^r$; 30, l. 13–30. 2. 10 to $C7^v$; 151. 3–152. 2. 2 to $M8^r$; 152. 2. 3–153. 1. 4 to $M8^v$; 178. 3. 4–179, l. 30 to $O8^r$; 179, l. 31–180. 3. 2 to $O8^v$.

G G. 11495, British Museum.
H Harvard University. (C7, M8, O8.)
Hn Henry E. Huntington Library, San Marino.
K1 South Kensington, Dyce A (with modern title-page).
K2 South Kensington, Dyce B (with original title-page).
M Malone 343, Bodleian Library. (M8.)
P Formerly owned by the Rev. C. P. Phinn. (C7, M8, O8.)[1]
S Stark copy, University of Texas.
U University of Illinois, Urbana. (C7, M8, O8.)
V University of Virginia.
We Wellesley College, Mass.
Wi Owned by Colonel C. H. Wilkinson. (C7, O8.)
Wo Worcester College, Oxford.
Wr Wrenn copy, University of Texas.
Y Yale University. (M8.)

The list of errata was a useful supplement to the corrections made in the text, but it was not complete. Of the errors which it passed over some are ordinary misprints, easily perceived and rectified; a few others, less obvious, have stayed in the text until now. In one instance an improvement is supplied by two manuscripts (not used by previous editors): 'madd' in 87. 2. 2 for 'made', a recorded form of 'mad', but probably a misprint here. Once *Hesperides* corrects itself, where the same line occurs in two different poems (126. 3. 14 and 231, l. 57), making sense the second time. There are a few other emendations peculiar to the present edition, none of which has been introduced without regard for its compatibility with Herrick's ways of thought and habits of expression, and with contemporary conventions in language, printing, and handwriting. Instances occur in 64. 3. 9 and 207, l. 61.

The copies of the 1648 volume used in preparing this edition were chiefly those listed above, especially F, H, and Wo; the last-mentioned[2] was used in reading the proofs. All the known variations in the text of 1648 are recorded in footnotes, as are all the present editor's departures from the copies chosen to represent that text, except that 's' replaces 'ſ' and that errors of spacing, wrong founts, and other merely typographical variations are as a rule normalized silently. In the Oxford text of 1915 there are about 100 deviations, more or less trifling, from the text of 1648 as represented by the copies listed above (excluding 'P', which was

1 Described by A. W. Pollard in *The Library*, New Series, iv, pp. 206–12 and 328–30.
2 Together with a working copy kindly lent by Mr. I. A. Shapiro.

not available). It was assumed that these deviations were inadvertent and they are not indicated here.

The original text (with the cancels) is designated *48* in the footnotes and elsewhere, '*X*' signifying the readings of the cancellanda. The typographical variants occasioned by cancelling are not recorded.

II. Other Printed Sources

A. *Before 1648*

Eight of the poems in *Hesperides* and two others accepted as Herrick's were published before 1648. They occur in the following seven volumes:

1. Stow's *Survey of London*, 1633. Contains 'Upon Elizabeth Herrick' (145. 1).
2. *A Description Of the King and Queene of Fayries, their habit, fare, their abode, pompe, and state. Beeing very delightfull to the sense, and full of mirth . . . London . . .* 1634 [and] 1635. Contains a shorter version of 'Oberons Feast' (119. 1). See Appendix B, p. 454.
3. *Poems. By Thomas Carew Esquire . . . London . . .* 1640. Contains 'Among the Mirtles, as I walkt' (106. 3) and 'The Primrose' (208. 1). Designated *C*.
4. *Poems: Written By Wil. Shake-speare. Gent. . . . London . . .* 1640. Contains 'Am I despis'd' (63. 1), 'The Apparition' (205. 5), and 'The Primrose' (208. 1). Designated *WS*.
5. *Recreation For Ingenious Head-peeces . . . London . . .* 1645. (*Witt's Recreations.*) Contains 'His fare-well to Sack' (45. 1) and 'The Description of a Woman' (404. 1). Designated *WR* (1645).
6. *The Academy Of Complements . . . London . . .* 1646. Contains 'To the Virgins' (84. 1) and 'Among the Mirtles' (106. 3). Designated *Ac46*.
7. *Comedies and Tragedies written by Francis Beaumont & Iohn Fletcher . . . London . . .* 1647. Contains 'Upon Master Fletchers Incomparable Playes' (415. 1).

B. *1649–1674*

After the publication of *Hesperides*, poems by Herrick appeared during his lifetime in the following:[1]

1. *Lachrymae Musarum. The Tears of the Muses . . . upon the death of the most hopefull Henry Lord Hastings . . . London . . .* 1649. Contains 'The New Charon' (416. 1).

[1] When there are two or more editions of the same work, only the first to contain poetry by Herrick is given, unless new Herrick material is added in a subsequent edition.

2. *Recreation For Ingenious Head-peeces . . . London* . . . 1650. (*Witt's Recreations.*) Contains 43. 1, 60. 4, 62. 1, 65. 3, 80. 1, 83. 2, 98. 3, 98. 5, 123. 5, 124. 1, 130. 1, 137. 2, 139. 6, 141. 1, 143. 2, 144. 4, 149. 2, 149. 3, 149. 4, 154. 1, 155. 3, 155. 4, 156. 1, 162. 2, 163. 3, 191. 2, 195. 5, 205. 2, 212. 3, 215. 2, 223. 2, 224. 2, 226. 1, 226. 5, 226. 6, 226. 7, 229. 3, 232. 2, 232. 5, 235. 1, 235. 2, 238. 5, 239. 3, 240. 4, 241. 6, 249. 4, 251. 3, 253. 3, 255. 4, 259. 2, 260. 4, 264. 5, 265. 2, 265. 3, 265. 4, 273. 2, 274. 2, 274. 4, 275. 5, 276. 2, 281. 1, 283. 2 (ll. 13–14 only), 284. 1, 287. 4, 289. 1, 296. 3, 298. 1, 315. 1, 327. 4, 327. 5, 331. 6, 333. 3, 334. 4; also 45. 1 and 404. 1 as in A. 5 above. (75 in all.)

Witt's Recreations has three sections: (1) Epigrams (the largest), (2) Epitaphs, and (3) Fancies and Fantasticks. The book is without pagination. The numbers given in the textual notes are those of the Epigrams except where the Epitaphs are mentioned. References to Fancies and Fantasticks are by signatures. The pieces by Herrick are scattered through the volume but there are runs of them having the same order as in *48*. Except 404. 1, there is apparently nothing that had not been published in *48*, and the few variants which occur do not necessarily imply the use of an independent manuscript. The textual notes do not record the numerous instances in which *Upon* in a *48* title appears as *On* in *Witt's Recreations*. Designated *WR*.

3. *The Academy Of Complements . . . London*. 1650. Contains 'To the Virgins' (84. 1); 'Among the Mirtles (106. 3); 'The Kisse' (130. 2); and 'The mad Maids song' (156. 4). Designated *Ac50*.

4. *Select Musicall Ayres, and Dialogues, For one and two Voyces . . . Composed by John Wilson, Charles Colman . . . Henry Lawes, William Webb . . . London, Printed for John Playford* . . . 1652. Contains 'The Bag of the Bee' (31. 2), 'To the Virgins' (84. 1), 'Among the Mirtles, as I walkt' (106. 3), 'To Anthea' (108. 2), 'The Willow Garland' (161. 2), 'Charon and Philomel' (248. 1), and 'The New Charon' (416. 1). Designated *P52*.

5. *Catch that Catch can, or A Choice Collection of Catches, Rounds, & Canōns . . . London printed for John Benson & John Playford* . . . 1652. [Hilton.] Contains 'On himselfe' (131. 2), 'How he would drinke his Wine' (187. 1), and 'Upon himselfe being buried' (199. 5). Designated *C52*.

6. *Select Musicall Ayres and Dialogues . . . London, Printed by T. H. for John Playford* . . . 1653. Contains the same pieces as *P52* except that 'The New Charon' (416. 1) is omitted. Designated *P53*.

7. *Ayres and Dialogues . . . By Henry Lawes . . . The First Book London, Printed by T. H. for John Playford* . . . 1653. Contains 'Am I despis'd' (63. 1), and 'The Primrose' (208. 1). Designated *L53*.

8. *Poems by Francis Beaumont Gent* 1653. Contains 'Upon Master Fletchers Incomparable Playes' (415. 1).

9. *The Marrow Of Complements* . . . *London* . . . 1655. Contains (pp. 157–61) 11. 1, 24. 1, 63. 3, 98. 2, 106. 2, 136. 1, 168. 3, 209. 2, 219. 2. Designated *MC.*

10. *Wits Interpreter, The English Parnassus* . . . By I. C[otgrave]. *London* . . . 1655. Contains 'Am I despis'd' (63. 1) and 'Among the Mirtles' (106. 3). Designated *WI.*

11. *The Second Book of Ayres, and Dialogues . . . By Henry Lawes . . . London, Printed by T. H. for John Playford* . . . 1655. Contains 'The Bag of the Bee' (31. 2) and 'Leander's Obsequies' (42. 1). Designated *L55.*

12. *An Introduction to the Skill of Musick . . . London, Printed for John Playford* . . . 1655. Contains 'To the Virgins' (84. 1) and 'The Willow Garland' (161. 2). Designated *P55.*

13. *Parnassus Biceps. Or Severall Choice Pieces Of Poetry* . . . *London* . . . 1656. Contains 'The Welcome to Sack' (77. 2), abbreviated. Designated *PB.*

14. *Wit a Sporting In A pleasant Grove Of New Fancies. By H. B.* [Henry Bold.] London . . . 1657. Contains 31. 2, 31. 4, 59. 2, 28. 3, 154. 4, 60. 2, 84. 1, 96. 1, 96. 2, 97. 3, 99. 2, 98. 2, 105. 3, 102. 3, 106. 2, 108. 2, 136. 1, 124. 4, 161. 2, 168. 3, 188. 3, 195. 5, 201. 2, 19. 1, 19. 2, 20. 3, 216. 1, 232. 3, 248. 1, 272. 3, 271. 2, 238. 2, 239. 1, 279. 3, 284. 3, 284. 4, 284. 5, 284. 6, 295. 3, 313. 2, 322. 4, 322. 5, 323. 1, 315. 2. The text is often corrupt and has not been collated with *48.*

15. *The English Parnassus: Or, A Helpe to English Poesie . . . By Josua Poole* . . . *London* . . . 1657. Contains 'A Nuptiall Song' (112. 2), 10 stanzas+5 lines; 'Oberons Feast (119. 1); and ll. 77–79 of 'His age' (132. 3). Text from MS. versions, not from *48.* Readings not found in MS. versions are recorded, but not those apparently due to corruption. Designated *EP.*

16. *Ayres, And Dialogues* . . . *By Henry Lawes* . . . *The Third Book. London* . . . 1658. Contains 'The Kisse' (130. 2). Reissued in 1669 as Book III of *The Treasury of Musick.* See 19 below. Designated *L58.*

17. *A Garden of Delight* [J. Tompson] . . . *London* . . . 1658. Contains 'The Vine' (16. 2); 'Cherry-pit' (19. 1); 'A Lyrick to Mirth' (39. 3); 'Upon Bunce' (83. 2); 'Upon Skrew' (149. 3); 'Upon Raspe' (154. 1); and 'Upon Lucia' (212. 2). Designated *GD.*

18. *The Mysteries Of Love and Eloquence, Or, the Arts of Wooing and Complementing* . . . *London* . . . 1658. Contains 'Loose no time' (442. 2). Designated *ML.*

19. *Select Ayres And Dialogues . . . Composed by John Wilson . . . Henry Lawes William Lawes . . . And other Excellent Masters of Musick . . . London* . . . 1659. Contains the pieces in *P52* (B. 4 above) minus 'The New Charon', and adds 'Not to love' (102. 3) and 'The Primrose' (208. 1). Reissued in 1669 as Book I of *The Treasury of Musick.* Designated *P59.*

20. *The Second Part Of Merry Drollery . . . London . . .* ? 1661. Contains 'To the Virgins' (84. 1). Designated *MD*.
21. *Recreation for Ingenious Head-Peeces . . . London . . .* 1663. (*Witt's Recreations.*) In addition to the seventy-five pieces in *WR* 1650 (B. 2 above) this volume contains the following: 19. 1, 28. 3, 31. 2, 84. 1, 97. 3, 98. 2, 102. 3, 105. 3, 136. 1, 168. 3. Designated *WR* (1663).
22. *Musick's Delight On The Cithren . . . London, Printed by W. G. and are sold by J. Playford . . .* 1666. Contains 'To the Virgins' (84. 1). Designated *P66*.
23. *Catch that Catch can: Or The Musical Companion . . . London, Printed by W. Godbid for J. Playford . . .* 1667. Contains 'To the Virgins' (84. 1), 'Among the Mirtles' (106. 3), and 'Charon and Philomel' (248. 1). Designated *P67*.
24. *Select Ayres And Dialogues . . . By Mr. Henry Lawes . . . And other Excellent Masters. The Second Book. London, Printed by William Godbid for John Playford . . .* 1669. Contains 'Am I despis'd' (63. 1), 'How Lillies came white' (74. 3), and 'The New Charon' (416. 1). This is Book II of *The Treasury of Musick*. It may consist of the sheets of an earlier issue (? 1663) with a new title-page. Designated *P69*.
25. *The New Help To Discourse . . . By W. W. . . . London . . .* 1669. Contains 'To the Virgins' (84. 1). Not seen by present editor.
26. *The New Academy Of Complements . . . London . . .* 1671. Contains 'The Bag of the Bee' (31. 2), 'Leanders Obsequies' (42. 1), and 'To Sycamores' (158. 5). Designated *Ac71*.
27. *Windsor Drollery . . . London . . .* 1672. Contains 'Leanders Obsequies' (42. 1), 'To the Virgins' (84. 1), and 'Among the Mirtles' (106. 3). Designated *WD*.
28. *The Loyal Garland . . . The fourth Edition . . . London . . .* 167? Contains 'To the Virgins' (84. 1). Designated *LG*.

III. Manuscripts

A. *Poems published in 'Hesperides'*

Only thirty-nine of the poems in *Hesperides* and one of *His Noble Numbers* are at present known to occur in manuscripts of the seventeenth century. The forty poems are the following (the number in square brackets shows how often the poem occurs[1]):

[1] With one exception the numbers do not include copies of these poems contained in commonplace-books listed by Messrs. Rosenbach, of New York, in their catalogue, *English Poetry to 1700* (1941). The exception is 85. 3, which occurs in one of these collections (No. 189 in the catalogue) and has not been found in any other manuscript. These commonplace-books have not been seen by the present editor.

'The Wounded Heart'	10. 5	[1]
'The Cheat of Cupid'	26. 3	[1]
'The Bag of the Bee'	31. 2	[2]
'A Country life'	34. 3	[2]
'Leanders Obsequies'	42. 1	[1]
'His fare-well to Sack'	45. 1	[7]
'Upon Mrs. Eliz: Wheeler	46. 2	[3]
'The Curse'	49. 2	[24][1]
'The wounded Cupid'	50. 1	[1]
'To Dewes'	50. 2	[1]
'An Epithalamie'	53. 2	[2]
'Am I despis'd'	63. 1	[4]
'How Lillies came white'	74. 2	[1]
'To Pansies'	74. 3	[1]
'The Lilly in a Christal'	75. 1	[1]
'The Welcome to Sack'	77. 2	[16][1]
'To the Virgins'	84. 1	[6]
'A Pastorall'	85. 3	[1]
'The Bubble'	87. 2	[2]
'The Present'	100. 3	[2]
'Not to love'	102. 3	[1]
'To Musick'	103. 1	[2]
'Upon the death of his Sparrow'	103. 3	[2]
'Among the Mirtles'	106. 3	[3]
'To Anthea'	108. 2	[2]
'A Nuptiall Song'	112. 3	[5]
'Oberons Feast'	119. 1	[8]
'The Kisse'	130. 2	[1]
'The admonition'	130. 3	[2]
'His age'	132. 3	[7]
'The mad Maids song'	156. 4	[1]
'To Sycamores'	158. 5	[2]
'The Willow Garland'	161. 2	[2]
'Oberons Palace'	165. 1	[5]
'The parting Verse'	174. 1	[6]
'The Apparition'	205. 5	[2]
'The Primrose'	208. 1	[1]
'The Night-piece, to Julia'	217. 1	[1]
'Charon and Phylomel'	248. 1	[5]
'To God: an Anthem'	342. 2	[1]

Most of the manuscripts containing these poems are common-

[1] In these instances it was found necessary to limit the number of manuscripts whose variants could be fully recorded.

place-books. The exceptions are song-collections and are marked with an asterisk in the following list:

Bodleian Library

Ashmole 38 (containing 34. 3, 49. 2 twice, 119. 1, 165. 1, 174. 1).
Firth e. 4 (45. 1, 77. 2, 112. 3, 119. 1, 132. 3, 165. 1).
Malone 16 (119. 1).
Rawlinson poet. 26 (77. 2).
65 (248. 1).
142 (77. 2).
160 (45. 1, 77. 2, 119. 1, 165. 1, 174. 1).
*Don. c. 57 (31. 2, 46. 2, 49. 2, 63. 1, 84. 1, 103. 1, 106. 3, 161. 2, 248. 1).
*Mus. b. 1 (49. 2).

Christ Church, Oxford

*Mus. 87 (103. 1).

Worcester College, Oxford

lviii (132. 3).

St. John's College, Cambridge

S. 23 (132. 3).

British Museum

Add. 15227 (49. 2, 100. 3).
19268 (49. 2, 77. 2).
*19759 (49. 2).
21433 (112. 3).
*22100 (49. 2).
22118 (119. 1).
22603 (77. 2, 119. 1, 165. 1, 174. 1).
25303 (112. 3, 165. 1).
25707 (49. 2).
*29396 (46. 2, 84. 1).
*29397 (49. 2, 248. 1).
*30382 (49. 2).
30982 (49. 2, 77. 2).
*31432 (William Lawes autograph) (50. 2, 74. 2, 74. 3, 84. 1, 102. 3, 158. 5, 248. 1).
*33234 (49. 2).
*33235 (49. 2).
33287 (49. 2).
33998 (10. 5, 45. 1, 77. 2, 130. 2).
35043 (248. 1).

Egerton 923 (119. 1).
*2013 (63. 1, 158. 5).
2421 (49. 2).
2725 (49. 2, 132. 3).

British Museum (*cont.*)

Harleian *3991 (84. 1).

6917 (112. 3, 156. 4).

6918 (53. 2, 84. 1, 87. 2, 103. 3, 132. 3).

6931 (77. 2).

Sloane 1446 (45. 1, 49. 2, 77. 2).

1792 (77. 2).

*Henry Lawes autograph (on loan) (26. 3, 31. 2, 42. 1, 46. 2, 50. 1, 63. 1, 106. 3, 108. 2, 130. 3, 161. 2, 208. 1, 217. 1).

Folger Shakespeare Library, Washington

1. 21 (45. 1, 49. 2 twice, 77. 2, 205. 5).

1. 27 (49. 2, 77. 2).

1. 8 (49. 2).

452. 1 (45. 1, 342. 2).

646. 4 (77. 2).

750. 1 (84. 1).

1669. 2 (77. 2).

Harvard Univ. Library

Eng. 626 F (49. 2, 53. 2, 75. 1, 87. 2, 103. 3, 112. 3, 130. 3, 132. 3, 174. 1).

Huntington Library, San Marino

HM 172 (205. 5).

HM 198 (34. 3, 45. 1, 49. 2, 77. 2, 119. 1, 132. 3, 174. 1).

New York Public Library. *Drexel 4257 (John Gamble's collection) (84. 1, 106. 3, 108. 2).

Other manuscripts:

Kingsborough-Hazelwood, referred to by Grosart (Memorial-Introduction to his edition of Herrick, p. cliv) as possessed by W. F. Cozens (174. 1). Not seen by present editor.

A manuscript cited by W. C. Hazlitt in his edition of Herrick, i, pp. 65–66 (63. 1). Not seen by present editor.

B. *Poems not published in 'Hesperides'*

All the 'additional poems' are found in manuscripts except 415. 1, 416. 1, and 419. 1. 404. 1, 442. 2, and 443. 1 occur both in manuscript and in print. The manuscripts in question are the following:

Bodleian Library

Ashmole 36–37 (413. 1).

38 (404. 1, 407. 1, 410. 1, 443. 1).

Don. c. 57 (421. 1, 421. 2, 442. 2).

Mus. b. 1 (440. 2, 442. 2, 443. 1).

Rawl. poet. 160 (404. 1, 410. 1, 417. 1).

British Museum
Add. 11811 (414. 1).
19268 (420. 2).
22603 (410. 1).
25707 (420. 2, 443. 1).
29396 (440. 2, 443. 1).
30982 (417. 1, 420. 2).
33998 (419. 2, 420. 1, 420. 2, 421. 1, first stanza).
41996, F (443. 1).
Egerton 2013 (420. 2, 421. 1).
2725 (420. 2).
Harleian 6057 (404. 1).
6917 (414. 2).
6918 (414. 1, 441. 1, 442. 1).
Sloane 1446 (417. 1, 420. 2).
1792 (417. 1).
Henry Lawes autograph (on loan) (420. 2, 440. 1).

Folger Shakespeare Library, Washington, 1. 21 (420. 2, twice).
1669. 2. (414. 2).
1. 8 (420. 2, 443. 1).

Harvard Univ. Library
Eng. 626 F (407. 1, 414. 1, 417. 1, 441. 1, 442. 1, 443. 2).

Huntington Library
HM 198 (404. 1, 410. 1, 420. 2, 422. 1).
904 (414. 2).

(Rosenbach Foundation Museum, Philadelphia, 423. 1–439. 1; see p. xxxiv).

IV. Revisions

Herrick's willingness to revise his poetry does not rest for proof on his own words,

> Better 'twere my Book were dead
> Than to live not perfected.

The perfecting process can in some degree be followed by comparing readings approved for publication in 1648 with others which appear to represent an earlier stage of composition.

These others are found in manuscript commonplace-books or manuscript song-books, printed books published before 1648, and a few collections published after that but containing lines by Herrick derived from a manuscript source and not from the authorized text. Some of the variants are plainly corruptions, due to misreading of what the copyist had before him. Some others may or may not be authentic. But many of them can by their nature be more reasonably attributed to Herrick than to anyone else and can therefore, in conjunction with the text of *Hesperides*, be used with some confidence to illustrate the art of revision as Herrick practised it.[1] That he revised to good purpose seems evident from the general superiority of the readings in *Hesperides* to those found elsewhere.[2] Many of the improvements are made by slight alterations, the substituted word or phrase giving clearer or fuller meaning, subtler emphasis, or better satisfaction for 'the sense of musical delight'. But very often the reformation is more drastic, and whole passages or stanzas are cut away to avoid superfluity and awkwardness. It seems likely that this method of exclusion or paring down was habitual; and generally that care and deliberation had more to do with Herrick's poetry, even with his effects of artless grace and unstudied finish, than might be supposed.

V. Additional Poems

As Herrick showed an inclusive spirit in deciding which of his poems might be worth publishing, it is the more surprising that he should have omitted some which on the whole are not below his average quality, though revision is sometimes obviously needed. There is no reason to suppose that any of the omitted pieces were written after 1648, though in some instances the possibility cannot be ruled out. A few may have been put aside as

[1] It need not be doubted, for example, that *The Academy of Complements*, 1646, preserves an authentic earlier reading of 'Gather ye rosebuds' (84. 1), ll. 11–12. In 1646 it is

Expect not then the last and worst,
Which still succeeds the former.

Elsewhere there is

Expect not then the last and worst
Time still succeeds the former.

As in some other instances it would be hard to pronounce on the relative merits and chronological order of these two versions; both of them are awkward, the former requiring 'time' to be understood after 'worst' and the other requiring 'which' to be understood after 'Time'. The authorized reading removes the difficulty:

But being spent, the worse, and worst
Times still succeed the former.

[2] That *Hesperides* has not always a monopoly of the superior readings is illustrated by the occurrence in some manuscripts of the improvement to 'Gather ye rosebuds' cited in the preceding note. The work of revision was probably not restricted to a narrow period but may have been intensive when publication was being seriously contemplated, round about 1640 and 1647.

drafts or studies which had later been superseded by something more fully developed or more deftly wrought; but others are not obviously related to any of the acknowledged ones. Carelessness may be part of the explanation; but it would be rash to infer that Herrick despised all that he failed to preserve.

It is most unlikely that all his unpublished poetry has now been assembled, and very questionable whether all the additional poems included in the present volume (41 as against 10 in the edition of 1915) are in fact from his hand. Where certainty was not to be had it seemed best to err on the side of comprehensiveness and admit some poems that may later have to be disclaimed. The grounds for admission were either (*a*) that the poem should have been attributed to Herrick in the seventeenth century, or (*b*) that the poem should carry with it some fairly convincing signs of his authorship. Often both these conditions appear to be satisfied. Internal evidence of style, so frequently misleading, is the more reliable here because of Herrick's many distinctive habits of mind and turns of expression.

Confirmation can sometimes be had from the position which a poem occupies in a manuscript collection. Thus the first six lines of 'Thou mayst be proud', which occur in Add. MS. 33998 without an ascription, could be recognized as probably by Herrick,[1] not because of their phrasing alone but because they are immediately preceded and followed by poems to which Herrick's name is attached. Another poem, 'Ile dote no more', found in MS. Harleian 6918, again without ascription, has several phrases of which any one or two might be thought too weak an indication of any particular poet's authorship, but which in their aggregate point to Herrick as a more likely author than anyone else; and here the case is strengthened by the fact that in the manuscript this poem immediately follows one of those in *Hesperides*, 'Upon the death of his Sparrow' (103. 3).

The same two poems appear in juxtaposition also in Harvard MS. Eng. 626 F, with thirteen others certainly or probably by Herrick though not there ascribed to him. This series is continuous save that the first poem (130. 3) occurs on f. 6^{v} and the last (49. 2) on f. 73; the rest being on ff. 22–39. The order is as follows (U = unpublished in *Hesperides*): 130. 3, 414. 1 (U), 53. 2, 112. 3, 132. 3, 407. 1 (U), 174. 1, 75. 1, 87. 2, 417. 1 (U), 443. 2 (U), 441. 1 (U), 442. 1 (U), 103. 3, 49. 2. Of the six poems un-

[1] They were so recognized by the present editor, before knowing that Herrick is named as the author of the whole poem in MS. Don. c. 57.

published by Herrick, 414. 1 and 407. 1 were first printed by Grosart, and 417. 1 by Delattre. The other three have not been attributed to Herrick until now. 441. 1 and 442. 1 occur with 103. 3 also in MS. Harleian 6918 but 443. 2 does not. In 443. 2, however, there is a fairly clear reference to two poems which Herrick included in *Hesperides* ('my teare And my late Primrose'), apparently 43. 1 and 208. 1.

'Stella wept' and the seventeen poems which follow it on pp. 423–39 below have been kindly made available by the Philip H. and A. S. W. Rosenbach Foundation from a manuscript commonplace-book in the Foundation's Library at Philadelphia. It was formerly owned by Sir Thomas Phillipps. The poems occur in two sections, the first ten on pp. 251–9 of the book and the remaining eight on pp. 287–97. The initials 'R. H.' are appended to all the poems except the first, which is obviously a companion piece to the second. The first poem is immediately preceded by a version of Herrick's acknowledged poem 'A Pastorall upon the birth of Prince Charles' (85. 3).

For internal evidence pointing to Herrick's authorship of the additional poems see Commentary, pp. 579–84.

VI. Modern Editions

No full account is attempted here of the numerous volumes containing selections from Herrick's poems. Nott's pioneering volume of 1814 is referred to above (p. xix). Conspicuous among the rest are those of Palgrave (*Chrysomela*, 1877), H. P. Horne (in The Canterbury Poets, 1887), and E. E. Hale (Athenaeum Press Series, 1895). A list of 'complete' editions is given in *The Cambridge Bibliography of English Literature*, i, p. 449. Chief among them are the following:

1. *Hesperides The Poems and other Remains of Robert Herrick now first collected.* Edited by W. Carew Hazlitt. London . . . 1869. 2 vols.

   This was the first edition to contain poems which were not in the original edition of 1648, and the first to include letters (14).

2. *The Complete Poems of Robert Herrick.* Edited, with Memorial-Introduction and Notes, by the Rev. Alexander B. Grosart. London . . . 1876. 3 vols.

   The introduction and notes added considerably to what was known about Herrick's life and writings. The information is not always accurate and later editors have sometimes put too much trust in the text as Grosart presented it.

3. *Hesperides: or Works both Human and Divine of Robert Herrick*. With an Introduction by Henry Morley. London . . . 1883. (Morley's Universal Library.)

A few expurgations are made.

4. *Robert Herrick The Hesperides and Noble Numbers*, ed. by Alfred Pollard with a Preface by A. C. Swinburne . . . London and New York . . . 1891. (The Muses' Library. 2 vols.)

The poems are for the first time numbered (*Hesperides* and *His Noble Numbers* separately). Some of the epigrams are placed apart, in an Appendix. On the accretions to the notes in the second edition (1898) see above, pp. v–vi.

5. *The Poetical Works of Robert Herrick*. Edited by George Saintsbury. London . . . 1893. (The Aldine Poets. 2 vols.)

Numbers the poems *through*.

6. *The Poetical Works of Robert Herrick*. Edited by F. W. Moorman. Oxford . . . 1915. (Oxford English Texts.) Humphrey Milford 1935 (2 vols.).

With textual introduction and notes. Text reissued, without Herrick's epigrams and without notes, in Oxford English Poets, 1921 (Preface by Percy Simpson).

VII. Abbreviations

A. *In Footnotes*

48 = *Hesperides* and *His Noble Numbers*, 1648. (Letters used to designate separate copies of this edition are explained by the alphabetical list on pp. xxii–xxiii). *rest* = copies in the list other than those specified in the same note. *X* = readings of the three cancellanda, C7, M8, O8. *ed.* = the present editor.

B. *In Critical Notes*

References to manuscripts are first by the library press-mark and thereafter by symbol. Thus Add. MS. 33998 becomes *A*, or *A33* if necessary to distinguish it from other Add. MSS. appearing in the same note, and Huntington MS. becomes *HM*. The titles of certain printed books (see pp. xxiv–xxvii above) are abbreviated as follows:

Ac46, *Ac50*, *Ac71* = *The Academy of Complements*, 1646, 1650, 1671.
C = *Poems* by Thomas Carew, 1640.
C52 = *Catch that Catch can* (Benson and Playford), 1652.
EP = *The English Parnassus* (Poole), 1657.
GD = *The Garden of Delight*, 1658.
L53 = *Ayres and Dialogues*, by Henry Lawes, Book I, 1653.
L55 = *The Second Book of Ayres and Dialogues*, by Henry Lawes, 1655.
L58 = *Ayres and Dialogues*, by Henry Lawes, Book III, 1658.
LG = *The Loyal Garland*, 167?.

MC = *The Marrow of Complements*, 1655.
MD = *The Second Part of Merry Drollery*, ? 1661, and *Merry Drollery*, Complete, 1670.
ML = *The Mysteries of Love and Eloquence*, 1658.
P52 = *Select Musicall Ayres and Dialogues* (Playford), 1652.
P53 = *Select Musicall Ayres and Dialogues* (Playford), 1653.
P55 = *An Introduction to the Skill of Musick* (Playford), 1655.
P59 = *Select Ayres and Dialogues* (Playford), 1659.
P66 = *Musicks Delight on the Cithern* (Playford), 1666.
P67 = *Catch that Catch can* (Playford), 1667.
P69 = *Select Ayres and Dialogues* (Playford), 1669.
(*P* stands for any one item in the series *P52–P69* where only one is in question; also for two or more items where these are in agreement.)
PB = *Parnassus Biceps*, 1656.
WD = *Windsor Drollery*, 1672.
WI = *Wits Interpreter*, 1655.
WR = *Recreation for Ingenious Head-peeces* (*Witt's Recreations*), 1650 (unless the edition of 1645 or that of 1663 is mentioned).
WS = *Poems written by Wil. Shake-speare*, 1640.

C. *In Commentary*

Besides standard abbreviations like *O.E.D.* and *D.N.B.* and others which explain themselves the following occur frequently:

Burton = Burton's *Anatomy of Melancholy*, with divisions and page-numbers as in the edition of 1638.
Jonson, *Works* = the edition by Herford and Simpson.
O.D.E. Prov. = *The Oxford Dictionary of English Proverbs.*
Prov. Eng. = *A Dictionary of the Proverbs in England in the Sixteenth and Seventeenth Centuries*, by M. P. Tilley.

Serial or line numbers used in references to the Anacreontea, the *Greek Anthology*, and Publilius Syrus are those of the Loeb editions.

In all parts of the book previous editions of Herrick are referred to by their editors' names.

III. CHRONOLOGICAL ORDER OF THE POEMS[1]

Only a small number of Herrick's poems can be dated with any confidence. About twenty of *His Noble Numbers* were almost

[1] The most useful suggestions are those of E. E. Hale, *Die chronologische Anordnung der Dichtungen Robert Herricks* (1892), of A. W. Pollard in a note in the Muses' Library edition of Herrick (1898, ii, pp. 298–9), and of F. Delattre, *Robert Herrick*, pp. 482–91.

certainly written no more than a year or two before they were published (see on 162. 3 in Commentary), but there is no reason to suppose that all the rest must have been of late composition. All are likely to be later than *c.* 1623, when Herrick was ordained. It was presumably in or near that year that he wrote 'his farwell unto Poetrie' (410. 1), with its intimation that Poetry might still hope for some part-time employment as a 'Mayde of Honor' to Religion; but as Poetry accepted neither the leave-taking nor the limitation, 1623 cannot be made a turning-point in Herrick's poetic career.

The poems in *Hesperides* (leaving aside *His Noble Numbers*) are put together with no obvious regard for the order in which they were written; nevertheless that order, intentionally or not, seems to have had some effect on the arrangement. There are also a few other considerations which, without pointing to particular dates for particular poems, suggest that certain kinds or classes of poems may be roughly assignable to certain periods, or at least regarded as 'early' or 'late' according as they fall before or after Michaelmas 1630, when Herrick's incumbency of Dean Prior officially began. But first it will be convenient to list the poems in *Hesperides* which can be attached more or less closely to identifiable occasions or circumstances. (For reasons see Commentary.)

Poems	*Dates*	*Reference in present edition*
A Country life: To his Brother, M. Tho: Herrick	*c.* 1610	34. 3
To my dearest Sister M. Mercie Herrick .	before 1612	269. 5
An Epithalamie to Sir Thomas Southwell and his Ladie	1618	53. 2
To his Brother in Law Master John Wingfield	before 1619	210. 3
A New-yeares gift sent to Sir Simeon Steward	1623	126. 3
A Nuptiall Song . . . on Sir Clipseby Crew and his Lady	1625	112. 3
To the High and Noble Prince, George, Duke . . . of Buckingham	1623–8	99. 4
A Dialogue betwixt Horace and Lydia . . .	1627	70. 1
To the reverend shade of his religious Father	1627	27. 1
Upon . . . Mistris Elizabeth Herrick .	1630	145. 2
A Pastorall upon the birth of Prince Charles .	1630	85. 3
His teares to Thamasis	? 1630	315. 4
On Tomasin Parsons	? 1625–30	304. 4
To his dying Brother, Master William Herrick	? 1632	73. 1
An Ode to Master Endymion Porter . .	? 1632	72. 2

Poems	*Dates*	*Reference in present edition*
The Poets good wishes for . . . the Duke of Yorke	1633	108. 1
To Doctor Alablaster	1633–4	256. 2
Upon the Bishop of Lincoln's Imprisonment	1637	52. 2
Upon Ben. Johnson.	1637	289. 1
An Ode for him	1637	289. 2
Upon M. Ben. Johnson	1637–?	150. 1
To the Lady Crew	1638	189. 4
On himself	1640	328. 1
To his Honoured Kinsman, Sir Richard Stone	1641	185. 3
To his Kinsman, Sir Tho. Soame	1641	176. 1
To M. Denham, on his Prospective Poem	? 1641	234. 3
To his honoured friend, Sir John Mynts	1642	194. 2
Upon his Sister-in-Law, Mistresse Elizab: Herrick	1643	23. 4
To the Lord Hopton, on his fight in Cornwall	1643	310. 1
To Sir John Berkley, Governour of Exeter	1643–6	251. 5
To the Lady Mary Villars, Governesse to the Princesse Henretta	1644–	137. 3
To the King Upon his comming with his Army into the West	1644	25. 2
To Sir George Parrie, Doctor of the Civill Law	1644	322. 3
To the King Upon his taking of Leicester	1645	271. 1
A Dirge upon the Death of the Right Valiant Lord, Bernard Stuart	1645	89. 1
To the right gratious Prince, Lodwick, Duke of . . . Lenox	1645	170. 2
Upon M. William Lawes, the rare Musitian	1645	288. 3
To Prince Charles upon his coming to Exeter	1645	254. 3
Ultimus Heroum . . . Henry, Marquesse of Dorchester	1647–	301. 1
Observation	1646–7	162. 3
To his worthy friend M. John Hall . . .	1647	299. 1
To the King Upon his welcome to Hampton-Court	1647	300. 2
To his Household gods	1647	111. 3
To Dean-bourn . . .	1647	29. 1
His returne to London	? 1647	242. 1

It will be seen from this list that in the first half of *Hesperides* (up to p. 168 in the present edition) the poems datable *before* the end of 1630 are rather more numerous than they are in the second half; but that the poems datable *after* 1630 are much more numerous in the second half than in the first. No general conclusions about the chronology of *Hesperides* can safely be drawn from this; but the following points seem relevant.

(*a*) Poems by Herrick occurring in manuscript commonplace-books and manuscript song-books are on the whole likely to have been written before his departure into Devonshire, after which there would presumably be fewer opportunities for him to show his new poems to his friends and for his friends to copy them out; and all the poems common to manuscripts and to *Hesperides* are found in the first half of the printed collection, with 5 exceptions out of 39 (174. 1, 205. 5, 208. 1, 217. 1, 248. 1). The 39 poems, together with one of *His Noble Numbers*, are listed on p. xxviii. Of those occurring in manuscripts but not published in 1648 (see pp. xxx–xxxi) only 413. 1 is clearly latc (1640).

(*b*) Herrick speaks more than once of his depression during the Civil War and in 84. 3 makes 'the untuneable Times' responsible for failing inspiration; so that when he connects Devonshire with specially successful composition (19. 3) it is reasonable to suppose that he is referring to the earlier rather than the later part of his sojourn there, before about 1640. Whether the poems that gave him so much satisfaction are to be identified with any of those which are most admired today may be questioned, but it is likely that 'ennobled numbers for the press' meant something rather more exciting than the generality of the *Noble Numbers* so called in his book.

(*c*) The indications already mentioned that there is some connexion, however tenuous and broken, between the order of the poems as they were printed in *Hesperides* and the order in which they were written can be supported by evidence that some of the influences on Herrick's poetry appear to be more pronounced in the earlier or later part of the secular volume. Thus the influence of Horace and Ovid is more noticeable in the first half, and of Martial and Tacitus in the second. That of Burton, unavailable before 1621, when the *Anatomy* was first published, cannot be very surely illustrated from any poems which are datable up to 1631 by their occasions or circumstances, and from few of the poems found in manuscripts. The influence is at least arguably at work in some of the best-known pieces, 'Delight in Disorder' (28. 1), 'Corinna's going a Maying' (67. 3, final stanza especially), and 'Bid me to live' (108. 2). It pervades *Hesperides* but is more frequently observable in the second half than in the first. The third and fourth editions of the *Anatomy* appeared in 1628 and 1632.[1]

[1] If Herrick derived from Burton the passage paraphrased from Ammianus in 194. 4 he must have been using the edition of 1632 or of 1638, as the passage is not in the earlier editions. It does not appear to be in Erasmus's *Adagia*. See also note in Commentary on 31. 1. 2.

(*d*) In the first half of *Hesperides*, as Delattre notices, there is a preponderance of longer poems, in the second of shorter ones. Correspondingly there is a fairly large proportion of longish poems among those occurring in manuscript collections.

(*e*) The same scholar agrees with Hale in observing that in poems more or less datable by other criteria, Herrick's verse becomes more tightly constructed as time goes on; and this, together with what is said above in connexion with Martial and Tacitus, favours the conclusion that Herrick was apt to write more diffusely and precipitately in his earlier years, more tersely and with more exacting self-criticism afterwards. Further evidence of this can be seen in the cuts he sometimes made when revising (see above, p. xxxii).

HESPERIDES:

OR,

THE WORKS

BOTH

HUMANE & DIVINE

OF

ROBERT HERRICK *Eſq.*

OVID.

Effugient avidos Carmina noſtra Rogos.

LONDON,

Printed for *John Williams,* and *Francis Eglesfield,* and are to be ſold at the Crown and Marygold in Saint *Pauls* Church-yard. 1648.

TO THE MOST

ILLVSTRIOVS,

AND

Most Hopefull PRINCE,

C H A R L E S,

Prince of *Wales*.

WELL may my Book come forth like Publique Day,
When such a *Light* as *You* are leads the way:
Who are my Works *Creator*, and alone
The *Flame* of it, and the *Expansion*.
And look how all those heavenly Lamps acquire
Light from the Sun, that *inexhausted Fire:*
So all my *Morne*, and *Evening Stars* from You
Have their *Existence*, and their *Influence* too.
Full is my Book of Glories; but all These
By You become *Immortall Substances*.

For these Transgressions which thou here dost see,
Condemne the Printer, Reader, and not me;
Who gave him forth good Grain, though he mistook
The Seed; so sow'd these Tares throughout my Book.

ERRATA

Page 33. line 10. read *Rods.* p. 41. l. 19. r. *Gotiere.* p. 65. l. 12. r. *only one.* p. 83. l. 28. r. *soft.* p. 88. l. 26. r. *the flowrie.* p. 91. l. 29. r. *such fears.* p. 136. l. 9. r. *to thee the.* p. 155. l. 10. r. *washt or's to tell.* p. 166. l. 10. r. *his Lachrimæ.* p. 181. l. 10. r. *Ah woe is me, woe, woe is me.* p. 183. l. 9. r. *and thy brest.* p. 201. l. 22. r. *let chast.* p. 230. l. 21. r. *and having drunk.* p. 260. l. 26. r. *to rise.* p. 335. l. 17. r. *a wife as.*

In the Divine.

Pag. 22. line 14. read *where so ere he sees.*

Errata. The page-numbers and line-numbers are those of the original text. The corresponding numbers in the present edition are 32.3.4; 39.3.13; 60.2.5; 75, l. 36; 80.2.3; 82.2.11; 119, l. 1; 134, l. 90; 144.1 (*heading*); 156.4.9; 158.2.3; 174, l. 8; 198, l. 10; 222.3.3; 283.4.8; 356.6.3. *The errata have been corrected in their places.*

HESPERIDES.

The Argument of his Book.

I SING of *Brooks*, of *Blossomes*, *Birds*, and *Bowers:*
Of *April*, *May*, of *June*, and *July*-Flowers.
I sing of *May-poles*, *Hock-carts*, *Wassails*, *Wakes*,
Of *Bride-grooms*, *Brides*, and of their *Bridall-cakes*.
I write of *Youth*, of *Love*, and have Accesse
By these, to sing of cleanly-*Wantonnesse*.
I sing of *Dewes*, of *Raines*, and piece by piece
Of *Balme*, of *Oyle*, of *Spice*, and *Amber-Greece*.
I sing of *Times trans-shifting*; and I write
How *Roses* first came *Red*, and *Lillies White*.
I write of *Groves*, of *Twilights*, and I sing
The Court of *Mab*, and of the *Fairie-King*.
I write of *Hell*; I sing (and ever shall)
Of *Heaven*, and hope to have it after all.

To his Muse.

WHITHER *Mad maiden* wilt thou roame?
Farre safer 'twere to stay at home:
Where thou mayst sit, and piping please
The poore and private *Cottages*.
Since *Coats*, and *Hamlets*, best agree
With this thy meaner Minstralsie.
There with the Reed, thou mayst expresse
The Shepherds Fleecie happinesse:
And with thy *Eclogues* intermixe
Some smooth, and harmlesse *Beucolicks*.
There on a Hillock thou mayst sing
Unto a handsome Shephardling;

Or to a Girle (that keeps the Neat)
With breath more sweet then Violet.
There, there, (perhaps) such Lines as These
May take the simple *Villages.*
But for the Court, the Country wit
Is despicable unto it.
Stay then at home, and doe not goe
Or flie abroad to seeke for woe.
Contempts in Courts and Cities dwell;
No *Critick* haunts the Poore mans Cell:
Where thou mayst hear thine own Lines read
By no one tongue, there, censured.
That man's unwise will search for Ill,
And may prevent it, sitting still.

To his Booke.

WHILE thou didst keep thy *Candor* undefil'd,
Deerely I lov'd thee; as my first-borne child:
But when I saw thee wantonly to roame
From house to house, and never stay at home;
I brake my bonds of Love, and bad thee goe,
Regardlesse whether well thou sped'st, or no.
On with thy fortunes then, what e're they be;
If good I'le smile, if bad I'le sigh for Thee.

Another.

TO read my Booke the Virgin shie
May blush, (while *Brutus* standeth by:)
But when He's gone, read through what's writ,
And never staine a cheeke for it.

Another.

WHO with thy leaves shall wipe (at need)
The place, where swelling *Piles* do breed:
May every Ill, that bites, or smarts,
Perplexe him in his hinder-parts.

To the soure Reader.

If thou dislik'st the Piece thou light'st on first;
Thinke that of All, that I have writ, the worst:
But if thou read'st my Booke unto the end,
And still do'st this, and that verse, reprehend:
O Perverse man! If All disgustfull be,
The Extreame Scabbe take thee, and thine, for me.

To his Booke.

Come thou not neere those men, who are like *Bread*
O're-leven'd; or like *Cheese* o're-renetted.

When he would have his verses read.

In sober mornings, doe not thou reherse
The holy incantation of a verse;
But when that men have both well drunke, and fed,
Let my Enchantments then be sung, or read.
When Laurell spirts 'ith fire, and when the Hearth
Smiles to it selfe, and guilds the roofe with mirth;
When up the * *Thyrse* is rais'd, and when the sound
Of sacred * *Orgies* flyes, A round, A round.
When the *Rose* raignes, and locks with ointments shine,
Let rigid *Cato* read these Lines of mine.

*A *Javelin* twind with *Ivy*.
* Songs to *Bacchus*.

Upon Julias *Recovery.*

Droop, droop no more, or hang the head
Ye *Roses* almost withered;
Now strength, and newer Purple get,
Each here declining *Violet*.
O *Primroses*! let this day be
A Resurrection unto ye;
And to all flowers ally'd in blood,
Or sworn to that sweet Sister-hood:
For Health on *Julia's* cheek hath shed
Clarret, and Creame commingled.
And those her lips doe now appeare
As beames of *Corrall*, but more cleare.

4.3 Now] New *conj.* Moorman

To Silvia *to wed.*

LET us (though late) at last (my *Silvia*) wed;
And loving lie in one devoted bed.
Thy Watch may stand, my minutes fly poste haste;
No sound calls back the yeere that once is past.
Then sweetest *Silvia*, let's no longer stay;
True love, we know, precipitates delay.
Away with doubts, all scruples hence remove;
No man at one time, can be wise, and love.

The Parliament of Roses to Julia.

I DREAMT the Roses one time went
To meet and sit in Parliament:
The place for these, and for the rest
Of flowers, was thy spotlesse breast:
Over the which a State was drawne
Of Tiffanie, or Cob-web Lawne;
Then in that *Parly*, all those powers
Voted the Rose; the Queen of flowers.
But so, as that her self should be
The maide of Honour unto thee.

No bashfulnesse in begging.

TO get thine ends, lay bashfulnesse aside;
Who feares to aske, doth teach to be deny'd.

The Frozen Heart.

I FREEZE, I freeze, and nothing dwels
In me but Snow, and *ysicles.*
For pitties sake give your advice,
To melt this snow, and thaw this ice;
I'le drink down Flames, but if so be
Nothing but love can supple me;
I'le rather keepe this frost, and snow,
Then to be thaw'd, or heated so.

To Perilla.

Ah my *Perilla*! do'st thou grieve to see
Me, day by day, to steale away from thee?
Age cals me hence, and my gray haires bid come,
And haste away to mine eternal home;
'Twill not be long (*Perilla*) after this,
That I must give thee the *supremest* kisse:
Dead when I am, first cast in salt, and bring
Part of the creame from that *Religious Spring*;
With which (*Perilla*) wash my hands and feet;
That done, then wind me in that very sheet
Which wrapt thy smooth limbs (when thou didst implore
The Gods protection, but the night before)
Follow me weeping to my Turfe, and there
Let fall a *Primrose*, and with it a teare:
Then lastly, let some weekly-strewings be
Devoted to the memory of me:
Then shall my *Ghost* not walk about, but keep
Still in the coole, and silent shades of sleep.

A Song to the Maskers.

1. Come down, and dance ye in the toyle
Of pleasures, to a Heate;
But if to moisture, Let the oyle
Of Roses be your sweat.

2. Not only to your selves assume
These sweets, but let them fly;
From this, to that, and so Perfume
E'ne all the standers by.

3. As Goddesse *Isis* (when she went,
Or glided through the street)
Made all that touch't her with her scent,
And whom she touch't, turne sweet.

To *Perenna.*

WHEN I thy Parts runne o're, I can't espie
In any one, the least indecencie:
But every Line, and Limb diffused thence,
A faire, and unfamiliar excellence:
So, that the more I look, the more I prove,
Ther's still more cause, why I the more should love.

Treason.

THE seeds of *Treason* choake up as they spring,
He Acts the Crime, that gives it Cherishing.

Two Things Odious.

TWO of a thousand things, are disallow'd,
A lying *Rich* man, and a *Poore* man proud.

To his Mistresses.

HELPE me! helpe me! now I call
To my pretty *Witchcrafts* all:
Old I am, and cannot do
That, I was accustom'd to.
Bring your *Magicks, Spels, and Charmes,*
To enflesh my thighs, and armes:
Is there no way to beget
In my limbs their former heat?
Æson had (as *Poets* faine)
Baths that made him young againe:
Find that *Medicine* (if you can)
For your drie-decrepid man:
Who would faine his strength renew,
Were it but to pleasure you.

The Wounded Heart.

COME bring your *sampler*, and with Art,
Draw in't a wounded Heart:
And dropping here, and there:
Not that I thinke, that any Dart,

Can make your's bleed a teare:
Or peirce it any where;
Yet doe it to this end: that I,
May by
This secret see,
Though you can make
That *Heart* to bleed, your's ne'r will ake
For me.

No Loathsomnesse in love.

WHAT I fancy, I approve,
No Dislike there is in love:
Be my Mistresse short or tall,
And distorted there-withall:
Be she likewise one of those,
That an *Acre* hath of Nose:
Be her forehead, and her eyes
Full of incongruities:
Be her cheeks so shallow too,
As to shew her *Tongue* wag through:
Be her lips ill hung, or set,
And her grinders black as jet;
Ha's she thinne haire, hath she none,
She's to me a *Paragon.*

To Anthea.

IF, deare *Anthea*, my hard fate it be
To live some few-sad-howers after thee:
Thy *sacred Corse* with *Odours* I will burne;
And with my *Lawrell* crown thy *Golden Urne.*
Then holding up (there) such religious Things,
As were (time past) thy holy *Filitings*:
Nere to thy *Reverend Pitcher* I will fall
Down dead for grief, and end my woes withall:
So three in one small plat of ground shall ly,
Anthea, Herrick, and his *Poetry.*

2.1 If,] *comma faint in ADM, absent in U*

The Weeping Cherry.

I SAW a *Cherry* weep, and why?
Why wept it? but for shame,
Because my *Julia's* lip was by,
And did out-red the same.
But pretty Fondling, let not fall
A teare at all for that:
Which *Rubies*, *Corralls*, *Scarlets*, all
For tincture, wonder at.

Soft Musick.

THE mellow touch of musick most doth wound
The soule, when it doth rather sigh, then sound.

The Difference Betwixt Kings and Subiects.

TWIXT Kings and Subjects ther's this mighty odds,
Subjects are taught by *Men*; Kings by the *Gods*.

His Answer to a Question.

SOME would know
Why I so
Long still doe tarry,
And ask why
Here that I
Live, and not marry?
Thus I those
Doe oppose;
What man would be here,
Slave to Thrall,
If at all
He could live free here?

Upon Julia's *Fall.*

JULIA was carelesse, and withall,
She rather took, then got a fall:
The wanton *Ambler* chanc'd to see
Part of her leggs sinceritie:

And ravish'd thus, It came to passe,
The Nagge (like to the *Prophets Asse*)
Began to speak, and would have been
A telling what rare sights h'ad seen:
And had told all; but did refraine,
Because his Tongue was ty'd againe.

Expences Exhaust.

LIVE with a thrifty, not a needy Fate;
Small shots paid often, waste a vast estate.

Love what it is.

LOVE is a circle that doth restlesse move
In the same sweet eternity of love.

Presence and Absence.

WHEN what is lov'd, is Present, love doth spring;
But being absent, Love lies languishing.

No Spouse but a Sister.

A BACHELOUR I will
Live as I have liv'd still,
And never take a wife
To crucifie my life:
But this I'le tell ye too,
What now I meane to doe;
A Sister (in the stead
Of Wife) about I'le lead;
Which I will keep embrac'd,
And kisse, but yet be chaste.

The Pomander Bracelet.

TO me my *Julia* lately sent
A Bracelet richly Redolent:
The Beads I kist, but most lov'd her
That did perfume the Pomander.

l. 9 And] (?) And, (*mark in some copies*)

The shooe tying.

ANTHEA bade me tye her shooe;
I did; and kist the Instep too:
And would have kist unto her knee,
Had not her Blush rebuked me.

The Carkanet.

INSTEAD of Orient Pearls, of Jet,
I sent my Love a Karkanet:
About her spotlesse neck she knit
The lace, to honour me, or it:
Then think how wrapt was I to see
My Jet t'enthrall such Ivorie.

His sailing from Julia.

WHEN that day comes, whose evening sayes I'm gone
Unto that watrie Desolation:
Devoutly to thy *Closet-gods* then pray,
That my wing'd Ship may meet no *Remora.*
Those Deities which circum-walk the Seas,
And look upon our dreadfull passages,
Will from all dangers, re-deliver me,
For one *drink-offering*, poured out by thee.
Mercie and *Truth* live with thee! and forbeare
(In my short absence) to unsluce a teare:
But yet for Loves-sake, let thy lips doe this,
Give my dead picture one engendring kisse:
Work that to life, and let me ever dwell
In thy remembrance (*Julia.*) So farewell.

How the Wall-flower came first, and why so called.

WHY this Flower is now call'd so,
List' sweet maids, and you shal know.
Understand, this First-ling was
Once a brisk and bonny Lasse,
Kept as close as *Danae* was:

Who a sprightly *Springall* lov'd,
And to have it fully prov'd,
Up she got upon a wall,
Tempting down to slide withall:
But the silken twist unty'd,
So she fell, and bruis'd, she dy'd.
Love, in pitty of the deed,
And her loving-lucklesse speed,
Turn'd her to this Plant, we call
Now, *The Flower of the Wall.*

Why Flowers change colour.

THESE fresh beauties (we can prove)
Once were Virgins sick of love,
Turn'd to Flowers. Still in some
Colours goe, and colours come.

To his Mistresse objecting to him neither Toying or Talking.

YOU say I love not, 'cause I doe not play
Still with your curles, and kisse the time away.
You blame me too, because I cann't devise
Some sport, to please those Babies in your eyes:
By *Loves Religion*, I must here confesse it,
The most I love, when I the least expresse it.
Small griefs find tongues: Full Casques are ever found
To give (if any, yet) but little sound.
Deep waters noyse-lesse are; And this we know,
That chiding streams betray small depth below.
So when Love speechlesse is, she doth expresse
A depth in love, and that depth, bottomlesse.
Now since my love is tongue-lesse, know me such,
Who speak but little, 'cause I love so much.

Upon the losse of his Mistresses.

I HAVE lost, and lately, these
Many dainty Mistresses:
Stately *Julia*, prime of all;
Sapho next, a principall:

Smooth *Anthea*, for a skin
White, and Heaven-like Chrystalline:
Sweet *Electra*, and the choice
Myrha, for the Lute, and Voice.
Next, *Corinna*, for her wit,
And the graceful use of it:
With *Perilla:* All are gone;
Onely *Herrick's* left alone,
For to number sorrow by
Their departures hence, and die.

The Dream.

ME thought, (last night) love in an anger came,
And brought a rod, so whipt me with the same:
Mirtle the twigs were, meerly to imply;
Love strikes, but 'tis with gentle crueltie.
Patient I was: Love pitifull grew then,
And stroak'd the stripes, and I was whole agen.
Thus like a Bee, *Love-gentle* stil doth bring
Hony to salve, where he before did sting.

The Vine.

I DREAM'D this mortal part of mine
Was Metamorphoz'd to a Vine;
Which crawling one and every way,
Enthrall'd my dainty *Lucia.*
Me thought, her long small legs & thighs
I with my *Tendrils* did surprize;
Her Belly, Buttocks, and her Waste
By my soft *Nerv'lits* were embrac'd:
About her head I writhing hung,
And with rich clusters (hid among
The leaves) her temples I behung:
So that my *Lucia* seem'd to me
Young *Bacchus* ravisht by his tree.
My curles about her neck did craule,
And armes and hands they did enthrall:
So that she could not freely stir,
(All parts there made one prisoner.)

But when I crept with leaves to hide
Those parts, which maids keep unespy'd,
Such fleeting pleasures there I took,
That with the fancie I awook;
And found (Ah me!) this flesh of mine
More like a *Stock*, then like a *Vine*.

To Love.

I'M free from thee; and thou no more shalt heare
My puling Pipe to beat against thine eare:
Farewell my shackles, (though of pearle they be)
Such precious thraldome ne'r shall fetter me.
He loves his bonds, who when the first are broke,
Submits his neck unto a second yoke.

On himselfe.

YOUNG I was, but now am old,
But I am not yet grown cold;
I can play, and I can twine
'Bout a Virgin like a Vine:
In her lap too I can lye
Melting, and in fancie die:
And return to life, if she
Claps my cheek, or kisseth me;
Thus, and thus it now appears
That our love out-lasts our yeeres.

Love's play at Push-pin.

LOVE and my selfe (beleeve me) on a day
At childish Push-pin (for our sport) did play:
I put, he pusht, and heedless of my skin,
Love prickt my finger with a golden pin:
Since which, it festers so, that I can prove
'Twas but a trick to poyson me with love:
Little the wound was; greater was the smart;
The finger bled, but burnt was all my heart.

The Rosarie.

ONE ask'd me where the Roses grew?
I bade him not goe seek;
But forthwith bade my *Julia* shew
A bud in either cheek.

Upon Cupid.

OLD wives have often told, how they
Saw *Cupid* bitten by a flea:
And thereupon, in tears half drown'd,
He cry'd aloud, Help, help the wound:
He wept, he sobb'd, he call'd to some
To bring him *Lint*, and *Balsamum*,
To make a *Tent*, and put it in,
Where the *Steletto* pierc'd the skin:
Which being done, the fretfull paine
Asswag'd, and he was well again.

The Parcæ, *or, Three dainty Destinies.*
The Armilet.

THREE lovely Sisters working were
(As they were closely set)
Of soft and dainty Maiden-haire,
A curious *Armelet.*
I smiling, ask'd them what they did?
(Faire *Destinies* all three)
Who told me, they had drawn a thred
Of Life, and 'twas for me.
They shew'd me then, how fine 'twas spun;
And I reply'd thereto,
I care not now how soone 'tis done,
Or cut, if cut by you.

Sorrowes succeed.

WHEN one is past, another care we have,
Thus woe succeeds a woe; as wave a wave.

Cherry-pit.

JULIA and I did lately sit
Playing for sport, at Cherry-pit:
She threw; I cast; and having thrown,
I got the Pit, and she the Stone.

To Robin Red-brest.

LAID out for dead, let thy last kindnesse be
With leaves and mosse-work for to cover me:
And while the Wood-nimphs my cold corps inter,
Sing thou my Dirge, sweet-warbling Chorister!
For Epitaph, in Foliage, next write this,
Here, here the Tomb of Robin Herrick is.

Discontents in Devon.

MORE discontents I never had
Since I was born, then here;
Where I have been, and still am sad,
In this dull *Devon-shire:*
Yet justly too I must confesse;
I ne'r invented such
Ennobled numbers for the Presse,
Then where I loath'd so much.

To his Paternall Countrey.

O EARTH! Earth! Earth heare thou my voice, and be
Loving, and gentle for to cover me:
Banish'd from thee I live; ne'r to return,
Unlesse thou giv'st my small Remains an Urne.

Cherrie-ripe.

CHERRIE-Ripe, Ripe, Ripe, I cry,
Full and faire ones; come and buy:
If so be, you ask me where
They doe grow? I answer, There,

1 *For variants see p.* 463

Where my *Julia*'s lips doe smile;
There's the Land, or Cherry-Ile:
Whose Plantations fully show
All the yeere, where Cherries grow.

To his Mistresses.

PUT on your silks; and piece by piece
Give them the scent of Amber-Greece:
And for your breaths too, let them smell
Ambrosia-like, or *Nectarell*:
While other Gums their sweets perspire,
By your owne jewels set on fire.

To Anthea.

NOW is the time, when all the lights wax dim;
And thou (*Anthea*) must withdraw from him
Who was thy servant. Dearest, bury me
Under that *Holy-oke*, or *Gospel-tree*:
Where (though thou see'st not) thou may'st think upon
Me, when thou yeerly go'st Procession:
Or for mine honour, lay me in that Tombe
In which thy sacred Reliques shall have roome:
For my Embalming (Sweetest) there will be
No Spices wanting, when I'm laid by thee.

The Vision to Electra.

I DREAM'D we both were in a bed
Of Roses, almost smothered:
The warmth and sweetnes had me there
Made lovingly familiar:
But that I heard thy sweet breath say,
Faults done by night, will blush by day:
I kist thee (panting,) and I call
Night to the Record! that was all.
But ah! if empty dreames so please,
Love give me more such nights as these.

Dreames.

HERE we are all, by day; By night w'are hurl'd
By dreames, each one, into a sev'rall world.

Ambition.

IN Man, Ambition is the common'st thing;
Each one, by nature, loves to be a King.

His request to Julia.

JULIA, if I chance to die
Ere I print my Poetry;
I most humbly thee desire
To commit it to the fire:
Better 'twere my Book were dead,
Then to live not perfected.

Money gets the masterie.

FIGHT thou with shafts of silver, and o'rcome,
When no force else can get the masterdome.

The Scar-fire.

WATER, water I desire,
Here's a house of flesh on fire:
Ope' the fountains and the springs,
And come all to Buckittings:
What ye cannot quench, pull downe;
Spoile a house, to save a towne:
Better tis that one shu'd fall,
Then by one, to hazard all.

Upon Silvia, *a Mistresse.*

WHEN some shall say, Faire once my *Silvia* was;
Thou wilt complaine, False now's thy Looking-glasse:
Which renders that quite tarnisht, which was green;
And Priceless now, what Peerless once had been:
Upon thy Forme more wrinkles yet will fall,
And comming downe, shall make no noise at all.

Cheerfulnesse in Charitie: or, *The sweet Sacrifice.*

'TIS not a thousand Bullocks thies
Can please those Heav'nly Deities,
If the Vower don't express
In his Offering, Cheerfulness.

Once poore, still penurious.

GOES the world now, it will with thee goe hard:
The fattest Hogs we grease the more with Lard.
To him that has, there shall be added more;
Who is penurious, he shall still be poore.

Sweetnesse in Sacrifice.

'TIS not greatness they require,
To be offer'd up by fire:
But 'tis sweetness that doth please
Those Eternall Essences.

Steame in Sacrifice.

IF meat the Gods give, I the steame
High-towring wil devote to them:
Whose easie natures like it well,
If we the roste have, they the smell.

Upon Julia's *Voice.*

SO smooth, so sweet, so silv'ry is thy voice,
As, could they hear, the Damn'd would make no noise,
But listen to thee, (walking in thy chamber)
Melting melodious words, to Lutes of Amber.

Againe.

WHEN I thy singing next shall heare,
Ile wish I might turne all to eare,
To drink in Notes, and Numbers; such
As blessed soules cann't heare too much:

Then melted down, there let me lye
Entranc'd, and lost confusedly:
And by thy Musique strucken mute,
Die, and be turn'd into a Lute.

All things decay and die.

ALL *things decay with Time*: The Forrest sees
The growth, and down-fall of her aged trees:
That Timber tall, which three-score *lusters* stood
The proud *Dictator* of the State-like wood:
I meane (the Soveraigne of all Plants) the Oke
Droops, dies, and falls without the cleavers stroke.

The succession of the foure sweet months.

FIRST, *April*, she with mellow showrs
Opens the way for early flowers;
Then after her comes smiling *May*,
In a more rich and sweet aray:
Next enters *June*, and brings us more
Jems, then those two, that went before:
Then (lastly) *July* comes, and she
More wealth brings in, then all those three.

No Shipwrack of Vertue. To a friend.

THOU sail'st with others, in this *Argus* here;
Nor wrack, or *Bulging* thou hast cause to feare:
But trust to this, my noble passenger;
Who swims with Vertue, he shall still be sure
(*Ulysses*-like) all tempests to endure;
And 'midst a thousand gulfs to be secure.

Upon his Sister-in-Law, Mistresse Elizab: Herrick.

FIRST, for Effusions due unto the dead,
My solemne Vowes have here accomplished:
Next, how I love thee, that my griefe must tell,
Wherein thou liv'st for ever. Deare farewell.

Of Love. A Sonet.

How Love came in, I do not know,
Whether by th'eye, or eare, or no:
Or whether with the soule it came
(At first) infused with the same:
Whether in part 'tis here or there,
Or, like the soule, whole every where:
This troubles me: but I as well
As any other, this can tell;
That when from hence she does depart,
The out-let then is from the heart.

To Anthea.

Ah my *Anthea!* Must my heart still break?
(*Love makes me write, what shame forbids to speak.*)
Give me a kisse, and to that kisse a score;
Then to that twenty, adde an hundred more:
A thousand to that hundred: so kisse on,
To make that thousand up a million.
Treble that million, and when that is done,
Let's kisse afresh, as when we first begun.
But yet, though Love likes well such Scenes as these,
There is an Act that will more fully please:
Kissing and glancing, soothing, all make way
But to the acting of this private Play:
Name it I would; but being blushing red,
The rest Ile speak, when we meet both in bed.

The Rock of Rubies: and The quarrie of Pearls.

Some ask'd me where the *Rubies* grew?
And nothing I did say:
But with my finger pointed to
The lips of *Julia.*
Some ask'd how *Pearls* did grow, and where?
Then spoke I to my Girle,
To part her lips, and shew'd them there
The Quarelets of Pearl.

Conformitie.

CONFORMITY was ever knowne
A foe to Dissolution:
Nor can we that a ruine call,
Whose crack gives crushing unto all.

TO THE KING,

Upon his comming with his Army into the West.

WELCOME, most welcome to our Vowes and us,
Most great, and universall *Genius!*
The Drooping West, which hitherto has stood
As one, in long-lamented-widow-hood;
Looks like a Bride now, or a bed of flowers,
Newly refresh't, both by the Sun, and showers.
War, which before was horrid, now appears
Lovely in you, brave Prince of Cavaliers!
A deale of courage in each bosome springs
By your accesse; (*O you the best of Kings!*)
Ride on with all white *Omens*; so, that where
Your Standard's up, we fix a Conquest there.

Upon Roses.

UNDER a Lawne, then skyes more cleare,
Some ruffled Roses nestling were:
And snugging there, they seem'd to lye
As in a flowrie Nunnery:
They blush'd, and look'd more fresh then flowers
Quickned of late by Pearly showers;
And all, because they were possest
But of the heat of *Julia*'s breast:
Which as a warme, and moistned spring,
Gave them their ever flourishing.

To the King and Queene, upon their unhappy distances.

WOE, woe to them, who (by a ball of strife)
Doe, and have parted here a Man and Wife:
CHARLS the best Husband, while MARIA strives
To be, and is, the very best of Wives:
Like Streams, you are divorc'd; but 'twill come, when
These eyes of mine shall see you mix agen.
Thus speaks the *Oke*, here; *C.* and *M.* shall meet,
Treading on *Amber*, with their silver-feet:
Nor wil't be long, ere this accomplish'd be;
The words found true, *C. M.* remember me.

Dangers wait on Kings.

AS oft as Night is banish'd by the Morne,
So oft, we'll think, we see a King new born.

The Cheat of Cupid: *Or, The ungentle guest.*

ONE silent night of late,
When every creature rested,
Came one unto my gate,
And knocking, me molested.

Who's that (said I) beats there,
And troubles thus the Sleepie?
Cast off (said he) all feare,
And let not Locks thus keep ye.

For I a Boy am, who
By Moonlesse nights have swerved;
And all with showrs wet through,
And e'en with cold half starved.

I pittifull arose,
And soon a Taper lighted;
And did my selfe disclose
Unto the lad benighted.

I saw he had a Bow,
  And Wings too, which did shiver;
And looking down below,
  I spy'd he had a Quiver.

I to my Chimney's shine
  Brought him, (as Love professes)
And chaf'd his hands with mine,
  And dry'd his dropping Tresses:

But when he felt him warm'd,
  Let's try this bow of ours,
And string if they be harm'd,
  Said he, with these late showrs.

Forthwith his bow he bent,
  And wedded string and arrow,
And struck me that it went
  Quite through my heart and marrow.

Then laughing loud, he flew
  Away, and thus said flying,
Adieu, mine Host, Adieu,
  Ile leave thy heart a dying.

To the reverend shade of his religious Father.

THAT for seven *Lusters* I did never come
To doe the *Rites* to thy Religious Tombe:
That neither haire was cut, or true teares shed
By me, o'r thee, (*as justments to the dead*)
Forgive, forgive me; since I did not know
Whether thy bones had here their Rest, or no.
But now 'tis known, Behold; behold, I bring
Unto thy Ghost, th'Effused Offering:
And look, what Smallage, Night-shade, Cypresse, Yew,
Unto the shades have been, or now are due,
Here I devote; And something more then so;
I come to pay a Debt of Birth I owe.
Thou gav'st me life, (but Mortall;) For that one
Favour, Ile make full satisfaction;
For my life mortall, Rise from out thy Herse,
And take a life immortall from my Verse.

Delight in Disorder.

A SWEET disorder in the dresse
Kindles in cloathes a wantonnesse:
A Lawne about the shoulders thrown
Into a fine distraction:
An erring Lace, which here and there
Enthralls the Crimson Stomacher:
A Cuffe neglectfull, and thereby
Ribbands to flow confusedly:
A winning wave (deserving Note)
In the tempestuous petticote:
A carelesse shooe-string, in whose tye
I see a wilde civility:
Doe more bewitch me, then when Art
Is too precise in every part.

To his Muse.

WERE I to give thee *Baptime*, I wo'd chuse
To *Christen* thee, the *Bride*, the *Bashfull Muse*,
Or *Muse* of *Roses:* since that name does fit
Best with those *Virgin-Verses* thou hast writ:
Which are so cleane, so chast, as none may feare
Cato the *Censor*, sho'd he scan each here.

Upon Love.

LOVE scorch'd my finger, but did spare
  The burning of my heart:
To signifie, in Love my share
  Sho'd be a little part.

Little I love; but if that he
  Wo'd but that heat recall:
That joynt to ashes burnt sho'd be,
  Ere I wo'd love at all.

3 *For variants see p.* 463   3.7 burnt sho'd be *WR*: sho'd be [*or* he] burnt *48*   be *HPUWi*: he *rest*

To Dean-bourn, *a rude River in* Devon, *by which sometimes he lived.*

DEAN-BOURN, farewell; I never look to see
Deane, or thy warty incivility.
Thy rockie bottome, that doth teare thy streams,
And makes them frantick, ev'n to all extreames;
To my content, I never sho'd behold,
Were thy streames silver, or thy rocks all gold.
Rockie thou art; and rockie we discover
Thy men; and rockie are thy wayes all over.
O men, O manners; Now, and ever knowne
To be *A Rockie Generation!*
A people currish; churlish as the seas;
And rude (almost) as rudest Salvages.
With whom I did, and may re-sojourne when
Rockes turn to Rivers, Rivers turn to Men.

Kissing Usurie.

BIANCHA, Let
Me pay the debt
I owe thee for a kisse
Thou lend'st to me;
And I to thee
Will render ten for this:

If thou wilt say,
Ten will not pay
For that so rich a one;
Ile cleare the summe,
If it will come
Unto a Million.

1 (*heading*) *To BPUVWiWr*: *om. rest.* Devon, *BPVWr*: Devon. *rest* (*stop uncertain in UWi*) 1.2 warty] watry *X* 1.6 thy . . . thy] thy . . . the *X* 1.9 Now] There *X* 1.12 rude (almost) as] rude as *P*

By this I guesse,
Of happinesse
Who has a little measure:
He must of right,
To th'utmost mite,
Make payment for his pleasure.

To Julia.

HOW rich and pleasing thou my *Julia* art
In each thy dainty, and peculiar part!
First, for thy *Queen-ship* on thy head is set
Of flowers a sweet commingled Coronet:
About thy neck a Carkanet is bound,
Made of the *Rubie*, *Pearle* and *Diamond:*
A golden ring, that shines upon thy thumb:
About thy wrist, the rich * *Dardanium.*
Between thy Breasts (then Doune of Swans more white)
There playes the *Saphire* with the *Chrysolite.*
No part besides must of thy selfe be known,
But by the *Topaz*, *Opal*, *Calcedon.*

* *A Bracelet, from Dardanus so call'd*

To Laurels.

A FUNERALL stone,
Or Verse I covet none;
But onely crave
Of you, that I may have
A sacred Laurel springing from my grave:
Which being seen,
Blest with perpetuall greene,
May grow to be
Not so much call'd a tree,
As the eternall monument of me.

His Cavalier.

GIVE me that man, that dares bestride
The active Sea-horse, & with pride,
Through that huge field of waters ride:

ll. 16–18 *precede* ll. 13–15 *X*   l. 13 this] this, *X*   l. 15 measure:] measure. *X*   l. 18 pleasure.] pleasure: *X*   1.9 Breasts *X*: Breast *48*   2.2 none;] none, *X*

Who, with his looks too, can appease
The ruffling winds and raging Seas,
In mid'st of all their outrages.
This, this a virtuous man can doe,
Saile against Rocks, and split them too;
I! and a world of Pikes passe through.

Zeal required in Love.

I'LE doe my best to win, when'ere I wooe:
That man loves not, who is not zealous too.

The Bag of the Bee.

ABOUT the sweet bag of a Bee,
  Two *Cupids* fell at odds;
And whose the pretty prize shu'd be,
  They vow'd to ask the Gods.

Which *Venus* hearing; thither came,
  And for their boldness stript them:
And taking thence from each his flame;
  With rods of *Mirtle* whipt them.

Which done, to still their wanton cries,
  When quiet grown sh'ad seen them,
She kist, and wip'd thir dove-like eyes;
  And gave the Bag between them.

Love kill'd by Lack.

LET me be warme; let me be fully fed:
  Luxurious Love by Wealth is nourished.
Let me be leane, and cold, and once grown poore,
I shall dislike, what once I lov'd before.

To his Mistresse.

CHOOSE me your Valentine;
  Next, let us marry:
Love to the death will pine,
  If we long tarry.

2 *For variants see p.* 463   2.2 odds *ACDGWeWoY*: ddos *rest*

Promise, and keep your vowes,
Or vow ye never:
Loves doctrine disallowes
Troth-breakers ever.

You have broke promise twice
(Deare) to undoe me;
If you prove faithlesse thrice,
None then will wooe ye.

To the generous Reader.

SEE, and not see; and if thou chance t'espie
Some Aberrations in my Poetry;
Wink at small faults, the greater, ne'rthelesse
Hide, and with them, their Fathers nakedness.
Let's doe our best, our Watch and Ward to keep:
Homer himself, in a long work, may sleep.

To Criticks.

ILE write, because Ile give
You Criticks means to live:
For sho'd I not supply
The Cause, th'effect wo'd die.

Duty to Tyrants.

GOOD Princes must be pray'd for: for the bad
They must be borne with, and in rev'rence had.
Doe they first pill thee, next, pluck off thy skin?
Good children kisse the rods, that punish sin.
Touch not the Tyrant; Let the Gods alone
To strike him dead, that but usurps a Throne.

Being once blind, his request to Biancha.

WHEN Age or Chance has made me blind,
So that the path I cannot find:
And when my falls and stumblings are
More then the stones i'th'street by farre:

l. 12 ye *ed.*: you *48*   3.2 must] mnst *48* (*? turned* u)   3.4 *rods K2 rod rest* (*corr. Errata to Rods*)

Goe thou afore; and I shall well
Follow thy Perfumes by the smell:
Or be my guide; and I shall be
Led by some light that flows from thee.
Thus held, or led by thee, I shall
In wayes confus'd, nor slip or fall.

Upon Blanch.

BLANCH swears her Husband's lovely; when a scald
Has blear'd his eyes: Besides, his head is bald.
Next, his wilde eares, like Lethern wings full spread,
Flutter to flie, and beare away his head.

No want where there's little.

TO Bread and Water none is poore;
And having these, what need of more?
Though much from out the Cess be spent,
Nature with little is content.

Barly-Break: or, *Last in Hell.*

WE two are last in Hell: what may we feare
To be tormented, or kept Pris'ners here?
Alas! If kissing be of plagues the worst,
We'll wish, in Hell we had been Last and First.

The Definition of Beauty.

BEAUTY, no other thing is, then a Beame
Flasht out between the Middle and Extreame.

To Dianeme.

DEARE, though to part it be a Hell,
Yet *Dianeme* now farewell:
Thy frown (last night) did bid me goe;
But whither, onely Grief do's know.
I doe beseech thee, ere we part,
(If mercifull, as faire thou art;

Or else desir'st that Maids sho'd tell
Thy pitty by Loves-Chronicle)
O *Dianeme*, rather kill
Me, then to make me languish stil!
'Tis cruelty in thee to'th'height,
Thus, thus to wound, not kill out-right:
Yet there's a way found (if thou please)
By sudden death to give me ease:
And thus devis'd, doe thou but this,
Bequeath to me one parting kisse:
So sup'rabundant joy shall be
The Executioner of me.

To Anthea *lying in bed.*

So looks *Anthea*, when in bed she lyes,
Orecome, or halfe betray'd by Tiffanies:
Like to a Twi-light, or that simpring Dawn,
That Roses shew, when misted o're with Lawn.
Twilight is yet, till that her Lawnes give way;
Which done, that Dawne, turnes then to perfect day.

To Electra.

MORE white then whitest Lillies far,
Or Snow, or whitest Swans you are:
More white then are the whitest Creames,
Or Moone-light tinselling the streames:
More white then *Pearls*, or *Juno's* thigh;
Or *Pelops* Arme of *Yvorie*.
True, I confesse; such Whites as these
May me delight, not fully please:
Till, like *Ixion's* Cloud you be
White, warme, and soft to lye with me.

A Country life: To his Brother, *M.* Tho: Herrick.

THRICE, and above, blest (my soules halfe) art thou,
In thy both Last, and Better Vow:

3 *For variants see pp.* 463–5

Could'st leave the City, for exchange, to see
    The Countries sweet simplicity:
And it to know, and practice; with intent
    To grow the sooner innocent:
By studying to know vertue; and to aime
    More at her nature, then her name:
The last is but the least; the first doth tell
    Wayes lesse to live, then to live well:
And both are knowne to thee, who now can'st live
    Led by thy conscience; to give
Justice to soone-pleas'd nature; and to show,
    Wisdome and she together goe,
And keep one Centre: This with that conspires,
    To teach Man to confine desires:
And know, that Riches have their proper stint,
    In the contented mind, not mint.
And can'st instruct, that those who have the itch
    Of craving more, are never rich.
These things thou know'st to'th'height, and dost prevent
    That plague; because thou art content
With that Heav'n gave thee with a warie hand,
    (More blessed in thy Brasse, then Land)
To keep cheap Nature even, and upright;
    To coole, not cocker Appetite.
Thus thou canst tearcely live to satisfie
    The belly chiefly; not the eye:
Keeping the barking stomach wisely quiet,
    Lesse with a neat, then needfull diet.
But that which most makes sweet thy country life,
    Is, the fruition of a wife:
Whom (Stars consenting with thy Fate) thou hast
    Got, not so beautifull, as chast:
By whose warme side thou dost securely sleep
    (While Love the Centinell doth keep)
With those deeds done by day, which n'er affright
    Thy silken slumbers in the night.
Nor has the darknesse power to usher in
    Feare to those sheets, that know no sin.
But still thy wife, by chast intentions led,
    Gives thee each night a Maidenhead.
The Damaskt medowes, and the peebly streames
    Sweeten, and make soft your dreames:

The Purling springs, groves, birds, and well-weav'd Bowrs,
With fields enameled with flowers,
Present their shapes; while fantasie discloses
Millions of *Lillies* mixt with *Roses*.
Then dream, ye heare the Lamb by many a bleat
Woo'd to come suck the milkie Teat:
While *Faunus* in the Vision comes to keep,
From rav'ning wolves, the fleecie sheep.
With thousand such enchanting dreams, that meet
To make sleep not so sound, as sweet:
Nor can these figures so thy rest endeare,
As not to rise when *Chanticlere*
Warnes the last Watch; but with the Dawne dost rise
To work, but first to sacrifice;
Making thy peace with heav'n, for some late fault,
With Holy-meale, and spirting-salt.
Which done, thy painfull Thumb this sentence tells us,
Jove for our labour all things sells us.
Nor are thy daily and devout affaires
Attended with those desp'rate cares,
Th'industrious Merchant has; who for to find
Gold, runneth to the Western Inde,
And back again, (tortur'd with fears) doth fly,
Untaught, to suffer Poverty.
But thou at home, blest with securest ease,
Sitt'st, and beleev'st that there be seas,
And watrie dangers; while thy whiter hap,
But sees these things within thy Map.
And viewing them with a more safe survey,
Mak'st easie Feare unto thee say,
A heart thrice wall'd with Oke, and Brasse, that man
Had, first, durst plow the Ocean.
But thou at home without or tyde or gale,
Canst in thy Map securely saile:
Seeing those painted Countries; and so guesse
By those fine Shades, their Substances:
And from thy Compasse taking small advice,
Buy'st Travell at the lowest price.
Nor are thine eares so deafe, but thou canst heare
(Far more with wonder, then with feare)
Fame tell of States, of Countries, Courts, and Kings;
And beleeve there be such things:

When of these truths, thy happyer knowledge lyes,
    More in thine eares, then in thine eyes.
And when thou hear'st by that too-true-Report,
    Vice rules the Most, or All at Court:
Thy pious wishes are, (though thou not there)
    Vertue had, and mov'd her Sphere.
But thou liv'st fearlesse; and thy face ne'r shewes
    Fortune when she comes, or goes.
But with thy equall thoughts, prepar'd dost stand,
    To take her by the either hand:
Nor car'st which comes the first, the foule or faire;
    A wise man ev'ry way lies square.
And like a surly *Oke* with storms perplext;
    Growes still the stronger, strongly vext.
Be so, bold spirit; Stand Center-like, unmov'd;
    And be not onely thought, but prov'd
To be what I report thee; and inure
    Thy selfe, if want comes to endure:
And so thou dost: for thy desires are
    Confin'd to live with private *Larr:*
Not curious whether Appetite be fed,
    Or with the first, or second bread.
Who keep'st no proud mouth for delicious cates:
    Hunger makes coorse meats, delicates.
Can'st, and unurg'd, forsake that Larded fare,
    Which Art, not Nature, makes so rare;
To taste boyl'd Nettles, Colworts, Beets, and eate
    These, and sowre herbs, as dainty meat?
While soft Opinion makes thy *Genius* say,
    Content makes all Ambrosia.
Nor is it, that thou keep'st this stricter size
    So much for want, as exercise:
To numb the sence of Dearth, which sho'd sinne haste it,
    Thou might'st but onely see't, not taste it.
Yet can thy humble roofe maintaine a Quire
    Of singing Crickits by thy fire:
And the brisk Mouse may feast her selfe with crums,
    Till that the green-ey'd Kitling comes.
Then to her Cabbin, blest she can escape
    The sudden danger of a Rape.
And thus thy little-well-kept-stock doth prove,
    Wealth cannot make a life, but Love.

Nor art thou so close-handed, but can'st spend
(Counsell concurring with the end)
As well as spare: still conning o'r this Theame,
To shun the first, and last extreame.
Ordaining that thy small stock find no breach,
Or to exceed thy Tether's reach:
But to live round, and close, and wisely true
To thine owne selfe; and knowne to few.
Thus let thy Rurall Sanctuary be
Elizium to thy wife and thee;
There to disport your selves with golden measure:
For seldome use commends the pleasure.
Live, and live blest; thrice happy Paire; Let Breath,
But lost to one, be th'others death.
And as there is one Love, one Faith, one Troth,
Be so one Death, one Grave to both.
Till when, in such assurance live, ye may
Nor feare, or wish your dying day.

Divination by a Daffadill.

WHEN a Daffadill I see,
Hanging down his head t'wards me;
Guesse I may, what I must be:
First, I shall decline my head;
Secondly, I shall be dead;
Lastly, safely buryed.

To the Painter, to draw him a Picture.

COME, skilfull *Lupo*, now, and take
Thy *Bice*, thy *Umber*, *Pink*, and *Lake*;
And let it be thy Pensils strife,
To paint a Bridgeman to the life:
Draw him as like too, as you can,
An old, poore, lying, flatt'ring man:
His cheeks be-pimpled, red and blue;
His nose and lips of mulbrie hiew.

Then for an easie fansie; place
A Burling iron for his face:
Next, make his cheeks with breath to swell,
And for to speak, if possible:
But do not so; for feare, lest he
Sho'd by his breathing, poyson thee.

Upon Cuffe. *Epig.*

CUFFE comes to Church much; but he keeps his bed
Those Sundayes onely, when as Briefs are read.
This makes *Cuffe* dull; and troubles him the most,
Because he cannot sleep i'th'Church, free-cost.

Upon Fone *a School-master.* Epig.

FONE sayes, those mighty whiskers he do's weare,
Are twigs of Birch, and willow, growing there:
If so, we'll think too, (when he do's condemne
Boyes to the lash) that he do's whip with them.

A Lyrick to Mirth.

WHILE the milder Fates consent,
Let's enjoy our merryment:
Drink, and dance, and pipe, and play;
Kisse our *Dollies* night and day:
Crown'd with clusters of the Vine;
Let us sit, and quaffe our wine.
Call on *Bacchus*; chaunt his praise;
Shake the *Thyrse*, and bite the *Bayes*:
Rouze *Anacreon* from the dead;
And return him drunk to bed:
Sing o're *Horace*; for ere long
Death will come and mar the song:
Then shall *Wilson* and *Gotiere*
Never sing, or play more here.

3 *For variants see p.* 465   3.13 *Gotiere*] *Coteire* 48 (*corr. Errata*)

To the Earle of Westmerland.

WHEN my date's done, and my gray age must die;
Nurse up, great Lord, this my posterity:
Weak though it be; long may it grow, and stand,
Shor'd up by you, (*Brave Earle of Westmerland.*)

Against Love.

WHEN ere my heart, Love's warmth, but entertaines,
O Frost! O Snow! O Haile forbid the Banes.
One drop now deads a spark; but if the same
Once gets a force, Floods cannot quench the flame.
Rather then love, let me be ever lost;
Or let me 'gender with eternall frost.

Upon Julia's *Riband.*

AS shews the Aire, when with a Rain-bow grac'd;
So smiles that Riband 'bout my *Julia*'s waste:
Or like——Nay 'tis that *Zonulet* of love,
Wherein all pleasures of the world are wove.

The frozen Zone: or, Julia *disdainfull.*

WHITHER? Say, whither shall I fly,
To slack these flames wherein I frie?
To the Treasures, shall I goe,
Of the Raine, Frost, Haile, and Snow?
Shall I search the under-ground,
Where all Damps, and Mists are found?
Shall I seek (for speedy ease)
All the floods, and frozen seas?
Or descend into the deep,
Where eternall cold does keep?
These may coole; but there's a Zone
Colder yet then any one:
That's my *Julia*'s breast; where dwels
Such destructive Ysicles;
As that the Congelation will
Me sooner starve, then those can kill.

An Epitaph upon a sober Matron.

WITH blamelesse carriage, I liv'd here,
To'th' (almost) sev'n and fortieth yeare.
Stout sons I had, and those twice three;
One onely daughter lent to me:
The which was made a happy Bride,
But thrice three Moones before she dy'd.
My modest wedlock, that was known
Contented with the bed of one.

To the Patron of Poets, *M.* End: Porter.

LET there be Patrons; Patrons like to thee,
Brave *Porter!* Poets ne'r will wanting be:
Fabius, and *Cotta*, *Lentulus*, all live
In thee, thou Man of Men! who here do'st give
Not onely subject-matter for our wit,
But likewise Oyle of Maintenance to it:
For which, before thy Threshold, we'll lay downe
Our Thyrse, for Scepter; and our Baies for Crown.
For to say truth, all Garlands are thy due;
The *Laurell*, *Mirtle*, *Oke*, and *Ivie* too.

The sadnesse of things for Sapho's *sicknesse.*

LILLIES will languish; Violets look ill;
Sickly the Prim-rose: Pale the Daffadill:
That gallant Tulip will hang down his head,
Like to a Virgin newly ravished.
Pansies will weep; and Marygolds will wither;
And keep a Fast, and Funerall together,
If *Sapho* droop; Daisies will open never,
But bid Good-night, and close their lids for ever.

Leanders *Obsequies.*

WHEN as *Leander* young was drown'd,
No heart by love receiv'd a wound;
But on a Rock himselfe sate by,
There weeping sup'rabundantly.
Sighs numberlesse he cast about,
And all his Tapers thus put out:
His head upon his hand he laid;
And sobbing deeply, thus he said,
Ah cruell Sea! and looking on't,
Wept as he'd drowne the Hellespont.
And sure his tongue had more exprest,
But that his teares forbad the rest.

Hope heartens.

NONE goes to warfare, but with this intent;
The gaines must dead the feare of detriment.

Foure things make us happy here.

HEALTH is the first good lent to men;
A gentle disposition then:
Next, to be rich by no by-wayes;
Lastly, with friends t'enjoy our dayes.

His parting from M[rs] Dorothy Keneday.

WHEN I did goe from thee, I felt that smart,
Which Bodies do, when Souls from them depart.
Thou did'st not mind it; though thou then might'st see
Me turn'd to tears; yet did'st not weep for me.
'Tis true, I kist thee; but I co'd not heare
Thee spend a sigh, t'accompany my teare.
Me thought 'twas strange, that thou so hard sho'dst prove,
Whose heart, whose hand, whose ev'ry part spake love.
Prethee (lest Maids sho'd censure thee) but say
Thou shed'st one teare, when as I went away;
And that will please me somewhat: though I know,
And Love will swear't, my Dearest did not so.

1 *For variants see p.* 465

The Teare sent to her from Stanes.

1. GLIDE gentle streams, and beare
Along with you my teare
To that coy Girle;
Who smiles, yet slayes
Me with delayes;
And strings my tears as Pearle.

2. See! see she's yonder set,
Making a Carkanet
Of Maiden-flowers!
There, there present
This Orient,
And Pendant Pearle of ours.

3. Then say, I've sent one more
Jem to enrich her store;
And that is all
Which I can send,
Or vainly spend,
For tears no more will fall.

4. Nor will I seek supply
Of them, the spring's once drie;
But Ile devise,
(Among the rest)
A way that's best
How I may save mine eyes.

5. Yet say; sho'd she condemne
Me to surrender them;
Then say; my part
Must be to weep
Out them, to keep
A poore, yet loving heart.

6. Say too, She wo'd have this;
She shall: Then my hope is,
That when I'm poore,
And nothing have
To send, or save;
I'm sure she'll ask no more.

Upon one Lillie, *who marryed with a maid call'd* Rose.

WHAT times of sweetnesse this faire day fore-shows,
When as the Lilly marries with the Rose!
What next is lookt for? but we all sho'd see
To spring from these a sweet Posterity.

An Epitaph upon a child.

VIRGINS promis'd when I dy'd,
That they wo'd each Primrose-tide,
Duely, Morne and Ev'ning, come,
And with flowers dresse my Tomb.
Having promis'd, pay your debts,
Maids, and here strew Violets.

Upon Scobble. *Epig.*

S*COBBLE* for Whoredome whips his wife; and cryes,
He'll slit her nose; But blubb'ring, she replyes,
Good Sir, make no more cuts i'th'outward skin,
One slit's enough to let Adultry in.

The Houre-glasse.

THAT Houre-glasse, which there ye see
With Water fill'd, (Sirs, credit me)
The humour was, (as I have read)
But Lovers tears inchristalled.
Which, as they drop by drop doe passe
From th'upper to the under-glasse,
Do in a trickling manner tell,
(By many a watrie syllable)
That Lovers tears in life-time shed,
Do restless run when they are dead.

His fare-well to Sack.

FAREWELL thou Thing, time-past so knowne, so deare
To me, as blood to life and spirit: Neare,
Nay, thou more neare then kindred, friend, man, wife,
Male to the female, soule to body: Life
To quick action, or the warme soft side
Of the resigning, yet resisting Bride.
The kisse of Virgins; First-fruits of the bed;
Soft speech, smooth touch, the lips, the Maiden-head:
These, and a thousand sweets, co'd never be
So neare, or deare, as thou wast once to me.
O thou the drink of Gods, and Angels! Wine
That scatter'st Spirit and Lust; whose purest shine,
More radiant then the Summers Sun-beams shows;
Each way illustrious, brave; and like to those
Comets we see by night; whose shagg'd portents
Fore-tell the comming of some dire events:
Or some full flame, which with a pride aspires,
Throwing about his wild, and active fires.
'Tis thou, above Nectar, O Divinest soule!
(Eternall in thy self) that canst controule
That, which subverts whole nature, grief and care;
Vexation of the mind, and damn'd Despaire.
'Tis thou, alone, who with thy Mistick Fan,
Work'st more then Wisdome, Art, or Nature can,
To rouze the sacred madnesse; and awake
The frost-bound-blood, and spirits; and to make
Them frantick with thy raptures, flashing through
The soule, like lightning, and as active too.
'Tis not *Apollo* can, or those thrice three
Castalian Sisters, sing, if wanting thee.
Horace, *Anacreon* both had lost their fame,
Had'st thou not fill'd them with thy fire and flame.
Phœbean splendour! and thou *Thespian* spring!
Of which, sweet Swans must drink, before they sing
Their true-pac'd-Numbers, and their Holy-Layes,
Which makes them worthy *Cedar*, and the *Bayes*.
But why? why longer doe I gaze upon
Thee with the eye of admiration?

1 *For variants see pp.* 465–7

Since I must leave thee; and enforc'd, must say
To all thy witching beauties, Goe, Away.
But if thy whimpring looks doe ask me why?
Then know, that Nature bids thee goe, not I.
'Tis her erroneous self has made a braine
Uncapable of such a Soveraigne,
As is thy powerfull selfe. Prethee not smile;
Or smile more inly; lest thy looks beguile
My vowes denounc'd in zeale, which thus much show thee,
That I have sworn, but by thy looks to know thee.
Let others drink thee freely; and desire
Thee and their lips espous'd; while I admire,
And love thee; but not taste thee. Let my Muse
Faile of thy former helps; and onely use
Her inadult'rate strength: what's done by me
Hereafter, shall smell of the Lamp, not thee.

Upon Glasco. *Epig.*

GLASCO had none, but now some teeth has got;
Which though they furre, will neither ake, or rot.
Six teeth he has, whereof twice two are known
Made of a Haft, that was a Mutton-bone.
Which not for use, but meerly for the sight,
He weares all day, and drawes those teeth at night.

Upon Mrs. Eliz: Wheeler, *under the name of Amarillis.*

SWEET *Amarillis*, by a Spring's
Soft and soule-melting murmurings,
Slept; and thus sleeping, thither flew
A *Robin-Red-brest*; who at view,
Not seeing her at all to stir,
Brought leaves and mosse to cover her:
But while he, perking, there did prie
About the Arch of either eye;
The lid began to let out day;
At which poore *Robin* flew away:
And seeing her not dead, but all disleav'd;
He chirpt for joy, to see himself disceav'd.

The Custard.

FOR second course, last night, a Custard came
To th'board, so hot, as none co'd touch the same:
Furze, three or foure times with his cheeks did blow
Upon the Custard, and thus cooled so:
It seem'd by this time to admit the touch;
But none co'd eate it, 'cause it stunk so much.

To Myrrha *hard-hearted.*

FOLD now thine armes; and hang the head,
Like to a Lillie withered:
Next, look thou like a sickly Moone;
Or like *Jocasta* in a swoone.
Then weep, and sigh, and softly goe,
Like to a widdow drown'd in woe:
Or like a Virgin full of ruth,
For the lost sweet-heart of her youth:
And all because, Faire Maid, thou art
Insensible of all my smart;
And of those evill dayes that be
Now posting on to punish thee.
The Gods are easie, and condemne
All such as are not soft like them.

The Eye.

MAKE me a heaven; and make me there
Many a lesse and greater spheare.
Make me the straight, and oblique lines;
The Motions, Lations, and the Signes.
Make me a Chariot, and a Sun;
And let them through a Zodiac run:
Next, place me Zones, and Tropicks there;
With all the Seasons of the Yeare.
Make me a Sun-set; and a Night:
And then present the Mornings-light
Cloath'd in her Chamlets of Delight.
To these, make Clouds to poure downe raine;
With weather foule, then faire againe.

And when, wise Artist, that thou hast,
With all that can be, this heaven grac't;
Ah! what is then this curious skie,
But onely my *Corinna's* eye?

Upon the much lamented, *Mr.* J. Warr.

WHAT Wisdome, Learning, Wit, or Worth,
Youth, or sweet Nature, co'd bring forth,
Rests here with him; who was the Fame,
The Volumne of himselfe, and Name.
If, Reader, then thou wilt draw neere,
And doe an honour to thy teare;
Weep then for him, for whom laments
Not one, but many Monuments.

Upon Gryll.

GRYLL eates, but ne're sayes Grace; To speak the troth,
Gryll either keeps his breath to coole his broth;
Or else because *Grill's* roste do's burn his Spit,
Gryll will not therefore say a Grace for it.

The suspition upon his over-much familiarity with a Gentlewoman.

AND must we part, because some say,
Loud is our love, and loose our play,
And more then well becomes the day?
Alas for pitty! and for us
Most innocent, and injur'd thus.
Had we kept close, or play'd within,
Suspition now had been the sinne,
And shame had follow'd long ere this,
T'ave plagu'd, what now unpunisht is.
But we as fearlesse of the Sunne,
As faultlesse; will not wish undone,
What now is done: since *where no sin*
Unbolts the doore, no shame comes in.

Then comely and most fragrant Maid,
Be you more warie, then afraid
Of these Reports; because you see
The fairest most suspected be.
The common formes have no one eye,
Or eare of burning jealousie
To follow them: but chiefly, where
Love makes the cheek, and chin a sphere
To dance and play in: (Trust me) there
Suspicion questions every haire.
Come, you are faire; and sho'd be seen
While you are in your sprightfull green:
And what though you had been embrac't
By me, were you for that unchast?
No, no, no more then is yond' Moone,
Which shining in her perfect Noone;
In all that great and glorious light,
Continues cold, as is the night.
Then, beauteous Maid, you may retire;
And as for me, my chast desire
Shall move t'wards you; although I see
Your face no more: So live you free
From Fames black lips, as you from me.

Single life most secure.

SUSPICION, Discontent, and Strife,
Come in for Dowrie with a Wife.

The Curse. A Song.

GOE perjur'd man; and if thou ere return
To see the small remainders in mine Urne:
When thou shalt laugh at my Religious dust;
And ask, Where's now the colour, forme and trust
Of Womans beauty? and with hand more rude
Rifle the Flowers which the Virgins strew'd:
Know, I have pray'd to Furie, that some wind
May blow my ashes up, and strike thee blind.

The wounded Cupid. *Song.*

CUPID as he lay among
Roses, by a Bee was stung.
Whereupon in anger flying
To his Mother, said thus crying;
Help! O help! your Boy's a dying.
And why, my pretty Lad, said she?
Then blubbering, replyed he,
A winged Snake has bitten me,
Which Country people call a Bee.
At which she smil'd; then with her hairs
And kisses drying up his tears:
Alas! said she, my Wag! if this
Such a pernicious torment is:
Come, tel me then, how great's the smart
Of those, thou woundest with thy Dart!

To Dewes. A Song.

I BURN, I burn; and beg of you
To quench, or coole me with your Dew.
I frie in fire, and so consume,
Although the Pile be all perfume.
Alas! the heat and death's the same;
Whether by choice, or common flame:
To be in Oyle of *Roses* drown'd,
Or water; where's the comfort found?
Both bring one death; and I die here,
Unlesse you coole me with a Teare:
Alas! I call; but ah! I see
Ye coole, and comfort all, but me.

Some comfort in calamity.

TO conquer'd men, some comfort 'tis to fall
By th'hand of him who is the Generall.

1 *and* 2 *For variants see p.* 468 1.14 Come,] *stop uncertain or abse*
in BCEUWi

The Vision.

SITTING alone (as one forsook)
Close by a Silver-shedding Brook;
With hands held up to Love, I wept;
And after sorrowes spent, I slept:
Then in a Vision I did see
A glorious forme appeare to me:
A Virgins face she had; her dresse
Was like a sprightly *Spartanesse.*
A silver bow with green silk strung,
Down from her comely shoulders hung:
And as she stood, the wanton Aire
Dandled the ringlets of her haire.
Her legs were such *Diana* shows,
When tuckt up she a hunting goes;
With Buskins shortned to descrie
The happy dawning of her thigh:
Which when I saw, I made accesse
To kisse that tempting nakednesse:
But she forbad me, with a wand
Of Mirtle she had in her hand:
And chiding me, said, Hence, Remove,
Herrick, thou art too coorse to love.

Love me little, love me long.

YOU say, to me-wards your affection's strong;
Pray love me little, so you love me long.
Slowly goes farre: The meane is best: Desire
Grown violent, do's either die, or tire.

Upon a Virgin kissing a Rose.

'TWAS but a single *Rose*,
Till you on it did breathe;
But since (me thinks) it shows
Not so much *Rose*, as Wreathe.

Upon a Wife that dyed mad with Jealousie.

IN this little Vault she lyes,
Here, with all her jealousies:
Quiet yet; but if ye make
Any noise, they both will wake,
And such spirits raise, 'twill then
Trouble Death to lay agen.

Upon the Bishop of Lincolne's *Imprisonment.*

NEVER was Day so over-sick with showres,
But that it had some intermitting houres.
Never was Night so tedious, but it knew
The Last Watch out, and saw the Dawning too.
Never was Dungeon so obscurely deep,
Wherein or Light, or Day, did never peep.
Never did Moone so ebbe, or seas so wane,
But they left Hope-seed to fill up againe.
So you, my Lord, though you have now your stay,
Your Night, your Prison, and your Ebbe; you may
Spring up afresh; when all these mists are spent,
And Star-like, once more, guild our Firmament.
Let but That Mighty *Cesar* speak, and then,
All bolts, all barres, all gates shall cleave; as when
That Earth-quake shook the house, and gave the stout
Apostles, way (unshackled) to goe out.
This, as I wish for, so I hope to see;
Though you (my Lord) have been unkind to me:
To wound my heart, and never to apply
(When you had power) the meanest remedy:
Well; though my griefe by you was gall'd, the more;
Yet I bring Balme and Oile to heal your sore.

Disswasions from Idlenesse.

CYNTHIUS pluck ye by the eare,
That ye may good doctrine heare.
Play not with the maiden-haire;
For each Ringlet there's a snare.
Cheek, and eye, and lip, and chin;
These are traps to take fooles in.

Armes, and hands, and all parts else,
Are but Toiles, or Manicles
Set on purpose to enthrall
Men, but Slothfulls most of all.
Live employ'd, and so live free
From these fetters; like to me
Who have found, and still can prove,
The lazie man the most doth love.

Upon Strut.

STRUT, once a Fore-man of a Shop we knew;
But turn'd a Ladies Usher now, ('tis true:)
Tell me, has *Strut* got ere a title more?
No; he's but Fore-man, as he was before.

An Epithalamie to Sir Thomas Southwell *and his Ladie.*

I.

NOW, now's the time; so oft by truth
Promis'd sho'd come to crown your youth.
Then Faire ones, doe not wrong
Your joyes, by staying long:
Or let Love's fire goe out,
By lingring thus in doubt:
But learn, that Time once lost,
Is ne'r redeem'd by cost.
Then away; come, *Hymen* guide
To the bed, the bashfull Bride.

II.

Is it (sweet maid) your fault these holy
Bridall-Rites goe on so slowly?
Deare, is it this you dread,
The losse of Maiden-head?
Beleeve me; you will most
Esteeme it when 'tis lost:
Then it no longer keep,
Lest Issue lye asleep.
Then away; come, *Hymen* guide
To the bed, the bashfull Bride.

III.

These Precious-Pearly-Purling teares,
But spring from ceremonious feares.
    And 'tis but Native shame,
    That hides the loving flame:
    And may a while controule
    The soft and am'rous soule;
    But yet, Loves fire will wast
    Such bashfulnesse at last.
Then away; come, *Hymen* guide
To the bed, the bashfull Bride.

IV.

Night now hath watch'd her self half blind;
Yet not a Maiden-head resign'd!
    'Tis strange, ye will not flie
    To Love's sweet mysterie.
    Might yon Full-Moon the sweets
    Have, promis'd to your sheets;
    She soon wo'd leave her spheare,
    To be admitted there.
Then away; come, *Hymen* guide
To the bed, the bashfull Bride.

V.

On, on devoutly, make no stay;
While *Domiduca* leads the way:
    And *Genius* who attends
    The bed for luckie ends:
    With *Juno* goes the houres,
    And Graces strewing flowers.
    And the boyes with sweet tunes sing,
    Hymen, O *Hymen* bring
Home the Turtles; *Hymen* guide
To the bed, the bashfull Bride.

VI.

Behold! how *Hymens* Taper-light
Shews you how much is spent of night.
    See, see the Bride-grooms Torch
    Halfe wasted in the porch.

And now those Tapers five,
That shew the womb shall thrive:
Their silv'rie flames advance,
To tell all prosp'rous chance
Still shall crown the happy life
Of the good man and the wife.

VII.

Move forward then your Rosie feet,
And make, what ere they touch, turn sweet.
May all, like flowrie Meads
Smell, where your soft foot treads;
And every thing assume
To it, the like perfume:
As *Zephirus* when he 'spires
Through *Woodbine*, and *Sweet-bryers*.
Then away; come *Hymen*, guide
To the bed the bashfull Bride.

VIII.

And now the yellow Vaile, at last,
Over her fragrant cheek is cast.
Now seems she to expresse
A bashfull willingnesse:
Shewing a heart consenting;
As with a will repenting.
Then gently lead her on
With wise suspicion:
For that, Matrons say, a measure
Of that Passion sweetens Pleasure.

IX.

You, you that be of her neerest kin,
Now o're the threshold force her in.
But to avert the worst;
Let her, her fillets first
Knit to the posts: this point
Remembring, to anoint
The sides: for 'tis a charme
Strong against future harme:
And the evil deads, the which
There was hidden by the Witch.

X.

O *Venus!* thou, to whom is known
The best way how to loose the Zone
Of Virgins! Tell the Maid,
She need not be afraid:
And bid the Youth apply
Close kisses, if she cry:
And charge, he not forbears
Her, though she wooe with teares.
Tel them, now they must adventer,
Since that Love and Night bid enter.

XI.

No Fatal Owle the Bedsted keeps,
With direful notes to fright your sleeps:
No Furies, here about,
To put the Tapers out,
Watch, or did make the bed:
'Tis *Omen* full of dread:
But all faire signs appeare
Within the Chamber here.
Juno here, far off, doth stand
Cooling sleep with charming wand.

XII.

Virgins, weep not; 'twill come, when,
As she, so you'l be ripe for men.
Then grieve her not, with saying
She must no more a Maying:
Or by Rose-buds devine,
Who'l be her Valentine.
Nor name those wanton reaks
Y'ave had at Barly-breaks.
But now kisse her, and thus say,
Take time Lady while ye may.

XIII.

Now barre the doors, the Bride-groom puts
The eager Boyes to gather Nuts.
And now, both Love and Time
To their full height doe clime:

O! give them active heat
And moisture, both compleat:
Fit Organs for encrease,
To keep, and to release
That, which may the honour'd Stem
Circle with a Diadem.

XIV.

And now, Behold! the Bed or Couch
That ne'r knew Brides, or Bride-grooms touch,
Feels in it selfe a fire;
And tickled with Desire,
Pants with a Downie brest,
As with a heart possest:
Shrugging as it did move,
Ev'n with the soule of love.
And (oh!) had it but a tongue,
Doves, 'two'd say, yee bill too long.

XV.

O enter then! but see ye shun
A sleep, untill the act be done.
Let kisses, in their close,
Breathe as the Damask Rose:
Or sweet, as is that gumme
Doth from *Panchaia* come.
Teach Nature now to know,
Lips can make Cherries grow
Sooner, then she, ever yet,
In her wisdome co'd beget.

XVI.

On your minutes, hours, dayes, months, years,
Drop the fat blessing of the sphears.
That good, which Heav'n can give
To make you bravely live;
Fall, like a spangling dew,
By day, and night on you.
May Fortunes Lilly-hand
Open at your command;
With all luckie Birds to side
With the Bride-groom, and the Bride.

XVII.

Let bounteous Fate your spindles full
Fill, and winde up with whitest wooll.
    Let them not cut the thred
    Of life, untill ye bid.
    May Death yet come at last;
    And not with desp'rate hast:
    But when ye both can say,
    Come, Let us now away.
Be ye to the Barn then born,
Two, like two ripe shocks of corn.

Teares are Tongues.

WHEN *Julia* chid, I stood as mute the while,
As is the fish, or tonguelesse Crocadile.
Aire coyn'd to words, my *Julia* co'd not heare;
But she co'd see each eye to stamp a teare:
By which, mine angry Mistresse might descry,
Teares are the noble language of the eye.
And when true love of words is destitute,
The Eyes by tears speak, while the Tongue is mute.

Upon a young mother of many children.

LET all chaste Matrons, when they chance to see
My num'rous issue: Praise, and pitty me.
Praise me, for having such a fruitfull wombe;
Pity me too, who found so soone a Tomb.

To Electra.

ILE come to thee in all those shapes
As *Jove* did, when he made his rapes:
Onely, Ile not appeare to thee,
As he did once to *Semele.*
Thunder and Lightning Ile lay by,
To talk with thee familiarly.
Which done, then quickly we'll undresse
To one and th'others nakednesse.

And ravisht, plunge into the bed,
(Bodies and souls commingled)
And kissing, so as none may heare,
We'll weary all the Fables there.

His wish.

IT is sufficient if we pray
To *Jove*, who gives, and takes away:
Let him the Land and Living finde;
Let me alone to fit the mind.

His Protestation to Perilla.

NOONE-day and Midnight shall at once be seene:
Trees, at one time, shall be both sere and greene:
Fire and water shall together lye
In one-self-sweet-conspiring sympathie:
Summer and Winter shall at one time show
Ripe eares of corne, and up to th'eares in snow:
Seas shall be sandlesse; Fields devoid of grasse;
Shapelesse the world, (as when all *Chaos* was)
Before, my deare *Perilla*, I will be
False to my vow, or fall away from thee.

Love perfumes all parts.

IF I kisse *Anthea's* brest,
There I smell the Phenix nest:
If her lip, the most sincere
Altar of Incense, I smell there.
Hands, and thighs, and legs, are all
Richly Aromaticall.
Goddesse *Isis* cann't transfer
Musks and Ambers more from her:
Nor can *Juno* sweeter be,
When she lyes with *Jove*, then she.

To Julia.

PERMIT me, *Julia*, now to goe away;
Or by thy love, decree me here to stay.
If thou wilt say, that I shall live with thee;
Here shall my endless Tabernacle be:
If not, (as banisht) I will live alone
There, where no language ever yet was known.

On himselfe.

LOVE-sick I am, and must endure
A desp'rate grief, that finds no cure.
Ah me! I try; and trying, prove,
No Herbs have power to cure Love.
Only one Soveraign salve, I know,
And that is Death, the end of Woe.

Vertue is sensible of suffering.

THOUGH a wise man all pressures can sustaine;
His vertue still is sensible of paine:
Large shoulders though he has, and well can beare,
He feeles when Packs do pinch him; and the where.

The cruell Maid.

AND Cruell Maid, because I see
You scornfull of my love, and me:
Ile trouble you no more; but goe
My way, where you shall never know
What is become of me: there I
Will find me out a path to die;
Or learne some way how to forget
You, and your name, for ever: yet
Ere I go hence; know this from me,
What will, in time, your Fortune be:
This to your coynesse I will tell;
And having spoke it once, Farewell.
The Lillie will not long endure;
Nor the Snow continue pure:

2.5 one] our *48* (*corr. Errata*)

The Rose, the Violet, one day
See, both these Lady-flowers decay:
And you must fade, as well as they.
And it may chance that Love may turn,
And (like to mine) make your heart burn
And weep to see't; yet this thing doe,
That my last Vow commends to you:
When you shall see that I am dead,
For pitty let a teare be shed;
And (with your Mantle o're me cast)
Give my cold lips a kisse at last:
If twice you kisse, you need not feare,
That I shall stir, or live more here.
Next, hollow out a Tombe to cover
Me; me, the most despised Lover:
And write thereon, *This, Reader, know,*
Love kill'd this man. No more but so.

To Dianeme.

SWEET, be not proud of those two eyes,
Which Star-like sparkle in their skies:
Nor be you proud, that you can see
All hearts your captives; yours, yet free:
Be you not proud of that rich haire,
Which wantons with the Love-sick aire:
When as that *Rubie*, which you weare,
Sunk from the tip of your soft eare,
Will last to be a precious Stone,
When all your world of Beautie's gone.

TO THE KING,

To cure the Evill.

TO find that Tree of Life, whose Fruits did feed,
And Leaves did heale, all sick of humane seed:
To finde *Bethesda*, and an Angel there,
Stirring the waters, I am come; and here,
At last, I find, (after my much to doe)
The Tree, Bethesda, and the Angel too:

And all in Your Blest Hand, which has the powers
Of all those suppling-healing herbs and flowers.
To that soft *Charm*, that *Spell*, that *Magick Bough*,
That high Enchantment I betake me now:
And to that Hand, (the Branch of Heavens faire Tree)
I kneele for help; O! lay that hand on me,
Adored *Cesar*! and my Faith is such,
I shall be heal'd, if that my *KING* but touch.
The Evill is not Yours: my sorrow sings,
Mine is the Evill, but the Cure, the KINGS.

His misery in a Mistresse.

WATER, Water I espie:
Come, and coole ye; all who frie
In your loves; but none as I.

Though a thousand showres be
Still a falling, yet I see
Not one drop to light on me.

Happy you, who can have seas
For to quench ye, or some ease
From your kinder Mistresses.

I have one, and she alone,
Of a thousand thousand known,
Dead to all compassion.

Such an one, as will repeat
Both the cause, and make the heat
More by Provocation great.

Gentle friends, though I despaire
Of my cure, doe you beware
Of those Girles, which cruell are.

Upon Jollies *wife.*

FIRST, *Jollies* wife is lame; then next, loose-hipt:
Squint-ey'd, hook-nos'd; and lastly, Kidney-lipt.

1 *For variant heading see p.* 468

To a Gentlewoman, objecting to him his gray haires.

AM I despis'd, because you say,
And I dare sweare, that I am gray?
Know, Lady, you have but your day:
And time will come when you shall weare
Such frost and snow upon your haire:
And when (though long it comes to passe)
You question with your Looking-glasse;
And in that sincere *Christall* seek,
But find no Rose-bud in your cheek:
Nor any bed to give the shew
Where such a rare Carnation grew.
Ah! then too late, close in your chamber keeping,
It will be told
That you are old;
By those true teares y'are weeping.

To Cedars.

IF 'mongst my many Poems, I can see
One, onely, worthy to be washt by thee:
I live for ever; let the rest all lye
In dennes of Darkness, or condemn'd to die.

Upon Cupid.

LOVE, like a Gypsie, lately came;
And did me much importune
To see my hand; that by the same
He might fore-tell my Fortune.

He saw my Palme; and then, said he,
I tell thee, by this score here;
That thou, within few months, shalt be
The youthfull Prince *D'Amour* here.

1 *For variants see p.* 468

I smil'd; and bade him once more prove,
And by some crosse-line show it;
That I co'd ne'r be Prince of Love,
Though here the Princely Poet.

How Primroses came green.

VIRGINS, time-past, known were these,
Troubled with Green-sicknesses,
Turn'd to flowers: Stil the hieu,
Sickly Girles, they beare of you.

To Jos: *Lo: Bishop of* Exeter.

WHOM sho'd I feare to write to, if I can
Stand before you, my learn'd *Diocesan?*
And never shew blood-guiltinesse, or feare
To see my Lines *Excathedrated* here.
Since none so good are, but you may condemne;
Or here so bad, but you may pardon them.
If then, (my Lord) to sanctifie my Muse
One onely Poem out of all you'l chuse;
And mark it for a Rapture nobly writ,
'Tis Good Confirm'd; for you have Bishop't it.

Upon a black Twist, rounding the Arme of the Countesse of Carlile.

I SAW about her spotlesse wrist,
Of blackest silk, a curious twist;
Which, circumvolving gently, there
Enthrall'd her Arme, as Prisoner.
Dark was the Jayle; but as if light
Had met t'engender with the night;
Or so, as Darknesse made a stay
To shew at once, both night and day.
I fancie none! but if there be
Such Freedome in Captivity;
I beg of Love, that ever I
May in like Chains of Darknesse lie.

3.9 none *ed.*: more *48* (*see Commentary, p. 513*)

On himselfe.

I FEARE no Earthly Powers;
But care for crowns of flowers:
And love to have my Beard
With Wine and Oile besmear'd.
This day Ile drowne all sorrow;
Who knowes to live to morrow?

Upon Pagget.

PAGGET, a School-boy, got a Sword, and then
He vow'd Destruction both to Birch, and Men:
Who wo'd not think this Yonker fierce to fight?
Yet comming home, but somewhat late, (last night)
Untrusse, his Master bade him; and that word
Made him take up his shirt, lay down his sword.

A Ring presented to Julia.

JULIA, I bring
To thee this Ring,
Made for thy finger fit;
To shew by this,
That our love is
(Or sho'd be) like to it.

Close though it be,
The joynt is free:
So when Love's yoke is on,
It must not gall,
Or fret at all
With hard oppression.

But it must play
Still either way;
And be, too, such a yoke,
As not too wide,
To over-slide;
Or be so strait to choak.

3 *For variants see p.* 469

So we, who beare,
This beame, must reare
Our selves to such a height:
As that the stay
Of either may
Create the burden light.

And as this round
Is no where found
To flaw, or else to sever:
So let our love
As endless prove;
And pure as Gold for ever.

To the Detracter.

WHERE others love, and praise my Verses; still
Thy long-black-Thumb-nail marks 'em out for ill:
A fellon take it, or some Whit-flaw come
For to unslate, or to untile that thumb!
But cry thee Mercy: Exercise thy nailes
To scratch or claw, so that thy tongue not railes:
Some numbers prurient are, and some of these
Are wanton with their itch; scratch, and 'twill please.

Upon the same.

I ASK'T thee oft, what Poets thou hast read,
And lik'st the best? Still thou reply'st, The dead.
I shall, ere long, with green turfs cover'd be;
Then sure thou't like, or thou wilt envie me.

Julia's *Petticoat.*

THY Azure Robe, I did behold,
As ayrie as the leaves of gold;
Which erring here, and wandring there,
Pleas'd with transgression ev'ry where:
Sometimes 'two'd pant, and sigh, and heave,
As if to stir it scarce had leave:

But having got it; thereupon,
'Two'd make a brave expansion.
And pounc't with Stars, it shew'd to me
Like a *Celestiall Canopie.*
Sometimes 'two'd blaze, and then abate,
Like to a flame growne moderate:
Sometimes away 'two'd wildly fling;
Then to thy thighs so closely cling,
That some conceit did melt me downe,
As Lovers fall into a swoone:
And all confus'd, I there did lie
Drown'd in Delights; but co'd not die.
That Leading Cloud, I follow'd still,
Hoping t'ave seene of it my fill;
But ah! I co'd not: sho'd it move
To Life Eternal, I co'd love.

To Musick.

BEGIN to charme, and as thou stroak'st mine eares
With thy enchantment, melt me into tears.
Then let thy active hand scu'd o're thy Lyre:
And make my spirits frantick with the fire.
That done, sink down into a silv'rie straine;
And make me smooth as Balme, and Oile againe.

Distrust.

TO safe-guard Man from wrongs, there nothing must
Be truer to him, then a wise Distrust.
And to thy selfe be best this sentence knowne,
Heare all men speak; but credit few or none.

Corinna's *going a Maying.*

GET up, get up for shame, the Blooming Morne
Upon her wings presents the god unshorne.
See how *Aurora* throwes her faire
Fresh-quilted colours through the aire:
Get up, sweet-Slug-a-bed, and see
The Dew-bespangling Herbe and Tree.

Each Flower has wept, and bow'd toward the East,
Above an houre since; yet you not drest,
    Nay! not so much as out of bed?
    When all the Birds have Mattens seyd,
    And sung their thankfull Hymnes: 'tis sin,
    Nay, profanation to keep in,
When as a thousand Virgins on this day,
Spring, sooner then the Lark, to fetch in May.

Rise; and put on your Foliage, and be seene
To come forth, like the Spring-time, fresh and greene;
    And sweet as *Flora*. Take no care
    For Jewels for your Gowne, or Haire:
    Feare not; the leaves will strew
    Gemms in abundance upon you:
Besides, the childhood of the Day has kept,
Against you come, some *Orient Pearls* unwept:
    Come, and receive them while the light
    Hangs on the Dew-locks of the night:
    And *Titan* on the Eastern hill
    Retires himselfe, or else stands still
Till you come forth. Wash, dresse, be briefe in praying:
Few Beads are best, when once we goe a Maying.

Come, my *Corinna*, come; and comming, marke
How each field turns a street; each street a Parke
    Made green, and trimm'd with trees: see how
    Devotion gives each House a Bough,
    Or Branch: Each Porch, each doore, ere this,
    An Arke a Tabernacle is
Made up of white-thorn neatly enterwove;
As if here were those cooler shades of love.
    Can such delights be in the street,
    And open fields, and we not see't?
    Come, we'll abroad; and let's obay
    The Proclamation made for May:
And sin no more, as we have done, by staying;
But my *Corinna*, come, let's goe a Maying.

There's not a budding Boy, or Girle, this day,
But is got up, and gone to bring in May.
    A deale of Youth, ere this, is come
    Back, and with *White-thorn* laden home.
    Some have dispatcht their Cakes and Creame,
    Before that we have left to dreame:
And some have wept, and woo'd, and plighted Troth,
And chose their Priest, ere we can cast off sloth:
    Many a green-gown has been given;
    Many a kisse, both odde and even:
    Many a glance too has been sent
    From out the eye, Loves Firmament:
Many a jest told of the Keyes betraying
This night, and Locks pickt, yet w'are not a Maying.

Come, let us goe, while we are in our prime;
And take the harmlesse follie of the time.
    We shall grow old apace, and die
    Before we know our liberty.
    Our life is short; and our dayes run
    As fast away as do's the Sunne:
And as a vapour, or a drop of raine
Once lost, can ne'r be found againe:
    So when or you or I are made
    A fable, song, or fleeting shade;
    All love, all liking, all delight
    Lies drown'd with us in endlesse night.
Then while time serves, and we are but decaying;
Come, my *Corinna*, come, let's goe a Maying.

On Julia's *breath.*

BREATHE, *Julia*, breathe, and Ile protest,
    Nay more, Ile deeply sweare,
That all the Spices of the East
    Are circumfused there.

Upon a Child. An Epitaph.

BUT borne, and like a short Delight,
I glided by my Parents sight.
That done, the harder Fates deny'd
My longer stay, and so I dy'd.

If pittying my sad Parents Teares,
You'l spil a tear, or two with theirs:
And with some flowrs my grave bestrew,
Love and they'l thank you for't. Adieu.

A Dialogue betwixt Horace *and* Lydia, *Translated* Anno 1627. *and set by Mr.* Ro: Ramsey.

Hor. WHILE, *Lydia*, I was lov'd of thee,
Nor any was preferr'd 'fore me
To hug thy whitest neck: Then I,
The Persian King liv'd not more happily.

Lyd. While thou no other didst affect,
Nor *Cloe* was of more respect;
Then *Lydia*, far-fam'd *Lydia*,
I flourish't more then Roman *Ilia*.

Hor. Now *Thracian Cloe* governs me,
Skilfull i'th'Harpe, and Melodie:
For whose affection, *Lydia*, I
(So Fate spares her) am well content to die.

Lyd. My heart now set on fire is
By *Ornithes* sonne, young *Calais*;
For whose commutuall flames here I
(To save his life) twice am content to die.

Hor. Say our first loves we sho'd revoke,
And sever'd, joyne in brazen yoke:
Admit I *Cloe* put away,
And love againe love-cast-off *Lydia*?

Lyd. Though mine be brighter then the Star;
Thou lighter then the Cork by far:
Rough as th'*Adratick sea*, yet I
Will live with thee, or else for thee will die.

The captiv'd Bee: or, *The little Filcher.*

As *Julia* once a slumb'ring lay,
It chanc't a Bee did flie that way,
(After a dew, or dew-like shower)
To tipple freely in a flower.
For some rich flower, he took the lip
Of *Julia*, and began to sip;
But when he felt he suckt from thence
Hony, and in the quintessence:
He drank so much he scarce co'd stir;
So *Julia* took the Pilferer.
And thus surpriz'd (as Filchers use)
He thus began himselfe t'excuse:
Sweet *Lady-Flower*, I never brought
Hither the least one theeving thought:
But taking those rare lips of yours
For some fresh, fragrant, luscious flowers:
I thought I might there take a taste,
Where so much sirrop ran at waste.
Besides, know this, I never sting
The flower that gives me nourishing:
But with a kisse, or thanks, doe pay
For Honie, that I beare away.
This said, he laid his little *scrip*
Of hony, 'fore her Ladiship:
And told her, (as some tears did fall)
That, that he took, and that was all.
At which she smil'd; and bade him goe
And take his bag; but thus much know,
When next he came a pilfring so,
He sho'd from her full lips derive,
Hony enough to fill his hive.

Upon Prig.

Prig now drinks Water, who before drank Beere:
What's now the cause? we know the case is cleere:
Look in *Prig's* purse, the chev'rell there tells you
Prig mony wants, either to buy, or brew.

Upon Batt.

BATT he gets children, not for love to reare 'em;
But out of hope his wife might die to beare 'em.

An Ode to Master Endymion Porter, *upon his Brothers death.*

NOT all thy flushing Sunnes are set,
Herrick, as yet:
Nor doth this far-drawn Hemisphere
Frown, and look sullen ev'ry where.
Daies may conclude in nights; and Suns may rest,
As dead, within the West;
Yet the next Morne, re-guild the fragrant East.

Alas for me! that I have lost
E'en all almost:
Sunk is my sight; set is my Sun;
And all the loome of life undone:
The staffe, the Elme, the prop, the shelt'ring wall
Whereon my Vine did crawle,
Now, now, blowne downe; needs must the old stock fall.

Yet, *Porter*, while thou keep'st alive,
In death I thrive:
And like a *Phenix* re-aspire
From out my *Narde*, and Fun'rall fire:
And as I prune my feather'd youth, so I
Doe mar'l how I co'd die,
When I had Thee, my chiefe Preserver, by.

I'm up, I'm up, and blesse that hand,
Which makes me stand
Now as I doe; and but for thee,
I must confesse, I co'd not be.
The debt is paid: for he who doth resigne
Thanks to the gen'rous Vine;
Invites fresh Grapes to fill his Presse with Wine.

To his dying Brother, Master William Herrick.

LIFE of my life, take not so soone thy flight,
But stay the time till we have bade Good night.
Thou hast both Wind and Tide with thee; Thy way
As soone dispatcht is by the Night, as Day.
Let us not then so rudely henceforth goe
Till we have wept, kist, sigh't, shook hands, or so.
There's paine in parting; and a kind of hell,
When once true-lovers take their last Fare-well.
What? shall we two our endlesse leaves take here
Without a sad looke, or a solemne teare?
He knowes not Love, that hath not this truth proved,
Love is most loth to leave the thing beloved.
Pay we our Vowes, and goe; yet when we part,
Then, even then, I will bequeath my heart
Into thy loving hands: For Ile keep none
To warme my Breast, when thou my Pulse art gone.
No, here Ile last, and walk (a harmless shade)
About this Urne, wherein thy Dust is laid,
To guard it so, as nothing here shall be
Heavy, to hurt those sacred seeds of thee.

The Olive Branch.

SADLY I walk't within the field,
To see what comfort it wo'd yeeld:
And as I went my private way,
An Olive-branch before me lay:
And seeing it, I made a stay.
And took it up, and view'd it; then
Kissing the *Omen*, said Amen:
Be, be it so, and let this be
A Divination unto me:
That in short time my woes shall cease;
And Love shall crown my End with Peace.

Upon Much-more. *Epig.*

MUCH-MORE, provides, and hoords up like an Ant;
Yet *Much-more* still complains he is in want.
Let *Much-more* justly pay his tythes; then try
How both his Meale and Oile will multiply.

To Cherry-blossomes.

Ye may simper, blush, and smile,
And perfume the aire a while:
But (sweet things) ye must be gone;
Fruit, ye know, is comming on:
Then, Ah! Then, where is your grace,
When as Cherries come in place?

How Lillies came white.

White though ye be; yet, Lillies, know,
From the first ye were not so:
But Ile tell ye
What befell ye;
Cupid and his Mother lay
In a Cloud; while both did play,
He with his pretty finger prest
The rubie niplet of her breast;
Out of the which, the creame of light,
Like to a Dew,
Fell downe on you,
And made ye white.

To Pansies.

Ah, cruell Love! must I endure
Thy many scorns, and find no cure?
Say, are thy medicines made to be
Helps to all others, but to me?
Ile leave thee, and to *Pansies* come;
Comforts you'l afford me some:
You can ease my heart, and doe
What Love co'd ne'r be brought unto.

On Gelli-flowers begotten.

What was't that fell but now
From that warme kisse of ours?
Look, look, by Love I vow
They were two *Gelli-flowers*.

Let's kisse, and kisse agen;
For if so be our closes
Make *Gelli-flowers*, then
I'm sure they'l fashion *Roses*.

2 and 3 For variants see p. 469

The Lilly in a Christal.

YOU have beheld a smiling *Rose*
When Virgins hands have drawn
O'r it a Cobweb-Lawne:
And here, you see, this Lilly shows,
Tomb'd in a *Christal* stone,
More faire in this transparent case,
Then when it grew alone;
And had but single grace.

You see how *Creame* but naked is;
Nor daunces in the eye
Without a Strawberrie:
Or some fine tincture, like to this,
Which draws the sight thereto,
More by that wantoning with it;
Then when the paler hieu
No mixture did admit.

You see how *Amber* through the streams
More gently stroaks the sight,
With some conceal'd delight;
Then when he darts his radiant beams
Into the boundlesse aire:
Where either too much light his worth
Doth all at once impaire,
Or set it little forth.

Put Purple Grapes, or Cherries in-
To Glasse, and they will send
More beauty to commend
Them, from that cleane and subtile skin,
Then if they naked stood,
And had no other pride at all,
But their own flesh and blood,
And tinctures naturall.

Thus Lillie, Rose, Grape, Cherry, Creame,
And Straw-berry do stir
More love, when they transfer
A weak, a soft, a broken beame;

l. 36 soft] foft *48* (*corr. Errata*)

Then if they sho'd discover
At full their proper excellence;
Without some Scean cast over,
To juggle with the sense.

Thus let this *Christal'd Lillie* be
A Rule, how far to teach,
Your nakednesse must reach:
And that, no further, then we see
Those glaring colours laid
By Arts wise hand, but to this end
They sho'd obey a shade;
Lest they too far extend.

So though y'are white as Swan, or Snow,
And have the power to move
A world of men to love:
Yet, when your Lawns & Silks shal flow;
And that white cloud divide
Into a doubtful Twi-light; then,
Then will your hidden Pride
Raise greater fires in men.

To his Booke.

LIKE to a Bride, come forth my Book, at last,
With all thy richest jewels over-cast:
Say, if there be 'mongst many jems here; one
Deservelesse of the name of *Paragon:*
Blush not at all for that; since we have set
Some *Pearls* on *Queens*, that have been counterfet.

Upon some women.

THOU who wilt not love, doe this;
Learne of me what Woman is.
Something made of thred and thrumme;
A meere Botch of all and some.
Pieces, patches, ropes of haire;
In-laid Garbage ev'ry where.
Out-side silk, and out-side Lawne;
Sceanes to cheat us neatly drawne.

False in legs, and false in thighes;
False in breast, teeth, haire, and eyes:
False in head, and false enough;
Onely true in shreds and stuffe.

Supreme fortune falls soonest.

WHILE leanest Beasts in Pastures feed,
The fattest Oxe the first must bleed.

The Welcome to Sack.

SO soft streams meet, so springs with gladder smiles
Meet after long divorcement by the Iles:
When Love (the child of likenesse) urgeth on
Their Christal natures to an union.
So meet stolne kisses, when the Moonie nights
Call forth fierce Lovers to their wisht Delights:
So *Kings* & *Queens* meet, when Desire convinces
All thoughts, but such as aime at getting Princes,
As I meet thee. Soule of my life, and fame!
Eternall Lamp of Love! whose radiant flame
Out-glares the Heav'ns **Osiris*; and thy gleams * The Sun
Out-shine the splendour of his mid-day beams.
Welcome, O welcome my illustrious Spouse;
Welcome as are the ends unto my Vowes:
I! far more welcome then the happy soile,
The Sea-scourg'd Merchant, after all his toile,
Salutes with tears of joy; when fires betray
The smoakie chimneys of his *Ithaca*.
Where hast thou been so long from my embraces,
Poore pittyed Exile? Tell me, did thy Graces
Flie discontented hence, and for a time
Did rather choose to blesse another clime?
Or went'st thou to this end, the more to move me,
By thy short absence, to desire and love thee?
Why frowns my Sweet? Why won't my Saint confer
Favours on me, her fierce Idolater?
Why are Those Looks, Those Looks the which have been
Time-past so fragrant, sickly now drawn in
Like a dull Twi-light? Tell me; and the fault
Ile expiate with Sulphur, Haire, and Salt:

For variants see pp. 469–73   2.9 As] A *48*   2.23 went'st] wentst'st *48*

And with the Christal humour of the spring,
Purge hence the guilt, and kill this quarrelling.
Wo't thou not smile, or tell me what's amisse?
Have I been cold to hug thee, too remisse,
Too temp'rate in embracing? Tell me, ha's desire
To thee-ward dy'd i'th'embers, and no fire
Left in this rak't-up Ash-heap, as a mark
To testifie the glowing of a spark?
Have I divorc't thee onely to combine
In hot Adult'ry with another Wine?
True, I confesse I left thee, and appeale
'Twas done by me, more to confirme my zeale,
And double my affection on thee; as doe those,
Whose love growes more enflam'd, by being Foes.
But to forsake thee ever, co'd there be
A thought of such like possibilitie?
When thou thy selfe dar'st say, thy Iles shall lack
Grapes, before *Herrick* leaves Canarie Sack.
Thou mak'st me ayrie, active to be born,
Like *Iphyclus*, upon the tops of Corn.
Thou mak'st me nimble, as the winged howers,
To dance and caper on the heads of flowers,
And ride the Sun-beams. Can there be a thing
Under the heavenly **Isis*, that can bring * The Moo
More love unto my life, or can present
My *Genius* with a fuller blandishment?
Illustrious Idoll! co'd th'*Ægyptians* seek
Help from the *Garlick*, *Onyon*, and the *Leek*,
And pay no vowes to thee? who wast their best
God, and far more transcendent then the rest?
Had *Cassius*, that weak Water-drinker, known
Thee in thy Vine, or had but tasted one
Small Chalice of thy frantick liquor; He
As the wise *Cato* had approv'd of thee.
Had not **Joves* son, that brave *Tyrinthian* Swain, * Hercu
(Invited to the *Thesbian* banquet) ta'ne
Full goblets of thy gen'rous blood; his spright
Ne'r had kept heat for fifty Maids that night.
Come, come and kisse me; Love and lust commends
Thee, and thy beauties; kisse, we will be friends
Too strong for Fate to break us: Look upon
Me, with that full pride of complexion,

As *Queenes*, meet *Queenes*; or come thou unto me,
As *Cleopatra* came to *Anthonie*;
When her high carriage did at once present
To the *Triumvir*, Love and Wonderment.
Swell up my nerves with spirit; let my blood
Run through my veines, like to a hasty flood.
Fill each part full of fire, active to doe
What thy commanding soule shall put it to.
And till I turne Apostate to thy love,
Which here I vow to serve, doe not remove
Thy Fiers from me; but *Apollo's* curse
Blast these-like actions, or a thing that's worse;
When these Circumstants shall but live to see
The time that I prevaricate from thee.
Call me *The sonne of Beere*, and then confine
Me to the Tap, the Tost, the Turfe; Let Wine
Ne'r shine upon me; May my Numbers all
Run to a sudden Death, and Funerall.
And last, when thee (deare Spouse) I disavow,
Ne'r may Prophetique *Daphne* crown my Brow.

Impossibilities to his friend.

MY faithful friend, if you can see
The Fruit to grow up, or the Tree:
If you can see the colour come
Into the blushing Peare, or Plum:
If you can see the water grow
To cakes of Ice, or flakes of Snow:
If you can see, that drop of raine
Lost in the wild sea, once againe:
If you can see, how Dreams do creep
Into the Brain by easie sleep:
Then there is hope that you may see
Her love me once, who now hates me.

Upon Luggs. *Epig.*

LUGGS, by the Condemnation of the Bench,
Was lately whipt for lying with a Wench.
Thus Paines and Pleasures turne by turne succeed:
He smarts at last, who do's not first take heed.

Upon Gubbs. *Epig.*

GUBBS call's his children *Kitlings:* and wo'd bound
(Some say) for joy, to see those Kitlings drown'd.

To live merrily, and to trust to Good Verses.

NOW is the time for mirth,
Nor cheek, or tongue be dumbe:
For with the flowrie earth,
The golden pomp is come.

The golden Pomp is come;
For now each tree do's weare
(Made of her Pap and Gum)
Rich beads of *Amber* here.

Now raignes the *Rose*, and now
Th'*Arabian* Dew besmears
My uncontrolled brow,
And my retorted haires.

Homer, this Health to thee,
In Sack of such a kind,
That it wo'd make thee see,
Though thou wert ne'r so blind.

Next, *Virgil*, Ile call forth,
To pledge this second Health
In Wine, whose each cup's worth
An Indian Common-wealth.

A Goblet next Ile drink
To *Ovid*; and suppose,
Made he the pledge, he'd think
The world had all *one Nose*.

Then this immensive cup
Of *Aromatike* wine,
Catullus, I quaffe up
To that Terce Muse of thine.

2.3 the] *om. 48* (*corr. Errata*)

Wild I am now with heat;
  O *Bacchus!* coole thy Raies!
Or frantick I shall eate
  Thy *Thyrse*, and bite the *Bayes.*

Round, round, the roof do's run;
  And being ravisht thus,
Come, I will drink a Tun
  To my *Propertius.*

Now, to *Tibullus*, next,
  This flood I drink to thee:
But stay; I see a Text,
  That this presents to me.

Behold, *Tibullus* lies
  Here burnt, whose smal return
Of ashes, scarce suffice
  To fill a little Urne.

Trust to good Verses then;
  They onely will aspire,
When Pyramids, as men,
  Are lost, i'th'funerall fire.

And when all Bodies meet
  In *Lethe* to be drown'd;
Then onely Numbers sweet,
  With endless life are crown'd.

Faire dayes: or, *Dawnes deceitfull.*

FAIRE was the Dawne; and but e'ne now the Skies
  Shew'd like to Creame, enspir'd with Strawberries:
But on a sudden, all was chang'd and gone
That smil'd in that first-sweet complexion.
Then Thunder-claps and Lightning did conspire
To teare the world, or set it all on fire.
What trust to things below, when as we see,
As Men, the Heavens have their Hypocrisie?

1.7 things below,] things, below *48*

Lips Tonguelesse.

For my part, I never care
For those lips, that tongue-ty'd are:
Tell-tales I wo'd have them be
Of my Mistresse, and of me.
Let them prattle how that I
Sometimes freeze, and sometimes frie:
Let them tell how she doth move
Fore- or backward in her love:
Let them speak by gentle tones,
One and th'others passions:
How we watch, and seldome sleep;
How by Willowes we doe weep:
How by stealth we meet, and then
Kisse, and sigh, so part agen.
This the lips we will permit
For to tell, not publish it.

To the Fever, not to trouble Julia.

Th'ast dar'd too farre; but Furie now forbeare
To give the least disturbance to her haire:
But lesse presume to lay a Plait upon
Her skins most smooth, and cleare expansion.
'Tis like a Lawnie-Firmament as yet
Quite dispossest of either fray, or fret.
Come thou not neere that Filmne so finely spred,
Where no one piece is yet unlevelled.
This if thou dost, woe to thee Furie, woe,
Ile send such Frost, such Haile, such Sleet, and Snow,
Such Flesh-quakes, Palsies, and such fears as shall
Dead thee to th'most, if not destroy thee all.
And thou a thousand thousand times shalt be
More shak't thy selfe, then she is scorch't by thee.

2.11 fears] Heates *48* (*corr. Errata*)

To Violets.

1. WELCOME Maids of Honour,
You doe bring
In the Spring;
And wait upon her.

2. She has Virgins many,
Fresh and faire;
Yet you are
More sweet then any.

3. Y'are the Maiden Posies,
And so grac't,
To be plac't,
'Fore Damask Roses.

4. Yet though thus respected,
By and by
Ye doe lie,
Poore Girles, neglected.

Upon Bunce. *Epig.*

MONY thou ow'st me; Prethee fix a day
For payment promis'd, though thou never pay:
Let it be Doomes-day; nay, take longer scope;
Pay when th'art honest; let me have some hope.

To Carnations. A Song.

1. STAY while ye will, or goe;
And leave no scent behind ye:
Yet trust me, I shall know
The place, where I may find ye.

2. Within my *Lucia*'s cheek,
(Whose Livery ye weare)
Play ye at *Hide* or *Seek*,
I'm sure to find ye there.

2 *For variants see p.* 473

To the Virgins, to make much of Time.

1. GATHER ye Rose-buds while ye may,
   Old Time is still a flying:
And this same flower that smiles to day,
   To morrow will be dying.

2. The glorious Lamp of Heaven, the Sun,
   The higher he's a getting;
The sooner will his Race be run,
   And neerer he's to Setting.

3. That Age is best, which is the first,
   When Youth and Blood are warmer;
But being spent, the worse, and worst
   Times, still succeed the former.

4. Then be not coy, but use your time;
   And while ye may, goe marry:
For having lost but once your prime,
   You may for ever tarry.

Safety to look to ones selfe.

FOR my neighbour Ile not know,
Whether high he builds or no:
Onely this Ile look upon,
Firm be my foundation.
Sound, or unsound, let it be;
'Tis the lot ordain'd for me.
He who to the ground do's fall,
Has not whence to sink at all.

To his Friend, on the untuneable Times.

PLAY I co'd once; but (gentle friend) you see
My Harp hung up, here on the Willow tree.
Sing I co'd once; and bravely too enspire
(With luscious Numbers) my melodious Lyre.
Draw I co'd once (although not stocks or stones,
Amphion-like) men made of flesh and bones,
Whether I wo'd; but (ah!) I know not how,
I feele in me, this transmutation now.
Griefe, (my deare friend) has first my Harp unstrung;
Wither'd my hand, and palsie-struck my tongue. [1]

[1] *For variants see p.* 473

His Poetrie his Pillar.

1. ONELY a little more
   I have to write,
   Then Ile give o're,
   And bid the world Good-night.

2. 'Tis but a flying minute,
   That I must stay,
   Or linger in it;
   And then I must away.

3. O time that cut'st down all!
   And scarce leav'st here
   Memoriall
   Of any men that were.

4. How many lye forgot
   In Vaults beneath?
   And piece-meale rot
   Without a fame in death?

5. Behold this living stone,
   I reare for me,
   Ne'r to be thrown
   Downe, envious Time by thee.

6. Pillars let some set up,
   (If so they please)
   Here is my hope,
   And my *Pyramides.*

Safety on the Shore.

WHAT though the sea be calme? Trust to the shore:
Ships have been drown'd, where late they danc't before.

A Pastorall upon the birth of Prince Charles, *Presented to the King, and Set by* *Mr.* Nic: Laniere.

The Speakers, Mirtillo, Amintas, *and* Amarillis.

Amin. GOOD day, *Mirtillo. Mirt.* And to you no lesse:
And all faire Signs lead on our Shepardesse.
Amar. With all white luck to you. *Mirt.* But say, What news
Stirs in our Sheep-walk? *Amin.* None, save that my Ewes,

My Weathers, Lambes, and wanton Kids are well,
Smooth, faire, and fat, none better I can tell:
Or that this day *Menalchas* keeps a feast
For his Sheep-shearers. *Mir.* True, these are the least.
But dear *Amintas*, and sweet *Amarillis*,
Rest but a while here, by this bank of Lillies.
And lend a gentle eare to one report
The Country has. *Amint.* From whence? *Amar.* From whence?
Mir. The Court.
Three dayes before the shutting in of *May*,
(With whitest Wool be ever crown'd that day!)
To all our joy, a sweet-fac't child was borne,
More tender then the childhood of the Morne.
Chor. Pan pipe to him, and bleats of lambs and sheep,
Let Lullaby the pretty Prince asleep!
Mirt. And that his birth sho'd be more singular,
At Noone of Day, was seene a silver Star,
Bright as the Wise-mens Torch, which guided them
To Gods sweet Babe, when borne at *Bethlehem*;
While Golden Angels (some have told to me)
Sung out his Birth with Heav'nly Minstralsie.
Amint. O rare! But is't a trespasse if we three
Sho'd wend along his Baby-ship to see?
Mir. Not so, not so. *Chor.* But if it chance to prove
At most a fault, 'tis but a fault of love.
Amar. But deare *Mirtillo*, I have heard it told,
Those learned men brought *Incense*, *Myrrhe*, and *Gold*,
From Countries far, with store of Spices, (sweet)
And laid them downe for Offrings at his feet.
Mirt. 'Tis true indeed; and each of us will bring
Unto our smiling, and our blooming King,
A neat, though not so great an Offering.
Amar. A Garland for my Gift shall be
Of flowers, ne'r suckt by th'theeving Bee:
And all most sweet; yet all lesse sweet then he.
Amint. And I will beare along with you
Leaves dropping downe the honyed dew,
With oaten pipes, as sweet, as new.
Mirt. And I a Sheep-hook will bestow,
To have his little King-ship know,
As he is Prince, he's Shepherd too.
Chor. Come let's away, and quickly let's be drest,

And quickly give, *The swiftest Grace is best.*
And when before him we have laid our treasures,
We'll blesse the Babe, Then back to Countrie pleasures.

To the Lark.

GOOD speed, for I this day
Betimes my Mattens say:
Because I doe
Begin to wooe:
Sweet singing Lark,
Be thou the Clark,
And know thy when
To say, *Amen.*
And if I prove
Blest in my love;
Then thou shalt be
High-Priest to me,
At my returne,
To Incense burne;
And so to solemnize
Love's, and my Sacrifice.

The Bubble. A Song.

TO my revenge, and to her desp'rate feares,
Flie thou madd Bubble of my sighs, and tears.
In the wild aire, when thou hast rowl'd about,
And (like a blasting Planet) found her out;
Stoop, mount, passe by to take her eye, then glare
Like to a dreadfull Comet in the Aire:
Next, when thou dost perceive her fixed sight,
For thy revenge to be most opposite;
Then like a Globe, or Ball of Wild-fire, flie,
And break thy self in shivers on her eye.

A Meditation for his Mistresse.

1. YOU are a *Tulip* seen to day,
But (Dearest) of so short a stay;
That where you grew, scarce man can say.

2. You are a lovely *July-flower*,
Yet one rude wind, or ruffling shower,
Will force you hence, (and in an houre.)

3. You are a sparkling *Rose* i'th'bud,
Yet lost, ere that chast flesh and blood
Can shew where you or grew, or stood.

4. You are a full-spread faire-set Vine,
And can with Tendrills love intwine,
Yet dry'd, ere you distill your Wine.

5. You are like Balme inclosed (well)
In *Amber*, or some *Chrystall* shell,
Yet lost ere you transfuse your smell.

6. You are a dainty *Violet*,
Yet wither'd, ere you can be set
Within the Virgins Coronet.

7. You are the *Queen* all flowers among,
But die you must (faire Maid) ere long,
As He, the maker of this Song.

The bleeding hand: or, *The sprig of Eglantine given to a maid.*

FROM this bleeding hand of mine,
Take this sprig of *Eglantine*.
Which (though sweet unto your smell)
Yet the fretfull bryar will tell,
He who plucks the sweets shall prove
Many thorns to be in Love.

Lyrick for Legacies.

GOLD I've none, for use or show,
Neither Silver to bestow
At my death; but thus much know,
That each Lyrick here shall be
Of my love a Legacie,
Left to all posterity.
Gentle friends, then doe but please,
To accept such coynes as these;
As my last Remembrances.

A Dirge upon the Death of the Right Valiant Lord, Bernard Stuart.

1. HENCE, hence, profane; soft silence let us have;
While we this *Trentall* sing about thy Grave.

2. Had Wolves or Tigers seen but thee,
They wo'd have shew'd civility;
And in compassion of thy yeeres,
Washt those thy purple wounds with tears.
But since th'art slaine; and in thy fall,
The drooping Kingdome suffers all.

Chor. This we will doe; we'll daily come
And offer Tears upon thy Tomb:
And if that they will not suffice,
Thou shalt have soules for sacrifice.

Sleepe in thy peace, while we with spice perfume thee,
And *Cedar* wash thee, that no times consume thee.

3. Live, live thou dost, and shalt; for why?
Soules doe not with their bodies die:
Ignoble off-springs, they may fall
Into the flames of Funerall:
When as the chosen seed shall spring
Fresh, and for ever flourishing.

Cho. And times to come shall, weeping, read thy glory,
Lesse in these Marble stones, then in thy story.

To Perenna, *a Mistresse.*

DEARE *Perenna,* prethee come,
And with *Smallage* dresse my Tomb:
Adde a *Cypresse*-sprig thereto,
With a teare; and so *Adieu.*

Great boast, small rost.

OF Flanks and Chines of Beefe doth *Gorrell* boast
He has at home; but who tasts boil'd or rost?
Look in his Brine-tub, and you shall find there
Two stiffe-blew-Pigs-feet, and a sow's cleft eare.

Upon a Bleare-ey'd woman.

WITHER'D with yeeres, and bed-rid *Mumma* lyes;
Dry-rosted all, but raw yet in her eyes.

The Fairie Temple: or, Oberons *Chappell.* *Dedicated to Mr.* John Merrifield, *Counsellor at Law.*

RARE Temples thou hast seen, I know,
And rich for in and outward show:
Survey this Chappell, built, alone,
Without or Lime, or Wood, or Stone:
Then say, if one th'ast seene more fine
Then this, the Fairies once, now *Thine.*

The Temple.

A WAY enchac't with glasse & beads
There is, that to the Chappel leads:
Whose structure (for his holy rest)
Is here the *Halcion's* curious nest:
Into the which who looks shall see
His *Temple of Idolatry:*
Where he of *God-heads* has such store,
As *Rome's Pantheon* had not more.
His house of *Rimmon*, this he calls,
Girt with small bones, instead of walls.
First, in a *Neech*, more black then jet,
His Idol-Cricket there is set:
Then in a Polisht Ovall by
There stands his *Idol-Beetle-flie*:
Next in an Arch, akin to this,
His *Idol-Canker* seated is:
Then in a Round, is plac't by these,
His golden god, *Cantharides.*
So that where ere ye look, ye see,
No *Capitoll*, no *Cornish* free,
Or *Freeze*, from this fine Fripperie.

Now this the Fairies wo'd have known,
Theirs is a mixt Religion.
And some have heard the Elves it call
Part Pagan, part Papisticall.
If unto me all Tongues were granted,
I co'd not speak the Saints here painted.
Saint *Tit*, Saint *Nit*, Saint *Is*, Saint *Itis*,
Who 'gainst *Mabs-state* plac't here right is.
Saint *Will o'th' Wispe* (of no great bignes)
But *alias* call'd here *Fatuus ignis*.
Saint *Frip*, Saint *Trip*, Saint *Fill*, S. *Fillie*,
Neither those other-Saint-ships will I
Here goe about for to recite
Their number (almost) infinite,
Which one by one here set downe are
In this most curious Calendar.
First, at the entrance of the gate,
A little-Puppet-Priest doth wait,
Who squeaks to all the commers there,
Favour your tongues, who enter here.
Pure hands bring hither, without staine.
A second pules, *Hence, hence, profane.*
Hard by, i'th'shell of halfe a nut,
The Holy-water there is put:
A little brush of Squirrils haires,
(Compos'd of odde, not even paires)
Stands in the Platter, or close by,
To purge the Fairie Family.
Neere to the Altar stands the Priest,
There off'ring up the Holy-Grist:
Ducking in Mood, and perfect Tense,
With (much-good-do't him) reverence.
The Altar is not here foure-square,
Nor in a forme Triangular;
Nor made of glasse, or wood, or stone,
But of a little Transverce bone;
Which boyes, and Bruckel'd children call
(Playing for Points and Pins) *Cockall.*
Whose Linnen-Drapery is a thin
Subtile and ductile Codlin's skin;
Which o're the board is smoothly spred,
With little Seale-work Damasked.

The Fringe that circumbinds it too,
Is Spangle-work of trembling dew,
Which, gently gleaming, makes a show,
Like Frost-work glitt'ring on the Snow.
Upon this fetuous board doth stand
Something for *Shew-bread*, and at hand
(Just in the middle of the Altar)
Upon an end, the *Fairie-Psalter*,
Grac't with the Trout-flies curious wings,
Which serve for watched Ribbanings.
Now, we must know, the Elves are led
Right by the Rubrick, which they read.
And if Report of them be true,
They have their Text for what they doe;
I, and their Book of Canons too.
And, as Sir *Thomas Parson* tells,
They have their Book of Articles:
And if that Fairie Knight not lies,
They have their Book of Homilies:
And other Scriptures, that designe
A short, but righteous discipline.
The Bason stands the board upon
To take the Free-Oblation:
A little Pin-dust; which they hold
More precious, then we prize our gold:
Which charity they give to many
Poore of the Parish, (if there's any)
Upon the ends of these neat Railes
(Hatcht, with the Silver-light of snails)
The Elves, in formall manner, fix
Two pure, and holy *Candlesticks:*
In either which a small tall bent
Burns for the Altars ornament.
For sanctity, they have, to these,
Their curious *Copes* and *Surplices*
Of cleanest *Cobweb*, hanging by
In their *Religious Vesterie.*
They have their *Ash-pans*, & their *Brooms*
To purge the Chappel and the rooms:
Their many *mumbling Masse-priests* here,
And many a dapper *Chorister.*
Their ush'ring *Vergers*, here likewise,

Their *Canons*, and their *Chaunteries:*
Of *Cloyster-Monks* they have enow,
I, and their *Abby-Lubbers* too:
And if their Legend doe not lye,
They much affect the *Papacie:*
And since the last is dead, there's hope,
Elve Boniface shall next be Pope.
They have their *Cups* and *Chalices*;
Their *Pardons* and *Indulgences:*
Their *Beads* of Nits, *Bels*, *Books*, & *Wax*
Candles (forsooth) and other knacks:
Their *Holy Oyle*, their *Fasting-Spittle*;
Their *sacred Salt* here, (not a little.)
Dry *chips*, old *shooes*, *rags*, *grease*, & *bones*;
Beside their *Fumigations*,
To drive the Devill from the Cod-piece
Of the Fryar, (of work an odde-piece.)
Many a trifle too, and trinket,
And for what use, scarce man wo'd think it.
Next, then, upon the *Chanters* side
An *Apples-core* is hung up dry'd,
With ratling Kirnils, which is rung
To call to Morn, and Even-Song.
The Saint, to which the most he prayes
And offers *Incense* Nights and dayes,
The *Lady* of the *Lobster* is,
Whose foot-pace he doth stroak & kisse;
And, humbly, chives of Saffron brings,
For his most cheerfull offerings.
When, after these, h'as paid his vows,
He lowly to the Altar bows:
And then he dons the Silk-worms shed,
(Like a *Turks Turbant* on his head)
And reverently departeth thence,
Hid in a cloud of *Frankincense:*
And by the glow-worms light wel guided,
Goes to the Feast that's now provided.

To Mistresse Katherine Bradshaw, *the lovely, that crowned him with Laurel.*

My Muse in Meads has spent her many houres,
Sitting, and sorting severall sorts of flowers,
To make for others garlands; and to set
On many a head here, many a Coronet:
But, amongst All encircled here, not one
Gave her a day of Coronation;
Till you (sweet Mistresse) came and enterwove
A *Laurel* for her, (ever young as love)
You first of all crown'd her; she must of due,
Render for that, a crowne of life to you.

The Plaudite, or end of life.

If after rude and boystrous seas,
My wearyed Pinnace here finds ease:
If so it be I've gain'd the shore
With safety of a faithful Ore:
If having run my Barque on ground,
Ye see the aged Vessell crown'd:
What's to be done? but on the Sands
Ye dance, and sing, and now clap hands.
The first Act's doubtfull, (but we say)
It is the last commends the Play.

To the most vertuous Mistresse Pot, *who many times entertained him.*

When I through all my many Poems look,
And see your selfe to beautifie my Book;
Me thinks that onely lustre doth appeare
A Light ful-filling all the Region here.
Guild still with flames this Firmament, and be
A Lamp Eternall to my Poetrie.
Which if it now, or shall hereafter shine,
'Twas by your splendour (Lady) not by mine.
The Oile was yours; and that I owe for yet:
He payes the halfe, who do's confesse the Debt.

To Musique, to becalme his Fever.

1. CHARM me asleep, and melt me so
With thy Delicious Numbers;
That being ravisht, hence I goe
Away in easie slumbers.
Ease my sick head,
And make my bed,
Thou Power that canst sever
From me this ill:
And quickly still:
Though thou not kill
My Fever.

2. Thou sweetly canst convert the same
From a consuming fire,
Into a gentle-licking flame,
And make it thus expire.
Then make me weep
My paines asleep;
And give me such reposes,
That I, poore I,
May think, thereby,
I live and die
'Mongst Roses.

3. Fall on me like a silent dew,
Or like those Maiden showrs,
Which, by the peepe of day, doe strew
A Baptime o're the flowers.
Melt, melt my paines,
With thy soft straines;
That having ease me given,
With full delight,
I leave this light;
And take my flight
For Heaven.

Upon a Gentlewoman with a sweet Voice.

SO long you did not sing, or touch your Lute,
We knew 'twas Flesh and Blood, that there sate mute.
But when your Playing, and your Voice came in,
'Twas no more you then, but a *Cherubin*.

1.22 Roses.] Roses, *48*

Upon Cupid.

As lately I a Garland bound,
'Mongst Roses, I there *Cupid* found:
I took him, put him in my cup,
And drunk with Wine, I drank him up.
Hence then it is, that my poore brest
Co'd never since find any rest.

Upon Julia's *breasts.*

DISPLAY thy breasts, my *Julia*, there let me
Behold that circummortall purity:
Betweene whose glories, there my lips Ile lay,
Ravisht, in that faire *Via Lactea.*

Best to be merry.

FOOLES are they, who never know
How the times away doe goe:
But for us, who wisely see
Where the bounds of black Death be:
Let's live merrily, and thus
Gratifie the *Genius.*

The Changes to Corinna.

BE not proud, but now encline
Your soft eare to Discipline.
You have changes in your life,
Sometimes peace, and sometimes strife:
You have ebbes of face and flowes,
As your health or comes, or goes;
You have hopes, and doubts, and feares
Numberlesse, as are your haires.
You have Pulses that doe beat
High, and passions lesse of heat.

You are young, but must be old,
And, to these, ye must be told,
Time, ere long, will come and plow
Loathed Furrowes in your brow:
And the dimnesse of your eye
Will no other thing imply,
But you must die
As well as I.

No Lock against Letcherie.

BARRE close as you can, and bolt fast too your doore,
To keep out the Letcher, and keep in the whore:
Yet, quickly you'l see by the turne of a pin,
The Whore to come out, or the Letcher come in.

Neglect.

ART quickens Nature; Care will make a face:
Neglected beauty perisheth apace.

Upon himselfe.

MOP-EY'D I am, as some have said,
Because I've liv'd so long a maid:
But grant that I sho'd wedded be,
Sho'd I a jot the better see?
No, I sho'd think, that Marriage might,
Rather then mend, put out the light.

Upon a Physitian.

THOU cam'st to cure me (Doctor) of my cold,
And caught'st thy selfe the more by twenty fold:
Prethee goe home; and for thy credit be
First cur'd thy selfe; then come and cure me.

3 *For variants see p.* 474

Upon Sudds *a Laundresse.*

SUDDS Launders Bands in pisse; and starches them
Both with her Husband's, and her own tough fleame.

To the Rose. Song.

1. GOE happy Rose, and enterwove
With other Flowers, bind my Love.
Tell her too, she must not be,
Longer flowing, longer free,
That so oft has fetter'd me.

2. Say (if she's fretfull) I have bands
Of Pearle, and Gold, to bind her hands:
Tell her, if she struggle still,
I have Mirtle rods, (at will)
For to tame, though not to kill.

3. Take thou my blessing, thus, and goe,
And tell her this, but doe not so,
Lest a handsome anger flye,
Like a Lightning, from her eye,
And burn thee'up, as well as I.

Upon Guesse. *Epig.*

GUESSE cuts his shooes, and limping, goes about
To have men think he's troubled with the Gout:
But 'tis no Gout (beleeve it) but hard Beere,
Whose acrimonious humour bites him here.

To his Booke.

THOU art a plant sprung up to wither never,
But like a Laurell, to grow green for ever.

Upon a painted Gentlewoman.

MEN say y'are faire; and faire ye are, 'tis true;
But (Hark!) we praise the Painter now, not you.

2 and 5 *For variants see p.* 474

Upon a crooked Maid.

CROOKED you are, but that dislikes not me;
So you be straight, where Virgins straight sho'd be.

Draw Gloves.

AT Draw-Gloves we'l play,
And prethee, let's lay
A wager, and let it be this;
Who first to the Summe
Of twenty shall come,
Shall have for his winning a kisse.

To Musick, to becalme a sweet-sick-youth.

CHARMS, that call down the moon from out her sphere,
On this sick youth work your enchantments here:
Bind up his senses with your numbers, so,
As to entrance his paine, or cure his woe.
Fall gently, gently, and a while him keep
Lost in the civill Wildernesse of sleep:
That done, then let him, dispossest of paine,
Like to a slumbring Bride, awake againe.

To the High and Noble Prince, GEORGE, *Duke, Marquesse, and Earle of* Buckingham.

NEVER my Book's perfection did appeare,
Til I had got the name of VILLARS here.
Now 'tis so full, that when therein I look,
I see a Cloud of Glory fills my Book.
Here stand it stil to dignifie our Muse,
Your sober Hand-maid; who doth wisely chuse,
Your Name to be a *Laureat Wreathe* to Hir,
Who doth both love and feare you *Honour'd Sir.*

His Recantation.

LOVE, I recant,
And pardon crave,
That lately I offended,
But 'twas,
Alas,
To make a brave,
But no disdaine intended.

No more Ile vaunt,
For now I see,
Thou onely hast the power,
To find,
And bind
A heart that's free,
And slave it in an houre.

The comming of good luck.

SO Good-luck came, and on my roofe did light,
Like noyse-lesse Snow; or as the dew of night:
Not all at once, but gently, as the trees
Are, by the Sun-beams, tickel'd by degrees.

The Present: or, *The Bag of the Bee.*

FLY to my Mistresse, pretty pilfring Bee,
And say, thou bring'st this Hony-bag from me:
When on her lip, thou hast thy sweet dew plac't,
Mark, if her tongue, but slily, steale a taste.
If so, we live; if not, with mournfull humme,
Tole forth my death; next, to my buryall come.

On Love.

LOVE bade me aske a gift,
And I no more did move,
But this, that I might shift
Still with my clothes, my Love:
That favour granted was;
Since which, though I love many,
Yet so it comes to passe,
That long I love not any.

The Hock-cart, or *Harvest home: To the Right Honourable*, Mildmay, *Earle of* Westmorland.

COME Sons of Summer, by whose toile,
We are the Lords of Wine and Oile:
By whose tough labours, and rough hands,
We rip up first, then reap our lands.
Crown'd with the eares of corne, now come,
And, to the Pipe, sing Harvest home.
Come forth, my Lord, and see the Cart
Drest up with all the Country Art.
See, here a *Maukin*, there a sheet,
As spotlesse pure, as it is sweet:
The Horses, Mares, and frisking Fillies,
(Clad, all, in Linnen, white as Lillies.)
The Harvest Swaines, and Wenches bound
For joy, to see the *Hock-cart* crown'd.
About the Cart, heare, how the Rout
Of Rurall Younglings raise the shout;
Pressing before, some coming after,
Those with a shout, and these with laughter.
Some blesse the Cart; some kisse the sheaves;
Some prank them up with Oaken leaves:
Some crosse the Fill-horse; some with great
Devotion, stroak the home-borne wheat:
While other Rusticks, lesse attent
To Prayers, then to Merryment,
Run after with their breeches rent.
Well, on, brave boyes, to your Lords Hearth,
Glitt'ring with fire; where, for your mirth,
Ye shall see first the large and cheefe
Foundation of your Feast, Fat Beefe:
With Upper Stories, Mutton, Veale
And Bacon, (which makes full the meale)
With sev'rall dishes standing by,
As here a Custard, there a Pie,
And here all tempting Frumentie.
And for to make the merry cheere,
If smirking Wine be wanting here,
There's that, which drowns all care, stout Beere;

Which freely drink to your Lords health,
Then to the Plough, (the Common-wealth)
Next to your Flailes, your Fanes, your Fatts;
Then to the Maids with Wheaten Hats:
To the rough Sickle, and crookt Sythe,
Drink frollick boyes, till all be blythe.
Feed, and grow fat; and as ye eat,
Be mindfull, that the lab'ring Neat
(As you) may have their fill of meat.
And know, besides, ye must revoke
The patient Oxe unto the Yoke,
And all goe back unto the Plough
And Harrow, (though they'r hang'd up now.)
And, you must know, your Lords word's true,
Feed him ye must, whose food fils you.
And that this pleasure is like raine,
Not sent ye for to drowne your paine,
But for to make it spring againe.

The Perfume.

To morrow, *Julia*, I betimes must rise,
For some small fault, to offer sacrifice:
The Altar's ready; Fire to consume
The fat; breathe thou, and there's the rich perfume.

Upon her Voice.

Let but thy voice engender with the string,
And Angels will be borne, while thou dost sing.

Not to love.

He that will not love, must be
My Scholar, and learn this of me:
There be in Love as many feares,
As the Summers Corne has eares:
Sighs, and sobs, and sorrowes more
Then the sand, that makes the shore:
Freezing cold, and firie heats,
Fainting swoones, and deadly sweats;

3 *For variants see p.* 474

Now an Ague, then a Fever,
Both tormenting Lovers ever.
Wod'st thou know, besides all these,
How hard a woman 'tis to please?
How crosse, how sullen, and how soone
She shifts and changes like the Moone.
How false, how hollow she's in heart;
And how she is her owne least part:
How high she's priz'd, and worth but small;
Little thou't love, or not at all.

To Musick. A Song.

MUSICK, thou *Queen of Heaven*, Care-charming-spel,
That strik'st a stilnesse into hell:
Thou that tam'st *Tygers*, and fierce storms (that rise)
With thy soule-melting Lullabies:
Fall down, down, down, from those thy chiming spheres,
To charme our soules, as thou enchant'st our eares.

To the Western wind.

1. SWEET Western Wind, whose luck it is,
(Made rivall with the aire)
To give *Perenn'as* lip a kisse,
And fan her wanton haire.

2. Bring me but one, Ile promise thee,
Instead of common showers,
Thy wings shall be embalm'd by me,
And all beset with flowers.

Upon the death of his Sparrow. An Elegie.

WHY doe not all fresh maids appeare
To work Love's Sampler onely here,
Where spring-time smiles throughout the yeare?
Are not here *Rose-buds*, *Pinks*, all flowers,
Nature begets by th'Sun and showers,
Met in one Hearce-cloth, to ore-spred
The body of the under-dead?

Phill, the late dead, the late dead Deare,
O! may no eye distill a Teare
For you once lost, who weep not here!
Had *Lesbia* (too-too-kind) but known
This Sparrow, she had scorn'd her own:
And for this dead which under-lies,
Wept out her heart, as well as eyes.
But endlesse Peace, sit here, and keep
My *Phill*, the time he has to sleep,
And thousand Virgins come and weep,
To make these flowrie Carpets show
Fresh, as their blood; and ever grow,
Till passengers shall spend their doome,
Not *Virgil's* Gnat had such a Tomb.

To Primroses fill'd with morning-dew.

1. WHY doe ye weep, sweet Babes? can Tears
Speak griefe in you,
Who were but borne
Just as the modest Morne
Teem'd her refreshing dew?
Alas you have not known that shower,
That marres a flower;
Nor felt th'unkind
Breath of a blasting wind;
Nor are ye worne with yeares;
Or warpt, as we,
Who think it strange to see,
Such pretty flowers, (like to Orphans young)
To speak by Teares, before ye have a Tongue.

2. Speak, whimp'ring Younglings, and make known
The reason, why
Ye droop, and weep;
Is it for want of sleep?
Or childish Lullabie?
Or that ye have not seen as yet
The *Violet*?
Or brought a kisse
From that Sweet-heart, to this?
No, no, this sorrow shown

By your teares shed,
Wo'd have this Lecture read,
That things of greatest, so of meanest worth,
Conceiv'd with grief are, and with teares brought forth.

How Roses came red.

1. ROSES at first were white,
Till they co'd not agree,
Whether my *Sapho's* breast,
Or they more white sho'd be.

2. But being vanquisht quite,
A blush their cheeks bespred;
Since which (beleeve the rest)
The *Roses* first came red.

Comfort to a Lady upon the Death of her Husband.

DRY your sweet cheek, long drown'd with sorrows raine;
Since Clouds disperst, Suns guild the Aire again.
Seas chafe and fret, and beat, and over-boile;
But turne soone after calme, as Balme, or Oile.
Winds have their time to rage; but when they cease,
The leavie-trees nod in a still-born peace.
Your storme is over; Lady, now appeare
Like to the peeping-spring-time of the yeare.
Off then with grave clothes; put fresh colours on;
And flow, and flame, in your *Vermillion.*
Upon your cheek sate *Ysicles* awhile;
Now let the Rose raigne like a Queene, and smile.

How Violets came blew.

LOVE on a day (wise Poets tell)
Some time in wrangling spent,
Whether the Violets sho'd excell,
Or she, in sweetest scent.

But *Venus* having lost the day,
Poore Girles, she fell on you;
And beat ye so, (as some dare say)
Her blowes did make ye blew.

3 *For variants see p.* 475

Upon Groynes. *Epig.*

G*ROYNES*, for his fleshly *Burglary* of late,
Stood in the *Holy-Forum Candidate*:
The word is *Roman*; but in English knowne:
Penance, and standing so, are both but one.

To the Willow-tree.

1. THOU art to all lost love the best,
The onely true plant found,
Wherewith young men and maids distrest,
And left of love, are crown'd.

2. When once the Lovers Rose is dead,
Or laid aside forlorne;
Then Willow-garlands, 'bout the head,
Bedew'd with teares, are worne.

3. When with Neglect, (the Lovers bane)
Poore Maids rewarded be,
For their love lost; their onely gaine
Is but a Wreathe from thee.

4. And underneath thy cooling shade,
(When weary of the light)
The love-spent Youth, and love-sick Maid,
Come to weep out the night.

Mrs. Eliz. Wheeler, *under the name of the lost Shepardesse.*

AMONG the *Mirtles*, as I walkt,
Love and my sighs thus intertalkt:
Tell me, said I, in deep distresse,
Where I may find my Shepardesse.
Thou foole, said Love, know'st thou not this?
In every thing that's sweet, she is.
In yond' *Carnation* goe and seek,
There thou shalt find her lip and cheek:

3 *For variants see p.* 475

In that ennamel'd *Pansie* by,
There thou shalt have her curious eye:
In bloome of *Peach*, and *Roses* bud,
There waves the Streamer of her blood.
'Tis true, said I, and thereupon
I went to pluck them one by one,
To make of parts an union;
But on a sudden all were gone.
At which I stopt; Said Love, these be
The true resemblances of thee;
For as these flowers, thy joyes must die,
And in the turning of an eye;
And all thy hopes of her must wither,
Like those short sweets ere knit together.

TO THE KING.

If when these Lyricks (CESAR) You shall heare,
And that *Apollo* shall so touch Your eare,
As for to make this, that, or any one
Number, Your owne, by free Adoption;
That Verse, of all the Verses here, shall be
The Heire to This *great Realme of Poetry.*

TO THE QUEENE.

GODDESSE *of Youth, and Lady of the Spring,*
(Most fit to be the Consort to a King)
Be pleas'd to rest you in *This Sacred Grove,*
Beset with *Mirtles*; whose each leafe drops Love.
Many a sweet-fac't *Wood-Nymph* here is seene,
Of which chast *Order You* are now the *Queene:*
Witness their *Homage*, when they come and strew
Your Walks with Flowers, and give their Crowns to you.
Your Leavie-Throne (with *Lilly*-work) possesse;
And be both *Princesse* here, and *Poetresse.*

The Poets good wishes for the most hopefull and handsome Prince, the Duke of Yorke.

MAY his pretty Duke-ship grow
Like t'a Rose of *Jericho*:
Sweeter far, then ever yet
Showrs or Sun-shines co'd beget.
May the Graces, and the Howers
Strew his hopes, and Him with flowers:
And so dresse him up with Love,
As to be the Chick of *Jove*.
May the thrice-three-Sisters sing
Him the Soveraigne of their Spring:
And entitle none to be
Prince of *Hellicon*, but He.
May his soft foot, where it treads,
Gardens thence produce and Meads:
And those Meddowes full be set
With the Rose, and Violet.
May his ample Name be knowne
To the last succession:
And his actions high be told
Through the world, but writ in gold.

To Anthea, *who may command him any thing.*

BID me to live, and I will live
  Thy Protestant to be:
Or bid me love, and I will give
  A loving heart to thee.

2. A heart as soft, a heart as kind,
  A heart as sound and free,
As in the whole world thou canst find,
  That heart Ile give to thee.

3. Bid that heart stay, and it will stay,
  To honour thy Decree:
Or bid it languish quite away,
  And't shall doe so for thee.

2 *For variants see p.* 476

4. Bid me to weep, and I will weep,
   While I have eyes to see:
And having none, yet I will keep
   A heart to weep for thee.

5. Bid me despaire, and Ile despaire,
   Under that *Cypresse* tree:
Or bid me die, and I will dare
   E'en Death, to die for thee.

6. Thou art my life, my love, my heart,
   The very eyes of me:
And hast command of every part,
   To live and die for thee.

Prevision, or Provision.

THAT Prince takes soone enough the Victors roome,
Who first provides, not to be overcome.

Obedience in Subjects.

THE Gods to Kings the Judgement give to sway:
The Subjects onely glory to obay.

More potent, lesse peccant.

HE that may sin, sins least; Leave to transgresse
Enfeebles much the seeds of wickednesse.

Upon a maid that dyed the day she was marryed.

THAT Morne which saw me made a Bride,
The Ev'ning witnest that I dy'd.
Those holy lights, wherewith they guide
Unto the bed the bashfull Bride;
Serv'd, but as Tapers, for to burne,
And light my Reliques to their Urne.
This *Epitaph*, which here you see,
Supply'd the *Epithalamie*.

Upon Pink *an ill-fac'd Painter. Epig.*

To paint the Fiend, *Pink* would the Devill see;
And so he may, if he'll be rul'd by me:
Let but *Pink*'s face i'th'Looking-glasse be showne,
And *Pink* may paint the Devill's by his owne.

Upon Brock. *Epig.*

To clense his eyes, *Tom Brock* makes much adoe,
But not his mouth (the fouler of the two.)
A clammie Reume makes loathsome both his eyes:
His mouth worse furr'd with oathes and blasphemies.

To Meddowes.

1. Ye have been fresh and green,
Ye have been fill'd with flowers:
And ye the Walks have been
Where Maids have spent their houres.

2. You have beheld, how they
With *Wicker Arks* did come
To kisse, and beare away
The richer Couslips home.

3. Y'ave heard them sweetly sing,
And seen them in a Round: 1
Each Virgin, like a Spring,
With Hony-succles crown'd.

4. But now, we see, none here,
Whose silv'rie feet did tread,
And with dishevell'd Haire,
Adorn'd this smoother Mead.

5. Like Unthrifts, having spent,
Your stock, and needy grown,
Y'are left here to lament
Your poore estates, alone. 2

Crosses.

Though good things answer many good intents;
Crosses doe still bring forth the best events.

Miseries.

THOUGH hourely comforts from the Gods we see,
No life is yet life-proofe from miserie.

Laugh and lie downe.

Y'AVE laught enough (sweet) vary now your Text;
And laugh no more; or laugh, and lie down next.

To his Houshold gods.

RISE, Houshold-gods, and let us goe;
But whither, I my selfe not know.
First, let us dwell on rudest seas;
Next, with severest Salvages;
Last, let us make our best abode,
Where humane foot, as yet, ne'r trod:
Search worlds of Ice; and rather there
Dwell, then in lothed *Devonshire.*

To the Nightingale, and Robin-Red-brest.

WHEN I departed am, ring thou my knell,
Thou pittifull, and pretty *Philomel:*
And when I'm laid out for a Corse; then be
Thou *Sexton* (*Red-brest*) for to cover me.

To the Yew and Cypresse to grace his Funerall.

1. BOTH you two have
Relation to the grave:
And where
The *Fun'rall-Trump* sounds, you are there.

2. I shall be made
Ere long a fleeting shade:
Pray come,
And doe some honour to my Tomb.

3. Do not deny
My last request; for I
Will be
Thankfull to you, or friends, for me.

I call and I call.

I CALL, I call, who doe ye call?
The Maids to catch this Cowslip-ball:
But since these Cowslips fading be,
Troth, leave the flowers, and Maids, take me.
Yet, if that neither you will doe,
Speak but the word, and Ile take you.

On a perfum'd Lady.

YOU say y'are sweet; how sho'd we know
Whether that you be sweet or no?
From *Powders* and *Perfumes* keep free;
Then we shall smell how sweet you be.

A Nuptiall Song, or Epithalamie, on Sir Clipseby Crew *and his Lady.*

1. WHAT's that we see from far? the spring of Day
Bloom'd from the East, or faire Injewel'd May
Blowne out of April; or some New-
Star fill'd with glory to our view,
Reaching at heaven,
To adde a nobler Planet to the seven?
Say, or doe we not descrie
Some Goddesse, in a cloud of Tiffanie
To move, or rather the
Emergent *Venus* from the Sea?

2. 'Tis she! 'tis she! or else some more Divine
Enlightned substance; mark how from the Shrine
Of holy Saints she paces on,
Treading upon *Vermilion*
And *Amber*; Spice-
ing the Chafte Aire with fumes of Paradise.
Then come on, come on, and yeeld
A savour like unto a blessed field,
When the bedabled Morne
Washes the golden eares of corne.

3 *For variants see pp.* 476–80

3. See where she comes; and smell how all the street
Breathes Vine-yards and Pomgranats: O how sweet!
As a fir'd Altar, is each stone,
Perspiring pounded Cynamon.
The Phenix nest,
Built up of odours, burneth in her breast.
Who therein wo'd not consume
His soule to Ash-heaps in that rich perfume?
Bestroaking Fate the while
He burnes to Embers on the Pile.

4. *Himen, O Himen!* Tread the sacred ground;
Shew thy white feet, and head with Marjoram crown'd:
Mount up thy flames, and let thy Torch
Display the Bridegroom in the porch,
In his desires
More towring, more disparkling then thy fires:
Shew her how his eyes do turne
And roule about, and in their motions burne
Their balls to Cindars: haste,
Or else to ashes he will waste.

5. Glide by the banks of Virgins then, and passe
The Shewers of Roses, lucky-foure-leav'd grasse:
The while the cloud of younglings sing,
And drown yee with a flowrie Spring:
While some repeat
Your praise, and bless you, sprinkling you with Wheat:
While that others doe divine;
Blest is the Bride, on whom the Sun doth shine;
And thousands gladly wish
You multiply, as doth a Fish.

6. And beautious Bride we do confess y'are wise,
In dealing forth these bashfull jealousies:
In Lov's name do so; and a price
Set on your selfe, by being nice:
But yet take heed;
What now you seem, be not the same indeed,
And turne *Apostate*: Love will
Part of the way be met; or sit stone-still.
On then, and though you slow-
ly go, yet, howsoever, go.

7. And now y'are enter'd; see the Codled Cook
Runs from his *Torrid Zone*, to prie, and look,
And blesse his dainty Mistresse: see,
The Aged point out, This is she,
Who now must sway
The House (Love shield her) with her Yea and Nay:
And the smirk Butler thinks it
Sin, in's Nap'rie, not to express his wit;
Each striving to devise
Some gin, wherewith to catch your eyes.

8. To bed, to bed, kind Turtles, now, and write
This the short'st day, and this the longest night;
But yet too short for you: 'tis we,
Who count this night as long as three,
Lying alone,
Telling the Clock strike Ten, Eleven, Twelve, One.
Quickly, quickly then prepare;
And let the Young-men and the Bride-maids share
Your Garters; and their joynts
Encircle with the Bride-grooms Points.

9. By the Brides eyes, and by the teeming life
Of her green hopes, we charge ye, that no strife
(Farther then Gentlenes tends) gets place
Among ye, striving for her lace:
O doe not fall
Foule in these noble pastimes, lest ye call
Discord in, and so divide
The youthfull Bride-groom, and the fragrant Bride:
Which Love fore-fend; but spoken,
Be't to your praise, no peace was broken.

10. Strip her of Spring-time, tender-whimpring-maids,
Now *Autumne*'s come, when all those flowrie aids
Of her Delayes must end; Dispose
That *Lady-smock*, that *Pansie*, and that *Rose*
Neatly apart;
But for *Prick-madam*, and for *Gentle-heart*;
And soft-*Maidens-blush*, the Bride
Makes holy these, all others lay aside:
Then strip her, or unto her
Let him come, who dares undo her.

11. And to enchant yee more, see every where
About the Roofe a *Syren* in a Sphere;
(As we think) singing to the dinne
Of many a warbling *Cherubin*:
O marke yee how
The soule of Nature melts in numbers: now
See, a thousand *Cupids* flye,
To light their Tapers at the Brides bright eye.
To Bed; or her they'l tire,
Were she an Element of fire.

12. And to your more bewitching, see, the proud
Plumpe Bed beare up, and swelling like a cloud,
Tempting the too too modest; can
Yee see it brusle like a Swan,
And you be cold
To meet it, when it woo's and seemes to fold
The Armes to hugge you? throw, throw
Your selves into the mighty over-flow
Of that white Pride, and Drowne
The night, with you, in floods of Downe.

13. The bed is ready, and the maze of Love
Lookes for the treaders; every where is wove
Wit and new misterie; read, and
Put in practise, to understand
And know each wile,
Each hieroglyphick of a kisse or smile;
And do it to the full; reach
High in your own conceipt, and some way teach
Nature and Art, one more
Play, then they ever knew before.

14. If needs we must for Ceremonies-sake,
Blesse a *Sack-posset*; Luck go with it; take
The Night-Charme quickly; you have spells,
And magicks for to end, and hells,
To passe; but such
And of such Torture as no one would grutch
To live therein for ever: Frie
And consume, and grow again to die,
And live, and in that case,
Love the confusion of the place.

15. But since It must be done, dispatch, and sowe
Up in a sheet your Bride, and what if so
It be with Rock, or walles of Brasse,
Ye Towre her up, as *Danae* was;
Thinke you that this,
Or hell it selfe a powerfull Bulwarke is?
I tell yee no; but like a
Bold bolt of thunder he will make his way,
And rend the cloud, and throw
The sheet about, like flakes of snow.

16. All now is husht in silence; *Midwife-moone*,
With all her *Owle-ey'd* issue begs a boon
Which you must grant; that's entrance; with
Which extract, all we can call pith
And quintiscence
Of Planetary bodies; so commence
All faire *Constellations*
Looking upon yee, that two Nations
Springing from two such Fires,
May blaze the vertue of their Sires.

The silken Snake.

FOR sport my *Julia* threw a Lace
Of silke and silver at my face:
Watchet the silke was; and did make
A shew, as if't'ad been a snake:
The suddenness did me affright;
But though it scar'd, it did not bite.

Upon himselfe.

I AM Sive-like, and can hold
Nothing hot, or nothing cold.
Put in Love, and put in too
Jealousie, and both will through:
Put in Feare, and hope, and doubt;
What comes in, runnes quickly out:
Put in secrecies withall,
What ere enters, out it shall:

l. 158 that two *K2Wi*: that, That *rest*

But if you can stop the Sive,
For mine own part I'de as lieve,
Maides sho'd say, or Virgins sing,
Herrick keeps, as holds nothing.

Upon Love.

LOVE'S a thing, (as I do heare)
Ever full of pensive feare;
Rather then to which I'le fall,
Trust me, I'le not like at all:
If to love I should entend,
Let my haire then stand an end:
And that terrour likewise prove,
Fatall to me in my love.
But if horrour cannot slake
Flames, which wo'd an entrance make;
Then the next thing I desire,
Is to love, and live i'th fire.

Reverence to Riches.

LIKE to the Income must be our expence;
Mans Fortune must be had in reverence.

Devotion makes the Deity.

WHO formes a Godhead out of Gold or Stone,
Makes not a God; but he that prayes to one.

To all young men that love.

I COULD wish you all, who love,
That ye could your thoughts remove
From your Mistresses, and be,
Wisely wanton (like to me.)
I could wish you dispossest
Of that *Fiend that marres your rest;*
And with Tapers comes to fright
Your weake senses in the night.
I co'd wish, ye all, who frie
Cold as Ice, or coole as I.

But if flames best like ye, then
Much good do't ye Gentlemen.
I a merry heart will keep,
While you wring your hands and weep.

The Eyes.

'Tis a known principle in War,
The eies be first, that conquer'd are.

No fault in women.

No fault in women to refuse
The offer, which they most wo'd chuse.
No fault in women, to confesse
How tedious they are in their dresse.
No fault in women, to lay on
The tincture of *Vermillion:*
And there to give the cheek a die
Of white, where nature doth deny.
No fault in women, to make show
Of largeness, when th'are nothing so:
(When true it is, the out-side swels
With inward Buckram, little else.)
No fault in women, though they be
But seldome from suspition free:
No fault in womankind, at all,
If they but slip, and never fall.

Upon Shark. *Epig.*

S*hark*, when he goes to any publick feast,
Eates to ones thinking, of all there, the least.
What saves the master of the House thereby?
When if the servants search, they may descry
In his wide Codpeece, (dinner being done)
Two Napkins cram'd up, and a silver Spoone.

Oberons *Feast.*

SHAPCOT! To thee the Fairy State
I with discretion, dedicate.
Because thou prizest things that are
Curious, and un-familiar.
Take first the feast; these dishes gone;
Wee'l see the Fairy-Court *anon.*

A LITTLE mushroome table spred,
After short prayers, they set on bread;
A Moon-parcht grain of purest wheat,
With some small glit'ring gritt, to eate
His choyce bitts with; then in a trice
They make a feast lesse great then nice.
But all this while his eye is serv'd,
We must not thinke his eare was sterv'd:
But that there was in place to stir
His Spleen, the chirring Grashopper;
The merry Cricket, puling Flie,
The piping Gnat for minstralcy.
And now, we must imagine first,
The Elves present to quench his thirst
A pure seed-Pearle of Infant dew,
Brought and besweetned in a blew
And pregnant violet; which done,
His kitling eyes begin to runne
Quite through the table, where he spies
The hornes of paperie Butterflies,
Of which he eates, and tastes a little
Of that we call the Cuckoes spittle.
A little Fuz-ball-pudding stands
By, yet not blessed by his hands,
That was too coorse; but then forthwith
He ventures boldly on the pith
Of sugred Rush, and eates the sagge
And well bestrutted Bees sweet bagge:
Gladding his pallat with some store
Of Emits eggs; what wo'd he more?
But Beards of Mice, a Newt's stew'd thigh,
A bloated Earewig, and a Flie;

1 *For variants see pp.* 480–1   1. 1 *the*] *om.* 48 (*corr. Errata*)

With the Red-capt worme, that's shut
Within the concave of a Nut,
Browne as his Tooth. A little Moth,
Late fatned in a piece of cloth:
With withered cherries; Mandrakes eares;
Moles eyes; to these, the slain-Stags teares:
The unctuous dewlaps of a Snaile;
The broke-heart of a Nightingale
Ore-come in musicke; with a wine,
Ne're ravisht from the flattering Vine,
But gently prest from the soft side
Of the most sweet and dainty Bride,
Brought in a dainty daizie, which
He fully quaffs up to bewitch
His blood to height; this done, commended
Grace by his Priest; *The feast is ended.*

Event of things not in our power.

BY Time, and Counsell, doe the best we can,
Th'event is never in the power of man.

Upon her blush.

WHEN *Julia* blushes, she do's show
Cheeks like to Roses, when they blow.

Merits make the man.

OUR Honours, and our Commendations be
Due to the Merits, not Authoritie.

To Virgins.

HEARE ye Virgins, and Ile teach,
What the times of old did preach.
Rosamond was in a Bower
Kept, as *Danae* in a Tower:
But yet Love (who subtile is)
Crept to that, and came to this.
Be ye lockt up like to these,
Or the rich *Hesperides*;

Or those Babies in your eyes,
In their Christall Nunneries;
Notwithstanding Love will win,
Or else force a passage in:
And as coy be, as you can,
Gifts will get ye, or the man.

Vertue.

EACH must, in vertue, strive for to excell;
That man lives twice, that lives the first life well.

The Bell-man.

FROM noise of Scare-fires rest ye free,
From Murders *Benedicitie.*
From all mischances, that may fright
Your pleasing slumbers in the night:
Mercie secure ye all, and keep
The Goblin from ye, while ye sleep.
Past one aclock, and almost two,
My Masters all, *Good day to you.*

Bashfulnesse.

OF all our parts, the eyes expresse
The sweetest kind of bashfulnesse.

To the most accomplisht Gentleman, Master Edward Norgate, *Clark of the Signet to His Majesty. Epig.*

FOR one so rarely tun'd to fit all parts;
For one to whom espous'd are all the Arts;
Long have I sought for: but co'd never see
Them all concenter'd in one man, but Thee.
Thus, thou, that man art, whom the Fates conspir'd
To make but One (and that's thy selfe) admir'd.

Upon Prudence Baldwin *her sicknesse.*

PRUE, my dearest Maid, is sick,
Almost to be Lunatick:
Æsculapius! come and bring
Means for her recovering;
And a gallant Cock shall be
Offer'd up by Her, to Thee.

To Apollo. *A short Hymne.*

PHŒBUS! when that I a Verse,
Or some numbers more rehearse;
Tune my words, that they may fall,
Each way smoothly Musicall:
For which favour, there shall be
Swans devoted unto thee.

A Hymne to Bacchus.

BACCHUS, let me drink no more;
Wild are Seas, that want a shore.
When our drinking has no stint,
There is no one pleasure in't.
I have drank up for to please
Thee, that great cup *Hercules:*
Urge no more; and there shall be
Daffadills g'en up to Thee.

Upon Bungie.

BUNGIE do's fast; looks pale; puts Sack-cloth on;
Not out of Conscience, or Religion:
Or that this Yonker keeps so strict a Lent,
Fearing to break the Kings Commandement:
But being poore, and knowing Flesh is deare,
He keeps not one, but many Lents i'th'yeare.

1 (*heading*) Prudence] Brudence *48* 2.2 Or] *Grosart records the reading* Of

On himselfe.

HERE down my wearyed limbs Ile lay;
My Pilgrims staffe; my weed of gray:
My Palmers hat; my Scallops shell;
My Crosse; my Cord; and all farewell.
For having now my journey done,
(Just at the setting of the Sun)
Here I have found a Chamber fit,
(God and good friends be thankt for it)
Where if I can a lodger be
A little while from Tramplers free;
At my up-rising next, I shall,
If not requite, yet thank ye all.
Meane while, the *Holy-Rood* hence fright
The fouler Fiend, and evill Spright,
From scaring you or yours this night.

Casualties.

GOOD things, that come of course, far lesse doe please,
Then those, which come by sweet contingences.

Bribes and Gifts get all.

DEAD falls the Cause, if once the Hand be mute;
But let that speak, the Client gets the suit.

The end.

IF well thou hast begun, goe on fore-right;
It is the End that crownes us, not the Fight.

Upon a child that dyed.

HERE she lies, a pretty bud,
Lately made of flesh and blood:
Who, as soone, fell fast asleep,
As her little eyes did peep.
Give her strewings; but not stir
The earth, that lightly covers her.

5 *For variant heading* *see p.* 481

Upon Sneape. *Epig.*

S*NEAPE* has a face so brittle, that it breaks
Forth into blushes, whensoere he speaks.

Content, not cates.

'TIS not the food, but the content
That makes the Tables merriment.
Where Trouble serves the board, we eate
The Platters there, as soone as meat.
A little Pipkin with a bit
Of Mutton, or of Veale in it,
Set on my Table, (Trouble-free)
More then a Feast contenteth me.

The Entertainment: or, *Porch-verse, at the Marriage of Mr.* Hen. Northly, *and the most witty Mrs.* Lettice Yard.

WEELCOME! but yet no entrance, till we blesse
First you, then you, and both for white successe.
Profane no Porch young man and maid, for fear
Ye wrong the *Threshold-god*, that keeps peace here:
Please him, and then all good-luck will betide
You, the brisk Bridegroome, you the dainty Bride.
Do all things sweetly, and in comely wise;
Put on your Garlands first, then Sacrifice:
That done; when both of you have seemly fed,
We'll call on Night, to bring ye both to Bed:
Where being laid, all Faire signes looking on,
Fish-like, encrease then to a million:
And millions of spring-times may ye have,
Which spent, one death, bring to ye both one Grave.

The good-night or Blessing.

BLESSINGS, in abundance come,
To the Bride, and to her Groome;
May the Bed, and this short night,
Know the fulness of delight!

3.14 one death] on death *48* (*see Commentary, p. 526*)

Pleasures, many here attend ye,
And ere long, a Boy Love send ye
Curld and comely, and so trimme,
Maides (in time) may ravish him.
Thus a dew of Graces fall
On ye both; Goodnight to all.

Upon Leech.

LEECH boasts, he has a Pill, that can alone,
With speed give sick men their salvation:
'Tis strange, his Father long time has been ill,
And credits Physick, yet not trusts his Pill:
And why? he knowes he must of Cure despaire,
Who makes the slie Physitian his Heire.

To Daffadills.

1. FAIRE Daffadills, we weep to see
You haste away so soone:
As yet the early-rising Sun
Has not attain'd his Noone.
Stay, stay,
Untill the hasting day
Has run
But to the Even-song;
And, having pray'd together, we
Will goe with you along.

2. We have short time to stay, as you,
We have as short a Spring;
As quick a growth to meet Decay,
As you, or any thing.
We die,
As your hours doe, and drie
Away,
Like to the Summers raine;
Or as the pearles of Mornings dew
Ne'r to be found againe.

To a Maid.

You say, you love me; that I thus must prove;
If that you lye, then I will sweare you love.

Upon a Lady that dyed in child-bed, and left a daughter behind her.

As Gilly flowers do but stay
To blow, and seed, and so away;
So you sweet Lady (sweet as May)
The gardens-glory liv'd a while,
To lend the world your scent and smile.
But when your own faire print was set
Once in a Virgin *Flosculet*,
(Sweet as your selfe, and newly blown)
To give that life, resign'd your own:
But so, as still the mothers power
Lives in the pretty Lady-flower.

A New-yeares gift sent to Sir Simeon Steward.

No newes of Navies burnt at Seas;
No noise of late spawn'd *Tittyries*:
No closset plot, or open vent,
That frights men with a Parliament:
No new devise, or late found trick,
To read by th'Starres, the Kingdoms sick:
No ginne to catch the State, or wring
The free-born Nosthrills of the King,
We send to you; but here a jolly
Verse crown'd with *Yvie*, and with *Holly*:
That tels of Winters Tales and Mirth,
That Milk-maids make about the hearth,
Of Christmas sports, the *Wassell-boule*,
That's tost up, after *Fox-i'th'hole*:
Of *Blind-man-buffe*, and of the care
That young men have to shooe the *Mare*:

3.8 Nosthrills *BEK1MPUWi*: Nosthrill *rest*

Of Twelf-tide Cakes, of Pease, and Beanes
Wherewith ye make those merry Sceanes,
When as ye chuse your King and Queen,
And cry out, *Hey, for our town green.*
Of Ash-heapes, in the which ye use
Husbands and Wives by streakes to chuse:
Of crackling Laurell, which fore-sounds,
A Plentious harvest to your grounds:
Of these, and such like things, for shift,
We send in stead of New-yeares gift.
Read then, and when your faces shine
With bucksome meat and capring Wine:
Remember us in Cups full crown'd,
And let our Citie-health go round,
Quite through the young maids and the men,
To the ninth number, if not tenne;
Untill the fired Chesnuts leape
For joy, to see the fruits ye reape,
From the plumpe Challice, and the Cup,
That tempts till it be tossed up:
Then as ye sit about your embers,
Call not to mind those fled Decembers;
But think on these, that are t'appeare,
As Daughters to the instant yeare:
Sit crown'd with Rose-buds, and carouse,
Till *Liber Pater* twirles the house
About your eares; and lay upon
The yeare (your cares) that's fled and gon.
And let the russet Swaines the Plough
And Harrow hang up resting now;
And to the Bag-pipe all addresse;
Till sleep takes place of wearinesse.
And thus, throughout, with Christmas playes
Frolick the full twelve Holy-dayes.

Mattens, or morning Prayer.

WHEN with the Virgin morning thou do'st rise,
Crossing thy selfe; come thus to sacrifice:
First wash thy heart in innocence, then bring
Pure hands, pure habits, pure, pure every thing.

Next to the Altar humbly kneele, and thence,
Give up thy soule in clouds of frankinsence.
Thy golden Censors fil'd with odours sweet,
Shall make thy actions with their ends to meet.

Evensong.

BEGINNE with *Jove*; then is the worke halfe done;
And runnes most smoothly, when tis well begunne.
Jove's is the first and last: The Morn's his due,
The midst is thine; But *Joves* the Evening too;
As sure as *Mattins* do's to him belong,
So sure he layes claime to the *Evensong*.

The Bracelet to Julia.

WHY I tye about thy wrist,
Julia, this my silken twist;
For what other reason is't,
But to shew thee how in part,
Thou my pretty Captive art?
But thy Bondslave is my heart:
'Tis but silke that bindeth thee,
Knap the thread, and thou art free:
But 'tis otherwise with me;
I am bound, and fast bound so,
That from thee I cannot go;
If I co'd, I wo'd not so.

The Christian Militant.

A MAN prepar'd against all ills to come,
That dares to dead the fire of martirdome:
That sleeps at home; and sayling there at ease,
Feares not the fierce sedition of the Seas:
That's counter-proofe against the Farms mis-haps,
Undreadfull too of courtly thunderclaps:
That weares one face (like heaven) and never showes
A change, when Fortune either comes, or goes:
That keepes his own strong guard, in the despight
Of what can hurt by day, or harme by night:

1 .5 as] a *48*   2 (*heading*) *Bracelet ed.*: *Braclet 48*

That takes and re-delivers every stroake
Of Chance, (as made up all of rock, and oake:)
That sighs at others death; smiles at his own
Most dire and horrid crucifixion.
Who for true glory suffers thus; we grant
Him to be here our *Christian militant.*

A short Hymne to Larr.

THOUGH I cannot give thee fires
Glit'ring to my free desires:
These accept, and Ile be free,
Offering *Poppy* unto thee.

Another to Neptune.

MIGHTY *Neptune*, may it please
Thee, the *Rector* of the Seas,
That my Barque may safely runne
Through thy watrie-region;
And a *Tunnie-fish* shall be
Offer'd up, with thanks to thee.

Upon Greedy. *Epig.*

AN old, old widow *Greedy* needs wo'd wed,
Not for affection to her, or her Bed;
But in regard, 'twas often said, this old
Woman wo'd bring him more then co'd be told,
He tooke her; now the jest in this appeares,
So old she was, that none co'd tell her yeares.

His embalming to Julia.

FOR my embalming, *Julia*, do but this,
Give thou my lips but their supreamest kiss:
Or else trans-fuse thy breath into the chest,
Where my small reliques must for ever rest:
That breath the *Balm*, the *myrrh*, the *Nard* shal be,
To give an *incorruption* unto me.

3.5 jest in this] jestn ithis *K1MPUWi*

Gold, before Goodnesse.

How rich a man is, all desire to know;
But none enquires if good he be, or no.

The Kisse. *A Dialogue.*

1. Among thy Fancies, tell me this,
   What is the thing we call a kisse?
2. I shall resolve ye, what it is.

It is a creature born and bred
Between the lips, (all cherrie-red,)
By love and warme desires fed,
Chor. And makes more soft the Bridall Bed.

2. It is an active flame, that flies,
First, to the Babies of the eyes;
And charmes them there with lullabies;
Chor. And stils the Bride too, when she cries.

2. Then to the chin, the cheek, the eare,
It frisks, and flyes, now here, now there,
'Tis now farre off, and then tis nere;
Chor. And here, and there, and every where.

1. Ha's it a speaking virtue? 2. Yes;
1. How speaks it, say? 2. Do you but this,
Part your joyn'd lips, then speaks your kisse;
Chor. And this loves sweetest language is.

1. Has it a body? 2. I, and wings
With thousand rare encolourings:
And as it flyes, it gently sings,
Chor. Love, honie yeelds; but never stings

The admonition.

Seest thou those *Diamonds* which she weares
In that rich Carkanet;
Or those on her dishevel'd haires,
Faire *Pearles* in order set?

1, 2, *and* 3 *For variants see pp.* 481–2

Beleeve young man all those were teares
By wretched Wooers sent,
In mournfull *Hyacinths* and *Rue*,
That figure discontent;
Which when not warmed by her view,
By cold neglect, each one,
Congeal'd to Pearle and stone;
Which precious spoiles upon her,
She weares as trophees of her honour.
Ah then consider! What all this implies;
She that will weare thy teares, wo'd weare thine eyes.

To his honoured kinsman Sir William Soame. *Epig.*

I CAN but name thee, and methinks I call
All that have been, or are canonicall
For love and bountie, to come neare, and see,
Their many vertues volum'd up in thee;
In thee Brave Man! Whose incorrupted fame,
Casts forth a light like to a Virgin flame:
And as it shines, it throwes a scent about,
As when a Rain-bow in perfumes goes out.
So vanish hence, but leave a name, as sweet,
As *Benjamin*, and *Storax*, when they meet.

On himselfe.

ASKE me, why I do not sing
To the tension of the string,
As I did, not long ago,
When my numbers full did flow?
Griefe (ay me!) hath struck my Lute,
And my tongue at one time mute.

To Larr.

NO more shall I, since I am driven hence,
Devote to thee my graines of Frankinsence:
No more shall I from mantle-trees hang downe,
To honour thee, my little Parsly crown:

No more shall I (I feare me) to thee bring
My chives of Garlick for an offering:
No more shall I, from henceforth, heare a quire
Of merry Crickets by my Country fire.
Go where I will, thou luckie *Larr* stay here,
Warme by a glit'ring chimnie all the yeare.

The departure of the good Dæmon.

WHAT can I do in Poetry,
Now the good Spirit's gone from me?
Why nothing now, but lonely sit,
And over-read what I have writ.

Clemency.

FOR punishment in warre, it will suffice,
If the chiefe Author of the faction dyes;
Let but few smart, but strike a feare through all:
Where the fault springs, there let the judgement fall.

His age, dedicated to his peculiar friend, M. John Wickes, *under the name of* Posthumus.

1. AH *Posthumus*! Our yeares hence flye,
And leave no sound; nor piety,
Or prayers, or vow
Can keepe the wrinkle from the brow:
But we must on,
As Fate do's lead or draw us; none,
None, *Posthumus*, co'd ere decline
The doome of cruell *Proserpine*.

2. The pleasing wife, the house, the ground
Must all be left, no one plant found
To follow thee,
Save only the *Curst-Cipresse* tree:
A merry mind
Looks forward, scornes what's left behind:
Let's live, my *Wickes*, then, while we may,
And here enjoy our Holiday.

1 *heading* Dæmon] Demon *BEK1MPUWi*   2.2 Author] auth *BEK1MUWiWr*   3 *For variants see pp.* 482–4

3. W'ave seen the past-best Times, and these
Will nere return, we see the Seas,
And Moons to wain;
But they fill up their Ebbs again:
But vanisht man,
Like to a Lilly-lost, nere can,
Nere can repullulate, or bring
His dayes to see a second Spring.

4. But on we must, and thither tend,
Where *Anchus* and rich *Tullus* blend
Their sacred seed:
Thus has *Infernall Jove* decreed;
We must be made,
Ere long, a song, ere long, a shade.
Why then, since life to us is short,
Lets make it full up, by our sport.

5. Crown we our Heads with Roses then,
And 'noint with *Tirian Balme*; for when
We two are dead,
The world with us is buried.
Then live we free,
As is the Air, and let us be
Our own fair wind, and mark each one
Day with the white and Luckie stone.

6. We are not poore; although we have
No roofs of Cedar, nor our brave
Baiæ, nor keep
Account of such a flock of sheep;
Nor Bullocks fed
To lard the shambles: Barbels bred
To kisse our hands, nor do we wish
For *Pollio's* Lampries in our dish.

7. If we can meet, and so conferre,
Both by a shining Salt-seller;
And have our Roofe,
Although not archt, yet weather proofe,
And seeling free,
From that cheape *Candle baudery*:
We'le eate our Beane with that full mirth,
As we were Lords of all the earth.

8. Well then, on what Seas we are tost,
Our comfort is, we can't be lost.
Let the winds drive
Our Barke; yet she will keepe alive
Amidst the deepes;
'Tis constancy (my *Wickes*) which keepes
The Pinnace up; which though she erres
I'th'Seas, she saves her passengers.

9. Say, we must part (sweet mercy blesse
Us both i'th'Sea, Camp, Wildernesse)
Can we so farre
Stray, to become lesse circular,
Then we are now?
No, no, that selfe same heart, that vow,
Which made us one, shall ne'r undoe;
Or ravell so, to make us two.

10. Live in thy peace; as for my selfe,
When I am bruised on the Shelfe
Of Time, and show
My locks behung with frost and snow:
When with the reume,
The cough, the ptisick, I consume
Unto an almost nothing; then,
The Ages fled, Ile call agen:

11. And with a teare compare these last
Lame, and bad times, with those are past,
While *Baucis* by,
My old leane wife, shall kisse it dry:
And so we'l sit
By'th'fire, foretelling snow and slit,
And weather by our aches, grown
Now old enough to be our own

12. True Calenders, as Pusses eare
Washt or's to tell what change is neare:
Then to asswage
The gripings of the chine by age;

l. 90 or's to] o're, to *48* (*corr. Errata*) neare:] neare *K1M*

I'le call my young
Iülus to sing such a song
I made upon my *Julia's* brest;
And of her blush at such a feast.

13. Then shall he read that flowre of mine
Enclos'd within a christall shrine:
A Primrose next;
A piece, then of a higher text:
For to beget
In me a more transcendant heate,
Then that insinuating fire,
Which crept into each aged Sire.

14. When the faire *Hellen*, from her eyes,
Shot forth her loving Sorceries:
At which I'le reare
Mine aged limbs above my chaire:
And hearing it,
Flutter and crow, as in a fit
Of fresh concupiscence, and cry,
No lust theres like to Poetry.

15. Thus frantick crazie man (God wot)
Ile call to mind things half forgot:
And oft between,
Repeat the Times that I have seen!
Thus ripe with tears,
And twisting my *Iülus* hairs;
Doting, Ile weep and say (In Truth)
Baucis, these were my sins of youth.

16. Then next Ile cause my hopefull Lad
(If a wild Apple can be had)
To crown the Hearth,
(*Larr* thus conspiring with our mirth)
Then to infuse
Our browner Ale into the cruse:
Which sweetly spic't, we'l first carouse
Unto the *Genius* of the house.

17. Then the next health to friends of mine
(Loving the brave *Burgundian wine*)

High sons of Pith,
Whose fortunes I have frolickt with:
Such as co'd well
Bear up the Magick bough, and spel:
And dancing 'bout the Mystick *Thyrse*,
Give up the just applause to verse:

18. To those, and then agen to thee
We'l drink, my *Wickes*, untill we be
Plump as the cherry,
Though not so fresh, yet full as merry
As the crickit;
The untam'd Heifer, or the Pricket,
Untill our tongues shall tell our ears,
W'are younger by a score of years.

19. Thus, till we see the fire lesse shine
From th'embers, then the kitlings eyne,
We'l still sit up,
Sphering about the wassail cup,
To all those times,
Which gave me honour for my Rhimes,
The cole once spent, we'l then to bed,
Farre more then night bewearied.

A short hymne to Venus.

GODDESSE, I do love a Girle
Rubie-lipt, and tooth'd with *Pearl:*
If so be, I may but prove
Luckie in this Maide I love:
I will promise there shall be
Mirtles offer'd up to Thee.

To a Gentlewoman on just dealing.

TRUE to your self, and sheets, you'l have me swear,
You shall; if righteous dealing I find there.
Do not you fall through frailty; Ile be sure
To keep my Bond still free from forfeiture.

1 *For variants see p.* 484

The hand and tongue.

TWO parts of us successively command;
The tongue in peace; but then in warre the hand.

Upon a delaying Lady.

COME come away,
Or let me go;
Must I here stay,
Because y'are slow;
And will continue so?
Troth Lady, no.

2. I scorne to be
A slave to state:
And since I'm free,
I will not wait,
Henceforth at such a rate,
For needy Fate.

3. If you desire
My spark sho'd glow,
The peeping fire
You must blow;
Or I shall quickly grow,
To Frost or Snow.

To the Lady Mary Villars, *Governesse to the Princesse* Henretta.

WHEN I of *Villars* doe but heare the name,
It calls to mind, that mighty *Buckingham*,
Who was your brave exalted Uncle here,
(Binding the wheele of Fortune to his Sphere)
Who spurn'd at Envie; and co'd bring, with ease,
An end to all his stately purposes.
For his love then, whose sacred Reliques show
Their Resurrection, and their growth in you:
And for my sake, who ever did prefer
You, above all Those *Sweets* of *Westminster:*
Permit my Book to have a free accesse
To kisse your hand, most Dainty Governesse.

Upon his Julia.

WILL ye heare, what I can say
Briefly of my *Julia?*
Black and rowling is her eye,
Double chinn'd, and forehead high:
Lips she has, all Rubie red,
Cheeks like Creame Enclarited:
And a nose that is the grace
And *Proscenium* of her face.
So that we may guesse by these,
The other parts will richly please.

To Flowers.

IN time of life, I grac't ye with my Verse;
Doe now your flowrie honours to my Herse.
You shall not languish, trust me: Virgins here
Weeping, shall make ye flourish all the yeere.

To my ill Reader.

THOU say'st my lines are hard;
And I the truth will tell;
They are both hard, and marr'd,
If thou not read'st them well.

The power in the people.

LET Kings Command, and doe the best they may,
The saucie Subjects still will beare the sway.

A Hymne to Venus, *and* Cupid.

SEA-BORN Goddesse, let me be,
By thy sonne thus grac't, and thee;
That when ere I wooe, I find
Virgins coy, but not unkind.
Let me when I kisse a maid,
Taste her lips, so over-laid
With Loves-sirrop; that I may,
In your Temple, when I pray,
Kisse the Altar, and confess
Ther's in love, no bitterness.

On Julia's *Picture.*

How am I ravisht! When I do but see,
The Painters art in thy *Sciography*?
If so, how much more shall I dote thereon,
When once he gives it incarnation?

Her Bed.

See'st thou that Cloud as silver cleare,
Plump, soft, & swelling every where?
Tis *Julia's* Bed, and she sleeps there.

Her Legs.

Fain would I kiss my *Julia's* dainty Leg,
Which is as white and hair-less as an egge.

Upon her Almes.

See how the poore do waiting stand,
For the expansion of thy hand.
A wafer Dol'd by thee, will swell
Thousands to feed by miracle.

Rewards.

Still to our gains our chief respect is had;
Reward it is, that makes us good or bad.

Nothing new.

Nothing is New: we walk where others went.
Ther's no vice now, but has his president.

The Rainbow.

Look, how the *Rainbow* doth appeare
But in one onely *Hemisphere:*
So likewise after our disseace,
No more is seen the Arch of Peace.
That Cov'nant's here; The under-bow,
That nothing shoots, but war and woe.

2.1 See'st] See'st, *48*

The meddow verse or Aniversary to Mistris Bridget Lowman.

COME with the Spring-time, forth Fair Maid, and be
This year again, the *medows Deity*.
Yet ere ye enter, give us leave to set
Upon your Head this flowry Coronet:
To make this neat distinction from the rest;
You are the Prime, and Princesse of the Feast:
To which, with silver feet lead you the way,
While sweet-breath Nimphs, attend on you this Day.
This is your houre; and best you may command,
Since you are Lady of this Fairie land.
Full mirth wait on you; and such mirth as shall
Cherrish the cheek, but make none blush at all.

The parting verse, the feast there ended.

LOTH to depart, but yet at last, each one
Back must now go to's habitation:
Not knowing thus much, when we once do sever,
Whether or no, that we shall meet here ever.
As for my self, since time a thousand cares
And griefs hath fil'de upon my silver hairs;
'Tis to be doubted whether I next yeer,
Or no, shall give ye a re-meeting here.
If die I must, then my last vow shall be,
You'l with a tear or two, remember me,
Your sometime Poet; but if fates do give
Me longer date, and more fresh springs to live:
Oft as your field, shall her old age renew,
Herrick shall make the meddow-verse for you.

Upon Judith. *Epig.*

JUDITH has cast her old-skin, and got new;
And walks fresh varnisht to the publick view.
Foule *Judith* was; and foule she will be known,
For all this fair *Transfiguration*.

Long and lazie.

THAT was the Proverb. Let my mistresse be
Lasie to others, but be long to me.

Upon Ralph. *Epig.*

CURSE not the mice, no grist of thine they eat:
But curse thy children, they consume thy wheat.

To the right honourable, Philip, *Earle of Pembroke, and Montgomerie.*

HOW dull and dead are books, that cannot show
A *Prince* of *Pembroke*, and that *Pembroke*, you!
You, who are High born, and a Lord no lesse
Free by your fate, then Fortunes mightinesse,
Who hug our Poems (Honourd Sir) and then
The paper gild, and Laureat the pen.
Nor suffer you the Poets to sit cold,
But warm their wits, and turn their lines to gold.
Others there be, who righteously will swear
Those smooth-pac't Numbers, amble every where;
And these brave Measures go a stately trot;
Love those, like these; regard, reward them not.
But you my Lord, are One, whose hand along
Goes with your mouth, or do's outrun your tongue;
Paying before you praise; and cockring wit,
Give both the Gold and Garland unto it.

An hymne to Juno.

STATELY Goddesse, do thou please,
Who art chief at marriages,
But to dresse the Bridall-Bed,
When my Love and I shall wed:
And a *Peacock* proud shall be
Offerd up by us, to thee.

1.2 *For variant see p.* 484 3.2 of *Hazlitt &c.*: or *48*

Upon Mease. *Epig.*

MEASE brags of Pullets which he eats: but *Mease*
Ne'r yet set tooth in stump, or rump of these.

Upon Sapho, *sweetly playing, and sweetly singing.*

WHEN thou do'st play, and sweetly sing,
Whether it be the voice or string,
Or both of them, that do agree
Thus to en-trance and ravish me:
This, this I know, I'm oft struck mute;
And dye away upon thy Lute.

Upon Paske *a Draper.*

PASKE, though his debt be due upon the day
Demands no money by a craving way;
For why sayes he, all debts and their arreares,
Have reference to the shoulders, not the eares.

Chop-Cherry.

THOU gav'st me leave to kisse;
Thou gav'st me leave to wooe;
Thou mad'st me thinke by this,
And that, thou lov'dst me too.

2. But I shall ne'r forget,
How for to make thee merry;
Thou mad'st me chop, but yet,
Another snapt the Cherry.

To the most learned, wise, and Arch-Antiquary, M. John Selden.

I WHO have favour'd many, come to be
Grac't (now at last) or glorifi'd by thee.
Loe, I, the Lyrick Prophet, who have set
On many a head the Delphick Coronet,

Come unto thee for Laurell, having spent,
My wreaths on those, who little gave or lent.
Give me the *Daphne*, that the world may know it,
Whom they neglected, thou hast crown'd a Poet.
A City here of *Heroes* I have made,
Upon the rock, whose firm foundation laid,
Shall never shrink, where making thine abode,
Live thou a *Selden*, that's a Demi-god.

Upon himself.

THOU shalt not All die; for while Love's fire shines
Upon his Altar, men shall read thy lines;
And learn'd Musicians shall to honour *Herricks*
Fame, and his Name, both set, and sing his Lyricks.

Upon wrinkles.

WRINKLES no more are, or no lesse,
Then beauty turn'd to sowernesse.

Upon Prigg.

P*RIGG*, when he comes to houses, oft doth use
(Rather then fail) to steal from thence old shoes:
Sound or unsound, be they rent or whole,
Prigg bears away the body and the sole.

Upon Moon.

MOON is an Usurer, whose gain,
Seldome or never, knows a wain,
Onely Moons conscience, we confesse,
That ebs from pittie lesse and lesse.

Pray and prosper.

FIRST offer Incense, then thy field and meads
Shall smile and smell the better by thy beads.
The spangling Dew dreg'd o're the grasse shall be
Turn'd all to Mell, and Manna there for thee.

2 *For variants see p.* 484 3.3 be] or be *Hazlitt*

Butter of *Amber*, *Cream*, and *Wine*, and *Oile*
Shall run, as rivers, all throughout thy soyl.
Wod'st thou to sincere-silver turn thy mold?
Pray once, twice pray; and turn thy ground to gold.

His Lachrimæ or Mirth, turn'd to mourning.

1. CALL me no more,
As heretofore,
The musick of a Feast;
Since now (alas)
The mirth, that was
In me, is dead or ceast.

2. Before I went
To banishment
Into the loathed West;
I co'd rehearse
A Lyrick verse,
And speak it with the best.

3. But time (Ai me)
Has laid, I see
My Organ fast asleep;
And turn'd my voice
Into the noise
Of those that sit and weep.

Upon Shift.

SHIFT now has cast his clothes: got all things new;
Save but his hat, and that he cannot mew.

Upon Cuts.

IF wounds in clothes, *Cuts* calls his rags, 'tis cleere,
His linings are the matter running there.

Gain and Gettings.

WHEN others gain much by the present cast,
The coblers getting time, is at the Last.

1 (*heading*) *Lachrimæ*] *Lacrime 48* (*corr. Errata*) 4.1 *For variant s*
p. 484

To the most fair and lovely Mistris, Anne Soame, *now Lady* Abdie.

So smell those odours that do rise
From out the wealthy spiceries:
So smels the flowre of *blooming Clove*;
Or *Roses* smother'd in the stove:
So smells the Aire of spiced wine;
Or *Essences* of *Jessimine*:
So smells the Breath about the hives,
When well the work of hony thrives;
And all the *busie Factours* come
Laden with wax and hony home:
So smell those neat and woven Bowers,
All over-archt with *Oringe flowers*,
And *Almond blossoms*, that do mix
To make rich these *Aromatikes*:
So smell those bracelets, and those bands
Of *Amber* chaf't between the hands,
When thus enkindled they transpire
A noble perfume from the fire.
The wine of cherries, and to these,
The cooling breath of Respasses;
The smell of mornings milk, and cream;
Butter of *Cowslips* mixt with them;
Of rosted warden, or bak'd peare,
These are not to be reckon'd here;
When as the meanest part of her,
Smells like the maiden-Pomander.
Thus sweet she smells, or what can be
More lik'd by her, or lov'd by mee.

Upon his kinswoman Mistris Elizabeth Herrick.

Sweet virgin, that I do not set
The pillars up of weeping *Jet*,
Or mournfull *Marble*; let thy shade
Not wrathfull seem, or fright the Maide,
Who hither at her wonted howers
Shall come to strew thy earth with flowers.

No, know (Blest Maide) when there's not one
Remainder left of Brasse or stone,
Thy living Epitaph shall be,
Though lost in them, yet found in me.
Dear, in thy *bed of Roses*, then,
Till this world shall dissolve as men,
Sleep, while we hide thee from the light,
Drawing thy curtains round: *Good night.*

A Panegerick to Sir Lewis Pemberton.

TILL I shall come again, let this suffice,
I send my salt, my sacrifice
To Thee, thy Lady, younglings, and as farre
As to thy *Genius* and thy *Larre*;
To the worn Threshold, Porch, Hall, Parlour, Kitchin,
The fat-fed smoking Temple, which in
The wholsome savour of thy mighty Chines
Invites to supper him who dines,
Where laden spits, warp't with large Ribbs of Beefe,
Not represent, but give reliefe
To the lanke-Stranger, and the sowre Swain;
Where both may feed, and come againe:
For no black-bearded *Vigil* from thy doore
Beats with a button'd-staffe the poore:
But from thy warm-love-hatching gates each may
Take friendly morsels, and there stay
To Sun his thin-clad members, if he likes,
For thou no Porter keep'st who strikes.
No commer to thy Roofe his *Guest-rite* wants;
Or staying there, is scourg'd with taunts
Of some rough Groom, who (yirkt with Corns) sayes, Sir
Y'ave dipt too long i'th Vinegar;
And with our Broth and bread, and bits; Sir, friend,
Y'ave farced well, pray make an end;
Two dayes y'ave larded here; a third, yee know,
Makes guests and fish smell strong; pray go
You to some other chimney, and there take
Essay of other giblets; make
Merry at anothers hearth; y'are here
Welcome as thunder to our beere:

l. 29 Merry] You merry *Hazlitt &c.*

Manners knowes distance, and a man unrude
        Wo'd soon recoile, and not intrude
His Stomach to a second Meale. No, no,
        Thy house, well fed and taught, can show
No such crab'd vizard: Thou hast learnt thy Train,
        With heart and hand to entertain:
And by the Armes-full (with a Brest unhid)
        As the old Race of mankind did,
When eithers heart, and eithers hand did strive
        To be the nearer Relative:
Thou do'st redeeme those times; and what was lost
        Of antient honesty, may boast
It keeps a growth in thee; and so will runne
        A course in thy Fames-pledge, *thy Sonne.*
Thus, like a *Roman Tribune*, thou thy gate
        Early setts ope to feast, and late:
Keeping no *currish Waiter* to affright,
        With blasting eye, the appetite,
Which fain would waste upon thy Cates, but that
        The *Trencher-creature* marketh what
Best and more suppling piece he cuts, and by
        Some private pinch tels danger's nie
A hand too desp'rate, or a knife that bites
        Skin deepe into the Porke, or lights
Upon some part of Kid, as if mistooke,
        When checked by the Butlers look.
No, no, thy bread, thy wine, thy jocund Beere
        Is not reserv'd for *Trebius* here,
But all, who at thy table seated are,
        Find equall freedome, equall fare;
And Thou, like to that *Hospitable God*,
        Jove, joy'st when guests make their abode
To eate thy Bullocks thighs, thy Veales, thy fat
        Weathers, and never grudged at.
The *Phesant*, *Partridge*, *Gotwit*, *Reeve*, *Ruffe*, *Raile*,
        The *Cock*, the *Curlew*, and the *quaile*;
These, and thy choicest viands do extend
        Their taste unto the lower end
Of thy glad table: not a dish more known
        To thee, then unto any one:
But as thy meate, so thy *immortall wine*
        Makes the smirk face of each to shine,

And spring fresh *Rose-buds*, while the salt, the wit
Flowes from the Wine, and graces it:
While Reverence, waiting at the bashfull board,
Honours my Lady and my Lord.
No scurrile jest; no open Sceane is laid
Here, for to make the face affraid;
But temp'rate mirth dealt forth, and so discreet-
ly that it makes the meate more sweet;
And adds perfumes unto the Wine, which thou
Do'st rather poure forth, then allow
By cruse and measure; thus devoting Wine,
As the *Canary* Isles were thine:
But with that wisdome, and that method, as
No One that's there his guilty glasse
Drinks of distemper, or ha's cause to cry
Repentance to his liberty.
No, thou know'st order, Ethicks, and ha's read
All Oeconomicks, know'st to lead
A House-dance neatly, and can'st truly show,
How farre a Figure ought to go,
Forward, or backward, side-ward, and what pace
Can give, and what retract a grace;
What Gesture, Courtship; Comliness agrees,
With those thy primitive decrees,
To give subsistance to thy house, and proofe,
What *Genii* support thy roofe,
Goodnes and *Greatnes*; not the oaken Piles;
For these, and marbles have their whiles
To last, but not their ever: Vertues Hand
It is, which builds, 'gainst Fate to stand.
Such is thy house, whose firme foundations trust
Is more in thee, then in her dust,
Or depth, these last may yeeld, and yearly shrinke,
When what is strongly built, no chinke
Or yawning rupture can the same devoure,
But fixt it stands, by her own power,
And well-laid bottome, on the iron and rock,
Which tryes, and counter-stands the shock,
And *Ramme* of time and by vexation growes
The stronger: *Vertue dies when foes*
Are wanting to her exercise, but great
And large she spreads by dust, and sweat.

Safe stand thy Walls, and Thee, and so both will,
Since neithers height was rais'd by th'ill
Of others; since no Stud, no Stone, no Piece,
Was rear'd up by the Poore-mans fleece:
No Widowes Tenement was rackt to guild
Or fret thy Seeling, or to build
A *Sweating-Closset*, to annoint the silke-
soft-skin, or bath in *Asses milke*:
No *Orphans* pittance, left him, serv'd to set
The Pillars up of *lasting Jet*,
For which their cryes might beate against thine eares,
Or in the dampe Jet read their Teares.
No *Planke* from *Hallowed* Altar, do's appeale
To yond' *Star-chamber*, or do's seale
A curse to Thee, or Thine; but all things even
Make for thy peace, and pace to heaven.
Go on directly so, as just men may
A thousand times, more sweare, then say,
This is that *Princely Pemberton*, who can
Teach man to keepe a God in man:
And when wise Poets shall search out to see
Good men, *They find them all in Thee*.

To his Valentine, *on S.* Valentines *day*.

OFT have I heard both Youths and Virgins say,
Birds chuse their Mates, and couple too, this day:
But by their flight I never can divine,
When I shall couple with my Valentine.

Upon Doll. *Epig.*

DOLL she so soone began the wanton trade;
She ne'r remembers that she was a maide.

Upon Skrew. *Epig.*

SKREW lives by shifts; yet sweares by no small oathes;
For all his shifts, he cannot shift his clothes.

Upon Linnit. Epig.

LINNIT playes rarely on the Lute, we know;
And sweetly sings, but yet his breath sayes no.

3 *For variants see p.* 485

Upon M. Ben. Johnson. *Epig.*

AFTER the rare Arch-Poet JOHNSON dy'd,
The Sock grew loathsome, and the Buskins pride,
Together with the Stages glory stood
Each like a poore and pitied widowhood.
The Cirque prophan'd was; and all postures rackt:
For men did strut, and stride, and stare, not act.
Then temper flew from words; and men did squeake,
Looke red, and blow, and bluster, but not speake:
No Holy-Rage, or frantick-fires did stirre,
Or flash about the spacious Theater.
No clap of hands, or shout, or praises-proofe
Did crack the Play-house sides, or cleave her roofe.
Artlesse the Sceane was; and that monstrous sin
Of deep and *arrant ignorance* came in;
Such ignorance as theirs was, who once hist
At thy unequal'd Play, the *Alchymist*:
Oh fie upon 'em! Lastly too, all witt
In utter darkenes did, and still will sit
Sleeping the lucklesse Age out, till that she
Her Resurrection ha's again with Thee.

Another.

THOU had'st the wreath before, now take the Tree;
That henceforth none be *Laurel crown'd but Thee.*

To his Nephew, to be prosperous in his art of Painting.

ON, as thou hast begunne, brave youth, and get
The Palme from *Urbin*, *Titian*, *Tintarret*,
Brugel and *Coxie*, and the workes out-doe,
Of *Holben*, and That mighty *Ruben* too.
So draw, and paint, as none may do the like,
No, not the glory of the World, *Vandike.*

3.3 *Coxie*] *Coxu 48*

Upon Glasse. *Epig.*

GLASSE, out of deepe, and out of desp'rate want,
Turn'd, from a Papist here, a Predicant.
A Vicarige at last *Tom Glasse* got here,
Just upon five and thirty pounds a yeare.
Adde to that thirty five, but five pounds more,
He'l turn a Papist, rancker then before.

A Vow to Mars.

STORE of courage to me grant,
Now I'm turn'd a combatant:
Helpe me so, that I my *shield*,
(Fighting) lose not in the field.
That's the greatest shame of all,
That in warfare can befall.
Do but this; and there shall be
Offer'd up a Wolfe to thee.

To his maid Prew.

THESE *Summer-Birds* did with thy Master stay
The times of warmth; but then they flew away;
Leaving their Poet (being now grown old)
Expos'd to all the comming Winters cold.
But thou *kind Prew* did'st with my Fates abide,
As well the Winters, as the Summers Tide:
For which thy Love, live with thy Master here,
Not two, but all the seasons of the yeare.

A Canticle to Apollo.

PLAY *Phœbus* on thy Lute;
And we will all sit mute:
By listning to thy Lire,
That sets all eares on fire.

2. Hark, harke, the God do's play!
And as he leads the way
Through heaven, the very Spheres,
As men, turne all to eares.

2.5 greatest] grearest *48*   3.8 two] one *X*   4.1 *Phœbus*] *Poehbus X*
2 will all sit] will sit all *X*: will, all sit *48* (*comma sometimes faint*)
7 Spheres] Speres *X*

A just man.

A JUST man's like a Rock that turnes the wroth
Of all the raging Waves, into a froth.

Upon a hoarse singer.

SING me to death; for till thy voice be cleare,
'Twill never please the pallate of mine eare.

How Pansies *or* Hearts-ease *came first.*

FROLLICK Virgins once these were,
Over-loving, (living here:)
Being here their ends deny'd
Ranne for Sweet-hearts mad, and dy'd.
Love in pitie of their teares,
And their losse in blooming yeares;
For their restlesse here-spent houres,
Gave them *Hearts-ease* turn'd to Flow'rs.

To his peculiar friend Sir Edward Fish, *Knight Baronet.*

SINCE for thy full deserts (with all the rest
Of these chaste spirits, that are here possest
Of Life eternall) Time has made Thee one,
For growth in this my rich Plantation:
Live here: But know 'twas vertue, & not chance,
That gave Thee this so high inheritance.
Keepe it for ever; grounded with the good,
Who hold fast here an endlesse lively-hood.

Larr's *portion, and the* Poets *part.*

AT my homely Country-seat,
I have there a little wheat;
Which I worke to Meale, and make
Therewithall a *Holy-cake*:
Part of which I give to *Larr*,
Part is my peculiar.

3 (*heading*) Hearts-ease] Hart-ease *X* 4.8 lively-hood] lively food
5 (*heading*) *and X*: *or 48*

Upon Man.

MAN is compos'd here of a two-fold part;
The first of Nature, and the next of Art:
Art presupposes Nature; Nature shee
Prepares the way to mans docility.

Liberty.

THOSE ills that mortall men endure,
So long are capable of cure,
As they of freedome may be sure:
But that deni'd; a griefe, though small,
Shakes the whole Roofe, or ruines all.

Lots to be liked.

LEARN this of me, where e'r thy Lot doth fall;
Short lot, or not, to be content with all.

Griefes.

J*OVE* may afford us thousands of reliefs;
Since man expos'd is to a world of griefs.

Upon Eeles. *Epig.*

E*ELES* winds and turnes, and cheats and steales; yet *Eeles*
Driving these sharking trades, is out at heels.

The Dreame.

BY Dream I saw, one of the three
Sisters of Fate appeare to me.
Close to my Beds side she did stand
Shewing me there a fire brand;
She told me too, as that did spend,
So drew my life unto an end.
Three quarters were consum'd of it;
Onely remaind a little bit,
Which will be burnt up by and by,
Then *Julia* weep, for I must dy.

1.4 to] for *X* 3.2 all.] all 48 5.2 heels.] heels, *48*
6.10 *Julia*] *Juha 48*

Upon Raspe *Epig.*

R*ASPE* playes at Nine-holes; and 'tis known he gets
Many a Teaster by his game, and bets:
But of his gettings there's but little sign;
When one hole wasts more then he gets by Nine.

Upon Center *a Spectacle-maker with a flat nose.*

C*ENTER* is known weak sighted, and he sells
To others store of helpfull spectacles.
Why weres he none? Because we may suppose,
Where *Leaven* wants, there *Levill* lies the nose.

Clothes do but cheat and cousen us.

AWAY with silks, away with Lawn,
Ile have no Sceans, or Curtains drawn:
Give me my Mistresse, as she is,
Drest in her nak't simplicities:
For as my Heart, ene so mine Eye
Is wone with flesh, not *Drapery.*

To Dianeme.

SHEW me thy feet; shew me thy legs, thy thighes;
Shew me Those *Fleshie Principalities*;
Shew me that Hill (where smiling Love doth sit)
Having a living Fountain under it.
Shew me thy waste; Then let me there withall,
By the *Assention* of thy Lawn, see All.

Upon Electra.

WHEN out of bed my Love doth spring,
'Tis but as day a kindling:
But when She's up and fully drest,
'Tis then *broad Day throughout the East.*

To his Booke.

HAVE I not blest Thee? Then go forth; nor fear
Or spice, or fish, or fire, or close-stools here.
But with thy fair Fates leading thee, Go on
With thy most white *Predestination.*
Nor thinke these Ages that do hoarcely sing
The *farting Tanner*, and *familiar King*;
The *dancing Frier*, tatter'd in the bush;
Those monstrous lies of little *Robin Rush*:
Tom Chipperfeild, and pritty-*lisping Ned*,
That doted on a Maide of *Gingerbred*:
The *flying Pilcher*, and the *frisking Dace*,
With all the rabble of *Tim-Trundells* race,
(Bred from the dung-hils, and adulterous rhimes,)
Shall live, and thou not superlast all times?
No, no, thy Stars have destin'd Thee to see
The whole world die, and turn to dust with thee.
He's greedie of his life, who will not fall,
When as a publick ruine bears down All.

Of Love.

I DO not love, nor can it be
Love will in vain spend shafts on me:
I did this God-head once defie;
Since which I freeze, but cannot frie.
Yet out alas! the deaths the same,
Kil'd by a frost or by a flame.

Upon himself.

I DISLIKT but even now;
Now I love I know not how.
Was I idle, and that while
Was I fier'd with a smile?
Ile to work, or pray; and then
I shall quite dislike agen.

Another.

LOVE he that will; it best likes me,
To have my neck from Loves yoke free.

3.5 to *WR* (*see p.* 485): too *48*

Upon Skinns. *Epig.*

S*KINNS* he din'd well to day; how do you think?
His Nails they were his meat, his Reume the drink.

Upon Pievish. Epig.

PIEVISH doth boast, that he's the very first
Of English Poets, and 'tis thought the Worst.

Upon Jolly *and* Jilly, *Epig.*

J*OLLY* and *Jillie*, bite and scratch all day,
But yet get children (as the neighbours say.)
The reason is, though all the day they fight,
They cling and close, some minutes of the night.

The mad Maids song.

1. GOOD morrow to the Day so fair;
   Good morning Sir to you:
Good morrow to mine own torn hair
   Bedabled with the dew.

2. Good morning to this Prim-rose too;
   Good morrow to each maid;
That will with flowers the *Tomb* bestrew,
   Wherein my Love is laid.

3. Ah woe is me, woe, woe is me,
   Alack and welladay!
For pitty, Sir, find out that Bee,
   Which bore my Love away.

4. I'le seek him in your *Bonnet* brave;
   Ile seek him in your eyes;
Nay, now I think th'ave made his grave
   I'th'bed of strawburies.

5. Ile seek him there; I know, ere this,
   The cold, cold Earth doth shake him;
But I will go, or send a kisse
   By you, Sir, to awake him.

4 *For variants see p.* 485. *(corr. Errata)*   4.9] Ah! woe woe woe woe woe is me 48

6. Pray hurt him not; though he be dead,
He knowes well who do love him,
And who with green-turfes reare his head,
And who do rudely move him.

7. He's soft and tender (Pray take heed)
With bands of Cow-slips bind him;
And bring him home, but 'tis decreed,
That I shall never find him.

To Springs and Fountains.

I HEARD ye co'd coole heat; and came
With hope you would allay the same:
Thrice I have washt, but feel no cold,
Nor find that true, which was foretold.
Me thinks like mine, your pulses beat;
And labour with unequall heat:
Cure, cure your selves, for I discrie,
Ye boil with Love, as well as I.

Upon Julia's *unlacing her self.*

TELL, if thou canst, (and truly) whence doth come
This *Camphire*, *Storax*, *Spiknard*, *Galbanum*:
These *Musks*, these *Ambers*, and those other smells
(Sweet as the *Vestrie of the Oracles*.)
Ile tell thee; while my *Julia* did unlace
Her silken bodies, but a breathing space:
The passive Aire such odour then assum'd,
As when to *Jove* Great *Juno* goes perfum'd.
Whose pure-Immortall body doth transmit
A scent, that fills both Heaven and Earth with it.

To Bacchus, *a Canticle.*

WHITHER dost thou whorry me,
Bacchus, being full of thee?
This way, that way, that way, this,
Here, and there a fresh Love is.
That doth like me, this doth please;
Thus a thousand Mistresses,
I have now; yet I alone,
Having All, injoy not *One*.

The Lawne.

WO'D I see Lawn, clear as the Heaven, and thin?
It sho'd be onely in my *Julia's* skin:
Which so betrayes her blood, as we discover
The blush of cherries, when a Lawn's cast over.

The Frankincense.

WHEN my off'ring next I make,
Be thy hand the hallowed Cake:
And thy brest the Altar, whence
Love may smell the *Frankincense.*

Upon Patrick *a footman, Epig.*

NOW *Patrick* with his footmanship has done,
His eyes and ears strive which sho'd fastest run.

Upon Bridget. *Epig.*

OF foure teeth onely *Bridget* was possest;
Two she spat out, a cough forc't out the rest.

To Sycamores.

I'M sick of Love; O let me lie
Under your shades, to sleep or die!
Either is welcome; so I have
Or here my Bed, or here my Grave.
Why do you sigh, and sob, and keep
Time with the tears, that I do weep?
Say, have ye sence, or do you prove
What *Crucifixions* are in Love?
I know ye do; and that's the why,
You sigh for Love, as well as I.

2.3 brest] bed *48* (*corr. Errata*)   5 *For variants see p.* 485

A Pastorall sung to the King: Montano, Silvio, *and* Mirtillo, *Shepheards.*

Mon. Bad are the times. *Sil.* And wors then they are we.
Mon. Troth, bad are both; worse fruit, and ill the tree:
The feast of Shepheards fail. *Sil.* None crowns the cup
Of *Wassaile* now, or sets the *quintell* up:
And He, who us'd to leade the Country-round,
Youthfull *Mirtillo*, Here he comes, Grief drownd.
Ambo Lets cheer him up. *Sil.* Behold him weeping ripe.
Mirt. Ah! *Amarillis*, farewell mirth and pipe;
Since thou art gone, no more I mean to play,
To these smooth Lawns, my mirthfull Roundelay.
Dear *Amarillis*! *Mon.* Hark! *Sil.* mark: *Mir.* this earth grew sweet
Where, *Amarillis*, Thou didst set thy feet.
Ambo. Poor pittied youth! *Mir.* And here the breth of kine
And sheep, grew more sweet, by that breth of Thine.
This flock of wooll, and this rich lock of hair,
This ball of *Cow-slips*, these she gave me here.
Sil. Words sweet as Love it self. *Montano*, Hark.
Mirt. This way she came, and this way too she went;
How each thing smells divinely redolent!
Like to a field of beans, when newly blown;
Or like a medow being lately mown.
Mont. A sweet-sad passion.——
Mirt. In dewie-mornings when she came this way,
Sweet Bents wode bow, to give my Love the day:
And when at night, she folded had her sheep,
Daysies wo'd shut, and closing, sigh and weep.
Besides (Ai me!) since she went hence to dwell,
The voices Daughter nea'r spake syllable.
But she is gone. *Sil. Mirtillo*, tell us whether,
Mirt. Where she and I shall never meet together.
Mont. Fore-fend it *Pan*, and *Pales* do thou please
To give an end: *Mir.* To what? *Scil.* such griefs as these.
Mirt. Never, O never! Still I may endure
The wound I suffer, never find a cure.
Mont. Love for thy sake will bring her to these hills
And dales again: *Mir.* No I will languish still;
And all the while my part shall be to weepe;
And with my sighs, call home my bleating sheep:

And in the Rind of every comely tree
Ile carve thy name, and in that name kisse thee:
Mont. Set with the Sunne, thy woes: *Scil.* The day grows old:
And time it is our full-fed flocks to fold.

Chor. The shades grow great; but greater growes our sorrow,
But lets go steepe
Our eyes in sleepe;
And meet to weepe
To morrow.

The Poet loves a Mistresse, but not to marry.

1. I DO not love to wed,
Though I do like to wooe;
And for a maidenhead
Ile beg, and buy it too.

2. Ile praise, and Ile approve
Those maids that never vary;
And fervently Ile love;
But yet I would not marry.

3. Ile hug, Ile kisse, Ile play,
And Cock-like Hens Ile tread:
And sport it any way;
But in the Bridall Bed:

4. For why? that man is poore,
Who hath but one of many;
But crown'd he is with store,
That single may have any.

5. Why then, say, what is he
(To freedome so unknown)
Who having two or three,
Will be content with one?

Upon Flimsey. *Epig.*

WHY walkes *Nick Flimsey* like a Male-content?
Is it because his money all is spent?
No, but because the Ding-thrift now is poore,
And knowes not where i'th world to borrow more.

Upon Shewbread. *Epig.*

LAST night thou didst invite me home to eate;
And shew'st me there much Plate, but little meat;
Prithee, when next thou do'st invite, barre State,
And give me meate, or give me else thy Plate.

The Willow Garland.

A WILLOW Garland thou did'st send
Perfum'd (last day) to me:
Which did but only this portend,
I was forsooke by thee.

Since so it is; Ile tell thee what,
To morrow thou shalt see
Me weare the Willow; after that,
To dye upon the Tree.

As Beasts unto the Altars go
With Garlands drest, so I
Will, with my Willow-wreath also,
Come forth and sweetly dye.

A Hymne to Sir Clipseby Crew.

'TWAS not Lov's Dart;
Or any blow
Of want, or foe,
Did wound my heart
With an eternall smart:

But only you,
My sometimes known
Companion,
(My dearest *Crew*,)
That me unkindly slew.

May your fault dye,
And have no name
In Bookes of fame;
Or let it lye
Forgotten now, as I.

.2 meat] meate *some copies including ACSUY. Reading (especially the stop)* *ncertain because of battered or broken type.* 2 *For variants see p.* 485

We parted are,
And now no more,
As heretofore,
By jocund Larr,
Shall be familiar. 2

But though we Sever
My *Crew* shall see,
That I will be
Here faithlesse never;
But love my *Clipseby* ever.

Upon Roots. *Epig.*

ROOTS had no money; yet he went o'th score
For a wrought Purse; can any tell wherefore?
Say, What sho'd *Roots* do with a Purse in print,
That h'ad nor Gold or Silver to put in't?

Upon Craw.

CRAW cracks in sirrop; and do's stinking say,
Who can hold that (my friends) that will away?

Observation.

WHO to the North, or South, doth set
His Bed, Male children shall beget.

Empires.

EMPIRES of Kings, are now, and ever were,
(As *Salust* saith) co-incident to feare.

Felicity, quick of flight.

EVERY time seemes short to be,
That's measur'd by felicity:
But one halfe houre, that's made up here
With griefe; seemes longer then a yeare.

Putrefaction.

PUTREFACTION is the end
Of all that Nature doth entend.

Passion.

WERE there not a Matter known,
There wo'd be no Passion.

Jack *and* Jill.

SINCE *Jack* and *Jill* both wicked be;
It seems a wonder unto me,
That they no better do agree.

Upon Parson Beanes.

OLD Parson *Beanes* hunts six dayes of the week,
And on the seaventh, he has his Notes to seek.
Six dayes he hollows so much breath away,
That on the seaventh, he can nor preach, or pray.

The crowd and company.

IN holy meetings, there a man may be
One of the crowd, not of the companie.

Short and long both likes.

THIS Lady's short, that Mistresse she is tall;
But long or short, I'm well content with all.

Pollicie in Princes.

THAT Princes may possesse a surer seat,
'Tis fit they make no One with them too great.

Upon Rook, Epig.

R*OOK* he sells feathers, yet he still doth crie
Fie on this pride, this Female vanitie.
Thus, though the Rooke do's raile against the sin,
He loves the gain that vanity brings in.

Upon the Nipples of Julia's *Breast.*

HAVE ye beheld (with much delight)
A red-Rose peeping through a white?
Or else a Cherrie (double grac't)
Within a Lillies Center plac't?
Or ever mark't the pretty beam,
A Strawberry shewes halfe drown'd in Creame?
Or seen rich Rubies blushing through
A pure smooth Pearle, and Orient too?
So like to this, nay all the rest,
Is each neate Niplet of her breast.

To Daisies, *not to shut so soone.*

1. SHUT not so soon; the dull-ey'd night
Ha's not as yet begunne
To make a seisure on the light,
Or to seale up the Sun.

2. No Marigolds yet closed are;
No shadowes great appeare;
Nor doth the early Shepheards Starre
Shine like a spangle here.

3. Stay but till my *Julia* close
Her life-begetting eye;
And let the whole world then dispose
It selfe to live or dye.

To the little Spinners.

YEE pretty Huswives, wo'd ye know
The worke that I wo'd put ye to?
This, this it sho'd be, for to spin,
A Lawn for me, so fine and thin,
As it might serve me for my skin.
For cruell Love ha's me so whipt,
That of my skin, I all am stript;
And shall dispaire, that any art
Can ease the rawnesse, or the smart;
Unlesse you skin again each part.

1.4 Lillies *ed.*: Lillie ? *48* 3.10 Unlesse] Uulesse *48*

Which mercy if you will but do,
I call all Maids to witnesse too
What here I promise, that no Broom
Shall now, or ever after come
To wrong a *Spinner* or her Loome.

Oberons *Palace.*

AFTER the Feast (my *Shapcot*) see,
The Fairie Court I give to thee:
Where we'le present our *Oberon* led
Halfe tipsie to the Fairie Bed,
Where *Mab* he finds; who there doth lie
Not without mickle majesty.
Which, done; and thence remov'd the light,
We'l wish both Them and Thee, good night.

Full as a Bee with Thyme, and Red,
As Cherry harvest, now high fed
For Lust and action; on he'l go,
To lye with *Mab*, though all say no.
Lust ha's no eares; He's sharpe as thorn;
And fretfull, carries Hay in's horne,
And lightning in his eyes; and flings
Among the Elves, (if mov'd) the stings
Of peltish wasps; well know his Guard
Kings though th'are hated, will be fear'd.
Wine lead him on. Thus to a Grove
(Sometimes devoted unto Love)
Tinseld with *Twilight*, He, and They
Lead by the shine of Snails; a way
Beat with their num'rous feet, which by
Many a neat perplexity,
Many a turn, and man' a crosse-
Track they redeem a bank of mosse
Spungie and swelling, and farre more
Soft then the finest Lemster Ore.
Mildly disparkling, like those fiers,
Which break from the Injeweld tyres
Of curious Brides; or like those mites
Of Candi'd dew in Moony nights.

1 *For variants see pp.* 485–7

Upon this *Convex*, all the flowers,
(Nature begets by th'Sun, and showers,)
Are to a wilde digestion brought,
As if Loves *Sampler* here was wrought:
Or *Citherea's Ceston*, which
All with temptation doth bewitch.
Sweet Aires move here; and more divine
Made by the breath of great-ey'd kine,
Who as they lowe empearl with milk
The four-leav'd grasse, or mosse like silk.
The breath of *Munkies* met to mix
With *Musk-flies*, are th'*Aromaticks*,
Which cense this Arch; and here and there,
And farther off, and every where,
Throughout that *Brave Mosaick* yard
Those Picks or Diamonds in the Card:
With peeps of Harts, of Club and Spade
Are here most neatly inter-laid.
Many a Counter, many a Die,
Half rotten, and without an eye,
Lies here abouts; and for to pave
The excellency of this Cave,
Squirrils and childrens teeth late shed,
Are neatly here enchequered
With brownest *Toadstones*, and the Gum
That shines upon the blewer Plum.
The nails faln off by Whit-flawes: Art's
Wise hand enchasing here those warts,
Which we to others (from our selves)
Sell, and brought hither by the Elves.
The tempting Mole, stoln from the neck
Of the shie Virgin, seems to deck
The holy Entrance; where within
The roome is hung with the blew skin
Of shifted Snake: enfreez'd throughout
With eyes of Peacocks Trains, & Trout-
flies curious wings; and these among
Those silver-pence, that cut the tongue
Of the red infant, neatly hung.
The glow-wormes eyes; the shining scales
Of silv'rie fish; wheat-strawes, the snailes

l. 40 great-ey'd kine] great ey'd-kine *48*

Soft Candle-light; the Kitling's eyne;
Corrupted wood; serve here for shine.
No glaring light of bold-fac't Day,
Or other over radiant Ray
Ransacks this roome; but what weak beams
Can make reflected from these jems,
And multiply; Such is the light,
But ever doubtfull Day, or night.
By this quaint Taper-light he winds
His Errours up; and now he finds
His Moon-tann'd *Mab*, as somewhat sick,
And (Love knowes) tender as a chick.
Upon six plump *Dandillions*, high-
Rear'd, lyes her Elvish-majestie:
Whose woollie-bubbles seem'd to drowne
Hir *Mab-ship* in obedient Downe.
For either sheet, was spread the Caule
That doth the Infants face enthrall,
When it is born: (by some enstyl'd
The luckie *Omen* of the child)
And next to these two blankets ore-
Cast of the finest *Gossamore*.
And then a Rug of carded wooll,
Which, *Spunge-like* drinking in the dull-
Light of the Moon, seem'd to comply,
Cloud-like, the *daintie Deitie*.
Thus soft she lies: and over-head
A *Spinners* circle is bespread,
With Cob-web-curtains: from the roof
So neatly sunck, as that no proof
Of any tackling can declare
What gives it hanging in the Aire.
The Fringe about this, are those *Threds*
Broke at the Losse of *Maiden-heads*:
And all behung with these pure Pearls,
Dropt from the eyes of *ravisht Girles*
Or writhing Brides; when, (panting) they
Give unto Love the straiter way.
For Musick now; He has the cries
Of fained-lost-Virginities;
The which the *Elves* make to excite
A more unconquer'd appetite.

The Kings undrest; and now upon
The Gnats-watch-word the *Elves* are gone.
And now the bed, and *Mab* possest
Of this great-little-kingly-Guest.
We'll nobly think, what's to be done,
He'll do no doubt; *This flax is spun.*

To his peculiar friend Master Thomas Shapcott, *Lawyer.*

I'VE paid Thee, what I promis'd; that's not All;
Besides I give Thee here a Verse that shall
(When hence thy Circum-mortall-part is gon)
Arch-like, hold up, *Thy Name's Inscription.*
Brave men can't die; whose Candid Actions are
Writ in the Poets Endlesse-Kalendar:
Whose *velome*, and whose *volumne* is the Skie,
And the pure Starres the praising Poetrie.
Farewell.

To Julia *in the Temple.*

BESIDES us two, i'th'Temple here's not one
To make up now a Congregation.
Let's to the *Altar of perfumes* then go,
And say short Prayers; and when we have done so,
Then we shall see, how in a little space,
Saints will come in to fill each Pew and Place.

To Oenone.

1. WHAT Conscience, say, is it in thee
When I a Heart had one,
To Take away that Heart from me,
And to retain thy own?

2. For shame or pitty now encline
To play a loving part;
Either to send me kindly thine,
Or give me back my heart.

3 *For variants see p.* 487

3. Covet not both; but if thou dost
Resolve to part with neither;
Why! yet to shew that thou art just,
Take me and mine together.

His weaknesse in woes.

I CANNOT suffer; And in this, my part
Of Patience wants. *Grief breaks the stoutest Heart.*

Fame makes us forward.

TO Print our Poems, the propulsive cause
Is Fame, (the breath of popular applause.)

To Groves.

YEE silent shades, whose each tree here
Some Relique of a Saint doth weare:
Who for some sweet-hearts sake, did prove
The fire, and martyrdome of love.
Here is the Legend of those Saints
That di'd for love; and their complaints:
Their wounded hearts; and names we find
Encarv'd upon the Leaves and Rind.
Give way, give way to me, who come
Scorch't with the selfe-same martyrdome:
And have deserv'd as much (Love knowes)
As to be canoniz'd 'mongst those,
Whose deeds, and deaths here written are
Within your *Greenie-Kalendar*:
By all those Virgins Fillets hung
Upon your Boughs, and Requiems sung
For Saints and Soules departed hence,
(Here honour'd still with Frankincense)
By all those teares that have been shed,
As a *Drink-offering*, to the dead:
By all those True-love-knots, that be
With Motto's carv'd on every tree,
By sweet S. *Phillis*; pitie me:
By deare S. *Iphis*; and the rest,
Of all those other Saints now blest;

Me, me, forsaken, here admit
Among your Mirtles to be writ:
That my poore name may have the glory
To live remembred in your story.

An Epitaph upon a Virgin.

HERE a solemne Fast we keepe,
While all beauty lyes asleep
Husht be all things; (no noyse here)
But the toning of a teare:
Or a sigh of such as bring
Cowslips for her covering.

To the right gratious Prince, Lodwick, *Duke of* Richmond *and* Lenox.

OF all those three-brave-brothers, faln i'th'Warre,
(Not without glory) Noble Sir, you are,
Despite of all concussions left the Stem
To shoot forth Generations like to them.
Which may be done, if (Sir) you can beget
Men in their substance, not in counterfeit.
Such Essences as those Three Brothers; known
Eternall by their own production.
Of whom, from Fame's white Trumpet, This Ile Tell,
Worthy their everlasting Chronicle,
Never since first *Bellona* us'd a Shield,
Such Three brave Brothers fell in Mars *his Field.*
These were those Three *Horatii Rome* did boast,
Rom's were these *Three Horatii* we have lost.
One *Cordelion* had that Age long since;
This, Three; which Three, you make up Foure *Brave Prince.*

To Jealousie.

O *JEALOUSIE*, that art
The Canker of the heart:
And mak'st all hell
Where thou do'st dwell;
For pitie be
No *Furie*, or no *Fire-brand* to me.

2.9 Fame's] Fam's *48* 2.14 were] where *48*

2\. Farre from me Ile remove
All thoughts of irksome Love:
And turn to snow,
Or Christall grow;
To keep still free
(O! Soul-tormenting Jealousie,) from Thee.

To live Freely.

LET'S live in hast; use pleasures while we may:
Co'd life return, 'twod never lose a day.

Upon Spunge. *Epig.*

SPUNGE makes his boasts that he's the onely man
Can hold of Beere and Ale an Ocean;
Is this his Glory? then his Triumph's Poore;
I know the *Tunne* of *Hidleberge* holds more.

His Almes.

HERE, here I live,
And somewhat give,
Of what I have,
To those, who crave.
Little or much,
My Almnes is such:
But if my deal
Of Oyl and Meal
Shall fuller grow,
More Ile bestow:
Mean time be it
E'en but a bit,
Or else a crum,
The scrip hath some.

Upon himself.

COME, leave this loathed Country-life, and then
Grow up to be a Roman *Citizen.*
Those mites of Time, which yet remain unspent,
Waste thou in that most Civill Government.

Get their comportment, and the gliding tongue
Of those mild Men, thou art to live among:
Then being seated in that smoother *Sphere*,
Decree thy everlasting *Topick* there.
And to the Farm-house nere return at all;
Though Granges do not love thee, Cities shall.

To enjoy the Time.

WHILE Fate permits us, let's be merry;
Passe all we must the fatall Ferry:
And this our life too whirles away,
With the Rotation of the Day.

Upon Love.

1. LOVE, I have broke
Thy yoke;
The neck is free:
But when I'm next
Love vext,
Then shackell me.

2. 'Tis better yet
To fret
The feet or hands;
Then to enthrall,
Or gall
The neck with bands.

To the right Honourable Mildmay, *Earle of* Westmorland.

YOU are a Lord, an Earle, nay more, a Man,
Who writes sweet Numbers well as any can:
If so, why then are not These Verses hurld,
Like *Sybels* Leaves, throughout the ample world?
What is a Jewell if it be not set
Forth by a Ring, or some rich Carkanet?
But being so; then the beholders cry,
See, see a Jemme (as rare as *Bælus* eye.)
Then publick praise do's runne upon the Stone,
For a most rich, a rare, a precious One.

Expose your jewels then unto the view,
That we may praise Them, or themselves prize You.
Vertue conceal'd (with *Horace* you'l confesse)
Differs not much from drowzie slothfullnesse.

The Plunder.

I AM of all bereft;
Save but some few Beanes left,
Whereof (at last) to make
For me, and mine a Cake:
Which eaten, they and I
Will say our grace, and die.

Littlenesse no cause of Leannesse.

ONE feeds on Lard, and yet is leane;
And I but feasting with a Beane,
Grow fat and smooth: The reason is,
Jove prospers my meat, more then his.

Upon one who said she was alwayes young.

YOU say y'are young; but when your Teeth are told
To be but three, Black-ey'd, wee'l thinke y'are old.

Upon Huncks. *Epig.*

H*UNCKS* ha's no money (he do's sweare, or say)
About him, when the Taverns shot's to pay.
If he ha's none in's pockets, trust me, *Huncks*
Ha's none at home, in Coffers, Desks, or Trunks.

The Jimmall Ring, or True-love-knot.

THOU sent'st to me a True-love-knot; but I
Return'd a Ring of Jimmals, to imply
Thy Love had one knot, mine a triple tye.

The parting Verse, or charge to his supposed Wife when he travelled.

Go hence, and with this parting kisse,
Which joyns two souls, remember this;
Though thou beest young, kind, soft, and faire,
And may'st draw thousands with a haire:
Yet let these glib temptations be
Furies to others, Friends to me.
Looke upon all; and though on fire
Thou set'st their hearts, let chaste desire
Steere Thee to me; and thinke (me gone)
In having all, that thou hast none.
Nor so immured wo'd I have
Thee live, as dead and in thy grave;
But walke abroad, yet wisely well
Stand for my comming, Sentinell.
And think (as thou do'st walke the street)
Me, or my shadow thou do'st meet.
I know a thousand greedy eyes
Will on thy Feature tirannize,
In my short absence; yet behold
Them like some Picture, or some Mould
Fashion'd like Thee; which though 'tave eares
And eyes, it neither sees or heares.
Gifts will be sent, and Letters, which
Are the expressions of that itch,
And salt, which frets thy Suters; fly
Both, lest thou lose thy liberty:
For that once lost, thou't fall to one,
Then prostrate to a million.
But if they wooe thee, do thou say,
(As that chaste Queen of *Ithaca*
Did to her suitors) this web done
(Undone as oft as done) I'm wonne;
I will not urge Thee, for I know,
Though thou art young, thou canst say no,
And no again, and so deny,
Those thy Lust-burning *Incubi*.

For variants see pp. 487–8 l. 8 let] yet *48* (*corr. Errata*)

Let them enstile Thee Fairest faire,
The Pearle of Princes, yet despaire
That so thou art, because thou must
Believe, Love speaks it not, but Lust;
And this their Flatt'rie do's commend
Thee chiefly for their pleasures end.
I am not jealous of thy Faith,
Or will be; for the Axiome saith,
He that doth suspect, do's haste
A gentle mind to be unchaste.
No, live thee to thy selfe, and keep
Thy thoughts as cold, as is thy sleep:
And let thy dreames be only fed
With this, that I am in thy bed.
And thou then turning in that Sphere,
Waking shalt find me sleeping there.
But yet if boundlesse Lust must skaile
Thy Fortress, and will needs prevaile;
And wildly force a passage in,
Banish consent, and 'tis no sinne
Of Thine; so *Lucrece* fell, and the
Chaste *Syracusian Cyane.*
So *Medullina* fell, yet none
Of these had imputation
For the least trespasse; 'cause the mind
Here was not with the act combin'd.
The body sins not, 'tis the Will
That makes the Action, good, or ill.
And if thy fall sho'd this way come,
Triumph in such a Martirdome.
I will not over-long enlarge
To thee, this my religious charge.
Take this compression, so by this
Means I shall know what other kisse
Is mixt with mine; and truly know,
Returning, if't be mine or no:
Keepe it till then; and now my Spouse,
For my wisht safety pay thy vowes,
And prayers to *Venus*; if it please
The *Great-blew-ruler* of the Seas;

Not many full-fac't-moons shall waine,
Lean-horn'd, before I come again
As one triumphant; when I find
In thee, all faith of Woman-kind.
Nor wo'd I have thee thinke, that Thou
Had'st power thy selfe to keep this vow;
But having scapt temptations shelfe,
Know vertue taught thee, not thy selfe.

To his Kinsman, Sir Tho. Soame.

SEEING Thee *Soame*, I see a Goodly man,
And in that Good, a great *Patrician.*
Next to which Two; among the City-Powers,
And Thrones, thy selfe one of Those Senatours:
Not wearing Purple only for the show;
(As many Conscripts of the Citie do)
But for True Service, worthy of that Gowne,
The *Golden* chain too, and the *Civick* Crown.

To Blossoms.

1. FAIRE pledges of a fruitfull Tree,
Why do yee fall so fast?
Your date is not so past;
But you may stay yet here a while,
To blush and gently smile;
And go at last.

2. What, were yee borne to be
An houre or half's delight;
And so to bid goodnight?
'Twas pitie Nature brought yee forth
Meerly to shew your worth,
And lose you quite.

3. But you are lovely Leaves, where we
May read how soon things have
Their end, though ne'r so brave:
And after they have shown their pride,
Like you a while: They glide
Into the Grave.

Mans dying-place uncertain.

MAN knowes where first he ships himselfe; but he
Never can tell, where shall his Landing be.

Nothing Free-cost.

NOTHING comes Free-cost here; *Jove* will not let
His gifts go from him; if not bought with sweat.

Few fortunate.

MANY we are, and yet but few possesse
Those Fields of everlasting happinesse.

To Perenna.

HOW long, *Perenna*, wilt thou see
Me languish for the love of Thee?
Consent and play a friendly part
To save; when thou may'st kill a heart.

To the Ladyes.

TRUST me Ladies, I will do
Nothing to distemper you;
If I any fret or vex,
Men they shall be, *not your sex.*

The old Wives Prayer.

HOLY-ROOD come forth and shield
Us i'th'Citie, and the Field:
Safely guard us, now and aye,
From the blast that burns by day;
And those sounds that us affright
In the dead of dampish night.
Drive all hurtfull Feinds us fro,
By the Time the Cocks first crow.

Upon a cheap Laundresse. Epig.

FEACIE (some say) doth wash her clothes i'th'Lie
That sharply trickles from her either eye.
The *Laundresses*, They envie her good-luck,
Who can with so small charges *drive the buck.*
What needs she fire and ashes to consume,
Who can scoure Linnens with her own salt *reeume*?

Upon his departure hence.

THUS I
Passe by,
And die:
As One,
Unknown,
And gon:
I'm made
A shade,
And laid
I'th grave,
There have
My Cave.
Where tell
I dwell,
Farewell.

The Wassaile.

1. GIVE way, give way ye Gates, and win
An easie blessing to your Bin,
And Basket, by our entring in.

2. May both with manchet stand repleat;
Your Larders too so hung with meat,
That though a thousand, thousand eat;

3. Yet, ere twelve *Moones* shall whirl about
Their silv'rie Spheres, ther's none may doubt,
But more's sent in, then was serv'd out.

4. Next, may your Dairies Prosper so,
As that your pans no Ebbe may know;
But if they do, the more to flow.

5. Like to a solemne sober Stream
Bankt all with Lillies, and the Cream
Of sweetest *Cow-slips* filling Them.

6. Then, may your Plants be prest with Fruit,
Nor Bee, or Hive you have be mute;
But sweetly sounding like a Lute.

7. Next may your Duck and teeming Hen
Both to the Cocks-tread say *Amen*;
And for their two egs render ten.

8. Last, may your Harrows, Shares and Ploughes,
Your Stacks, your Stocks, your sweetest Mowes,
All prosper by your Virgin-vowes.

9. Alas! we blesse, but see none here,
That brings us either Ale or Beere;
In a drie-house all things are neere.

10. Let's leave a longer time to wait,
Where Rust and Cobwebs bind the gate;
And all live here with *needy Fate.*

11. Where Chimneys do for ever weepe,
For want of warmth, and Stomachs keepe
With noise, the servants eyes from sleep.

12. It is in vain to sing, or stay
Our free-feet here; but we'l away:
Yet to the Lares this we'l say,

13. The time will come, when you'l be sad,
And reckon this for fortune bad,
T'ave lost the good ye might have had.

14 Lillies,] Lillies *X* l. 17 you] ye *X* l. 22 Last,] Last *X*; oughes, *X*: Ploughes. *48* l. 24 your] our *X* ll. 31–33] *om. X save* r *catchword* Where *on preceding page* (207) l. 36 say,] say *X*

Upon a Lady faire, but fruitlesse.

TWICE has *Pudica* been a Bride, and led
By holy *Himen* to the Nuptiall Bed.
Two Youths sha's known, thrice two, and twice 3. yeares;
Yet not a Lillie from the Bed appeares;
Nor will; for why, *Pudica*, this may know,
Trees never beare, unlesse they first do blow.

How Springs came first.

THESE Springs were Maidens once that lov'd,
But lost to that they most approv'd:
My Story tells, by Love they were
Turn'd to these Springs, which wee see here:
The pretty whimpering that they make,
When of the Banks their leave they take;
Tels ye but this, they are the same,
In nothing chang'd but in their name.

To Rosemary and Baies.

MY wooing's ended: now my wedding's neere;
When Gloves are giving, *Guilded be you there.*

Upon Skurffe.

SKURFFE by his Nine-bones sweares, and well he may,
All know a Fellon eate the Tenth away.

Upon a Scarre in a Virgins *Face.*

'TIS Heresie in others: In your face
That Scarr's no *Schisme*, but the *sign of grace.*

Upon his eye-sight failing him.

I BEGINNE to waine in sight;
Shortly I shall bid goodnight:
Then no gazing more about,
When the Tapers once are out.

2.2 that] that, *X* 2.3 tells,] tels *X* 2.4 here:] here; *X*

To his worthy Friend, M. Tho. Falconbirge.

STAND with thy Graces forth, Brave man, and rise
High with thine own *Auspitious Destinies*:
Nor leave the search, and proofe, till Thou canst find
These, or those ends, to which Thou wast design'd.
Thy lucky *Genius*, and thy guiding *Starre*,
Have made Thee prosperous in thy wayes, thus farre:
Nor will they leave Thee, till they both have shown
Thee to the World a *Prime* and *Publique One*.
Then, when Thou see'st thine Age all turn'd to gold,
Remember what thy *Herrick* Thee foretold,
When at the holy Threshold of thine house,
He Boded good-luck to thy Selfe and Spouse.
Lastly, be mindfull (when thou art grown great)
That Towrs high rear'd dread most the lightnings threat:
When as the humble Cottages not feare
The cleaving Bolt of Jove *the Thunderer.*

Upon Julia's *haire fill'd with Dew.*

DEW sate on *Julia's* haire,
And spangled too,
Like Leaves that laden are
With trembling Dew:
Or glitter'd to my sight,
As when the Beames
Have their reflected light,
Daunc't by the Streames.

Another on her.

HOW can I choose but love, and follow her,
Whose shadow smels like milder *Pomander*!
How can I chuse but kisse her, whence do's come
The *Storax*, *Spiknard*, *Myrrhe*, and *Ladanum*.

Losse from the least.

GREAT men by small meanes oft are overthrown:
He's Lord of thy life, who contemnes his own.

Rewards and punishments.

ALL things are open to these two events,
Or to Rewards, or else to Punishments.

Shame, no Statist.

SHAME is a bad attendant to a State:
He rents his Crown, That feares the Peoples hate.

To Sir Clipsebie Crew.

SINCE to th'Country first I came,
I have lost my former flame:
And, methinks, I not inherit,
As I did, my ravisht spirit.
If I write a Verse, or two,
'Tis with very much ado;
In regard I want that Wine,
Which sho'd conjure up a line.
Yet, though now of Muse bereft,
I have still the manners left
For to thanke you (Noble Sir)
For those gifts you do conferre
Upon him, who only can
Be in Prose a *gratefull man.*

Upon himselfe.

I CO'D never love indeed;
Never see mine own heart bleed:
Never crucifie my life;
Or for Widow, Maid, or Wife.

2. I co'd never seeke to please
One, or many Mistresses:
Never like their lips, to sweare
Oyle of Roses still smelt there.

3. I co'd never breake my sleepe,
Fold mine Armes, sob, sigh, or weep:
Never beg, or humbly wooe
With oathes, and lyes, (as others do.)

4. I co'd never walke alone;
Put a shirt of sackcloth on:
Never keep a fast, or pray
For good luck in love (that day.)

5. But have hitherto liv'd free,
As the aire that circles me:
And kept credit with my heart,
Neither broke i'th whole, or part.

Fresh Cheese and Cream.

WO'D yee have fresh Cheese and Cream?
Julia's Breast can give you them:
And if more; Each *Nipple* cries,
To your *Cream*, here's *Strawberries*.

An Eclogue, or Pastorall between Endimion Porter *and* Lycidas Herrick, *set and sung*.

Endym. AH! *Lycidas*, come tell me why
Thy whilome merry Oate
By thee doth so neglected lye;
And never purls a Note?

2. I prithee speake: *Lyc.* I will. *End.* Say on:
Lyc. 'Tis thou, and only thou,
That art the cause *Endimion*;
End. For Loves-sake, tell me how.

3. *Lyc.* In this regard, that thou do'st play
Upon an other Plain:
And for a Rurall Roundelay,
Strik'st now a Courtly strain.

4. Thou leav'st our Hills, our Dales, our Bowers,
Our finer fleeced sheep:
(Unkind to us) to spend thine houres,
Where Shepheards sho'd not keep.

5. I meane the Court: Let *Latmos* be
My lov'd *Endymions* Court;
End. But I the Courtly State wo'd see:
Lyc. Then see it in report.

6. What ha's the Court to do with Swaines,
Where *Phillis* is not known?
Nor do's it mind the Rustick straines
Of us, or *Coridon*.

7. *End.* Breake, if thou lov'st us, this delay;
Dear *Lycidas*, e're long,
I vow by *Pan*, to come away
And Pipe unto thy Song.

8. Then *Jessimine*, with *Florabell*;
And dainty *Amarillis*,
With handsome-handed *Drosomell*
Shall pranke thy Hooke with Lillies.

9. *Lyc.* Then *Tityrus*, and *Coridon*,
And *Thyrsis*, they shall follow
With all the rest; while thou alone
Shalt lead, like young *Apollo*.

10. And till thou com'st, thy *Lycidas*,
In every *Geniall* Cup,
Shall write in Spice, *Endimion* 'twas
That kept his Piping up.

And my most luckie Swain, when I shall live to see
Endimions Moon to fill up full, remember me:
Mean time, let *Lycidas* have leave to Pipe to thee.

To a Bed of Tulips.

1. BRIGHT Tulips, we do know,
You had your comming hither;
And Fading-time do's show,
That Ye must quickly wither.

2. Your *Sister-hoods* may stay,
And smile here for your houre;
But dye ye must away:
Even as the meanest Flower.

3. Come Virgins then, and see
Your frailties; and bemone ye;
For lost like these, 'twill be,
As Time had never known ye.

A Caution.

THAT Love last long; let it thy first care be
To find a Wife, that is most fit for Thee.
Be She too wealthy, or too poore; be sure,
Love in extreames, can never long endure.

To the Water Nymphs, drinking at the Fountain.

1. REACH, with your whiter hands, to me,
Some Christall of the Spring;
And I, about the Cup shall see
Fresh Lillies flourishing.

2. Or else sweet Nimphs do you but this;
To'th'Glasse your lips encline;
And I shall see by that one kisse,
The Water turn'd to Wine.

To his Honoured Kinsman, Sir Richard Stone.

TO this *white Temple* of my *Heroes*, here
Beset with stately Figures (every where)
Of such rare *Saint-ships*, who did here consume
Their lives in sweets, and left in death perfume.
Come thou *Brave man*! And bring with Thee a Stone
Unto thine own *Edification.*
High are These Statues here, besides no lesse
Strong then the Heavens for everlastingnesse:
Where build aloft; and being fixt by These,
Set up Thine own *eternall Images.*

Upon a Flie.

A GOLDEN Flie one shew'd to me,
Clos'd in a Box of Yvorie:
Where both seem'd proud; the Flie to have
His buriall in an yvory grave:
The yvorie tooke State to hold
A Corps as bright as burnisht gold.
One Fate had both; both equall Grace;
The Buried, and the Burying-place.

Not *Virgils Gnat*, to whom the Spring
All Flowers sent to'is burying.
Not *Marshals Bee*, which in a Bead
Of *Amber* quick was buried.
Nor that fine Worme that do's interre
Her selfe i'th'*silken Sepulchre*.
Nor my rare **Phil*, that lately was
With Lillies Tomb'd up in a Glasse;
More honour had, then this same *Flie*;
Dead, and clos'd up in *Yvorie*.

* Sparrow

Upon Jack *and* Jill. *Epig.*

When *Jill* complaines to *Jack* for want of meate;
Jack kisses *Jill*, and bids her freely eate:
Jill sayes, of what? sayes *Jack*, on that sweet kisse,
Which full of Nectar and Ambrosia is,
The food of Poets; so I thought sayes *Jill*,
That makes them looke so lanke, so Ghost-like still.
Let Poets feed on aire, or what they will;
Let me feed full, till that I fart, sayes *Jill*.

To Julia.

Julia, when thy *Herrick* dies,
Close thou up thy Poets eyes:
And his last breath, let it be
Taken in by none but Thee.

To Mistresse Dorothy Parsons.

If thou aske me (Deare) wherefore
I do write of thee no more:
I must answer (Sweet) thy part
Lesse is here, then in my heart.

Upon Parrat.

Parrat protests 'tis he, and only he
Can teach a man the *Art of memory*:
Believe him not; for he forgot it quite,
Being drunke, who 'twas that Can'd his Ribs last night.

How he would drinke his Wine.

FILL me my Wine in Christall; thus, and thus
I see't in's *puris naturalibus*:
Unmixt. I love to have it smirke and shine,
'Tis sin I know, 'tis sin to throtle Wine.
What Mad-man's he, that when it sparkles so,
Will coole his flames, or quench his fires with snow?

How Marigolds *came yellow.*

JEALOUS *Girles* these sometimes were,
While they liv'd, or lasted here:
Turn'd to *Flowers*, still they be
Yellow, markt for Jealousie.

The broken Christall.

TO Fetch me Wine my *Lucia* went,
Bearing a Christall *continent*:
But making haste, it came to passe,
She brake in two the purer Glasse,
Then smil'd, and sweetly chid her speed;
So with a blush, beshrew'd the deed.

Precepts.

GOOD Precepts we must firmly hold,
By daily *Learning* we wax old.

To the right Honourable Edward *Earle of* Dorset.

IF I dare write to You, my Lord, who are,
Of your own selfe, a *Publick Theater*.
And sitting, see the wiles, wayes, walks of wit,
And give a righteous judgement upon it.
What need I care, though some dislike me sho'd,
If *Dorset* say, what *Herrick* writes, is good?
We know y'are learn'd i'th'Muses, and no lesse
In our *State-sanctions*, deep, or bottomlesse.
Whose smile can make a Poet; and your glance
Dash all bad Poems out of countenance.

So, that an Author needs no other Bayes
For Coronation, then Your onely Praise.
And no one mischief greater then your frown,
To null his Numbers, and to blast his Crowne.
Few live the life immortall. He ensures
His Fame's long life, who strives to set up Yours.

Upon himself.

TH'ART hence removing, (like a Shepherds Tent)
And walk thou must the way that others went:
Fall thou must first, then rise to life with These,
Markt in thy Book for faithfull Witnesses.

Hope well and Have well: or, Faire after Foule weather.

WHAT though the Heaven be lowring now,
And look with a contracted brow?
We shall discover, by and by,
A Repurgation of the Skie:
And when those clouds away are driven,
Then will appeare a cheerfull Heaven.

Upon Love.

I HELD Love's head while it did ake;
But so it chanc't to be;
The cruell paine did his forsake,
And forthwith came to me.

2. Ai me! How shal my griefe be stil'd?
Or where else shall we find
One like to me, who must be kill'd
For being too-too-kind?

To his Kinswoman, Mrs. Penelope Wheeler.

NEXT is your lot (Faire) to be number'd one,
Here, in my Book's Canonization:
Late you come in; but you a Saint shall be,
In Chiefe, in this Poetick Liturgie.

Another upon her.

FIRST, for your shape, the curious cannot shew
Any one part that's dissonant in you:
And 'gainst your chast behaviour there's no Plea,
Since you are knowne to be *Penelope.*
Thus faire and cleane you are, although there be
A mighty strife 'twixt Forme and Chastitie.

Kissing and Bussing.

KISSING and bussing differ both in this;
We busse our Wantons, but our Wives we kisse.

Crosse and Pile.

FAIRE and foule dayes trip Crosse and Pile; The faire
Far lesse in number, then our foule dayes are.

To the Lady Crew, *upon the death of her Child.*

WHY, Madam, will ye longer weep,
When as your Baby's lull'd asleep?
And (pretty Child) feeles now no more
Those paines it lately felt before.
All now is silent; groanes are fled:
Your Child lyes still, yet is not dead:
But rather like a flower hid here
To spring againe another yeare.

His Winding-sheet.

COME thou, who art the Wine, and wit
Of all I've writ:
The Grace, the Glorie, and the best
Piece of the rest.
Thou art of what I did intend
The All, and End.

2 (*heading*) *Bussing.*] *Bussing..* *48*

And what was made, was made to meet
Thee, thee my sheet.
Come then, and be to my chast side
Both Bed, and Bride.
We two (as Reliques left) will have
One Rest, one Grave.
And, hugging close, we will not feare
Lust entring here:
Where all Desires are dead, or cold
As is the mould:
And all Affections are forgot,
Or Trouble not.
Here, here the Slaves and Pris'ners be
From Shackles free:
And weeping Widowes long opprest
Doe here find rest.
The wronged Client ends his Lawes
Here, and his Cause.
Here those long suits of Chancery lie
Quiet, or die:
And all Star-chamber-Bils doe cease,
Or hold their peace.
Here needs no Court for our Request,
Where all are best;
All wise; all equall; and all just
Alike i'th'dust.
Nor need we here to feare the frowne
Of Court, or Crown.
Where Fortune bears no sway o're things,
There all are Kings.
In this securer place we'l keep,
As lull'd asleep;
Or for a little time we'l lye,
As Robes laid by;
To be another day re-worne,
Turn'd, but not torn:
Or like old Testaments ingrost,
Lockt up, not lost:
And for a while lye here conceal'd,
To be reveal'd
Next, at that great Platonick yeere,
And then meet here.

To Mistresse Mary Willand.

ONE more by Thee, Love, and Desert have sent,
T'enspangle this expansive Firmament.
O Flame of Beauty! come, appeare, appeare
A Virgin Taper, ever shining here.

Change gives content.

WHAT now we like, anon we disapprove:
The new successor drives away old Love.

Upon Magot *a frequenter of Ordinaries.*

MAGOT frequents those houses of good-cheere,
Talkes most, eates most, of all the Feeders there.
He raves through leane, he rages through the fat;
(What gets the master of the Meal by that?)
He who with talking can devoure so much,
How wo'd he eate, were not his hindrance such?

On himselfe.

BORNE I was to meet with Age,
And to walke Life's pilgrimage.
Much I know of Time is spent,
Tell I can't, what's Resident.
Howsoever, cares, adue;
Ile have nought to say to you:
But Ile spend my comming houres,
Drinking wine, & crown'd with flowres.

Fortune favours.

FORTUNE did never favour one
Fully, without exception;
Though free she be, ther's something yet
Still wanting to her Favourite.

3.6 not] nor *48*

To Phillis *to love, and live with him.*

LIVE, live with me, and thou shalt see
The pleasures Ile prepare for thee:
What sweets the Country can afford
Shall blesse thy Bed, and blesse thy Board.
The soft sweet Mosse shall be thy bed,
With crawling Woodbine over-spread:
By which the silver-shedding streames
Shall gently melt thee into dreames.
Thy clothing next, shall be a Gowne
Made of the Fleeces purest Downe.
The tongues of Kids shall be thy meate;
Their Milke thy drinke; and thou shalt eate
The Paste of Filberts for thy bread
With Cream of Cowslips buttered:
Thy Feasting-Tables shall be Hills
With *Daisies* spread, and *Daffadils*;
Where thou shalt sit, and *Red-brest* by,
For meat, shall give thee melody.
Ile give thee Chaines and Carkanets
Of *Primroses* and *Violets*.
A Bag and Bottle thou shalt have;
That richly wrought, and This as brave;
So that as either shall expresse
The Wearer's no meane Shepheardesse.
At Sheering-times, and yearely Wakes,
When *Themilis* his pastime makes,
There thou shalt be; and be the wit,
Nay more, the Feast, and grace of it.
On Holy-dayes, when Virgins meet
To dance the Heyes with nimble feet;
Thou shalt come forth, and then appeare
The *Queen of Roses* for that yeere.
And having danc't ('bove all the best)
Carry the Garland from the rest.
In Wicker-baskets Maids shal bring
To thee, (my dearest Shephardling)
The blushing Apple, bashfull Peare,
And shame-fac't Plum, (all simp'ring there).
Walk in the Groves, and thou shalt find
The name of *Phillis* in the Rind

Of every straight, and smooth-skin tree;
Where kissing that, Ile twice kisse thee.
To thee a Sheep-hook I will send,
Be-pranckt with Ribbands, to this end,
This, this alluring Hook might be
Lesse for to catch a sheep, then me.
Thou shalt have Possets, Wassails fine,
Not made of Ale, but spiced Wine;
To make thy Maids and selfe free mirth,
All sitting neer the glitt'ring Hearth.
Thou sha't have Ribbands, Roses, Rings,
Gloves, Garters, Stockings, Shooes, and Strings
Of winning Colours, that shall move
Others to Lust, but me to Love.
These (nay) and more, thine own shal be,
If thou wilt love, and live with me.

To his Kinswoman, Mistresse Susanna Herrick.

WHEN I consider (Dearest) thou dost stay
But here awhile, to languish and decay;
Like to these Garden-glories, which here be
The Flowrie-sweet resemblances of Thee:
With griefe of heart, methinks, I thus doe cry,
Wo'd thou hast ne'r been born, or might'st not die.

Upon Mistresse Susanna Southwell *her cheeks.*

RARE are thy cheeks *Susanna*, which do show
Ripe Cherries smiling, while that others blow.

Upon her Eyes.

CLEERE are her eyes,
Like purest Skies.
Discovering from thence
A Babie there
That turns each Sphere,
Like an Intelligence.

Upon her feet.

Her pretty feet
Like snailes did creep
A little out, and then,
As if they started at Bo-peep,
Did soon draw in agen.

To his honoured friend, Sir John Mynts.

For civill, cleane, and circumcised wit,
And for the comely carriage of it;
Thou art The Man, the onely Man best known,
Markt for the *True-wit* of a Million:
From whom we'l reckon. Wit came in, but since
The *Calculation* of thy Birth, *Brave Mince.*

Upon his gray haires.

Fly me not, though I be gray,
Lady, this I know you'l say;
Better look the Roses red,
When with white commingled.
Black your haires are; mine are white;
This begets the more delight,
When things meet most opposite:
As in Pictures we descry,
Venus standing *Vulcan* by.

Accusation.

If Accusation onely can draw blood,
None shall be guiltlesse, be he ne'r so good.

Pride allowable in Poets.

As thou deserv'st, be proud; then gladly let
The Muse give thee the Delphick Coronet.

1.4 started *FGHnK2SU*: played *rest* 2 (*heading*) Mynts *FGHnK2*[illegible]
Mince *rest*

A Vow to Minerva.

GODDESSE, I begin an Art;
Come thou in, with thy best part,
For to make the Texture lye
Each way smooth and civilly:
And a broad-fac't Owle shall be
Offer'd up with Vows to Thee.

On Jone.

JONE wo'd go tel her haires; and well she might,
Having but seven in all; three black, foure white.

Upon Letcher. *Epig.*

LETCHER was Carted first about the streets,
For false Position in his neighbours sheets:
Next, hang'd for Theeving: Now the people say,
His Carting was the *Prologue* to this Play.

Upon Dundrige.

DUNDRIGE his Issue hath; but is not styl'd
For all his Issue, Father of one Child.

To Electra.

'TIS Ev'ning, my Sweet,
And dark; let us meet;
Long time w'ave here been a toying:
And never, as yet,
That season co'd get,
Wherein t'ave had an enjoying.

2. For pitty or shame,
Then let not Love's flame,
Be ever and ever a spending;
Since now to the Port
The path is but short;
And yet our way has no ending.

3. Time flyes away fast;
Our houres doe waste:
The while we never remember,
How soone our life, here,
Growes old with the yeere,
That dyes with the next *December*.

Discord not disadvantageous.

FORTUNE no higher Project can devise,
Then to sow Discord 'mongst the Enemies.

Ill Government.

PREPOSTEROUS is that Government, (and rude)
When Kings obey the wilder Multitude.

To Marygolds.

GIVE way, and be ye ravisht by the Sun,
(And hang the head when as the Act is done)
Spread as He spreads; wax lesse as He do's wane;
And as He shuts, close up to Maids again.

To Dianeme.

GIVE me one kisse,
And no more;
If so be, this
Makes you poore;
To enrich you,
Ile restore
For that one, two
Thousand score.

To Julia, *the* Flaminica Dialis, *or* Queen-Priest.

THOU know'st, my *Julia*, that it is thy turne
This Mornings Incense to prepare, and burne.
The Chaplet, and **Inarculum* here be,
With the white Vestures, all attending Thee.

* A twig of a Pomgranat, which the queen-priest did use to weare on her head at sacrificing. (*note in 48*)

This day, the *Queen-Priest*, thou art made t'appease
Love for our very-many Trespasses.
One chiefe transgression is among the rest,
Because with Flowers her Temple was not drest:
The next, because her Altars did not shine
With daily Fyers: The last, neglect of Wine:
For which, her wrath is gone forth to consume
Us all, unlesse preserv'd by thy Perfume.
Take then thy Censer; Put in Fire, and thus,
O *Pious-Priestresse!* make a Peace for us.
For our neglect, Love did our Death decree,
That we escape. *Redemption comes by Thee.*

Anacreontike.

BORN I was to be old,
And for to die here:
After that, in the mould
Long for to lye here.
But before that day comes,
Still I be Bousing;
For I know, in the Tombs
There's no Carousing.

Meat without mirth.

EATEN I have; and though I had good cheere,
I did not sup, because no friends were there.
Where Mirth and Friends are absent when we Dine
Or Sup, there wants the Incense and the Wine.

Large Bounds doe but bury us.

ALL things o'r-rul'd are here by Chance;
The greatest mans Inheritance,
Where ere the luckie Lot doth fall,
Serves but for place of Buriall.

Upon Ursley.

U*RSLEY*, she thinks those Velvet Patches grace
The Candid Temples of her comely face:
But he will say, who e'r those Circlets seeth,
They be but signs of *Ursleys* hollow teeth.

An Ode to Sir Clipsebie Crew.

1. HERE we securely live, and eate
The Creame of meat;
And keep eternal fires,
By which we sit, and doe Divine
As Wine
And Rage inspires.

2. If full we charme; then call upon
Anacreon
To grace the frantick Thyrse:
And having drunk, we raise a shout
Throughout
To praise his Verse.

3. Then cause we *Horace* to be read,
Which sung, or seyd,
A Goblet, to the brim,
Of Lyrick Wine, both swell'd and crown'd,
A Round
We quaffe to him.

4. Thus, thus, we live, and spend the houres
In Wine and Flowers:
And make the frollick yeere,
The Month, the Week, the instant Day
To stay
The longer here.

5. Come then, brave Knight, and see the Cell
Wherein I dwell;
And my Enchantments too;
Which Love and noble freedome is;
And this
Shall fetter you.

6. Take Horse, and come; or be so kind,
To send your mind
(Though but in Numbers few)
And I shall think I have the heart,
Or part
Of *Clipseby Crew*.

l. 10 having] havink *48* (*corr. Errata*)

To his worthy Kinsman, Mr. Stephen Soame.

NOR is my Number full, till I inscribe
Thee sprightly *Soame*, one of my righteous Tribe:
A Tribe of one Lip, Leven, and of One
Civil Behaviour, and Religion.
A Stock of Saints; where ev'ry one doth weare
A stole of white, (and Canonized here)
Among which Holies, be Thou ever known,
Brave Kinsman, markt out with the whiter stone:
Which seals Thy Glorie; since I doe prefer
Thee here in my eternall Calender.

To his Tomb-maker.

GO I must; when I am gone,
Write but this upon my Stone;
Chaste I liv'd, without a wife,
That's the Story of my life.
Strewings need none, every flower
Is in this word, Batchelour.

Great Spirits supervive.

OUR mortall parts may wrapt in Seare-cloths lye:
Great Spirits never with their bodies dye.

None free from fault.

OUT of the world he must, who once comes in:
No man exempted is from Death, or sinne.

Upon himselfe being buried.

LET me sleep this night away,
Till the Dawning of the day:
Then at th'opening of mine eyes,
I, and all the world shall rise.

Pitie to the prostrate.

TIS worse then barbarous cruelty to show
No part of pitie on a conquer'd foe.

Way in a crowd.

ONCE on a Lord-Mayors day, in Cheapside, when
Skulls co'd not well passe through that scum of men.
For quick dispatch, *Sculls* made no longer stay,
Then but to breath, and every one gave way:
For as he breath'd, the People swore from thence
A Fart flew out, or a *Sir-reverence.*

His content in the Country.

HERE, here I live with what my Board,
Can with the smallest cost afford.
Though ne'r so mean the Viands be,
They well content my *Prew* and me.
Or Pea, or Bean, or Wort, or Beet,
What ever comes, content makes sweet:
Here we rejoyce, because no Rent
We pay for our poore Tenement:
Wherein we rest, and never feare
The Landlord, or the Usurer.
The Quarter-day do's ne'r affright
Our Peacefull slumbers in the night.
We eate our own, and batten more,
Because we feed on no mans score:
But pitie those, whose flanks grow great,
Swel'd with the Lard of others meat.
We blesse our Fortunes, when we see
Our own beloved privacie:
And like our living, where w'are known
To very few, or else to none.

The credit of the Conquerer.

HE who commends the vanquisht, speaks the Power,
And glorifies the worthy Conquerer.

On himselfe.

SOME parts may perish; dye thou canst not all:
The most of Thee shall scape the funerall.

Upon one-ey'd Broomsted. *Epig.*

BROOMSTED a lamenesse got by cold and Beere;
And to the *Bath* went, to be cured there:
His feet were helpt, and left his Crutch behind:
But home return'd, as he went forth, halfe blind.

The Fairies.

If ye will with *Mab* find grace,
Set each Platter in his place:
Rake the Fier up, and get
Water in, ere Sun be set.
Wash your Pailes, and clense your Dairies;
Sluts are loathsome to the Fairies:
Sweep your house: Who doth not so,
Mab will pinch her by the toe.

To his honoured friend, M. John Weare, *Councellour.*

Did I or love, or could I others draw
To the indulgence of the rugged Law:
The first foundation of that zeale sho'd be
By Reading all her *Paragraphs* in Thee.
Who dost so fitly with the Lawes unite,
As if You Two, were one *Hermophrodite*:
Nor courts thou Her because she's well attended
With wealth, but for those ends she was entended:
Which were, (and still her offices are known)
Law is to give to ev'ry one his owne.
To shore the Feeble up, against the strong;
To shield the Stranger, and the Poore from wrong:
This was the Founders grave and good intent,
To keepe the out-cast in his Tenement:
To free the Orphan from that Wolfe-like-man,
Who is his *Butcher* more then *Guardian.*
To drye the Widowes teares; and stop her Swoones,
By pouring Balme and Oyle into her wounds.
This was the old way; and 'tis yet thy course,
To keep those pious Principles in force.
Modest I will be; but one word Ile say
(Like to a sound that's vanishing away)

Sooner the in-side of thy hand shall grow
Hisped, and hairie, ere thy Palm shall know
A *Postern-bribe* tooke, or a *Forked-Fee*
To fetter Justice, when She might be free.
Eggs Ile not shave: But yet brave man, if I
Was destin'd forth to golden Soveraignty:
A Prince I'de be, that I might Thee preferre
To be my Counsell both, and Chanceller.

The Watch.

Man is a Watch, wound up at first, but never
Wound up again: Once down, He's down for ever.
The Watch once downe, all motions then do cease;
And Mans Pulse stopt, *All passions sleep in Peace.*

Lines have their Linings, and Bookes their Buckram.

As in our clothes, so likewise he who lookes,
Shall find much farcing Buckram in our Books.

Art above Nature, to Julia.

When I behold a Forrest spread
With silken trees upon thy head;
And when I see that other Dresse
Of flowers set in comlinesse:
When I behold another grace
In the ascent of curious Lace,
Which like a Pinacle doth shew
The top, and the top-gallant too.
Then, when I see thy Tresses bound
Into an Ovall, square, or round;
And knit in knots far more then I
Can tell by tongue; or true-love tie:
Next, when those Lawnie Filmes I see
Play with a wild civility:
And all those airie silks to flow,
Alluring me, and tempting so:
I must confesse, mine eye and heart
Dotes less on Nature, then on Art.

Upon Sibilla.

WITH paste of Almonds, *Syb* her hands doth scoure;
Then gives it to the children to devoure.
In Cream she bathes her thighs (more soft then silk)
Then to the poore she freely gives the milke.

Upon his kinswoman Mistresse Bridget Herrick.

SWEET *Bridget* blusht, & therewithall,
Fresh blossoms from her cheekes did fall.
I thought at first 'twas but a dream,
Till after I had handled them;
And smelt them, then they smelt to me,
As Blossomes of the *Almond* Tree.

Upon Love.

I PLAID with Love, as with the fire
The wanton Satyre did;
Nor did I know, or co'd descry
What under there was hid.

2. That Satyre he but burnt his lips;
(But min's the greater smart)
For kissing Loves dissembling chips,
The fire scorcht my heart.

Upon a comely, and curious Maide.

IF Men can say that beauty dyes;
Marbles will sweare that here it lyes.
If Reader then thou canst forbeare,
In publique loss to shed a Teare:
The Dew of griefe upon this stone
Will tell thee *Pitie* thou hast none.

Upon the losse of his Finger.

ONE of the five straight branches of my hand
Is lopt already; and the rest but stand
Expecting when to fall: which soon will be;
First dyes the Leafe, the Bough next, next the Tree.

Upon Irene.

ANGRY if *Irene* be
But a Minutes life with me:
Such a fire I espie
Walking in and out her eye,
As at once I freeze, and frie.

Upon Electra's *Teares.*

UPON her cheekes she wept, and from those showers
Sprang up a sweet *Nativity* of Flowres.

Upon Tooly.

THE Eggs of Pheasants wrie-nos'd *Tooly* sells;
But ne'r so much as licks the speckled shells:
Only, if one prove addled, that he eates
With superstition, (as the Cream of meates.)
The Cock and Hen he feeds; but not a bone
He ever pickt (as yet) of any one.

A Hymne to the Graces.

WHEN I love, (as some have told,
Love I shall when I am old)
O ye Graces! Make me fit
For the welcoming of it.
Clean my Roomes, as Temples be,
T'entertain that Deity.
Give me words wherewith to wooe,
Suppling and successefull too:
Winning postures; and withall,
Manners each way musicall:
Sweetnesse to allay my sowre
And unsmooth behaviour.
For I know you have the skill
Vines to prune, though not to kill,
And of any wood ye see,
You can make a *Mercury.*

To Silvia.

NO more my *Silvia*, do I mean to pray
For those good dayes that ne'r will come away.
I want beliefe; O gentle *Silvia*, be
The patient Saint, and send up vowes for me.

Upon Blanch. *Epig.*

I HAVE seen many Maidens to have haire;
Both for their comely need, and some to spare:
But *Blanch* has not so much upon her head,
As to bind up her chaps when she is dead.

Upon Umber. *Epig.*

UMBER was painting of a Lyon fierce,
And working it, by chance from *Umbers* Erse
Flew out a crack, so mighty, that the Fart,
(As *Umber* sweares) did make his Lyon start.

The Poet hath lost his pipe.

I CANNOT pipe as I was wont to do,
Broke is my Reed, hoarse is my singing too:
My wearied Oat Ile hang upon the Tree,
And give it to the *Silvan Deitie.*

True Friendship.

WILT thou my true Friend be?
Then love not mine, but me.

The Apparition of his Mistresse calling him to Elizium.

Desunt nonnulla———

COME then, and like two Doves with silv'rie wings,
Let our soules flie to'th'shades, where ever springs
Sit smiling in the Meads; where Balme and Oile,
Roses and Cassia crown the untill'd soyle.
Where no disease raignes, or infection comes
To blast the Aire, but *Amber-greece* and *Gums.*
This, that, and ev'ry Thicket doth transpire
More sweet, then *Storax* from the hallowed fire:
Where ev'ry tree a wealthy issue beares
Of fragrant Apples, blushing Plums, or Peares:
And all the shrubs, with sparkling spangles, shew
Like Morning-Sun-shine tinsilling the dew.

5 *For variants see pp.* 488–9

Here in green Meddowes sits eternall May,
Purfling the Margents, while perpetuall Day
So double gilds the Aire, as that no night
Can ever rust th'Enamel of the light.
Here, naked Younglings, handsome Striplings run
Their Goales for Virgins kisses; which when done,
Then unto Dancing forth the learned Round
Commixt they meet, with endlesse Roses crown'd.
And here we'l sit on Primrose-banks, and see
Love's *Chorus* led by *Cupid*; and we'l be
Two loving followers too unto the Grove,
Where Poets sing the stories of our love.
There thou shalt hear Divine *Musæus* sing
Of *Hero*, and *Leander*; then Ile bring
Thee to the Stand, where honour'd *Homer* reades
His *Odisees*, and his high *Iliades*.
About whose Throne the crowd of Poets throng
To heare the incantation of his tongue:
To *Linus*, then to *Pindar*; and that done,
Ile bring thee *Herrick* to *Anacreon*,
Quaffing his full-crown'd bowles of burning Wine,
And in his Raptures speaking Lines of Thine,
Like to His subject; and as his Frantick-
Looks, shew him truly *Bacchanalian* like,
Besmear'd with Grapes; welcome he shall thee thither,
Where both may rage, both drink and dance together.
Then stately *Virgil*, witty *Ovid*, by
Whom faire *Corinna* sits, and doth comply
With Yvorie wrists, his Laureat head, and steeps
His eye in dew of kisses, while he sleeps.
Then soft *Catullus*, sharp-fang'd *Martial*,
And towring *Lucan*, *Horace*, *Juvenal*,
And Snakie *Perseus*, these, and those, whom Rage
(Dropt from the jarres of heaven) fill'd t'engage
All times unto their frenzies; Thou shalt there
Behold them in a spacious Theater.
Among which glories, (crown'd with sacred Bayes,
And flatt'ring Ivie) Two recite their Plaies,
Beumont and *Fletcher*, Swans, to whom all eares
Listen, while they (like Syrens in their Spheres)
Sing their *Evadne*; and still more for thee
There yet remaines to know, then thou can'st see

By glim'ring of a fancie: Doe but come,
And there Ile shew thee that capacious roome
In which thy Father *Johnson* now is plac't,
As in a Globe of Radiant fire, and grac't
To be in that Orbe crown'd (that doth include
Those Prophets of the former Magnitude)
And be our chiefe; But harke, I heare the Cock,
(The Bell-man of the night) proclaime the clock
Of late struck one; and now I see the prime
Of Day break from the pregnant East, 'tis time
I vanish; more I had to say;
But Night determines here, Away.

Life is the Bodies Light.

LIFE is the Bodies light; which once declining,
Those crimson clouds i'th'cheeks & lips leave shining.
Those counter-changed *Tabbies* in the ayre,
(The Sun once set) all of one colour are.
So, when Death comes, *Fresh tinctures* lose their place,
And dismall Darknesse then doth smutch the face.

Upon Urles. *Epig.*

URLES had the Gout so, that he co'd not stand;
Then from his Feet, it shifted to his Hand:
When 'twas in's Feet, his Charity was small;
Now tis in's Hand, he gives no Almes at all.

Upon Franck.

FRANCK ne'r wore silk she sweares; but I reply,
She now weares silk to hide her blood-shot eye.

Love lightly pleased.

LET faire or foule my Mistresse be,
Or low, or tall, she pleaseth me:
Or let her walk, or stand, or sit,
The posture hers, I'm pleas'd with it.
Or let her tongue be still, or stir,
Gracefull is ev'ry thing from her.
Or let her Grant, or else Deny,
My Love will fit each Historie.

The Primrose.

Aske me why I send you here
This sweet *Infanta* of the yeere?
Aske me why I send to you
This Primrose, thus bepearl'd with dew?
I will whisper to your eares,
The sweets of Love are mixt with tears.

2. Ask me why this flower do's show
So yellow-green, and sickly too?
Ask me why the stalk is weak
And bending, (yet it doth not break?)
I will answer, These discover
What fainting hopes are in a Lover.

The Tythe. To the Bride.

If nine times you your Bride-groome kisse;
The tenth you know the Parsons is.
Pay then your Tythe; and doing thus,
Prove in your Bride-bed numerous.
If children you have ten, Sir *John*
Won't for his tenth part ask you one.

A Frolick.

Bring me my Rose-buds, Drawer come;
So, while I thus sit crown'd;
Ile drink the aged *Cecubum*,
Untill the roofe turne round.

Change common to all.

All things subjected are to Fate;
Whom this Morne sees most fortunate,
The Ev'ning sees in poore estate.

1 *For variants see p.* 489

To Julia.

THE Saints-bell calls; and, *Julia*, I must read
The Proper Lessons for the Saints now dead:
To grace which Service, *Julia*, there shall be
One *Holy Collect*, said or sung for Thee.
Dead when thou art, Deare *Julia*, thou shalt have
A *Trentall* sung by Virgins o're thy Grave:
Meane time we two will sing the Dirge of these;
Who dead, deserve our best remembrances.

No luck in Love.

I DOE love I know not what;
Sometimes this, & sometimes that:
All conditions I aime at.

2. But, as lucklesse, I have yet
Many shrewd disasters met,
To gaine her whom I wo'd get.

3. Therefore now Ile love no more,
As I've doted heretofore:
He who must be, shall be poore.

In the darke none dainty.

NIGHT hides our thefts; all faults then pardon'd be:
All are alike faire, when no spots we see.
Lais and *Lucrece*, in the night time are
Pleasing alike; alike both singular:
Jone, and my *Lady* have at that time one,
One and the selfe-same priz'd complexion.
Then please alike the Pewter and the Plate;
The chosen *Rubie*, and the *Reprobate*.

A charme, or an allay for Love.

IF so be a Toad be laid
In a Sheeps-skin newly flaid,
And that ty'd to man 'twil sever
Him and his affections ever.

1.6 *Trentall*] *Tentrall 48*   2 *For variants see p.* 489

Upon a free Maid, with a foule breath.

You say you'l kiss me, and I thanke you for it:
But stinking breath, I do as hell abhorre it.

Upon Coone. *Epig.*

What is the reason *Coone* so dully smels?
His Nose is over-cool'd with Isicles.

To his Brother in Law Master John Wingfield.

For being comely, consonant, and free
To most of men, but most of all to me:
For so decreeing, that thy clothes expence
Keepes still within a just circumference:
Then for contriving so to loade thy Board,
As that the Messes ne'r o'r-laid the Lord:
Next for Ordaining, that thy words not swell
To any one unsober *syllable*.
These I co'd praise thee for beyond another,
Wert thou a *Winckfield* onely, not a Brother.

The Head-ake.

My head doth ake,
O *Sappho*! take
Thy fillit,
And bind the paine;
Or bring some bane
To kill it.

2. But lesse that part,
Then my poore heart,
Now is sick:
One kisse from thee
Will counsell be,
And Physick.

On himselfe.

Live by thy Muse thou shalt; when others die
Leaving no Fame to long Posterity:
When Monarchies trans-shifted are, and gone;
Here shall endure thy vast Dominion.

Upon a Maide.

HENCE a blessed soule is fled,
Leaving here the body dead:
Which (since here they can't combine)
For the Saint, we'l keep the Shrine.

Upon Spalt.

OF Pushes *Spalt* has such a knottie race,
He needs a Tucker for to burle his face.

Of Horne *a Comb-maker.*

H*ORNE* sells to others teeth; but has not one
To grace his own Gums, or of Box, or bone.

Upon the troublesome times.

O! TIMES most bad,
Without the scope
Of hope
Of better to be had!

2. Where shall I goe,
Or whither run
To shun
This publique overthrow?

3. No places are
(This I am sure)
Secure
In this our wasting Warre.

4. Some storms w'ave past;
Yet we must all
Down fall,
And perish at the last.

Cruelty base in Commanders.

NOTHING can be more loathsome, then to see
Power conjoyn'd with Natures *Crueltie.*

Upon a sowre-breath Lady. Epig.

FIE, (quoth my Lady) what a stink is here?
When 'twas her breath that was the *Carrionere.*

Upon Lucia.

I ASKT my *Lucia* but a kisse;
And she with scorne deny'd me this:
Say then, how ill sho'd I have sped,
Had I then askt her Maidenhead?

Little and loud.

LITTLE you are; for Womans sake be proud;
For my sake next, (though little) *be not loud.*

Ship-wrack.

HE, who has suffer'd Ship-wrack, feares to saile
Upon the Seas, though with a gentle gale.

Paines without profit.

A LONG-LIFES-DAY I've taken paines
For very little, or no gaines:
The Ev'ning's come; here now Ile stop,
And work no more; but shut up Shop.

To his Booke.

BE bold my Booke, nor be abasht, or feare
The cutting Thumb-naile, or the Brow severe.
But by the *Muses* sweare, all here is good,
If but well read; or ill read, understood.

His Prayer to Ben. Johnson.

WHEN I a Verse shall make,
Know I have praid thee,
For old *Religions* sake,
Saint *Ben* to aide me.

2. Make the way smooth for me,
When I, thy *Herrick*,
Honouring thee, on my knee
Offer my *Lyrick*.

3. Candles Ile give to thee,
And a new Altar;
And thou Saint *Ben*, shalt be
Writ in my *Psalter*.

Poverty and Riches.

GIVE *Want* her welcome if she comes; we find,
Riches to be but burthens to the mind.

Again.

WHO with a little cannot be content,
Endures an everlasting punishment.

The Covetous still Captives.

LET'S live with that smal pittance that we have;
Who covets more, is evermore a slave.

Lawes.

WHEN Lawes full power have to sway, we see
Little or no part there of Tyrannie.

Of Love.

ILE get me hence,
Because no fence,
Or Fort that I can make here;
But Love by charmes,
Or else by Armes
Will storme, or starving take here.

Upon Cock.

COCK calls his Wife his Hen: when *Cock* goes too't,
Cock treads his Hen, but treads her under-foot.

To his Muse.

GO wooe young *Charles* no more to looke,
Then but to read this in my Booke:
How *Herrick* beggs, if that he can-
Not like the Muse; to love the man,
Who by the Shepheards, sung (long since)
The Starre-led-birth of Charles the *Prince.*

The bad season makes the Poet sad.

DULL to my selfe, and almost dead to these
My many fresh and fragrant Mistresses:
Lost to all Musick now; since every thing
Puts on the semblance here of sorrowing.
Sick is the Land to'th'heart; and doth endure
More dangerous faintings by her desp'rate cure.
But if that golden Age wo'd come again,
And *Charles* here Rule, as he before did Raign;
If smooth and unperplext the Seasons were,
As when the *Sweet Maria* lived here:
I sho'd delight to have my Curles halfe drown'd
In *Tyrian Dewes*, and Head with Roses crown'd.
And once more yet (ere I am laid out dead)
Knock at a Starre with my exalted Head.

To Vulcan.

THY sooty *Godhead*, I desire
Still to be ready with thy fire:
That sho'd my Booke despised be,
Acceptance it might find of thee.

Like Pattern, like People.

THIS is the height of Justice, that to doe
Thy selfe, which thou put'st other men unto.
As great men lead; the meaner follow on,
Or to the good, or evill action.

Purposes.

No wrath of Men, or rage of Seas
Can shake a just mans purposes:
No threats of Tyrants, or the Grim
Visage of them can alter him;
But what he doth at first entend,
That he holds firmly to the end.

To the Maids to walke abroad.

Come sit we under yonder Tree,
Where merry as the Maids we'l be.
And as on *Primroses* we sit,
We'l venter (if we can) at wit:
If not, at *Draw-gloves* we will play;
So spend some minutes of the day:
Or else spin out the thread of sands,
Playing at *Questions* and *Commands*:
Or tell what strange Tricks Love can do,
By quickly making one of two.
Thus we will sit and talke; but tell
No cruell truths of *Philomell*,
Or *Phillis*, whom hard Fate forc't on,
To kill her selfe for *Demophon*.
But Fables we'l relate; how *Jove*
Put on all shapes to get a Love:
As now a *Satyr*, then a *Swan*;
A *Bull* but then; and now a man.
Next we will act, how young men wooe;
And sigh, and kiss, as Lovers do:
And talke of Brides; & who shall make
That wedding-smock, this Bridal-Cake;
That Dress, this Sprig, that Leaf, this Vine;
That smooth and silken Columbine.
This done, we'l draw lots, who shall buy
And guild the Baies and Rosemary:

For variant heading *see p.* 490 2.14 for] *Moorman observes that* [so]*me copies' of 48 read* from *but no such copy has been located* 2.19 act,] [co]*mma very faint 48*

What Posies for our Wedding Rings;
What Gloves we'l give, and Ribanings:
And smiling at our selves, decree,
Who then the joyning *Priest* shall be.
What short sweet Prayers shall be said;
And how the Posset shall be made
With Cream of Lillies (not of Kine)
And *Maiden's-blush*, for spiced wine.
Thus, having talkt, we'l next commend
A kiss to each; and *so we'l end.*

His own Epitaph.

As wearied *Pilgrims*, once possest
Of long'd-for lodging, go to rest:
So I, now having rid my way;
Fix here my Button'd Staffe and stay.
Youth (I confess) hath me mis-led;
But Age hath brought me right to Bed.

A Nuptiall Verse to Mistresse Elizabeth Lee, *now Lady* Tracie.

SPRING with the Larke, most comely Bride, and meet
Your eager Bridegroome with *auspitious* feet.
The Morn's farre spent; and the immortall Sunne
Corrols his cheeke, to see those Rites not done.
Fie, *Lovely maid*! Indeed you are too slow,
When to the Temple Love sho'd runne, not go.
Dispatch your dressing then; and quickly wed:
Then feast, and coy't a little; then to bed.
This day is Loves day; and this busie night
Is yours, in which you challeng'd are to fight
With such an arm'd, but such an easie Foe,
As will if you yeeld, lye down conquer'd too.
The Field is pitcht; but such must be your warres,
As that your kisses must out-vie the Starres.
Fall down together vanquisht both, and lye
Drown'd in the bloud of Rubies there, not die.

The Night-piece, to Julia.

HER Eyes the Glow-worme lend thee,
The Shooting Starres attend thee;
And the Elves also,
Whose little eyes glow,
Like the sparks of fire, befriend thee.

2. No *Will-o'th'-Wispe* mis-light thee;
Nor Snake, or Slow-worme bite thee:
But on, on thy way
Not making a stay,
Since Ghost ther's none to affright thee.

3. Let not the darke thee cumber;
What though the Moon do's slumber?
The Starres of the night
Will lend thee their light,
Like Tapers cleare without number.

4. Then *Julia* let me wooe thee,
Thus, thus to come unto me:
And when I shall meet
Thy silv'ry feet,
My soule Ile poure into thee.

To Sir Clipseby Crew.

GIVE me wine, and give me meate,
To create in me a heate,
That my Pulses high may beate.

2. Cold and hunger never yet
Co'd a noble Verse beget;
But your Boules with Sack repleat.

3. Give me these (my Knight) and try
In a Minutes space how I
Can runne mad, and Prophesie.

4. Then if any Peece proves new,
And rare, Ile say (my dearest *Crew*)
It was full enspir'd by you.

For variants see p. 490 2 (*heading*) Clipseby *SWeY*: Cilpseby *rest*

Good Luck not lasting.

If well the Dice runne, lets applaud the cast:
The happy fortune will not alwayes last.

A Kisse.

What is a Kisse? Why this, as some approve;
The sure sweet-Sement, Glue, and Lime of Love.

Glorie.

I make no haste to have my Numbers read.
Seldome comes Glorie till a man be dead.

Poets.

Wantons we are; and though our words be such,
Our Lives do differ from our Lines by much.

No despight to the dead.

Reproach we may the living; not the dead:
'Tis cowardice to bite the buried.

To his Verses.

What will ye (my poor Orphans) do
When I must leave the World (and you)
Who'l give ye then a sheltring shed,
Or credit ye, when I am dead?
Who'l let ye by their fire sit?
Although ye have a stock of wit,
Already coin'd to pay for it.
I cannot tell; unlesse there be
Some Race of old humanitie
Left (of the large heart, and long hand)
Alive, as Noble *Westmorland*;
Or gallant *Newark*; which brave two
May fost'ring fathers be to you.
If not; expect to be no lesse
Ill us'd, then Babes left fatherless.

His charge to Julia *at his death.*

DEAREST of thousands, now the time drawes neere,
That with my Lines, my Life must full-stop here.
Cut off thy haires; and let thy Teares be shed
Over my Turfe, when I am buried.
Then for *effusions*, let none wanting be,
Or other Rites that doe belong to me;
As Love shall helpe thee, when thou do'st go hence
Unto thy everlasting residence.

Upon Love.

IN a Dreame, Love bad me go
To the Gallies there to Rowe;
In the Vision I askt, why?
Love as briefly did reply;
'Twas better there to toyle, then prove
The turmoiles they endure that love.
I awoke, and then I knew
What Love said was too too true:
Henceforth therefore I will be
As from Love, from trouble free.
None pities him that's in the snare,
And warn'd before, wo'd not beware.

The Coblers Catch.

COME sit we by the fires side;
And roundly drinke we here;
Till that we see our cheekes Ale-dy'd
And noses tann'd with Beere.

Upon Bran. *Epig.*

WHAT made that mirth last night? the neighbours say,
That *Bran* the Baker did his Breech bewray:
I rather thinke (though they may speake the worst)
'Twas to his Batch, but Leaven laid there first.

Upon Snare, *an Usurer.*

S*NARE*, ten i'th'hundred calls his wife; and why?
Shee brings in much, by carnall usury.
He by extortion brings in three times more:
Say, who's the worst, th'exactor, or the whore?

Upon Grudgings.

GRUDGINGS turnes bread to stones, when to the Poore
He gives an almes, and chides them from his doore.

Connubii Flores, *or the well-wishes at Weddings.*

Chorus Sacerdotum.

1. FROM the Temple to your home
May a thousand blessings come!
And a sweet concurring stream
Of all joyes, to joyn with them.

Chorus Juvenum.

2. Happy day
Make no long stay
Here
In thy Sphere;
But give thy place to night,
That she,
As Thee,
May be
Partaker of this sight.
And since it was thy care
To see the Younglings wed;
'Tis fit that Night, the Paire,
Sho'd see safe brought to Bed.

Chorus Senum.

3. Go to your banquet then, but use delight,
So as to rise still with an appetite.
Love is a thing most nice; and must be fed
To such a height; but never surfeited.
What is beyond the mean is ever ill:
'Tis best to feed Love; but not over-fill:
Go then discreetly to the Bed of pleasure;
And this remember, *Vertue keepes the measure.*

Chorus Virginum.

4. Luckie signes we have discri'd
To encourage on the Bride;
And to these we have espi'd,
Not a kissing *Cupid* flyes
Here about, but has his eyes,
To imply your Love is wise.

Chorus Pastorum.

5. Here we present a fleece
To make a peece
Of cloth;
Nor Faire, must you be loth
Your Finger to apply
To huswiferie.
Then, then begin
To spin:
And (Sweetling) marke you, what a Web will come
Into your Chests, drawn by your painfull Thumb.

Chorus Matronarum.

6. Set you to your Wheele, and wax
Rich, by the Ductile Wool and Flax.
Yarne is an Income; and the Huswives thread
The Larder fils with meat; the Bin with bread.

Chorus Senum.

7. Let wealth come in by comely thrift,
And not by any sordid shift:
'Tis haste
Makes waste;
Extreames have still their fault;
The softest Fire makes the sweetest Mault.
Who gripes too hard the dry and slip'rie sand,
Holds none at all, or little in his hand.

Chorus Virginum.

8. Goddesse of Pleasure, Youth and Peace,
Give them the blessing of encrease:
And thou *Lucina*, that do'st heare
The vowes of those, that children beare:
When as her Aprill houre drawes neare,
Be thou then propitious there.

Chorus Juvenum.

9. Farre hence be all speech, that may anger move:
Sweet words must nourish soft and gentle Love.

Chorus omnium.

10. Live in the Love of Doves, and having told
The Ravens yeares, go hence more Ripe then old.

To his lovely Mistresses.

ONE night i'th'yeare, my dearest Beauties, come
And bring those *dew-drink-offerings* to my Tomb.
When thence ye see my reverend Ghost to rise,
And there to lick th'effused sacrifice:
Though palenes be the Livery that I weare,
Looke ye not wan, or colourlesse for feare.
Trust me I will not hurt ye; or once shew
The least grim looke, or cast a frown on you:
Nor shall the Tapers when I'm there, burn blew.
This I may do (perhaps) as I glide by,
Cast on my Girles a glance, and loving eye:
Or fold mine armes, and sigh, because I've lost
The world so soon, and in it, you the most.
Then these, no feares more on your Fancies fall,
Though then I smile, and speake no words at all.

Upon Love.

A CHRISTALL Violl *Cupid* brought,
Which had a juice in it:
Of which who drank, he said no thought
Of Love he sho'd admit.

2. I greedy of the prize, did drinke,
And emptied soon the glasse;
Which burnt me so, that I do thinke
The fire of hell it was.

3. Give me my earthen Cups again,
The Christall I contemne;
Which, though enchas'd with Pearls, contain
A deadly draught in them.

3.3 rise] kisse *48* (*corr. Errata*)

4. And thou O *Cupid*! come not to
   My Threshold, since I see,
For all I have, or else can do,
   Thou still wilt cozen me.

Upon Gander. *Epig.*

SINCE *Gander* did his prettie Youngling wed;
Gander (they say) doth each night pisse a Bed:
What is the cause? Why *Gander* will reply,
No Goose layes good eggs that is trodden drye.

Upon Lungs. *Epig.*

LUNGS (as some say) ne'r sets him down to eate,
But that his breath do's Fly-blow all the meate.

The Beggar to Mab, *the* Fairie Queen.

PLEASE your Grace, from out your Store,
Give an Almes to one that's poore,
That your mickle, may have more.
Black I'm grown for want of meat;
Give me then an Ant to eate;
Or the cleft eare of a Mouse
Over-sowr'd in drinke of Souce:
Or *sweet Lady* reach to me
The *Abdomen* of a Bee;
Or commend a *Crickets-hip*,
Or his *Huckson*, to my Scrip.
Give for bread, a little bit
Of a Pease, that 'gins to chit,
And my full thanks take for it.
Floure of Fuz-balls, that's too good
For a man in needy-hood:
But the Meal of Mill-dust can
Well content a craving man.
Any Orts the Elves refuse
Well will serve the Beggars use.
But if this may seem too much
For an Almes; then give me such

2 *For variants see p.* 490   2.1 some] some, *48*

Little bits, that nestle there
In the Pris'ners *Panier*.
So a blessing light upon
You, and mighty *Oberon*:
That your plenty last till when,
I return your Almes agen.

An end decreed.

LET'S be jocund while we may;
All things have an ending day:
And when once the Work is done;
Fates revolve no Flax th'ave spun.

Upon a child.

HERE a pretty Baby lies
Sung asleep with Lullabies:
Pray be silent, and not stirre
Th'easie earth that covers her.

Painting sometimes permitted.

IF Nature do deny
Colours, let Art supply.

Farwell Frost, or welcome the Spring.

FLED are the Frosts, and now the Fields appeare
Re-cloth'd in fresh and verdant Diaper.
Thaw'd are the snowes, and now the lusty Spring
Gives to each Mead a neat enameling.
The Palms put forth their Gemmes, and every Tree
Now swaggers in her Leavy gallantry.
The while the *Daulian Minstrell* sweetly sings,
With warbling Notes, her *Tyrrean* sufferings.
What gentle Winds perspire? As if here
Never had been the *Northern Plunderer*
To strip the Trees, and Fields, to their distresse,
Leaving them to a pittied nakednesse.

And look how when a frantick Storme doth tear
A stubborn Oake, or Holme (long growing there)
But lul'd to calmnesse, then succeeds a breeze
That scarcely stirs the nodding leaves of Trees:
So when this War (which tempest-like doth spoil
Our salt, our Corn, our Honie, Wine, and Oile)
Falls to a temper, and doth mildly cast
His inconsiderate Frenzie off (at last)
The gentle Dove may, when these turmoils cease,
Bring in her Bill, once more, *the Branch of Peace.*

The Hag.

THE Hag is astride,
This night for to ride;
The Devill and shee together:
Through thick, and through thin,
Now out, and then in,
Though ne'r so foule be the weather.

2. A Thorn or a Burr
She takes for a Spurre:
With a lash of a Bramble she rides now,
Through Brakes and through Bryars,
O're Ditches, and Mires,
She followes the Spirit that guides now.

3. No Beast, for his food,
Dares now range the wood;
But husht in his laire he lies lurking:
While mischeifs, by these,
On Land and on Seas,
At noone of Night are a working.

4. The storme will arise,
And trouble the skies;
This night, and more for the wonder,
The ghost from the Tomb
Affrighted shall come,
Cal'd out by the clap of the Thunder.

1.18 working.] working, *48*

Upon an old man a Residenciarie.

TREAD, Sirs, as lightly as ye can
Upon the grave of this old man.
Twice fortie (bating but one year,
And thrice three weekes) he lived here.
Whom gentle fate translated hence
To a more happy Residence.
Yet, Reader, let me tell thee this
(Which from his ghost a promise is)
If here ye will some few teares shed,
He'l never haunt ye now he's dead. 1

Upon Teares.

TEARES, though th'are here below the sinners brine,
Above they are the Angels spiced wine.

Physitians.

PHYSITIANS fight not against men; but these
Combate for men, by conquering the disease.

The Primitiæ *to Parents.*

OUR *Houshold-gods* our Parents be;
And manners good requires, that we
The first Fruits give to them, who gave
Us hands to get what here we have.

Upon Cob. *Epig.*

COB clouts his shooes, and as the story tells,
His thumb-nailes-par'd, afford him sperrables.

Upon Lucie. *Epig.*

SOUND Teeth has *Lucie*, pure as Pearl, and small,
With mellow Lips, and luscious there withall.

Upon Skoles. *Epig.*

SKOLES stinks so deadly, that his Breeches loath
His dampish Buttocks furthermore to cloath:
Cloy'd they are up with Arse; but hope, one blast
Will whirle about, and blow them thence at last.

To Silvia.

I AM holy, while I stand
Circum-crost by thy pure hand:
But when that is gone; Again,
I, as others, am *Prophane*.

To his Closet-Gods.

WHEN I goe Hence ye *Closet-Gods*, I feare
Never againe to have ingression here:
Where I have had, what ever thing co'd be
Pleasant, and precious to my Muse and me.
Besides rare sweets, I had a Book which none
Co'd reade the Intext but my selfe alone.
About the Cover of this Book there went
A curious-comely clean *Compartiement*:
And, in the midst, to grace it more, was set
A blushing-pretty-peeping Rubelet:
But now 'tis clos'd; and being shut, & seal'd,
Be it, O be it, never more reveal'd!
Keep here still, *Closet-Gods*, 'fore whom I've set
Oblations oft, of sweetest Marmelet.

A Bacchanalian Verse.

FILL me a mighty Bowle
Up to the brink:
That I may drink
Unto my *Johnsons* soule.

2. Crowne it agen agen;
And thrice repeat
That happy heat;
To drink to Thee my *Ben*.

3. Well I can quaffe, I see,
To th'number five,
Or nine; but thrive
In frenzie ne'r like thee.

.8 *Compartiement*] *Compartlement 48 (see Commentary, p.* 547) 3.2 brink] rim *48*

Long lookt for comes at last.

THOUGH long it be, yeeres may repay the debt;
None loseth that, which he in time may get.

To Youth.

DRINK Wine, and live here blithefull, while ye may:
The morrowes life too late is, Live to day.

Never too late to dye.

NO man comes late unto that place from whence
Never man yet had a regredience.

A Hymne to the Muses.

O! YOU the Virgins nine!
That doe our soules encline
To noble Discipline!
Nod to this vow of mine:
Come then, and now enspire
My violl and my lyre
With your eternall fire:
And make me one entire
Composer in your Quire.
Then I'le your Altars strew
With Roses sweet and new;
And ever live a true
Acknowledger of you.

On himselfe.

ILE sing no more, nor will I longer write
Of that sweet Lady, or that gallant Knight:
Ile sing no more of Frosts, Snowes, Dews and Showers;
No more of Groves, Meades, Springs, and wreaths of Flowers:
Ile write no more, nor will I tell or sing
Of *Cupid*, and his wittie coozning:
Ile sing no more of death, or shall the grave
No more my Dirges, and my Trentalls have.

4.7 eternall] etetnall *48*

Upon Jone *and* Jane.

J*ONE* is a wench that's painted;
Jone is a Girle that's tainted;
Yet *Jone* she goes
Like one of those
Whom purity had Sainted.

Jane is a Girle that's prittie;
Jane is a wench that's wittie;
Yet, who wo'd think,
Her breath do's stinke,
As so it doth? that's pittie.

To Momus.

WHO read'st this Book that I have writ,
And can'st not mend, but carpe at it:
By all the muses! thou shalt be
Anathema to it, and me.

Ambition.

IN wayes to greatnesse, think on this,
That slippery all Ambition is.

The Country life, to the honoured M. End. Porter, *Groome of the Bed-Chamber to His Maj.*

SWEET Country life, to such unknown,
Whose lives are others, not their own!
But serving Courts, and Cities, be
Less happy, less enjoying thee.
Thou never Plow'st the Oceans foame
To seek, and bring rough Pepper home:
Nor to the Eastern Ind dost rove
To bring from thence the scorched Clove.
Nor, with the losse of thy lov'd rest,
Bring'st home the Ingot from the West.
No, thy Ambition's Master-piece
Flies no thought higher then a fleece:

Or how to pay thy Hinds, and cleere
All scores; and so to end the yeere:
But walk'st about thine own dear bounds,
Not envying others larger grounds:
For well thou know'st, *'tis not th'extent*
Of Land makes life, but sweet content.
When now the Cock (the Plow-mans Horne)
Calls forth the lilly-wristed Morne;
Then to thy corn-fields thou dost goe,
Which though well soyl'd, yet thou dost know,
That the best compost for the Lands
Is the wise Masters Feet, and Hands.
There at the Plough thou find'st thy Teame,
With a Hind whistling there to them:
And cheer'st them up, by singing how
The Kingdoms portion *is the Plow.*
This done, then to th'enameld Meads
Thou go'st; and as thy foot there treads,
Thou seest a present God-like Power
Imprinted in each Herbe and Flower:
And smell'st the breath of great-ey'd Kine,
Sweet as the blossomes of the Vine.
Here thou behold'st thy large sleek Neat
Unto the Dew-laps up in meat:
And, as thou look'st, the wanton Steere,
The Heifer, Cow, and Oxe draw neere
To make a pleasing pastime there.
These seen, thou go'st to view thy flocks
Of sheep, (safe from the Wolfe and Fox)
And find'st their bellies there as full
Of short sweet grasse, as backs with wool.
And leav'st them (as they feed and fill)
A Shepherd piping on a hill.
For Sports, for Pagentrie, and Playes,
Thou hast thy Eves, and Holydayes:
On which the young men and maids meet,
To exercise their dancing feet:
Tripping the comely country round,
With Daffadils and Daisies crown'd.
Thy Wakes, thy Quintels, here thou hast,
Thy May-poles too with Garlands grac't:
Thy Morris-dance; thy Whitsun-ale;

Thy Sheering-feast, which never faile.
Thy Harvest home; thy Wassaile bowle,
That's tost up after Fox i'th'Hole.
Thy Mummeries; thy Twelfe-tide Kings
And Queenes; thy Christmas revellings:
Thy Nut-browne mirth; thy Russet wit;
And no man payes too deare for it.
To these, thou hast thy times to goe
And trace the Hare i'th'trecherous Snow:
Thy witty wiles to draw, and get
The Larke into the Trammell net:
Thou hast thy Cockrood, and thy Glade
To take the precious Phesant made:
Thy Lime-twigs, Snares, and Pit-falls then
To catch the pilfring Birds, not Men.
O happy life! if that their good
The Husbandmen but understood!
Who all the day themselves doe please,
And Younglings, with such sports as these.
And, lying down, have nought t'affright
Sweet sleep, that makes more short the night.

Cætera desunt———

To *Electra.*

I DARE not ask a kisse;
I dare not beg a smile;
Lest having that, or this,
I might grow proud the while.

2. No, no, the utmost share
Of my desire, shall be
Onely to kisse that Aire,
That lately kissed thee.

To his worthy friend, M. Arthur Bartly.

WHEN after many Lusters thou shalt be
Wrapt up in Seare-cloth with thine Ancestrie:
When of thy ragg'd *Escutcheons* shall be seene
So little left, as if they ne'r had been:
Thou shalt thy Name have, and thy Fames best trust,
Here with the Generation of my Just.

What kind of Mistresse he would have.

BE the Mistresse of my choice,
Cleane in manners, cleere in voice:
Be she witty, more then wise;
Pure enough, though not Precise:
Be she shewing in her dresse,
Like a civill Wilderness;
That the curious may detect
Order in a sweet neglect:
Be she rowling in her eye,
Tempting all the passers by:
And each Ringlet of her haire,
An Enchantment, or a Snare,
For to catch the Lookers on;
But her self held fast by none.
Let her *Lucrece* all day be,
Thais in the night, to me.
Be she such, as neither will
Famish me, nor over-fill.

Upon Zelot.

IS *Zelot* pure? he is: ye see he weares
The signe of *Circumcision* in his eares.

The Rosemarie branch.

GROW for two ends, it matters not at all,
Be't for my *Bridall*, or my *Buriall*.

Upon Madam Ursly, *Epig.*

FOR ropes of pearle, first Madam *Ursly* showes
A chaine of Cornes, pickt from her eares and toes:
Then, next, to match *Tradescant's* curious shels,
Nailes from her fingers mew'd, she shewes: what els?
Why then (forsooth) a Carcanet is shown
Of teeth, as deaf as nuts, and all her own.

Upon Crab, *Epigr.*

CRAB faces gownes with sundry Furres; 'tis known,
He keeps the Fox-furre for to face his own.

A Paranæticall, or Advisive Verse, to his friend, M. John Wicks.

Is this a life, to break thy sleep?
To rise as soon as day doth peep?
To tire thy patient Oxe or Asse
By noone, and let thy good dayes passe,
Not knowing This, that *Jove* decrees
Some mirth, t'adulce mans miseries?
No; 'tis a life, to have thine oyle,
Without extortion, from thy soyle:
Thy faithfull fields to yeeld thee Graine,
Although with some, yet little paine:
To have thy mind, and nuptiall bed,
With feares, and cares uncumbered:
A Pleasing Wife, that by thy side
Lies softly panting like a Bride.
This is to live, and to endeere
Those minutes, Time has lent us here.
Then, while Fates suffer, live thou free,
(As is that ayre that circles thee)
And crown thy temples too, and let
Thy servant, not thy own self, sweat,
To strut thy barnes with sheafs of Wheat.
Time steals away like to a stream,
And we glide hence away with them.
No sound recalls the houres once fled,
Or Roses, being withered:
Nor us (my Friend) when we are lost,
Like to a Deaw, or melted Frost.
Then live we mirthfull, while we should,
And turn the iron Age to Gold.
Let's feast, and frolick, sing, and play,
And thus lesse last, then live our Day.
Whose life with care is overcast,
That man's not said to live, but last:
Nor is't a life, seven yeares to tell,
But for to live that half seven well:
And that wee'l do; as men, who know,
Some few sands spent, we hence must go,
Both to be blended in the Urn,
From whence there's never a return.

Once seen, and no more.

THOUSANDS each day passe by, which wee,
Once past and gone, no more shall see.

Love.

THIS Axiom I have often heard,
Kings ought to be more lov'd, then fear'd.

To M. Denham, *on his Prospective Poem.*

OR lookt I back unto the Times hence flown,
To praise those Muses, and dislike our own?
Or did I walk those *Pean*-Gardens through,
To kick the Flow'rs, and scorn their odours too?
I might (and justly) be reputed (here)
One nicely mad, or peevishly severe.
But by *Apollo!* as I worship wit,
(Where I have cause to burn perfumes to it:)
So, I confesse, 'tis somwhat to do well
In our high art, although we can't excell,
Like thee; or dare the Buskins to unloose
Of thy brave, bold, and sweet *Maronian* Muse.
But since I'm cal'd (rare *Denham*) to be gone,
Take from thy *Herrick* this conclusion:
'Tis dignity in others, if they be
Crown'd Poets; yet live Princes under thee:
The while their wreaths and Purple Robes do shine,
Lesse by their own jemms, then those beams of thine.

A Hymne, to the Lares.

IT was, and still my care is,
To worship ye, the *Lares*,
With crowns of greenest Parsley,
And Garlick chives not scarcely:
For favours here to warme me,
And not by fire to harme me.
For gladding so my hearth here,
With inoffensive mirth here;

That while the Wassaile Bowle here
With *North-down* Ale doth troule here,
No sillable doth fall here,
To marre the mirth at all here.
For which, ô *Chimney-keepers!*
(I dare not call ye Sweepers)
So long as I am able
To keep a countrey-table,
Great be my fare, or small cheere,
I'le eat and drink up all here.

Deniall in women no disheartning to men.

WOMEN, although they ne're so goodly make it,
Their fashion is, but to say no, to take it.

Adversity.

LOVE is maintain'd by wealth; when all is spent,
Adversity then breeds the discontent.

To Fortune.

TUMBLE me down, and I will sit
Upon my ruines (smiling yet:)
Teare me to tatters; yet I'le be
Patient in my necessitie.
Laugh at my scraps of cloaths, and shun
Me, as a fear'd infection:
Yet scarre-crow-like I'le walk, as one,
Neglecting thy derision.

To Anthea.

COME *Anthea*, know thou this,
Love at no time idle is:
Let's be doing, though we play
But at push-pin (half the day:)
Chains of sweet bents let us make,
Captive one, or both, to take:
In which bondage we will lie,
Soules transfusing thus, and die.

1 *For variants see p.* 490

Cruelties.

NERO commanded; but withdrew his eyes
From the beholding Death, and cruelties.

Perseverance.

HAST thou begun an act? ne're then give o're:
No man despaires to do what's done before.

Upon his Verses.

WHAT off-spring other men have got,
The how, where, when, I question not.
These are the Children I have left;
Adopted some; none got by theft.
But all are toucht (like lawfull plate)
And no Verse illegitimate.

Distance betters Dignities.

KINGS must not oft be seen by publike eyes;
State at a distance adds to dignities.

Health.

HEALTH is no other (as the learned hold)
But a just measure both of Heat and Cold.

To Dianeme. A Ceremonie in Glocester.

I'LE to thee a Simnell bring,
'Gainst thou go'st a *mothering*,
So that, when she blesseth thee,
Half that blessing thou'lt give me.

To the King.

GIVE way, give way, now, now my *Charles* shines here,
A Publike Light (in this immensive Sphere.)
Some starres were fixt before; but these are dim,
Compar'd (in this my ample Orbe) to Him.
Draw in your feeble fiers, while that He
Appeares but in His Meaner Majestie.

Where, if such glory flashes from His Name,
Which is His Shade, who can abide His Flame!
Princes, and such like Publike Lights as these,
Must not be lookt on, but at distances:
For, if we gaze on These brave Lamps too neer,
Our eyes they'l blind, or if not blind, they'l bleer.

The Funerall Rites of the Rose.

THE Rose was sick, and smiling di'd;
And (being to be sanctifi'd)
About the Bed, there sighing stood
The sweet, and flowrie Sisterhood.
Some hung the head, while some did bring
(To wash her) water from the Spring.
Some laid her forth, while other wept,
But all a solemne Fast there kept.
The holy Sisters some among
The sacred *Dirge* and *Trentall* sung.
But ah! what sweets smelt every where,
As Heaven had spent all perfumes there.
At last, when prayers for the dead,
And Rites were all accomplished;
They, weeping, spread a Lawnie Loome,
And clos'd her up, as in a Tombe.

The Rainbow: or curious Covenant.

MINE eyes, like clouds, were drizling raine,
And as they thus did entertaine
The gentle Beams from *Julia's* sight
To mine eyes level'd opposite:
O Thing admir'd! there did appeare
A curious Rainbow smiling there;
Which was the Covenant, that she
No more wo'd drown mine eyes, or me.

The last stroke strike sure.

THOUGH by well-warding many blowes w'ave past,
That stroke most fear'd is, which is struck the last.

Fortune.

FORTUNE's a blind profuser of her own,
Too much she gives to some, enough to none.

Stool-ball.

1 AT Stool-ball, *Lucia*, let us play,
For Sugar-cakes and Wine;
Or for a Tansie let us pay,
The losse or thine, or mine.

2 If thou, my Deere, a winner be
At trundling of the Ball,
The wager thou shalt have, and me,
And my misfortunes all.

3 But if (my Sweetest) I shall get,
Then I desire but this;
That likewise I may pay the Bet,
And have for all a kisse.

To Sappho.

LET us now take time, and play,
Love, and live here while we may;
Drink rich wine; and make good cheere,
While we have our being here:
For, once dead, and laid i'th grave,
No return from thence we have.

On Poet Prat, *Epigr.*

PRAT He writes Satyres; but herein's the fault,
In no one Satyre there's a mite of salt.

Upon Tuck, *Epigr.*

AT Post and Paire, or Slam, *Tom Tuck* would play
This Christmas, but his want wherwith, sayes Nay.

Biting of Beggars.

WHO, railing, drives the Lazar from his door,
Instead of almes, sets dogs upon the poor.

The May-pole.

THE May-pole is up,
Now give me the cup;
I'le drink to the Garlands a-round it:
But first unto those
Whose hands did compose
The glory of flowers that crown'd it.

A health to my Girles,
Whose husbands may Earles
Or Lords be, (granting my wishes)
And when that ye wed
To the Bridall Bed,
Then multiply all, like to Fishes.

Men mind no state in sicknesse.

THAT flow of Gallants which approach
To kisse thy hand from out the coach;
That fleet of Lackeyes, which do run
Before thy swift Postilion;
Those strong-hoof'd Mules, which we behold,
Rein'd in with Purple, Pearl, and gold,
And shod with silver, prove to be
The drawers of the *axeltree.*
Thy Wife, thy Children, and the state
Of *Persian* Loomes, and *antique* Plate:
All these, and more, shall then afford
No joy to thee their sickly Lord.

Adversity.

ADVERSITY hurts none, but onely such
Whom whitest Fortune dandled has too much.

Want.

NEED is no vice at all; though here it be,
With men, a loathed inconveniencie.

Griefe.

SORROWES divided amongst many, lesse
Discruciate a man in deep distresse.

Love palpable.

I PREST my *Julia's* lips, and in the kisse
Her Soule and Love were palpable in this.

No action hard to affection.

NOTHING hard, or harsh can prove
Unto those that truly love.

Meane things overcome mighty.

BY the weak'st means things mighty are o'rethrown,
He's Lord of thy life, who contemnes his own.

Upon Trigg, *Epig.*

TRIGG having turn'd his sute, he struts in state,
And tells the world, he's now regenerate.

Upon Smeaton.

HOW co'd *Luke Smeaton* weare a shoe, or boot,
Who two and thirty cornes had on a foot.

The Bracelet of Pearle: to Silvia.

I BRAKE thy Bracelet 'gainst my will;
And, wretched, I did see
Thee discomposed then, and still
Art discontent with me.

One jemme was lost; and I will get
A richer pearle for thee,
Then ever, dearest *Silvia*, yet
Was drunk to *Antonie*.

Or, for revenge, I'le tell thee what
Thou for the breach shalt do;
First, crack the strings, and after that,
Cleave thou my heart in two.

How Roses came red.

'TIS said, as *Cupid* danc't among
The *Gods*, he down the Nectar flung;
Which, on the white *Rose* being shed,
Made it for ever after red.

Kings.

MEN are not born Kings, but are men renown'd;
Chose first, confirm'd next, & at last are crown'd.

First work, and then wages.

PREPOST'ROUS is that order, when we run
To ask our wages, e're our work be done.

Teares, and Laughter.

KNEW'ST thou, one moneth wo'd take thy life away,
Thou'dst weep; but laugh, sho'd it not last a day.

Glory.

GLORY no other thing is (*Tullie* sayes)
Then a mans frequent Fame, spoke out with praise.

Possessions.

THOSE possessions short-liv'd are,
Into the which we come by warre.

Laxare fibulam.

TO loose the button, is no lesse,
Then to cast off all bashfulnesse.

His returne to London.

FROM the dull confines of the drooping West,
To see the day spring from the pregnant East,
Ravisht in spirit, I come, nay more, I flie
To thee, blest place of my Nativitie!
Thus, thus with hallowed foot I touch the ground,
With thousand blessings by thy Fortune crown'd.
O fruitfull Genius! that bestowest here
An everlasting plenty, yeere by yeere.
O *Place!* O *People!* Manners! fram'd to please
All *Nations*, *Customes*, *Kindreds*, *Languages!*
I am a free-born *Roman*; suffer then,
That I amongst you live a Citizen.
London my home is: though by hard fate sent
Into a long and irksome banishment;
Yet since cal'd back; henceforward let me be,
O native countrey, repossest by thee!
For, rather then I'le to the West return,
I'le beg of thee first here to have mine Urn.
Weak I am grown, and must in short time fall;
Give thou my sacred Reliques Buriall.

Not every day fit for Verse.

'TIS not ev'ry day, that I
Fitted am to prophesie:
No, but when the Spirit fils
The fantastick Pannicles:
Full of fier; then I write
As the Godhead doth indite.
Thus inrag'd, my lines are hurl'd,
Like the *Sybells*, through the world.
Look how next the holy fier
Either slakes, or doth retire;
So the Fancie cooles, till when
That brave Spirit comes agen.

Poverty the greatest pack.

TO mortall men great loads allotted be,
But of all packs, no pack like poverty.

A Beucolick, or discourse of Neatherds.

1 COME blithefull Neatherds, let us lay
A wager, who the best shall play,
Of thee, or I, the Roundelay,
That fits the businesse of the Day.

Chor. And *Lallage* the Judge shall be,
To give the prize to thee, or me.

2 Content, begin, and I will bet
A Heifer smooth, and black as jet,
In every part alike compleat,
And wanton as a Kid as yet.

Chor. And *Lallage* (with cow-like eyes)
Shall be Disposeresse of the prize.

1 Against thy Heifer, I will here
Lay to thy stake a lustie Steere,
With gilded hornes, and burnisht cleere.

Chor. Why then begin, and let us heare
The soft, the sweet, the mellow note
That gently purles from eithers Oat.

2 The stakes are laid: let's now apply
Each one to make his melody:

Lal. The equall Umpire shall be I,
Who'l hear, and so judge righteously.

Chor. Much time is spent in prate; begin,
And sooner play, the sooner win. [*He playes.*

1 That's sweetly touch't, I must confesse:
Thou art a man of worthinesse:
But hark how I can now expresse
My love unto my Neatherdesse. [*He sings.*

Chor. A suger'd note! and sound as sweet
As Kine, when they at milking meet.

1 Now for to win thy Heifer faire,
I'le strike thee such a nimble Ayre,
That thou shalt say (thy selfe) 'tis rare;
And title me without compare.

Chor. Lay by a while your Pipes, and rest,
Since both have here deserved best.

2 To get thy Steerling, once again,
I'le play thee such another strain;
That thou shalt swear, my Pipe do's raigne
Over thine Oat, as Soveraigne.
[*He sings.*

Chor. And *Lallage* shall tell by this,
Whose now the prize and wager is.

1 Give me the prize: 2. The day is mine:
1 Not so; my Pipe has silenc't thine:
And hadst thou wager'd twenty Kine,
They were mine own. *Lal.* In love combine.

Chor. And lay we down our Pipes together,
As wearie, not o'recome by either.

True safety.

'TIS not the Walls, or purple, that defends
A Prince from Foes; but 'tis his Fort of Friends.

A Prognostick.

AS many Lawes and Lawyers do expresse
Nought but a Kingdoms ill-affectednesse:
Ev'n so, those streets and houses do but show
Store of diseases, where Physitians flow.

Upon Julia's *sweat.*

WO'D ye oyle of Blossomes get?
Take it from my *Julia's* sweat:
Oyl of Lillies, and of Spike,
From her moysture take the like:
Let her breath, or let her blow,
All rich spices thence will flow.

Proof to no purpose.

YOU see this gentle streame, that glides,
Shov'd on, by quick succeeding Tides:
Trie if this sober streame you can
Follow to th'wilder Ocean:

And see, if there it keeps unspent
In that congesting element.
Next, from that world of waters, then
By poares and cavernes back agen
Induc't that inadultrate same
Streame to the Spring from whence it came.
This with a wonder when ye do,
As easie, and els easier too:
Then may ye recollect the graines
Of my particular Remaines;
After a thousand Lusters hurld,
By ruffling winds, about the world.

Fame.

'TIS still observ'd, that Fame ne're sings
The order, but the Sum of things.

By use comes easinesse.

OFT bend the Bow, and thou with ease shalt do,
What others can't with all their strength put to.

To the Genius of his house.

COMMAND the Roofe great *Genius*, and from thence
Into this house powre downe thy influence,
That through each room a golden pipe may run
Of living water by thy *Benizon.*
Fulfill the Larders, and with strengthning bread
Be evermore these Bynns replenished.
Next, like a Bishop consecrate my ground,
That luckie Fairies here may dance their Round:
And after that, lay downe some silver pence,
The Masters charge and care to recompence.
Charme then the chambers; make the beds for ease,
More then for peevish pining sicknesses.
Fix the foundation fast, and let the Roofe
Grow old with time, but yet keep weather-proofe.

His Grange, or private wealth.

THOUGH Clock,
To tell how night drawes hence, I've none,
A Cock,
I have, to sing how day drawes on.
I have
A maid (my *Prew*) by good luck sent,
To save
That little, Fates me gave or lent.
A Hen
I keep, which creeking day by day,
Tells when
She goes her long white egg to lay.
A goose
I have, which, with a jealous eare,
Lets loose
Her tongue, to tell what danger's neare.
A Lamb
I keep (tame) with my morsells fed,
Whose Dam
An Orphan left him (lately dead.)
A Cat
I keep, that playes about my House,
Grown fat,
With eating many a miching Mouse.
To these
A **Trasy* I do keep, whereby * His Spaniel.
I please
The more my rurall privacie:
Which are
But toyes, to give my heart some ease:
Where care
None is, slight things do lightly please.

Good precepts, or counsell.

IN all thy need, be thou possest
Still with a well-prepared brest:
Nor let the shackles make thee sad;
Thou canst but have, what others had.

And this for comfort thou must know,
Times that are ill wo'nt still be so.
Clouds will not ever powre down raine;
A sullen day will cleere againe.
First, peales of Thunder we must heare,
Then Lutes and Harpes shall stroke the eare.

Money makes the mirth.

WHEN all Birds els do of their musick faile,
Money's the still-sweet-singing *Nightingale.*

Up tailes all.

BEGIN with a kisse,
Go on too with this:
And thus, thus, thus let us smother
Our lips for a while,
But let's not beguile
Our hope of one for the other.

This play, be assur'd,
Long enough has endur'd,
Since more and more is exacted;
For love he doth call
For his Uptailes all;
And that's the part to be acted.

Upon Franck.

F*RANCK* wo'd go scoure her teeth; and setting to't,
Twice two fell out, all rotten at the root.

Upon Lucia *dabled in the deaw.*

MY *Lucia* in the deaw did go,
And prettily bedabled so,
Her cloaths held up, she shew'd withall
Her decent legs, cleane, long and small.
I follow'd after to descrie
Part of the nak't sincerity;
But still the envious Scene between
Deni'd the Mask I wo'd have seen.

Charon *and* Phylomel, *a Dialogue sung.*

Ph. CHARON! O gentle *Charon*! let me wooe thee,
By tears and pitie now to come unto mee.
Ch. What voice so sweet and charming do I heare?
Say what thou art. *Ph.* I prithee first draw neare.
Ch. A sound I heare, but nothing yet can see,
Speak where thou art. *Ph.* O *Charon* pittie me!
I am a bird, and though no name I tell,
My warbling note will say I'm *Phylomel.*
Ch. What's that to me, I waft nor fish or fowles,
Nor Beasts (fond thing) but only humane soules.
Ph. Alas for me! *Ch.* Shame on thy witching note,
That made me thus hoist saile, and bring my Boat:
But Ile returne; what mischief brought thee hither?
Ph. A deale of Love, and much, much Griefe together.
Ch. What's thy request? *Ph.* that since she's now beneath
Who fed my life, I'le follow her in death.
Ch. And is that all? I'm gone. *Ph.* By love I pray thee,
Ch. Talk not of love, all pray, but few soules pay me.
Ph. Ile give thee vows & tears. *Ch.* can tears pay skores
For mending sails, for patching Boat and Oares?
Ph. I'le beg a penny, or Ile sing so long,
Till thou shalt say, I've paid thee with a song.
Ch. Why then begin, and all the while we make
Our slothfull passage o're the Stygian Lake,
Thou & I'le sing to make these dull Shades merry,
Who els with tears wo'd doubtles drown my ferry.

Upon Paul. *Epigr.*

PAULS hands do give, what give they bread or meat,
Or money? no, but onely deaw and sweat.
As stones and salt gloves use to give, even so
Pauls hands do give, nought else for ought we know.

1 *For variants see pp.* 490–1 1.21 *Ph.*] *Ch. 48* 1.26 ferry.] ferry *48*
2.3 gloves] shores *conj. ed.* (*see Commentary, p.* 551)

Upon Sibb. *Epigr.*

SIBB when she saw her face how hard it was,
For anger spat on thee her Looking-glasse:
But weep not *Christall*; for the shame was meant
Not unto thee, but That thou didst present.

A Ternarie of littles, upon a pipkin of Jellie sent to a Lady.

1 A LITTLE Saint best fits a little Shrine,
A little prop best fits a little Vine,
As my small Cruse best fits my little Wine.

2 A little Seed best fits a little Soyle,
A little Trade best fits a little Toyle:
As my small Jarre best fits my little Oyle.

3 A little Bin best fits a little Bread,
A little Garland fits a little Head:
As my small stuffe best fits my little Shed.

4 A little Hearth best fits a little Fire,
A little Chappell fits a little Quire,
As my small Bell best fits my little Spire.

5 A little streame best fits a little Boat;
A little lead best fits a little Float;
As my small Pipe best fits my little note.

6 A little meat best fits a little bellie,
As sweetly Lady, give me leave to tell ye,
This little Pipkin fits this little Jellie.

Upon the Roses in Julias *bosome.*

THRICE happie Roses, so much grac't, to have
Within the Bosome of my Love your grave.
Die when ye will, your sepulchre is knowne,
Your Grave her Bosome is, the Lawne the Stone.

Maids nay's are nothing.

MAIDS nay's are nothing, they are shie
But to desire what they denie.

The smell of the Sacrifice.

THE Gods require the thighes
Of Beeves for sacrifice;
Which rosted, we the steam
Must sacrifice to them:
Who though they do not eat,
Yet love the smell of meat.

Lovers how they come and part.

A *GYGES* Ring they beare about them still,
To be, and not seen when and where they will.
They tread on clouds, and though they sometimes fall,
They fall like dew, but make no noise at all.
So silently they one to th'other come,
As colours steale into the Peare or Plum,
And Aire-like, leave no pression to be seen
Where e're they met, or parting place has been.

To women, to hide their teeth, if they be rotten or rusty.

CLOSE keep your lips, if that you meane
To be accounted inside cleane:
For if you cleave them, we shall see
There in your teeth much Leprosie.

In praise of women.

O *JUPITER*, sho'd I speake ill
Of woman-kind, first die I will;
Since that I know, 'mong all the rest
Of creatures, woman is the best.

The Apron of Flowers.

TO gather Flowers *Sappha* went,
And homeward she did bring
Within her Lawnie Continent,
The treasure of the Spring.

She smiling blusht, and blushing smil'd,
And sweetly blushing thus,
She lookt as she'd been got with child
By young *Favonius*.

Her Apron gave (as she did passe)
An Odor more divine,
More pleasing too, then ever was
The lap of *Proserpine*.

The Candor of Julias *teeth.*

WHITE as *Zenobias* teeth, the which the Girles
Of Rome did weare for their most precious Pearles.

Upon her weeping.

SHE wept upon her cheeks, and weeping so,
She seem'd to quench loves fires that there did glow.

Another upon her weeping.

SHE by the River sate, and sitting there,
She wept, and made it deeper by a teare.

Delay.

BREAK off Delay, since we but read of one
That ever prosper'd by *Cunctation*.

To Sir John Berkley, *Governour of Exeter.*

STAND forth brave man, since Fate has made thee here
The *Hector* over *Aged Exeter*;
Who for a long sad time has weeping stood,
Like a *poore Lady* lost in Widdowhood:
But feares not now to see her safety sold
(As other Townes and Cities were) for gold,
By those ignoble *Births*, which shame the stem
That gave Progermination unto them:

3 *For variant heading see p.* 491

Whose restlesse *Ghosts* shall heare their children sing,
Our Sires betraid their Countrey and their King.
True, if this Citie seven times rounded was
With rock, and seven times circumflankt with brasse,
Yet if thou wert not, *Berkley*, loyall proofe,
The Senators down tumbling with the Roofe,
Would into prais'd (but pitied) ruines fall,
Leaving no shew, where stood the *Capitoll.*
But thou art just and itchlesse, and dost please
Thy *Genius* with two strength'ning *Buttresses,*
Faith, and *Affection:* which will never slip
To weaken this thy great *Dictator-ship.*

To Electra. *Love looks for Love.*

LOVE love begets, then never be
Unsoft to him who's smooth to thee.
Tygers and Beares (I've heard some say)
For profer'd love will love repay:
None are so harsh, but if they find
Softnesse in others, will be kind;
Affection will affection move,
Then you must like, because I love.

Regression spoiles Resolution.

HAST thou attempted greatnesse? then go on,
Back-turning slackens Resolution.

Contention.

DISCREET and prudent we that Discord call,
That either profits, or not hurts at all.

Consultation.

CONSULT ere thou begin'st, that done, go on
With all wise speed for execution.

Love dislikes nothing.

WHATSOEVER thing I see,
Rich or poore although it be;
'Tis a Mistresse unto mee.

Be my Girle, or faire or browne,
Do's she smile, or do's she frowne:
Still I write a Sweet-heart downe.

Be she rough, or smooth of skin;
When I touch, I then begin
For to let Affection in.

Be she bald, or do's she weare
Locks incurl'd of other haire;
I shall find enchantment there.

Be she whole, or be she rent,
So my fancie be content,
She's to me most excellent.

Be she fat, or be she leane,
Be she sluttish, be she cleane,
I'm a man for ev'ry Sceane.

Our own sinnes unseen.

OTHER mens sins wee ever beare in mind;
None sees the fardell of his faults behind.

No Paines, no Gaines.

IF little labour, little are our gaines:
Mans fortunes are according to his paines.

Upon Slouch.

SLOUCH he packs up, and goes to sev'rall Faires,
And weekly Markets for to sell his wares:
Meane time that he from place to place do's rome,
His wife her owne ware sells as fast at home.

3.1 labour] lalour *48*

Vertue best united.

BY so much, vertue is the lesse,
By how much, neere to singlenesse.

The eye.

A WANTON and lascivious eye
Betrayes the Hearts Adulterie.

To Prince Charles *upon his coming to Exeter.*

WHAT Fate decreed, Time now ha's made us see
A Renovation of the West by Thee.
That Preternaturall Fever, which did threat
Death to our Countrey, now hath lost his heat:
And calmes succeeding, we perceive no more
Th'unequall Pulse to beat, as heretofore.
Something there yet remaines for Thee to do;
Then reach those ends that thou wast destin'd to.
Go on with *Sylla's* Fortune; let thy Fate
Make Thee like Him, this, that way fortunate,
Apollos Image side with Thee to blesse
Thy Warre (discreetly made) with white successe.
Meane time thy Prophets Watch by Watch shall pray;
While young *Charles* fights, and fighting wins the day.
That done, our smooth-pac't Poems all shall be
Sung in the high *Doxologie* of Thee.
Then maids shall strew Thee, and thy Curles from them
Receive (with Songs) a flowrie Diadem.

A Song.

BURNE, or drowne me, choose ye whether,
So I may but die together:
Thus to slay me by degrees,
Is the height of Cruelties.
What needs twenty stabs, when one
Strikes me dead as any stone?
O shew mercy then, and be
Kind at once to murder mee.

Princes and Favourites.

PRINCES and Fav'rites are most deere, while they
By giving and receiving hold the play:
But the Relation then of both growes poor,
When These can aske, and Kings can give no more.

Examples, or like Prince, like People.

EXAMPLES lead us, and wee likely see,
Such as the Prince is, will his People be.

Potentates.

LOVE and the *Graces* evermore do wait
Upon the man that is a Potentate.

The Wake.

COME *Anthea* let us two
Go to Feast, as others do.
Tarts and Custards, Creams and Cakes,
Are the Junketts still at Wakes:
Unto which the Tribes resort,
Where the businesse is the sport:
Morris-dancers thou shalt see,
Marian too in Pagentrie:
And a Mimick to devise
Many grinning properties.
Players there will be, and those
Base in action as in clothes:
Yet with strutting they will please
The incurious Villages.
Neer the dying of the day,
There will be a *Cudgell*-Play,
Where a *Coxcomb* will be broke,
Ere a good *word* can be spoke:
But the anger ends all here,
Drencht in Ale, or drown'd in Beere.
Happy Rusticks, best content
With the cheapest Merriment:
And possesse no other feare,
Then to want the Wake next Yeare.

The Peter-*penny.*

FRESH strowings allow
To my Sepulcher now,
To make my lodging the sweeter;
A staffe or a wand
Put then in my hand,
With a pennie to pay S. *Peter.*

Who has not a Crosse,
Must sit with the losse,
And no whit further must venture;
Since the Porter he
Will paid have his fee,
Or els not one there must enter.

Who at a dead lift,
Can't send for a gift
A Pig to the Priest for a Roster,
Shall heare his Clarke say,
By yea and by nay,
No pennie, no Pater Noster.

To Doctor Alablaster.

NOR art thou lesse esteem'd, that I have plac'd
(Amongst mine honour'd) Thee (almost) the last:
In great Processions many lead the way
To him, who is the triumph of the day,
As these have done to Thee, who art the one,
One onely glory of a million,
In whom the spirit of the Gods do's dwell,
Firing thy soule, by which thou dost foretell
When this or that vast *Dinastie* must fall
Downe to a *Fillit* more *Imperiall.*
When this or that *Horne* shall be broke, and when
Others shall spring up in their place agen:
When times and seasons and all yeares must lie
Drown'd in the Sea of wild Eternitie:
When the *Black Dooms-day Bookes* (as yet unseal'd)
Shall by the mighty *Angell* be reveal'd:

And when the Trumpet which thou late hast found
Shall call to Judgment; tell us when the sound
Of this or that great Aprill day shall be,
And next the Gospell wee will credit thee.
Meane time like Earth-wormes we will craule below,
And wonder at Those Things that thou dost know.

Upon his Kinswoman Mrs. M. S.

HERE lies a Virgin, and as sweet
As ere was wrapt in winding sheet.
Her name if next you wo'd have knowne,
The Marble speaks it *Mary Stone*:
Who dying in her blooming yeares,
This Stone, for names sake, melts to teares.
If fragrant Virgins you'l but keep
A Fast, while Jets and Marbles weep,
And praying, strew some Roses on her,
You'l do my *Neice* abundant honour.

Felicitie knowes no Fence.

OF both our Fortunes good and bad we find
Prosperitie more searching of the mind:
Felicitie flies o're the Wall and Fence,
While misery keeps in with patience.

Death ends all woe.

TIME is the Bound of things, where e're we go,
Fate gives a meeting. Death's the end of woe.

A Conjuration, to Electra.

BY those soft Tods of wooll
With which the aire is full:
By all those Tinctures there,
That paint the *Hemisphere*:
By Dewes and drisling Raine,
That swell the Golden Graine:
By all those sweets that be
I'th flowrie Nunnerie:

By silent Nights, and the
Three Formes of *Heccate*:
By all Aspects that blesse
The sober *Sorceresse*,
While juice she straines, and pith
To make her Philters with:
By Time, that hastens on
Things to perfection:
And by your self, the best
Conjurement of the rest:
O my *Electra*! be
In love with none, but me.

Courage cool'd.

I CANNOT love, as I have lov'd before:
For, I'm grown old; &, with mine age, grown poore:
Love must be fed by wealth: this blood of mine
Must needs wax cold, if wanting bread and wine.

The Spell.

HOLY Water come and bring;
Cast in Salt, for seasoning:
Set the Brush for sprinkling:
Sacred Spittle bring ye hither;
Meale and it now mix together;
And a little Oyle to either:
Give the Tapers here their light,
Ring the *Saints-Bell*, to affright
Far from hence the evill Sp'rite.

His wish to privacie.

GIVE me a Cell
To dwell,
Where no foot hath
A path:
There will I spend,
And end
My wearied yeares
In teares.

A good Husband.

A MASTER of a house (as I have read)
Must be the first man up, and last in bed:
With the Sun rising he must walk his grounds;
See this, View that, and all the other bounds:
Shut every gate; mend every hedge that's torne,
Either with old, or plant therein new thorne:
Tread ore his gleab, but with such care, that where
He sets his foot, he leaves rich *compost* there.

A Hymne to Bacchus.

I SING thy praise *Iacchus*,
Who with thy *Thyrse* dost thwack us:
And yet thou so dost back us
With boldness that we feare
No *Brutus* entring here;
Nor *Cato* the severe.
What though the *Lictors* threat us,
We know they dare not beate us;
So long as thou dost heat us.
When we thy *Orgies* sing,
Each Cobler is a King;
Nor dreads he any thing:
And though he doe not rave,
Yet he'l the courage have
To call my *Lord Maior* knave;
Besides too, in a brave,
Although he has no riches,
But walks with dangling breeches,
And skirts that want their stiches,
And shewes his naked flitches;
Yet he'le be thought or seen,
So good as *George-a-Green*;
And calls his Blouze, his Queene;
And speaks in language keene:
O *Bacchus*! let us be
From cares and troubles free;
And thou shalt heare how we
Will chant new *Hymnes* to thee.

2 *For variants see p.* 491

Upon Pusse *and her Prentice. Epig.*

PUSSE and her Prentice both at Draw-gloves play;
That done, they kisse, and so draw out the day:
At night they draw to Supper; then well fed,
They draw their clothes off both, so draw to bed.

Blame the reward of Princes.

AMONG disasters that discention brings,
This not the least is, which belongs to Kings.
If Wars goe well; each for a part layes claime:
If ill, then Kings, not Souldiers beare the blame.

Clemency in Kings.

KINGS must not only cherish up the good,
But must be niggards of the meanest bloud.

Anger.

WRONGS if neglected, vanish in short time;
But heard with anger, we confesse the crime.

A Psalme or Hymne to the Graces.

GLORY be to the Graces!
That doe in publike places,
Drive thence what ere encumbers,
The listning to my numbers.

Honour be to the Graces!
Who doe with sweet embraces,
Shew they are well contented
With what I have invented.

Worship be to the Graces!
Who do from sowre faces,
And lungs that wo'd infect me,
For evermore protect me.

An Hymne to the Muses.

HONOUR to you who sit!
Neere to the well of wit;
And drink your fill of it.

Glory and worship be!
To you sweet Maids (thrice three)
Who still inspire me.

And teach me how to sing
Unto the *Lyrick* string
My measures ravishing.

Then while I sing your praise,
My *Priest-hood* crown with bayes
Green, to the end of dayes.

Upon Julia's *Clothes.*

WHEN as in silks my *Julia* goes,
Then, then (me thinks) how sweetly flowes
That liquefaction of her clothes.

Next, when I cast mine eyes and see
That brave Vibration each way free;
O how that glittering taketh me!

Moderation.

IN things a moderation keepe,
Kings ought to sheare, not skin their sheepe.

To Anthea.

LETS call for *Hymen* if agreed thou art;
Delays in love but crucifie the heart.
Loves thornie Tapers yet neglected lye:
Speak thou the word, they'l kindle by and by.
The nimble howers wooe us on to wed,
And *Genius* waits to have us both to bed.
Behold, for us the *Naked Graces* stay
With maunds of roses for to strew the way:

Besides, the most religious Prophet stands
Ready to joyne, as well our hearts as hands.
Juno yet smiles; but if she chance to chide,
Ill luck 'twill bode to th'Bridegroome and the Bride.
Tell me *Anthea*, dost thou fondly dread
The loss of that we call a Maydenhead?
Come, Ile instruct thee. Know, the vestall fier
Is not by mariage quencht, but flames the higher.

Upon Prew *his Maid.*

In this little Urne is laid
Prewdence Baldwin (once my maid)
From whose happy spark here let
Spring the purple Violet.

The Invitation.

To sup with thee thou didst me home invite;
And mad'st a promise that mine appetite
Sho'd meet and tire, on such lautitious meat,
The like not *Heliogabalus* did eat:
And richer Wine wo'dst give to me (thy guest)
Then Roman *Sylla* powr'd out at his feast.
I came; (tis true) and lookt for Fowle of price,
The bastard *Phenix*; bird of *Paradice*;
And for no less then Aromatick Wine
Of *Maydens-blush*, commixt with *Jessimine*.
Cleane was the herth, the mantle larded jet;
Which wanting *Lar*, and smoke, hung weeping wet;
At last, i'th'noone of winter, did appeare
A ragd-soust-neats-foot with sick vineger:
And in a burnisht Flagonet stood by
Beere small as Comfort, dead as Charity.
At which amaz'd, and pondring on the food,
How cold it was, and how it child my blood;
I curst the master; and I damn'd the souce;
And swore I'de got the ague of the house.
Well, when to eat thou dost me next desire,
I'le bring a Fever; since thou keep'st no fire.

Ceremonies for Christmasse.

COME, bring with a noise,
My merrie merrie boyes,
The Christmas Log to the firing;
While my good Dame, she
Bids ye all be free;
And drink to your hearts desiring.

With the last yeeres brand
Light the new block, And
For good successe in his spending,
On your Psaltries play,
That sweet luck may
Come while the Log is a teending.

Drink now the strong Beere,
Cut the white loafe here,
The while the meat is a shredding
For the rare Mince-Pie;
And the Plums stand by
To fill the Paste that's a kneading.

Christmasse-Eve, another Ceremonie.

COME guard this night the Christmas-Pie,
That the Thiefe, though ne'r so slie,
With his Flesh-hooks, don't come nie
To catch it

From him, who all alone sits there,
Having his eyes still in his eare,
And a deale of nightly feare
To watch it.

Another to the Maids.

WASH your hands, or else the fire
Will not teend to your desire;
Unwasht hands, ye Maidens, know,
Dead the Fire, though ye blow.

Another.

WASSAILE the Trees, that they may beare
You many a Plum, and many a Peare:
For more or lesse fruits they will bring,
As you doe give them Wassailing.

Power and Peace.

'TIS never, or but seldome knowne,
Power and Peace to keep one Throne.

To his deare Valentine, Mistresse Margaret Falconbrige.

NOW is your turne (my Dearest) to be set
A Jem in this eternall Coronet:
'Twas rich before; but since your Name is downe,
It sparkles now like *Ariadne's* Crowne.
Blaze by this Sphere for ever: Or this doe,
Let Me and It shine evermore by you.

To Oenone.

SWEET *Oenone*, doe but say
Love thou dost, though Love sayes Nay.
Speak me faire; for Lovers be
Gently kill'd by Flatterie.

Verses.

WHO will not honour Noble Numbers, when
Verses out-live the bravest deeds of men?

Happinesse.

THAT Happines do's still the longest thrive,
Where Joyes and Griefs have Turns Alternative.

Things of choice, long a comming.

WE pray 'gainst Warre, yet we enjoy no Peace;
Desire deferr'd is, that it may encrease.

Poetry perpetuates the Poet.

HERE I my selfe might likewise die,
And utterly forgotten lye,
But that eternall Poetrie
Repullulation gives me here
Unto the thirtieth thousand yeere,
When all now dead shall re-appeare.

Upon Bice.

BICE laughs, when no man speaks; and doth protest
It is his own breech there that breaks the jest.

Upon Trencherman.

TOM shifts the Trenchers; yet he never can
Endure that luke-warme name of Serving-man:
Serve or not serve, let *Tom* doe what he can,
He is a serving, who's a Trencher-man.

Kisses.

GIVE me the food that satisfies a Guest:
Kisses are but dry banquets to a Feast.

Orpheus.

ORPHEUS he went (as Poets tell)
To fetch *Euridice* from Hell;
And had her; but it was upon
This short but strict condition:
Backward he should not looke while he
Led her through Hells obscuritie:
But ah! it hapned as he made
His passage through that dreadfull shade:
Revolve he did his loving eye;
(For gentle feare, or jelousie)
And looking back, that look did sever
Him and *Euridice* for ever.

Upon Comely *a good speaker but an ill singer*, Epig.

COMELY Acts well; and when he speaks his part,
He doth it with the sweetest tones of Art:
But when he sings a *Psalme*, ther's none can be
More curst for singing out of tune then he.

Any way for wealth.

E'ENE all Religious courses to be rich
Hath been reherst, by *Joell Michelditch*:
But now perceiving that it still do's please
The sterner Fates, to cross his purposes;
He tacks about, and now he doth profess
Rich he will be by all unrighteousness:
Thus if our ship fails of her Anchor hold,
We'l love the Divell, so he lands the gold.

Upon an old Woman.

OLD widdow *Prouse* to do her neighbours evill
Wo'd give (some say) her soule unto the Devill.
Well, when sh'as kild, that Pig, Goose, Cock or Hen,
What wo'd she give to get that soule agen?

Upon Pearch. *Epig.*

THOU writes in Prose, how sweet all Virgins be;
But ther's not one, doth praise the smell of thee.

To Sapho.

SAPHO, I will chuse to go
Where the Northern winds do blow
Endlesse Ice, and endlesse Snow:
Rather then I once wo'd see,
But a Winters face in thee,
To benumme my hopes and me.

To his faithfull friend, Master John Crofts, *Cup-bearer to the King.*

FOR all thy many courtesies to me,
Nothing I have (my *Crofts*) to send to Thee
For the requitall; save this only one
Halfe of my just remuneration.
For since I've travail'd all this Realm throughout
To seeke, and find some few *Immortals* out
To *circumspangle* this my spacious Sphere,
(As Lamps for everlasting shining here:)
And having fixt Thee in mine *Orbe* a Starre
(Amongst the rest) both bright and singular;
The present Age will tell the world thou art
If not to th'whole, yet satisfy'd in part.
As for the rest, being too great a summe
Here to be paid; Ile pay't i'th'world to come.

The Bride-Cake.

THIS day my *Julia* thou must make
For Mistresse Bride, the wedding Cake:
Knead but the Dow and it will be
To paste of Almonds turn'd by thee:
Or kisse it thou, but once, or twice,
And for the Bride-Cake ther'l be Spice.

To be merry.

LETS now take our time;
While w'are in our Prime;
And old, old Age is a farre off:
For the evill evill dayes
Will come on apace;
Before we can be aware of.

Buriall.

MAN may want Land to live in; but for all,
Nature finds out some place for buriall.

Lenitie.

'Tis the Chyrurgions praise, and height of Art,
Not to cut off, but cure the vicious part.

Penitence.

Who after his transgression doth repent,
Is halfe, or altogether innocent.

Griefe.

Consider sorrowes, how they are aright:
Griefe, if't be great, 'tis short; if long, 'tis light.

The Maiden-blush.

So look the mornings when the Sun
Paints them with fresh Vermilion:
So Cherries blush, and Kathern Peares,
And Apricocks, in youthfull yeares:
So Corrolls looke more lovely Red,
And Rubies lately polished:
So purest Diaper doth shine,
Stain'd by the Beames of Clarret wine:
As *Julia* looks when she doth dress
Her either cheeke with bashfullness.

The Meane.

Imparitie doth ever discord bring:
The Mean the Musique makes in every thing.

Haste hurtfull.

Haste is unhappy: What we Rashly do
Is both unluckie; I, *and foolish too.*
Where War with rashnesse is attempted, there
The Soldiers leave the Field with equall feare.

Purgatory.

READERS wee entreat ye pray
For the soule of *Lucia*;
That in little time she be
From her *Purgatory* free:
In th'*intrim* she desires
That your teares may coole her fires.

The Cloud.

SEEST thou that Cloud that rides in State
Part *Ruby-like*, part *Candidate*?
It is no other then the Bed
Where *Venus* sleeps (halfe smothered.)

Upon Loach.

SEEAL'D up with Night-gum, *Loach* each morning lyes,
Till his Wife licking, so unglews his eyes.
No question then, but such a lick is sweet,
When a warm tongue do's with such Ambers meet.

The Amber Bead.

I SAW a Flie within a Beade
Of Amber cleanly buried:
The Urne was little, but the room
More rich then *Cleopatra's* Tombe.

To my dearest Sister M. Mercie Herrick.

WHEN ere I go, or what so ere befalls
Me in mine Age, or forraign Funerals,
This Blessing I will leave thee, ere I go,
Prosper thy Basket, and therein thy Dow.
Feed on the paste of Filberts, or else knead
And Bake the floure of Amber for thy bread.
Balm may thy Trees drop, and thy Springs runne oyle
And everlasting Harvest crown thy Soile!
These I but wish for; but thy selfe shall see,
The Blessing fall in mellow times on Thee.

1.1 entreat] enteat *48*

The Transfiguration.

IMMORTALL clothing I put on,
So soone as *Julia* I am gon
To mine eternall Mansion.

Thou, thou art here, to humane sight
Cloth'd all with incorrupted light;
But yet how more admir'dly bright

Wilt thou appear, when thou art set
In thy refulgent Thronelet,
That shin'st thus in thy counterfeit?

Suffer that thou canst not shift.

DO'S Fortune rend thee? Beare with thy hard Fate:
Vertuous instructions ne'r are delicate.
Say, do's she frown? still countermand her threats:
Vertue best loves those children that she beates.

To the Passenger.

IF I lye unburied Sir,
These my Reliques, (pray) interre:
'Tis religions part to see
Stones, or turfes to cover me.
One word more I had to say;
But it skills not; go your way;
He that wants a buriall roome
For a Stone, ha's Heaven his Tombe.

Upon Nodes.

WHERE ever *Nodes* do's in the Summer come,
He prayes his Harvest may be well brought home.
What store of Corn has carefull *Nodes*, thinke you,
Whose Field his foot is, and whose Barn his shooe?

3.3 religions *Pollard*: religious *48* (*? turned* n) 3.8 *Tombe.*] *Tombe* *48*

TO THE KING,
Upon his taking of *Leicester*.

THIS Day is Yours *Great CHARLES*! and in this War
 Your Fate, and Ours, alike Victorious are.
In her white Stole; now Victory do's rest
Enspher'd with Palm on Your Triumphant Crest.
Fortune is now Your Captive; other Kings
Hold but her hands; You hold both hands and wings.

To Julia, *in her Dawn, or Day-breake.*

BY the next kindling of the day
 My *Julia* thou shalt see,
Ere *Ave-Mary* thou canst say
 Ile come and visit thee.

Yet ere thou counsel'st with thy Glasse,
 Appeare thou to mine eyes
As smooth, and nak't, as she that was
 The prime of *Paradice.*

If blush thou must, then blush thou through
 A Lawn, that thou mayst looke
As purest Pearles, or Pebles do
 When peeping through a Brooke.

As Lillies shrin'd in Christall, so
 Do thou to me appeare;
Or Damask Roses, when they grow
 To sweet acquaintance there.

Counsell.

'TWAS *Cesars* saying: *Kings no lesse Conquerors are*
 By their wise Counsell, then they be by Warre.

Bad Princes pill their People.

LIKE those infernall Deities which eate
The best of all the sacrificed meate;
And leave their servants, but the smoak & sweat:
So many *Kings*, and *Primates* too there are,
Who claim the Fat, and Fleshie for their share,
And leave their Subjects but the starved ware.

Most Words, lesse Workes.

IN desp'rate cases, all, or most are known
Commanders, *few for execution.*

To Dianeme.

I CO'D but see thee yesterday
Stung by a fretfull Bee;
And I the Javelin suckt away,
And heal'd the wound in thee.

A thousand thorns, and Bryars & Stings,
I have in my poore Brest;
Yet ne'r can see that salve which brings
My Passions any rest.

As Love shall helpe me, I admire
How thou canst sit and smile,
To see me bleed, and not desire
To stench the blood the while.

If thou compos'd of gentle mould
Art so unkind to me;
What dismall Stories will be told
Of those that cruell be?

Upon Tap.

TAP (better known then trusted) as we heare
Sold his old Mothers Spectacles for Beere:
And not unlikely; rather too then fail,
He'l sell her Eyes, and Nose, for Beere and Ale.

His Losse.

ALL has been plundered from me, but my wit;
Fortune her selfe can lay no claim to it.

Draw, and Drinke.

MILK stil your Fountains, and your Springs, for why?
The more th'are drawn, the lesse they wil grow dry.

Upon Punchin. *Epig.*

GIVE me a reason why men call
Punchin a dry *plant-animall.*
Because as Plants by water grow,
Punchin by Beere and Ale, spreads so.

To Oenone.

THOU sayest Loves Dart
Hath prickt thy heart;
And thou do'st languish too:
If one poore prick,
Can make thee sick,
Say, what wo'd many do?

Upon Blinks. *Epig.*

TOM *Blinks* his Nose is full of wheales, and these
Tom calls not pimples, but *Pimpleides*:
Sometimes (in mirth) he sayes each whelk's a sparke
(When drunke with Beere) to light him home, i'th'dark.

Upon Adam Peapes. *Epig.*

PEAPES he do's strut, and pick his Teeth, as if
His jawes had tir'd on some large Chine of Beefe.
But nothing so; The Dinner *Adam* had,
Was cheese full ripe with Teares, with Bread as sad.

To Electra.

SHALL I go to Love and tell,
Thou art all turn'd isicle?
Shall I say her Altars be
Disadorn'd, and scorn'd by thee?
O beware! in time submit;
Love has yet no wrathfull fit:
If her patience turns to ire,
Love is then consuming fire.

To Mistresse Amie Potter.

AI me! I love, give him your hand to kisse
Who both your wooer, and your Poet is.
Nature has pre-compos'd us both to Love;
Your part's to grant; my Scean must be to move.
Deare, can you like, and liking love your Poet?
If you say (I) Blush-guiltinesse will shew it.
Mine eyes must wooe you; (though I sigh the while)
True Love is tonguelesse as a Crocodile.
And you may find in Love these differing Parts;
Wooers have Tongues of Ice, *but burning hearts.*

Upon a Maide.

HERE she lyes (in Bed of Spice)
Faire as *Eve* in Paradice:
For her beauty it was such
Poets co'd not praise too much.
Virgins Come, and in a Ring
Her supreamest *Requiem* sing;
Then depart, but see ye tread
Lightly, lightly ore the dead.

Upon Love.

LOVE is a Circle, and an Endlesse Sphere;
From good to good, revolving here, & there.

Beauty.

BEAUTIE'S no other but a lovely Grace
Of lively colours, flowing from the face.

Upon Love.

SOME salve to every sore, we may apply;
Only for my wound there's no remedy.
Yet if my *Julia* kisse me, there will be
A soveraign balme found out to cure me.

Upon Hanch *a Schoolmaster. Epig.*

HANCH, since he (lately) did interre his wife,
He weepes and sighs (as weary of his life.)
Say, is't for reall griefe he mourns? not so;
Teares have their springs from joy, as well as woe.

Upon Peason. *Epig.*

LONG Locks of late our Zelot *Peason* weares,
Not for to hide his high and mighty eares;
No, but because he wo'd not have it seen,
That Stubble stands, where once large eares have been.

To his Booke.

MAKE haste away, and let one be
A friendly Patron unto thee:
Lest rapt from hence, I see thee lye
Torn for the use of Pasterie:
Or see thy injur'd Leaves serve well,
To make loose Gownes for Mackarell:
Or see the Grocers in a trice,
Make hoods of thee to serve out Spice.

Readinesse.

THE readinesse of doing, doth expresse
No other, but the doers willingnesse.

Writing.

WHEN words we want, Love teacheth to endite;
And what we blush to speake, she bids us write.

Society.

TWO things do make society to stand;
The first *Commerce* is, & the next *Command.*

Upon a Maid.

GONE she is a long, long way,
But she has decreed a day
Back to come, (and make no stay.)
So we keepe till her returne
Here, her ashes, or her Urne.

Satisfaction for sufferings.

FOR all our workes, a recompence is sure:
'Tis sweet to thinke on what was hard t'endure.

The delaying Bride.

WHY so slowly do you move
To the centre of your love?
On your niceness though we wait,
Yet the houres say 'tis late:
Coynesse takes us to a measure;
But o'racted deads the pleasure.
Go to Bed, and care not when
Cheerfull day shall spring agen.
One *Brave Captain* did command
(By his word) the Sun to stand:
One short charme if you but say
Will enforce the Moon to stay,
Till you warn her hence (away)
T'ave your blushes seen by day.

To M. Henry Lawes, *the excellent Composer of his Lyricks.*

TOUCH but thy Lire (my *Harrie*) and I heare
From thee some raptures of the rare *Gotire.*
Then if thy voice commingle with the String
I heare in thee rare *Laniere* to sing;
Or curious *Wilson*: Tell me, canst thou be
Less then *Apollo*, that usurp'st such Three?
Three, unto whom the whole world give applause;
Yet their Three praises, praise but One; that's *Lawes.*

2 *For variant heading see p.* 491

Age unfit for Love.

MAIDENS tell me I am old;
Let me in my Glasse behold
Whether smooth or not I be,
Or if haire remaines to me.
Well, or be't or be't not so,
This for certainty I know;
Ill it fits old men to play,
When that Death bids come away.

The Bed-man, or Grave-maker.

THOU hast made many Houses for the Dead;
When my Lot calls me to be buried,
For Love or Pittie, prethee let there be
I'th'Church-yard, made, one Tenement for me.

To Anthea.

ANTHEA I am going hence
With some small stock of innocence:
But yet those blessed gates I see
Withstanding entrance unto me.
To pray for me doe thou begin,
The Porter then will let me in.

Need.

WHO begs to die for feare of humane need,
Wisheth his body, not his soule, good speed.

To Julia.

I AM zeallesse, prethee pray
For my well-fare (*Julia*)
For I thinke the gods require
Male perfumes, but Female fire.

On Julias *lips.*

SWEET are my *Julia's* lips and cleane,
As if or'e washt in Hippocrene.

Twilight.

TWILIGHT, no other thing is, Poets say,
Then the last part of night, and first of day.

To his Friend, Master J. Jincks.

LOVE, love me now, because I place
Thee here among my righteous race:
The bastard Slips may droop and die
Wanting both Root, and Earth; but thy
Immortall selfe, shall boldly trust
To live for ever, with my Just.

On himselfe.

IF that my Fate has now fulfill'd my yeere,
And so soone stopt my longer living here;
What was't (ye Gods!) a dying man to save,
But while he met with his Paternall grave;
Though while we living 'bout the world do roame,
We love to rest in peacefull Urnes at home,
Where we may snug, and close together lye
By the dead bones of our deare Ancestrie.

Kings and Tyrants.

'TWIXT Kings & Tyrants there's this difference known;
Kings seek their Subjects good: Tyrants their owne.

Crosses.

OUR Crosses are no other then the rods,
And our Diseases, Vultures of the Gods:
Each griefe we feele, that likewise is a Kite
Sent forth by them, our flesh to eate, or bite.

Upon Love.

LOVE brought me to a silent Grove,
And shew'd me there a Tree,
Where some had hang'd themselves for love,
And gave a Twist to me.

The Halter was of silk, and gold,
That he reacht forth unto me:
No otherwise, then if he would
By dainty things undo me.

He bade me then that Neck-lace use;
And told me too, he maketh
A glorious end by such a Noose,
His Death for Love that taketh.

'Twas but a dream; but had I been
There really alone;
My desp'rate feares, in love, had seen
Mine Execution.

No difference i'th'dark.

NIGHT makes no difference 'twixt the Priest and Clark;
Jone as my Lady is as good i'th'dark.

The Body.

THE Body is the Soules poore house, or home,
Whose Ribs the Laths are, & whose Flesh the Loame.

To Sapho.

THOU saist thou lov'st me *Sapho*; I say no;
But would to Love I could beleeve 'twas so!
Pardon my feares (sweet *Sapho*,) I desire
That thou be righteous found; and I the Lyer.

Out of Time, out of Tune.

WE blame, nay we despise her paines
That wets her Garden when it raines:
But when the drought has dri'd the knot;
Then let her use the watring pot.
We pray for showers (at our need)
To drench, but not to drown our seed.

To his Booke.

TAKE mine advise, and go not neere
Those faces (sower as Vineger.)
For these, and Nobler numbers can
Ne'r please the *supercillious* man.

To his Honour'd friend, Sir Thomas Heale.

STAND by the *Magick* of my powerfull Rhymes
'Gainst all the indignation of the Times.
Age shall not wrong thee; or one jot abate
Of thy both Great, and everlasting fate.
While others perish, here's thy life decreed
Because begot of my *Immortall* seed.

The Sacrifice, by way of Discourse betwixt himselfe and Julia.

Herr. COME and let's in solemn wise
Both addresse to sacrifice:
Old Religion first commands
That we wash our hearts, and hands.
Is the beast exempt from staine,
Altar cleane, no fire prophane?
Are the Garlands, Is the Nard
Jul. Ready here? All well prepar'd,
With the Wine that must be shed
(Twixt the hornes) upon the head
Of the holy Beast we bring
For our Trespasse-offering.
Herr. All is well; now next to these
Put we on pure Surplices;
And with Chaplets crown'd, we'l rost
With perfumes the Holocaust:
And (while we the gods invoke)
Reade acceptance by the smoake.

To Apollo.

THOU mighty Lord and master of the Lyre,
Unshorn *Apollo*, come, and re-inspire
My fingers so, the Lyrick-strings to move,
That I may play, and sing a Hymne to Love.

On Love.

LOVE is a kind of warre; Hence those who feare,
No cowards must his royall Ensignes beare.

1.5 here's] her'es *48*

Another.

WHERE love begins, there dead thy first desire:
A sparke neglected makes a mighty fire.

An Hymne to Cupid.

THOU, thou that bear'st the sway
With whom the Sea-Nimphs play;
And *Venus*, every way:
When I embrace thy knee;
And make short pray'rs to thee:
In love, then prosper me.
This day I goe to wooe;
Instruct me how to doe
This worke thou put'st me too.
From shame my face keepe free,
From scorne I begge of thee,
Love to deliver me:
So shall I sing thy praise;
And to thee Altars raise,
Unto the end of daies.

To Electra.

LET not thy Tomb-stone er'e be laid by me:
Nor let my Herse, be wept upon by thee:
But let that instant when thou dy'st be known,
The minute of minc *expiration.*
One knell be rung for both; and let one grave
To hold us two, an endlesse honour have.

How his soule came ensnared.

MY soule would one day goe and seeke
For Roses, and in *Julia's* cheeke,
A richess of those sweets she found,
(As in an other *Rosamond.*)
But gathering Roses as she was;
(Not knowing what would come to passe)
It chanst a ringlet of her haire,
Caught my poore soule, as in a snare:
Which ever since has been in thrall,
Yet freedome, shee enjoyes withall.

Factions.

THE factions of the great ones call,
To side with them, the Commons all.

Kisses Loathsome.

I ABHOR the slimie kisse,
(Which to me most loathsome is.)
Those lips please me which are plac't
Close, but not too strictly lac't:
Yeilding I wo'd have them; yet
Not a wimbling Tongue admit:
What sho'd poking-sticks make there,
When the ruffe is set elsewhere?

Upon Reape.

R*EAPES* eyes so rawe are, that (it seemes) the flyes
Mistake the flesh, and flye-blow both his eyes;
So that an Angler, for a daies expence,
May baite his hooke, with maggots taken thence.

Upon Teage.

T*EAGE* has told lyes so long, that when *Teage* tells
Truth, yet *Teages* truths are untruths, (nothing else.)

Upon Julia's *haire, bundled up in a golden net.*

TELL me, what needs those rich deceits,
These golden Toyles, and Trammel-nets,
To take thine haires when they are knowne
Already tame, and all thine owne?
'Tis I am wild, and more then haires
Deserve these Mashes and those snares.
Set free thy Tresses, let them flow
As aires doe breathe, or winds doe blow:
And let such curious Net-works be
Lesse set for them, then spred for me.

Upon Truggin.

TRUGGIN a Footman was; but now, growne lame,
Truggin now lives but to belye his name.

The showre of Blossomes.

LOVE in a showre of Blossomes came
Down, and halfe drown'd me with the same:
The Blooms that fell were white and red;
But with such sweets commingled,
As whether (this) I cannot tell
My sight was pleas'd more, or my smell:
But true it was, as I rowl'd there,
Without a thought of hurt, or feare;
Love turn'd himselfe into a Bee,
And with his Javelin wounded me:
From which mishap this use I make,
Where most sweets are, there lyes a Snake.
Kisses and Favours are sweet things;
But Those have thorns, and These have stings.

Upon Spenke.

SPENKE has a strong breath, yet short Prayers saith:
Not out of want of breath, but want of faith.

A defence for Women.

NAUGHT are all Women: I say no,
Since for one Bad, one Good I know:
For *Clytemnestra* most unkind,
Loving *Alcestis* there we find:
For one *Medea* that was bad,
A good *Penelope* was had:
For wanton *Lais*, then we have
Chaste *Lucrece*, or a wife as grave:
And thus through Woman-kind we see
A Good and Bad. *Sirs credit me.*

2 *For variant heading see p.* 491 4.8 wife] wise *48* (*corr. Errata*)

Upon Lulls.

LULLS swears he is all heart; but you'l suppose
By his *Probossis* that he is all nose.

Slavery.

'TIS liberty to serve one Lord; but he
Who many serves, serves base servility.

Charmes.

BRING the holy crust of Bread,
Lay it underneath the head;
'Tis a certain Charm to keep
Hags away, while Children sleep.

Another.

LET the superstitious wife
Neer the childs heart lay a knife:
Point be up, and Haft be downe;
(While she gossips in the towne)
This 'mongst other mystick charms
Keeps the sleeping child from harms.

Another to bring in the Witch.

TO house the Hag, you must doe this;
Commix with Meale a little Pisse
Of him bewitcht: then forthwith make
A little Wafer or a Cake;
And this rawly bak't will bring
The old Hag in. No surer thing.

Another Charme for Stables.

HANG up Hooks, and Sheers to scare
Hence the Hag, that rides the Mare,
Till they be all over wet,
With the mire, and the sweat:
This observ'd, the Manes shall be
Of your horses, all knot-free.

Ceremonies for Candlemasse Eve.

DOWN with the Rosemary and Bayes,
Down with the Misleto;
In stead of Holly, now up-raise
The greener Box (for show.)

The Holly hitherto did sway;
Let Box now domineere;
Untill the dancing Easter-day,
Or Easters Eve appeare.

Then youthfull Box which now hath grace,
Your houses to renew;
Grown old, surrender must his place,
Unto the crisped Yew.

When Yew is out, then Birch comes in,
And many Flowers beside;
Both of a fresh, and fragrant kinne
To honour Whitsontide.

Green Rushes then, and sweetest Bents,
With cooler Oken boughs;
Come in for comely ornaments,
To re-adorn the house.
Thus times do shift; each thing his turne do's hold;
New things succeed, as former things grow old.

The Ceremonies for Candlemasse day.

KINDLE the Christmas Brand, and then
Till Sunne-set, let it burne;
Which quencht, then lay it up agen,
Till Christmas next returne.

Part must be kept wherewith to teend
The Christmas Log next yeare;
And where 'tis safely kept, the Fiend,
Can do no mischiefe (there.)

Upon Candlemasse day.

END now the White-loafe, & the Pye,
And let all sports with Christmas dye.

Surfeits.

BAD are all surfeits: but Physitians call
That surfeit tooke by bread, the worst of all.

Upon Nis.

N*IS*, he makes Verses; but the Lines he writes,
Serve but for matter to make Paper-kites.

To Biancha, *to blesse him.*

WO'D I wooe, and wo'd I winne,
Wo'd I well my worke begin?
Wo'd I evermore be crown'd
With the end that I propound?
Wo'd I frustrate, or prevent
All Aspects malevolent?
Thwart all Wizzards, and with these
Dead all black contingencies:
Place my words, and all works else
In most happy Parallels?
All will prosper, if so be
I be kist, or blest by thee.

Julia's *Churching, or Purification.*

PUT on thy *Holy Fillitings*, and so
To th'Temple with the sober *Midwife* go.
Attended thus (in a most solemn wise)
By those who serve the Child-bed misteries.
Burn first thine incense; next, when as thou see'st
The candid Stole thrown ore the *Pious Priest*;
With reverend Curtsies come, and to him bring
Thy free (and not decurted) offering.
All Rites well ended, with faire Auspice come
(As to the breaking of a Bride-Cake) home:
Where ceremonious *Hymen* shall for thee
Provide a second *Epithalamie*.
She who keeps chastly to her husbands side
Is not for one, but every night his Bride:
And stealing still with love, and feare to Bed,
Brings him not one, but many a Maiden-head.

To his Book.

BEFORE the Press scarce one co'd see
A little-peeping-part of thee:
But since th'art Printed, thou dost call
To shew thy nakedness to all.
My care for thee is now the less;
(Having resign'd thy shamefac'tness:)
Go with thy Faults and Fates; yet stay
And take this sentence, then away;
Whom one belov'd will not suffice,
She'l runne to all adulteries.

Teares.

TEARES most prevaile; with teares too thou mayst move
Rocks to relent, and coyest maids to love.

To his friend to avoid contention of words.

WORDS beget Anger; Anger brings forth blowes:
Blowes make of dearest friends immortall Foes.
For which prevention (Sociate) let there be
Betwixt us two no more *Logomachie.*
Farre better 'twere for either to be mute,
Then for to murder friendship, by dispute.

Truth.

TRUTH is best found out by the time, and eyes;
Falsehood winnes credit by uncertainties.

Upon Prickles. *Epig.*

PRICKLES is waspish, and puts forth his sting,
For Bread, Drinke, Butter, Cheese; for every thing
That *Prickles* buyes, puts *Prickles* out of frame;
How well his nature's fitted to his name!

The Eyes before the Eares.

WE credit most our sight; one eye doth please
Our trust farre more then ten eare-witnesses.

6.2 then ten] ten then *48*

Want.

WANT is a softer Wax, that takes thereon,
This, that, and every base impression.

To a Friend.

LOOKE in my Book, and herein see,
Life endlesse sign'd to thee and me.
We o're the tombes, and Fates shall flye;
While other generations dye.

Upon M. William Lawes, *the rare Musitian.*

SHO'D I not put on Blacks, when each one here
Comes with his Cypresse, and devotes a teare?
Sho'd I not grieve (my *Lawes*) when every Lute,
Violl, and Voice, is (by thy losse) struck mute?
Thy loss brave man! whose Numbers have been hurl'd,
And no less prais'd, then spread throughout the world.
Some have Thee call'd *Amphion*; some of us,
Nam'd thee *Terpander*, or sweet *Orpheus*:
Some this, some that, but all in this agree,
Musique had both her birth, and death with Thee.

A song upon Silvia.

FROM me my *Silvia* ranne away,
And running therewithall;
A *Primrose* Banke did cross her way,
And gave my Love a fall.

But trust me now I dare not say,
What I by chance did see;
But such the Drap'ry did betray
That fully ravisht me.

The Hony-combe.

IF thou hast found an honie-combe,
Eate thou not all, but taste on some:
For if thou eat'st it to excess;
That sweetness turnes to Loathsomness.
Taste it to Temper; then 'twill be
Marrow, and Manna unto thee.

Upon Ben. Johnson.

HERE lyes *Johnson* with the rest
Of the Poets; but the Best.
Reader, wo'dst thou more have known?
Aske his Story, not this Stone.
That will speake what this can't tell
Of his glory. *So farewell.*

An Ode for him.

AH *Ben*!
Say how, or when
Shall we thy Guests
Meet at those *Lyrick* Feasts,
Made at the *Sun*,
The *Dog*, the triple *Tunne?*
Where we such clusters had,
As made us nobly wild, not mad;
And yet each Verse of thine
Out-did the meate, out-did the frolick wine.

My *Ben*
Or come agen:
Or send to us,
Thy wits great over-plus;
But teach us yet
Wisely to husband it;
Lest we that Tallent spend:
And having once brought to an end
That precious stock; the store
Of such a wit the world sho'd have no more.

Upon a Virgin.

SPEND Harmless shade thy nightly Houres,
Selecting here, both Herbs, and Flowers;
Of which make Garlands here, and there,
To dress thy silent sepulchre.
Nor do thou feare the want of these,
In everlasting Properties.
Since we fresh strewings will bring hither,
Farre faster then the first can wither.

Blame.

IN Battailes what disasters fall,
The King he beares the blame of all.

A request to the Graces.

PONDER my words, if so that any be
Known guilty here of incivility:
Let what is graceless, discompos'd, and rude,
With sweetness, smoothness, softness, be endu'd.
Teach it to blush, to curtsie, lisp, and shew
Demure, but yet, full of temptation too.
Numbers ne'r tickle, or but lightly please,
Unlesse they have some wanton carriages.
This if ye do, each Piece will here be good,
And gracefull made, by your neate Sisterhood.

Upon himselfe.

I LATELY fri'd, but now behold
I freeze as fast, and shake for cold.
And in good faith I'd thought it strange
T'ave found in me this sudden change;
But that I understood by dreames,
These only were but Loves extreames;
Who fires with hope the Lovers heart,
And starves with cold the self-same part.

Multitude.

WE Trust not to the multitude in Warre,
But to the stout; and those that skilfull are.

Feare.

MAN must do well out of a good intent;
Not for the servile feare of punishment.

To M. Kellam.

WHAT can my *Kellam* drink his Sack
In Goblets to the brim,
And see his *Robin Herrick* lack,
Yet send no Boules to him?

For love or pitie to his Muse,
(That she may flow in Verse)
Contemne to recommend a Cruse,
But send to her a Tearce.

Happinesse to hospitalitie, or a hearty wish to good house-keeping.

FIRST, may the hand of bounty bring
Into the daily offering
Of full provision; such a store,
Till that the Cooke cries, Bring no more.
Upon your hogsheads never fall
A drought of wine, ale, beere (at all)
But, like full clouds, may they from thence
Diffuse their mighty influence.
Next, let the Lord, and Ladie here
Enjoy a Christning yeare by yeare;
And this *good blessing* back them still,
T'ave Boyes, and Gyrles too, as they will.
Then from the porch may many a Bride
Unto the Holy Temple ride:
And thence return, (short prayers seyd)
A wife most richly married.
Last, may the Bride and Bridegroome be
Untoucht by cold *sterility*;
But in their springing blood so play,
As that in *Lusters* few they may,
By laughing too, and lying downe,
People a *City* or a *Towne*.

Cunctation in Correction.

THE *Lictors* bundl'd up their rods: beside,
Knit them with knots (with much adoe unty'd)
That if (unknitting) men wo'd yet repent,
They might escape the lash of punishment.

Present Government grievous.

MEN are suspicious; prone to discontent:
Subjects still loath the present Government.

Rest Refreshes.

LAY by the good a while; a resting field
Will, after ease, a richer harvest yeild:
Trees this year beare; next, they their wealth with-hold:
Continuall reaping makes a land wax old.

Revenge.

MANS disposition is for to requite
An injurie, before a benefite:
Thanksgiving is a burden, and a paine;
Revenge is pleasing to us, as our gaine.

The first marrs or makes.

IN all our high designments, 'twill appeare,
The first event breeds confidence or feare.

Beginning, difficult.

HARD are the two first staires unto a Crowne;
Which got, the third, bids him a King come downe.

Faith four-square.

FAITH is a thing that's four-square; let it fall
This way or that, it not declines at all.

The present time best pleaseth.

PRAISE they that will Times past, I joy to see
My selfe now live: *this age best pleaseth mee.*

Cloathes, are conspirators.

THOUGH from without no foes at all we feare;
We shall be wounded by the cloathes we weare.

Cruelty.

TIS but a dog-like madnesse in bad Kings,
For to delight in wounds and murderings.
As some plants prosper best by cuts and blowes;
So Kings by killing doe encrease their foes.

Faire after foule.

TEARES *quickly drie: griefes will in time decay:*
A cleare will come after a cloudy day.

Hunger.

ASKE me what hunger is, and Ile reply,
'Tis but a fierce desire of hot and drie.

Bad wages for good service.

IN this misfortune Kings doe most excell,
To heare the worst from men, when they doe well.

The End.

CONQUER we shall, but we must first contend;
'Tis not the Fight that crowns us, but the end.

The Bondman.

BIND me but to thee with thine haire,
And quickly I shall be
Made by that fetter or that snare
A bondman unto thee.

Or if thou tak'st that bond away,
Then bore me through the eare;
And by the Law I ought to stay
For ever with thee here.

Choose for the best.

GIVE house-roome to the best; *'Tis never known*
Vertue and pleasure, both to dwell in one.

To Silvia.

PARDON my trespasse (*Silvia*) I confesse,
My kisse out-went the bounds of shamfastnesse:
None is discreet at all times; no, *not Jove*
Himselfe, at one time, can be wise, and Love.

Faire shewes deceive.

SMOOTH was the Sea, and seem'd to call
Two prettie girles to play withall:
Who padling there, the Sea soone frown'd,
And on a sudden both were drown'd.
What credit can we give to seas,
Who, kissing, kill such Saints as these?

His wish.

FAT be my Hinde; unlearned be my wife;
Peacefull my night; my day devoid of strife:
To these a comely off-spring I desire,
Singing about my everlasting fire.

Upon Julia's *washing her self in the river.*

HOW fierce was I, when I did see
My *Julia* wash her self in thee!
So *Lillies* thorough Christall look:
So purest pebbles in the brook:
As in the River *Julia* did,
Halfe with a Lawne of water hid,
Into thy streames my self I threw,
And strugling there, I kist thee too;
And more had done (it is confest)
Had not thy waves forbad the rest.

2.2 Two] To *48*   3.2 my night] by night *48* (*see Commentary, p.* 56c

A Meane in our Meanes.

THOUGH Frankinsense the *Deities* require,
We must not give all to the hallowed fire.
Such be our gifts, and such be our expence,
As for our selves to leave some frankinsence.

Upon Clunn.

A ROWLE of Parchment *Clunn* about him beares,
Charg'd with the Armes of all his Ancestors:
And seems halfe ravisht, when he looks upon
That *Bar*, this *Bend*; that *Fess*, this *Cheveron*;
This *Manch*, that *Moone*; this *Martlet*, and that *Mound*;
This counterchange of *Perle* and *Diamond*.
What joy can *Clun* have in that Coat, or this,
When as his owne still out at elboes is?

Upon Cupid.

LOVE, like a Beggar, came to me
With Hose and Doublet torne:
His Shirt bedangling from his knee,
With Hat and Shooes out-worne.

He askt an almes; I gave him bread,
And meat too, for his need:
Of which, when he had fully fed,
He wisht me all *Good speed.*

Away he went, but as he turn'd
(In faith I know not how)
He toucht me so, as that I burn'd,
And am tormented now.

Love's silent flames, and fires obscure
Then crept into my heart;
And though I saw no Bow, I'm sure,
His finger was the dart.

Upon Blisse.

BLISSE (last night drunk) did kisse his mothers knee:
Where he will kisse (next drunk) conjecture ye.

Upon Burr.

BURR is a smell-feast, and a man alone,
That (where meat is) will be a hanger on.

Upon Megg.

MEGG yesterday was troubled with a Pose,
Which, this night hardned, sodders up her nose.

An Hymne to Love.

I WILL confesse
With Cheerfulnesse,
Love is a thing so likes me,
That let her lay
On me all day,
Ile kiss the hand that strikes me.

2. I will not, I,
Now blubb'ring, cry,
It (Ah!) too late repents me,
That I did fall
To love at all,
Since love so much contents me.

3. No, no, Ile be
In fetters free;
While others they sit wringing
Their hands for paine;
Ile entertaine
The wounds of love with singing.

4. With Flowers and Wine,
And Cakes Divine,
To strike me I will tempt thee:
Which done; no more
Ile come before
Thee and thine Altars emptie.

*To his honoured and most Ingenious friend M*r. Charles Cotton.

FOR brave comportment, wit without offence,
Words fully flowing, yet of influence:
Thou art that man of men, the man alone,
Worthy the Publique Admiration:
Who with thine owne eyes read'st what we doe write,
And giv'st our Numbers *Euphonie*, and weight.
Tel'st when a Verse springs high, how understood
To be, or not borne of the Royall-blood.
What State above, what *Symmetrie* below,
Lines have, or sho'd have, thou the best canst show.
For which (my *Charles*) it is my pride to be,
Not so much knowne, as to be lov'd of thee.
Long may I live so, and my wreath of *Bayes*,
Be lesse anothers *Laurell*, then thy praise.

Women uselesse.

WHAT need we marry Women, when
Without their use we may have men?
And such as will in short time be,
For murder fit, or mutinie;
As *Cadmus* once a new way found,
By throwing teeth into the ground:
(From which poore seed, and rudely sown)
Sprung up a War-like Nation.
So let us Yron, Silver, Gold,
Brasse, Leade or Tinne, throw into th'mould;
And we shall see in little space
Rise up of men, a fighting race.
If this can be, say then, what need
Have we of Women or their seed?

Love is a sirrup.

L*OVE is a sirrup*; and who er'e we see
Sick and surcharg'd with this sacietie:
Shall by this pleasing trespasse quickly prove,
Ther's loathsomnesse e'en in the sweets of love.

Leven.

LOVE is a Leven, and a loving kisse
The Leven of a loving sweet-heart is.

Repletion.

PHYSITIANS say Repletion springs
More from the sweet then sower things.

On Himselfe.

WEEPE for the dead, for they have lost this light:
And weepe for me, lost in an endlesse night.
Or mourne, or make a Marble Verse for me,
Who writ for many. *Benedicite.*

No man without Money.

NO man such rare parts hath, that he can swim,
If favour or occasion helpe not him.

On Himselfe.

LOST to the world; lost to my selfe; alone
Here now I rest under this Marble stone:
In depth of silence, heard, and seene of none.

To M. Leonard Willan *his peculiar friend.*

I WILL be short, and having quickly hurl'd
This line about, live Thou throughout the world;
Who art a man for all Sceanes; unto whom
(What's hard to others) nothing's troublesome.
Can'st write the *Comick*, *Tragick* straine, and fall
From these to penne the pleasing Pastorall:
Who fli'st at all heights: Prose and Verse run'st through;
Find'st here a fault, and mend'st the trespasse too:
For which I might extoll thee, but speake lesse,
Because thy selfe art comming to the Presse:
And then sho'd I in praising thee be slow,
Posterity will pay thee what I owe.

To his worthy friend M. John Hall, *Student of Grayes-Inne.*

TELL me young man, or did the Muses bring
Thee lesse to taste, then to drink up their spring;
That none hereafter sho'd be thought, or be
A Poet, or a Poet-like but Thee.
What was thy Birth, thy starre that makes thee knowne,
At twice ten yeares, a prime and publike one?
Tell us thy Nation, kindred, or the whence
Thou had'st, and hast thy *mighty influence*,
That makes thee lov'd, and of the men desir'd,
And no lesse prais'd, then of the maides admir'd.
Put on thy Laurell then; and in that trimme
Be thou *Apollo*, or the type of him:
Or let the *Unshorne God* lend thee his Lyre,
And next to him, be Master of the Quire.

To Julia.

OFFER thy gift; but first the Law commands
Thee *Julia*, first, to *sanctifie* thy hands:
Doe that my *Julia* which the rites require,
Then boldly give thine incense to the fire.

To the most comely and proper M. Elizabeth Finch.

HANSOME you are, and Proper you will be
Despight of all your infortunitie:
Live long and lovely, but yet grow no lesse
In that your owne prefixed comelinesse:
Spend on that stock: and when your life must fall,
Leave others Beauty, to set up withall.

Upon Ralph.

R*ALPH* pares his nayles, his warts, his cornes, and *Raph*
In sev'rall tills, and boxes keepes 'em safe;
Instead of Harts-horne (if he speakes the troth)
To make a lustie-gellie for his broth.

To his Booke.

IF hap it must, that I must see thee lye
Absyrtus-like all torne confusedly:
With solemne tears, and with much grief of heart,
Ile recollect thee (weeping) part by part;
And having washt thee, close thee in a chest
With spice; that done, Ile leave thee to thy rest.

TO THE KING,

Upon his welcome to Hampton-Court.

Set and Sung.

WELCOME, *Great Cesar*, welcome now you are,
As dearest Peace, after destructive Warre:
Welcome as slumbers; or as beds of ease
After our long, and peevish sicknesses.
O *Pompe of Glory!* Welcome now, and come
To re-possess once more your long'd-for home.
A thousand Altars smoake; a thousand thighes
Of Beeves here ready stand for Sacrifice.
Enter and prosper; while our eyes doe waite
For an *Ascendent* throughly *Auspicate*:
Under which signe we may the former stone
Lay of our safeties new foundation:
That done; *O Cesar*, live, and be to us,
Our *Fate*, our *Fortune*, and our *Genius*;
To whose free knees we may our temples tye
As to a still protecting Deitie.
That sho'd you stirre, we and our Altars too
May (*Great Augustus*) *goe along with You.*
Chor. Long live the King; and to accomplish this,
We'l from our owne, adde far more years to his.

2.9 prosper;] *stop uncertain 48, possibly comma*

Ultimus Heroum:

OR,

To the most learned, and to the right Honourable, Henry, *Marquesse of* Dorchester.

AND as time past when *Cato* the Severe
Entred the circumspacious Theater;
In reverence of his person, every one
Stood as he had been turn'd from flesh to stone:
E'ne so my numbers will astonisht be
If but lookt on; struck dead, if scan'd by Thee.

To his Muse, another to the same.

TELL that Brave Man, fain thou wo'dst have access
To kiss his hands, but that for fearfullness;
Or else because th'art like a modest Bride,
Ready to blush to death, sho'd he but chide.

Upon Vineger.

VINEGER is no other I define,
Then the dead Corps, or carkase of the Wine.

Upon Mudge.

M*UDGE* every morning to the Postern comes,
(His teeth all out) to rince and wash his gummes.

To his learned friend M. Jo. Harmar, *Phisitian to the Colledge of* Westminster.

WHEN first I find those Numbers thou do'st write;
To be most soft, terce, sweet, and perpolite:
Next, when I see Thee towring in the skie,
In an expansion no less large, then high;
Then, in that compass, sayling here and there,
And with Circumgyration every where;
Following with love and active heate thy game,
And then at last to truss the Epigram;
I must confess, distinction none I see
Between *Domitians Martiall* then, and Thee.
But this I know, should *Jupiter* agen
Descend from heaven, to re-converse with men;
The Romane Language full, and superfine,
If *Iove* wo'd speake, he wo'd accept of thine.

Upon his Spaniell Tracie.

NOW thou art dead, no eye shall ever see,
For shape and service, *Spaniell* like to thee.
This shall my love doe, give thy sad death one
Teare, that deserves of me a million.

The deluge.

DROWNING, drowning, I espie
Coming from my *Julia's* eye:
'Tis some solace in our smart,
To have friends to beare a part:
I have none; but must be sure
Th'inundation to endure.
Shall not times hereafter tell
This for no meane *miracle*;
When the waters by their fall
Threatn'd ruine unto all?
Yet the deluge here was known,
Of a world to drowne but One.

Upon Lupes.

LUPES for the outside of his suite has paide;
But for his heart, he cannot have it made:
The reason is, his credit cannot get
The inward carbage for his cloathes as yet.

Raggs.

WHAT are our patches, tatters, raggs, and rents,
But the base dregs and lees of vestiments?

Strength to support Soveraignty.

LET Kings and Rulers, learne this line from me;
Where power is weake, unsafe is Majestie.

Upon Tubbs.

FOR thirty yeares, *Tubbs* has been proud and poor,
'Tis now his habit, which he can't give ore.

Crutches.

THOU seest me *Lucia* this year droope,
Three *Zodiaks* fill'd more I shall stoope;
Let Crutches then provided be
To shore up my debilitie.
Then while thou laugh'st; Ile, sighing, crie,
A *Ruine underpropt* am I:
Do'n will I then my *Beadsmans* gown,
And when so feeble I am grown,
As my weake shoulders cannot beare
The burden of a *Grashopper*:
Yet with the bench of aged sires,
When I and they keep tearmly fires;
With my weake voice Ile sing, or say
Some Odes I made of *Lucia*:
Then will I heave my wither'd hand
To *Jove* the Mighty for to stand
Thy faithfull friend, and to poure downe
Upon thee many a *Benizon.*

To Julia.

HOLY waters hither bring
For the sacred sprinkling:
Baptize me and thee, and so
Let us to the Altar go.
And (ere we our rites commence)
Wash our hands in innocence.
Then I'le be the *Rex Sacrorum*,
Thou the Queen of *Peace and Quorum.*

Upon Case.

CASE is a Lawyer, that near pleads alone,
But when he hears the like confusion,
As when the disagreeing Commons throw
About their House, their clamorous I, or No:
Then *Case*, as loud as any *Serjant* there,
Cries out (my Lord, my Lord) the Case is clear:
But when all's husht, *Case* then a fish more mute,
Bestirs his Hand, but starves in hand the Suite.

To Perenna.

I A *Dirge* will pen for thee;
Thou a *Trentall* make for me:
That the Monks and Fryers together,
Here may sing the rest of either:
Next, I'm sure, the Nuns will have
Candlemas to grace the Grave.

To his Sister in Law, M. Susanna Herrick.

THE Person crowns the Place; your lot doth fall
Last, yet to be with These a Principall.
How ere it fortuned; know for Truth, I meant
You a fore-leader in this Testament.

Upon the Lady Crew.

THIS Stone can tell the storie of my life,
What was my Birth, to whom I was a Wife:
In teeming years, how soon my Sun was set,
Where now I rest, these may be known by *Jet.*
For other things, my many Children be
The best and truest *Chronicles* of me.

On Tomasin Parsons.

GROW up in Beauty, as thou do'st begin,
And be of all admired, *Tomasin.*

Ceremony upon Candlemas Eve.

DOWN with the Rosemary, and so
Down with the Baies, & misletoe:
Down with the Holly, Ivie, all,
Wherewith ye drest the Christmas Hall:
That so the superstitious find
No one least Branch there left behind:
For look how many leaves there be
Neglected there (maids trust to me)
So many *Goblins* you shall see.

5.5 superstitious] superstious *48*

Suspicion makes secure.

HE that will live of all cares dispossest,
Must shun the bad, I, and suspect the best.

Upon Spokes.

SPOKES when he sees a rosted Pig, he swears
Nothing he loves on't but the chaps and ears:
But carve to him the fat flanks; and he shall
Rid these, and those, and part by part eat all.

To his kinsman M. Tho: Herrick, *who desired to be in his Book.*

WELCOME to this my Colledge, and though late
Tha'st got a place here (standing candidate)
It matters not, since thou art chosen one
Here of my great and good foundation.

A Bucolick betwixt Two: Lacon *and* Thyrsis.

Lacon. FOR a kiss or two, confesse,
What doth cause this pensiveness?
Thou most lovely Neat-heardesse:
Why so lonely on the hill?
Why thy pipe by thee so still,
That ere while was heard so shrill?

Tell me, do thy kine now fail
To fulfill the milkin-paile?
Say, what is't that thou do'st aile?

Thyr. None of these; but out, alas!
A mischance is come to pass,
And I'le tell thee what it was:
See mine eyes are weeping ripe,
Lacon. Tell, and I'le lay down my Pipe.

Thyr. I have lost my lovely steere,
That to me was far more deer
Then these kine, which I milke here.
Broad of fore-head, large of eye,
Party colour'd like a Pie;
Smooth in each limb as a die;

Clear of hoof, and clear of horn;
Sharply pointed as a thorn:
With a neck by yoke unworn.
From the which hung down by strings,
Balls of Cowslips, Daisie rings,
Enterplac't with ribbanings.
Faultless every way for shape;
Not a straw co'd him escape;
Ever gamesome as an ape:
But yet harmless as a sheep.
(Pardon, *Lacon* if I weep)
Tears will spring, where woes are deep.
Now (ai me) (ai me.) Last night
Came a mad dog, and did bite,
I, and kil'd my dear delight.

Lacon. Alack for grief!
Thyr. But I'le be brief,

Hence I must, for time doth call
Me, and my sad Play-mates all,
To his Ev'ning Funerall.
Live long, *Lacon*, so *adew*.
Lacon. Mournfull maid farewell to you;
Earth afford ye flowers to strew.

Upon Sapho.

LOOK upon *Sapho's* lip, and you will swear,
There is a love-like-leven rising there.

Upon Faunus.

WE read how *Faunus*, he the shepheards *God*,
His wife to death whipt with a *Mirtle Rod*.
The Rod (perhaps) was better'd by the name;
But had it been of Birch, the death's the same.

The Quintell.

UP with the Quintill, that the Rout,
May fart for joy, as well as shout:
Either's welcome, Stinke or Civit,
If we take it, as they give it.

A Bachanalian Verse.

DRINKE up
Your Cup,
But not spill Wine;
For if you
Do,
'Tis an ill signe;

2. That we
Foresce,
You are cloy'd here,
If so, no
Hoe,
But avoid here.

Care a good keeper.

CARE keepes the Conquest; 'tis no lesse renowne,
To keepe a Citie, then to winne a Towne.

Rules for our reach.

MEN must have Bounds how farre to walke; for we
Are made farre worse, by lawless liberty.

To Biancha.

AH *Biancha!* now I see,
It is Noone and past with me:
In a while it will strike one;
Then *Biancha*, I am gone.
Some *effusions* let me have,
Offer'd on my holy Grave;
Then, *Biancha*, let me rest
With my face towards the East.

To the handsome Mistresse Grace Potter.

AS is your name, so is your comely face,
Toucht every where with such diffused grace,
As that in all that *admirable round*,
There is not one least *solecisme* found;
And as that part, so every portion else,
Keepes line for line with *Beauties Parallels*.

Anacreontike.

I MUST
Not trust
Here to any;
Bereav'd,
Deceiv'd
By so many:
As one
Undone
By my losses;
Comply
Will I
With my crosses.
Yet still
I will
Not be grieving;
Since thence
And hence
Comes relieving.
But this
Sweet is
In our mourning;
Times bad
And sad
Are a turning:
And he
Whom we
See dejected;
Next day
Wee may
See erected.

More modest, more manly.

'Tis still observ'd, those men most valiant are,
That are most modest ere they come to warre.

Not to covet much where little is the charge.

Why sho'd we covet much, when as we know,
W'ave more to beare our charge, then way to go?

Anacrontick Verse.

BRISK methinks I am, and fine,
When I drinke my capring wine:
Then to love I do encline;
When I drinke my wanton wine:
And I wish all maidens mine,
When I drinke my sprightly wine:
Well I sup, and well I dine,
When I drinke my frolick wine:
But I languish, lowre, and Pine,
When I want my fragrant wine.

Upon Pennie.

BROWN bread *Tom Pennie* eates, and must of right,
Because his stock will not hold out for white.

Patience in Princes.

K*INGS must not use the Axe for each offence:*
Princes cure some faults by their patience.

Feare gets force.

D*ESPAIRE takes heart, when ther's no hope to speed:*
The Coward then takes Armes, and do's the deed.

Parcell-gil't-Poetry.

LET'S strive to be the best; the Gods, we know it,
Pillars and men, hate an indifferent Poet.

Upon Love, by way of question and answer.

I BRING ye love, *Quest.* What will love do?
Ans. Like, and dislike ye:
I bring ye love: *Quest.* What will love do?
Ans. Stroake ye to strike ye.
I bring ye love: *Quest.* What will Love do?
Ans. Love will be-foole ye:
I bring ye love: *Quest.* What will love do?
Ans. Heate ye to coole ye:

I bring ye love: *Quest.* What will love do?
Ans. Love gifts will send ye:
I bring ye love: *Quest.* What will love do?
Ans. Stock ye to spend ye:
I bring ye love: *Quest.* What will love do?
Ans. Love will fulfill ye:
I bring ye love: *Quest.* What will love do?
Ans. Kisse ye, to kill ye.

To the Lord Hopton, *on his fight in* Cornwall.

GO on brave *Hopton*, to effectuate that
Which wee, and times to come, shall wonder at.
Lift up thy Sword; next, suffer it to fall,
And by that *One blow* set an end to all.

His Grange.

HOW well contented in this private *Grange*
Spend I my life (that's subject unto change:)
Under whose Roofe with *Mosse-worke* wrought, there I
Kisse my *Brown wife*, and *black Posterity.*

Leprosie in houses.

WHEN to a House I come, and see
The *Genius* wastefull, more then free:
The servants *thumblesse*, yet to eat,
With lawlesse tooth the floure of wheate:
The Sonnes to suck the milke of Kine,
More then the teats of Discipline:
The Daughters wild and loose in dresse;
Their cheekes unstain'd with shamefac'tnesse:
The Husband drunke, the Wife to be
A Baud to incivility:
I must confesse, I there descrie,
A House spred through with *Leprosie.*

Good manners at meat.

THIS rule of manners I will teach my guests,
To come with their own bellies unto feasts:
Not to eat equall portions; but to rise
Farc't with the food, that may themselves suffice.

Anthea's *Retractation.*

ANTHEA laught, and fearing lest excesse
Might stretch the cords of civill comelinesse:
She with a dainty blush rebuk't her face;
And cal'd each line back to his *rule* and *space.*

Comforts in Crosses.

BE not dismaide, though crosses cast thee downe;
Thy fall is but the rising to a Crowne.

Seeke and finde.

ATTEMPT the end, and never stand to doubt;
Nothing's so hard, but search will find it out.

Rest.

ON with thy worke, though thou beest hardly prest;
Labour is held up, by the hope of rest.

Leprosie in Cloathes.

WHEN flowing garments I behold
Enspir'd with *Purple, Pearle,* and *Gold;*
I think no other but I see
In them a glorious leprosie
That do's infect, and make the rent
More mortall in the vestiment.
As flowrie vestures doe descrie
The wearers rich immodestie;
So plaine and simple cloathes doe show
Where vertue walkes, not those that flow.

Upon Buggins.

BUGGINS is Drunke all night, all day he sleepes;
This is the Levell-coyle that *Buggins* keeps.

Great Maladies, long Medicines.

To an old soare a long cure must goe on;
Great faults require great satisfaction.

His Answer to a friend.

You aske me what I doe, and how I live?
And (Noble friend) this answer I must give:
Drooping, I draw on to the vaults of death,
Or'e which you'l walk, when I am laid beneath.

The Begger.

Shall I a daily Begger be,
For loves sake asking almes of thee?
Still shall I crave, and never get
A hope of my desired bit?
Ah cruell maides! Ile goe my way,
Whereas (perchance) my fortunes may
Finde out a Threshold or a doore,
That may far sooner speed the poore:
Where thrice we knock, and none will heare,
Cold comfort still I'm sure lives there.

Bastards.

Our Bastard-children are but like to Plate,
Made by the Coyners illegitimate.

His change.

My many cares and much distress,
Has made me like a wilderness:
Or (discompos'd) I'm like a rude,
And all confused multitude:
Out of my comely manners worne;
And as in meanes, in minde all torne.

5.3 discompos'd] discompo'sd *48*

The Vision.

ME thought I saw (as I did dreame in bed)
A crawling Vine about *Anacreon's* head:
Flusht was his face; his haires with oyle did shine;
And as he spake, his mouth ranne ore with wine.
Tipled he was; and tipling lispt withall;
And lisping reeld, and reeling like to fall.
A young *Enchantresse* close by him did stand
Tapping his plump thighes with a *mirtle* wand:
She smil'd; he kist; and kissing, cull'd her too;
And being cup-shot, more he co'd not doe.
For which (me thought) in prittie anger she
Snatcht off his Crown, and gave the wreath to me:
Since when (me thinks) my braines about doe swim,
And I am wilde and wanton like to him.

A vow to Venus.

HAPPILY I had a sight
Of my dearest deare last night;
Make her this day smile on me,
And Ile Roses give to thee.

On his Booke.

THE bound (almost) now of my book I see,
But yet no end of those therein or me:
Here we begin new life; while thousands quite
Are lost, and theirs, in everlasting night.

A sonnet of Perilla.

THEN did I live when I did see
Perilla smile on none but me.
But (ah!) by starres malignant crost,
The life I got I quickly lost:
But yet a way there doth remaine,
For me embalm'd to live againe;
And that's to love me; in which state
Ile live as one *Regenerate*.

Bad may be better.

MAN may at first transgress, but next do well:
Vice doth in some but lodge a while, not dwell.

Posting to Printing.

LET others to the Printing Presse run fast,
Since after death comes glory, *Ile not haste.*

Rapine brings Ruine.

WHAT'S got by Justice is establisht sure;
No Kingdomes got by Rapine long endure.

Comfort to a youth that had lost his Love.

WHAT needs complaints,
When she a place
Has with the race
Of Saints?
In endlesse mirth,
She thinks not on
What's said or done
In earth:
She sees no teares,
Or any tone
Of thy deep grone
She heares:
Nor do's she minde,
Or think on't now,
That ever thou
Wast kind.
But chang'd above,
She likes not there,
As she did here,
Thy Love.
Forbeare therefore,
And Lull asleepe
Thy woes and weep
No more.

Upon Boreman. *Epig.*

BOREMAN takes tole, cheats, flatters, lyes, yet *Boreman*,
For all the Divell helps, will be a poore man.

Saint Distaffs day, or the morrow after Twelth day.

PARTLY worke and partly play
Ye must on S. *Distaffs* day:
From the Plough soone free your teame;
Then come home and fother them.
If the Maides a spinning goe,
Burne the flax, and fire the tow:
Scorch their plackets, but beware
That ye singe no maiden-haire.
Bring in pailes of water then,
Let the Maides bewash the men.
Give S. *Distaffe* all the right,
Then bid Christmas sport *good-night*.
And next morrow, every one
To his owne vocation.

Sufferance.

IN the hope of ease to come,
Let's endure one Martyrdome.

His tears to Thamasis.

I SEND, I send here my supremest kiss
To thee my *silver-footed Thamasis.*
No more shall I reiterate thy Strand,
Whereon so many Stately Structures stand:
Nor in the summers sweeter evenings go,
To bath in thee (as thousand others doe.)
No more shall I a long thy christall glide,
In Barge (with boughes and rushes beautifi'd)
With soft-smooth Virgins (for our chast disport)
To *Richmond*, *Kingstone*, and to *Hampton-Court:*
Never againe shall I with Finnie-Ore
Put from, or draw unto the faithfull shore:

And Landing here, or safely Landing there,
Make way to my *Beloved Westminster:*
Or to the *Golden-cheap-side*, where the earth
Of *Julia Herrick* gave to me my Birth.
May all clean *Nimphs* and curious water Dames,
With Swan-like-state, flote up & down thy streams:
No drought upon thy wanton waters fall
To make them Leane, and languishing at all.
No ruffling winds come hither to discease
Thy pure, and *Silver-wristed Naides.*
Keep up your state ye streams; and as ye spring,
Never make sick your Banks by surfeiting.
Grow young with Tydes, and though I see ye never,
Receive this vow, *so fare-ye-well for ever.*

Pardons.

THOSE ends in War the best contentment bring,
Whose Peace is made up with a Pardoning.

Peace not Permanent.

GREAT Cities seldome rest: If there be none
T'invade from far: They'l finde worse foes at home.

Truth and Errour.

TWIXT Truth and Errour, there's this difference known,
Errour is fruitfull, Truth is onely one.

Things mortall still mutable.

THINGS are uncertain, and the more we get,
The more on ycie pavements we are set.

Studies to be supported.

STUDIES themselves will languish and decay,
When either price, or praise is ta'ne away.

Wit punisht, prospers most.

DREAD not the shackles: on with thine intent;
Good wits get more fame by their punishment.

Twelfe night, or King *and* Queene.

NOW, now the mirth comes
With the cake full of plums,
Where Beane's the *King* of the sport here;
Beside we must know,
The Pea also
Must revell, as *Queene*, in the Court here.

Begin then to chuse,
(This night as ye use)
Who shall for the present delight here,
Be a *King* by the lot,
And who shall not
Be Twelfe-day *Queene* for the night here.

Which knowne, let us make
Joy-sops with the cake;
And let not a man then be seen here,
Who unurg'd will not drinke
To the base from the brink
A health to the King and the Queene here.

Next crowne the bowle full
With gentle lambs-wooll;
Adde sugar, nutmeg and ginger,
With store of ale too;
And thus ye must doe
To make the wassaile a swinger.

Give then to the King
And Queene wassailing;
And though with ale ye be whet here;
Yet part ye from hence,
As free from offence,
As when ye innocent met here.

His desire.

GIVE me a man that is not dull,
When all the world with rifts is full:
But unamaz'd dares clearely sing,
When as the roof's a tottering:
And, though it falls, continues still
Tickling the *Citterne* with his quill.

Caution in Councell.

KNOW when to speake; for many times it brings
Danger to give the best advice to Kings.

Moderation.

LET moderation on thy passions waite
Who loves too much, too much the lov'd will hate.

Advice the best actor.

STILL take advice; though counsels when they flye
At randome, sometimes hit most happily.

Conformity is comely.

CONFORMITY gives comelinesse to things.
And equall shares exclude all murmerings.

Lawes.

WHO violates the Customes, hurts the Health,
Not of one man, but all the Common-wealth.

The meane.

TIS much among the filthy to be clean;
Our heat of youth can hardly keep the mean.

Like loves his like.

LIKE will to like, each Creature loves his kinde;
Chaste words proceed still from a bashfull minde.

His hope or sheat-Anchor.

AMONG these Tempests great and manifold
My Ship has here one only Anchor-hold;
That is my hope; which if that slip, I'm one
Wildred in this vast watry *Region*.

Comfort in Calamity.

TIS no discomfort in the world to fall,
When the great Crack not Crushes one, but all.

Twilight.

THE Twi-light is no other thing (we say)
Then Night now gone, and yet not sprung the Day.

False Mourning.

HE who wears Blacks, and mournes not for the Dead,
Do's but deride the Party buried.

The will makes the work, or consent makes the Cure.

NO grief is grown so desperate, but the ill
Is halfe way cured, if the party will.

Diet.

IF wholsome Diet can re-cure a man,
What need of Physick, or Physitian?

Smart.

STRIPES justly given yerk us (with their fall)
But causelesse whipping smarts the most of all.

The Tinkers Song.

ALONG, come along,
Let's meet in a throng
Here of Tinkers;
And quaffe up a Bowle
As big as a Cowle
To Beer Drinkers.
The pole of the Hop
Place in the Ale-shop
to Bethwack us;
If ever we think
So much as to drink
Unto *Bacchus.*
Who frolick will be,
For little cost he
Must not vary,
From Beer-broth at all,
So much as to call
For Canary.

His Comfort.

THE only comfort of my life
Is, that I never yet had wife;
Nor will hereafter; since I know
Who Weds, ore-buyes his weal with woe.

Sincerity.

WASH clean the Vessell, lest ye soure
What ever Liquor in ye powre.

To Anthea.

SICK is *Anthea*, sickly is the spring,
The Primrose sick, and sickly every thing:
The while my deer *Anthea* do's but droop,
The *Tulips*, *Lillies*, *Daffadills* do *stoop*;
But when again sh'as got her healthfull houre,
Each bending then, will rise a proper flower.

Nor buying or selling.

Now, if you love me, tell me,
For as I will not sell ye,
So not one cross to buy thee
Ile give, if thou deny me.

To his peculiar friend M. Jo: Wicks.

Since shed or Cottage I have none,
I sing the more, that thou hast one;
To whose glad threshold, and free door
I may a Poet come, though poor;
And eat with thee a savory bit,
Paying but common thanks for it.
Yet sho'd I chance, (my *Wicks*) to see
An over-leven-looke in thee,
To soure the Bread, and turn the Beer
To an exalted vineger;
Or sho'dst thou prize me as a Dish
Of thrice-boyl'd-worts, or third dayes fish;
I'de rather hungry go and come,
Then to thy house be Burdensome;
Yet, in my depth of grief, I'de be
One that sho'd drop his *Beads* for thee.

The more mighty, the more mercifull.

Who may do most, do's least: The bravest will
Shew mercy there, where they have power to kill.

After Autumne, Winter.

Die ere long I'm sure, I shall;
After leaves, the tree must fall.

A good death.

For truth I may this sentence tell,
No man dies ill, that liveth well.

2.8 looke] looks *48*

Recompence.

Who plants an Olive, but to eate the Oile?
Reward, we know, is the chiefe end of toile.

On Fortune.

This is my comfort, when she's most unkind,
She can but spoile me of my Meanes, not Mind.

To Sir George Parrie, *Doctor of the Civill Law.*

I have my Laurel Chaplet on my head,
If 'mongst these many Numbers to be read,
But one by you be hug'd and cherished.

Peruse my Measures thoroughly, and where
Your judgement finds a guilty Poem, there
Be you a Judge; but not a Judge severe.

The meane passe by, or over, none contemne;
The good applaud: the peccant lesse condemne,
Since *Absolution* you can give to them.

Stand forth Brave Man, here to the publique sight;
And in my Booke now claim a two-fold right:
The first as *Doctor*, and the last as *Knight*.

Charmes.

This Ile tell ye by the way,
Maidens when ye Leavens lay,
Crosse your Dow, and your dispatch,
Will be better for your Batch.

Another.

In the morning when ye rise
Wash your hands, and cleanse your eyes.
Next be sure ye have a care,
To disperse the water farre.
For as farre as that doth light,
So farre keepes the evill Spright.

Another.

IF ye feare to be affrighted
When ye are (by chance) benighted:
In your Pocket for a trust,
Carrie nothing but a Crust:
For that holy piece of Bread,
Charmes the danger, and the dread.

Upon Gorgonius.

UNTO *Pastillus* ranke *Gorgonius* came,
To have a tooth twitcht out of's native frame.
Drawn was his tooth; but stanke so, that some say,
The Barber stopt his Nose, and ranne away.

Gentlenesse.

THAT Prince must govern with a gentle hand,
Who will have love comply with his command.

A Dialogue betwixt himselfe and Mistresse Eliza: Wheeler, *under the name of* Amarillis.

MY dearest Love, since thou wilt go,
And leave me here behind thee;
For love or pitie let me know
The place where I may find thee.

Amaril. In country Meadowes pearl'd with Dew,
And set about with Lillies;
There filling Maunds with Cowslips, you
May find your *Amarillis.*

Her. What have the Meades to do with thee,
Or with thy youthfull houres?
Live thou at Court, where thou mayst be
The *Queen* of men, not flowers.

Let Country wenches make 'em fine
With Poesies, since 'tis fitter
For thee with richest Jemmes to shine,
And like the Starres to glitter.

Amaril. You set too high a rate upon
 A Shepheardess so homely;
 Her. Believe it (dearest) ther's not one
 I'th'Court that's halfe so comly. 2●

 I prithee stay. (*Am.*) I must away,
 Lets kiss first, then we'l sever.
Ambo. And though we bid adieu to day,
 Wee shall not part for ever.

To Julia.

HELP me, *Julia*, for to pray,
 Mattens sing, or Mattens say:
This I know, the Fiend will fly
Far away, if thou beest by.
Bring the Holy-water hither;
Let us wash, and pray together:
When our Beads are thus united,
Then the Foe will fly affrighted.

To Roses in Julia's *Bosome.*

ROSES, you can never die,
 Since the place wherein ye lye,
Heat and moisture mixt are so,
As to make ye ever grow.

To the Honoured, Master
Endimion Porter.

WHEN to thy Porch I come, and (ravisht) see
 The State of Poets there attending Thee:
Those *Bardes*, and I, all in a *Chorus* sing,
We are Thy *Prophets Porter*; *Thou our King.*

Speake in season.

WHEN times are troubled, then forbeare; but speak,
 When a cleare day, out of a Cloud do's break.

Obedience.

THE Power of Princes rests in the Consent
Of onely those, who are obedient:
Which if away, proud Scepters then will lye
Low, and of Thrones the Ancient *Majesty.*

Another on the same.

NO man so well a Kingdome Rules, as He,
Who hath himselfe obaid the Soveraignty.

Of Love.

1. INSTRUCT me now, what love will do;
2. 'Twill make a tongless man to wooe.
1. Inform me next, what love will do;
2. 'Twill strangely make a one of too.
1. Teach me besides, what love wil do;
2. 'Twill quickly mar, & make ye too.
1. Tell me, now last, what love will do;
2. 'Twill hurt and heal a heart pierc'd through.

Upon Trap.

TRAP, of a Player turn'd a Priest now is;
Behold a suddaine *Metamorphosis.*
If Tythe-pigs faile, then will he shift the scean,
And, from a Priest, turne Player once again.

Upon Grubs.

GRUBS loves his Wife and Children, while that they
Can live by love, or else grow fat by Play:
But when they call or cry on *Grubs* for meat;
Instead of Bread, *Grubs* gives them stones to eat.
He raves, he rends, and while he thus doth tear,
His Wife and Children fast to death for fear.

Upon Dol.

NO question but *Dols* cheecks wo'd soon rost dry,
Were they not basted by her either eye.

Upon Hog.

HOG has a place i'th'Kitchen, and his share
The flimsie Livers, and blew Gizzards are.

The School or Perl of Putney, *the Mistress of all singular manners, Mistresse* Portman.

WHETHER I was my selfe, or else did see
Out of my self that *Glorious Hierarchie*!
Or whether those (in orders rare) or these
Made up One State of *Sixtie Venuses*;
Or whether *Fairies*, *Syrens*, *Nymphes* they were,
Or *Muses*, on their mountaine sitting there;
Or some enchanted Place, I do not know
(Or *Sharon*, where eternall Roses grow.)
This I am sure; I Ravisht stood, as one
Confus'd in utter Admiration.
Me thought I saw them stir, and gently move,
And look as all were capable of Love:
And in their motion smelt much like to flowers
Enspir'd by th'Sun-beams after dews & showers.
There did I see the *Reverend Rectresse* stand,
Who with her eyes-gleam, or a glance of hand,
Those spirits rais'd; and with like precepts then
(As with a *Magick*) laid them all agen:
(*A happy Realme! When no compulsive Law,*
Or fear of it, but Love keeps all in awe.)
Live you *great Mistresse* of your Arts, and be
A nursing Mother so to Majesty;
As those your Ladies may in time be seene,
For Grace and Carriage, every one a Queene.
One Birth their Parents gave them; but their new,
And better Being, they receive from You.
Mans former Birth is grace-lesse; but the state
Of life comes in, when he's Regenerate.

2.19 *compulsive*] *compulsine P*: *compulsinve rest* 2.22 A] A a *48*
2.24 For] Fot *48*

To Perenna.

THOU say'st I'm dull; if edge-lesse so I be,
Ile whet my lips, and sharpen Love on thee.

On himselfe.

LET me not live, if I not love,
Since I as yet did never prove,
Where Pleasures met; at last, doe find,
All Pleasures meet in Woman-kind.

On Love.

THAT love 'twixt men do's ever longest last
Where War and Peace the Dice by turns doe cast.

Another on Love.

LOVE'S of it self, too sweet; the best of all
Is, when loves hony has a dash of gall.

Upon Gut.

SCIENCE puffs up, sayes *Gut*, when either Pease
Make him thus swell, or windy Cabbages.

Upon Chub.

WHEN *Chub* brings in his harvest, still he cries,
Aha my boyes! heres wheat for Christmas Pies!
Soone after, he for beere so scores his wheat,
That at the tide, he has not bread to eate.

Pleasures Pernicious.

WHERE Pleasures rule a Kingdome, never there
Is sober virtue, seen to move her sphere.

4 *and* 5 *For variants see p.* 492   5.2 Cabbages.] Cabbages, *48*

On himself.

A WEARIED Pilgrim, I have wandred here
Twice five and twenty (bate me but one yeer)
Long I have lasted in this world; (tis true)
But yet those yeers that I have liv'd, but few.
Who by his gray Haires, doth his lusters tell,
Lives not those yeers, but he that lives them well.
One man has reatch't his sixty yeers, but he
Of all those three-score, has not liv'd halfe three:
He lives, who lives to virtue: men who cast
Their ends for Pleasure, do not live, but last.

To M. Laurence Swetnaham.

READ thou my Lines, my *Swetnaham*, if there be
A fault, tis hid, if it be voic't by thee.
Thy mouth will make the sourest numbers please;
How will it drop pure hony, speaking these?

His Covenant or Protestation to Julia.

WHY do'st thou wound, & break my heart?
As if we sho'd for ever part?
Hast thou not heard an Oath from me,
After a day, or two, or three,
I wo'd come back and live with thee?
Take, if thou do'st distrust that Vowe;
This second Protestation now.
Upon thy cheeke that spangel'd Teare,
Which sits as Dew of Roses there:
That Teare shall scarce be dri'd before
Ile kisse the Threshold of thy dore.
Then weepe not sweet; but thus much know,
I'm halfe return'd before I go.

On himselfe.

I WILL no longer kiss,
I can no longer stay;
The way of all Flesh is,
That I must go this day:
Since longer I can't live,
My frolick Youths adieu;
My Lamp to you Ile give,
And all my troubles too.

3.6 distrust] distrust, *48*

To the most accomplisht Gentleman Master Michael Oulsworth.

NOR thinke that Thou in this my Booke art worst,
Because not plac't here with the midst, or first.
Since Fame that sides with these, or goes before
Those, that must live with Thee for evermore.
That Fame, and Fames rear'd Pillar, thou shalt see
In the next sheet *Brave Man* to follow Thee.
Fix on That Columne then, and never fall;
Held up by Fames *eternall Pedestall.*

To his Girles who would have him sportfull.

ALAS I can't, for tell me how
Can I be gamesome (aged now)
Besides ye see me daily grow
Here Winter-like, to Frost and Snow.
And I ere long, my Girles, shall see,
Ye quake for cold to looke on me.

Truth and falsehood.

TRUTH by her own simplicity is known,
Falsehood by Varnish and Vermillion.

His last request to Julia.

I HAVE been wanton, and too bold I feare,
To chafe o're much the Virgins cheek or eare:
Beg for my Pardon *Julia*; *He doth winne*
Grace with the Gods, who's sorry for his sinne.
That done, my *Julia*, dearest *Julia*, come,
And go with me to chuse my Buriall roome:
My Fates are ended; when thy *Herrick* dyes,
Claspe thou his Book, then close thou up his Eyes.

On himselfe.

ONE Eare tingles; some there be,
That are snarling now at me:
Be they those that *Homer* bit,
I will give them thanks for it.

Upon Kings.

KINGS must be dauntlesse: Subjects will contemne
Those, who want Hearts, and weare a Diadem.

To his Girles.

WANTON Wenches doe not bring
For my haires black colouring:
For my Locks (Girles) let 'em be
Gray or white, all's one to me.

Upon Spur.

S*PUR* jingles now, and sweares by no meane oathes,
He's double honour'd, since h'as got gay cloathes:
Most like his Suite, and all commend the Trim;
And thus they praise the Sumpter; but not him:
As to the Goddesse, people did conferre
Worship, and not to'th'Asse that carried her.

To his Brother Nicolas Herrick.

WHAT others have with cheapnesse seene, and ease,
In Varnisht maps; by'th'helpe of Compasses:
Or reade in Volumes, and those Bookes (with all
Their large Narrations, *Incanonicall*)
Thou hast beheld those seas, and Countries farre;
And tel'st to us, what once they were, and are.
So that with bold truth, thou canst now relate
This Kingdomes fortune, and that Empires fate:
Canst talke to us of *Sharon*; where a spring
Of Roses have an endlesse flourishing.
Of *Sion*, *Sinai*, *Nebo*, and with them,
Make knowne to us the now *Jerusalem.*
The Mount of *Olives*; *Calverie*, and where
Is (and hast seene) *thy Saviours Sepulcher.*
So that the man that will but lay his eares,
As *Inapostate*, to the thing he heares,
Shall by his hearing quickly come to see
The truth of Travails lesse in bookes then Thee.

3.2 honour'd,] *comma uncertain 48* 4.17 by] be *48*

The Voice and Violl.

RARE is the voice it selfe; but when we sing
To'th Lute or Violl, then 'tis ravishing.

Warre.

IF Kings and kingdomes, once distracted be,
The sword of war must trie the Soveraignty.

A King and no King.

THAT *Prince, who may doe nothing but what's just,*
Rules but by leave, and takes his Crowne on trust.

Plots not still prosperous.

ALL are not ill Plots, that doe sometimes faile;
Nor those false vows, which oft times don't prevaile.

Flatterie.

WHAT is't that wasts a Prince? example showes,
'Tis flatterie spends a King, more then his foes.

Upon Rumpe.

RUMPE is a Turne-broach, yet he seldome can
Steale a swolne sop out of the Dripping pan.

Upon Shopter.

OLD Widow *Shopter*, when so ere she cryes,
Lets drip a certain Gravie from her eyes.

Upon Deb.

IF felt and heard, (unseen) thou dost me please;
If seen, thou lik'st me, *Deb*, in none of these.

Excesse.

EXCESSE is sluttish: keepe the meane; for why?
Vertue's clean Conclave is sobriety.

Upon Croot.

ONE silver spoon shines in the house of *Croot*;
Who cannot buie, or steale a second to't.

The soul is the salt.

THE body's salt, the soule is; which when gon,
The flesh soone sucks in putrifaction.

Upon Flood, *or a thankfull man.*

FLOOD, if he has for him and his a bit,
He sayes his fore and after Grace for it:
If meate he wants, then Grace he sayes to see
His hungry belly borne by Legs *Jaile-free.*
Thus have, or have not, all alike is good,
To this our poore, yet ever patient *Flood.*

Upon Pimpe.

WHEN *Pimpes* feet sweat (as they doe often use)
There springs a sope-like-lather in his shoos.

Upon Luske.

IN Den'-shire Kerzie *Lusk* (when he was dead)
Wo'd shrouded be, and therewith buried.
When his Assignes askt him the reason why?
He said, because he got his wealth thereby.

Foolishnesse.

IN'S *Tusc'lanes, Tullie* doth confesse,
No plague ther's like to foolishnesse.

Upon Rush.

R*USH* saves his shooes, in wet and snowie wether;
And feares in summer to weare out the lether:
This is strong thrift that warie *Rush* doth use
Summer and Winter still to save his shooes.

5.2 therewith] there with *P* 6.1 *Tusc'lanes*] *Tusc'luanes P*

Abstinence.

AGAINST diseases here the strongest fence
Is the defensive vertue, Abstinence.

No danger to men desperate.

WHEN feare admits no hope of safety, then
Necessity makes dastards valiant men.

Sauce for sorrowes.

ALTHOUGH our suffering meet with no reliefe,
An equall mind is the best sauce for griefe.

To Cupid.

I HAVE a leaden, thou a shaft of gold;
Thou kil'st with heate, and I strike dead with cold.
Let's trie of us who shall the first expire;
Or thou by frost, or I by quenchlesse fire:
Extreames are fatall, where they once doe strike,
And bring to'th'heart destruction both alike.

Distrust.

WHAT ever men for Loyalty pretend,
'*Tis Wisdomes part to doubt a faithfull friend.*

The Hagg.

THE staffe is now greas'd,
And very well pleas'd,
She cockes out her Arse at the parting,
To an old Ram Goat,
That rattles i'th'throat,
Halfe choakt with the stink of her farting.

In a dirtie Haire-lace
She leads on a brace
Of black-bore-cats to attend her;
Who scratch at the Moone,
And threaten at noone
Of night from Heaven for to rend her.

3 *For variants see p.* 492 4.4 by frost] be frost *48*

A hunting she goes;
A crackt horne she blowes;
At which the hounds fall a bounding;
While th'Moone in her sphere
Peepes trembling for feare,
And night's afraid of the sounding.

The mount of the Muses.

AFTER thy labour take thine ease,
Here with the sweet *Pierides.*
But if so be that men will not
Give thee the Laurell Crowne for lot;
Be yet assur'd, thou shalt have one
Not subject to corruption.

On Himselfe.

IL'E write no more of Love; but now repent
Of all those times that I in it have spent.
Ile write no more of life; but wish twas ended,
And that my dust was to the earth commended.

To his Booke.

GOE thou forth my booke, though late;
Yet be timely fortunate.
It may chance good-luck may send
Thee a kinsman, or a friend,
That may harbour thee, when I,
With my fates neglected lye.
If thou know'st not where to dwell,
See, the fier's by: *Farewell.*

The end of his worke.

PART of the worke remaines; one part is past:
And here my ship rides having Anchor cast.

To Crowne it.

MY wearied Barke, O Let it now be Crown'd!
The Haven reacht to which I first was bound.

On Himselfe.

THE worke is done: young men, and maidens set
Upon my curles the *Mirtle Coronet*,
Washt with sweet ointments; Thus at last I come
To suffer in the Muses *Martyrdome:*
But with this comfort, if my blood be shed,
The Muses will weare blackes, when I am dead.

The pillar of Fame.

FAMES pillar here, at last, we set,
Out-during *Marble*, *Brasse*, or *Jet*,
Charm'd and enchanted so,
As to withstand the blow
Of overthrow:
Nor shall the seas,
Or OUTRAGES
Of storms orebear
What we up-rear,
Tho Kingdoms fal,
This pillar never shall
Decline or waste at all;
But stand for ever by his owne
Firme and well fixt foundation.

To his Book's end this last line he'd have plac't,
Jocond his Muse was; but his Life was chast.

FINIS.

HIS
NOBLE NUMBERS:
OR,
HIS PIOUS PIECES,
Wherein (amongſt other things)
he ſings the Birth of his CHRIST:
and ſighes for his *Saviours* ſuffe-
ring on the *Croſſe*.

HESIOD.

Ἴδμεν ψεύδεα πολλὰ λέγειν ἐτύμοισιν ὁμοῖα.
Ἴδμεν δ', εὖτ' ἐθέλωμεν, ἀληθέα μυθήσασθαι.

LONDON.
Printed for *John Williams*, and *Francis Eglesfield*.
1647.

HIS
Noble Numbers:
OR,
His pious Pieces.

His Confession.

LOOK how our foule Dayes do exceed our faire;
And as our bad, more then our good Works are:
Ev'n so those Lines, pen'd by my wanton Wit,
Treble the number of these good I've writ.
Things precious are least num'rous: Men are prone
To do ten Bad, for one Good Action.

His Prayer for Absolution.

FOR Those my unbaptized Rhimes,
Writ in my wild unhallowed Times;
For every sentence, clause and word,
That's not inlaid with Thee, (my Lord)
Forgive me God, and blot each Line
Out of my Book, that is not Thine.
But if, 'mongst all, thou find'st here one
Worthy thy Benediction;
That One of all the rest, shall be
The Glory of my Work, and Me.

To finde God.

WEIGH me the Fire; or, canst thou find
A way to measure out the Wind;
Distinguish all those Floods that are
Mixt in that watrie Theater;
And tast thou them as saltlesse there,
As in their Channell first they were.

Tell me the People that do keep
Within the Kingdomes of the Deep;
Or fetch me back that Cloud againe,
Beshiver'd into seeds of Raine;
Tell me the motes, dust, sands, and speares
Of Corn, when Summer shakes his eares;
Shew me that world of Starres, and whence
They noiselesse spill their Influence:
This if thou canst; then shew me Him
That rides the glorious *Cherubim*.

What God is.

GOD is above the sphere of our esteem,
And is the best known, not defining Him.

Upon God.

GOD is not onely said to be
An *Ens*, but *Supraentitie*.

Mercy and Love.

GOD hath two wings, which He doth ever move,
The one is Mercy, and the next is Love:
Under the first the Sinners ever trust;
And with the last he still directs the Just.

Gods Anger without Affection.

GOD when He's angry here with any one,
His wrath is free from perturbation;
And when we think His looks are sowre and grim,
The alteration is in us, not Him.

God not to be comprehended.

'TIS hard to finde God, but to comprehend
Him, as He is, is labour without end.

Gods part.

PRAYERS and Praises are those spotlesse two
Lambs, by the Law, which God requires as due.

Affliction.

GOD n'ere afflicts us more then our desert,
Though He may seem to over-act His part:
Somtimes He strikes us more then flesh can beare;
But yet still lesse then Grace can suffer here.

Three fatall Sisters.

THREE fatall Sisters wait upon each sin;
First, Fear and Shame without, then Guilt within.

Silence.

SUFFER thy legs, but not thy tongue to walk:
God, the most Wise, is sparing of His talk.

Mirth.

TRUE mirth resides not in the smiling skin:
The sweetest solace is to act no sin.

Loading and unloading.

GOD loads, and unloads, (thus His work begins)
To load with blessings, and unload from sins.

Gods Mercy.

GODS boundlesse mercy is (to sinfull man)
Like to the ever-wealthy Ocean:
Which though it sends forth thousand streams, 'tis ne're
Known, or els seen to be the emptier:
And though it takes all in, 'tis yet no more
Full, and fild-full, then when full-fild before.

Prayers must have Poise.

GOD He rejects all Prayers that are sleight,
And want their Poise: words ought to have their weight.

To God: an Anthem, sung in the Chappell at White-Hall, before the King.

Verse. MY God, I'm wounded by my sin,
And sore without, and sick within:
Ver. Chor. I come to Thee, in hope to find
Salve for my body, and my mind.
Verse. In *Gilead* though no Balme be found,
To ease this smart, or cure this wound;
Ver. Chor. Yet, Lord, I know there is with Thee
All saving health, and help for me.
Verse. Then reach Thou forth that hand of Thine,
That powres in oyle, as well as wine.
Ver. Chor. And let it work, for I'le endure
The utmost smart, so Thou wilt cure.

Upon God.

GOD is all fore-part; for, we never see
Any part backward in the Deitie.

Calling, and correcting.

GOD is not onely mercifull, to call
Men to repent, but when He strikes withall.

No escaping the scourging.

GOD scourgeth some severely, some He spares;
But all in smart have lesse, or greater shares.

The Rod.

GODS Rod doth watch while men do sleep; & then
The Rod doth sleep, while vigilant are men.

God has a twofold part.

GOD when for sin He makes His Children smart,
His own He acts not, but anothers part:
But when by stripes He saves them, then 'tis known,
He comes to play the part that is His own.

God is One.

GOD, as He is most Holy knowne;
So He is said to be most One.

Persecutions profitable.

AFFLICTIONS they most profitable are
To the beholder, and the sufferer:
Bettering them both, but by a double straine,
The first by patience, and the last by paine.

To God.

DO with me, God! as Thou didst deal with *Iohn*,
(Who writ that heavenly *Revelation*)
Let me (like him) first cracks of thunder heare;
Then let the Harps inchantments strike mine eare;
Here give me thornes; there, in thy Kingdome, set
Upon my head the golden coronet;
There give me day; but here my dreadfull night:
My sackcloth here; but there my *Stole* of white.

Whips.

GOD has his whips here to a twofold end,
The bad to punish, and the good t'amend.

Gods Providence.

IF all transgressions here should have their pay,
What need there then be of a reckning day:
If God should punish no sin, here, of men,
His Providence who would not question then?

Temptation.

THOSE Saints, which God loves best,
The Devill tempts not least.

His Ejaculation to God.

MY God! looke on me with thine eye
Of pittie, not of scrutinie;
For if thou dost, thou then shalt see
Nothing but loathsome sores in mee.
O then! for mercies sake, behold
These my irruptions manifold;
And heale me with thy looke, or touch:
But if thou wilt not deigne so much,
Because I'me odious in thy sight,
Speak but the word, and cure me quite.

Gods gifts not soone granted.

GOD heares us when we pray, but yet defers
His gifts, to exercise Petitioners:
And though a while He makes Requesters stay,
With Princely hand He'l recompence delay.

Persecutions purifie.

GOD strikes His Church, but 'tis to this intent,
To make, not marre her, by this punishment:
So where He gives the bitter Pills, be sure,
'Tis not to poyson, but to make thee pure.

Pardon.

GOD pardons those, who do through frailty sin;
But never those that persevere therein.

An Ode of the Birth of our Saviour.

1. IN Numbers, and but these few,
I sing Thy Birth, Oh JESU!
Thou prettie Babie, borne here,
With sup'rabundant scorn here:
Who for Thy Princely Port here,
Hadst for Thy place
Of Birth, a base
Out-stable for thy Court here.

2. Instead of neat Inclosures
Of inter-woven Osiers;
Instead of fragrant Posies
Of Daffadills, and Roses;
Thy cradle, Kingly Stranger,
As Gospell tells,
Was nothing els,
But, here, a homely manger.

3. But we with Silks, (not Cruells)
With sundry precious Jewells,
And Lilly-work will dresse Thee;
And as we dispossesse thee
Of clouts, wee'l make a chamber,
Sweet Babe, for Thee,
Of Ivorie,
And plaister'd round with Amber.

4. The Jewes they did disdaine Thee,
But we will entertaine Thee
With Glories to await here
Upon Thy Princely State here,
And more for love, then pittie.
From yeere to yeere
Wee'l make Thee, here,
A Free-born of our Citie.

Lip labour.

IN the old Scripture I have often read,
The calfe without meale n'ere was offered;
To figure to us, nothing more then this,
Without the heart, lip-labour nothing is.

The Heart.

IN Prayer the Lips ne're act the winning part,
Without the sweet concurrence of the Heart.

Eare-rings.

WHY wore th'Egyptians Jewells in the Eare?
But for to teach us, all the grace is there,
When we obey, by acting what we heare.

Sin seen.

WHEN once the sin has fully acted been,
Then is the horror of the trespasse seen.

Upon Time.

TIME was upon
The wing, to flie away;
And I cal'd on
Him but a while to stay;
But he'd be gone,
For ought that I could say.

He held out then,
A Writing, as he went;
And askt me, when
False man would be content
To pay agen,
What God and Nature lent.

An houre-glasse,
In which were sands but few,
As he did passe,
He shew'd, and told me too,
Mine end near was,
And so away he flew.

His Petition.

IF warre, or want shall make me grow so poore
As for to beg my bread from doore to doore;
Lord! let me never act that beggars part,
Who hath thee in his mouth, not in his heart.
He who asks almes in that so sacred Name,
Without due reverence, playes the cheaters game.

To God.

THOU hast promis'd, Lord, to be
With me in my miserie;
Suffer me to be so bold,
As to speak, Lord, say and hold.

His Letanie, to the Holy Spirit.

1. IN the houre of my distresse,
When temptations me oppresse,
And when I my sins confesse,
Sweet Spirit comfort me!

2. When I lie within my bed,
Sick in heart, and sick in head,
And with doubts discomforted,
Sweet Spirit comfort me!

3. When the house doth sigh and weep,
And the world is drown'd in sleep,
Yet mine eyes the watch do keep;
Sweet Spirit comfort me!

4. When the artlesse Doctor sees
No one hope, but of his Fees,
And his skill runs on the lees;
Sweet Spirit comfort me!

5. When his Potion and his Pill,
His, or none, or little skill,
Meet for nothing, but to kill;
Sweet Spirit comfort me!

3.18 His] Has *editors*

6. When the passing-bell doth tole,
And the Furies in a shole
Come to fright a parting soule;
Sweet Spirit comfort me!

7. When the tapers now burne blew,
And the comforters are few,
And that number more then true;
Sweet Spirit comfort me!

8. When the Priest his last hath praid,
And I nod to what is said,
'Cause my speech is now decaid;
Sweet Spirit comfort me!

9. When (God knowes) I'm tost about,
Either with despaire, or doubt;
Yet before the glasse be out,
Sweet Spirit comfort me!

10. When the Tempter me pursu'th
With the sins of all my youth,
And halfe damns me with untruth;
Sweet Spirit comfort me!

11. When the flames and hellish cries
Fright mine eares, and fright mine eyes,
And all terrors me surprize;
Sweet Spirit comfort me!

12. When the Judgment is reveal'd,
And that open'd which was seal'd,
When to Thee I have appeal'd;
Sweet Spirit comfort me!

Thanksgiving.

THANKSGIVING for a former, doth invite
God to bestow a second benefit.

Cock-crow.

BELL-MAN of Night, if I about shall go
For to denie my Master, do thou crow.
Thou stop'st S. *Peter* in the midst of sin;
Stay me, by crowing, ere I do begin;
Better it is, premonish'd, for to shun
A sin, then fall to weeping when 'tis done.

All things run well for the Righteous.

ADVERSE and prosperous Fortunes both work on
Here, for the righteous mans salvation:
Be he oppos'd, or be he not withstood,
All serve to th'Augmentation of his good.

Paine ends in Pleasure.

AFFLICTIONS bring us joy in times to come,
When sins, by stripes, to us grow wearisome.

To God.

I'LE come, I'le creep, (though Thou dost threat)
Humbly unto Thy Mercy-seat:
When I am there, this then I'le do,
Give Thee a Dart, and Dagger too;
Next, when I have my faults confest,
Naked I'le shew a sighing brest;
Which if that can't Thy pittie wooe,
Then let Thy Justice do the rest,
And strike it through.

A Thanksgiving to God, for his House.

LORD, Thou hast given me a cell
Wherein to dwell;
And little house, whose humble Roof
Is weather-proof;
Under the sparres of which I lie
Both soft, and drie;
Where Thou my chamber for to ward
Hast set a Guard

Of harmlesse thoughts, to watch and keep
Me, while I sleep.
Low is my porch, as is my Fate,
Both void of state;
And yet the threshold of my doore
Is worn by'th poore,
Who thither come, and freely get
Good words, or meat:
Like as my Parlour, so my Hall
And Kitchin's small:
A little Butterie, and therein
A little Byn,
Which keeps my little loafe of Bread
Unchipt, unflead:
Some brittle sticks of Thorne or Briar
Make me a fire,
Close by whose living coale I sit,
And glow like it.
Lord, I confesse too, when I dine,
The Pulse is Thine,
And all those other Bits, that bee
There plac'd by Thee;
The Worts, the Purslain, and the Messe
Of Water-cresse,
Which of Thy kindnesse Thou hast sent;
And my content
Makes those, and my beloved Beet,
To be more sweet.
'Tis thou that crown'st my glittering Hearth
With guiltlesse mirth;
And giv'st me Wassaile Bowles to drink,
Spic'd to the brink.
Lord, 'tis thy plenty-dropping hand,
That soiles my land;
And giv'st me, for my Bushell sowne,
Twice ten for one:
Thou mak'st my teeming Hen to lay
Her egg each day:
Besides my healthfull Ewes to beare
Me twins each yeare:
The while the conduits of my Kine
Run Creame, (for Wine.)

All these, and better Thou dost send
Me, to this end,
That I should render, for my part,
A thankfull heart;
Which, fir'd with incense, I resigne,
As wholly Thine;
But the acceptance, that must be,
My Christ, by Thee.

To God.

MAKE, make me Thine, my gracious God,
Or with thy staffe, or with thy rod;
And be the blow too what it will,
Lord, I will kisse it, though it kill:
Beat me, bruise me, rack me, rend me,
Yet, in torments, I'le commend Thee:
Examine me with fire, and prove me
To the full, yet I will love Thee:
Nor shalt thou give so deep a wound,
But I as patient will be found.

Another, to God.

LORD, do not beat me,
Since I do sob and crie,
And swowne away to die,
Ere Thou dost threat me.

Lord, do not scourge me,
If I by lies and oaths
Have soil'd my selfe, or cloaths,
But rather purge me.

None truly happy here.

HAPPY'S that man, to whom God gives
A stock of Goods, whereby he lives
Neer to the wishes of his heart:
No man is blest through ev'ry part.

To his ever-loving God.

CAN I not come to Thee, my God, for these
So very-many-meeting hindrances,
That slack my pace; but yet not make me stay?
Who slowly goes, rids (in the end) his way.
Cleere Thou my paths, or shorten Thou my miles,
Remove the barrs, or lift me o're the stiles:
Since rough the way is, help me when I call,
And take me up; or els prevent the fall.
I kenn my home; and it affords some ease,
To see far off the smoaking Villages.
Fain would I rest; yet covet not to die,
For feare of future-biting penurie:
No, no, (my God) Thou know'st my wishes be
To leave this life, not loving it, but Thee.

Another.

THOU bidst me come; I cannot come; for why,
Thou dwel'st aloft, and I want wings to flie.
To mount my Soule, she must have pineons given;
For, 'tis no easie way from Earth to Heaven.

To Death.

THOU bidst me come away,
And I'le no longer stay,
Then for to shed some teares
For faults of former yeares;
And to repent some crimes,
Done in the present times:
And next, to take a bit
Of Bread, and Wine with it:
To d'on my robes of love,
Fit for the place above;
To gird my loynes about
With charity throughout;
And so to travaile hence
With feet of innocence:
These done, I'le onely crie
God mercy; and so die.

Neutrality loathsome.

GOD will have all, or none; serve Him, or fall
Down before *Baal*, *Bel*, or *Belial:*
Either be hot, or cold: God doth despise,
Abhorre, and spew out all Neutralities.

Welcome what comes.

WHATEVER comes, let's be content withall:
Among Gods Blessings, there is no one small.

To his angrie God.

THROUGH all the night
Thou dost me fright,
And hold'st mine eyes from sleeping;
And day, by day,
My Cup can say,
My wine is mixt with weeping.

Thou dost my bread
With ashes knead,
Each evening and each morrow:
Mine eye and eare
Do see, and heare
The coming in of sorrow.

Thy scourge of steele,
(Ay me!) I feele,
Upon me beating ever:
While my sick heart
With dismall smart
Is disacquainted never.

Long, long, I'm sure,
This can't endure;
But in short time 'twill please Thee,
My gentle God,
To burn the rod,
Or strike so as to ease me.

Patience, or Comforts in Crosses.

ABUNDANT plagues I late have had,
Yet none of these have made me sad:
For why, my Saviour, with the sense
Of suffring gives me patience.

Eternitie.

1 O YEARES! and Age! Farewell:
Behold I go,
Where I do know
Infinitie to dwell.

2 And these mine eyes shall see
All times, how they
Are lost i'th'Sea
Of vast Eternitie.

3 Where never Moone shall sway
The Starres; but she,
And Night, shall be
Drown'd in one endlesse Day.

To his Saviour, a Child; a Present, by a child.

GO prettie child, and beare this Flower
Unto thy little Saviour;
And tell Him, by that Bud now blown,
He is the *Rose of Sharon* known:
When thou hast said so, stick it there
Upon his Bibb, or Stomacher:
And tell Him, (for good handsell too)
That thou hast brought a Whistle new,
Made of a clean strait oaten reed,
To charme his cries, (at time of need:)
Tell Him, for Corall, thou hast none;
But if thou hadst, He sho'd have one;
But poore thou art, and knowne to be
Even as monilesse, as He.
Lastly, if thou canst win a kisse
From those mellifluous lips of his;
Then never take a second on,
To spoile the first impression.

The New-yeeres Gift.

LET others look for Pearle and Gold,
Tissues, or Tabbies manifold:
One onely lock of that sweet Hay
Whereon the blessed Babie lay,
Or one poore Swadling-clout, shall be
The richest New-yeeres Gift to me.

To God.

IF any thing delight me for to print
My Book, 'tis this; that *Thou, my God, art in't.*

God, and the King.

HOW am I bound to Two! God, who doth give
The mind; the King, the meanes whereby I live.

Gods mirth, Mans mourning.

WHERE God is merry, there write down thy fears:
What He with laughter speaks, heare thou with tears.

Honours are hindrances.

GIVE me Honours: what are these,
But the pleasing hindrances?
Stiles, and stops, and stayes, that come
In the way 'twixt me, and home:
Cleer the walk, and then shall I
To my heaven lesse run, then flie.

The Parasceve, or Preparation.

TO a Love-Feast we both invited are:
The figur'd Damask, or pure Diaper,
Over the golden Altar now is spread,
With Bread, and Wine, and Vessells furnished;
The *sacred Towell*, and the *holy Eure*
Are ready by, to make the Guests all pure:
Let's go (my *Alma*) yet e're we receive,
Fit, fit it is, we have our *Parasceve.*
Who to that *sweet Bread* unprepar'd doth come
Better he starv'd, then but to tast one crumme.

To God.

GOD gives not onely corne, for need,
But likewise sup'rabundant seed;
Bread for our service, bread for shew;
Meat for our meales, and fragments too:
He gives not poorly, taking some
Between the finger, and the thumb;
But, for our glut, and for our store,
Fine flowre prest down, and running o're.

A will to be working.

ALTHOUGH we cannot turne the fervent fit
Of sin, we must strive 'gainst the streame of it:
And howsoe're we have the conquest mist;
'Tis for our glory, that we did resist.

Christs part.

CHRIST, He requires still, wheresoere He comes,
To feed, or lodge, to have the best of Roomes:
Give Him the choice; grant Him the nobler part
Of all the House: the best of all's the Heart.

Riches and Poverty.

GOD co'd have made all rich, or all men poore;
But why He did not, let me tell wherefore:
Had all been rich, where then had Patience been?
Had all been poore, who had His Bounty seen?

Sobriety in Search.

TO seek of God more then we well can find,
Argues a strong distemper of the mind.

Almes.

GIVE, if thou canst, an Almes; if not, afford,
Instead of that, a sweet and gentle word:
God crowns our goodnesse, where so ere He sees,
On our part, wanting all abilities.

6.3 *where so ere*] *when* 48 (*corr. Errata*)

To his Conscience.

CAN I not sin, but thou wilt be
My private *Protonotarie*?
Can I not wooe thee to passe by
A short and sweet iniquity?
I'le cast a mist and cloud, upon
My delicate transgression,
So utter dark, as that no eye
Shall see the hug'd impietie:
Gifts blind the wise, and bribes do please,
And winde all other witnesses:
And wilt not thou, with gold, be ti'd
To lay thy pen and ink aside?
That in the mirk and tonguelesse night,
Wanton I may, and thou not write?
It will not be: And, therefore, now,
For times to come, I'le make this Vow,
From aberrations to live free;
So I'le not feare the Judge, or thee.

To his Saviour.

LORD, I confesse, that Thou alone art able
To purifie this my *Augean* stable:
Be the Seas water, and the Land all Sope,
Yet if Thy Bloud not wash me, there's no hope.

To God.

GOD is all-sufferance here; here He doth show
No Arrow nockt, onely a stringlesse Bow:
His Arrowes flie; and all his stones are hurl'd
Against the wicked, in another world.

His Dreame.

I DREAMT, last night, Thou didst transfuse
Oyle from Thy Jarre, into my creuze;
And powring still, Thy wealthy store,
The vessell full, did then run ore:

Me thought, I did Thy bounty chide,
To see the waste; but 'twas repli'd
By Thee, Deare God, God gives man seed
Oft-times for wast, as for his need.
Then I co'd say, that house is bare,
That has not bread, and some to spare.

Gods Bounty.

GODS Bounty, that ebbs lesse and lesse,
As men do wane in thankfulnesse.

To his sweet Saviour.

NIGHT hath no wings, to him that cannot sleep;
And Time seems then, not for to flie, but creep;
Slowly her chariot drives, as if that she
Had broke her wheele, or crackt her axeltree.
Just so it is with me, who list'ning, pray
The winds, to blow the tedious night away;
That I might see the cheerfull peeping day.
Sick is my heart; O Saviour! do Thou please
To make my bed soft in my sicknesses:
Lighten my candle, so that I beneath
Sleep not for ever in the vaults of death:
Let me Thy voice betimes i'th morning heare;
Call, and I'le come; say Thou, the when, and where:
Draw me, but first, and after Thee I'le run,
And make no one stop, till my race be done.

His Creed.

I DO believe, that die I must,
And be return'd from out my dust:
I do believe, that when I rise,
Christ I shall see, with these same eyes:
I do believe, that I must come,
With others, to the dreadfull Doome:
I do believe, the bad must goe
From thence, to everlasting woe:

I do believe, the good, and I,
Shall live with Him eternally:
I do believe, I shall inherit
Heaven, by Christs mercies, not my merit:
I do believe, the One in Three,
And Three in perfect Unitie:
Lastly, that JESUS is a Deed
Of Gift from God: *And heres my Creed.*

Temptations.

TEMPTATIONS hurt not, though they have accesse:
Satan o'recomes none, but by willingnesse.

The Lamp.

WHEN a mans Faith is frozen up, as dead;
Then is the Lamp and oyle extinguished.

Sorrowes.

SORROWES our portion are: Ere hence we goe,
Crosses we must have; or, hereafter woe.

Penitencie.

A MANS transgression God do's then remit,
When man he makes a Penitent for it.

The Dirge of Jephthahs *Daughter: sung by the Virgins.*

1 O THOU, the wonder of all dayes!
O Paragon, and Pearle of praise!
O Virgin-martyr, ever blest
Above the rest
Of all the Maiden-Traine! We come,
And bring fresh strewings to thy Tombe.

2 Thus, thus, and thus we compasse round
Thy harmlesse and unhaunted Ground;
And as we sing thy Dirge, we will
The Daffadill,
And other flowers, lay upon
(The Altar of our love) thy Stone.

3 Thou wonder of all Maids, li'st here,
Of Daughters all, the Deerest Deere;
The eye of Virgins; nay, the Queen
Of this smooth Green,
And all sweet Meades; from whence we get
The Primrose, and the Violet.

4 Too soon, too deere did *Jephthah* buy,
By thy sad losse, our liberty:
His was the Bond and Cov'nant, yet
Thou paid'st the debt,
Lamented Maid! he won the day,
But for the conquest thou didst pay.

5 Thy Father brought with him along
The Olive branch, and Victors Song:
He slew the Ammonites, we know,
But to thy woe;
And in the purchase of our Peace,
The Cure was worse then the Disease.

6 For which obedient zeale of thine,
We offer here, before thy Shrine,
Our sighs for Storax, teares for Wine;
And to make fine,
And fresh thy Herse-cloth, we will, here,
Foure times bestrew thee ev'ry yeere.

7 Receive, for this thy praise, our teares:
Receive this offering of our Haires:
Receive these Christall Vialls fil'd
With teares, distil'd
From teeming eyes; to these we bring,
Each Maid, her silver Filleting,

8 To guild thy Tombe; besides, these Caules,
These Laces, Ribbands, and these Faules,
These Veiles, wherewith we use to hide
The Bashfull Bride,
When we conduct her to her Groome:
All, all we lay upon thy Tombe.

9 No more, no more, since thou art dead,
Shall we ere bring coy Brides to bed;

No more, at yeerly Festivalls
We Cowslip balls,
Or chaines of Columbines shall make,
For this, or that occasions sake.

10 No, no; our Maiden-pleasures be
Wrapt in the winding-sheet, with thee:
'Tis we are dead, though not i'th grave:
Or, if we have
One seed of life left, 'tis to keep
A Lent for thee, to fast and weep.

11 Sleep in thy peace, thy bed of Spice;
And make this place all Paradise:
May Sweets grow here! & smoke from hence,
Fat Frankincense:
Let Balme, and Cassia send their scent
From out thy Maiden-Monument.

12 May no Wolfe howle, or Screech-Owle stir
A wing about thy Sepulcher!
No boysterous winds, or stormes, come hither,
To starve, or wither
Thy soft sweet Earth! but (like a spring)
Love keep it ever flourishing.

13 May all shie Maids, at wonted hours,
Come forth, to strew thy Tombe with flow'rs:
May Virgins, when they come to mourn,
Male-Incense burn
Upon thine Altar! then return,
And leave thee sleeping in thy Urn.

To God, on his sicknesse.

WHAT though my Harp, and Violl be
Both hung upon the Willow-tree?
What though my bed be now my grave,
And for my house I darknesse have?
What though my healthfull dayes are fled,
And I lie numbred with the dead?
Yet I have hope, by Thy great power,
To spring; though now a wither'd flower.

Sins loath'd, and yet lov'd.

SHAME *checks our first attempts*; but then 'tis prov'd,
Sins first dislik'd, are after that belov'd.

Sin.

SIN leads the way, but as it goes, it feels
The following plague still treading on his heels.

Upon God.

GOD when He takes my goods and chattels hence,
Gives me a portion, giving patience:
What is in God is God; if so it be,
He patience gives; He gives himselfe to me.

Faith.

WHAT here we hope for, we shall once inherit:
By Faith we all walk here, not by the Spirit.

Humility.

HUMBLE we must be, if to Heaven we go:
High is the roof there; but the gate is low:
When e're thou speak'st, look with a lowly eye:
Grace is increased by humility.

Teares.

OUR present Teares here (not our present laughter)
Are but the handsells of our joyes hereafter.

Sin and Strife.

AFTER true sorrow for our sinnes, our strife
Must last with Satan, to the end of life.

1.1 prov'd,] prov'd. *S*

An Ode, or Psalme, to God.

DEER God,
If thy smart Rod
Here did not make me sorrie,
I sho'd not be
With Thine, or Thee,
In Thy eternall Glorie.

But since
Thou didst convince
My sinnes, by gently striking;
Add still to those
First stripes, new blowes,
According to Thy liking.

Feare me,
Or scourging teare me;
That thus from vices driven,
I may from Hell
Flie up, to dwell
With Thee, and Thine in Heaven.

Graces for Children.

WHAT God gives, and what we take,
'Tis a gift for Christ His sake:
Be the meale of Beanes and Pease,
God be thank'd for those, and these:
Have we flesh, or have we fish,
All are Fragments from His dish.
He His Church save, and the King,
And our Peace here, like a Spring,
Make it ever flourishing.

God to be first serv'd.

HONOUR thy Parents; but good manners call
Thee to adore thy God, the first of all.

Another Grace for a Child.

HERE a little child I stand,
Heaving up my either hand;
Cold as Paddocks though they be,
Here I lift them up to Thee,
For a Benizon to fall
On our meat, and on us all. *Amen.*

A Christmas Caroll, *sung to the King in the Presence at* White-Hall.

Chor. WHAT sweeter musick can we bring,
Then a Caroll, for to sing
The Birth of this our heavenly King?
Awake the Voice! Awake the String!
Heart, Eare, and Eye, and every thing
Awake! the while the active Finger
Runs division with the Singer.

From the Flourish they came to the Song.

1 Dark and dull night, flie hence away,
And give the honour to this Day,
That sees *December* turn'd to *May*.

2 If we may ask the reason, say;
The why, and wherefore all things here
Seem like the Spring-time of the yeere?

3 Why do's the chilling Winters morne
Smile, like a field beset with corne?
Or smell, like to a Meade new-shorne,
Thus, on the sudden? 4. Come and see
The cause, why things thus fragrant be:
'Tis He is borne, whose quickning Birth
Gives life and luster, publike mirth,
To Heaven, and the under-Earth.

Chor. We see Him come, and know him ours,
Who, with His Sun-shine, and His showers,
Turnes all the patient ground to flowers.

1 The Darling of the world is come,
And fit it is, we finde a roome
To welcome Him. 2. The nobler part
Of all the house here, is the heart,

Chor. Which we will give Him; and bequeath
This Hollie, and this Ivie Wreath,
To do Him honour; who's our King,
And Lord of all this Revelling.

The Musicall Part was composed by
M. Henry Lawes.

The New-yeeres Gift, or Circumcisions Song, sung to the King in the Presence at White-Hall.

1 PREPARE for Songs; He's come, He's come;
And be it sin here to be dumb,
And not with Lutes to fill the roome.

2 Cast Holy Water all about,
And have a care no fire gos out,
But 'cense the porch, and place throughout.

3 The Altars all on fier be;
The Storax fries; and ye may see,
How heart and hand do all agree,
To make things sweet. *Chor.* Yet all less sweet then He.

4 Bring Him along, most pious Priest,
And tell us then, when as thou seest
His gently-gliding, Dove-like eyes,
And hear'st His whimp'ring, and His cries;
How canst thou this Babe circumcise?

5 Ye must not be more pitifull then wise;
For, now unlesse ye see Him bleed,
Which makes the Bapti'me; 'tis decreed,
The Birth is fruitlesse: *Chor.* Then the *work God speed.*

1 Touch gently, gently touch; and here
Spring Tulips up through all the yeere;
And from His sacred Bloud, here shed,
May Roses grow, to crown His own deare Head.

Chor. Back, back again; each thing is done
With zeale alike, as 'twas begun;
Now singing, homeward let us carrie
The Babe unto His Mother *Marie*;
And when we have the Child commended
To her warm bosome, then our Rites are ended.

Composed by M. *Henry Lawes.*

Another New-yeeres Gift, or Song for the Circumcision.

1 HENCE, hence prophane, and none appeare
With any thing unhallowed, here:
No jot of Leven must be found
Conceal'd in this most holy Ground:

2 What is corrupt, or sowr'd with sin,
Leave that without, then enter in;
Chor. But let no Christmas mirth begin
Before ye purge, and circumcise
Your hearts, and hands, lips, eares, and eyes.

3 Then, like a perfum'd Altar, see
That all things sweet, and clean may be:
For, here's a Babe, that (like a *Bride*)
Will *blush to death*, if ought be spi'd
Ill-scenting, or unpurifi'd.

Chor. The room is cens'd: help, help t'invoke
Heaven to come down, the while we choke
The Temple, with a cloud of smoke.

4 Come then, and gently touch the Birth
Of Him, who's Lord of Heav'n and Earth;

5 And softly handle Him: y'ad need,
Because the *prettie Babe* do's bleed.
Poore-pittied Child! who from Thy Stall
Bring'st, in Thy Blood, a Balm, that shall
Be the best New-yeares Gift to all.

1 Let's blesse the Babe: And, as we sing
His praise; so let us blesse the King:

Chor. Long may He live, till He hath told
His New-yeeres trebled to His old:
And, when that's done, to re-aspire
A new-borne *Phœnix* from His own chast fire.

Gods Pardon.

WHEN I shall sin, pardon my trespasse here;
For, once in hell, none knowes Remission there.

Sin.

SIN once reacht up to Gods eternall Sphere,
And was committed, not remitted there.

Evill.

EVILL no Nature hath; the losse of good
Is that which gives to sin a livelihood.

The Star-Song: A Caroll to the King; sung at White-Hall.

The Flourish of Musick: then followed the Song.

1 TELL us, thou cleere and heavenly Tongue,
Where is the Babe but lately sprung?
Lies He the Lillie-banks among?

2 Or say, if this new Birth of ours
Sleeps, laid within some Ark of Flowers,
Spangled with deaw-light; thou canst cleere
All doubts, and manifest the where.

3 Declare to us, bright Star, if we shall seek
Him in the Mornings blushing cheek,
Or search the beds of Spices through,
To find him out?
Star. No, this ye need not do;
But only come, and see Him rest
A Princely Babe in's Mothers Brest.

Chor. He's seen, He's seen, why then a Round,
Let's kisse the sweet and holy ground;
And all rejoyce, that we have found
A King, before conception crown'd.

4 Come then, come then, and let us bring
Unto our prettie *Twelfth-Tide King*,
Each one his severall offering;

Chor. And when night comes, wee'l give Him wassailing:
And that His treble Honours may be seen,
Wee'l chuse Him King, and make His Mother Queen.

To God.

WITH golden Censers, and with Incense, here,
Before Thy Virgin-Altar I appeare,
To pay Thee that I owe, since what I see
In, or without; all, all belongs to Thee:
Where shall I now begin to make, for one
Least loane of Thine, half Restitution?
Alas! I cannot pay a jot; therefore
I'le kisse the Tally, and confesse the score.
Ten thousand Talents lent me, Thou dost write:
'Tis true, my God; *but I can't pay one mite.*

To his deere God.

I'LE hope no more,
For things that will not come;
And, if they do, they prove but cumbersome;
Wealth brings much woe:
And, since it fortunes so;
'Tis better to be poore,
Then so t'abound,
As to be drown'd,
Or overwhelm'd with store.

Pale care, avant,
I'le learn to be content
With that small stock, Thy Bounty gave or lent.
What may conduce
To my most healthfull use,

Almighty God me grant;
But that, or this,
That hurtfull is,
Denie Thy suppliant.

To God, his good will.

GOLD I have none, but I present my need,
O Thou, that crown'st the will, where wants the deed.
Where Rams are wanting, or large Bullocks thighs,
There a poor Lamb's a plenteous sacrifice.
Take then his Vowes, who, if he had it, would
Devote to Thee, both incense, myrrhe, and gold,
Upon an Altar rear'd by Him, and crown'd
Both with the *Rubie*, *Pearle*, and *Diamond*.

On Heaven.

PERMIT mine eyes to see
Part, or the whole of Thee,
O happy place!
Where all have Grace,
And Garlands shar'd,
For their reward;
Where each chast Soule
In long white stole,
And Palmes in hand,
Do ravisht stand;
So in a ring,
The praises sing
Of Three in One,
That fill the Throne;
While Harps, and Violls then
To Voices, say, *Amen.*

The Summe, and the Satisfaction.

LAST night I drew up mine Account,
And found my Debits to amount
To such a height, as for to tell
How I sho'd pay,'s impossible:
Well, this I'le do; my mighty score
Thy mercy-seat I'le lay before;

2.15 Violls] Vlolls *48*

But therewithall I'le bring the Band,
Which, in full force, did daring stand,
Till my Redeemer (on the Tree)
Made void for millions, as for me.
Then, if Thou bidst me pay, or go
Unto the prison, I'le say, no;
Christ having paid, I nothing owe:
For, this is sure, the Debt is dead
By Law, the Bond once *cancelled.*

Good men afflicted most.

GOD makes not good men wantons, but doth bring
Them to the field, and, there, to skirmishing;
With trialls those, with terrors these He proves,
And hazards those most, whom the most He loves:
For *Sceva*, darts; for *Cocles*, dangers; thus
He finds a fire for mighty *Mutius*;
Death for stout *Cato*; and besides all these,
A poyson too He has for *Socrates*;
Torments for high *Attilius*; and, with want,
Brings in *Fabricius* for a Combatant:
But, bastard-slips, and such as He dislikes,
He never brings them once to th'push of Pikes.

Good Christians

PLAY their offensive and defensive parts,
Till they be hid o're with a wood of darts.

The Will the cause of Woe.

WHEN man is punisht, he is plagued still,
Not for the fault of Nature, but of will.

To Heaven.

OPEN thy gates
To him, who weeping waits,
And might come in,
But that held back by sin.
Let mercy be
So kind, to set me free,
And I will strait
Come in, or force the gate.

The Recompence.

ALL I have lost, that co'd be rapt from me;
And fare it well: yet *Herrick*, if so be
Thy Deerest Saviour renders thee but one
Smile, that one smile's full restitution.

To God.

PARDON me God, (once more I Thee intreat)
That I have plac'd Thee in so meane a seat,
Where round about Thou seest but all things vaine,
Uncircumcis'd, unseason'd, and prophane.
But as Heavens publike and immortall Eye
Looks on the filth, but is not soil'd thereby;
So Thou, my God, may'st on this impure look,
But take no tincture from my sinfull Book:
Let but one beame of Glory on it shine,
And that will make me, and my Work divine.

To God.

LORD, I am like to *Misletoe*,
Which has no root, and cannot grow,
Or prosper, but by that same tree
It clings about; so I by Thee.
What need I then to feare at all,
So long as I about Thee craule?
But if that Tree sho'd fall, and die,
Tumble shall heav'n, and down will I.

His wish to God.

I WOULD to God, that mine old age might have
Before my last, but here a living grave,
Some one poore Almes-house; there to lie, or stir,
Ghost-like, as in my meaner sepulcher;
A little piggin, and a pipkin by,
To hold things fitting my necessity;
Which, rightly us'd, both in their time and place,
Might me excite to fore, and after-grace.
Thy Crosse, my *Christ*, fixt 'fore mine eyes sho'd be,
Not to adore that, but to worship Thee.
So, here the remnant of my dayes I'd spend,
Reading Thy Bible, and my Book; *so end.*

Satan.

WHEN we 'gainst Satan stoutly fight, the more
He teares and tugs us, then he did before;
Neglecting once to cast a frown on those
Whom ease makes his, without the help of blowes.

Hell.

HELL is no other, but a soundlesse pit,
Where no one beame of comfort peeps in it.

The way.

WHEN I a ship see on the Seas,
Cuft with those watrie savages,
And therewithall, behold, it hath
In all that way no beaten path;
Then, with a wonder, I confesse,
Thou art our way i'th wildernesse:
And while we blunder in the dark,
Thou art our candle there, or spark.

Great grief, great glory.

THE lesse our sorrowes here and suffrings cease,
The more our Crownes of Glory there increase.

Hell.

HELL is the place where whipping-cheer abounds,
But no one Jailor there to wash the wounds.

The Bell-man.

ALONG the dark, and silent night,
With my Lantern, and my Light,
And the tinkling of my Bell,
Thus I walk, and this I tell:

Death and dreadfulnesse call on,
To the gen'rall Session;
To whose dismall Barre, we there
All accompts must come to cleere:
Scores of sins w'ave made here many,
Wip't out few, (God knowes) if any.
Rise ye Debters then, and fall
To make paiment, while I call.
Ponder this, when I am gone;
By the clock 'tis almost *One*.

The goodnesse of his God.

WHEN Winds and Seas do rage,
  And threaten to undo me,
Thou dost their wrath asswage,
  If I but call unto Thee.

A mighty storm last night
  Did seek my soule to swallow,
But by the peep of light
  A gentle calme did follow.

What need I then despaire,
  Though ills stand round about me;
Since mischiefs neither dare
  To bark, or bite, without Thee?

The Widdowes teares: or, Dirge of Dorcas.

1. COME pitie us, all ye, who see
Our Harps hung on the Willow-tree:
Come pitie us, ye Passers by,
Who see, or heare poor Widdowes crie:
Come pitie us; and bring your eares,
And eyes, to pitie Widdowes teares.
  Chor. And when you are come hither;
          Then we will keep
          A Fast, and weep
      Our eyes out all together.

2. For *Tabitha*, who dead lies here,
Clean washt, and laid out for the Beere;
O modest Matrons, weep and waile!
For now the Corne and Wine must faile:
The Basket and the Bynn of Bread,
Wherewith so many soules were fed
Chor. Stand empty here for ever:
And ah! the Poore,
At thy worne Doore,
Shall be releeved never.

3. Woe worth the Time, woe worth the day,
That reav'd us of thee *Tabitha!*
For we have lost, with thee, the Meale,
The Bits, the Morsells, and the deale
Of gentle Paste, and yeelding Dow,
That Thou on Widdowes didst bestow.
Chor. All's gone, and Death hath taken
Away from us
Our Maundie; thus,
Thy Widdowes stand forsaken.

4. Ah *Dorcas*, *Dorcas!* now adieu
We bid the Creuse and Pannier too:
I and the flesh, for and the fish,
Dol'd to us in That Lordly dish.
We take our leaves now of the Loome,
From whence the house-wives cloth did come:
Chor. The web affords now nothing;
Thou being dead,
The woosted thred
Is cut, that made us clothing.

5. Farewell the Flax and Reaming wooll,
With which thy house was plentifull.
Farewell the Coats, the Garments, and
The Sheets, the Rugs, made by thy hand.
Farewell thy Fier and thy Light,
That ne're went out by Day or Night:
Chor. No, or thy zeale so speedy,
That found a way
By peep of day,
To feed and cloth the Needy.

6. But, ah, alas! the Almond Bough,
And Olive Branch is wither'd now.
The Wine Presse now is ta'ne from us,
The Saffron and the Calamus.
The Spice and Spiknard hence is gone,
The Storax and the Cynamon,
Chor. The Caroll of our gladnesse
Ha's taken wing,
And our late spring
Of mirth is turn'd to sadnesse.

7. How wise wast thou in all thy waies!
How worthy of respect and praise!
How Matron-like didst thou go drest!
How soberly above the rest
Of those that prank it with their Plumes;
And jet it with their choice purfumes.
Chor. Thy vestures were not flowing:
Nor did the street
Accuse thy feet
Of mincing in their going.

8. And though thou here li'st dead, we see
A deale of beauty yet in thee.
How sweetly shewes thy smiling face,
Thy lips with all diffused grace!
Thy hands (though cold) yet spotlesse, white,
And comely as the Chrysolite.
Chor. Thy belly like a hill is,
Or as a neat
Cleane heap of wheat,
All set about with Lillies.

9. Sleep with thy beauties here, while we
Will shew these garments made by thee;
These were the Coats, in these are read
The monuments of *Dorcas* dead.
These were thy Acts, and thou shalt have
These hung, as honours o're thy Grave,
Chor. And after us (distressed)
Sho'd fame be dumb;
Thy very Tomb
Would cry out, *Thou art blessed.*

To God, in time of plundering.

RAPINE has yet tooke nought from me;
But if it please my God, I be
Brought at the last to th'utmost bit,
God make me thankfull still for it.
I have been gratefull for my store:
Let me say grace when there's no more.

To his Saviour. The New yeers gift.

THAT little prettie bleeding part
Of Foreskin send to me:
And Ile returne a bleeding Heart,
For New-yeers gift to thee.

Rich is the Jemme that thou did'st send,
Mine's faulty too, and small:
But yet this Gift Thou wilt commend,
Because I send Thee *all*.

Doomes-Day.

LET not that Day Gods Friends and Servants scare:
The Bench is then their place; and not the Barre.

The Poores Portion.

THE sup'rabundance of my store,
That is the portion of the poore:
Wheat, Barley, Rie, or Oats; what is't
But he takes tole of ? all the Griest.
Two raiments have I: *Christ* then makes
This Law; that He and I part stakes.
Or have I two loaves; then I use
The poore to cut, and I to chuse.

The white Island: or place of the Blest.

IN this world (the *Isle of Dreames*)
While we sit by sorrowes streames,
Teares and terrors are our theames
Reciting:

But when once from hence we flie,
More and more approaching nigh
Unto young Eternitie
Uniting:

In that *whiter Island*, where
Things are evermore sincere;
Candor here, and lustre there
Delighting:

There no monstrous fancies shall
Out of hell an horrour call,
To create (or cause at all)
Affrighting.

There in calm and cooling sleep
We our eyes shall never steep;
But eternall watch shall keep,
Attending

Pleasures, such as shall pursue
Me immortaliz'd, and you;
And fresh joyes, as never too
Have ending.

To Christ.

I CRAWLE, I creep; my *Christ*, I come
To Thee, for curing *Balsamum:*
Thou hast, nay more, Thou art the Tree,
Affording salve of Soveraigntie.
My mouth I'le lay unto Thy wound
Bleeding, that no Blood touch the ground:
For, rather then one drop shall fall
To wast, my JESU, I'le take all.

To God.

GOD! to my little meale and oyle,
Add but a bit of flesh, to boyle:
And Thou my Pipkinnet shalt see,
Give a *wave-offring* unto Thee.

Free Welcome.

GOD He refuseth no man; but makes way
For All that now come, or hereafter may.

Gods Grace.

GODS Grace deserves here to be daily fed,
That, thus increast, it might be perfected.

Coming to Christ.

TO him, who longs unto his CHRIST to go,
Celerity even it self is slow.

Correction.

GOD had but one Son free from sin; but none
Of all His sonnes free from correction.

Gods Bounty.

GOD, as He's potent, so He's likewise known,
To give us more then Hope can fix upon.

Knowledge.

SCIENCE in God, is known to be
A Substance, not a Qualitie.

Salutation.

CHRIST, I have read, did to His Chaplains say,
Sending them forth, *Salute no man by'th way:*
Not, that He taught His Ministers to be
Unsmooth, or sowre, to all civilitie;
But to instruct them, to avoid all snares
Of tardidation in the Lords Affaires.
Manners are good: but till his errand ends,
Salute we must, nor Strangers, Kin, or Friends.

Lasciviousnesse.

LASCIVIOUSNESSE is known to be
The sister to saturitie.

Teares.

GOD from our eyes all teares hereafter wipes,
And gives His Children kisses then, not stripes.

Gods Blessing.

IN vain our labours are, whatsoe're they be,
Unlesse God gives the *Benedicite.*

God, and Lord.

GOD, is His Name of Nature; but that word
Implies His Power, *when He's cal'd the LORD.*

The Judgment-Day.

GOD hides from man the reck'ning Day, that He
May feare it ever for uncertaintie:
That being ignorant of that one, he may
Expect the coming of it ev'ry day.

Angells.

ANGELLS are called Gods; yet of them, none
Are Gods, but by *participation*:
As Just Men are intitled Gods, yet none
Are Gods, of them, but by Adoption.

Long life.

THE longer thred of life we spin,
The more occasion still to sin.

Teares.

THE teares of Saints more sweet by farre,
Then all the songs of sinners are.

Manna.

THAT Manna, which God on His people cast,
Fitted it self to ev'ry Feeders tast.

Reverence.

TRUE rev'rence is (as *Cassiodore* doth prove)
The feare of God, commixt with cleanly love.

Mercy.

MERCY, the wise Athenians held to be
Not an Affection, but a *Deitie*.

Wages.

AFTER this life, the wages shall
Not shar'd alike be unto all.

Temptation.

GOD tempteth no one (as S. *Aug'stine* saith)
For any ill; but, for the proof of Faith:
Unto temptation God exposeth some;
But none, of purpose, to be overcome.

Gods hands.

GODS Hands are round, & smooth, that gifts may fall
Freely from them, and hold none back at all.

Labour.

LABOUR we must, and labour hard
I'th *Forum* here, or *Vineyard*.

Mora Sponsi, *the stay of the Bridegroome.*

THE time the Bridegroom stayes from hence,
Is but the time of penitence.

Roaring.

ROARING is nothing but a weeping part,
Forc'd from the mighty dolour of the heart.

1.1 is (as *Cassiodore*] is as (*Cassiodore* G

The Eucharist.

HE *that is hurt seeks help:* sin is the wound;
The salve for this i'th Eucharist is found.

Sin severely punisht.

GOD in His own Day will be then severe,
To punish great sins, who small faults whipt here.

Montes Scripturarum, *the Mounts of the Scriptures.*

THE Mountains of the Scriptures are (some say)
Moses, and *Iesus*, called *Ioshua:*
The *Prophets* Mountains of the Old are meant;
Th' *Apostles* Mounts of the *New Testament.*

Prayer.

A PRAYER, that is said alone,
Starves, having no companion.
Great things ask for, when thou dost pray,
And those great are, which ne're decay.
Pray not for silver, rust eats this;
Ask not for gold, which metall is:
Nor yet for houses, which are here
But earth: *such vowes nere reach Gods eare.*

Christs sadnesse.

CHRIST was not sad, i'th garden, for His own
Passion, but for His sheeps dispersion.

God heares us.

GOD, who's in Heav'n, will hear from thence;
If not to'th sound, yet, to the sense.

God.

GOD (as the learned *Damascen* doth write)
A *Sea of Substance* is, *Indefinite.*

Clouds.

HE that ascended in a cloud, shall come
In clouds, descending to the publike *Doome.*

Comforts in contentions.

THE same, who crownes the Conquerour, will be
A Coadjutor in the Agonie.

Heaven.

HEAV'N is most faire; but fairer He
That made that fairest Canopie.

God.

IN God there's nothing, but 'tis known to be
Ev'n God Himself, in perfect *Entitie.*

His Power.

GOD can do all things, save but what are known
For to imply a contradiction.

Christs words on the Crosse, My God, My God.

CHRIST, when He hung the dreadfull Crosse upon,
Had (as it were) a *Dereliction;*
In this regard, in those great terrors He
Had no one *Beame* from Gods sweet Majestie.

JEHOVAH.

JEHOVAH, as *Boëtius* saith,
No number of the *Plurall* hath.

Confusion of face.

GOD then confounds mans face, when He not hears
The Vowes of those, who are Petitioners.

Another.

THE shame of mans face is no more
Then prayers repel'd, (sayes *Cassiodore.*)

Beggars.

JACOB Gods Beggar was; and so we wait
(Though ne're so rich) all beggars at His Gate.

Good, and bad.

THE Bad among the Good are here mixt ever:
The Good without the Bad are here plac'd never.

Sin.

SIN no Existence; Nature none it hath,
Or Good at all, (as learn'd *Aquinas* saith.)

Martha, Martha.

THE repetition of the name made known
No other, then *Christs* full Affection.

Youth, and Age.

GOD on our Youth bestowes but little ease;
But on our Age most sweet *Indulgences.*

Gods Power.

GOD is so potent, as His Power can
Draw out of *bad* a soveraigne *good* to man.

Paradise.

PARADISE is (as from the Learn'd I gather)
A quire of blest Soules circling in the Father.

Observation.

THE Jewes, when they built Houses (I have read)
One part thereof left still unfinished:
To make them, thereby, mindfull of their own
Cities most sad and dire destruction.

The Asse.

GOD did forbid the Israelites, to bring
An Asse unto Him, for an *offering*:
Onely, by this dull creature, to expresse
His detestation to all slothfulnesse.

Observation.

THE Virgin-Mother stood at distance (there)
From her Sonnes Crosse, not shedding once a teare:
Because the Law forbad to sit and crie
For those, who did as malefactors die.
So she, to keep her mighty woes in awe,
Tortur'd her love, not to transgresse the Law.
Observe we may, how *Mary Joses* then,
And th'other *Mary* (*Mary Magdalen*)
Sate by the Grave; and sadly sitting there,
Shed for their Master many a bitter teare:
But 'twas not till their *dearest Lord* was dead;
And then to weep they both were licensed.

Tapers.

THOSE Tapers, which we set upon the grave,
In fun'rall pomp, but this importance have;
That soules departed are not put out quite;
But, as they walk't here in their *vestures* white,
So live in Heaven, in everlasting light.

Christs Birth.

ONE Birth our Saviour had; the like none yet
Was, or will be a *second* like to it.

The Virgin Mary.

TO work a *wonder*, God would have her shown,
At once, a Bud, and yet a *Rose full-blowne*.

Another.

As Sun-beames pierce the glasse, and streaming in,
No crack or Schisme leave i'th subtill skin:
So the Divine Hand work't, and brake no thred,
But, in a *Mother*, kept a *maiden-head.*

God.

God, in the *holy Tongue*, they call
The Place that filleth *All in all.*

Another of God.

God's said to leave this place, and for to come
Nearer to that place, then to other some:
Of locall motion, in no least respect,
But only by impression of effect.

Another.

God is *Jehovah* cal'd; which name of His
Implies or *Essence*, or the *He* that Is.

Gods presence.

God's evident, and may be said to be
Present with just men, to the veritie:
But with the wicked if He doth comply,
'Tis (as S. *Bernard* saith) but seemingly.

Gods Dwelling.

God's said to dwell there, wheresoever He
Puts down some prints of His high Majestie:
As when to man He comes, and there doth place
His *holy Spirit*, or doth plant His *Grace.*

The Virgin Mary.

The *Virgin Marie* was (as I have read)
The *House of God*, by *Christ* inhabited;
Into the which He enter'd: but, the Doore
Once shut, was never to be open'd more.

To God.

GOD'S undivided, *One* in *Persons Three*;
And *Three* in *Inconfused Unity*:
Originall of Essence there is none
'Twixt God the *Father*, *Holy Ghost*, and *Sonne:*
And though the *Father* be the first of *Three*,
'Tis but by *Order*, not by *Entitie*.

Upon Woman and Mary.

SO long (it seem'd) as *Maries* Faith was small,
Christ did her *Woman*, not her *Mary* call:
But no more *Woman*, being strong in Faith;
But *Mary* cal'd then (as S. *Ambrose* saith.)

North and South.

THE *Jewes* their beds, and offices of ease,
Plac't *North* and *South*, for these cleane purposes;
That mans uncomely froth might not molest
Gods wayes and walks, which lie still East and West.

Sabbaths.

S*ABBATHS* are threefold, (as S. *Austine* sayes:)
The first of Time, or Sabbath here of Dayes;
The second is a Conscience trespasse-free;
The last the *Sabbath of Eternitie*.

The Fast, or Lent.

N*OAH* the first was (as Tradition sayes)
That did ordaine the Fast of forty Dayes.

Sin.

THERE is no evill that we do commit,
But hath th'extraction of some good from it:
As when we sin; God, the great *Chymist*, thence
Drawes out th'*Elixar* of true penitence.

God.

GOD is more here, then in another place,
Not by His *Essence*, but commerce of *Grace.*

This, and the next World.

GOD hath this world for many made; 'tis true:
But He hath made the world to come for few.

Ease.

GOD gives to none so absolute an Ease,
As not to know, or feel some *Grievances.*

Beginnings and Endings.

PAUL, he began ill, but he ended well;
Judas began well, but he foulely fell:
In godlinesse, not the beginnings, so
Much as the ends are to be lookt unto.

Temporall goods.

THESE temp'rall goods God (the most Wise) commends
To th'good and bad, in common, for two ends:
First, that these goods none here may o're esteem,
Because the wicked do partake of them:
Next, that these ills none cowardly may shun;
Being, oft here, the just mans portion.

Hell fire.

THE fire of Hell this strange condition hath,
To burn, not shine (as learned *Basil* saith.)

Abels *Bloud.*

SPEAK, did the Bloud of *Abel* cry
To God for vengeance? yes say I;
Ev'n as the sprinkled bloud cal'd on
God, for an expiation.

6.2 as] a *G*

Another.

THE bloud of *Abel* was a thing
Of such a rev'rend reckoning,
As that the old World thought it fit,
Especially to sweare by it.

A Position in the Hebrew Divinity.

ONE man repentant is of more esteem
With God, then one, that never sin'd 'gainst Him.

Penitence.

THE Doctors, in the Talmud, say,
That in this world, one onely day
In true repentance spent, will be
More worth, then Heav'ns Eternitie.

Gods presence.

GOD'S present ev'ry where; but most of all
Present by Union *Hypostaticall:*
God, He is there, where's nothing else (Schooles say)
And nothing else is there, *where He's away.*

The Resurrection possible, and probable.

FOR each one Body, that i'th earth is sowne,
There's an up-rising but of one for one:
But for each Graine, that in the ground is thrown,
Threescore or fourescore spring up thence for one:
So that the wonder is not halfe so great,
Of ours, as is the rising of the wheat.

Christs suffering.

JUSTLY our *dearest Saviour* may abhorre us,
Who hath more suffer'd by us farre, then for us.

Sinners.

SINNERS confounded are a twofold way,
Either as when (the learned Schoolemen say)
Mens sins destroyed are, when they repent;
Or when, for sins, men suffer punishment.

Temptations.

NO man is tempted so, but may o'recome,
If that he has a will to Masterdome.

Pittie, and punishment.

GOD doth embrace the good with love; & gaines
The good by mercy, as the bad by paines.

Gods price, and mans price.

GOD bought man here with his hearts blood expence;
And man sold God here for base *thirty pence.*

Christs Action.

CHRIST never did so great a work, but there
His humane Nature did, in part, appeare:
Or, ne're so meane a peece, but men might see
Therein some beames of His Divinitie:
So that, in all He did, there did combine
His Humane Nature, and His Part Divine.

Predestination.

P*REDESTINATION* is the Cause alone
Of many standing, but of fall to none.

Another.

ART thou not destin'd? then, with hast, go on
To make thy faire *Predestination:*
If thou canst change thy life, God then will please
To change, or call back, His past *Sentences.*

Sin.

SIN never slew a soule, unlesse there went
Along with it some tempting blandishment.

Another.

SIN is an act so free, that if we shall
Say, 'tis not free, 'tis then no sin at all.

Another.

SIN is the cause of death; and sin's alone
The cause of Gods *Predestination:*
And from Gods *Prescience* of mans sin doth flow
Our *Destination* to eternall woe.

Prescience.

GODS *Prescience makes none sinfull*; but th'offence
Of man's the chief cause of Gods *Prescience.*

Christ.

TO all our wounds, here, whatsoe're they be,
Christ is the one sufficient *Remedie.*

Christs Incarnation.

CHRIST took our Nature on Him, not that He
'Bove all things lov'd it, for the puritie:
No, but He drest Him with our humane Trim,
Because our flesh stood most in need of Him.

Heaven.

HEAVEN is not given for our good works here:
Yet it is given to the *Labourer.*

Gods keyes.

GOD has *foure keyes*, which He reserves alone;
The first of *Raine*, the key of *Hell* next known:
With the third key He opes and shuts the wombe;
And with the *fourth key* He unlocks the tombe.

Sin.

THERE'S no constraint to do amisse,
Whereas but one enforcement is.

Almes.

GIVE unto all, lest he, whom thou deni'st,
May chance to be no other man, but *Christ.*

Hell fire.

ONE onely fire has Hell; but yet it shall,
Not after one sort, there excruciate all:
But look, how each transgressor onward went
Boldly in sin, shall feel more punishment.

To keep a true Lent.

1 IS this a Fast, to keep
The Larder leane?
And cleane
From fat of Veales, and Sheep?

2 Is it to quit the dish
Of Flesh, yet still
To fill
The platter high with Fish?

3 Is it to fast an houre,
Or rag'd to go,
Or show
A down-cast look, and sowre?

4 No: 'tis a Fast, to dole
Thy sheaf of wheat,
And meat,
Unto the hungry Soule.

5 It is to fast from strife,
From old debate,
And hate;
To circumcise thy life.

6 To shew a heart grief-rent;
To sterve thy sin,
Not Bin;
And that's to keep thy Lent.

No time in Eternitie.

By houres we all live here, in Heaven is known
No spring of Time, or Times succession.

His Meditation upon Death.

Be those few hours, which I have yet to spend,
Blest with the Meditation of my end:
Though they be few in number, I'm content;
If otherwise, I stand indifferent:
Nor makes it matter, *Nestors* yeers to tell,
If man lives long, and if he live not well.
A multitude of dayes still heaped on,
Seldome brings order, but confusion.
Might I make choice, long life sho'd be with-stood;
Nor wo'd I care how short it were, if good:
Which to effect, let ev'ry passing Bell
Possesse my thoughts, next comes my dolefull knell:
And when the night perswades me to my bed,
I'le thinke I'm going to be buried:
So shall the Blankets which come over me,
Present those Turfs, which once must cover me:
And with as firme behaviour I will meet
The sheet I sleep in, as my Winding-sheet.
When sleep shall bath his body in mine eyes,
I will believe, that then my body dies:
And if I chance to wake, and rise thereon,
I'le have in mind my Resurrection,
Which must produce me to that *Gen'rall Doome*,
To which the Pesant, so the Prince must come,
To heare the Judge give sentence on the Throne,
Without the least hope of affection.
Teares, at that day, shall make but weake defence;
When Hell and Horrour fright the Conscience.
Let me, though late, yet at the last, begin
To shun the least Temptation to a sin;
Though to be tempted be no sin, untill
Man to th'alluring object gives his will.
Such let my life assure me, when my breath
Goes theeving from me, I am safe in death;
Which is the height of comfort, when I fall,
I rise triumphant in my Funerall.

Cloaths for Continuance.

THOSE Garments lasting evermore,
Are works of mercy to the poore,
Which neither Tettar, Time, or Moth
Shall fray that silke, or fret this cloth.

To God.

COME to me God; but do not come
To me, as to the gen'rall Doome,
In power; or come Thou in that state,
When Thou Thy Lawes didst promulgate,
When as the Mountaine quak'd for dread,
And sullen clouds bound up his head.
No, lay thy stately terrours by,
To talke with me familiarly;
For if Thy thunder-claps I heare,
I shall lesse swoone, then die for feare.
Speake thou of love and I'le reply
By way of *Epithalamie*,
Or sing of *mercy*, and I'le suit
To it my Violl and my Lute:
Thus let Thy lips but love distill,
Then come my God, and hap what will.

The Soule.

WHEN once the Soule has lost her way,
O then, how restlesse do's she stray!
And having not her God for light,
How do's she erre in endlesse night!

The Judgement day.

IN doing justice, God shall then be known,
Who shewing mercy here, few priz'd, or none.

Sufferings.

WE merit all we suffer, and by far
More stripes, then God layes on the sufferer.

2.5 Mountaine *Pollard*: Mountains *48*

Paine and pleasure.

GOD suffers not His Saints, and Servants deere,
To have continuall paine, or pleasure here:
But look how night succeeds the day, so He
Gives them by turnes their grief and jollitie.

Gods presence.

GOD is *all-present* to what e're we do,
And as *all-present*, so *all-filling* too.

Another.

THAT there's a God, we all do know,
But what God is, we cannot show.

The poore mans part.

TELL me rich man, for what intent
Thou load'st with gold thy vestiment?
When as the poore crie out, to us
Belongs all gold superfluous.

The right hand.

GOD has a Right Hand, but is quite bereft
Of that, which we do nominate the Left.

The Staffe and Rod.

TWO instruments belong unto our God;
The one a *Staffe* is, and the next a *Rod*:
That if the twig sho'd chance too much to smart,
The staffe might come to play the friendly part.

God sparing in scourging.

GOD still rewards us more then our desert:
But when He strikes, He quarter-acts His part.

Confession.

CONFESSION twofold is (as *Austine* sayes,)
The first of *sin* is, and the next of *praise:*
If ill it goes with thee, thy faults confesse:
If well, then chant Gods praise with cheerfulnesse.

Gods descent.

GOD is then said for to descend, when He
Doth, here on earth, some thing of novitie;
As when, in humane nature He works more
Then ever, yet, the like was done before.

No coming to God without Christ.

GOOD *and great God!* How sho'd I feare
To come to Thee, if *Christ* not there!
Co'd I but think, He would not be
Present, to plead my cause for me;
To Hell I'd rather run, then I
Wo'd see Thy Face, and He not by.

Another, to God.

THOUGH Thou beest all that *Active Love*,
Which heats those ravisht Soules above;
And though all joyes spring from the glance
Of Thy most winning countenance;
Yet sowre and grim Thou'dst seem to me;
If through my *Christ* I saw not Thee.

The Resurrection.

THAT *Christ* did die, the *Pagan* saith;
But that He rose, that's *Christians* Faith.

Coheires.

WE are Coheires with *Christ*; nor shall His own
Heire-ship be lesse, by our adoption:
The number here of Heires, shall from the state
Of His great *Birth-right* nothing derogate.

The number of two.

GOD hates the *Duall Number*; being known
The lucklesse number of division:
And when He blest each sev'rall Day, whereon
He did His *curious operation*;
'Tis never read there (as the Fathers say,)
God blest His work done on the *second day:*
Wherefore two prayers ought not to be said,
Or by our selves, or from the Pulpit read.

Hardning of hearts.

GOD'S said our hearts to harden then,
When as His grace not supples men.

The Rose.

BEFORE Mans fall, the Rose was born
(S. *Ambrose* sayes) without the Thorn:
But, for Mans fault, then was the Thorn,
Without the fragrant Rose-bud, born;
But ne're the Rose without the Thorn.

Gods time must end our trouble.

GOD doth not promise here to man, that He
Will free him quickly from his miserie;
But in His own time, and when He thinks fit,
Then He will give a happy end to it.

Baptisme.

THE strength of *Baptisme*, that's within;
It saves the soule, by drowning sin.

Gold and Frankincense.

GOLD serves for Tribute to the King;
The *Frankincense* for Gods Offring.

To God.

GOD, who me gives a will for to repent,
Will add a power, to keep me innocent;
That I shall ne're that trespasse recommit,
When I have done true Penance here for it.

The chewing the Cud.

WHEN well we speak, & nothing do that's good,
We not divide the *Hoof*, but chew the *Cud*:
But when good words, by good works, have their proof,
We then both chew the *Cud*, and cleave the *Hoof*.

Christs twofold coming.

THY former coming was to cure
My soules most desp'rate *Calenture*;
Thy second *Advent*, that must be
To heale my Earths infirmitie.

To God, his gift.

AS my little Pot doth boyle,
We will keep this *Levell-Coyle*;
That a *Wave*, and I will bring
To my God, a *Heave-offering*.

Gods Anger.

GOD can't be wrathfull; but we may conclude,
Wrathfull He may be, by similitude:
God's wrathfull said to be, when He doth do
That without *wrath*, which wrath doth *force us* to.

Gods Commands.

IN Gods Commands, ne're ask the reason why;
Let thy *obedience* be the best Reply.

To God.

If I have plaid the *Truant*, or have here
Fail'd in my part; O! Thou that art my *deare*,
My *mild*, my *loving Tutor*, *Lord and God!*
Correct my errors gently with Thy Rod.
I know, that faults will many here be found,
But where sin swells, there let Thy grace abound.

To God.

The work is done; now let my *Lawrell* be
Given by none, but by Thy selfe, to me:
That done, with Honour Thou dost me create
Thy *Poet*, and Thy *Prophet Lawreat*.

Good Friday: Rex Tragicus, *or Christ going to His Crosse.*

Put off Thy Robe of *Purple*, then go on
To the sad place of execution:
Thine houre is come; and the Tormentor stands
Ready, to pierce Thy tender Feet, and Hands.
Long before this, the base, the dull, the rude,
Th'inconstant, and unpurged Multitude
Yawne for Thy coming; some e're this time crie,
How He deferres, how loath He is to die!
Amongst this scumme, the Souldier, with his speare,
And that sowre Fellow, with his *vineger*,
His *spunge*, and *stick*, do ask why Thou dost stay?
So do the *Skurfe* and *Bran* too: Go Thy way,
Thy way, Thou guiltlesse man, and satisfie
By Thine approach, each their beholding eye.
Not as a thief, shalt Thou ascend the mount,
But like a Person of some high account:
The *Crosse* shall be Thy *Stage*; and Thou shalt there
The spacious field have for Thy *Theater*.
Thou art that *Roscius*, and that markt-out man,
That must this day act the Tragedian,
To wonder and affrightment: Thou art He,

Whom all the flux of Nations comes to see;
Not those poor Theeves that act their parts with Thee:
Those act without regard, when once a *King*,
And *God*, as Thou art, comes to suffering.
No, No, this *Scene* from Thee takes life and sense,
And soule and spirit, plot, and excellence.
Why then begin, great King! ascend Thy Throne,
And thence proceed, to act Thy Passion
To such an height, to such a period rais'd,
As Hell, and Earth, and Heav'n may stand amaz'd.
God, and good Angells guide Thee; and so blesse
Thee in Thy severall parts of bitternesse;
That those, who see Thee nail'd unto the Tree,
May (though they scorn Thee) praise and pitie Thee.
And we (Thy Lovers) while we see Thee keep
The Lawes of Action, will both sigh, and weep;
And bring our Spices, to embalm Thee dead;
That done, wee'l see Thee sweetly buried.

His words to Christ, going to the Crosse.

WHEN Thou wast taken, Lord, I oft have read,
All Thy Disciples Thee forsook, and fled.
Let their example not a pattern be
For me to flie, but now to follow Thee.

Another, to his Saviour.

IF Thou beest taken, *God* forbid,
I flie from Thee, as others did:
But if Thou wilt so honour me,
As to accept my companie,
I'le follow Thee, hap, hap what shall,
Both to the *Judge*, and *Judgment-Hall*:
And, if I see Thee posted there,
To be all-flayd with whipping-cheere,
I'le take my share; or els, my God,
Thy stripes I'le kisse, or burn the *Rod*.

l. 27 spirit,] spirit *48*   1.4 now] now, *P*

His Saviours words, going to the Crosse.

HAVE, have ye no regard, all ye
Who passe this way, to pitie me,
Who am a man of miserie!

A man both bruis'd, and broke, and one
Who suffers not here for mine own,
But for my friends *transgression!*

Ah! *Sions Daughters*, do not feare
The *Crosse*, the *Cords*, the *Nailes*, the *Speare*,
The *Myrrhe*, the *Gall*, the *Vineger:*

For *Christ*, your loving Saviour, hath
Drunk up the wine of Gods fierce wrath;
Onely, there's left a little froth,

Lesse for to tast, then for to shew,
What bitter cups had been your due,
Had He not drank them up for *you.*

His Anthem, to Christ on the Crosse.

WHEN I behold Thee, almost slain,
With one, and all parts, full of pain:
When I Thy gentle Heart do see
Pierc't through, and dropping bloud, for me,
I'le call, and cry out, Thanks to Thee.

Vers. But yet it wounds my soule, to think,
That for my sin, Thou, Thou must drink,
Even Thou alone, the *bitter cup*
Of *furie*, and of *vengeance* up.

Chor. Lord, I'le not see Thee to drink all
The *Vineger*, the *Myrrhe*, the *Gall*:

Ver. Chor. But I will sip a little wine;
Which done, Lord say, *The rest is mine.*

This Crosse-Tree here
Doth JESUS *beare,*
Who sweet'ned first,
The Death accurs't.
Here all things ready are, make hast, make hast away;
For, long this work wil be, & very short this Day.
Why then, go on to act: Here's wonders to be done,
Before the last least sand of Thy ninth houre be run;
Or e're dark Clouds do dull, or dead the Mid-dayes Sun.
Act when Thou wilt,
Bloud will be spilt;
Pure Balm, that shall
Bring Health to All.
Why then, Begin
To powre first in
Some Drops of Wine,
In stead of Brine,
To search the Wound,
So long unsound:
And, when that's done,
Let Oyle, next, run,
To cure the Sore
Sinne made before.
And O! Deare Christ,
E'en as Thou di'st,
Look down, and see
Us weepe for Thee.
And tho (Love knows)
Thy dreadfull Woes
Wee cannot ease;
Yet doe Thou please,
Who Mercie art,
T'accept each Heart,
That gladly would
Helpe, if it could.
Meane while, let mee,
Beneath this Tree,
This Honour have,
To make my grave.

To his Saviours Sepulcher: his Devotion.

HAILE holy, and all-honour'd Tomb,
By no ill haunted; here I come,
With shoes put off, to tread thy Roome.
I'le not prophane, by soile of sin,
Thy Doore, as I do enter in:
For I have washt both hand and heart,
This, that, and ev'ry other part;
So that I dare, with farre lesse feare,
Then full affection, enter here.
Thus, thus I come to kisse Thy Stone
With a warm lip, and solemne one:
And as I kisse, I'le here and there
Dresse Thee with flowrie Diaper.
How sweet this place is! as from hence
Flow'd all *Panchaia's* Frankincense;
Or rich *Arabia* did commix,
Here, all her rare *Aromaticks*.
Let me live ever here, and stir
No one step from this *Sepulcher*.
Ravisht I am! and down I lie,
Confus'd, in this brave Extasie.
Here let me rest; and let me have
This for my *Heaven*, that was Thy *Grave*:
And, coveting no higher sphere,
I'le my Eternitie spend here.

His Offering, with the rest, at the Sepulcher.

TO joyn with them, who here confer
Gifts to my Saviours Sepulcher;
Devotion bids me hither bring
Somwhat for my Thank-Offering.
Loe! Thus I give a Virgin-Flower,
To dresse my Maiden-Saviour.

His coming to the Sepulcher.

HENCE they have born my Lord: Behold! the Stone
Is rowl'd away; and my sweet Saviour's gone!
Tell me, white Angell; what is now become
Of Him, we lately seal'd up in this Tombe?
Is He, from hence, gone to the shades beneath,
To vanquish Hell, as here He conquer'd Death?
If so; I'le thither follow, without feare;
And live in Hell, if that my *Christ* stayes there.

OF all the good things whatsoe're we do,
God is the ΑΡΧΗ, and the ΤΕΛΟΣ too.

ADDITIONAL POEMS CHIEFLY FROM MANUSCRIPTS

A. INCLUDED IN PREVIOUS MODERN EDITIONS

The Descripcion: of a Woman.

WHOSE head befringed with bescattered tresses
Seemes like Apollo's when the morne he blesses
Or like vnto Aurora when shee setts
her long disheuel'd rose=crown'd tramaletts
Her forehead smooth full polisht bright and high
bares in it selfe a gracefull maiestye
Vnder the which twoe crawling eyebrowes twine
like to the tendrells of a flattring vine
Vnder whose shades Twoe starry sparkling eyes
are beawtifi'd with faire fring'd canopies
Her comly nose with vniformall grace
like purest white stands in the middle place
Parting the paire as wee may well suppose
each cheeke resembling still a damaske rose
Which like a garden manifestly showe
how roses lillies and carnations grow
which sweetly mixed both with white and redd
like rose leaues, white and redd seeme mingled
Ther nature for a sweet allurement setts
twoe smelling swelling bashful Cherriletts
The which with ruby rednes being tipt
doe speake a virgin merry cherry=lip't
Over the which a meet sweet skin is drawne
Which makes them shewe like roses vnder lawne
These be the Ruby portalls and devine
Which ope themselves to shewe an holy shrine
Whose breath is rich perfume, that to the sence
smells like the burnt Sabæan ffrankinsense
In which the tongue, though but a member small
stands garded with a rosy hilly wall

1 From MS. Rawlinson poet. 160, f. 105. For variants see pp. 492–3.

And her white teeth which in the gumms are sett
Like pearle and gold make one rich Carcenett
Next doth her chinne with dimpled beawty striue
ffor his plumpe white and smooth prerogatiue
At whose faire topp to please the sight there growes
the blessed Image of a blushing rose
mou'd by the chinne whose motion causeth this
That both her lipps doe part doe meete doe kisse.
Her eares which like twoe Laborinths are plac'd
on either side with rich rare Jewells grac'd
mooving a question whether that by them
the Jem is grac'd? or they grac'd by the Jemme
But the foundacion of this Architect
is the swan=stayning faire rare stately neck
which with ambitious humblenes stands vnder
bearing aloft this rich round world of wonder
In which the veynes ymplanted seeme to lye
like loving vines hid vnder Ivorye
Soe full of clarrett that whoe soe pricks a vine
may see it sprout forth streames of muscadine
Her brest (a place for beawtyes throne most fitt)
beares vp twoe globes where loue and pleasure sitt
Which headed with twoe rich round rubies showe
like wanton rose buds growing out of snowe
And in the milky vally that's betweene
sits Cupid kissing of his mother Queene
Fingring the paps that feele like sleeded silke
And prest a little they will weepe new milke
Then comes the belly seated next belowe
like a faire mountaine of Riphean snowe
Where nature in a whitenes without spott
hath in the middle ty'de a Gordian knott
Or ells that she on that white waxen hill
hath seal'd the promise of her vtmost skill
But now my muse hath spi'de a darke descent
from this soe peereles pretious prominent,
A milky high waye that direction yeilds
Vnto the port mouth of th'Elisian feilds
A place desir'd of all but got by theis
whome loue admitts to this Hesperides
Heres golden fruit that farre exceeds all price
growing in this loue garded paradice

Aboue the entrance there is written this
this is the portall to the bowre of bliss
Through mid'st thereof a christall stream there flowes
passing the sweet sweet of a musky rose
Now loue invites me to survey her thighes
swelling in likenes like twoe christall skyes
With plumpe soft flesh of mettle pure & fine
Resembling sheilds both smooth and christalline
Hence rise those twoe ambitious hills that looke
into the middle moste sight pleasing crooke
Which for the better beawtifying shrowdes
its humble selfe twixt twoe aspiring cloudes
Which to the knees by nature fastned on
deriue their ever well grac'd motion
her leggs with twoe cleire calues like silver tride
Kindly swell vp with little pretty pride
Leaving a distance for the beawtious small
to beawtify the legg and foote withall
Then lowly yet most louely stand the feete
Round short and cleire, like pounded spices sweete
And whatsoever thing they tread vpon
They make it scent like bruized Cinnamon
The lovely shoulders now allure the eye
To see two tablets of pure Ivory
from which two armes like branches seem to spread
With tender ryne and silver coloured,
With little hands & fingers long and small
To grace a Lute a vyall Virginall.
In length each finger doth his next excell
Each richly headed with a pearly shell
Richer then that faire pretious virtuos horne
That armes the forehead of the Vnicorne
Thus every part in contrariety
Meets in the whole and maks a harmony
As divers strings do singly disagree
But form'd by number make sweet melody
Vnto the Idoll of the work devine
I consecrate this loving work of mine
Bowing my lips vnto that stately root
Whence beawty springs, and thus I kisse thy foot

. . . .

Mr Hericke his daughter's Dowrye

ERE I goe hence and bee noe more
Seene to the world, Ile giue the skore
I owe vnto A female Child,
And that is this, A uerse Instylde
My daughters Dowrye; haueing which
Ile leaue thee then Compleatly riche
Insteade of gould *Pearle Rubies Bonds*
Longe forfaite pawnèd diamonds
Or Antique pledges, House or Lande
I giue thee this that shall with stande
The blow of Ruine and of Chance
Theis hurte not thyne Inheritance
for tis ffee simple, and noe rent
Thou *Fortune* ow'st for tenement
how euer after tymes will praise,
This Portion my Prophetique Bayes
Cannot deliuer vpp to'th rust
Yett I keepe peacefull in my dust
As for thy birth, and better seeds
(Those which must growe to *Vertuous deeds*)
Thou didst deriue from that old steem
(*Loue*, *Peace*, and *Mercie*, cherrish them)
which like a *Vestall Virgine* ply
with holye fier least that itt dye
Growe vpp with Mylder Lawes to knowe
Att what tyme to say I, or noe,
Lett Manners teach the whear to bee
More Comely flowing: where les free
Theis bringe thy husband, like to those
Old Coynes and Meddals, wee expose
To'th shew, but Neuer part with; next
As In a more Conspicuous Text
(Thy fore=head) lett therin bee sign'd
The Mayden Candour of thy Mynde:

1 From MS. Ashmole 38, p. 94. For variants see p. 493.

And vnder it two Chast borne spyes
To barr out, bolde Adulteryes
ffor through those Optickes, fly the dartes
Of Lust, which setts on fier our hartes
On eyther side of theis, quicke Eares
Ther must bee plac'd, for season'd feares
which sweeten Loue, yett ner'e come nighe
The Plague of wilder Jelousie
Then lett each Cheeke of thyne intice
his soule as to a bedd of spice
wheare hee may roule, and loose his sence
As in a bedd of Frankensence
A Lipp Inkyndled with that Coale
with which Loue Chafes and warmes the soule
Bringe to hym next, and in it shew
Loues Cherries from such fyers growe
And haue their haruest, which must stand
The Gathering of the Lipp: not hand
Then vnto theis, bee it thy Care
To cloath thy words in gentle Ayre
That smooth as Oyle, sweet softe and Cleane
As is the Childish Bloome of Beane
Thay may fall downe and stroake as the
Beames of the sunn, the peacefull sea
White handes as smooth, as Mercies, bring
hym for his better Cherrishing
That when thou doest his necke Insnare
Or with thy wrist or flattering Hayre
hee may (a prisoner) ther discrye
Bondage more Loued then Lybertye
A Nature, soe well form'd, soe wrought
Too Calme A tempest lett bee brought
with thee; that should hee but Inclyne
To Roughnes, Claspe hym lyke a Vine
Or lyke as woole meetes steele, giue way
Vnto the passion, not to stay;
Wrath yf resisted ouer boyles
Iff not, it dyes, or eles recoyles
And Lastly, see thou bring to hym
Somewhat peculiar to each lymm

And I charge thee to bee knowne
By n' other Face, but by thyne owne,
Lett itt (in Loues name) bee keept sleeke
Yett to bee found when hee shall seeke
It, and not Instead of Saint
Giue vpp his worshipp to the painte
ffor (trust me Girle) shee ouer-does
who by a double Proxie woes
But Least I should forgett his bedd
Bee sure thou bringe A Mayden head
That is *A Margarite*, which Lost
Thou bring'st vnto his bedd A frost
Or A colde Poyson, which his blood
Benummes like the forgettfull floode
Now for some Jewells to supplye
The Wante of Eare rings brauerye
ffor puplike Eyes, take onlye theis
Ne're trauylde for beyonde the Seas,
Theyre Nobly=home=bread, yett haue price
beyound the fare-fetch Marchandize
Obedience, *Wise=Distrust*, *Peace*; shey
Distance, and sweet *Vrbanitie*
Safe Modestie, *Lou'd Patience*, *feare*
Of offending, *Temperance*, *Deare*
Constancie, *Bashfullnes*, and all
The *Vertues Lesse*, or *Cardinall*
Take with my blessinge; and goe forth
In Jewelld, with thy Natiue worthe,
And now yf ther A man bee founde
That Lookes for such prepared grownd
Lett hym but with indifferent skill
Soe good a soile bee=stocke and till
  Hee may ere longe haue such a wyfe
  Nourish in's breast, a Tree of Life

finis Robt: Hericke

Mr Robert Hericke his farwell vnto Poetrie.

I HAVE behelde two louers in a night
(Hatch't o're with Moone=shine, from their stolen delight)
When this to that, and That, to This, had giuen
A kisse to such a Jewell of the heauen:
Or while that each from other's breath, did drincke
Healthes to the Rose, the Violet, or Pinke,
Call'd on the suddayne by the Jealouse Mother
Some strickter Mistris or suspitious other
Vrging diuorcement (worse then death to Theis)
By the soone gingling of some sleepy keyes
Parte with a hastye kisse; and in that shew
how stay thay would, yet forc't thay are to goe.
Euen such are wee; and in our parting, doe
Noe otherwise then as those former, two
Natures, like ours, wee who haue spent our tyme
Both from the Morning to the Euening Chyme;
Nay tell the Bell-man of the Night had tould
past Noone of night, yett weare the howers not old
Nor dull'd with Iron sleepe; but haue out-worne
The fresh and fayrest flourish of the Morne
With Flame, and Rapture; drincking to the ode
Number of Nyne, which makes vs full with God
And In that Misticke frenzie, wee haue hurl'de
(As with a Tempest) Nature through the worlde
And In a Whirl=wynd twirld her home, agast
Att that which in her extasie had past;
Thus Crownd with Rose Budds, Sacke, thou mad'st mee flye
Like fier-drakes, yett did'st mee no harme therby.
O thou Allmightye Nature, who did'st giue
True heate, whear with humanitie doth Liue
Beyond its stinted Circle; giueing foode
(While Fame) and Resurrection to the Good
Soaring them vpp, boue Ruyne, till the doome
(The generall Aprill of the world dothe Come)

[1] From MS. Ashmole 38, p. 106. For variants see pp. 493–4.

That makes all æquall, manye thowsands should
(wert not for thee) haue Crumbled Into Mould
And with thayr Ceareclothes rotted, not to shew
whether the world such Sperritts had or noe
whear as by Thee, Those, and A Million since
Nor Fate, nor Enuye, cann theyr Fames Conuince,
Homer, *Musæus*, *Ouid*, *Maro*, more
Of those god-full Prophetts longe before
Holde there Eternall fiers; and ours of Late
(Thy Mercie helping) shall resist stronge fate
nor stoope to'th Center, but suruiue as Longe
As Fame or Rumour, hath or Trumpe or Tongue
But vnto mee, bee onlye hoarse, since now
(Heauen and my soule beare Record of my Vowe)
I, my desires screw from thee, and directe
Them and my Thoughts to that sublim'd respecte
And Conscience vnto Preist-hood, tis not Need
(The skarcrow vnto Mankinde) that doth breed
Wiser Conclusions in mee, since I knowe
I'ave more to beare my Chardge, then way to goe
Or had I not, I'de stopp the spreading itch
Off craueing more: soe In Conceipt bee ritch,
But tis the god of Nature, who Intends
And shaps my Functions for more glorious ends
Guesse, soe departe; yett stay A while too see
The Lines of Sorrowe, that lye drawne in mee
In speach, in Picture; noe otherwise then when
(Judgment and Death, denounc'd gainst Guilty men)
Each takes A weeping farwell, rackt in mynde
With Joyes before, and Pleasures left behind:
Shakeing the head, whilst each, to each dothe mourne
With thought thay goe, whence thay must ner returne
Soe with like lookes, as once the *Ministrell*
Cast, leading his *Euredice* through hell
I stricke thy loues, and greedyly persue
Thee, with myne Eyes, or in, or out, of View
Soe look't the Grecian Oratour when sent
ffroms Natiue Cuntrye, in to Banishment
Throwing his eye balls backward, to suruaye
The smoake of his beloued *Attica*

59 *Guesse*] see Commentary, p. 580.

Soe Tullye look't, when from the Brest's of Rome
The sad soule went, not with his Loue, but doome;
Shooting his Eye-darts 'gainst it, to surprise
It, or to drawe the Cittie to his Eyes
Such is my parting with thee; and to proue
Ther was not Varnish (only) in my loue
But substance, to! receaue this Pearlye Teare
ffrozen with Greife; and place it in thyne eare
Then Parte in name of peace; & softely on
With Numerous feete to Hoofy Helicon
And when thou art vppon that forked Hill
Amongest the thrice, three, sacred Virgins, fill
A full brimm'd bowle of Furye and of rage
And quafe it to the Prophets of our Age;
when drunck with Rapture; Curse the blind & lame
Base Ballad=mongers, who vsurpe thy name
And fowle thy Altar, Charme some Into froggs
Some to bee Ratts, and others to bee hoggs:
Into the Loathsomst shapps, thou Canst deuise
To make ffooles hate them, onlye by disguise;
Thus with a kisse of warmth, and loue, I parte
Not soe, but that some Relique In my Harte
Shall stand for euer, though I doe addresse
Cheifelye my selfe to what I must proffess:
Knowe yet (rare soule) when my diuiner Muse
Shall want a Hand-mayde, (as she ofte will vse)
Bee readye, thou In mee, to wayte vppon her
Thoughe as a seruant, yet a Mayde of Honor
  The Crowne of dutye is our dutye; well
  Doing's, the Fruite of Doinge well, Farwell

finis M[r] Rob[t] Herricke

A Charroll presented to Dr: Williams Bp. of Lincolne as a Newyears guift.

FLY hence Pale Care, noe more remember
Past Sorrowes with the fled December
But let each present Cheeke appeare
Smooth as the Childhood of the yeare
And sing a Caroll here.
T'was braue, t'was braue could we comand the hand
Of Youths swift watch to stand
As yow haue done your day
Then should we not decay
But all we wither & our Light
Is spilt in euerlasting night
When as your Sight
Shewes like the Heavens aboue the Moone
Like an Eternall Noone
That sees noe setting Sunn.

Keepe vp those flames, & though you shroud
A while your forehead in a Cloude
Doe it like the Sun to write
I'th ayre, a greater Text of light
Welcome to all our vowes
And since you pay
To vs the day
Soe longe desir'd
See we haue fyr'd
Our holy Spicknard & ther's none
But brings his stick of Cynamon
His eager Eye, or Smoother Smyle
And layes it gently on the Pyle
Which thus enkindled we invoke
Your name amidst the sacred smoke.

Chorus

Come then greate Lord
And see our Alter burne
With Loue of your Returne
And not a man here but consumes
His soule to glad you in perfumes.

Rob: Herrick.

[1] From MS. Ashmole 36–37, f. 298.

His Mistris to him at his farwell

YOU may vow Ile not forgett
To pay the debt,
Which to thy Memorie stands as due
As faith can seale It you
Take then tribute of my teares
So long as I haue feares
To prompt mee, I shall euer
Languish and looke but thy returne see neuer
Oh then to lessen my dispaire
Print thy lips Into the ayre
So by this
Meanes I may kisse thy kisse
When as some kinde
winde
Shall hither waft it and In leiu
My lipps shall send a 1000 back to you

Ro: herrick.

Vpon parting:

GOE hence away, and in thy parting know
tis not my voice, but heauens, that bidds thee goe;
Spring hence thy faith, nor thinke it ill desert
I finde in thee, that makes me thus to part,
But voice of fame, and voice of heauen haue thunderd
we both were lost, if both of us not sunderd;
fould now thine armes, and in thy last looke reare
one Sighe of loue, and coole it with a teare;
Since part we must Let's kisse, that done retire
with as cold frost, as erst we mett with fire;
With such white vowes as fate can nere dissever
but truth knitt fast; and so farewell for euer.

R: Herrick:

1 From Add. MS. 11811, f. 37. For variants see p. 494.
2 From MS. Harl. 6917, f. 82^{v}. For variants see p. 494.

Upon Master FLETCHERS *Incomparable Playes.*

APOLLO sings, his harpe resounds; give roome,
For now behold the golden Pompe is come,
Thy Pompe of Playes which thousands come to see,
With admiration both of them and thee,
O Volume worthy leafe, by leafe and cover
To be with juice of Cedar washt all over;
Here's words with lines, and lines with Scenes consent,
To raise an Act to full astonishment;
Here melting numbers, words of power to move
Young men to swoone, and Maides to dye for love.
Love lyes a bleeding here, *Evadne* there
Swells with brave rage, yet comely every where,
Here's a *mad lover*, there that high designe
Of *King and no King* (and the rare Plott thine)
So that when 'ere wee circumvolve our Eyes,
Such rich, such fresh, such sweet varietyes,
Ravish our spirits, that entranc't wee see
None writes lov's passion in the world, like Thee.

ROB. HERRICK.

From *Comedies and Tragedies*, by Beaumont and Fletcher (1647), f.e. See p. 494.

The New Charon,

Upon the death of *Henry* Lord *Hastings.*

The Musical part being set by M. Henry Lawes.

The Speakers,

Charon and Eucosmeia.

Euc. Charon, O *Charon*, draw thy Boat to th' shore,
And to thy many, take in one soul more.
Cha. Who calls? who calls? *Euc.* One overwhelm'd with ruth;
Have pity either on my Tears or Youth,
And take me in, who am in deep Distress;
But first cast off thy wonted Churlishness.
Cha. I will be gentle as that Air which yeelds
A breath of Balm along th'*Elizean* fields.
Speak, what art thou? *Euc.* One, once that had a lover,
Then which, thy self ne'er wafted sweeter over.
He was—— *Cha.* Say what. *Eu.* Ay me, my woes are deep.
Cha. Prethee relate, while I give ear and weep.
Euc. He was an *Hastings*; and that one Name has
In it all Good, that is, and ever was.
He was my *Life*, my *Love*, my *Joy*; but di'd
Some hours before I shou'd have been his Bride.
Chorus. *Thus, thus the Gods celestial still decree,*
For Humane Joy, Contingent Misery.
Euc. The *hallowed Tapers* all prepared were,
And *Hymen* call'd to bless the Rites. *Cha.* Stop there.
Euc. Great are my woes. *Cha.* And great must that Grief be,
That makes grim *Charon* thus to pity thee.
But now come in. *Euc.* More let me yet relate.
Cha. I cannot stay; more souls for waftage wait,
And I must hence. *Eu.* Yet let me thus much know,
Departing hence, where Good and Bad souls go.

From *Lachrymæ Musarum; The Tears of the Muses: exprest in Elegies . . . Upon the death of . . . Henry Lord Hastings. . . . Collected and set forth b[y]* R[*ichard*] B[*rome*]. . . . 1649, p. 38. For variants see pp. 494–5.

Cha. Those souls which ne'er were drencht in pleasures stream,
The Fields of *Pluto* are reserv'd for them;
Where, drest with garlands, there they walk the ground,
Whose blessed Youth with endless flow'rs is crown'd.
But such as have been drown'd in this wilde Sea,
For those is kept the Gulf of *Hecate*;
Where, with their own contagion they are fed;
And there do punish, and are punished.
This known, the rest of thy sad story tell,
When on the Flood that nine times circles Hell
Chorus. *We sail along, to visit mortals never;*
But there to live, where Love shall last for ever.

ROB. HERRICK.

Vpon a Cherrystone sent to the tip of the Lady Jemmonia Walgraves eare.

LADY I intreate yow weare
this little pendant on your eare
Tis noe Jewell of great prize
Or in respect of Merchandize
But deepe mistery not the stone
gives it estimation.
Take it then and in a veiwe
See th'Epitomè of yow
ffor what life and death confines
Looks through the passage of theis lines
Whose incarvements doe descrye
A scripture how yow liue and dye
Read it then before your lipp
Comends it to your eares soft tipp
And the while yow doe surveye
this Janus looking double waye
With a teare yow may compare
to that yow must be; what yow are
know time past this cherrystone
had a sweet complexion

1 From MS. Rawl. poet. 160, f. 28. For variants see p. 495.

Skynne and colour flesh and blood
daintye tast for ladyes food
All's now fledd saue this alone
Poore relique of the beawty, bone
And that soe little we despaire
It ever dangling smil'd i'th'aire.
Soe must that faire face of yours
(As this looking=glasse assures)
ffaile and scarce leaue to be showne
there ever lived such a one
And when an other age shall bring
Your leane scalp to sensuring
though the Sextons truly sweare
Here Jemmonia's titles were
In this rag'd Escutcheon
most maye smile beleiue will none
Or there thought of faith may growe
But to this to think 'twas soe
This lesson you must pearse to'th'truth
And know (faire mistris) of your youth
death with it still walkes along
ffrom Mattins to the Euensong,
from the Pickaxe to the spade
To the tombe wher't must be layd
Whether in the morne of noone
Of your beawty death comes soone
And though his visage hung i'th'eare
doth not to the sight appeare
At each warning hees as much
know, to'th'hearing as the touch.
Place then this mirror to the veiw
Of those virgins whose briske hew
Of lines and colours make them scorne
This livery which the *greeke hath worne
Let them read this booke and learne
their ayry coulors to discerne
Twixt this and them this Gorgon showne
Turnes the beholders into stone.

ffinis R: Herricke:

53 *greeke] *The asterisk marks an intended note which was not supplied.*

[Epitaph on the Tomb of Sir Edward Giles and his wife in the South Aisle of Dean Prior Church.]

NO trust to Metals nor to Marbles, when
These have their Fate, and wear away as Men;
Times, Titles, Trophies, may be lost and Spent;
But Vertue Rears the eternal Monument.
What more than these can Tombs or Tomb-stones Say
But here's the Sun-set of a Tedious day:
These Two asleep are: I'll but be Vndrest
And so to Bed: Pray wish us all Good Rest.

B. NOT INCLUDED IN PREVIOUS EDITIONS

(*For sources see pp.* 496–7.)

(i) ATTRIBUTED TO HERRICK IN THE SEVENTEENTH CENTURY

To a Mayd.

1. FAYRE Mayd, you did but cast your eyes erewhile
your ripening eyes
Upon a Banke of Camomile,
And straight a blushing Birth
of Strawberryes
began to smile
and all to gild the earth.

2. Would you have Cherry harvest here
still last? then doe no more
but kisse yon Sicamore
that Mirtle, or that Bay;
And Cherryes will appeare
not onely ripe for that one day
but dangling all the yeare. Rob: Herricke.

Epitaph on a man who had a Scold to his Wife.

1. NAY, read & spare not, Passenger,
my sence is now past feeling,
who to my Grave a wound did beare
within, past Physicks healing.

2. But doe not, if thou be to wed,
to read my story tarry;
least thou envy me this cold Bed,
rather then live to marry.

3. For a long strife with a leud Wife
(worst of all Ills beside)
made me grow weary of my life,
so I fell sicke & dyde. Rob:
Herricke.

To his false Mistris.

1. WHITHER are all her false oathes blowne,
or in what region doe they live?
I'me sure no place where faith is knowne
dare any harbour to them give.

2. My withered heart, which Love did burne,
shall venture one sigh with the wind,
Oh may it never home returne
till one of her false oathes it find.

3. Then lett them wrestle in the sky
till they shall both one Lightning prove,
and falling may they pierce her eye
that was thus periurd in her love. Rob:
Herricke.

[*To a disdaynefull fayre.*]

THOU maist be proud and be thou so for me
yet know there is a death for me & thee
when as poore souls our softer frailties must
be lost in blended dust,
That Charnell house that keepes us both shall signe
no neat distinction twixt thy bones & mine.

2. And when to Hell our two lean soules
Where that just iudge shall giue to each his doome
Think'st thou thy pride forme colour there can fee
Him not to censure thee
Know wretched soule a judge thou there shalt finde
Who not respects the body but the minde.

3. And for my plea in acorne cups Ile show
Those two last teares which from mine eyes did flow
And all my sighs through silke-worme bags shall sound
Thou gau'st me deadly wound.
Can Justice then when these haue sworne thy guilt,
Ah! not reuenge the blood that thou hast spilt.

Herick

[*Orpheus and Pluto.*]

[Or.] HOWLE not you Ghosts & furies while I sing
Accents of greife to your infernall King
Pluto oh! Pluto pitty my sad teares!
[Pl.] What heavenly rapture this doth peirce our eares
Hark hark what art that cal'st to Hell
[Or.] Orpheus the poore Thracian Minstrell
What cam'st thou here for! [Or.] Justice. [Pl.] Whats thy plea
[Or.] To crave againe my deare Euridice
[Pl.] Com'st thou for her whom fates too hasty sheares
cut of but in the blossome of her yeares
[Or.] for her I come [Pl.] fond man she 's our's by fate
[Or.] Yet Love's intreaty never comes too Late
[Pl.] What should infernall Jove doe [Or.] Deigne to warne
the fatall Sisters to retwist the yarne
But oh! it is in Pluto's power to doe it
If he but nodd & put the Parcae to it

Let Love move Pluto let my greife tormenting
And jointly both move Pluto to repenting
[Pl.] Can we in justice do it [Or.] Jove may & who
dares speak 'gainst that which Jove is pleased to doe
Call back her fate and give a new beginning
to the cut web & blesse the thread in spinning
[Pl.] Why then triumph go take her hence & tell
Thy Music fetch't Euridice from Hell.
Such are thy measures Musick such thy charmes
that it the Furies of their brands disarmes
Such were thy active numbers Musick then
when thou build'st Thebes & cast it downe agen.

Mr Robt Ramsy
Mr. Heyrick

Parkinsons shade to the house of mr Pallauicine takeing his death ill

WILL you still lament and rayse
A shade from rest
doe you loue and will molest
A harmles Ghost with Ayes
Babram, by my loue forbeare
to shed A teare
or spend A groane, unless for Tombes
youle haue me come to haunt your romes
ah should I proue
A Goblin to the place I loue
no, no rather lett me keepe
my peacefull vrne
Then to the Comon light returne
and want my silken sleepe
I am ould and loue to bee
mongst Auncestry
wher in charnels we compare
our Grandsires bones to those which are
in theis dayes when
the Age breeds boyes not men
but howsoeuer theyse defaults
haue fate alike in uaults.

1. 17 wher in] wherin *MS.*

this from the dead: prepare to come,
for me and you benignant Earth has rome
    meane while Gods benison and good mens vowes
    preuent your Acts, Peace guard this house
        Exit Parkenson:

R: Herricke

(ii) ATTRIBUTED TO 'R.H.' IN A SEVENTEENTH-CENTURY MANUSCRIPT

Stella wept.

HEERE & there teares gently strewinge
One her rosy cheekes bedewinge
Stella wept.
(As raine descends when Phaebus shines)
In siluer showres from the eyne
Stella wept.
As if her dimpled cheeke had meant
To be inlayd with Orient
Stella wept.
(Like starres downe bendinge from there spheare)
Droppinge many a siluer teare.

Stellaes smile.

THOSE watery gemmes by Loues force charm'd
Vanish away. soe teares scarse warm'd
By the morninge sunne doe reeke
Upon the startled Lillyes cheeke
And vanish; soone the sunne gan rise
Which had sett in Stella'es eyes
To cashiere those churlish cloudes
From of her brow where sorrow shrowdes
Herselfe; which done I boldly say
Stella's growne the fairer day. R.H.

Sweet Bett.

SINCE fame speakes thee a Linguist I shall wronge
Thee, not to write the mistris of the tongues
As well as hearts, since judgement's proud to weare
Each word of thine a jewell in her eare

For an inrichinge; yett I know a man
Would putt thee downe for an Hebritian
Durst Bett encounter, hauinge learn't the trick
That women can not read without a *prick*. (Hebrew
R.H.

An anagram one Mistris Maria. H.

MARIA sounds amarj, then soe writt
A Mary to be lou'd I english itt
If soe, then for to be noe tedious debtor
Vnto your fortunes, borrow the first letter
Of my name in yours then giue itt place
Where your best wishes best shall find a space
This done I doubt not but that Maries head
Shall weare the Nuptiall wreath well marryed.
R.H.

The Tobacconist.

KNOW you the garbe? thus I accost you, what?
My noble blades will yee evaporate?
Will you exchange a whiffe or two! come smother,
In cloudes of smoake envelope one another;
A match; you sirra, bringe the best you can
Or else I sweare as I am a gentleman.
sitt round boone blades; shaver light the taper
How like a child thou suckst? more ample vapour
must steame to such excesse, as when the sunne
Changes the ayre to exhalation.
Phaugh; by Joue this rellishes plaine Kitt
A St and brooke such bastard counterfeit
Tobacco? sure good man thou hast beene priz'd
Att higher rates when thou wert canoniz'd.
Better't you villaine else (would I were dead)
Thy shoulders shall goe bare vnto thy head;
Why this is right: itt hath a dainty touch
Verinahs selfe could neuer boast of such.
Y'faith weele smoake itt, I must see itt spread,
The ayre blew coated, whiff about my head.
Could I but feed vpon such ayre alone
I'de quitt my nature, turne Camelion

see how the azure vapour rythes the skies
Weele smoake out all those vulgar dietyes
Which lurke soe close; as you haue seene them driue
The silly drones from there vnpeopled hiue.
For this Prometheus ransackt heauen, these fires
Entic'd his hands to second his desires
Eu'ne to a sacriledge; diuinest flame;
Why then a fye upon all such prophane
Tobacco? satans hearbe, soe vile will pose
All the rhetoricall language of the nose.
Thou varlett, how thy stinkinge breath doth staine
An herbe of vertue stiled soueraigne
It is the poets Moly, richest nectar
The gods Ambrosia, our pure Elixar,
It is most pretious. know itt will reuiue
Decayinge nature, tis restoratiue
For wasted spiritts, shames the Emperick
And his cauterian for the rheumatick;
This head with Cataracts of Nile did runne
I stopt the streames by salivation
It prompts the memory, invention
Cleares, itt quickens apprehension;
Good for obstructions, itt opes the veines
Fills them with spiritts, closeth them againe
Provokes an appetite, itt whetteth on
The stomack, helpes all crude digestion
My grannam sure Birlady us'd to call
The ashes for kibd heeles a Cordiall
Exchangeth mirth for greife, doth antidate
Presuminge hopes, it doth exhilerate
Preuents all poison (though old Gallen wrote
Of noe such hearbe) this the best antidote
This I dare say soe good to kill the fleas
Theres noe Collyrium in Hippocrates.
The fire a Vestall flame, the ruby nose
God Bacchus altar, whereon incense glowes
It is all spiritt, but to force beleefe
It is the life of ayre, the ayre of life. R.H.

The Censure.

This vice robs vertue of her name, that done
Pleads an excuse, this is the fashion.
Such are the times, hee thinkes hees out o'th list
Of Gentlemen, thats noe Tobacconist
Walke but the streets, twill savour of noe newes
To meet a Buffon reekinge from the stewes.
Your eye needs noe great search, I doe presume
You may e'ene smell him ont by that perfume.
see how he tosseth as he reelinge goes
A new Meteor, a beacon att his nose
Of such a pretty size, to goe about
To measures nose itt must bee by his foot.
You can not see his face for itt, itt jetts
Out like a promontory, itt is sett
In steed of an Umbella to encrease
A shaddow like the strange sciopedes
Its a conueniency tis, that he goes
To light his pipe noe further then his nose
For sure the sparke thereof doth farr surpasse
All touchwood, tinder, or the burning glasse.
Could I perswade him this without demurre
It should be cas't with an exstinguisher
Me thinkes itt should be dangerous to carry
soe nigh his beard that dire incendiary
Which if itt scape the fire, that bush
Of sooty coulour, well may make a brush
To sweepe the chimney of his nose, may bee
In time a dainty mirkin for a Lady.
Those pearely pimples of his face giue light
As doe the glowormes in the darkest night,
He needs noe other eyes, his owne would feare
A burninge, should they but come once soe neere,
And therefore sinke into his head, yett hunge
A smoakinge like a withered onion.
with what a grace he puffs: yett I averr
He giues a mouth but a suppositer
Feele how he stinkes? his tongue is but a mop
To cleanse his mouth that fowle Tobacco=shop
A man? a beast, a diuell, not to blurr
Mans nature with soe fowle a character

My chimist turnes all things to smoake, & by
A rule that crosseth all Philosophy
Can proue himselfe compos'd of aery breath
And then to vanish is the only death. R.H.

The Novice Loues blind.

NOE sooner had Loues gentle fire begunne
To warme my breast with wanton motions,
Then fond desires temptinge Venus doues
To shed there plumes to wing my tender loue
Withall; I like a novice which had beene
A tedious votary at Dian's shrine
Now master of my art a dareinge fly
Att the bright mirrours of faire Stella's eye
Yett like the silly larke which mounts the ayre
Hoveringe aloft till stoopinge to the snare
Is taken captiue, first I did but play
With some delightfull fancy, & att bay
I courted amorous thoughts att last my hart
A bleeding's stuck full of loues fiery darts
Which copy out to mee my fatall doome
To be betrayed thus to passion
Ay mee ~ ~ ~ ~ ~ ~
But cannot teares allay this heat, dispence
You louely cruell eyes an influence
Of lesse disaster, come you little suns
Draw vp a cloude of exhalations
Upon my brow, & from those starrlight spheares
Dissolue those vapours into showres of teares
To quench these flames; those eyes some ease impart
who could strike fire vpon a flinty heart,
O lett these balls of ebony be spent
In teares makinge themselues the punishment
who were the authours, till an equall hate
Proportion'd to my Loue can expiate
The crime; would itt auayle mee ought these eyes
Should suffer an Ecclipse; twill not suffice
Alas itt cannot; though that I should proue
Starke blind yett would that blindnesse argue Loue.
R.H.

The Heliotrope

Of all the flowry traine I hope
To choose my wife the Heliotrope
Which risinge
Springeth as the day is borne
A constant bride vnto the morne
Which settinge
Suffreth a kind of gentle rape
With the sunne coucht in her Lapp. R.H.

On a gentlewoman risinge earely in the morninge.

Fancy how the fairest morne
Casts of (in a pretty scorne)
Her night attire trimly dresses
Her dissheueld haire in tresses
Neatly dight, whose trimme array
Is sunshine purity of day
Assumes her vayle, wherewith beclad
Her bewtye's in a cloudy shade
Yett att the last will not disdaine
To show the world her face againe.

ffairer then the morne my loue
As innocent as is the doue
Lately stole from of her bed
In a blushinge maiden red
Stept to her glasse there to conferr
With beawtyes best interpreter;
And findinge there those graces whence
Glory might begg an influence
Her sparklinge eye had ne're outshone
The Christall in reflexion
As if sha'd striued to outvye
Venus selfe in victorye
Soe faire as if from thence the sunne
Had borrowed a complexion.
Tis done the hand of art gan dresse
Her in the choicest comelinesse

A snow white stole best suited her
With whom the snow scarse dur[s]t compare
Nay in disdaine of Orient
Her owne selfe was an ornament
Attired thus att last descends
From out her closet, straightway sends
Amidst the thronginge troopes her eye
In Embassage of curtesy.
Those bewtyes each stroue to inhance
Which fell from of her countenance
But least that some vulgar eye
might surfeit one such raritye
She maskt her bewty in a shrine
of modesty, but yett her eyne
Had power enough to rauish sense
In a tender violence.
The rest her enuious maske withdrew
In Ecclipses from our view
Till att last being overcome
To giue each satisfaction
She courteously her maske lett fall
And became more prodigall
Of that, which my thought might commence
A wonder for its excellence
That since my muse is strucken dumbe
In an admiration. R.H.

On a Limmer drawing a Gentle-womans picture vnawares.

CONCEIUE with mee the fairest, sweetest dame
That euer meritt honour'd with the name
Of bewtyous; conceiue a virgine, one
Where graces thronge for a possession
Imagine such a one as could haue lent
The proudest eye a rare astonishment
Thence to admire how nature had outdone
Her selfe in giuinge her perfection
Conceiue the goddesse portraited in jett
By curious hand yett say twas counterfeit

When Chloris shall appeare, whom euery sense
Welcomes within there eyes circumference ~ ~ ~
~ ~ ~ ~ ~ ~ ~ ~
Conceiue a painter vnawares did stand
With pensill & his table in his hand
Ready to limme; within whose actiue eye
Yow reade the art of Phisiognomy
Yett stands amaz'd beinge dazeled by some glance
Of bewty to the height of ignorance
Noe sooner is himselfe but straight his eye
Hath taught him to committ Idolatry.
That curious peece of nature was my sunne
My Loue, which cast such a reflection
Shee is that archtype wherein is that all
Of bewty couch'd in the originall;
That theife of bewty came to filch from thence
The face, Epitome of excellence
The which with too too sacrilegious hand
The puny would haue drawne without command
But faylinge by th'inchantment of her eye
Was planett strucken to an extasy;
Nay soe he was as one that scarce did know
Whither his picture or him selfe did owe
Most right to humane nature, yett att last
Awaked to himselfe a flourish cast
Vpon his worke, but since I know theres none
Can second him to a perfection. R.H.

A dreame one a snow.

YOU impes of glory, daughters of delight
Sisters to bewty, hither I invite
You (in the height of vertue) to become
Interpreters of this my vision ~ ~ ~
Erst when a snowy garment cladd the night
In whitest liuery & had bedight
His sable shades as in a trimme array
Of whitest wooll about to cloath the day,
Soft slumber had my senses gently prest
To what my wandringe fancy might suggest,
Me thoughts I saw the earth in virgine dye
Right neatly drest in maiden purity,

The snow vpon her seem'd a vesture sent
From heauens rich wardrobe for an ornament,
Or as the night=reale, when the moone had wedd
Herselfe unto the Cynthian Maydenhead,
Soe faire, soe bright, as if the swarthy night
Had borrowed of the day a purer light.
The snow came downe, as if the heauens had went
To shivers, in soe sumptuous a descent
As though the goddesse in her coach of snow
Drawne by her milke white swans descended low,
Or as the thisly downe that whiflinge playes
The dandled wantons one a summers day,
Soe one a snowy winge I saw them flye
In scattered flakes of whitest Iuory
And houeringe in the ayre could take noe rest
Vntill they lay'd within her snowy breast.
Soe soft, soe faire soe bewtifull was shee
Invested with soe pure a sanctitye.
Mee thoughts twas pitty that shee e're should bee
Dismantled of that innocence but see
Before that time could well diuide asunder
The day & night vnto a ninth dayes wonder,
Her bewty faded, comelinesse & grace
Felt a consumption like a haggish face
Whereon the hand of art, had cast a dye
To dresse itt in a curious vanitye,
Breath but vpon itt & itt will abate
Its bewty, melt away, annihilate;
Looke wistly one itt, and behold all's gone,
But thickskind bewty, hard complexion:
Euen soe the earth, her face had lost her dye
Vnmasked to her owne deformitye.
Whereat I startled, att my first awake
I was resolu'd, itt was but a mistake,
Shee is not now soe faire, time seem'd to plow,
And age to furrow in her wrinkeled brow
Her hoary locks from of her raueld head
Farre different from the snow were scattered,
In stead of beawtyes right, her vncoth skinne
Was spotted with a Leprosy of sinne,
In sheets of snow in stead of finer dresse
The earth did penance as adulteresse,

The melted snow fell from her guilty eye
As though shee wept for her iniquitye,
Soe sad that euer since mee thinkes shee stood
As one forsaken in her widdowhood. R.H.

One a paire of gloues.

FAIRE Cloris, faire, if that your courteous eye
Vouchsafe to find an opportunitye
To question mee, what I within mee beare
Hearken, Ile tell you gently in your eare.
Within inclos'd, I here present a gloue
Perfumed onely with the doners Loue,
To make itt odoriferous I presume
A kisse from of your hands a rich perfume;
Are they not white enough? the doner sent
Them in there purity deficient
One purpose for to gaine a purer dye
By borrowinge a fairer Liuery
From of your snowy hand, whose vertue's such
That itt will clarify euen with a touch.
Are they too bigg? & will not neatly fitt
Your hand, draw them but one & they will sitt
Soe close vnto your hand as if they meant
To keepe itt in a soft imprisonment,
Are they too little for your hand, they proue
Farre lesser as a gift, then as a gloue,
Your gracious acceptance may preuent
The one, the other beare vnto euent,
Rather then they should be casheer'd your hand
They would enlarge themselues without commande
They're very plaine, the plainer that they bee
The lesse endebted to curiositye,
Noe wanton needle busily hath trac't
The hand of art in trimme deuises, grac't
With rich embroderings as if
The tender needle tooke itt as a greife
To wound the harmelesse gloue; know this the rose
Betweene the Lillyes durst not interpose
Herselfe; your hand they durst not come to nigh
Least they should blush to a deformitye.

But why doe I excuse there plainenesse, thence
Fondly to make a slender recompence;
My masters will is this, that they should bee
Plaine as the embleme of sinceritye.
These are the faults which may the gloue befall
Accept them and there is noe fault att all.
Here then I tender them to your acceptance, take
Them not for theres, but for the doner's sake.
But question not who sent mee, for his name
Must be concealed from the eare of fame,
Knowe onely this, he scorneth to bee knowne
Onely in the height of admiration
Of your vertues, least he should expresse
In your true worth his owne vnworthinesse
Which craues your pardon then you may vnseale
What in my treasury I doe conceale,
Disdaine itt not, & you accept itt, thrift
Hath allmost vndervalued the gift
Unlesse you honour itt with acceptance, which
The doner knowes his present shall enrich
Beyond a present, sett a price vpon
A higher price, vpon affection
And, now I'ue done my message, free from blame
Come sacrifice mee to the greedy flame,
Preserue my ashes, and as some diuine
Relique of affection enshrine
Them in your fauour, wherein if I dye
Yett I shall liue to an eternitye. R.H.

On a paire of kniues.

PRETTY paper doe a freind
A curtesy, and recommend
My seruice to thy mistresse, runne
Without a salutation
And say itt was not my intent
To preface in a complement,
Goe sacrifice my loue vpon
The altar of affection.
And beare with thee this little thinge
To offer for an offeringe.

To know what tis doe but vnshrine
Them of there sheathy magazine
And you shall finde them neere ally'de
Whose property is to diuide,
Yett can they neuer vs disseuer
Whom loue and nature joyn'de together.
Tis saide a knifes vnlucky; see
It is but there false augury;
Were not loue aboue a fate
Twere ominous to dedicate
A knife, which though itt should disjoyne
Vs, loue would vs vnite againe,
Loue is a Hydra, for one head
By strikinge off, anothers bredd;
Though winter nipp itt in the bud, twill thriue
And with a second flourishinge reuiue.
Here my muse gaue (in a nod
Of grauity) a period
Yett if you haue an idle time
To cast away vpon my rime
Spend a little leisure one
This there commendation.
A wonder first they will bestowe
vpon beeliefe, for you shall knowe,
Them onely fitt for vse, and grace
When that they are out of case:
Beleeue mee they are noble blades
To slash, & cutt one purpose made
They scorne to turne there steely backs
To quakinge custards, or flapjacks,
Nay I know a little thinge
Would make them stabb a bagpuddinge
They're mettle, doe but whett them one
And a whole battalion
Of marshalld dishes cannot stand
Before them, for the vpper hand
Is all wayes theres, they made the flawe
In the bowells of Bread—a
midst vs also they will bee
Pycorners greatest enemye.
In sadnesse, they will skirmish best
When they are sharpe sett att a feast.

There wellcome I must needs commend
Farre better att the latter end
Of a feast the prouerbe sayes
Then the beginninge of a fray,
Yett doe you them but take in hand—
They will be seruants att command,
When you haue done, lay them aside
And thinke how freindly they abide
Putt them vp safe, & without doubt
They will not presently fall out,
But louingely together lye
Nestlinge in an vnitye.

~ ~ ~ ~ ~ ~ ~
~ ~ ~ ~ ~ ~ ~

One case two kniues containes, vpon
Each knife 2 hearts impression
Two hearts in one you see combinde
But one in both of vs I finde
Blest be that constellation
That wrought in vs this vnion,
Blest be the time, thrice blessed since
Our hearts enjoy'd loues influence. R.H.

On a false freind, shaddowed vnder the propertye of a shaddow.

WHY hast thou left mee all alone
my shaddowy companion
And thus disdainefully deny
Mee, once thy dearest company.
See; whilst the glory of my sunne
Gaue mee but a reflexion
Att that my noone tide of delight,
Thou, thou wert neuer out of sight,
But now my night o're casts my day
And shadow=like thou flyest away.
Nothinge once might vs disseuer
Nothinge now may joynes together,
Yett should my sunne once more appeare
In height of glory to cashiere
These cloudes of fortune, I should see
The time when thou wouldst waite one mee,

Goe then my freind, goe freindly goe,
Whilst I in these my teares will flow,
In swellinge tides, that may expresse
Mine in thine vnhappinesse,
Flow then my teares to wash away
The sad remembrance of the day
When first wee lou'de, hereafter I
Will neuer know an vnity
Ne're will I be embraced by
The shaddow of inconstancy
Fly fast away, yett lett desire
Beg this one thinge I require
That sith my sunne ecclipsd my light
Come make mee of the shade of night
A mantle of thy sable dye
To wrapp me in obscurity
Vntill my morninge sunne shall deigne
To bringe my happy day againe
My Genius then shall haue the sence
Of a happier influence. R.H.

On a faire Gentlewoman married to a blackman likened to the night & day.

THE burnisht rayes beganne to multiply
Themselues vnto a dayes serenitie
Of such a maiden lustre; sure his spheare
The sunne dismounted to inhabite here;
A day all sunne, when pleasures did inuite
Diuidinge numbers into infinite;
These were the nuptialls, when the day the light
It selfe espoused, went to bed with night.
The heauens there curtaines of a sable dye
Noe sooner spred about there Canopy
Then each partakinge of the choisest blisses
Had made a twilight of exchanged kisses,
Stella with all her starry traine did rise
As if the heauens had meant to turne all eyes
To gaze vpon them, quite forgatt to runne
There course, as fixt in admiration;
Each had a burninge taper which in stead
Of blazinge torches watcht the marriage bedd

Vntill the morne; when gently they arose
And part in kisses, feareinge to disclose
There bashfull heads; the day without offence
Did blush the guilt of true loues innocence
But when her bewty could noe longer lye
Vnder the vayle of nights obscuritye
Her first approachinge glory gaue vs sight
And blindnesse, strucken by the selfe same light,
The starrs beganne to twinkle, durst not stay
Could not behold the breakinge of the day
But straight went out, soe sneakinge in there heads
That euer since they lye extinguished.

R.H.

One the same.

WHEN faire Apollo, when the worlds bright eye
You (as another sunne) did last espye
Imagine why our shaddow crouchinge nigh
Soe nee're allyde did beare you company
From thence discouer, why loue often tyes
Those hands which might perswade antipathyes
Peruse mee, yea before you haue begunne
You reade the cause of this there vnion.
You need not bee inquisitiue, your eye
Vpon each letter best will satisfye
That harmelesse riddle; marke how black & white
Are reconcilde yett both are opposite,
The snow=white paper doth receaue noe blurr
From blacknesse which hath dy'de this character
But like soe many moales on Venus face
Receaue & giue a most peculiar grace
True blacknesse hath a treasury, where lyes
A generall collection of eyes
Where pilgrime like they safe arriue, yea tary
There and rejoyce to take vp sanctuary,
Behold the tender puple of your eye
Most full of light, though black as Ebony
Imagine his to be true beads of jett
Which Venus tooke from of her Carcanett
Sett there one purpose to entice your eye
(As well acquainted with that propertye)

That comely blacknesse ore his face dispred
May seeme to be the maske he borrowed
Of you, which now he weares, as tw'ere, a shrine
Betweene his bewty & your sparklinge eyne,
Least that your bewtyes with a bleakinge ray
Should strangely make a night in stead of day
By lookinge one him, like the sunne which canne
Create a Negro of an Englishman.
Those locks of haire, which once were golden thread
Turne black, because they were vnsheltered
If thus your selues, you study to compare
Thinke he must needs be blacke you are soe faire

R.H.

On a gentlewoman blushinge

WHAT blush? nay then blush one; since tis begun
Thus I allay such high dy'de passion
Tis but lip=labour, this, & this alone
Takes off which gaue thee that complection.
Why dost thou hide that which one purpose rose
(sent from thy heart one message) to disclose
Some mistery of loue, if soe take this
And smother itt with pressures of a kisse
The startled blood into that place did runne
To giue & take, (I want expression)
But thus & thus you may conceiue itt, thence
Steales downe to giue your heart intelligence.
Vpon your cheeke flowes a redd sea of blood
Striuinge to winne a neerer neighbourhood
mingleth her streames with mine, did not a skreene
Of skinne in kisses interpose betweene.
You blush because you blush, you know not why
Your face is damaskt with that sanguine dye,
I read the cause, most part of itt in sight
Did blush to see the borderinge parts soe white
And beinge spredd doe here & there bedecke
Those louely dimples with a purple specke
As if the goddesse spunne fine scarlett thread
To interweaue those azure veines with redd,
Of such a sweet composure, sure vpon
That ruddy white dwells the Carnation.

* Kisse

You smile a rose, your touch a flower setts
You speake hearts=ease, you breath the violett
I spend noe praise vpon your eye of Jett
Your lip with Corall & the ruby sett
A knott of Lillyes one your browe, a bedd
Of maiden haire that groweth one your head
I add but this which doth my heart ingraue
Each glance eu'ne of your eye doth kill or saue
Your snow=white neck & soe I should descend
Where each peculiar grace itt selfe commends
But since that nature hath conceald from vs
Such secresies as too mysterious
I thus excuse my selfe, & make itt good
What may bee wantinge shall be vnderstood R.H.

A ringe sent a Gentlew: with this posy Still beginninge, neuer endinge.

NOT the posy of your ringe
Not the choise enamellinge
Tempts affection, these moue
More like bribes, then suites of loue
The richnesse promiseth to mee
Not soe much loue as curtesye
Had each letter beene arrayde
With a pearely teare inlay'de
They could pleade with loue noe more
Then a silent oratour;
Women loue not to conferre
In soe dead a character.
Lett mee read thee what thou art
From the Motto of thine heart
Speake to mee as to the sect
Of a bussinge dialect
Who still Comma itt with kisses
Till they period there blisses. R.H.

(iii) ATTRIBUTED TO HERRICK IN 1941

[*The Showre of Roses.*]

MY Mistris blush'de, and therewithall,
as that Rich Crimson Spred,
from either cheeke, A showre did fall,
of blossoms whyte and Red.

2 the More she blush'de, the More the grace
did Make the Softe bloomes grow,
which Guilded there, fell downe a pace,
like flakes of winters snow.

3 had she not cast her Eye beneath
and Seene a Realme of flowr's
Ah doubtles she had bloomde to death
with Rayninge Rosye showr's

4 but when she stopt A sent soe blest
I Smelt, that I did sweare
that parradice had lefte the East
to spend his spices there.

(iv) NOT ATTRIBUTED TO HERRICK HITHERTO

[*The Eclipse.*]

VAILE thou thine eyes a while my Deare,
and muffle vp those twins of light,
Suns which euery day appeare
surfeit the eye and dimne the sight
preserve those fyers
till vennom'd age shall me benight
of my desires
sights seene aloofe more strictly tye the sence
to due observance of their Excellence,

The Lilly or the blushing rose
wrappt in a mantle of pure lawne
more gently strokes the sight of those
whose eyes by that Eclipse are drawne,

then should they lye
tendring themselv's a naked pawne
to every eye
Beauty still gaz'd on dyes, but somtimes hid
doth strike amazement & cheape eyes forbid

The farewell:

SWEETEST Loue since wee must part
by meere constraint, not heart,
stay a kissing while to know
what are my vowes, then goe:
Let that day when you goe hence
with other care dispence,
only busied to descrye
this happy Augury
that as she doth part us twaine
she will neuer meete againe:
Let the free, and gentle ayre
a teare or two declare,
and the sadd and passing Bell
bee dolefull Philomell;
to whose ruthfull tones wee'll weepe
that teares true time may keepe:
Let noe Churlish winde once dare
to awake the quiet ayre
as you ride, but still bee they
as to *Alcione*;
Let the stroaking sunne first aske
leaue of your vailing maske,
Ere his rayes through that Ecclipse
dare come to kisse your lipps:
Let the soft, the sweet the kinde
breath of the westerne winde
Calmely spire a kisse, not blowe
yet make your Tresses flowe
Like to Daphnes, when shee fledd
the losse of maydenhead:
Let your steede noe other pace
haue, nor noe other grace
then the Bull that bare the sweete
Europa into Creete:

Let our parting still the scope
keepe of a meeting hope,
though not this day, or the next
A third may make loue vext,
yet a fourth may issue when
wee two shall meete againe;
Then faire mistrisse, though delayes
make two seeme twenty dayes,
Let truth number them in sport
our absence will bee short.

A Sonnet:

ILE dote noe more, nor shall mine eyes
againe
maintaine
my former Jealousies,
If I can feare
noe more her haire
to fetter mee, twill bee the best
the noblest Trophy I can reare
unto my rest:
Thus perish in mee all my fire of Lust
only a Just
desire keepe heate in mee
to bee
A looker on yet still Liue free.

[*A Song*]

LOOSE no time nor youth but be
kinde to men as they to thee
the faire Lyllyes that now grow
in thy cheekes & purely show
the cherry & the rose that blow
if too long they hang & wast
winter comes & all will blast
thou art ripe full ripe for men
in thy sweet be gathred then.

[*Advice to a Maid.*]

LOUE in thy youth fayre Mayde bee wise
Ould time will make thee colder
and thoughe each Morneinge newe arise
yett wee each daye growe oulder,

Thou as heauen art faire, and younge,
thine Eyes like twynn Starrs shineinge,
but ere an other daye bee sprunge
all theise will bee declineinge.

Then winter comes with all his feares,
and all thy sweetes shall borrowe,
too Late then wilt thou showre thy teares,
and I too Late shall sorrowe.

ffinis

[*Elegy.*]

SINCE louely sweete, much like vnto a Dewe
Of pearle thou art lost vnto our View
Or like a vanish't dreame, this ground
When wee haue pray'd and censt it, lett it round
In our wild eares, whether thou art gone,
If to thine endlesse habitation,
Or to insoule some starre till that great yeare
Fills vp the motion of the Maister speare
And to returne att All soules daye, when wee
Att that great Aprill shall reviue and bee
Those verie same wee are, or yf not soe
Yett lett thy shade enforme, that wee maie knowe
If in the Orient, or the spice'd West
Thou lyest conceal'd, rowl'd vp in a nest
Of   and spiknard, that some wind
Maie fann thine odours hither; soe to find
Thee, and fall downe to worshipp, like as when
That siluer candle lead those wiser men,
To that they sought for: soe lett some one thing
What e're it bee (soe true) guide vs and bring
Where wee may thinke and bee: this by my teare

And my late Primrose tell I charge thee where
Thou settlest thine abode: saye do'st thou looke
Nymph-like into some glibb, and pratling brooke
Hemm'd all about with lillies, or sowest reames
Amidds't the pibbly murmure of her streames?
Speake by thy purling accent, and make knowne
Thou liu'st a swann there, or some Halcion,
Or yf some Meadowe Nymph thou art, declare
Thy Goddhead in some flower, that wee may spare
The plucking to adore it; or if in
None of these shapes thou wilt bee worshipp't, spynne
This to our madd thoughts, thou art become
The Genius to some Cittie great, as Rome
Had hirs, whose   but revealed name
Did overturne the very Fate and frame
Of all her Building, or if like some shield
Or fallne Palladium thou do'st sway and weild
Some farre Republique, wee dare name thee And
With reverence to our wellfare laye an hand
Of holy rigour on thee, and thy Powers
Charme forth, and soe reduce thee wholy ours
But thou art lost, and whether will th'excesse
Of hudwinkt passions lead vs? What Wi'ldernesse
Is this soe vast, soe boundlesse, in whose straye
Wee wind and looke, yett neuer find a waye
That leads vs to a Saboth, thou art lost
O thou art lost for ever, like a frost
Dissolu'd and fledd n'ere to bee found againe
Noe more then broaken blisters, dropps of raine
Rais'd to vndoe. whoe guides vs, where our eies
May on the tombe stone paie the sacrifice
Due to soe iust a greife, and there wee'le lie
Weeping our eies out dropp by dropp and die.

Finis

APPENDIXES

APPENDIX A

LETTERS TO SIR WILLIAM HERRICK FROM CAMBRIDGE

(*All the letters, formerly at Beaumanor, are now in the County Archives at Leicester, except* XIIA, *which is owned by Mr. Arthur A. Houghton, Jr.*, 718 *Fifth Avenue, New York.*)

I

S^{r} syth the quallitie of the Time, and extreamitie of my Brothers occasions forse me; I first show my deutie, and next entreat you to furnish my Brother with 15 pounds which he would needes borrow of me, and because his vrgent occasions stand in so vehement a manner I am willing to pleasure him, still relying vpon your worships fauour, and trusting that I shall not seem offensiue to you nor engender any cause of dislike in my proceeding: I haue writ thus much at the request of my Brother; though indeed I was vnwilling to acquaint you in this busines yet pray S^{r} iustly waigh each thing in equall ballances: I still runn headlong into your worships debt, I trust you will be pleased, though I vnwillingly acquaint you with this. Thus hauing rudely made known the effect of the matter, I with my endles deutie take my leaue: liuing to be comanded by you and yours for euer:

Robert Herick:

[*Endorsed*] To the right wor^{ll} Sr William Hearick at Beaumeanor or els where.

[Receipted by Thomas Heyrick, 1 Oct. 1613.]

II

Cambridg: St Johns:

S^{r}: considering the importunitie of my own affaires and the last testimonie of your so euident Loue makes me to run head long between two ineuitable difficulties, but desirous of equall performance, the shortness of this, shall not hinder the one, nor I trust detract from the other: S^{r} vnderstand that my hart (more feruently then my pen can express) speakes my deuout thanks, and ioye's in no greater thing then this, that it can see some sparkes of your conceald affection: I haue not as hitherto acquainted you with the chardg I liue in, but your self can iudg, by my often (as now at this time) writing for mony, which when I doe, it is for no impertinent expens, but for constraind necessitie:

for be your self the iudg, when aboue twentie pounds will not suffice the house (not reckoning with it commoditie for my self (I meane apparell nor other complements) nor tuition mony nor other sundrie occasions for chardges, this but considered, there is no reasonable soule, but will kindly and indulgently censure of my lyfe and me. Had I but a competent estate to mayntayne my self, to my title, I could presume of as soone atayning to ye end of the efficient cause (my com̃ing as he that hath stronger cause and fortune: S^r^ I know you vnderstand me, and did you but know how disfurnished I came to Cambridg, without bedding (which I yet want) and other necessaries, you would (as I now trust you will) better your thoughts towards me, considering of my forc't expence. S^r^ I entreat you to furnish me with ten pounds this quarter, for the last mony which I receaud came not till the last quarter had almost spent it self, which now constraines me so suddenly to write for more, good S^r^ forbeare to censure me as prodigall for I endeuour rather to strengthen (then debilitate) my feeble and familiar Fortune. I should fill much paper, yf I should follow my passions, but I will break off, only entreating you (yf there be no waye for me to leade a lyfe here, that then you would write me your counsell how I maye learn to liue, in hope that you will some waye effectuate my desires, with all respect of deutie and obseruance I forstop my passage:

euer to be at com̃and and studeous to please

R Hearick:

[*Endorsed*] To his most carefull Vncle Sr Will̄ Hearick dwelling at London in wood-streete

III

From S^t^: Johns in Cambridg

Qui timide rogat,
negare docet?

Are the minds of men immutable? and will they rest in only one opinion without the least perspicuous shewe of chaing? O no they cannot, for Tempora mutantur et nos mutamur in illis: it is an old but yet yoong saying in our age: as times chaing so mens minds are altered: o would † weere seene for then some pittying Planet would with a dr † deaw refreash my withered hopes, and giue a lyfe to that which is † to die, the bodie is preserued by foode, and lyfe by hope, which but wanting either of these conseruers,) faint, feare, fall, freese and die, tis in your power to cure all to infuse by (a profusion a duble lyf into a single bodie) Homo homini Deus) man should be soe and he is commanded so, but fraile, and glasslik man proues brittle in many things How kind Arcisilaus the philosopher was vnto Apelles the painter Plutark in his morals will tell you, which should I heere depaint the length of my letter would hide the sight of my labour, which that it may not, I bridle in my Quill and mildly, and yet I feare to rasly, and to boldly, make knowne and discouer, which modestie would conceale, and this is all, my studie craues but your assistance to furnish hir with bookes wherein she is most desirous to laboure, blame not hir modest boldnes, but suffer the aspertions of your loue to distill vpon hir, and next to Heauen, she will consecrate hir laboures vnto you, and because that Time hath deuoured some yeeres, I am the more importunate in the crauing, suffer not the distance to hinder, that which I know your disposition will not denie, and now is the time, (that florida ætas) which promises frutifulness for hir former barrenness and wisheth all to hope: As euery thing will haue in time an end, so this, which though it would extend it self and ouerflow its bounds, I forcesibly withstand it, wishing this worlds happines to follow and attend you in this lyf, and that with a triumphant crown of glorie, you maye be crowned in the best world to come — —

Robert Hearick

[*Endorsed*] To ye viry worshipf† his Vncle Sr Wi† Hearicke dwelling at London in woodstreete These

IV

Cambridg.

Sr your prosperitie desired and the good success of your issue, I pronounce my deutie and wish some felicitie to my self (as all other creatures do). I entreat you (as heretofore) so now to paye to Mr Adrian Marius bookseller in the black fryers the some of tenn pounds who hath payd the same some at Cambridg: I cannot auert the expence for want of primarie consideration, be you but pleasd and I shall iustifie the expectation (which I trust is religious) of all men. My prayers begin at home but end at you there obiect, bless me with your countenance and I shall liue triumphant and my weake hopes will receaue vigour yf you reflect vpon † I am all youres and completly yours for euer— obsequious

Robin Hearick

[*Endorsed*] To the right worll his louing vncle Sr William Hearick dwelling at London in great Wood-street ths.
[Receipted by Robert Martine for Adrian Marius, 24 Jan. 1615.]

V

Cambridge

Before you vnceald my letter (right worll) it cannot be doubted but you had perfect knowledg of the essence of my writing, before you reade it, for custome hath made you expect in my playne songe (mitte pecuniam) that beeing the, causa sine quâ non; or the forme that giues lyfe and beeing to each matter; I delight not to draw your imagination to inextricable perplexities, or knit vp my sence in indissoluable

knotts, but neede no other exposition but the literall sence, which is t
entreat you to paye to Mr Adrian Morice the some of tenn pounds a
customarily, and to take a note of his hand for the receit. which I desir
may be effected brefly, because the circumstance of the time must b
respected. I perceaue I must crie with the afflicted (vsquequo vsquequ
Domine, yet I haue confidence that I liue in your memorie, howsoeue
Time brings not the thing hope't for to its iust maturity, but m
beleef is stronge and I do establish my hopes on rocks and feare n
quick sands. be you my forme assistant and good effects (produce
from virtuous causes) follow. so shall my wishes pace with yours, fo
the suplement of your owne happiness and the perfection of your own
posterity.

Euer to be commanded
R Hearick

to paye to Mr Blunt book seller in Paules church yarde the som
aboue named:

postscriptũ.

[Receipted by Ed. Blunt, 13 Jan. 1616.]

VI

Chambridge

Because my commencment is at hand (worthie Sir) I am compeld t
write though it be with a violent reluctation; for what hermonie ca
be effected when there is diuision twixt the hart and hand; want an
chardge admit no sympathie because they are of diffring natures; no
conuertibles. yet Volens, nolens, it must be done, and as heretofore s
now I desire your worship to paye to this bearer mr Hotchkin, the dev
of tenn pounds for my vse at Chambridge. I haue runn thorough th
most of the expense which is not much but in respect of disabilitie
yf it may please you to remember me like a trew Mæcenas, I shall glor
in that my Fate hath raysed me vp a Frend to share in my passions
multorum manibus grande leuatur onus many hands make light worke
your healp can make my burden light, I attend your pleasure and as
hope such wilbe my hap. I haue fayth in the goodness of your Nature
attending with patience the complement and consummation of m
hopes.
Bis dat qui cito dat.

Euer obseruant to your benignan
fauours R Hearick.

[*Endorsed*] To the right worll his loving vncle Sr William Hearic
dwelling at London in great woodstreet Ths

[Receipted by John Hotchkin, 20 Feb. 1616.]

VII

Camb†

S^{r} that which makes my letter to be abortiue and borne before maturitie, is and hath been my commencment, which I haue now ouergonn though I confess with many a throe and pinches of the purse, but it was necessarie and the prize was worthie the hazarde which makes me less sensible of the expence by reason of a titular prerogatiue. et bonum est prodire in bono: the essence of my writing is (as heretofore) to entreat you to paye for my vse to m^{r}. Arthour Johnson bookseller in Paules church yard the ordinarie sume of tenn pounds and that with as much sceleritie you maye, though I could wish chardges had leaden wings and Tortice feete to come vpon me; sed votis puerilibus opto; S^{r} I fix my hopes on Time and you, still gazing for an happie flight of birdes, and the refreshing blast of a second winde, doubtfull as yet of either Fortuens I liue hoarding vp prouision against the assault of either. Thus I salute your Vertues—.

Hopefull R Hearick

[*Endorsed*] To the right wor^{ll}: his louing vncle Sr William Hearicke dwelling at London in Greate Woodstreet giue this,

[Receipted for Arthur Johnson, 11 April 1617.]

VIII

Health from Heauen
Chambridg

S^{r} I haue long since expected your return, in that your long absence hath made me want that, which your presence could haue remedied, (I trust you are not ignorant what my meaning is) may it therefore please you to send me 10^{li} for my ocasions require so much, and the long time that your worship hath been absent from London hath compelled me to runn somewhat deepe into my Tailours debt: I entreat your Worship to send me a part of my stipend, with all possible sceleritie for want of which so necessarie helpe, cares greatly posses me, and force me contrarie to my will, in some sort to neglect my study, whereas yf you would be pleased to furnish me with so much, that I might keepe before hand with my Tutor, I doubt not but with quicker dispatch to attaine to what I ayme: Thus trusting that you will in some sort be mindfull of me in sending me that which I haue writ for, with my eternall deutie to your self for euer, togeither with my Ladie—I finish.

For euer readie to be com̄anded during mortallitie
Robert Hearick

I entrate your worship to furnish me with so much as will serue me till the natiuitie:—

[*Endorsed*] To the right wor^{ll} his carefull vncle Sr William Hearick these be delired at his house in London.

IX

From Cambridg

S^{r}; I am loath, yet ꝑforce I must, beeing ouerruled by necessitie (trouble you) I haue before the birth of this letter sent others, which peraduenture haue been stayed by infortunitie, but I trust this will manifest it self: let it not seeme offensiue though I exceede a little in length, for your worships long beeing in the Cuntrie, hath constrained me contrarie to my will to become a debter to my instructer wherfore let me entreat your worship to be mindfull of me, and that this weeke I may receaue it, for my extreames be such that vnless I obtaine what now I desire, I shalbe constrained to make a iourney to London to satisfie the mind of my Tutour, good S^{r} consider this and redress it, and I shall for euer in deutie show my self most abundantly thankfull. I trust this little will suffice to explain my great want, and I hope you will in some sorte bee carefull for my credit, which wilbe weak except I here from your worship this weeke. I will not extend two farr, but with my deutie to you and my Ladie I for this time cease:

beeing euer obsequious to both:
Robert Hearick.

[*Endorsed*] To the Right worshipfull his louing vncle Sr Williã Hearick dwelling at London in g[r]eate woodstreet giue this.

X

Chambridge.

Sr

Though my seruice be late, yet better thus then neuer, it is in you to pardon what I haue so long neglected, and I beleeue you will, I will come speedily and personally to attend you at London, and bring your bond along; to which end (necessitie constrayning me) I entreate you out of my litle possession to deliuer to this bearer the customarye 10^{li}. without which I cannot create my ioyrney; I vnderstand it is troublesome to you for the quarterly dispatch and I am honestly sorrowfull for your disease, pardon me and mayntayne some good opinion of me, that what I haue lost heretofore in your estimation, time and my endeuours may redeeme it trusting to which I offer vp to them, and to your self the sacrifice of my vowes.

Robert Hearicke.

[*Endorsed*] To his louinge Vncle Sr William Hearicke dwellinge at Westminster this del: del.

[Receipted 9 July.]

XI

from St Johns in Cambridg:

Sr I presume againe to present an other Embassador, who in the best eloquence that was taught him, aboundly thanks you for the larg extent of your fauor and kindness, which though present time denies to mak any ostentation of desert, yet future † crownes the expectation of the hopefull; and because the vrgent extreamite and vnexpected occasion of chamber roome instigats me to such importunate demands, I am bold to entreat you that the mony might this week be sent me, for necessitie feruently requires it and I am sorrie to be the subiect of so great a molestation to your worship, but trusting on your patience, I am bold to saye that generous minds still haue the best contentment, and willingly healp where there is an euidencie of want: Thus hoping to triumph in the victorie of my wishes, by being not frustrated in my expectatiõ I tak my leaue, and eternally thank you; liuing to be comanded by you and yours to the end of mortalitie:

euer most—obsequious
Robert Hearick

Be it known to all) that I Robert Hearick fellow Commoner of St Johns colledg in Cambridg, acknowledg my self to stand indebited vnto my vncle Sr Will Hearick of London † the some of tenn pounds, for so much receaued of him, to be repayde vnto him, a all times I saye receaued tenn pounds by me Robert Hearick

I hope this sufficient for the acknowledgment of the aboue borrowed ome: . . .

Endorsed] To the right Worll his Vncle Sr Will Hearicke dwelling at London in great Wood-streete giue this.

Receipted by William Peirson for Sir William Herrick, 21 June.]

XII

Cambridg: 11th of October.

r my deutie remembred to your self and La: the cause essentiall is this: That I would entreat you to paye to this bringer to Mr Adrian Marius book seller in the black friers the some of xli: the which my Tutor hath receaued, to be payde at London I haue business that drawes me from prolixitie, and I craue pardon for this rudeness, still xpecting the sun-shine of your fauour and the daye of happiness. end with my prayers for your preseruation. and health the best terrestriall good. Long lyf and the aspertions of Heauen fall vpon you

Yours euer obsequious
R. Hearick.

Endorsed] To the right worll his louing vncle Sr William Hearick welling at London in great woodstreet.

XIIA

Cambridg St Johns

Sr the first place testifies my deutie the second only reiterats the forme letter, of which (as I may iustly wonder) I heard no answeare, nethe concerning the payment or receat of the letter (It is best knowne to your self) Upon which ignorance I haue sent this oratour, entreating you to paye to mr Adrian marius bookseller of the black fryers the some of 10li from whome so soone as it is payd I shall receaue a dew acknowledgment: I shall not need to amplyfy my sense for this warrant sufficiencie. I expect your countenance and your furtherance to my well beeing who hath power to command my seruice to eternitie Heauen be your guide to direct you to pfection which is the end o mans endeuour:

Robin Hearick
obliged to your
Virtue eternally:

I expect an answeare from mr Adrian concerning the recipt:

XIII

After my abundant thanks for your last great loue (worthie sir) prou of your fauoure and kindness shewne by my Ladie to my vnworthi self) thus I laye open my self; that for, as much as my continuanc will not long consist in the spheare where I now moue I make know my thoughts and modestly craue your counsell whether it were bette for me to direct my study towards the lawe or not, which yf I shoul (as it will not be impertinent) I can with facilitie laboure my self int another colledg appointed for the like end and studyes, where I assur my self the charge will not be so great as where I now exist; I make bol freely to acquaint you with my thoughts and I entreat you to answear me, this beeing most which checks me that my time (I trust) beein short) it maye be to a lesser end and smaller purpose; but that shalb as you shall lend direction, nothing now remaines but my perfec thankfullness, and remembrance of your hopefull promises which whe Heauen working with you shall bring them to performance I sha triumph in the victorie of my wishes, till when my prayers shall in uocate heauen to powre vpon you and your posteritie the vtmost c all essentiall happiness:

Yours euer seruicabl
R Hearick.

XIV

Trinitie Hall: Cam

Sr) the confidence I haue of your, both virtuous, and generous disposi tion, makes me (though with some honest reluctation) the seldome to solicite you, for I haue so incorporated beleef into me, that I canno chuse, but perswade my self that (though absent) I stand imprinted in your memorie; and the remembrance of my last beeing at London serud for an earnest motiue (which I trust liues yet vnperisht) to the effectuating of my desire, which is not, but in modesty ambitious, and consequently virtuous: but where freeness is euident there needs no feere for forwardness, and I doubt not (because fayth giues boldness) but that Heauen togeither with your self, will bring my ebbing estate, to an indifferent tyde; meane while I hope: I haue (as I presume you know) changd my colledg, for one, where the quantie of expence wilbe shortned, by reason of the priuacie of the house, where I purpose to liue recluce, till Time contract me to some other calling, striuing now with my self (retayning vpright thoughts) both sparingly to liue, thereby to shun the current of expence. this is my desire (which I entreat maye be ꝑformd) that Mr Adrian Marius book seller of the black fryers maye be payd ten pounds as heretofore and to take his acquittance, trusting whereto, Ile terminate your sight, and end; hoping to see your dayes many, and good, and prosperitie to crown your self and issue.

Euer seruiceable to your Virtues
R Hearick.

APPENDIX B

VARIANT VERSIONS OF THREE POEMS

1. *A Description of his Dyet.* This appears, expanded, in *Hesperides* as *Oberons Feast* (see p. 119). It occurs in 'A Description Of the King and Queene of *Fayries*, their habit, fare, their abode, pompe, and state. Beeing very delightfull to the sense, and full of mirth . . .' 1635. The copy of this in the Bodleian Library is said to be unique, but in the catalogue of *English Poetry to 1700* issued by the Rosenbach Company in 1941 item 408*a* appears to be the same work with date 1634. Herrick's verses are preceded (pp. 1–3) by 'A Description of the Kin[g] of *Fayries* Clothes, brought to hi[m] on New-yeares day in the morning, 1626. by his Queenes Chamber-maids'. This is by Sir Simeon Steward and an expanded version of it is in MS. Ashmole 38, pp. 99–100: 'King Oberons Apparell'. Herrick's verses are on pp. 4–5 (misprinted 6) as follows:

A Description of his Dyet.

Now they the Elves within a trice,
Prepar'd a feast lesse great than nice.
Where you may imagine first,
The Elves prepare to quench his thirst,
In pure seed Pearle of Infant dew
Brought and sweetned with a blew
And pregnant Violet; which done,
His killing eies begin to runne
Quite ore the table, where hee spyes
The hornes of water'd Butter-flies.
Of which he eats, but with a little
Neat coole allay of Cuckows spittle.
Next this the red cap worme thats shut
Within the concave of a nut.
Moles eyes he tastes, then Adders eares;
To these for sauce the slaine stagges teares
A bloted earewig, and the pith
Of sugred rush he glads him with.
Then he takes a little Mothe,
Late fatted in a scarlet cloth,
A Spinners ham, the beards of mice,
Nits carbonado'd, a device
Before unknowne; the blood of fleas
Which gave his Elveships stomacke ease.

8 killing] *read* kitling

The unctious dew tops of a Snaile,
The broake heart of a Nightingale,
Orecome in musicke, with the sagge
And well bestrowted Bees sweet bagge.
Conserves of Atomes, and the mites,
The silke wormes sperme, and the delights
Of all that ever yet hath blest
Fayrie land: so ends his feast.

These verses are followed by another set entitled 'The Fairies Fegaries', but there is nothing to connect them with Herrick except that they contain some lines about the diet resembling his:

The tongues of Nightingales,
With unctious iuyce of Snailes,
. . . .
. . . .
. . . . the beards of mice
. . . .

2. *An Epithalamium*. From MS. Harl. 6918, ff. 43^{v}–47. Compare *An Epithalamie to Sir* Thomas Southwell *and his Ladie*, pp. 53–58 above. The version in this Harleian MS. is also in Harvard MS. Eng. 626 F, f. 23, with the slight variants noted.

An Epithalamium:

NOW, now's the time soe oft by truth
promised should come to crowne your youth;
then faire ones doe not wrong
your Joyes by staying long;
or let your fires goe out
by lingring still in doubt
love not admitts delay,
then haste and come away,
night with all her children starres
waite to light you to the warres:

Faire virgin enter Cupids field
and though you doe resist, yet yeeld:
It is noe shame at all
for you to take the fall,
When thousands like to you
could nere the foyle eschew,
nor in their strict defence
depart unconquerd hence:
then faire Maide now adventer
Since Time and Loue bidds enter:

25 dew tops] *read* dewlops   19 Maide *Hv*: maides *Hari.*

Is it your fault, that these soe holy
Bridall Rites goe on soe slowly?
or is it that you dread
the losse of maydenhead?
Know virgin you will most
love it when it is lost;
then it noe longer keepe
Least issue lye asleepe;
Come, come Hymen, Hymen guide
to the bedd the bashfull Bride:

These pretious pearly purling teares
but spring from Ceremonious feares,
and tis but natiue shame
that hides the louing flame;
Loues fire, faire maide, will waste
all bashfullnesse at last,
then trust that night will couer
what the Rosy Cheekes discouer:

Night now hath watcht her selfe halfe blinde
yet not a maydenhead resigned;
tis strange yee will not trye
Loues sacred mistery;
might yon full moone the sweetes
haue, promis'd to your sheetes
Shee soone would leaue her spheare
to be admitted there;
Then away faire virgin come,
haste least Luna take your roome:

Behold the Bridegroome in the porch
Expects you with his pinie Torch,
and Hymens Taper light
tells what is spent of night;
fiue Boyes with torches five,
that shew the wombe shall thriue,
their golden flames advance,
and tell all prosperous Chance,
still shall Crowne the happy life
of the Goodman, and the wife:

Now forward then your Rosy feete
to make each thing you touch turne sweete;
and where your shooe you sett
there spring a Violet;

59 Now forward] Moue forward *Hv*

Let all the Balmy meades
Smell, where your soft foote treades,
make Earth as flourishing,
as in the painted spring,
when Zephirus, and warme May
pranke the fields in sweete arraye:

Now on devoutly, make noe stay
for domiduca leades the way,
and Genius that attends
the bedd for lucky ends;
with Juno goe thy howers
And Graces scattering flowers,
while Boyes with soft tunes singe
Hymen, oh Hymen bringe,
bring oh Hymen, bringe the Bride,
or the winged Boy will Chide:

See, see the yellow Vayle at last
ore her fragrant Cheeke is cast,
now seemes she to expresse
a bashfull willingnesse,
and hath a will thereto
without a minde to doe,
then softly leade her on
with wise suspition,
wise matrons say a measure
of it, will sweeten pleasure:

You, you that bee her nearest Kinne
ore the Threshold force her in,
But to avert the worst
let her, her fillets first
knitt to the post, this poynt
remembering to annoynt
the last, for tis a Charme
strong against future harme;
and poyson kills, the which
there was hidden by the witch:

Now quickly Venus leade them to it,
and then instruct them how to doe it
first let them meete with kisses,
then shew them other blisses;

72 lucky] luckier *Hv* 73 thy howers] the howres *Hv* 79 See, see] See the *Hv* 80 Cheeke] cheekes *Hv* 83 hath] ha's *Hv* 97 kills] kill *Hv*

fullnesse of pleasure giue and Joy,
may Comfort neuer cloye
Thou mistrisse of these games
double in them their flames;
oh bidd thou them undresse,
and tell them nakednesse,
suits thy sports, bidd them venter
for Loue, Time, place bids enter:

Noe fatall owle the Bedsted keepes
with direfull note to fright your sleepes,
nor furies full of dread
made this your Bridall bedd,
nor with their Brands doe watch
the lights away to snatch;
but all good omen there
doth at the bedd appeare;
Juno here, aloofe doth stand
soft sleepe with his Charming wand:

Oh now behold the longing Couch
that nere yet felt a virgins touch,
feeles in it selfe a fire,
and tickled with desire,
pants with its downy breast
as with a heart possest;
shrugging as if it moued
with passions as it loued,
Then undoe your selues and venter
for the dimpling bedd bidds enter:

Virgins weepe not, twill come when
as she, soe you'll be ripe for men;
then grieue her not with saying
she must noe more a maying;
or by her dreame divine
who'll be her valentine,
or kisse a Rose budd ouer,
And wish it were her Louer;
But kisse her, and embrace her,
and twixt the soft sheets place her:

Now shutt the doores, the husband putts
the eager boyes to gather nutts,
and now both Loue and Time
to their full heigth doe climbe,

115 Brands doe watch] Brands watch *Hv* 120 with his Charming] charming with his *Hv*

giue them both actiue heate,
with moisture good and neate,
and organs for encrease,
to keepe and to release,
that may the honourd stemme
Circle with a diadem:

Oh Venus thou to whom the Zone
of virgins is soe truly knowne,
Cherish, and blesse this deede,
and with a mellow speede,
bring to the parents Joy,
their first fruite bee a Boy
soe sprightfull, that the Earth
may swell with such a birth;
and her time of reckoning come
thou Lucina helpe the wombe:

Not a slumber, much more shunne
a sleepe, untill the act be done;
not the least breath expire
but let it urge desire;
flye slowly, slowly howers
now while their lipps make flowers;
Each kisse in its warme Close
smells like a damaske Rose,
or like that pretious Gumme
doth from Panchaia come;
soules, and breaths, and lipps excite
sweetes, to rouze up appetite:

On you minuts, howers, dayes, moneths, yeares
dropp the full blessing of the spheares,
what good to man, and wife
to build an happy life
benignant heauen allowes
follow your prayers and vowes;
may fortunes Lilly hand
open at your command:

Oh Venus thou to whom is knowne
the best way how to loose the Zone
of virgins; tell the maide
she neede not be afraid;
and teach the youth to apply
close kisses if she crye;

173 On you] On your *Hv*

and Charge hee not forbeares
although shee wooe with teares
Then tell them now they must adventer
while yet Time and Loue bidds enter:

May bounteous fates your spindle full-
fill, and winde up with whiter wooll;
let them not cutt the thread
of life, untill you bidd;
Let Death yet come at last
with slow, not desperate haste,
But when yee both can say
fate wee will now away;
Bee yee to the Barne then borne
Two, like two ripe shocks of Corne.

Rob: Herrick:

3. *A dialogue.* From a manuscript in the Rosenbach Foundation Library; see Introduction, p. xxxiv. Compare *A Pastorall* (85.3).

A dialogue on Prince Charles his birth, betwene 3 sheapherds; Amintas, Martillo, Ambo.

Amint: Good day Martillo; Mar: And to you noe lesse
Amb: And crownes of wheate fall one our shepherdesse
Mar: And mirthfull pipes to you, but say what newes
Stirs in our sheepewalkes? Amar: None saue that mine ewes
Wethers, lambs, & kids are well
I nothinge else can tell.
Amin: Or that this day Menalcas makes a feast
To his sheepeshearers. Mar: Tut these are the least
Come deere Aminta'nd faire Amarillis
Rest a while here one thy banke of lillyes
And lend an eare to a report
The country ha's; Amb: from whence? Mar: the Court
Two dayes before the shuttinge vp of May
When whitest woole beclad the day
To Englands joy a Prince was borne
Soft as the childhood of the morne
Amb: Pan pipe to him, & bleates of lambs and sheepe
Lett Lullaby the pretty Prince asleepe
Mar: And that his birth might be more singular
At noone of day appear'd a starr

200 Two, like] Twoe, like *Hv* Two like, *H*

Bright as the wisemens torch that lighted them
To Gods babe borne at Bethleem
Amar: And ist a sinne if we
Should goe this child to see
Mar: Not soe, not soe, but if soe bee itt proue
Almost a fault, tis but a fault of loue;
Amin: Yea but martillo I haue heard itt told
Those learned men brought incense, mirrh & gold
And spices sweet
And laid them downe att there kings feet
Mart: Tis true Amar, tis true. Omnes. And each of vs will bring
Vnto our bloominge kinge
A neat, though not soe great an offeringe.

Offerings.

Amint: A garland for my gift shall be
Of flowers nere suckt by theevinge bee
And all most sweet, yett all less sweet then hee
Amar: And I will lay before his view
Leaues droppinge downe the hony dew
Mar: And I a sheepehooke will bestow
To make his little kingship know
As hees a Prince, hees sheapheard too.

Chorus.

Come letts make hast & trimly letts be drest
And quickly giue; the swiftest grace is best
And when before him wee haue laid our treasure
Weele blesse his face, then back to country pleasure R.H

ADDITIONAL FOOTNOTES

(Placed here because of the need to preserve the pagination of 1915 down to p. 419.)

THE following poems have variants recorded in the Critical Notes or in Appendix B: 10. 5, 11. 1, 16. 2, 24. 1, 26. 3, 43. 1, 46. 2, 49. 2, 53. 2, 85. 3, 87. 2, 100. 3, 103. 1, 103. 3, 137. 2, 145. 2, 154. 1, 155. 4, 191. 2, 195. 5, 212. 2 and 3, 219. 2, 226. 1, 6, and 7, 232. 2, 238. 5, 249. 4, 255. 4, 281. 1, 331. 6, 334. 4, 342. 2.

The following notes refer to the printed text of 1648: 46. 2. 10 away] amay *48*　　67. 1. 6 Oile *DK1 (? corrected by hand)*: Oiie *rest*　　69, l. 50 Priest] Ptiest *48*　　79. 1. 2 up, or] (*?*) upon　　86, l. 10 Lillies.] *stop uncertain in 48, (?) broken comma*　　87. 2. 2 madd *MSS.*: made *48*　　110. 2. 2 mouth] *followed by space, as for comma 48*　　115, l. 104 *Cherubin MSS.*: *Cherubim 48*　　115, l. 113 too too *MSS.*: two too *48*　　115, l. 117 you *MSS.*: it *48*　　126. 3. 8 the] tke *48*　　126. 3. 14 That's *ed.*: That *48 (see Commentary)*　　137. 3. 9 who ever] whoever *48*　　148, l. 114 *sweat.*] *sweat 48*　　155. 4. 2 yoke free] yoke-free *48*　　165. 1. 17 well know] we'l know *48*: well knowne *MSS.*　　Guard] Guard. *some MSS.*　　172. 1. 1 Fate *ed.*: Fates *48*　　172. 3 (*heading*) Westmorland.] Westmorland.. *48*　　175, l. 45 doth] *Moorman observes that 'some copies' of 48 read* 'doth still' *but no such copy has been located*　　182. 1 (*heading*) *Rewards ed.*: *Reward (with space) 48*　　182. 3 (*heading*) Clipsebie] Clisebie *48 (see* 161. 3)　　183. 1. 4 here's *ed.*: her's *48*　　183. 2 (*heading*) Herrick,] Herrick,, *48*　　191. 5 (*heading*) *Fortune*] (*?*) *Fortunes*　　192. 1. 36 Shephardling] Sheparling *48*　　192. 1. 38 there).] there) *48*　　197. 3. 2 Inheritance,] Inheritance. *48*　　199. 1. 3 Lip, *ed.*: Lip; *48*　　203. 3. 8 scorcht] scorctht *48*　　204. 4. 7 wooe,] *comma raised and turned 48*　　206, l. 28 *Iliades F G Hn K2 S U*: *Iliads rest*　　206, l. 46 from *MSS.*: for *48*　　207, l. 61 be our *ed.*: he one *48 (see Commentary)*　　213. 4. 2 Tyrannie.] Tyrannie, *48*　　218. 6. 5 sit] fit (*doubtful*) *48*　　219. 1. 8 residence.] residence, *48*　　229. 1. 5 Sainted.] *stop uncertain 48*　　237. 3 (*heading*) *strike*] (*?*) *strikes*　　243. 1. 31 1] 4 *48*　　263. 1. 15–16] *The semicolon is at the end of* 15 *in 48*　　263. 2. 4 it *ed.*: it. *48*　　274. 4. 1 Beautie's] Beauti's *48*　　285. 2. 4 Till] Tiil *48*　　288. 5. 6 thee.] thee *48*　　290. 2. 7 *tickle,*] *full stop or broken comma 48*　　295. 3. 11 burn'd] burn *48*　　296. 1 (*heading*) *and* l. 1 Burr] *In F erased in ink and* Job *substituted*　　315. 3. 2 one] (*?*) our (*see Commentary*)　　322. 3. 11 fold] folrd *48*　　324. 1. 3 fly] fiy *48*　　329. 2. 5 Girles, *ed.*: Girles *48*　　331. 8. 2 these.] these, *48*　　335. 2. 10 Kingdoms fal] Kingdom fals *P*　　345. 1. 29 pittie.] (*?*) pittie,　　374, l. 40 clothing.] clothing: *48*　　375, l. 81 9.] *om. 48*

CRITICAL NOTES

(*Obvious scribal errors in manuscripts are, as a rule, not recorded.*)

10. 5. The Wounded Heart. In Add. MS. 33998, f. 61^{v}, headed To his Mistresse 2 in't] in it *A* 5 bleed] shed *A* 7 Yet] But *A* 9 This] That *A* 11 ne'r will] will not *A*

11. 1. No Loathsomnesse in love. In *MC*, p. 157, headed A SONG. 10 *Tongue* wag] tongue-way *MC* 13 hath] has *MC*

16. 2. The Vine. In *GD*, p. 108, headed *A Dream.* 3 Which . . . and] Spreading his branches *GD* 4 Enthrall'd my dainty] To enthrall my prety *GD* 5 long small] Cedry *GD* 9–12 About . . . my]

Her curious parts I so did twine
With the rich clusters of my Vine,
That my sweet *GD*

14–15 curles . . . hands] curling Branches did so crall, That hands and arms *GD* 16–17 could . . . one] lay and could not stir, But yield her self my *GD*

19. 1. Cherry-pit. In *GD*, p. 108 and *WR*(1663), f. Cc4^{v} 1 *Julia*] Lucia *GD* *Julia* and I] Nicholas and Nell *WR* 3 She threw; I cast] They both did throw *WR* 4 I] He *WR* and she] she got *GD*

24. 1. Of Love. In *MC*, p. 157, headed A SONNET.

26. 3. The Cheat of Cupid. In H. Lawes autograph MS., p. 138. 5 beats] knocks *HL* 13 pittifull] pitty'ng him *HL* 14 soon] streight *HL* 21 Chimney's] Chimney *HL* 28 Said] Quoth *HL* 29 Forthwith] Then streight *HL* 36 Ile . . . heart] but thy poore Hart's *HL*

28. 3. Upon Love. In *WR* (1663), f. Dd1; not in stanzas. 3 signifie] tell me that *WR* 7 burnt sho'd be] See footnote

31. 2. The Bag of the Bee. In *P52*, *P53*, *L55*, *P59*, and *P69*; MS. Don. c. 57, f. 95^{v}; H. Lawes autograph MS., p. 145; *WR* (1663), f. Dd5^{v}; and *Ac71*. Headings: *A Strife betwixt two* Cupids, *reconciled. P59 The Bag of a Bee. WR* Song 119 *Ac71* 1 About] To have *WR* 3 prize] pray *Don* 7 thence from each] then from each *Don* from them each *WR* 8 rods of Mirtle] myrtle rods she *WR* 9 done] love *P52* 10 When] and *P L Don HL Ac71* 11 wip'd] dry'd *P L Don HL Ac71*

34. 3. A Country life. In MS. Ashmole 38, p. 90 and Huntington MS. (*HM*) 198, p. 12. Headings: In praise of the Country Life *Ash* M^{r}: Herricks Country Life *HM* 3 Could'st] Canst *Ash HM* for] wth *Ash* 7 to know] how to knowe *Ash* 10 lesse to live, then] not to live, but *Ash HM* 12 Led] Lett *Ash* 17 And] To *Ash HM*

18 In] And *Ash* 19 those] such *Ash HM* 22 plague] Mange *Ash HM* 23 thee] *om. HM* warie] sparing *Ash HM* 24 then Land] the sand *Ash* then Sand *HM* 25 cheap] weake *Ash HM* 26 coole] quench *Ash HM* 27–30] replaced in *Ash* and *HM* by two lines:

The first is Naturs end: this doth imparte
Least thankes to Nature, most to Art

31 most . . . country] next Creates thy happye *Ash HM* 40 those] the *HM* After 42 *Ash* and *HM* insert:

And in thy sence, her Chaster thoughtes Commend
not halfe so much the Act, as end

43 damaskt] damaske *Ash HM* peebly] Crawling *Ash HM* 49 ye . . . by] you . . . w^th^ *Ash* 50 Woo'd]woe *HM* 51 While] whilst *HM* comes] vowes *Ash HM* 52 rav'ning wolves] Rau'nous Wolfe *Ash* rauenous wolues *HM* fleecie] wolly *Ash HM* 55 rest] selfe *Ash* 57 Warnes] Crowes *Ash HM* dost] doth *Ash* to *HM* 60 spirting] Crackling *Ash HM* 61 this sentence] thus *Ash* this *HM* 62 *Jove*] God *Ash HM* 65 has] hath *Ash HM* 66 Western] farthest *Ash HM* 67 fears] feare *Ash HM* fly] hye *Ash HM* 69 securest] securer *Ash HM* 70 that there be] there are *Ash* that theere are *HM* 71 while thy whiter] when thy better *Ash HM* 72 sees these] see'st those *Ash HM* 79 Seeing] Veiwing *Ash HM* those] the *HM* 80 those fine Shades] their shadowes *Ash HM* 81 taking small] borrowing *Ash HM* 83 thine] thy *Ash HM* deafe] seal'd *Ash HM* 85 tell . . . Kings] tells the [of *HM*] states of Courtes of kinges *Ash HM* 86 And] thow *HM* beleeve] beleu'st *Ash HM* 87 these truths, thy] those states the [thy *HM*] *Ash HM* 89 too-] twice *HM* 90 rules . . . at] is Vicgerent, att the *Ash HM* 91 pious] Godly *Ash HM* 92 had, and mov'd] had moved In *Ash* After 92 *Ash* and *HM* insert

Nor [no, *HM*] knowe thy happye, and vn-enuey'de state
  Owes more to *Vertue* then too *Fate*
Or [And *HM*] *Fortune* too, for what the first secures
  That as her selfe, or Heauen indures
The two last fayle, and by experience make
  knowne, [what] they giue againe, they take

93 liv'st fearlesse] not fearest them *Ash HM* 95 thoughts] hopes *Ash* prepar'd] (strong built) *HM Ash* 96 To take her by the] for to salute her *Ash HM* 97 the first] first *Ash* 99 surly] sturdye *Ash HM* 100 Growes still] still growes *Ash HM* 101 bold] brave *Ash HM* unmov'd] immou'd *HM* 104 comes] come *Ash HM* 105 are] now are *Ash* 106 *Larr*] fare *Ash HM* 109 keep'st . . . mouth] keepes . . . tooth *Ash HM* 111 fare] Cheer *Ash HM* 112 rare] dearr *Ash HM* 113 Col-

worts . . . eate] Colewort, mynte & date [eate *HM*] *Ash HM* 114 sowre] such *HM* as] is *Ash* 115 While] whilst *HM* makes thy] bids my *Ash* bids thy *HM* 116 After this line *Ash* and *HM* insert

Canst drinke in Earthen Cupps, w^{c}h ne're Contayne
Cold Hemlocke, or the Libbards bane

117 Nor . . . keep'st] nor doest thow kepe *HM* that] fitt *Ash* 119 sho'd sinne] since sins *HM* 120 see't] see *Ash* 122 thy] the *Ash HM* 123 And the brisk] [And *HM*] The Bristle *Ash HM* feast] feed *Ash* 126 a] the *HM* 128 *make*] build *Ash HM* 132 shun] flye *Ash HM* 133 find] knowe *Ash HM* 135 close . . . true] neate, firme Close, & true *Ash HM* 139 to . . . selves] doe disporte you^{r} [thy *HM*] thoughtes *Ash HM* 142 one] th'one *HM* 144 one Grave] and graue *HM* 145 when . . . live] then lett Faith soe prompt you^{r} liues *Ash HM* ye] you *HM* 146 Nor feare, or] Not feare, nor *Ash HM* After this line *Ash* adds: finis Mr Robt Hericke

39. 3. A Lyrick to Mirth. In *GD*, p. 25. 4 *Dollies*] lasses *GD* 13 *Gotiere*] *Coteire GD*

42. 1. Leanders Obsequies. In H. Lawes autograph MS., p. 322; *L53*, headed *Leander* Drownd; *Ac71* (*Song* 47); and *WD* (*Song* 241). 5–6] *om. HL L53 Ac71 WD* 8 sobbing] sighing *HL L53 Ac71 WD* 9 Sea] Fate *L53 Ac71 WD* 12 But that] had not *HL L53 Ac71 WD*

43. 1. The Teare sent to her from Stanes. In *WR*, f. S6, headed *A Teare sent his Mistresse*

45. 1. His fare-well to Sack. In Add. MS. 33998, f. 5; MS. Sloane 1446, f. 17^{v}; MS. Firth e. 4, p. 18; MS. Rawl. poet. 160, f. 165; MSS. Folger 1. 21, f. 56 and Folger 452. 1, p. 23; Huntington MS. 198, p. 16; and *WR* (1645), f. Z8^{v}. Headings: Herricks Farewell to Sacke *A33* The farewell to sacke *S14* Mr Hearick his farwell to Sacke *F* M^{r}: Herick his farewell to Sacke *R* M^{r}: Rob: Herricks Farwell to Sacke *Fol1* Herrick's farewell to Sacke *Fol4* M^{r}: Herricks farwell to Sacke *HM* *A Farewell to Sack. WR* 1 thou] the *A33 R Fol4 HM* Thing] lacuna in *F* knowne, so] true and *WR* 2 blood to life] life to th' bloud *A33* blood to'th'life *R* to] of *S14* and] to *HM* spirit:] spirit, and *WR* to life . . . Neare] as ye life & spirits were *Fol4* 3 man] or *A33 WR* & *F* 4 to the] to a *A33* soule to] soule to the *F Fol4 WR* soule and *Fol1* 5 To] vnto *A33* 6 resigning, yet resisting] resisting, yet resigning *A33 S14 R Fol1 Fol4 HM* yet chast, and undefiled *WR* 7–8] *om. WR* 7 Virgins] maydens *Fol 4* First-fruits] first fruite *S14 Fol4* 8 Soft . . . lips] sweet speech, sweet [soft *Fol1*] Touch, ye Lipps [lip *Fol4*] *A33 F R Fol1 Fol4 HM* sweet lipps sweete speech, the touch *S14* 9 sweets] such *A33 R Fol1 Fol4 HM* more *F WR* 10 So] More *WR* or] soe *S14 F Fol1 Fol4* more *WR* as] then *WR* wast] wert *S14 WR* once to] unto *Fol4* 11–22] *om. WR* 12 Spirit] spirits *A33 S14 F R Fol4 HM* and Lust;] & lastly *A33* purest] pure A33 purer *F R Fol1 Fol4 HM* warmer *S14* 13 then the] then *A33* Summers] summer *S14* 14 brave;] *om. A33 Fol4* 15 shagg'd] shagg *S14 R Fol4* sad *A33* sage *HM* 16 Fore tell] Foreshew *A33 S14 F R Fol4 HM* fforespeake *Fol1* 17 full] feirce *F* full of *R* a] her *F* 18 Throwing] Spirting *Fol1* about] abroad *A33 S14 R Fol1 Fol4 HM* his] her *F* wild, and active] wild & piercing *A33 F R Fol1 Fol4 HM* calde & peirceing *S14* 19 thou] thou thou *Fol1 F* thee *R* the *HM* above] lov'd *A33 S14 R HM* Nectar] Nature *Fol1* Divinest] diviner *A33 R Fol1 Fol4 HM* diuined *S14* sweete *F* 21 subverts] subiects *A33* 22 of the] of *A33* damn'd] deepe *F* 23 thou, alone] Thou above *F WR* who] wch *S14* Fan] faln *WR* 24–31] *om. S14* 24 Work'st] Works *Fol1* Wisdome, Art] wise Art *HM* 25 rouze] raise *WR* the sacred] the holy *A33 R Fol4 HM WR* this secreet *Fol1* and] to *F* 26 to] can *Fol1* 27 Them] The *F* flashing] striking *A33 F R Fol1 Fol4 HM* stretching *WR* 28 The soule] The souls *WR* Their Soules *F* 29–36] *om. WR* 29 or] nor *R Fol1* 30 if] it *R* 31 *Horace,*] Horace & *Fol1* 32 fire and] mighty *F* 33 thou] yᵉ *A33 R Fol1 HM* 34 Of which] of whose *R HM* All whose *A33* 35 true-pac'd] time past *Fol4* and their] and your *HM* Holy-] sacred *A33 S14 F R Fol1 Fol4 HM* 36 makes] made *A33* make *F R Fol1* worthy] wynne the *Fol1* 37 longer doe I] longer do we *F* doe I longer *WR* 38 eye] eyes *A33 S14 F R Fol1 Fol4 HM* admiration] Adoration *A33 S14 F R Fol1 Fol4 HM* 39 Since] When *F Fol1 WR* enforc'd] forc'd now *F* 40 witching] wished *F* Goe, Away] goe away *A33 S14 F R Fol4 HM WR* 41 But] And *WR* 42 Then . . . goe] Know then, 'tis Nature biddeth thee hence *WR* thee] me *HM* 43 has] hath *A33 S14 F R HM WR* made] forg'd *A33 S14 F R Fol1 Fol4 HM* form'd *WR* a] my *WR* 45 selfe] rule *Fol1* Prethee] I prethee *WR* not smile] draw in *A33 S14 R Fol1 Fol4 HM WR* 45–54] *om. F* After 45 *A33 S14 R Fol1 Fol4 HM WR* insert:

> thy glaring fires, least in yᵉⁱʳ sight yᵉ sin
> Of Idolatry steale vpon me, and
> I turne Apostate to yᵉ strict comand
> Of Nature; bid me now farewell, or smile

Thus A33. There are the following variants: glaring] gazing *WR* fires] eyes *R* in]at *WR* yᵉⁱʳ] thy *Fol1* Of] Of feirce *S14 R Fol1 Fol4 HM WR* steale vpon] shute into *S14 R Fol1 Fol4 HM WR* 46 Or smile] *om. MSS. and WR* inly] mildlie *S14 Fol4* ugly *WR* thy] thy tempting *A33 S14 R Fol1 Fol4 HM WR* 47 denounc'd] pronounc't *WR* thus much] thus must *A33 R HM* must *S14* show] shows *WR* thee] mee *Fol1* 49 freely; and] and wth mayne *A33 S14 R Fol4 HM* boldly, and *WR* 50 espous'd] espouse *A33 S14 R Fol4 HM* while] whilst *Fol1* 51 thee; but not] thee, yet not *A33 S14 R Fol1 Fol4 HM* but yet not *WR* 52 thy] her *S14* 53 inadult'rate] in adulterate *S14 R HM* 54 Hereafter, shall smell] shall smell hereafter *S14 WR* Hereafter] *om. Fol1*

46. 2. Upon Mrs. Eliz: Wheeler &c. In MS. Don. c. 57, f. 94^v (as follows); also in H. Lawes autograph MS., p. 140 and Add. MS. 29396, f. 27^v, with variants from *Don* as shown:

Amarillis by a spring's [springe *A*]
soft & soul melting murmerings [murmuringe *A*]
slept unto whom a redbreast fled
who simply thinking she was dead
to bury her brought Speermint [spearmints *A*] fine
& leaues of sweetest Eglantine
where [when *HL*] placeing them he saw her stirre
at wch amaz'd [affraid *HL A*] he flew from her
unto a Myrtle growing by
where [whence *HL A*] marking from her little [ejther *HL*] eye
a thousand flames of Love to fly
poore Robin redbreast y^n [he *A*] drew nigh
& seeing her not dead but all disleav'd
he chirpt for joy to see himselfe deceivd

49. 2. The Curse. In Add. MSS. 15227, f. 3; 19268, f. 22; 25707, f. 110^v; 30982, f. 42^v; 33234, f. 49; and 33287, f. 2; MSS. Egerton 2421, f. 22^v and 2725, f. 69; MS. Sloane 1446, f. 74^v; MS. Don. c. 57, f. 11 and MS. Mus. b. 1, f. 45. Also in MS. Ashmole 38 twice, pp. 4 and 179 ('*Ash* (1 and 2)'); MS. Folger 1. 21 twice, ff. 46^v and 72 ('*FolA*' and '*FolB*'); MS. Folger 1. 27, p. 107; MS. Folger 1. 8, f. 8^v; Harvard MS. Eng. 626 F, f. 73; Huntington MS. 198, p. 53; and (set by John Blow) in Add. MSS. 19759, 22100, 29397, 30382, and 33235. Account is taken of these last thirteen versions only in so far as they present variants not found in the rest. Headings: Her Answere (sc. to 420. 2) *A19* On hir periur'd sirvant. *A257 E27* The answare. *A30 Fol B* Goe perjur'd Man *A33234* A forsaken Lady that died for loue *E24 S14* An Epitaphe made by A Gentelwoman att her Death, her louer prouing Inconstant *Ash*(2) 1 Goe] Goe goe *Don* thou] you *A309 A33287* if] when *Ash* (1 and 2) ere] doest *A15 Ash*(1) ner *A19* shalt *Ash*(2) 2 To] And *A15* see] view *A309 Don* the] these *Hv* small] sad *Ash*(2) remainders] remainder *A15 A33234 E24 S14 Don* in] of *A33234 E24* mine] my *A15 A25 A33287 E24 E27 Don Mus* Urne] toombe *E24* 3 thou] you *A30382* shalt] wilt *Don* shall *A30382* laugh] *om. A30982* off *E24 S14* Religious] forsaken *Ash* (1 and 2) 4 ask] say *A15*

Where's] where is *A257* colour] colours *A33235* and] or *Don* 5 Of] In *S14* Womans] womens *A15 A19 A257 E27 S14 Don* beauty] beautys *E24 S14* and] or *Don* with hand more perhaps with *A15 A257 A33234 A33287 E27 S14 Don Mus* perhaps what *E24* with hands too *A30982* with hands most *Ash* (1 and 2) 6 Rifle] Wiffle *A30982* Ruffell *Ash* (1 and 2) Hands scatter *A1*… *Don* hands teare *E24* hands, stro'y *S14* hands rifle *A33234 A3328*… Hands ruffle *FolA* hand rifle *A257 E27 Mus* which] that *Ash*(1… Virgins] virgin *E24* 7 Know] Then *Fol. 1. 27* I have] I'v… *A33287 A33234* Furie] pittie *all MSS.* some] the *A3323*… *A33287* same *Harvard* 8 may] might *A33234 A33287* my mine *A15* *E24* adds four lines (indented) as follows:

Reader stay let fall a teare
For much beauty lyeth here;
Thou art if thou sheddest none
As very marble as the stone.

50. 1. The wounded Cupid. In H. Lawes autograph MS., p. 13… 6 Lad] wagge *HL* 8 winged Snake] serpent wing'd *HL* 1… then] & *HL* 12 Wag] Lad *HL* 13 Such a pernicious] so ffeirce a *HL* 14 Come] *om. HL*

50. 2. To Dewes. In Add. MS. 31432, f. 33, headed To the Dewe… 3 so] quite *A* 4 the] my *A* 5 Alas!] for both *A* Oyle] dew *A* 10 coole] ease *A*

53. 2. An Epithalamie. See Appendix B, p. 455, for variant versio… of this poem in MS. Harl. 6918 and in Harvard MS. Eng. 626 F.

60. 4. The cruell Maid. In *WR*, f. S7ᵛ.

62. 1. His misery in a Mistresse. In *WR*, f. T1, with heading: H… Misery.

63. 1. To a Gentlewoman. In *WS*, f. M2ᵛ, *L53*, *WI*, p. 50 (secon… pagination), *P69*, MS. Egerton 2013, f. 16ᵛ, MS. Don. c. 57, f. 28… H. Lawes autograph MS., p. 134, and a manuscript cited but u… specified by W. C. Hazlitt (i, p. 65). Headings: *To his Mistress objecti… his Age. L53, E P69* *Age not to be rejected WI* An old Man to his your… Mrˢ *Hazlitt* 2 dare sweare] believe *all other versions* 4–1… All other versions differ here; that in *L53* follows, with the varian… therefrom:

And night will come, when men will [shall *E*] swear
Time has spilt snow upon your hair: [hath spilt *WS E D*…
hath spitt *Hazlitt*] [on your *WS*]
Then when in your Glass you seek, [see below for *E*]
But find no Rose-bud in your cheek, [Rose buds *WS* roses …
Hazlitt]
No, nor the bed to give the [thee *WS* a *WI*] shew, [Barke to gi…
E bedd (bud *Hazlitt*) at lest to shew *Don Hazlitt*]
Where such a rare [fayre *Hazlitt*] Carnation grew;
And such a smiling Tulip too.

After l. 5 *E* proceeds:

And when though longe it come to passe,
that you shall call your looking glasse,
and in that seeke

12 Ah!] O *WS* close in] Ah close in *E* in close *WS* 15 those] these *Don* y'are] you'r *E*

63. 3. Upon Cupid. In *MC*, p. 157, headed A SONG *Upon Cupid.* 2 me] *om. MC* 11 That] For *MC*

65. 3. A Ring presented to Julia. In *WR*, f. R3^v, headed *With A* ◎ *to* Julia. 8 The] Thy *WR*

74. 2. How Lillies came white. In Add. MS. 31432, f. 33^v, headed: On the Lillyes; in *P69*, headed: *The* Lilly. 1 ye] you *P* 8 niplet] Nipple *A P* 12 ye] you *P*

74. 3. To Pansies. In Add. MS. 31432, f. 32. 2 Thy many scorns, and] all thy scorne yet *A* 3 Say, are] are *A* 4 Helps] help *A* *A* has second stanza:

Ah Cruell fate, enraged Lust
Of Tyrants proues most Just
For thy Conquests are with losse
Just are the Gods that thus dispose
Thy Ensigne then noe More Ile reare
all thy Victor's makes me feare
If my Wounds I can but heale
all future flame I will conceale

75. 1. The Lilly in a Christal. In Harvard MS. Eng. 626 F, f. 34^v (*Hv*). 9–16 and 17–24] order reversed in *Hv* 9 how] that *Hv* 10 daunces] dannceth *Hv* 12 fine . . . to] soft shade, which gleames *Hv* 13 draws] doth *Hv* thereto] renewe *Hv* 14 that . . . with] vniting vnto *Hv* 16 mixture] mixtion *Hv* 20 darts] shootes *Hv* radiant] pointed *Hv* 24 set] setts *Hv* 28 cleane] cleare *Hv* 33 Thus] The *Hv* 41 *Christal'd*] Cristall *Hv* 50 have . . . move] like a Paphian doue *Hv* 51 A world of men] Maie charme the soule *Hv*

77. 2. The Welcome to Sack. In Add. MSS. 19268, f. 39^v; 22603, f. 37; 30982, f. 140; and 33998, f. 5^v; MS. Harl. 6931, f. 61; MSS. Sloane 1446, f. 18^v and 1792, f. 125^v; MS. Firth e. 4, p. 14; MSS. Rawl. poet. 160, f. 165^v and 26, f. 89. '*all*' in notes signifies agreement between these ten MSS. There is also a short version (62 ll.) in *PB*, evidently from a manuscript (variants not occurring elsewhere recorded), and a short and corrupt version in MS. Rawl. poet. 142, f. 44^v (variants not recorded). Variant headings: Mr Herrickes welcome to Sacke *A19 A30 H S17* Mr Hearick his welcome to Sack. *F* The time expired, he Welcomes his M^{rs} (Sacke) as followeth. *A22* R*1* The Time of his vow expird, he thus welcomes it againe *A33* Herick's Welcome to Sack *R2* A welcome to Sack *PB* The poem also occurs in the following MSS.: Folger 1. 21; 1. 27 (incomplete); 646. 4; 1669. 2; Huntington 198. These present few readings not found elsewhere. Folger MS. 1669. 2, however, gives six additional lines. See after note on l. 92, below.

1–2] Soe swift streames meete, so meete with gladder smiles
Springs after long divorcem^{t}. made by Iles, *H*

1 gladder] gladsome *A33* 2 Meet] ioine *HM* by the] made by *A19 A30 S14 S17 R2* 3 urgeth] leadeth *PB* 4 natures] waters *A19 A30 H* water *S17* an] a *S14* 5 Moonie] mooneshine *A22 A33 R1* nights] night *A19 A22 A30 H S17* 6 Call] Calls *A19 A30 H S17* forth] for *A22* fierce] faire *S14 R2* Delights] delight *A19 A30 H S17* 8 but such as aime at] saue those that ayme at *S14 R2* saue those y^{t} tende to *A19 A30 H S17* 9 meet] mett *S14* 10 of Love] *om. A19* of Joue *F* of . . . radiant] whose most irradiant *Fol. 1. 27* 11 Out-glares] Out-stares *A22 A33 F R1 R2 HM* Out starrs *S14* Outdarts *A19 A30 H S17* 11 *Osiris*] *om. H* gleams] gemmes *A19 A30 H S17* 12 Out-shine] Dash forth *A22 A33 S14 F R1 R2* Dart forth *A30 S17* Darken *A19 H* Darkens *PB* his] the *A33* 14 are the ends] is ye end *A22 A33 R1* 15 I] Nay *A19 A22 A30 A33 H S17 R1* Yea *S14 R2* 16 The] To th' *F* 17 betray] display *all* 18 smoakie] smoakinge *A19 A22 A30 A33 H S17 F R1* chimneys] Chymney *R2* of] in *A30 S17* 19 so] thus *A22 A33 R1 R2* 20 Exile? Tell] Ile (why tell *H* Isle, ô tell *A19* 22 Did rather choose] Choose [Chase *A30*] rather for *A19 A30 H S17* another] some other *A19 A22 A30 H S17 R1* some forreigne *A33* 23–24] *om. A19 A30 H S17* 23–24 Or went'st . . . absence]

Or was it to the [that *A22 R1*] end thou mean'st to move me
more, by thy absence *A22 A33 R1*
Or was it to this end thou wentst to moue mee
more by thy [thine *R2*] absence *S14 F R2*

24 and] to *R2* 25 Why frowns . . . confer] O then noe longer let my sweet deferre *A19 A30 H S17* Why won't . . . confer] why does [doth *S14*] my Saint defer *A22 A33 S14 F R1 R2* 26 Favours . . . Idolater?] Her buxome [Bosome *A22 A33 R1* buxomes *S14*] smiles from me her worshipper: *all* 27 are Those Looks, Those Looks] are those happy [cloudy *F*] [sullen *Fol.1.21*] lookes *A22 A33 F R1 Fol.1.21* haue [are *H R2*] those amber lookes *A19 A30 H S14 S17 R2* are those amber locks *Fol. 646. 4* 28 Time] Tymes *S14 R2* drawn] calld *A19* 29 Tell . . . fault] *all MSS. read:*

tell me hath [has *A22 A33 F R1*] my soule
Prophan'd in speech or done an act y^{t} is [act more *A22 A33 R1*] fowle
Against thy purer essence, [purer nature *A22 A33 F R1*] for y^{t} fault

30 Sulphur] fire, with *PB* Haire] fyre *Fol.1.21* 32 kill] purge *R2* (*corr. to* kill *in another hand*) aire, *PB* this] y^{e} *all except F* 33 Wo't] Wilt *all* or] and *A30 S14* nor *A19 H S17 R2* ô *Fol.1.21* 35 in] *om. A19* embracing] embraces *A19 A30 H S17* embracinges *A22 R1* Tell me] *om. all* ha's] hath *A19 S14* 36 thee-ward] thee wards *A19 A30 H S17 F* i'th'] in the *A19 A22 S14 S17* in th' *H R1* in *A30* with *F* no] not *R1* 37 this rak't-up Ash-heap] y^{e} rakt up ashes *A19 A30 H S14 S17 R2* 39–40] *om. A19 A30 H S17* 39 divorc't] deuour'd *S14 R2* 40] Or [And *PB*] quench't [quench *A33 R1 PB*] my lust vpon some other [another *F*] wine *A22 A33 F R1 PB* or quench my last thirst with another wine *S14* Or quench my lust=sopp in an other wine *R2* 41 True, I] I must *A19 A30 H S17* 42 confirme] increase *H* 43 my affection on thee] my affection *A19 A30 A33 H R1* mine affection *S17 F* my affections *A22* m'affection on thee *S14* mine affection on thee *R2* 44 love growes] loues growe *A19* Foes] froze *H* 45 thee ever, co'd there] thee, euer could there *A22* thee! Could there euer *H* thee cold there evere *A19 A30 S17* 46 like possibilitie] like probabilitie *S14 R2* impossibility *Fol. 646. 4* 47 dar'st] durst *A22 A33 R1* dares *F* darest *R2* dost *PB* say] sweare *F* thy Iles] the Iles *A33 S14 F R1 R2* shall] should *A22 A33 R1*

47] When all the world shall know ye Vine shall lacke *A30*
W^{n} all the world may know, y^{t} Vines must lacke *H*
When all the world may know ye vines [vine *S17*] shall lack *A19 S17*

48 before] ere that *PB* *Herrick*] Ile *S14* I will *R2* leaves] leaue *A19 A30 A33 H S14 S17 R2* After 48 *all* (+*PB*) insert four lines as follows (reading of *A19*):

Sack is my life my leauen, salt to all
My dearest Dainties tis the principall
Fier to all my functions, giues me blod
An actiue spirit full marrow and w^{t} is good

There are the following variants: Sack is] Thou art *A22 A33 S14 F R1 R2 PB* leauen] Heaven *PB* dearest] dearer *A22 A33 R1* best of *F* better *Fol.1.21* tis the] nay tis y^{e} *A30 H S17* thou the *PB* nauill *A22 A33 S14 F R1 R2* to] vnto *A33 H* functions] actions *R1* giues] giuest (*or* giu'st) *A22 A33 S14 F R1 PB* Fier . . . blod] Fire to my functions all, thou giv'st me blood *R2* An actiue . . . good] Chine, [T'haue *F*] spirit, and marrow, and w^{t} els is good *A22 A33 S14 F R1 R2* (*S14 R1 R2* omit first 'and') *PB* 49 Thou mak'st] Sack makes *A19 A30 H S17* and mak'st *S14 R2* ayrie, active] sprightfull, aery *A19 S17* spiritfull, aery *A30* actiue, aiery *S14 F R2* sprightly, aery *H* 50 *Iphyclus*, upon] Iphiclus on *A22* Iphycus uppon *A19 S14 S17 H R2* Ipitus vpon *A30* (*R1* omits name) tops] eares *A33* 51 Thou mak'st] And makest (*or* mak'st) *A22 F R1* Sack makes *A19 A30 H S17* 51 nimble, as the winged] winged like [as *F*] ye nimble *A22 A33 F R1* 52 on] o're *A19 A30 H S17* heads] tops *A19 A30 A33 S14 S17 R2* toppe *H* 53 a] any *S14* 54 *Isis*] Iris *A30 S17* heavenly *Isis*] Cope of heauen *H* 55 love unto my life] joy unto my soule *A19* joy vnto my loue *A30 H S17* loue vnto my loue *S14 R2* 57 co'd] can *all except F* *Ægyptians*] Egyptian *A19 A22 A33 H S14 R1 R2* 58 *Garlick, Onyon*] Onion, Garlick *A30* *Onyon,* and] Limon or *S14* Onyon or *A33* 59 who wast] who art *A19 H S17* wch art *A30* who was *A22 R1 R2* who wert *F* their] the *A19 A30 H S17* 60 transcendent] transcending *H* 61 weak] great *R1* 62 or had] had he *A22 A33 R1* 63 Small] Full *A22 A33 R1* frantick liquor; He] purer nectar, hee *A22 A33 R1* Nectar, hee, even hee *A19 A30 H S14 S17 F R2* 64 had approv'd] would approu'd *A30* 65 Had] Or had *F* not] but *S14* *Joves* son] Joue found *R1* that brave] that vast *A22 A33 R1* the vast *A19 A30 H S14 S17 R2* 66 *Thesbian*] Thespian *all except A22 R1* 67 gen'rous blood; his] bloud, his Jouiall *A22 A33 R1* bloud, his lustfull *A19 A30 H S14 S17 R2* flaminge blood, his *F* 68 Ne'r had] had not *A19 A30 H S17* Had neere *S14 F R2* 69–72] *om. A19 A30 H S17* 69 Love and lust] heate of lust *A22 A33 R1* heat of loue *S14 R2* heat, & lust *F* 70 beauties] beautie *S14* we will] and wee'le *A22 A33 S14 F R1* mee, wee'l *R2* 71 Fate to break us] hate to sunder *S14 R2* 73 As *Queenes*] as Kings *A30* meet] see *A22 A33 R1* or come thou unto] so let sack come to *A19 A30 H S17* 74 As *Cleopatra* came to] As Cleopatra to Marke *A22 A33 R1* Or as Cleopatra vnto *A19 A30 H S17* As Cleopatra did to *S14* 75 carriage] visage *all* except *S14* linage *S14* 76 *Triumvir*] Triumviri *A33 R1* Wonderment] blandisment *A30* merriment *A33* 77 nerves with spirit] feeble sinewes *A19 A30 H S17* 78 Run . . . hasty] Flow, as did Nilus in hir purple *Fol. 646. 4* my] y^e^ *R1* veines] braines *S14* a] an *A30 S17 F* hasty] lustie *S14 R2* winter *Fol. 1. 27* 78–79 Run . . . fire,]

Fill each part full of Fire, let all my good
Parts be encouraged, *H*

79 fire, active to doe] active fire to doe *A30* fire, apt to do *A33* 80 soule] state *A33 R1* it] me *A19 A33 H S14 S17 R1* thee *A30* 82 doe not] never *A19 A30 H S17* 83 Fiers] blessings *A19 A30 H S17* me; but] lacuna in *S14* but] but let *A22 R1 R2* 84 theselike] all my *A22 A30 A33 H S14 R1* all mine *A19 S17 F R2* or] and *A30* that's] y^t^ is *A19* 85 Circumstants] circumstances *R1* shall but live] shall haue power *A22 A33 R1* shall haue fate *A30 S14 S17 F R2* haue ye Fate *A19 H* 86 that] when *all except A33 and R1* 87 and then] and *S14* 88 the Tap,

the Tost, the Turfe] ye turffe, ye tost, ye tappe [lap *R1*] *A22 A33 R1* 89 Ne'r shine upon] never shine on *A33* May my Numbers] let my verses *all* 90 Run] Hast *all* Death] change *F* 91 when thee (deare Spouse) I] (Deare Spouse) w^n^ I thee *A19 A22 A30 A33 H S17 R1* 91 disavowe] disallow *A19 A30 H S17* 92 Ne'r may] May ne're *A19 H* After this line MS. Folger 1669. 2, f. 270^v^, has the following additional lines:

Grant my request this once you powers deuine
lett this Canary poet wante no wine
Nature I pray thee doe his yeares recall
And lett him bee an Infant but withall
Blesse so this suckling that his mother pappe
May bee the nourishing Canary tapp

80. 1. Upon Gubbs. In *WR*, No. 84.

83. 2. Upon Bunce. In *WR*, No. 89 and *GD*, p. 86, headed *On the same* (referring to 149. 3, which precedes it). 2 payment promis'd] payment, promise *GD*.

84. 1. To the Virgins. In Add. MSS. 31432, f. 33^v^ and 29396, f. 18; MS. Harl. 6918, f. 25; MS. Don. c. 57, f. 72^v^; MS. Folger 750. 1 (ll. 1–4 only), p. 49; *Ac46*, p. 228 (same text in *Ac50*); corrupt versions in MS. Harl. 3991, f. 145^v^, MS. Drexel 4257, *MD*, and *WD* (variants not recorded here). Also in *P52*, *P53*, *P55*, *P59*, *P66*, *P67*, and in *WR* (1663), f. Dd6. Headings: *A Sonnet*: Harl. 6918 *A Song. Ac46 MD* To make much of Time. *WR* Loose No time *Harl. 3991* Good Advice. *LG* 1 Gather ye] Gather your *A29 H Don Fol P WR Ac46 LG* Rose-buds] roses *Fol* while ye] while you *A20 H Don P* whilst you *Fol WR LG* 2 Old] for *LG* 3] And those sweet flowers that smell to day *Fol* Those blossomes which doe bloome to day *Ac46* this] that *A29 H Don P WR LG* that smiles] that smells *H* which grows *LG* 4 will] may *H WR* 5 Heaven] light *Don* 6 he's a] he is *WR P53 P55 P59 LG* he is a *P52 P56 P66 P67* 7 run] done *Don* 8 neerer he's to] hee's the neerer *A29 H* neerer to his *WR* he's] is *LG* 9–12] *om. H* 9 which] that *A29 Don Ac46 P* (except *P67*) *LG* 10 When] While *Don P* Blood] old *WR* 11 But] And *WR* spent] past *A29* fled *A31 LG* 11 the worse, and worst] the worst, and worst *A31* grows worse and worse *LG*
11–12] Expect not the [not then y^e^ *Don Ac46 P66 P67*] last and worst
Time [Which *Ac46*] still succeeds the former *Don Ac46 P*
12 Times] Time *A29 A31 LG* still] ill *LG* succeed] succeeds *A29 A31 LG* 13 use] spend *LG* 14 And while ye] While ye [*or* you] *P* (*except P66 and P67*) And whilst you *A29 H Ac46 P67 LG* And while you *WR P66* 15 lost but once] once but lost *A29 Ac46 P LG* prime] tyme *A31* 13–16 *om. Don* 16 may] must *Ac46*

85. 3. A Pastorall. See Appendix B, p. 460, for variant version of this poem in a seventeenth-century manuscript. See also Introduction, p. xxvii, footnote.

87. 2. The Bubble. In MS. Harl. 6918, f. 50, headed To his Scornefull mistris: and in Harvard MS. Eng. 626 F, f. 35^{v} 2 Flie] haste *H Hv*   madd *H Hv*: made *48*   5 Stoop, mount] Mount, stay *H* Mount, stoope *Hv*   take] catch *H Hv*   6 Like to a dreadfull] Like a dire *H Hv*   7–10] *H* and *Hv* read:

And when thy shaking fires, and her sight [fight *Hv*]
Are thus, and thus, and truely opposite,
then like a ball of wildfire flye,
and breake thy selfe upon her eye.

97. 3. Upon himselfe. In *WR* (1663), f. Dd1, headed *On an old Batchelour.*   3 wedded] married *WR*   4 a] one *WR*   6 mend, put out the light] mend me, blind me quite *WR*

98. 2. To the Rose. In *MC*, p. 160, headed A SONG TO THE ROSE. Also in *WR* (1663), f. Cc5^{v}, headed *Another* (referring to a preceding poem not by Herrick).   4 flowing] peevish *WR*   5 oft has] long hath *WR*   6 she's fretfull)] she frets, that *WR*   8 struggle] struggles *WR*   10 For to tame, though not to] That can tame, although not *WR*   11 thus] now *WR*   12 but] yet *MC*

98. 3. Upon Guesse. In *WR*, No. 97.

98. 5. Upon a painted Gentlewoman. In *WR*, No. 102, headed *On a Painted Madam.*

100. 3. The Present. In Add. MS. 15227, f. 3^{v}, headed 'Nuncius amoris Apes', and in MS. Ashmole 38, p. 152.   1 pretty pilfring] yellowfooted *A Ash*   2 bring'st] brought'st *Ash*   3] When on her lips thy sweet dew thou hast plac't *A Ash*   4 but] doth *Ash*   but slily] willingly *A*   5 we] I *A Ash*   6 next,] so *A Ash*   buryall] funerall *Ash*

102. 3. Not to love. In Add. MS. 31432, f. 32^{v}, headed Perswasions Not to loue. In *P59* headed *On the Vicissitudes of Love.* Also in *WR* (1663), f. Dd3, headed *Counsel not to love.*   4 Summers] Sum̃er *A P*   has] haue *A*   hath *P WR*   5 sobs] tears *WR*   sorrowes] troubles *P*   6 makes] make *WR*   7–8] *om. A P*   7 Freezing cold] Fiery colds *WR*   firie heats] freezing heats *WR*   13–16] *om. A P*   16 her own least] in every *WR*   17 and worth] whose worth's *P*   18 thou't] thou'lt *A P*   not] nought *A P*   *A* has a second stanza, with corruption in l. 2:

He that will not loue must be
more colder then that he or thee
tis a cryme I would not name
sure the able haue a flame
sleepy man forbeare to say
thou hast a soule, thou'rt nought but clay
else a fyer growing higher

soone would burne thee with desire
prithy know tis but disease
take this Cure it giues all ease
Gaze on those eyes and thou must proue
if not lasciuious strong in loue.

103. 1. To Musick. A Song. In MS. Don. c. 57, f. 52v and in Christ Church MS. Mus. 87, f. 13v. 1 *Queen*] soul *Don Ch* 2, 3] Between these lines *Don* and *Ch* have:

yu whose soft accents & alluring tones
give [giues *Ch*] life & motion unto stones

3 tam'st] calm'st *Don* 5 down, down, down,] downe *Don* downe Come downe *Ch* chiming] shyning *Ch* 6 To] & *Don Ch*

103. 3. Upon the death of his Sparrow. In MS. Harl. 6918, f. 51, headed *A Sonnet*: and in Harvard MS. Eng. 626 F, f. 38v. 2 work] make *Hv* Love's Sampler onely] true Samplers duly *H Hv* 4 all] and *Hv* 6 Met] meete *H Hv* one] our *Hv* 7 body] ashes *H Hv* 9 distill] befriend *H Hv* 10 For you once lost] to you once dead *H* to you once [hiatus] *Hv* 11 Had] Hast *Hv* 13–14]

and for the death of this Lyes
Entombed here, wept out hir Eyes: *H Hv*

15 sit] dwell *H Hv* 16]the time my Phill has here to sleep *H Hv* 19 blood] blouds *H* 20 their] this *H Hv*

105. 3. How Violets came blew. In *WR* (1663), f. Cc7, headed *How the Violets came blew*. Not in stanzas in *WR*.
1–2]

The Violets, as Poets tell,
With *Venus* wrangling went

3 sho'd] did *WR* 6 Girles] Girle *WR* 7 ye] you *WR* dare] do *WR* 8 ye] you *WR*

106. 2. To the Willow-tree. In *MC*, p. 158, headed A SONG. *Upon the Willow-Tree.* 10 Maids] hearts *MC*

106. 3. Mrs. Eliz. Wheeler &c. In *Poems by Thomas Carew*, 1640, p. 170; see Appendix B in edition by R. Dunlap, 1949, pp. 195–6. Occurs also in MS. Don. c. 57, f. 97 (four four-lined stanzas, and a fifth of six lines); H. Lawes autograph MS., p. 150; MS. Drexel 4257, f. 38 (= *D*); *Ac46*, p. 200, headed *A Song*; *Ac50*, p. 192, same heading and text as *Ac46*; *WI*, p. 103 (second pagination); *P52*, *P53*, *P59*, *P67* (first four lines only); and *WD*, where it is *Song* 133 (same text as *Ac46* and *Ac50*). Headings elsewhere: *The Enquiry*. *C* Loves sweet Repose. *P59* 1 Among] Amongst *C Ac46* Amidst *P D* Amid *WI* walkt] walke *P WI* 2] Alone, I with my sighs thus talkt *Ac46* sighs] selfe *D* intertalkt] entertalke *WI P except P67* entred talke *P67 D* 4 I may] may I *C* 5 Thou] Then *Ac46 P WI* 6 sweet] good *C Don HL Ac46 P D WI* 7 yond' Carnation] yonder tulip *C Don HL Ac46 P D WI* 8 thou shalt] thou maist *C Don* thou shall *P53* find] haue *HL* and] her *HL D* 9 that] you *C* (*for* yon) yon *D* Pansie] pausie *C* Fancy

P WI 10 thou shalt] thou maist *Don* shalt thou *P WI* have] find *Don Ac46 P D WI* 11 bloome] balme *D* and] in *HL Don D* 12 waves the Streamer] wave [waves *Ac46*] the streamers *C Ac46* wave the streames *P* run the Streamers *D* 12] There do wave the streames &c. *WI* 12, 13] Between these lines *C* has:

In brightest lillies that there stands (? *for* that *read* leaf)
The emblems of her whiter hands.
In yonder rising hill there smells
Such sweets as in her bosome dwells.

14 I] And *P* to pluck] and pluckt *Ac46 P WI* 15 To . . . parts] Of parts to make *D* of parts an union] a part a union *P* an] a *C* 16 a] the *D* were] was *C Ac46 P WI* 17 At which] With that *C* And then *D* At the which *WI* 18 The true] (Fond man) *C HL Ac46 P WI D* 19 For] And *C* joyes] Joy *P* ways *D* must] shall *C* 20 And . . . turning] Even [And *D*] in the twinkling *C D* Even [As *Don*] in the turning *Ac46 Don P WI* 21 And] Then D must] shall *C* 22 ere] thus *C* ere knit] in link *D* 22] As doe those flowers, when knit together *Ac46 P WI* those] these *HL*

108. 2. To Anthea. In H. Lawes autograph MS., p. 144 and MS. Drexel 4257, f. 133. Also in *P52*, *P53*, *P59*. Heading in *P59*: *Loves Votary.* 1 to] but *HL P D* 2 Protestant] vottary *HL P D* 6 sound and] soundly *P* 7 whole . . . canst] world thou canst not *P* 9 will] shall *HL P D* 10 To] and *HL P D* 12 And't shall doe so] And it shall do't *P* 15 And] Or *P* 17–20] *om. HL P D* 21 life, my love] love, my life *P D* 22 eyes] eye *P* 24 and] or *HL D*

112. 3. A Nuptiall Song &c. In MS. Harl. 6917, f. 10; Add. MSS. 21433, f. 126 and 25303, f. 141^v (designated *A* when in agreement); MS. Firth e. 4, p. 75 and MS. Harvard Eng. 626 F, f. 26. 10 stanzas + 5 lines in *EP*, p. 279 (Y5). Headings: An Epithalamium: *H* Epithalamie *A* Epithalamium *F* An Epithalamie *Hv*. Seven extra stanzas in *H* and *A*, three of them also in *F* and four in *Hv*. Order of stanzas in *H* and *A* (compared with *48*): 1, 2, additional (A), 3, 4, additional (B), 5, (C), 6, (D), (E), 7, (F), 14, 8, 9, 10, 11, 12, 13, (G), 15, 16 (23 stanzas). Order in *F*: 1, 2, (A), 3, 4, 5, (C), (E), 7, 14, 8, 9, 10, 11, 12, 13 (16 stanzas). Order in *Hv* same as in *F*, with addition, at end, of (G), 15, 16 (19 stanzas). (*all* = all MSS.) 2 Injewel'd] enamelld *all* 6 nobler] noble *H A* 10 Emergent] Emerging *all* 11 else some more] rather some *F* 12 mark] Se *F Hv* 13 paces] passes *F* 14 Treading upon] Throwing about *all* 16 Chafte] chast *H F Hv* After 20 all MSS. have the following stanza (A):

3. Lead on faire paranymphs, the while her eyes, [payre of Nymphs, ye whilest *F Hv*]

guilty of [to *A F Hv*] somewhat, ripe [guild *F Hv*] the Strawberries
and Cherries in her cheekes, there's Creame
allready spillt, her rayes must gleame
gently thereon,
And soe begett [create *F Hv*] lust and temptation
to surfeit and to hunger;
helpe on her pace, and though she lagg, yet stirre
her homewards, [homeward *F Hv*] well she knowes
her heart's at home howere she goes: [There is her [his *Hv*] heart where ere *F Hv*]

21 street] sheet *F* 22 O] & *F* 24 Perspiring] Spirting forth *H A21* spiring forth *A25 F Hv* pounded] powdred *F* 26 of] with *F* 27 therein wo'd not] would not then *H A* 28 Ash-heaps] ashes *H* Cindars *F Hv* that] This *F Hv* 30 burnes] burne *A* Embers] Cindars *F* 31 ground] round *H* 34 Display the] Display thy *H A* 36 More towring, more disparkling] More towring, and besparckling [desparkling *A*] *H A* Towring more, more sparkling *F* Towring more, more disparkling *Hv* 39 Cindars] ash-heapes *F* ashes *Hv* 40 else to ashes] like a firebrand *H A* else to nothing *F Hv* After 40 *H A* have the following stanza (B):

6. See how he waves his hand, and through his eyes
Shootes forth his Jealous soule, for to surprize
And ravish you his Bride, doe you
not now perceiue the soule of C: C:
Your Mayden Knight [*lacuna of three lines*]
with kisses to inspire
you with [of *A*] his Just and holy Ire:

41 by] through *F Hv* 41] If so glide through the rankes [bankes *A25*] of Virgins, passe *H A* 43 cloud] clouds *F Hv* 44 yee] you *H A Hv* 45 some repeat] Fame repeates *F Hv* 46 you] yee *Hv* sprinkling] couering *F Hv* 47 While that] While *F Hv* 50 doth a] doe the *H F* doth the *A* After 50 all MSS. have the following stanza (C):

8. Why then goe forward sweet [on forward faire *F Hv*] Auspicious Bride
and come upon your [y^e^ *F*] Bridegroome like a Tyde
bearing downe Time before you, hye
swell, mixe, and loose your soules; implye
like streames which [y^t^ *F*] flow
Encurlld together, and noe difference show
In their siluer waters; runne [their mo'lt [most *A*] siluer, run, run *F A Hv*]
Into your selues like wooll together spunne;
or [And *F Hv*] blend so as the sight [blende as that ye sight *A*]

of two makes one Hermaphrodite: [Hermophrodite *A F Hv*]

51–60] *om. F*   51 y'are] you *H* yor *A21* you'r *A25*   52 dealing] drawing *H*   dolinge *A*   these] those *H A*   57 *Apostate*] Apostata *H*   59 you slow-] y'are slow *H*   60 ly go] in going *H*   howsoever] however *H*   After 60 *H A* have the two following stanzas (D) and (E); *F* and *Hv* have (E) only, following (C):

10. How long soft Bride shall your deare   make [*A* has 'C:'
instead of lacuna]
loue to your welcome with the mistick Cake,
how long, oh [ah *A*] pardon, shall the house
and the smooth Hand maides pay their Vowes
with oyle and wine,
for your approach, yet see their Altars pine?
how long shall the page, to please
you, stand for to surrender up the keyes
of the glad house? come come
or Lar will freeze to death at home:

11. Welcome at last unto [into *Hv*] the Threshold, Time
throaned in a saffron Evening, seemes to chyme [throaned *om. F Hv*]
All in, kisse and so enter, If
a prayer must be said, be briefe;
The easy Gods
For such neglect [contempt *EP*], haue only Myrtle rodds,
to stroake not strike; feare you
Not [No *F*] more, milde nymph, then they would [will *Hv*] haue you doe;
But dread that you doe more offend [dread you more offend *A F*   dread you more t'offend *Hv*]
In that [In what *F Hv*] you doe beginne, then end:

61 y'are] you'r *A*   you are *F*   yee are *Hv*   Codled] codshead *Hv*   62 Runs . . . prie] from his Torrid zone doth pray *F Hv*   64 The Aged] how th'aged *all*   point out] whisper *F Hv*   66 The House] us *all*   Love shield her] and God shield her *H A*   peace shield vs *F*   Peace sheild her *Hv*   67 smirk] smirking *F Hv*   68 in's] in his *H*   70] Some Ginns [ginne *Hv*], wherby to Take her eyes *F Hv*   your] her *all*   After 70 *H A* have the following stanza (F):

13. What though your laden Altar now has [hath *A25*] wonne
the creditt from the table of the Sunne
for earth and sea; this Cost
on you is altogether lost,
because you feede
not on the flesh of beasts, but on the seede
of contemplation, your,
your eyes are they, wherewith you draw the pure

elixar to the minde,
which sees the body fedd, yet pined:

71 kind] sweet *all* 72 This . . . longest] This the shortest day, this, the longest *H A* This longest day, & This ye Shortest *F* This the longest daye, and this the longest *Hv* 73 But] and *all* 74 Who] Which *F Hv* 75 Lying alone] When you are gone: *F* 76 Telling] hearing *H A* Numbring *F Hv* strike] goe *all* 81–82 Note in right-hand margin: [t]o the Maide *A21* To ye Maides *A25* 82 we] I *F Hv* ye] you *H F* 83 Farther then Gentlenes tends] further then vertue lends [teach *F Hv*] *all* 84 ye] you *H F* striving for] catching at *all* 86 ye] you *H* 88 youthfull] gentle *all* fragrant] fragrous *H A* 89 fore-fend] forbid *F* 91 tender-] soft, & *F Hv* 97 *Maidens*-] mayden *H A* And soft-*Maidens*-] Soft Maide, & *F* Soft maides, and *Hv* 98 others] other *F Hv* 99 Then] Thus *H A* 101 yee] you *H A25 F Hv* see] view *all* 104 *Cherubin all*: *Cherubim 48* 105 O marke yee] List' oh list *all* 106] Euen heauen giues up his soule betweene you [yee *A25 Hv*] now, *all* 107 See, a] marke how *H A* Marke; A *F Hv* thousand] thousands *A21* 108 at] on *F* 109] To bed, to bed, or They will tire, *F* To bedd, or they will tire *Hv* 110 Were she an] Her, were sh'an *F Hv* 111 bewitching] bewitchings *F Hv* 112 beare . . . swelling] beares vp, & rises *F Hv* swelling] rising *H A* 113 too too *all*: two too *48* 114 Yee] you *all* brusle] lusty *F* 116 woo's] comes *Hv* 117 you *all*: it *48* 118 the mighty over-flow] that mayne, in the full flow *H A* the Sea in the full-flowe *Hv* this sea, into ye flowe *F* 119 that] the *all* 120 night] starrs *all* 121 The bed is] You see tis *all* 127 do it to the full; reach] doe it in [to *A*] the full reach, *H A* to it, to the full reach *F Hv* 128 conceipt] conceipts *all* and some way teach] and rather teach *H A* Teach *F Hv* 130 Play] sport *all* After 130 *H A Hv* have the following stanza (G) and *A* has the marginal note: To the maides:

And now y'haue wept enough, depart you [? yon *H*] [yee
A21 y^e *A25 Hv*] starres,
begin to pinke, as weary that the warres [of these warres *Hv*]
know so long Treaties; beate the drumme
aloft, and like two armies, come
and guild the field;
fight brauely for the flame of mankinde, yeeld
not to this, or that [that, or this *Hv*] assault,
for that would proue more Heresy then fault,
In Combatants to flye
fore this or that hath [had *Hv*] gott the victory:

131 If needs we must] If you must needs *H* But if you must needes *A* Now if we must *F Hv* 132 it] you *H A* 134 magicks]

magick *H A21* 136 one] God *all* 138 And] I and *all* 140 confusion] damnation *all* the] that *H A* that *altered to* the *Hv* 143] With ribbs of rocke, or brasse *Hv* Rock, or walles of] Ribbe [ribbs *A25*] of Rocke and *H A* 144 Ye] Yea *H* You *Hv* Towre] fold *Hv* 145 you] yee *A Hv* 147 yee] yo^{u} *A21 H* no] nay *Hv* (end of line) 148 Bold bolt] bolt *Hv* his] *om. A* will make] *om. Hv* 149] Will make and throwe *Hv* 150 sheet] sheetes *H Hv* 153] And you must grannt it, entrance with *Hv* 154 can] *om. H A* 158 yee] yo^{u} *H A* that two] that, that *A Hv* that] the *H*

119. 1. Oberons Feast. In Add. MSS. 22603 (*26*), f. 61 and 22118 (*21*), f. 1 (first four lines (ll. 7–10 of text) partly torn off and some lines omitted); also in MS. Egerton 923, f. 43; MS. Ashmole 38, p. 100; MS. Firth e. 4, p. 23; MS. Malone 16, f. 3; MS. Rawlinson F. poet. 160, f. 169^{v}; MS. *HM* 198, p. 27; and *EP*, p. 294. For an earlier printed version see Appendix, p. 454: Headings: Kinge Oberons his feast. *A26* Oberons † *A21* The fayries feast att his mariage *E* Kinge Obrons Feast *Ash* Oberon his Banquet. *F* Oberons feast. *M* King Oberons Feast *R* 1–6] *om. all MSS.* 8 short prayers] ye daunce *all MSS.* a dance *EP* 9 A . . . grain] A yellow corne *all MSS.* purest] Perky *all MSS.* 10 glit'ring] sandy *all MSS.* gritt] gretes *A26 E Ash R HM* 11 choyce] choysest *Ash* with; then] with which *A26 Ash R* with and *A21 E F M* wch with- *HM* 12 nice] mise *E* mice *R* 13–18] *om. A21* 13 this] the *all MSS. except E* his eye] that this *HM* is] was *A26 Ash F M R* 14 must not] dare not *all MSS. except F* cannot *EP* eare was] eares were *A26 R HM* 15 there was] he had *E* 16 Spleen] eares *EP* Spleen . . . chirring] fire [fires *F*] y^{e} [this *E*] pitteringe *A26 E Ash F R HM* fires, the pitying *M* 17 puling] pusinge *A26 HM* (bussing *in margin*) Puissing *Ash* passing *R* 18 Gnat] *om. HM* gnats *EP* minstralcy] *om. E* After 18 (in *A21* after 12) the MSS. have:

The Hum̃inge Dorre, y^{e} [and *E R HM*] dyinge Swan
And each a choyse musitian.

19 And] Butt *A22 F M* we] y^{u} *E* 21 Infant] instant *E* 22 besweetned] besweeted *Ash* beswetted *A26 R HM* 24 kitling] killing *A21* begin] (?) begane *Ash* 25 where] with which *E* 27 and tastes] butt with *all MSS.* 28 Of that we call] Neate=coole Allay [array *R*] *all MSS.* Cuckoes] Coockoe *F HM* 30 By,] And *EP* blessed] bless'd *E* by] wth *A21 Ash F M R* 31 was] seem'd *A21 F M* then forthwith] he not spares *all MSS.*, substituting for 32–33:

To feed vpon y^{e} Candid hares
Of a dryed Cancker [Caker *F*], with a [the *E*] sagg [& ye lagg *A21 M* with ye lagge *F*]

34 bestrutted] bestuffed *A26* bee strutted *Ash* 35 Gladding]

Strokinge *all MSS.* 36 what wo'd] nor would *Ash* what will *A21 F M* 37 But] and *M* a Newt's] an Eu'ts *A26 Ash R* a Gnats *A21 E F M* and Eughts *HM* and gnats *EP* 38] A Pickled maggot and a dry *all MSS. except E, which omits the line* 39
With the Red-capt] Hippe, with a red=cap *A26 R HM* [red-capt *A21 Ash*] Hipps, with y^{e} redcapt *F M* hipps, & y^{e} red Capt *E* 41
Tooth] tooth is *EP* 41 After 'Tooth' all MSS. have:

and [*om. A F M HM*] with y^{e} [a *A21*] fat
And well-boyled inkepin of a Batt. [well broyld *E Ash R* Well rooted Eye-ball *A21 F* well-rated eyeball *M* Inspin *E*]
A bloated earewigge with ye Pith [bloter *A21* and y^{e} *E*]
Of sugered rush a glads him with. [*A21 omits the line* he glads *E Ash F M HM*]
But most of all the glowwormes fire
As much beticklinge his desire [bewitching *Ash R* belickling *E*]
To know [burn *EP*] his Queene mixt [and *E*] with y^{e} farre-
ffetcht bindinge ielly of a starre [fetch *Ash* gliding gelly *E*]

A F M continue at l. 43; the other MSS. add

The silke=wormes seed, a little moth

and continue at l. 42 42 Late fatned] Lately fatted *A26* Late fatted *E Ash R HM* 43 With] *om. A26 Ash R HM* 44 to] wth *A21* teares] teaer *E* 45 dewlaps] dewlop *M* dewlapp *HM* 47 Ore-come in] orecoming *HM* in] wth *A21 E M* a] the *E* 48 flattering] Hallowing *A21* fruitfull *Ash* clustered *EP* 49 orest] strayned *A21 F M* soft] *om. A21* 50 the] a *E* dainty] tender *F* 51 a daintie daizie] a Dazy challice *all MSS. except M* (a challice) 52 up] of *A26 E Ash R HM* 53 to height] too high *A26* 54 Grace by] Grac't by *A26 Ash R HM* (lacuna in F) After 54 *M* has: ffinis. Rich: Hiericke of Clare Hall

123. 5. Upon a child that dyed. In *WR*, *Epitaphs*, No. 120, headed *On a Childe.*

124. 1. Upon Sneape. *In WR*, No. 111.

130. 1. Gold, before Goodnesse. In *WR*, No. 115, headed *A Foolish Querie.*

130. 2. The Kisse. In Add. MS. 33998, f. 82. Also in *Ac50*, p. 164, headed *Upon a Kisse.* (No prefixes of 'Chor.') and in *L58*, headed *A Dialogue on a* Kisse. 1 thy] the *Ac50* 3 ye] you *A Ac50 L58* 5 Between] betwixt *A Ac50 L58* 6 desires] desire tis *A* 7, 11 &c. *Chor.*] *om. A* 7 soft] sweet *L58* 9 Babies of] Baby in *A* 10 them] it *A Ac50 L58* 12 chin, the cheek] cheek, the chin *Ac50* 13 and] it *L58* 14 then] now *A Ac50 L58* 15 And] 'Tis *L58* 16 Ha's] Hath *Ac50* speaking] voycing *A L58* noysing *Ac50* 17 say] then *L58* 18 speaks] speak *Ac50* your kisse] the kiss *L58* 21 rare] various *L58* more *Ac50* encolourings] colourings *L58* 22 gently] sweetly *L58*

130. 3. The admonition. In Harvard MS. Eng. 626 F, f. 6^{v} and

H. Lawes autograph MS., p. 53. 1 *Diamonds* which] Jewells that *Hv* 2 In] on *HL* 3 Or] And *Hv HL* 5 those] these *Hv HL* 6 By] of *HL* wretched] sondrie *Hv HL* 7 mournfull] bubbles, *Hv HL* 8 That figure] Emblems of *Hv* all Embling *HL* 10 By] through *HL* 11 Congeal'd] Of them, did Turne *Hv* and] or *Hv HL* 12 Which precious spoiles] These [wch *HL*] now the spoiles of loue *Hv HL* 13 trophees] titles *Hv* both readings in *HL* 14 Ah] O *HL* consider . . . implies] beware, fond youth [man *HL*], and thus surmise, *Hv HL* 15 will] could *Hv*

131. 2. On himselfe. In *C52*. 5 ay] ah *C52*

132. 3. His age &c. In MSS. Egerton 2725, f. 72v; Harl. 6918, f. 47; Firth e. 4, p. 7; St. John's Coll. Camb., S 23, f. 77v ('*J*'); Worcester Coll. Oxford, lviii, p. 275 ('*W*'); Harvard Eng. 626 F, f. 29; Huntington 198, p. 23. Ll. 77–79 in *EP*, p. 430. Headings: Mr Herrickes old age to Mr. Weekes. *E* His old age to Mr Weekes: *H Hv* To his peculiar frend Mr John Weekes his Age he dedicates *HM* Mr Herick to his friend Mr Weeks *J* Mr Hericks Age, dedicated to his peculiar friend Mr John Wicks, under the name of Posthumus. *W* (which adds 'pag: 152', the page-number in *48*). *W* has few differences from *48*. '*all*' in notes means all MSS. except *W*. 3 Or prayers, or] nor prayer nor *E H Hv J* Nor prayer or *F HM* 6 do's] doe *E* doth *H F HM Hv J* 7 decline] *om. F* 10 no] not *E H Hv* nor *F* 14 Looks . . . left] Dislikes to care for what's *all* 15 Wickes] Weekes *all* while] whilst *H HM* 16 here] thus *all* 17 W'ave] Wee haue *all* Wee've *W* the] our *E H Hv* past-best] past best *E Hv* past, best *W* past *H J* best past- *F* past-best Times] best Pastimes *HM* 20 they] they'll *H Hv* 22 to a Lilly-lost] a lost mayden-head *all* 24 dayes] life *J* a second] another *Hv* 25 on we must] we must on *E H F HM Hv W* 26 *Anchus . . . Tullus*] Tullus . . . Ancus *all* 28 Thus has] Thus *E H* This *Hv* Thus hath *F HM J* 29 must] shall *J* should *HM Hv* 31] Then since our life time is but short *J* 32 by] with *W* 33 Roses] rose buds *all* 36 buried] perished *F HM* 37] Liue we then free *HM* 39 wind] winds *all* 40 white and Luckie] best and whitest *all* 41 We are not] Wee'l not be *all* 42 roofs] roofe *all* nor our] nor no *J* 43 *Baiæ*] Bayes *E H HM Hv* Buildings *J* 45 fed] feed *E H* 46 bred] breed *E H* 47 hands] hand *HM J* do] will *H I HM Hv* can *J* 48 For *Pollio's*] Apollo's *F* After 48 *all* insert:

Wee haue noe vinyards [vineyard *HM*] which [that *J*] doe beare
Their lustfull [pleasant *F*] Clusters all the yeare
Nor [Noe *F HM*] odoriferous
Orchards, like to Alcinous
Nor gall [gull *F*] the seas,
Our witty appetites to please,

With mullet [mulletts *HM*], Turbot, guilthead [Guilt heads *H*] [guilthead, Turbet, *J*] bought
At a high [deare *F HM*] rate, and further [farther *F J*] brought.
Nor can we glory of a great
And stuffed [strutted *H F HM Hv J*] Magazine of wheat
Wee have noe bath
Of oyle, but onely rich in faith,
Ore which the hand
Of fortune can have no command
ffor what she gives not, she not [nere *J*] takes
But of her owne [one *HM*] a spoile she makes

50 Both] Close *all* 51 have] see *all* 52 Although not archt] Though not of gold *all* 54 that cheape] open *E H F Hv J* 54] *om. HM after* From 55 Beane] Cates *HM* full] same *E H F HM Hv* that full] as much *J* 57 then . . . we] on what seas then we [wee then *HM*] *E H F HM Hv* then on what seas so ere we *J* 60 Barke] barkes *all* she] they *all* 61 Amidst] Middst *H Hv* 62 Wickes] Weekes *all* which] that *all* 63 she] it *all* 64 she] yet *E H* it *F HM J* 66 both . . . Wildernesse] both in [i'th *H F HM* in the *Hv*] Campe and Wildernesse *all* 70 No, no] Oh noe *all* 71 Which] that *HM J* 74 bruised] banished *W* 75 show] read *all* 76] Eternall daylight ore [on *H F Hv J*] my head *all* 78 The cough, the] With Cough and *E H Hv* The Cough, and *F HM J* 79 Unto . . . nothing] Into an [A *HM Hv*] heap of cinders *all* 81 these] those *HM* 82 Lame . . . with] And cold times unto [to *H Hv*] *E H Hv* Lame & cold lines to [with *J*] *F HM J* 84 My . . . it] With her leane lips shall kisse them [it *J*] *all* 85 And so we'l] Then [Thus *F*] [And then *J*] will we *all* 86 By'th'] by the *H Hv* and slit] *om. F* slit] sleete *H HM* fleet *E* 88 Now old] Old *all* own] owne. *E H F* 89 Calenders] Kalender *E H Hv* as Pusses eare] *om. E* 90 Washt or's to tell] Is [Are *J*] for to know *all* change] chance *F J* 92 gripings] griping *all* of] in *all except F J* 94 *Iülus*] Iullus *E* Julus *H F HM J* sing] sing me *F J* 95 *Julia's*] Mistris *all* 96 And of her] Or such a *all* blush] smile *HM* 97 that flowre of mine] my Lilly-fine *all* 98 Enclos'd] Entomb'd *all* 99 A] My *E H F Hv* 100 then] much *J* a] an *HM* 104 crept] stole *all* aged] Reverend *all* 105–12] *all read:*

When the high Hellen [When as Helene *F*] her faire cheekes
Shew'd to the Army of the Greekes
At which Ile rise
(Blind though as [at *J*] midnight in mine [my *W*] eyes)
And hearing it
Flutter [Chatter *J*] and crow, as [and *E*] in a fit
Of young concupiscence, and feele
New flames within the aged steele

113 Thus . . . crazie] Then like a frantik *J* man] now *H* more *F* 114 things half] the times *E H HM Hv* the lines *F* the dayes *J* 116 Repeat] Sigh out *E F HM Hv J* Sigh at *H* I] wee *all except J* 117] *om. HM* And shed a teare *E H Hv* And wth a teare *F* Then shed a teare, *J* 118 my] up my *Hv J* of my *F* *Iülus*] Iullus *E* Julus *H F J* Julius *HM* hairs] haire *all* 120 my] the *E H F HM Hv W* our *J* 121 next Ile] will I *all* 123 Hearth] health *J* 124 (*Larr* thus] and Lar *J* *Larr*] *om. HM* thus] this *HM* mirth] health *J* 125 Then] Next *all* except *W* There *W* 126 browner Ale] better beare *all* 127 sweetly] neatly *all* first] *om. J* 128 *Genius*] Vesta *all* 129 the next] next the *F* 130 Loving the brave] In oysters and *all* 131–6] *all read:*

Hind, Goderiske [Godderick *H Hv* Goodricke *HM* Goodrich *J*], Smith
And Nansagge [Nansogg *H Hv* *om. HM* Mansog *J*] sonnes of chine [clune *E*] and pith
Such who [That do *J*] know [knew *HM* knows *Hv*] well
To beare the Magicke bowle [bowe *H Hv J* bough *F HM*], and spill [spell *H F HM*]
All mighty [Immortall *J*] blood, and can [who canst *HM* that canst *H F Hv* that can *J*] doe more
Then Jove and [or *F J*] Chaos them [him *F HM Hv J* did *H*] before

131–2 *F* has 'Nansogge' in 131 and 'Goodrick' in 132 137 To those, and then] To theys then and *HM* To these and then *F J* 138 We'l] I *J* *Wickes*] weekes *F HM Hv J* 139 the] a *F* 140 yet full] but yet *all* 141 As] As is *all* (*including W*) 142 or] and *J* 143 shall] do *J* 144 W'are] wee are *H Hv J* we're *HM W* 150 Which] That *J* for] to *HM* from *H Hv* 151 The . . . spent] The fire out *F HM* The fire being out *J* once] much *E* we'l] wee will *HM* 152 Farre] Much *E* night] night- *F*

136. 1. A short hymne to Venus. In *MC*, p. 159, headed A SONG TO VENUS. Also in *WR* (1663), f. Cc5, headed *A vow to Cupid.* 1 *Goddesse*] *Cupid WR* 2 with] like *WR* 3 I may but] that I may *WR* 5 will] do *WR*

137. 2. Upon a delaying Lady. In *WR*, f. T2, headed *A Check to her delay.*

139. 6. Nothing new. In *WR*, No. 119.

141. 1. Long and lazie. In *WR*, No. 123. 2 be long] belong *WR*

143. 2. Upon wrinkles. In *WR*, No. 128, headed *To a stale Lady.* 1] Thy wrinkles are no more, nor less *WR*

144. 4. Gain and Gettings. In *WR*, No. 139. 1 others] other *WR*

145. 2. Upon . . . Elizabeth Herrick. See p. 585.

149. 2. Upon Doll. In *WR*, No. 141.

149. 3. Upon Skrew. In *WR*, No. 145 and in *GD*, p. 86, headed *On* C. Hill. 1 *Skrew*] *Hill GD*

149. 4. Upon Linnit. In *WR*, No. 154.

154. 1. Upon Raspe. In *WR*, No. 197 and in *GD*, p. 87, headad *Epigram*. 1 *Raspe*] Dick *GD*

155. 3. Upon himself. In *WR*, No. 418.

155. 4. Another. In *WR*, No. 270, headed *Love and Libertie*. 2 yoke free *WR*: yoke-free *48*

156. 1. Upon Skinns. In *WR*, No. 159.

156. 4. The mad Maids song. In MS. Harl. 6917, f. 48, headed A Songe Also in *Ac50*, p. 232, headed *A Song*. 2 morning] morrow *H Ac50* 4 Bedabled with] all dabbled in *H Ac50* 5 morning] morrow *H Ac50* Prim-rose] Cowslip *H Ac50* 7 flowers] teares *H* the] this *Ac50* 8 is] was *H Ac50* 11 Bee] he *Ac50* 12 Which] That *Ac50* 13 *Bonnet*] Cities *Ac50* 17 know] hope *H Ac50* 22 do] doth *H Ac50* 23 reare] reares *H Ac50* 24 do] doth *H Ac50* 26 Cow-slips] Balsome *H Ac50* 27 home] back *Ac50* 28 I] you *Ac50*

158. 5. To Sycamores. In Add. MS. 31432, f. 34 (*headed* To the Sicamour); MS. Egerton 2013, f. 21v; and *Ac71*, where it is *Song* 77. 3 so] so heere *A E* I] I may *Ac71* 6 with] to *Ac71* that] whilst *Ac71* 7 Say, have ye] Can ye haue *A* can you haue *E Ac71* do] can *E* you] yee *A E* 9 ye] you *Ac71* 10] ye [you *E*] weepe, being sick of loue as I *A E* Y'are weeping sick of Love as I *Ac71*

161. 2. The Willow Garland. In *P52*, *P53*, *P55*; *P59*, headed A. Willow Garland sent for a Newyeers-gift. Also in MS. Don. c. 57, f. 72v and H. Lawes autograph MS., penultimate fol. 2 Perfum'd (last day)] Last day perfum'd *P Don HL* 4 by] of *P* 5 so] thus *P* (*except P59*) that *P59* thus *Don HL* Ile] I *Don* 9 Altars] altar *P Don HL* 10 drest, so] so go *Don* (go *partly erased, but* drest *is not inserted before* so)

162. 2. Upon Craw. In *WR*, No. 192.

163. 3. Jack and Jill. In *WR*, No. 202.

165. 1. Oberons Palace. In Add. MSS. 22603, f. 59 and 25303, f. 157; also in MSS. Ashmole 38, p. 101; Firth e. 4, p. 52; and Rawl. poet. 160, f. 167. Headings: Kinge Oberons his Pallace. *A26* Oberons Pallace *A25* King Oberons Pallace *Ash and R* Oberon his Pallace: by Mr Hearick. *F* In MS. Ashmole 38 pp. 101–2 give ll. 9–69 (69 erased) including the additional verses noted below; ll. 69–107 were first copied on p. 105, the writer having inadvertently turned over two pages. On discovering the mistake he copied ll. 69–107 again on p. 103 (*Ash²* in notes). The poem was finished in another hand on p. 105 (*Ash³*). 1–8] *om. all MSS.* 10 high] full *F* 11 he'l go] hee goes *A25* 13 ha's] hath *A22 A25 Ash F* eares] eare *F* 16 Among] Amonst *F* 17 peltish] pettish *A22* hellish *F* well know] well knowne *all MSS.*

we'l know *48* Guard] guard. *A22 A25* 19 lead] led *all MSS.* on. Thus] on thus *A22 A25 F R* one, thus *Ash* 20 Sometimes] Sometime *A22 Ash* 22 shine] shines *Ash* a way] away *A22 A25 R* 23 with] by *A22* 24 perplexity] perplexed eye *F* 25 and man'] many *all MSS.* 27 Spungie and swelling] Swellinge, and spungy *all MSS.* 28 finest] grasse of *A22 A25 Ash F* grosse of *R* 29 Mildly disparkling] Soberly sparklinge *A22 A25 Ash F* Seemely sparkling *R* 30 break] breaking *Ash* from] *om. F* 31 those] y^e^ *all MSS.* 33 this] his *A22* 34 and] or *A25* 35 to] in *all MSS.* 36 here was] here were *A22 Ash F* there was *R* 37 *Ceston*] girdle *all MSS.* 38] The eyes of all doth strayte bewitch *all* 39 Aires move] ayre moues *A22 F* 41 lowe] plough *Ash* empearl] in pearle *A22 Ash R* 42 or] and *all* 45 cense] cause *Ash* lacuna in *F* 46–54] Expanded in all MSS. as follows (text from *Ash*; the italicized words are distinguished in the MS.):

And further [farther *A25 F*] of, some Orte of peare
Apple or plume is neatly Layde
(as yff yt were [was *A22 R*] a tribute payde)
By the [this *F*] round *Vrchin*, some mixt [nipte *A25*] wheat
The [That *A22 R* In *F*] which the Ant did tast, not Eate
Deafe *Nutts* soft *Iewes=eares*, and some thine
Chipping [chippings *A25 F*], the *Mice* filcht from the Binn
Of the graye Farmer; and to theis
The scrappes of *Lintells* Chitted *Pease* [Lintells chitted, Pease | Dryed, *A22*]
Dryed *Hony=combes*, browne *Acorne Cupps*
Out of the which hee sometymes [sometime *R*] Sups
His hearby=broath: and theis [then *F* there *A22*] Close by
Are puckered [*lacuna in F*] *Bullas*, *Cankers*, and dry
kernells, and withered *Hawes*: the rest
Are trinketts falne from the [*om. F*] Kytes neast
As butter'd Bread the w^c^h the wilde
Birde, snach't away from the Crying [*om. A25*] Childe
Blew Pynes, Taggs, Fescas, Beades, and things
Of higher [greater *F*] price, as halfe *Iett* rings
Ribands; and then some silken shreakes [streaks *A25* shreake *F*]
The Virgins lost att Barlye breakes [breake *F*]
Many a Purse stringe, many a Threade } [*om. A25*]
Of gould and siluer, ther is spread, }
Manye a Counter, Manye a Dye
Halfe Rotten and w^t^hout an [*om. F*] eye
Lyes here about; and as wee ghesse
Some bitts of *Thymbles* seeme [seemes *R*] to dresse
The braue cheape worke [Workes *F*]; and for to paue
The Easie Excellence [excellency *A22 R*] of the Caue

56 Are neatly here] Serue here, both which *all MSS.* 57] Expanded in all MSS. as follows:

W^th Castors doucetts (wch poore thay
Bite [Bitt *Ash*] of them selves to scape away)
Browne *Toade=stones*, *Ferretts* eyes, the Gumm

60 Wise hand] Hand *all* 62 the] those *Ash* 64 the shie] the [a *F*] sly *A22 Ash F R* Virgin] mayden *all* 65 where] and *all* 66 the] a *F* 67 Snake] snakes *all* 68 eyes] the Eyes *Ash* 70 silver-pence] Punyes are *A22 F* peñyes are *A25* Puisneirs are *Ash* Puisneirs, *Ash²* cut] cutts *A25* 71 neatly] choycely *A22 A25 R* Richlye *Ash* closely *F* 73 silv'rie fish] syluer Roach *all* 74 Kitling's] Kittling *Ash²* 75 here] there *F* for] to *A25* 76 glaring] glassing *Ash²* 77 Or] nor *A25 Ash F* Noe *A22 R* 78 roome] Caue *all* what] with *F* 79 Can] *om. F* make reflected] get reflection *A22 Ash R* gett reflected *A25* Comes reflexion *F* these] those *Ash* 80 multiply] multiplyes *F* 81 ever] euen *F* 82 Taper-light] Candlemas *all* 83 Errours] errour *F* 84 tann'd] tane *A22* as] and *A22 Ash R* 85 tender] as tender *A22* 87 Rear'd] Rays'd *all* lyes] was *F* 88 seem'd] seeme *all* 89 obedient] Conuenient *Ash* 91 face] head *all* 93 luckie] whiter *all except F* better *F* 94 And] but *Ash²* 96 carded] lockes of *all* 97 *Spunge-like*] spungie and *A22 A25 F R* spungie *Ash* 98 seem'd] seemes *all* comply] imply *all* 99 the] her *Ash* 101 *Spinners*] Spinsters *A22 Ash F R* spinters *A25* 103 sunck] hung *F* 106 those] the *all* *Threds*] heads *F* 107 Broke at the Losse] We call ye ffyles *all* 108 these] those *A22 Ash³ F R* pure] soft *all* 109 Dropt] Which *all* 110 Or] And *all* writhing] waytinge *A22* when, (panting)] are shed when *all* 112 has] hath *all* 114 The which] Which *Ash³* to excite] for to accite *Ash³* 118 *Mab*] mab's *F* 121 *This*] his *F* *flax*] yarne *all*

168. 3. To Oenone. In *MC*, p. 159, headed A SONG. Also in *WR* (1663), f. Dd6^v, headed *The Farewell to Love, and to his Mistresse*; not in stanzas. 1] What conscience say, Is it in thee, *WR* 5 or] and *WR* 8 give] send *WR* 9 Covet] Court *WR* but] for *WR*

174. 1. The parting Verse &c. In Add. MS. 22603, f. 41^v; MS. Ashmole 38, p. 93; MS. Rawl. poet. 160, f. 47^v; Huntington MS. 198, p. 5; and Harvard MS. Eng. 626 F, f. 33^v. '*all*' signifies agreement between these five versions. Grosart, Memorial-Introduction, pp. cliv–clvi, gives readings from another manuscript (Kingsborough-Hazelwood), then owned by W. F. Cozens. Present location unknown. The readings in general closely follow those of the other manuscripts and are not recorded here. Headings: Mr Herickes Charge to his Wife *A* Mr Hericke his charge to his wife *Ash* The husband charge departing from home, to his wife, *HM* R: Herrick: his charge vnto his wife *R* My charge *Hv* 1 Go hence] Goe *all* 2 joyns] ioyes *HM* 3 beest] bee *Ash* kind, soft] soft, kind *A Ash R* 4 thousands with a] wooers by thy *A Ash R Hv* wooers by the *Ash* 8 let] by *R* 10 that] things *HM* 11–16 and 17–28 in reverse order in *all* 11 immured] iniured *A* 12 and] or *all* thy] the *Hv* 14 Stand for] Keepe, 'gainst *all*

15–16] And thinke each man thou seest doth doome
Thy thoughts to say, I backe am come. *all*

18 Feature] beauty *all* 21 'tave] th'aue *A* they'haue *R* itt haue *HM* 22 it] yet *all except HM* or] nor *all* 24] As Emblemes will expresse yᵉ itch, *all* 25 thy] yᵉ *A R HM Hv* 27 thou't fall to one] thou needst [needs *Ash R HM*] must fall *all* 28] To one, then prostitute to all. *all* 29 But if they] Let them *all* 30 that] the *HM* 31 web] wilbe *HM Hv* 34 art] beest *all except HM* 35 so] still *all* 36 Those] These *all* 37 enstile] call thee *all* Fairest] wondrous *all* 38 The Pearle of Princes] Crowne of women *all* 39 so thou art] thow art soe *all* 41 And this] And *all* their Flatt'rie] theis flatterers *Ash* their flatteries *R* do's] doth *A Ash HM Hv* doe *R* 42 pleasures] pleasur'd *A* 44 Or] Nor *all* the] *om. Ash* ('our' inserted over caret) 45 do's] doth *all* 46 gentle] vertuous *all* 47 thee] *om. Ash* thow *HM* then *Hv* 49 And let] Let *all* 51 thou then] thow *HM Hv* then *rest* that] thy *Ash* 52 shalt find] find *HM* findst *rest* 53 But yet] But *all* must] will *HM Hv* 54 will] must *all* 55 And wildly] 'Gainst thee, and *all* 58 *Syracusian*] Syracusan *A Ash HM* *Cyane*] Cyone *A Ash HM Hv* Cynoë *R* 59 *Medullina*] Medullino *A* 60 these] those *A R Hv* had] knew *all* 61 For] of *HM* 62 Here was] Was *all* 64 *That makes*] Creates *all* 66 Triumph] Glory *all* such a] such *Ash* 69 this compression] this my last signet *A* my last signett *Ash HM* this my signet *R* this last signet *Hv* 73 till] still *Hv* 74 my] thy *R* wisht] *om. HM* 78 Lean-horn'd] Sharp-horn'd *HM* before I come] before I turne *A HM Hv* ere I returne *Ash R* 79 As one triumphant] In my full triumph *all* 80 all faith] yᵉ height *all* Woman-kind] women kind *A Hv* 82 Had'st] Hast *A Ash HM* 83 shelfe] selfe *HM*

187. 1. How he would drinke his Wine. In *C52*.

191. 2. Change gives content. In *WR*, No. 253, headed *Change*.

195. 5. To Electra. In *WR*, f. T3ᵛ, headed *To Julia*.

199. 5. Upon himselfe being buried. In *C52*.

205. 2. Upon Umber. In *WR*, No. 228.

205. 5. The Apparition. In *WS*, f. L5, headed *His Mistris Shade*. Also in MS. Folger 1. 21, f. 15 and Huntington MS. 172, f. 9ᵛ. '*all*' in notes signifies agreement between these three versions. *Desunt* *nonnulla*——] *om. WS Fol* 1 with silv'rie] of silver *WS* with silver *Fol HM* 3 in the Meads] on the bankes *all* 8 *Storax*] Spicknard *all* from] through *all* hallowed] hallow *WS* 9 wealthy] fruitefull *Fol HM* 10 fragrant . . . or] mellow Apples, ripened Plumbs and *all* 17 naked Younglings, handsome Striplings] handsome striplings, naked younglings *all* 18 Virgins] Virgin *all* 20 Commixt . . . Roses] So soone as each his dangling locks hath [has *Fol HM*] *all* After this line *all* add

With Rosie Chaplets, Lillies, Pansies red
Soft Saffron Circles to perfume the head.

23 too unto] to *WS* 24 our] their *all* 25 thou shalt] shalt thou *all* 28 *Iliades* or *Iliads*] Illiades *all*

29–30] Vnto the Prince of Shades, whom once his Pen
Entituled the Greecian Prince of men. *all*

31 and that done] thereupon *all* 33 bowles] Cups *all* 36 Looks, shew him truly] Lookes renders him, true *all* 37 shall] will *all* 38 Where] Whence *Fol HM* rage] laugh *all* and dance] both rage *all* 40 sits] stands *all* 42 eye] eyes *all* 46 from *all*: for *48* jarres] Iarre *all* t'engage] to enrage *WS* 48 a spacious Theater] an Amphitheater *all* 49 Among which glories] Amongst [Amonge *Fol HM*] which Synod *all* 50 Ivie] joy *WS* Two] weele have to *WS* weele haue *Fol HM* 51 *Beumont* and *Fletcher*] *Shakespeare* and *Beamond all* all eares] the Spheares *all*

52–53] Listen, while they call backe the former yeare [yeares *Fol HM*]
To teach the truth of Seenes, and more for thee, *all*

54 to know] brave soule *WS* *om. Fol HM* thou] thou as yet *HM* 56 capacious] illustrious *all* 57 now is plac't] shall be plac'd *all*

59–61] To be of that high Hyrarchy, where none
But brave soules take illumination
Immediatly from heaven, but harke the Cocke *all*

62 proclaime] proclaimes *all* 63 see] feele *all* 64 from] through *all*

208. 1. The Primrose. In *WS*, f. L8[v]; *Poems by Thomas Carew*, 1640, p. 188 (see note to 106. 3, p. 475 above); *L53*; *P59*; and in H. Lawes autograph MS., p. 155. 2 sweet *Infanta* of the] firstling of the Winter *WS* firstling of the Infant *C L P HL* 4 thus] all *all* 5 will] straight will *WS* strait *C* must *L P HL* to] in *WS* 6 mixt] wash'd *all* 7 flower] Rose *L P HL* do's] doth *WS L P HL* 8 So yellow-green] So yellow, greene *WS* So yellow greene *C* All yellow, green *L P HL* 10] And yielding each way, yet not break? *L P HL* 11 will answer] must tell you *all* 12 fainting hopes] doubts and fears *all*

209. 2. No luck in Love. In *MC*, p. 160, headed A SONG. 9 who] that *MC*

212. 2. Upon Lucia. In *GD*, p. 109. 1 *Lucia*] *Julia GD* 3 Say then] Then think *GD*

212. 3. Little and loud. In *WR*, No. 176. 1 Womans] Womens *WR*

215. 2. To the Maids. In *WR*, f. V5, headed *Abroad with the Maids.*

217. 1. The Night-piece, to Julia. In H. Lawes autograph MS., p. 337. 2 attend] to Atend *HL* 12 do's] doe *HL* 15 Tapers] Taper *HL* 20 Ile] I will *HL*

219. 2. Upon Love. In *MC*, p. 159, headed A SONG VPON LOVE.

223. 2. Upon Lungs. In *WR*, No. 214. 1 sets] sits *WR* (1663) 2 do's] doth *WR* the] his *WR*

224. 2. Upon a child. In *WR*, Epitaphs, No. 92.

226. 1. Upon an old man &c. In *WR*, Epitaphs, No. 134. 1 ye] you *WR*

226. 5. Upon Cob. In *WR*, No. 231.

226. 6. Upon Lucie. In *WR*, No. 244, headed *On Betty.* 1 *Lucie*] *Betty WR*

226. 7. Upon Skoles. In *WR*, No. 281. 3 one] and *WR*

229. 3. Ambition. In *WR*, No. 292.

232. 2. Upon Zelot. In *WR*, No. 296. 1 ye] yet *WR* (1663)

232. 5. Upon Crab. In *WR*, No. 300.

235. 1. Deniall in women &c. In *WR*, No. 304, headed *On Womens Deniall.* 2 to take] and take *WR*

235. 2. Adversity. In *WR*, No. 319.

238. 5. Upon Tuck. In *WR*, No. 329. 2 wherwith] therewith *WR* 1654 *and* 1663

239. 3. Adversity. In *WR*, No. 358.

240. 4. Upon Trigg. In *WR*, No. 365.

241. 6. Possessions. In *WR*, No. 369.

248. 1. Charon and Phylomel &c. In MS. Rawl. poet. 65, f. 32; Add. MS. 29397, f. 27, headed A dialogue between Phylomel & Charon; Add. MS. 31432, f. 34ᵛ, headed Dialogue, Charon, and yᵉ Nitingale; Add. MS. 35043, f. 22ᵛ; and MS. Don. c. 57, f. 57ᵛ. Also in *P52*, *P53*, *P59*, *P67*. MSS. omit speech-prefixes *Ph.* and *Ch.*, as do *P52* and *P53*. 2 By] With *all* unto] to *A29 A35 P59* 3 charming] warbling *Don* 4 Say] Speak *R* prithee] pray thee *Don* 5 sound] voice *R* yet can] doe I *R Don* yet I *P A29 A31 A35* 6 where] what *R Don* 7 bird] shade *all* 8 warbling note] mournful note *R* mournful voyce *A29 A31 A35 Don P* 9 nor] no *R* or] nor *all* fowles] foul *R A29 A31 A35 P* 10 Beasts] beast *A31 P* except *P67* but only] only *R* 11 witching] warbling *R A29 A31 A35 P* charming *Don* 12 thus hoist] hoist up *R* hoyse my *P A29 A35* hoise up my *A31* hoyst my *Don* saile] sayles *Don* 13 returne] be gone *R* 15 she's] he's *R Don* 16 Who] that *all* Ile] I'de *R Don* I *A31 A35 P* her] h *R Don* in] to *A29* 17 And is] Ands *A29 A31 A35* is that all] that's all *R P* By] For *R A29 A31 A35 P* 17] If y[ts] all I am gone for Love I pray thee *Don* 18 pray] praise *R* few] no *all* soules] fowls *A29* pay] pays *R* 19 vows] sighs *all* 20 mending] patching *all* for] or *all* patching] mending *all* Boat] boats *R A35* and] or *R Don P* 22 shalt] shall *A35* with] in *all* . 23 begin,] *P* gives remaining words to 'Chorus' 24 Our slothfull] Our *R* o're] through *R* 25 these] the *Don* 26 wo'd] will *A29 A31 A35 Don P* my] our *A29 A31 A35* y[e] *Don P* ferry] underlined and 'wherry' written above *Don* wherry *R* 25–26] Thus in *R*:

Thou & Ile sing, thou & Ile sing
To make those dull shades merry
Who els with teares
Would doubtless drowne our wherry.

There follows in *R* the dialogue song in Fletcher's *The Mad Lover*, IV. i.

249. 4. Maids nay's are nothing. In *WR*, No. 382, headed *Maides Nay's.*

251. 3. Another upon her weeping. In *WR*, No. 386, headed *On Julias weeping.*

253. 3. No Paines, no Gaines. In *WR*, No. 399.

255. 4. The Wake. In *WR*, f. V8[v], headed *Alvar and Anthea.* 3 Creams] Cream *WR*

259. 2. A Hymne to Bacchus. In *WR*, f. X7[v] (four 3-lined stanzas followed by four 4-lined) 1 *Iacchus*] *Bacchus WR* 13 doe] doth *WR* 15 *Maior*] *Major WR* 16 brave,] brave. *WR* 24 in] in a *WR*

260. 4. Anger. In *WR*, No. 422.

264. 5. Verses. In *WR*, No. 442.

265. 2. Upon Bice. In *WR*, No. 451.

265. 3. Upon Trencherman. In *WR*, No. 459.

265. 4. Kisses. In *WR*, No. 472.

273. 2. Upon Punchin. In *WR*, No. 483.

274. 2. Upon a Maide. In *WR*, Epitaphs, No. 135.

274. 4. Beauty. In *WR*, No. 498.

275. 5. Writing. In *WR*, No. 503.

276. 2. Satisfaction for sufferings. In *WR*, No. 505, headed *Satisfaction.*

281. 1. Another. In *WR*, No. 631, headed *On Love.* 1 dead] dread *WR*

283. 2. The showre of Blossomes, ll. 13–14. In *WR*, No. 653, headed *Sharpe Sauce.*

284. 1. Upon Lulls. In *WR*, No. 660.

287. 4. Truth. In *WR*, No. 667.

289. 1. Upon Ben. Johnson. In *WR*, Epitaphs, No. 174.

296. 3. An Hymne to Love. In *WR*, f. S4[v].

298. 1. Leven. In *WR*, No. 672.

315. 1. Upon Boreman. In *WR*, No. 677.

327. 4. Another on Love. In *WR*, No. 394, headed *On Love.*

327. 5. Upon Gut. In *WR*, No. 377.

331. 6. Upon Rumpe. In *WR*, No. 324. 1 -broach] -spit *WR*

333. 3. Sauce for sorrowes. In *WR*, No. 223. 1 suffering] sufferings *WR*

334. 4. The end of his worke. In *WR*, No. 706, headed *Of his Booke.*

342. 2. To God: an Anthem. In MS. Folger 452. 1, p. 22, headed An Anthem by M[r]. Herricke. 6 this . . . this] my . . . my *Fol*

ADDITIONAL POEMS

Headings of poems from manuscripts are italicized in the text, whether underlined in the manuscripts or not; and manuscript contractions have been expanded.

404. 1. The Description of a Woman. Also in MS. Harl. 6057, f. 42; MS. Ashmole 38, p. 88; Huntington MS. 198, p. 8; *WR* (1645), f. X4 ('V4'), under Fancies and Fantasticks (engraving precedes poem). *WR* omits ll. 47–50, 57–58, 63–76, 79–84, 103–4, and 109–12. Headings: A description of a woman *H* The Description of Women *WR* 2 Seemes] Shews *WR* Apollo's] Appollo *HM* blesses] dresses *WR* 3 like vnto] like *WR Ash HM* when] when with pearle *WR Ash HM* 4 tramaletts] Corronetts *H* 6 Bares] Bears *WR Ash* 10 with faire] with *H* fring'd] frindge *Ash* 14 a] the *H* 15–16 show . . . grow] shown . . . grown *WR* 17 mixed] mixeth *H* 18 like] the *HM* seeme] lye *Ash* 19 Ther] Then *WR Ash HM* 20 smelling swelling] seming smiling *HM* bashfull *WR Ash HM*: *om. R H* 23 meet] neat *WR HM* 24 shewe] selues *Ash* 25 portalls] Portall *HM* 26 an] a *Ash* 27 rich] sweet *HM* that] w[ch] *H* 31 the] her *Ash H* 32 pearle] pearles *H* Carcenett] Cabinet *WR Ash HM* 33–37 with . . . chinne] *om. H* 34 plumpe white] white, plumpe *WR* 35 faire] white *Ash* 36 blessed] fairest *WR* 41 by] bee *Ash* 43 of this] of the *WR H* 47 veynes] veyne *H* 49 a] this *Ash* vine] vayne *H HM* 50 of] lyke *Ash HM* 52 beares] Beare *Ash HM* 57 Fingring the *Ash*: (*lacuna*) the *R*: But when theis *H* Fingring that *HM* sleeded] sleued *Ash* (?) slesy *HM* 58 And] w[ch] *HM* 60 of] in *WR* *om. H* Riphean] Riphdan *H* 63 on] in *Ash* 64 promise] primrose *Ash* 66 peereles pretious] pretious pearly *Ash HM* prominent *ed.*: permanent *R Ash H HM* promanent (*margin*) *HM* 67 direction] directions *H HM* 69 by] of *H* 70 this] the *Ash* 71 Here's] her *HM* farre exceeds] doth excede *Ash* 72 loue] loues *H* 74 to] of *HM* 76 sweet sweet] sweet sweetes *H* a] the *H* 77 me] for *H* 78 like twoe] like to *Ash* vnto *H* 80 smooth] pure *Ash* 82 moste *H*: sweet- *Ash HM* *om. R* sight] high *HM* 84 its] Itt *Ash HM* 85 knees] kne *HM* 86 ever well grac'd *Ash H HM*: overwell grac'd *R* ever well 'greed *WR* 88] *om. H* 89 beawtious] comely *WR* 90 legg and foote] leggs and feet *Ash* 91 Then] though (*margin*) *HM* 92 pounded] powred *Ash* 95 lovely] lowly *Ash* allure] allures *HM* 97 seem] seem'd *H* 98 ryne] rinde *H* Rin'de *Ash* vein'd *WR* (?) vine *HM* 99 hands] hand *H* 106 Meets] Meet *WR Ash H HM* maks] make *WR H Ash HM* a] an *WR Ash* 108 melody] harmonye *HM* 110 work] life *Ash HM* 112 Whence] Wheare *Ash* thy] *om. Ash* At end: finis Robt Herick *Ash* R: W H

407. 1. Mr Hericke his daughter's Dowry. Also in MS. Harvard Eng. 626 F, f. 31^v, headed My (The *erased*) Daughters Dowry 2 giue] quitt *Hv* 6 thee] her *Hv* 8 forfaite] forfeited *Hv* 14 Fortune] for time *Hv* 15 praise,] praise *Ash Hv* 16 Bayes] layes *Hv* 17 rust] trust *Hv* 18 keepe peacefull] sleepe pleased *Hv* 21 that] this *Hv* 22 Loue, Peace, and *Hv*: *Loue* and *Ash* 24 that] *om. Hv* 25 with Mylder Lawes] by mild meanes *Hv* 26 or] and *Hv* 27 the] thee *Hv* 31 To th'shew] To the sight *Hv* 33 Thy] The *Hv* 35 it] those *Hv* 37 fly] passe *Hv* 38 setts] sett *Hv* 39 theis, *ed.*: theis *Ash Hv* 40 for season'd] to season *Hv* 42 Plague] brands *Hv* 46 bedd] cloude *Hv* 47 Inkyndled] vnkindled *Hv* 48 Chafes and warmes] warmes and chafes *Hv* 56 As is] (As (is *Ash* 57 stroake] stroake) *Ash* 59 White *conj. P. Simpson*: W^th *Ash* With *Hv* 62 flattering] fettering *Hv* 66 A tempest] and temper *Hv* 70 to] it *Hv* 74 to] in *Hv* 75 I] I doe *Hv* 76 but] then *Hv* 80 worshipp *Hv*: wor^pp. *Ash* (*misread* worth *by editors*) 81 ffor] And *Hv* shee] hee *Hv* 84 bringe] bring'st *Hv* 86 vnto] into *Hv* 88 the] that *Hv* 90 Eare rings] earing *Hv* 92 trauylde for] travaile far *Hv* 93 price] prize *Hv* 94 fetch] fetch't *Hv* 95 shey] shie *Hv* 97 *Lou'd*] Loue *Hv* 97–98 feare Of offending] *not distinguished as for italics in Ash or Hv* 107 haue] with *Hv*

410. 1. Mr Robert Hericke his farwell vnto Poetrie. Also in Add. MS. 22603, f. 30^v; MS. Rawl. poet. 160, f. 46^v; and Huntington MS. HM 198, p. 14. Headings: Herickes Farewell to Poetrie *A* R: Herricks ffarewell to Poesye. *R* Mr Herricks farwell to Poetry *HM* 1 I haue behelde] Euen as yow see *R* 5 that each] ye Earth *A* 6 Healthes] Health *A R HM* 10 some sleepy] ye sleepiğe *A HM* ye parting *R* 12 yet forc't they are] and yet are forc'd *A* 13] *om. HM* 14 those] theis *R* 17 tell] till *A R* 20 fresh] first *HM* 22 Nyne *A R HM*: wyne *Ash* makes] made *A R* with God] of Gods *A* 29 who did'st] who doest *A HM* which do'st *R* 32 While] White *conj. W. C. Hazlitt*

39 Those] theis *R* 40 Fames] fame *A* 41 *Ouid, Maro*] Maro, Ovid *R* 42 those] the same *HM* 45 nor . . . suruiue] not stouping downe, but she suruiues *HM* 46 or] a *A R HM* 48 of] to *A R HM* 50 that] thy *HM* sublim'd] sublime *A R HM* 51–52 tis . . . Mankinde)] *om. A* 58 Functions] (?) Function, *Ash* 59 *Guesse*] Ghesse *A HM* Kisse *conj. W. C. Hazlitt* 60 that lye drawne] wch lye drawne *R HM* 61 in] and *A R HM* 64 Joyes] ioy *HM* Pleasures] pleasure *HM* 65 whilst] while *R* 68 through] from *HM* 69 loues]loue *A* 70 myne] my *R HM* 74 *Attica*] Africa *A* 75 Brest's] brest *HM* 80 Varnish (only)] onely varnish *A R HM* 82 thyne] thy *A HM* 84 Hoofy] holly *HM* 85 that] y^e *A* 91 thy] thine *HM* 93 Loathsomst *A R HM*: Loathsoms *Ash* shapps] shape *R* 98 must] doe *A HM* 99 rare] deare *A* diuiner] deuinest *HM* 100 a] an *A R* 101 thou] then *HM* 102 Thoughe as] Though *A* At end *R* has 'ffinis' without name

414. 1. His Mistris &c. Also in MS. Harl. 6918, f. 23 and MS. Harvard Eng. 626 F, f. 22^v. 1 vow] vow, *H* Ile] I *H Hv* 3 thy] your *H Hv* 4 can] could *H Hv* It] to *H Hv* 5 Take then] Clame then a *H Hv* 8, 10, 12 thy] your *H Hv* 9 Oh] Ah *H Hv* 13 When as] Whereas *Hv* 15 and] as *H Hv* 16 shall] will *Hv* Ascription at end in *Ash* only

414. 2. Vpon parting. Also in MS. Folger 1669. 2, f. 270^v (a few scribal errors; ll. 5 and 6 are indented, as if for a stanzaic arrangement, but not ll. 11 and 12); and in Huntington MS. 904, f. 13. 1 in] at *HM* 2 tis] T'was *HM* 3–4] *om. HM* 5 But] For *HM* 6 were] are *HM* 7 now] then *HM* 8 and] then *HM* 10 cold] much *HM* 11 With] And *HM* fate] time *HM* can nere] canot *HM* 12 But truth] With Fath *HM* Ascription in *Fol. 1669. 2*: Ro Herrick (not in *HM*)

415. 1. Upon Master Fletchers Incomparable Playes. Also in *Poems* by Francis Beaumont (1653), f. A5. The present text gives italics for roman and vice versa.

416. The New Charon. Also in *P52* headed *A Dialogue.* Charon and Eucosmia. *Occasioned by the death of the yong Lord* Hastings, *Heire apparent to the Earle of* Huntington, *who dyed some few dayes before he was to have been marryed to Sir* Theodore Meiherns *Daughter, in* June, 1649. Also in *P69* with title abbreviated. 3 overwhelm'd] or'e whelm'd *P* 5 who am in deep] a Virgin in *P* 7 I will be] I'd be as *P* 8 *Elizean*] Elizium *P* 9 Speak] Tell *P* art thou] thou art *P* One, once] A Mayd *P* 11 Ay] Ah *P* 13 He was an Hastings] Hastings, Hastings, was his name *P* 15 my Love, my Joy] my joy, my love *P* 18 *For Humane Joy*] To humane joyes *P* 22 That] Which *P* thus] here *P* 23 let me] I would *P* 24 waftage] wafting *P* 27 stream] streams *P* 31 this] the *P69* 35 known] know *P* 37 We sail along] We sayl from hence *P*

417. 1. Vpon a Cherrystone. Also in MSS. Sloane 1446, f. 62v, and 1792, f. 20; Add. MS. 30982, f. 66; and Harvard MS. Eng. 626 F, f. 35v. '*all*' in notes signifies agreement among these four versions. Headings: On a cherry stone sent to weare in his Mrs eare, a deaths head on the one side & her face on the other *S 14* A cherry stone sent to weare in his Mris eare a deaths head on one side her owne face on ye other *S17* On a cherry stone haveing a deaths head one ye one side & a Gentle woman on ye other side. *A* Vpon a Carued Cherriestone *Hv* 2 on] in *all* 3 of great] for ye *all* 4 respect] regard *all* except *Hv* 5] ffor the Morrall on't alone *S14* 6 it] it an *A* 7–10 follow 58 in *Hv* 7 Take] reade *all except Hv* in a] in *A* 10 Looks] looke *A* theis] those *S14* 11–12 *om. Hv* 11 incarvements] carved mesures *all* 12 yow] wee *A* 13 Read] Kisse *all* except *Hv* 14 Comends] commend *A* Convey *S14 S17* 17 may] must *A* 18 that] what *all* 19 time] times *A* this] the *S14* 20 had] Like *Hv* 23 All's now fledd] All nowe is gone *Hv* 24 Poore] The *Hv* the] a *A* beawty, bone] beautie stone *S14* 25–26] *om. S14* 26 ever . . . aire.] *om. S17* i'th'] in the *A* 29 ffaile] fade *all* to] for to *A* 30 ever] ere *A* a] an *A* 31 And] Then *S14 S17* 32 leane] bare *A* to] to the *A* 33 Sextons] Sexton *all* except *Hv* sweare] sweares *A* 34 Here] that heer *S14* Jemmonia's] Jeminias *A* all yor *S14* Gemmenayath's *S17* Jemimihs *Hv* titles were] title are *S14* 35 rag'd Escutcheon] raged escutcheon showne *A* ragged Scutchion showne *S14 S17 Hv* 36 maye] will *Hv* beleiue] beeleeu't *S14* 37 there thought] theire height (*?*leight *A*) *all* may] will *S14 S17* 40 your] the *A* 41 with it still] still with it *A* 42 Euensong] Eveninge songe *S14 A Hv* 43 Pickaxe] Pike, axe *A* 46 your] yō faire *S14* 47 though *all*: through *R* his] this *S14 Hv* hung] hang *A* i'th'] in the *A* 48 doth not to] and doth not in *A* doth not so to *S14* 49 hees] ther's *S14 S17* it's *Hv* 50 know] knowne *A S14 Hv* to'th'] in the *A Hv* i'the *S14 S17* as] as in *A* and *S14 Hv* 51–53] *R* omits l. 52 and reads:

Place then this mirror whose briske hue
Of lines and colors make them scorne

51 Place] Placed *A* this] his *A* the *S14 S17* 51–52 to the veiw Of *A Hv*: of this view To *S14 S17* 52 those . . . hew] *all*, except that *A* reads 'brisky' and *Hv* 'those chast virgins' 53 lines] limbs *A S14 S17* (*?*) liues *Hv* colours] coulour *A* make] makes *Hv* 54 This] the *A* that *S14 S17* greeke hath] Greeks haue *A S14* Greek haue *S17* 55–58] *om. A* 55] lett them then, o lett them learne *S14* Let them learne *S17* booke] verse *Hv* 56 to] do *S17* 58 beholders] beholder *Hv* At end *S14* has Rog: Hericke.

419. 1. Epitaph in Dean Prior Church. The engraver put 'f' for long 's' passim, terminally as well elsewhere. Line 5 overran the length of the stone and the final word 'Pay' is inserted above the line over a caret. It is not followed by a question-mark. See Commentary. 5 Say *ed.*: Pay *engraver*

419. 2. To a Mayd. From Add. MS. 33998, f. 82^{v}. Also in *Ac50*, p. 231. 8 Cherry] every *Ac50* 10 yon] your *Ac50* 12 Cherryes] Berries *Ac50* 13 that one] this whole *Ac50*

420. 1. Epitaph. From Add. MS. 33998, f. 33^{v}.

420. 2. To his false Mistris. From Add. MS. 33998, f. 82^{v}. Also in Add. MSS. 19268, f. 22, 25707, f. 110^{v}, and 30982, f. 42^{v}; MSS. Egerton 2013, f. 8^{v}, and 2725, f. 68^{v}; MS. Sloane 1446, f. 88; H. Lawes autograph MS., p. 86; MS. Folger 1. 21 twice, ff. 44 and 72 ('*Fol A*' and '*Fol B*'); Huntington MS. 198, p. 63. Headings: A complaint of his piurd M^{rs} *A19* on his periur'd M.^{ris} *A25* A complaint *A30* On a periured M.$^{ris.}$ *E27* On a false Ms̃ *S*. No division into stanzas in *A19 A25 A30 E20 E27 Fol A Fol B* and *HM*. The verses often occur together with 49. 2 ('The Curse'), q.v. They are attributed to Herrick again in *A19*, unless the attribution there is meant for 49. 2, as by its position it may be. 1 Whither] Whether *A19 A30 S FolA and B* Wheer *HM* her] those *E20* ower *HM* oathes] Oath *HM* 2 they] the *A25* 3 I'me sure] I know *A25 E20 E27 HL* faith] Loue *Fol A* 4 dare] Dares *A19 A25 E20 E27 HL Fol A* 5 which] that *A25 E27 HL Fol A* w^{t}h *A30* did] doth *S* 6 one] on *A19* sigh] sight *A30* 7] and never back againe returne *S* 7 never] euer *A 30* 8 one] once *A30* till . . . false] Vntill one of her *A25 E20 E27 HL Fol A* false] lost *S* oathes] vowes *S* 10 shall] *om. A19 Fol B* shall both] *om. A30* 9–12] *A25 E20 E27 S HL Fol A* and *HM* read as follows, with exceptions noted:

There may they [it *Fol A*] wrastle in the skyes
Till [untill *HM*] they both [do both *S*] one Lightninge proue
Then [and *HM*] falling Lett it [may they *HM*] blast hir eyes
That is thus periur'd in hir loue. [was thus *HL HM* was so *S Fol A*

421. 1. To a disdaynefull fayre. From MS. Don. c. 57, f. 41. First stanza also in Add. MS. 33998, f. 82^{v} (whence the heading) and MS. Egerton 2013, f. 10 (music by John Hilton). Attributed to Herrick in *Don* only. The complete poem is in Ault's *A Treasury of Unfamiliar Lyrics* (1938). 2 is] rests *A* me & thee *A*: thee & me *Don E20* (corrected in pencil in *E20*) 3 softer] weaker *A* 5 that] w^{ch} *E* 6 neat] neare *E* 7] line incomplete in MS.

421. 2. Orpheus and Pluto. From MS. Don. c. 57, f. 53^{v}. In Ault, op. cit. No heading and no speech-prefixes in *Don*.

422. 1. Parkinsons shade &c. From MS. HM 198, p. 30. 22 uaults.] uaults *HM* 23 dead:] dead *HM* come,] come *HM*

423. 1. to **439.** 1. From a manuscript commonplace-book in the Rosenbach Foundation Library. See Introduction, p. xxxiv.

440. 1. The Showre of Roses. From H. Lawes autograph MS., p. 139 (between 26. 3 and 46. 2). First printed and attributed to Herrick by Willa M. Evans in her biography, *Henry Lawes*, 1941, pp. 157–8. Heading supplied by present editor.

440. 2. The Eclipse. From MS. Mus. b. 1, f. 110^{v}. Heading supplied by present editor. Also in Add. MS. 29396, f. 80^{v}. In Ault, op. cit., under 'Anon.'   8 seene *A*: seeme *Mus*

441. 1. The farewell. From MS. Harl. 6918, f. 50^{v}. Also in Harvard MS. Eng. 626 F, f. 37^{v}, where it is arranged in stanzas of four and six lines as follows: 4, 6, 6, 4+4 or 8 (end of page after first 4), 6, 4, 6, 4. No heading in *Hv*.   10 neuer] ne're *Hv*   33 bare] bore *Hv*   35 parting] partings *Hv*

442. 1. A Sonnet. From MS. Harl. 6918, f. 51^{v}. Also in Harvard MS. Eng. 626 F, f. 38, without heading.   8 noblest] noble *Hv*

442. 2. A Song. From MS. Don. c. 57, f. 17^{v}, without heading. Also in MS. Mus. b. 1, f. 39^{v}; *Ac50*, p. 240, headed *A Song*; and *ML*, p. 78, headed *Lose no time.*   1 no] not *Mus*   2 men] then *Mus*   6 &] they'l *Ac50*   7 &] y^{t} *Mus ML*   which *Ac50*   9 in] In all *Ac50*   sweet] sweetes *Mus Ac50 ML*

443. 1. Advice to a Maid. From Add. MS. 25707, f. 149. Also in Add. MS. 29396, f. 93^{v}; Add. MS. 41996, F; MS. Ashmole 38, p. 141; MS. Mus. b. 1, f. 33^{v}; W. Porter's *Madrigales and Airs* (1632), f. C2^{v}, whence Ault, op. cit., gives it under 'Anon.'; and *C52*. Heading supplied by present editor.   2 time] Age *Ash*   4 yett . . . growe] yet thou each day growes *Ash*   oulder] colder *C52*   5 Thou as heauen] As heauen thou *Ash*   8 will] may *Ash*   9 Then] when *Ash*   10 shall] may *Ash*   will *C52*   11 too . . . showre] Then thou to late wilt sheed *Ash*

443. 2. Elegy. From Harvard MS. Eng. 626 F, f. 36^{v}. Heading supplied by editor.   5 gone, *ed.*: gone *Hv*   15 hiatus in MS.   21 bee: *ed.*: bee *Hv*   35 hiatus in MS.   51 vndoe. *ed.*: vndoe, *Hv*   our *ed.*: are *Hv*

APPENDIX A. LETTERS

All of these appear to be in Herrick's hand. Manuscript contractions are not expanded. † signifies manuscript defect.

COMMENTARY

HESPERIDES

Frontispiece. The initials at the foot of the Latin verses, I. H. C. W. M., almost certainly stand for John Harmar, of Westminster College. See note to 301. 5. For the engraver, William Marshall, see *D.N.B.*

Title-page. Hesperides. The name was applied not only to the daughters of Hesperus but also to their garden in the Fortunate Isles at the western extremity of the earth. See *O.E.D.* s.v., 1. *c*. Herrick implies that his poems, fruits of the west country, are to be associated with the golden apples which the mythical garden contained. For other possible associations see a note by G. C. Moore Smith in *Mod. Lang. Rev.* ix, July 1914, pp. 373–4.

Title-page. Motto. Ovid has three lines resembling this one: *Amores*, iii. 9. 28; *Tristia*, iii. 7. 54; and *Ex Ponto*, iii. 2. 32. The nearest to Herrick's version, which is also on the title-page of Drayton's *The Shepheards Garland*, 1593, is the first of these:

Diffugiunt [*or* Effugiunt] avidos carmina sola rogos.

3. 1. *Charles, Prince of Wales*. This address may have been intended for the volume of Herrick's poems entered in 1640 (see Introduction, p. xv). Charles, born in 1630, was made Prince of Wales in 1638.

3. 1. 4. *Expansion*. See 82. 2. 4–5 and note. See also 67, l. 8, 191. 1. 2, and 301. 5. 4.

5. 1. *The Argument*. For a similar catalogue in fourteen lines see Th. Bastard, *Chrestoleros, Seuen Bookes of Epigrames*, 1598, p. 1 (Spenser Soc., 1888, p. 7): *Epigr.* 1 *de subiecto operis sui*:

I speake of wants, of frauds, of policies,
Of manners, and of vertues and of times,
Of vnthrifts and of friends, and enemies,
Poets, Physitions, Lawyers, and Diuines . . .

5. 2. 1–2. Cf. Martial, i. 3. 11–12:

aetherias, lasciva, cupis volitare per auras:
i, fuge; sed poteras tutior esse domi.

6, ll. 17–18. Cf. Martial, loc. cit., l. 3:

nescis, heu, nescis dominae fastidia Romae.

6. 1. See Horace, *Ep.* i. 20. 3, 5, 14.

6. 1. 4. *house to house*. Luke x. 7.

6. 1. 5. *bonds of Love*. Hosea xi. 4.

6. 2. Cf. Martial, xi. 16. 9–10:

erubuit posuitque meum Lucretia librum,
sed coram Bruto; Brute, recede, leget.

(Quoted by Burton, 3. 1. 1. 1, but not in editions prior to 1651.)

6. 3. 2. Cf. Juvenal, ii. 13: 'tumidae . . . mariscae'.

6. 3. 4. See Ps. lxxviii. 67.

7. 1. 6. A blurred reminiscence of Hor. *Ars Poet.* 417: 'occupet extremum scabies'.

7. 2. 2. *O're-leven'd.* Cf. 321. 2. 8.

7. 3. 1–2, 7–10. Cf. Martial, x. 20 (19). 18–21:

> Seras tutior ibis ad lucernas:
> haec hora est tua, cum furit Lyaeus,
> cum regnat rosa, cum madent capilli:
> tunc me vel rigidi legant Catones.

Also Martial, xiii. 2. 9–10; and iv. 82. 5–6.

7. 3. 3. Cf. John ii. 10.

7. 4. 9–10. Cf. 138. 1. 6.

8. 1. 4. Cf. 233. 1. 24.

8. 1. 8. *No man &c.* See 294. 1. 4. Cf. Publilius Syrus, 22: 'Amare et sapere vix deo conceditur.' See Burton, 'Democritus to the Reader', p. 72, and 3. 2. 3. 1, p. 514. Plutarch attributes a similar saying to Agesilaus: 'O how hard is it, both to loue and to be wise!' (North, *Tudor Trans.* iv, p. 174.) Quoted by Montaigne, iii. 5 (Florio, *Tudor Trans.*, p. 121).

8. 2. 5. *State.* Canopy. *O.E.D.* s.v., 2. *b.*

8. 3. 2. From Seneca, *Hippol.* 593–4: 'qui timide rogat docet negare'.

9. 1. In this poem Herrick may have been influenced by Tibullus, iii. 2. 9 sqq.

9. 1. 6. Cf. 129. 4. 2 and Ovid, *Met.* vi. 278: 'Oscula . . . suprema.'

9. 2. 9–12. Cf. Plutarch, *Isis and Osiris*, 15 (*Morals*, transl. Holland, 1603, p. 1293): 'onely the Queenes waiting maids and women that came by, she saluted and made much of . . . casting from her into them a marvellous sweet . . . sent issuing from her body, whiles she dressed them.'

10. 1. 1–2. Cf. Ovid, *Am.* 1. 5. 17–18: 'Ut stetit &c.'

10. 2. 1. Cf. Seneca, *Ep.* lxxxv. 9: 'Facilius est enim initia illorum [sc. affectuum] prohibere quam impetum regere.'

10. 2. 2. Juvenal, xiii. 209–10: 'nam scelus &c.'

10. 3. See Ecclus. xxv. 2.

11. 1. 3. *short or tall.* Ovid, *Am.* ii. 4. 36: 'longa brevisque'.

11. 1. 3–14. Cf. Burton, 3. 2. 3. 1 (p. 515): 'Every Lover admires his mistris, though shee be very deformed of her selfe, ill favored, . . . a thin, leane, chitty face . . . crooked . . . a nose like a promontory . . . black, uneven, browne teeth . . . he had rather have her then any woman in the world . . .' See also 207. 4; 253. 1.

13. 2. *Love what it is.* See 274. 3 and note.

13. 4. 7–8. 1 Cor. ix. 5.

14. 3. 9. 2 Sam. xv. 20.

15. 2. 7–8. See *O.D.E. Prov.*, 'Small sorrows speak . . .' and 'Empty vessels make the greatest sound.'

15. 2. 9–10. See *O.D.E. Prov.*, 'Still waters run deep.'

15. 2. 9–14. Cf. Ralegh, 'Sir Walter Ralegh to the Queen', ll. 1–6 &c. (*Poems*, ed. Latham, pp. 104–5.)

16. 1. 7–8. Cf. Anacreontea, 28. 5–7.

16. 2. Cf. Secundus, *Basia*, 2.

17. 1. 5–6. See 219. 2. 11–12; also Hor. *Sat.* ii. 7. 70–71 and Burton, 3. 2. 5. 3 (p. 562): 'What shall I say to him that marries againe and againe,

Stulta maritali qui porrigit ora capistro' (Juv. vi. 43).

17. 2. 1–2. Possibly a reminiscence of Anacreontea, 39.

17. 2. 7–8. Cf. Burton, 3. 2. 2. 2 (p. 455): 'One such a kisse would recover a man if he were a dying . . .'

18. 4. 2. Cf. Hor. *Ep.* ii. 2. 176: '. . . velut unda supervenit undam'.

19. 2. 6. *Robin Herrick.* Altered in *Wit a Sporting* (H. Bold, 1657) to *William Ridley.*

19. 4. 1. *O Earth.* Jer. xxii. 29.

20. 2. 4. *Holy-oke, or Gospel-tree.* See *O.E.D.* s.v. 'Holy'.

20. 3. 10. Cf. Ovid, *Am.* i. 5. 26, transl. Marlowe: 'Jove send me more such afternoons as this.'

21. 1. 1–2. Cf. Joseph Hall, *Meditations*, 1616, iii. 20 (*Works*, 1837, viii, p. 63): 'It was a witty and true speech of . . . Heraclitus, That all men, awaking, are in one common world; but, when we sleep, each man goes into a several world by himself.' (Heraclitus, *Fragm.*, ed. Bywater, No. 95.) The saying is quoted in *Spectator*, No. 487, as one 'which *Plutarch* ascribes to Heraclitus'. (Plutarch, *De Superst.* 3, transl. Holland, *Morals*, 1603, p. 262.)

21. 3. 5–6. Cf. Ecclus. Prologue: 'leaving this book almost perfected'.

21. 4. *heading.* See Tilley, *Prov. Eng.*, M1075, 'Money makes masteries' (1602).

21. 4. 1. Cf. Erasmus, *Adagia*, 'Munerum Corruptela': 'Argenteis hastis pugnare.'

21. 6. Cf. *Greek Anthol.* v. 21 (Rufinus).

22. 1. See Isa. i. 11; 1 Chron. xxix. 21; 2 Cor. ix. 7.

22. 2. 3–4. Cf. Martial, v. 81, and Matt. xxv. 29.

22. 3. Cf. Hor. *Carm.* iii. 23. 17–20.

22. 5. 4. *Lutes of amber.* See observations on this phrase in *N. and Q.*, 9th S., ix–x, 1902, beginning 24 May, pp. 408–9. As suggested there by F. G. Stephens, 5 July, p. 17, Herrick probably refers to lutes inlaid with amber, the resin, not the metal. See *O.E.D.* s.v. 'Amber'.

23. 2. 1–2. *April . . . Opens.* Cf. Ovid, *Fasti*, iv. 87, 89:

Nam quia ver aperit tunc omnia . . .
Aprilem memorant ab aperto tempore dictum.

23. 4. *heading.* Elizabeth Herrick was probably the widow of Herrick's brother William, but may have been the widow of the elder brother, Thomas. See notes to 73. 1. heading and 34. 3. heading; also 13. 4. Elizabeth Herrick was buried at Dean Prior, 11 April 1643.

24. 1. 3–4. Cf. Browne, *Religio Medici*, 1642, pp. 86–87: 'that Rhetoricall sentence, and *Antanaclasis* of *Augustine*, *creando infunditur, infundendo creatur*'.

24. 1. 5–6. Cf. Burton, 1. 1. 2. 5 (p. 20): 'Others make a doubt, whether it be all in all, and all in every part.' Cf. St. Augustine, *Ep.* clxvi. 4 (*Opera*, Migne, ii, col. 722), and see T. W. Baldwin, *On the Literary Genetics of Shakespeare's Poems & Sonnets*, pp. 157 sqq.

24. 2. 2. From Ovid, *Heroides*, iv. 10:

Dicere quae puduit, scribere iussit amor.

24. 2. 3–8. Cf. Catullus, v. 7–9.

25. 1. 1–2. Cf. Florio's *Montaigne*, iii. 9 (*Tudor Trans.* iii, p. 205): 'nothing falleth, where all things fall: a generall disease is a particular health: Conformitie is a quality enemie to dissolution.' See also 318. 5.

25. 1. 3–4. See 155. 1. 17–18 and note; also 319. 3. Cf. Seneca, *Troades*, 162–4:

felix quisquis
bello moriens omnia secum
consumpta tulit [videt].

Id. *De Prov.* 5: 'Grande solacium est cum universo rapi.' Cf. the proverb (of uncertain authorship) 'Solamen miseris socios habuisse doloris', quoted by Marlowe in *Dr. Faustus*, II. i. 42, and twice by Burton (2. 3. 1. 1, p. 304, and 3. 3. 4. 1, p. 616). See also 239. 5 and note; and 302. 2. 3–4.

25. 2. *The King . . . comming . . . into the West*. This was in 1644. See Clarendon, *Hist.* viii. 71–148; also note to 137. 3.

25. 2. 7. *horrid*. Virg. *Aen.* vi. 86: 'horrida bella'.

25. 2. 11. *Ride on*. Ps. xlv. 5. *white omens*. Propertius iv. 1. 67–68: 'candida . . . omina'.

26. 1. *heading*. A speech in Parliament by Sir B. Rudyerd of 9 July, 1642 (*Harl. Misc.* v. 77) was entitled 'The present unhappy Distance between His Majesty & ye Parliament'.

26. 1. 7. A reference to the talking oaks of Dodona. Seneca, *Herc. Oet.* 1473–4: 'quercus hanc sortem &c.'.

26. 2. Seneca, *Herc. Oet.* 614–15:

noctem quoties summovet Eos,
regem totiens credite nasci.

26. 3. Anacreontea, 33. But the following Latin version by H. Estienne (in *Anacreontis Teij odae*, 1554, pp. 86–87) is, as shown by Delattre, sometimes closer to Herrick's:

Nuper silente nocte,
Quum iam rotatur Vrsa
Circa manum Bootae,
Et corpus omne somnos,
Fessum labore, carpit:

Superuenit, forésque
Meas Cupido pulsat.
Quis tundit ostium, inquam,
Turbâtque somniantem?
Reclude, clamat ille,
Fores, metúmque pone.
Nam sum puellus, & per
Illunem oberro noctem,
Madens ab imbre totus.
Vt audij haec, misertus
Accendo lumen, atque
Meos recludo postes.
Tunc conspicor puellum,
Sed arcum habentem & alas,
Sed pendulam pharetram.
Foco admouetur à me,
Manibus manus & eius
Foueo vt calescat, imbrem
Et exprimo capillis.
Ille, vt recessit algor,
Probemus, inquit, arcum,
An laesus imbre neruus.
Statímque tendit illum,
Ferit & mihi sagitta
Medium iecur, quasi oestrum.
Tunc exilit cachinnans,
Aítque, Gratulare
O hospes: ecce, saluus
Meus quidem mihi arcus,
At cor tibi dolebit.

27. 1. *heading. religious.* Revered, sacred. See *O.E.D.* s.v., A. 1. *c.*

27. 1. 3. *neither haire was cut.* See 219. 1. 3 and note.

27. 1. 4. *justments. O.E.D.* quotes only this example.

27. 1. 5–6. See Introduction, p. xii. It may well have been thought inadvisable to let the precise place of burial be generally known.

28. 1. *Delight in Disorder.* This poem develops the song in Jonson's *Epicoene*, I. i. 91–102, 'Still to be neat &c.', itself based upon a poem of unknown authorship which has sometimes been attributed to Jean de Bonnefon, 'Semper munditias &c.' There are classical anticipations, as in Ovid's 'neglecta decens' (*Am.* i. 14. 21). Cf. Aemil. Magn. Arborius, *Ad Nympham Nimis Cultam*, and see Aelian, *Var. Hist.* xiv, on the 'adulteries of art'. Cf. also Jonson, *Masque of Blacknesse*, l. 29: 'imitating that orderly disorder, which is common in nature'. As a principle in literary composition the 'brave disorder', or its appearance, is recognized in Cicero's *Orator ad M. Brutum*, xxiii. 78: 'quaedam etiam neglegentia est diligens', and in Boileau's *L'Art poétique*, ii. 72 (on the Ode):

Chez elle un beau désordre est un effet de l'art.

See also 66. 3, 202. 3. 13–14, and 232. i. 6, 8.

28. 1. 2. *wantonnesse*. See 290. 2. 8.

28. 1. 4. *distraction*. Displacement, divagation.

28. 1. 5. *erring*. See 66. 3. 4.

28. 1. 5–8. Burton, 3. 2. 2. 3 (p. 465): 'costly stomachers, guarded and loose garments'.

28. 1. 8. Jonson, *Epicœne*, I. i. 99: 'Robes loosely flowing.' Arborius, op. cit. 21–22:

Ne toga fluxa volet, reprimit tibi fascia corpus;
  Sat corpus veneror, sit toga fluxa licet.

28. 1. 12. *wilde civility*. See 202. 3. 14, 99. 3. 6, and 232. 1. 6.

29. 1. 6. *Two Gent. of Verona*, II. iv. 170–2:

as rich . . .
As twenty seas, if all their sand were pearl,
The water nectar, and the rocks pure gold.

29. 1. 11–12. Burton, 2. 3. 2 (p. 314): 'those ordinary boores & pesants . . . a rude, brutish, uncivill, wilde, a currish generation . . .' Jer. v. 3: 'made their faces harder than a rock'.

30. 1. 8. *Dardanium*. Pliny, *Hist. Nat.* xxxiii. 12, transl. Holland, 1601, ii, pp. 461–2 (of men wearing gold bracelets): 'which devise and ornament of the arme is called Dardanium, because the invention came from the Dardanians'.

30. 3. Cf. Hor. *Carm.* 1. 3. and Wither, *Hallelujah*, 1641, 'When we are upon the Seas', st. 2:

A stirring courser now I sit,
  A headstrong steed I ride . . .

31, l. 9. Cf. Massinger, *The Unnatural Combat*, III. iii (ed. Gifford, 1813, i, p. 183):

This hath past through
A wood of pikes.

31. 1. 2. St. Augustine, *Contra Adimantum*, 13. 2: 'Non enim frustra vulgo dici solet: Qui non zelat, non amat.' (*Opera*, Migne, viii, col. 147.) In Erasmus, *Adagia*, s.v. 'Amor'. Cited by Burton, 3. 3. 1. 1 (p. 591), but not earlier than in the edition of 1632.

31. 2. 8. *rods of Mirtle*. Ovid, *Am.* iii. 1. 34: 'myrtea virga' (also Martial, iii. 82. 12).

31. 2. 11. *dove-like eyes*. Song of Sol. i. 15, &c.

31. 3. 2. Ovid, *Rem. Am.* 746:

Divitiis alitur luxuriosus amor.

32, l. 5. *Promise &c.* Ps. lxxvi. 11: 'Promise . . . and keep it.'

32, ll. 5–6. Eccles. v. 4–5.

32. 1. 1–3. Cf. John Taylor, *Works*, 1630, 'To the Reader' (Spenser

Soc., 1869, p. 6): '(*as you meet with faults*) *see, and not see*'; and Hor. *Ars Poet.* 351–3.

32. 1. 2. *Aberrations.* Cf. Joseph Hall, *Meditations*, 1616, Dedicatory Letter (ed. cit. viii, p. 4): 'so many men as I live amongst, so many monitors I shall have; which shall point me to my own rules, and upbraid me with my aberrations'. See also 357. 1. 17.

32. 1. 3. See *O.D.E. Prov.*, 'Wink at small faults.' In Burton, 3. 1. 1. 1 (p. 407).

32. 1. 4. Gen. ix. 22–23.

32. 1. 6. Hor. *Ars Poet.* 359.

33. 2. *heading.* Cf. Tilley, *Prov. Eng.*, L346, 'He is not poor that has little &c.'

33. 2. 1. Seneca, *Ep.* xxv. 4: 'panem et aquam natura desiderat. nemo ad haec pauper est'. Quoted Burton, 2. 3. 3 (p. 323, Latin in margin).

33. 2. 4. Id., *Ep.* xvi. 8: 'exiguum natura desiderat'. Cf. *Ep.* xvii. 9 and lx. 3.

33. 3. *heading. Barly-Break.* See the account of this game in *O.E.D.* s.v.

33. 4. 1. Cf. Burton, 3. 1. 1. 2 (p. 408): 'Beauty shines, *Plato* saith.'

34. 1. 3–4. Cf. Shakespeare, *Venus and Adonis*, 590: 'Like lawn being spread upon the blushing rose.' See also 75. 1 and notes.

34. 2. 1. *More white &c.* Propertius, ii. 3. 10.

34. 2. 9. Cf. Plautus, *Casina*, IV. iv. 21 (Burton, 3. 2. 2. 2, p. 460): '*Nebula haud est mollior &c.*' Also Jonson, *Cynthias Reuells*, V. iv. 435.

34. 3. *heading. M. Tho: Herrick.* See Introd., p. xii, and Appendix A, p. 445 (1). 'Thomas, baptized May 12, 1588, was placed by his uncle and guardian sir William, with Mr. Massam, a merchant in London; but in 1610 appears to have returned into the country and to have been afterwards settled in a small farm.' (Nichols, *Leicestershire*, II. ii, p. 631.) In *Leicestershire Marriage Bonds and Allegations*, 1570–1729, i, f. 82, it is recorded that in 1611 Thomas Eyricke, of London, married Elizabeth Stanford, of Loasbey (the document itself is missing from the Leicester Records). See note to 23. 4.

34. 3. The whole poem is indebted to Jonson's address 'To Sir Robert Wroth' (*Forest*, iii); and directly or secondarily to Hor. *Epod.* ii; Martial, i. 49 and iii. 58; and Virgil, *Georg.* ii. 493–540.

34. 3. 1. Cf. Hor. *Carm.* i. 13. 17 and i. 3. 8.

35, l. 10. Seneca, *Ep.* lxx. 4: 'non enim vivere bonum est, sed bene vivere'. Cf. 121. 1. 2 and note.

35, ll. 19–20. Hor. *Ep.* i. 12. 14: 'scabiem . . . lucri'.

35, l. 20. Cf. Hor. loc. cit., l. 4.

35, l. 23. Hor. *Carm.* iii. 16. 43–44.

35, l. 25. *cheap Nature.* See 33. 2. 1, 4 and notes.

35, l. 33. Hor. *Carm.* ii. 17. 22: 'consentit astrum'.

36, ll. 47–48. Cf. Daniel, *Civil Wars*, ii. 52. 7: 'Millions of figures fantasy presents.'

36, l. 55. *figures*. Imaginary forms. See note to 36, ll. 47–48, and *O.E.D.* s.v. II. 9.†*b*.

36, ll. 59–60. Hor. *Carm.* iii. 23. 19–20.

36, l. 62. Quoted in Montaigne, ii. 20, from Epicharmus in Xenophon, *Memorabilia*, ii. 1. 20 (Florio, *Tudor Trans.*, p. 409): 'The gods sell us all the goods they give us.' Cf. *O.D.E. Prov.*, 'Pains is the price that God putteth upon all things', and Hor. *Sat.* i. 9. 59–60:

Nil sine magno
Vita labore dedit mortalibus.

See a note by J. Gwyn Griffiths ('A Saying of Leonardo') in *T.L.S.*, 17 April 1953 (p. 253).

36, ll. 65–66. Hor. *Ep.* i. 1. 45: 'impiger extremos &c.'

36, ll. 67–68. Hor. *Carm.* i. 1. 16–18.

36, l. 71. *whiter hap*. Cf. Tibullus, iii. 6. 50: 'candida fata'.

36, ll. 75–76. Hor. *Carm.* i. 3. 9–12.

36, ll. 77–79. Cf. Burton, 'Democritus to the Reader' (p. 3): 'I never travelled but in Map or Card'; and Jonson, *Cynthia's Revels*, II. ii. 25–26.

37, l. 90. Cf. the lines translated by Jonson (Ungathered Verse, *Works*, viii, p. 423) from Lucan, viii. 493–5:

he that will honest be, may quitt the Court,
Virtue, and Soveraigntie, they not consort.

Cp. Seneca, *Hippol.* 982: 'fraus sublimi regnat in aula'. See also 327. 7 and note.

37, l. 92. *mov'd*. Kept in motion. See *O.E.D.* s.v. 'Move', vb. 2. *b*. and cf. 327. 7. 2.

37, l. 94. Cf. Hor. *Carm.* iii. 29. 53–54: 'laudo manentem &c.'

37, l. 95. Cf. Hor. *Carm.* ii. 3. 1–2: 'Aequam memento &c.'

37, ll. 95–98. *equall . . . square*. Cf. Puttenham, *Arte of English Poesie*, ii. 12 (*Elizabethan Critical Essays*, ed. Gregory Smith, ii, p. 104): '. . . the Prince of Philosophers, in his first booke of the *Ethicks* [ch. x], termeth a constant minded man euen egal and direct on all sides, and not easily ouerthrowne by euery litle aduersitie, *hominem quadratum*, a square man'. Herrick's phrasing is nearer to Puttenham's than to Aristotle's.

37, l. 108. *second bread*. Hor. *Ep.* ii. 1. 123: 'pane secundo'.

37, l. 113. Hor. *Ep.* i. 12. 7–8: 'herbis . . . et urtica'.

37, l. 117. *size*. Rule, standard, ration.

37, l. 128. Prov. xv. 17; Luke xii. 15; Tibullus, iii. 3. 21–24.

38, ll. 135–6. *true To thine owne selfe*. Perhaps a reminiscence of *Hamlet*, I. iii. 78.

38, l. 140. Juvenal, xi. 208: 'voluptates commendat rarior usus'. For Herrick's phrasing cf. Taverner, *Proverbes*, 1539, f. 24: 'A seldom vse of pleasures maketh the same more pleasaunt.'

38, l. 144. Cf. Ovid, *Met.* viii. 709–10 and Fletcher, *The Elder Brother*, III. v. 175–6:

one hour of death
Shall shut our eyes, and one grave make us happy.

38, l. 146. Martial, x. 47. 13, trans. Jonson, *Und.* xc. 13:

Nor feare thy latest day, nor wish therfore.

Martial's line is quoted by Montaigne, ii. 37 (*Tudor Trans.* ii, p. 506) and by Burton, 2. 3. 5 (p. 342).

38. 2. 3–4. *strife &c.* Cf. Jonson in *Shakespeare*, F1, 1623, 'To the Reader':

Wherein the Grauer had a strife
With Nature, to out-doo the life.

39. 3. 1. Cf. Tibullus, i. 1. 69: 'dum fata sinunt'; also Propertius, ii. 15. 23.

39. 3. 8. *bite the Bayes.* Cf. 81, l. 32; Lycophron, *Alexandra*, 6: δαφνηφάγων. Also Juvenal, vii. 18–19, and Martial, v. 4. 2.

39. 3. 13. The references are to Dr. John Wilson (1595–1674), Professor of Music at Oxford, 1656, and to James Gouter or Gualtier ('*fl.* 1636'), French lutanist. For fuller accounts see *D.N.B.* A book of musical settings by Wilson (Bodleian MS. Mus. b. 1) includes Herrick's 'The Curse' (49. 2) and some other poems of which Herrick may be the author. See pp. xxix and xxx. Herrick refers to these two musicians again in 276. 4.

40. 1. *heading.* Mildmay Fane succeeded the first Earl in 1628. Author of *Otia Sacra*, 1648. See *D.N.B.* Herrick addresses him again in 101. 1 and 172. 3.

40. 2. 3. *deads.* For this verb see also 42. 2. 2; 55, l. 89; and 286. 3. 8.

40. 4. 3–4. *Treasures, &c.* Job xxxviii. 22.

40. 4. 9 *descend . . . deep.* Rom. x. 7.

41. 1. Cf. Martial, x. 63.

41. 1. 8. Cf. Catullus, cxi. 1: 'Aufilena, viro contentam vivere solo . . .', and *Greek Anth.* vii. 331 (anon.).

41. 2. *heading.* For Endymion Porter (1587–1649) see *D.N.B.* and *The Life and Letters of Mr. Endymion Porter*, by D. Townshend, 1897. Herrick addresses him also in 72. 2, 183. 2, 229. 4, and 324. 3.

41. 2. 1–2. Martial's line (viii. 56. 5), 'Sint Maecenates, non deerunt, Flacce, Marones', is twice quoted by Burton (1628 onwards), 1. 2. 3. 15 (pp. 138 and 139) and on p. 138 is paraphrased 'Let there be bountifull Patrons, and there will be painfull Schollers in all Sciences.' On p. 139 the quotation is preceded by references to the poverty of scholars and there is a marginal quotation of Juvenal, vii. 222–4. This may have recalled to Herrick the names of the patrons mentioned in the same satire, l. 95, the Fabius, Cotta, and Lentulus of Herrick's l. 3.

42. 1. 2. Sc. because Love ('himselfe' in l. 3) was disarmed by grief. Here and in ll. 4–9 Herrick adapts Ovid, *Amores*, iii. 9. 7–12 (on the death of Tibullus):

Ecce puer Veneris fert eversamque pharetram
Et fractos arcus, et sine luce facem . . .

42. 3. See Bergk, *Anth. Lyr.*, Scol. 6, p. 329, for the anonymous Greek original (attributed to Simonides). Herrick, however, as Delattre suggests (pp. 404–5), may have translated from the Latin version by H. Estienne in *Carminum poet. novem . . . fragmenta* (1586, p. 201):

> Bene valere praestantissimum est viro mortali,
> Secundum autem, pulchrum indole esse,
> Tertium verò, divitem essé non dolosè,
> Quartum, pubertate frui unà cum amicis.

42. 4. *heading. Mrs Dorothy Keneday.* Not identified.

44. 3. The name 'Scobell' occurs frequently in the Dean Prior Parish Register.

44. 4. Cf. Jonson, *Und.* viii, 'The Houre-glasse', based on Girolamo Amaltei's 'Horologium Pulverum' (quoted in *Works*, xi, p. 53).

44. 4. 3. *as I have read.* Sc. in Jonson or in the Latin.

45. 1. 2. *blood to . . . spirit.* Cf. Featley, *Clavis Mystica*, 1636, p. 188: 'The spirits runne along in the arteries with the purer and refined blood, yet the spirits are not the blood.'

45. 1. 3–6. Herrick has not made all his meaning clear. Phinn connects 'Life to quick action' with 'the activity of the man' and the rest of that clause with 'the receptivity of the woman'. It is possible that the sentence ending at l. 10 begins with 'Life' in l. 4.

45. 1. 23. *Mistick Fan.* Virg. *Georg.* i. 166: 'mystica vannus Iacchi'.

45. 1. 33. *Thespian spring.* Cf. Jonson, *Every Man Out of his Humour*, Induct. 70; Drayton, 'To Reynolds', l. 106.

45. 1. 36. *Cedar.* Cf. 63. 2, 89. 1. 14, and 415. 1. 6; where the references are to the use of cedar-oil as a preservative of papyri; see Hor. *Ars Poet.* 332: 'carmina linenda cedro'.

46. 2. *heading.* Elizabeth Wheeler was Martha Herrick, daughter of Robert Herrick, of Leicester, the poet's uncle and godfather. She married John Wheeler, goldsmith of London, in 1606. (*Leic. Marriage Bonds*, 1570–1729, i, f. 22; *Visitation of London*, 1633, ii, p. 341.)

47. 1. Martial, iii. 17.

47. 2. 1. *Fold now thine armes.* In token of grief or melancholy. See *Love's Labour's Lost*, III. 1. 191 and the figure of Inamorato on the engraved title of Burton, 1628 onwards.

47. 2. 4. *Jocasta in a swoone.* The reference may be to some representation of Jocasta in graphic or plastic form.

47. 2. 5. *softly goe.* Cf. Isa. xxxviii. 15.

47. 2. 13. Ovid, *Her.* xvi (Paridis). 280: 'faciles . . . deos'. Cf. Martial, i. 103. 4.

48. 1. *heading. Mr. J. Warr.* Probably John Warre, who matriculated from Exeter College 21 May 1619 (at the age of 14). B.A. 1621/2. M.A. 1624. (*Al. Oxon.*) Admitted to Gray's Inn 1627 as 'son and heir of Edward Warre, of Chipley, Somerset'. Randolph also wrote an elegy on his death (*Poems*, ed. Thorn-Drury, p. 56).

49, l. 19. *eare of . . . jealousie*. See Wisd. of Sol. i. 10.

49, l. 24. Cf. Daniel, *Rosamond*, st. 73: 'For what is beauty if it be not seen?' Cited by Burton, 3. 2. 3. 3 (p. 471). Cf. also Milton, *Comus*, 745–6.

49. 1. Jonson, *Epicoene*, IV. iv. 23–24: 'Strife and tumult are the dowrie that comes with a wife'. Cf. Ovid, *Ars Am.* ii. 155: 'dos est uxoria lites'.

49. 2. In some manuscripts (see Critical Notes) this poem is described as the 'answer'; sc. to 420. 2, which is found in manuscripts only. With the lines added to 49. 2 in MS. Egerton 2421 (see p. 468) cf. 203. 4. 3–6. 'The Curse' was set to music by R. Ramsay (MS. Don. c. 57 and Add. MS. 15227), John Wilson (MS. Mus. b. 1), and John Blow (Add. MS. 19759 &c.).

49. 2. 3. Cf. Corbet, 'An Elegie . . . upon the death of Dr. Ravis', l. 19: 'thy religious dust'.

49. 2. 4. Hor. *Carm.* iv. 13. 17: 'quo fugit Venus, heu, quove color?' Cf. Virg. *Ecl.* ii. 17.

50. 1. Anacreontea, 35. The Latin version by H. Estienne (see note to 26. 3) follows:

Inter rosas Cupido
Apiculam iacentem
Non vidit, éstque punctus.
Manúmque sauciatus,
Mox eiulare coepit.
Et cursitans volánsque
Ad candidam Cytherem,
Heu óccidi, óccidi, inquit,
Vitamque, mater, efflo.
En me minuta serpens
Pennata vulnerauit:
Apem vocant coloni.
Tunc illa, Apis si acumen
Tantum facit dolorem,
Quantum putas dolere
Quos tu feris Cupido?
(1554, pp. 104–5.)

50. 1. 10–11. *with her hairs*. The phrasing is probably influenced by Luke vii. 38, 44.

50. 3. Cf. Ovid, *Met.* xii. 80–81:

solamen habeto
Mortis, ab Haemonio quod sis iugulatus Achille.

and Publilius Syrus, 689: 'Superari a superiore pars est gloriae.'

51. 1. 7–16. Imitated from Virg. *Aen.* i. 315–20.

51. 1. 16. *dawning*. Cf. 271. 2. heading, 'To Julia, in her Dawn, or Day-breake.'

51. 2. *heading and* 2. See *O.D.E. Prov.*, 'Love me little &c.'

51. 2. 1–4. Cf. *Romeo and Juliet*, II. vi. 9–15.

51. 2. 3. *Slowly goes farre.* See *O.D.E. Prov.*, 'Soft pace goes far'; also Tilley, *Prov. Eng.*, S601, 'Soft and fair goes far' and S544, 'Slow but sure.' Cf. 352. 1. 4.

51. 2. 3. *The meane is best.* See Tilley. *Prov. Eng.*, M793, 'The mean is the best.'

51. 3. 4. *Wreathe.* Garland or cluster, a number as opposed to the single rose of l. 1.

52. 2. *heading.* John Williams, 1582–1650; Lord Keeper, 1621–5; Bishop of Lincoln, 1621. He was charged with betraying the king's secrets and with subornation of perjury; and was imprisoned in the Tower 1637–40. Archbishop of York 1641–50. For further information see *D.N.B.* Herrick wrote the 'Charroll' on p. 413 to celebrate his release. Cowley also wrote a poem ('*Miscellanies*', pp. 12–13, in *Works*, 1681) 'Upon his Enlargement out of the Tower'. Jonson's *Underwoods*, lxi, is addressed to him.

52. 2. 8. *Hope-seed.* Not in *O.E.D.*

52. 2. 15–16. See Acts xvi. 26.

52. 2. 18–20. The nature of this unkindness is not known.

52. 3. 1. *Cynthius, &c.* Virg. *Ecl.* vi. 3. Cited by Burton, 3. 4. 2. 6 (p. 718) with transl. 'God pulls them by the eare.'

52. 3. 4. See 232. 1. 11–12; 281. 4. 7–8; 282. 5. Cf. Burton, 3. 2. 3. 2 (p. 460): 'In a word, *The haires are* Cupids *nets, to catch all commers.*' Cf. also *The Merchant of Venice*, III. ii. 122: 'A golden mesh to entrap the hearts of men.'

53, ll. 10–14. Ovid, *Rem. Am.* 139–44, &c. Cf. Burton, 3. 2. 2. 1 (p. 446): 'Idlenesse overthrowes all . . . love tyrannizeth in an idle person . . . For love as *Theophrastus* defines it, is *otiosi animi affectus*, an affection of an idle minde.' Burton also quotes the Ovid passage in 3. 2. 5. 1 (p. 541). See note on 155. 3. 3–6.

53. 2. *heading. Sir Thomas Southwell.* Son of Sir Robert Southwell of Wood Rising, Norfolk. See Blomefield, ed. Parkin, *Hist. of Norfolk*, x, pp. 275 and 277–8, where it appears that T. S. was about five months old when his father died in 1599. Knighted at Whitehall in 1615 (Shaw, *Knights of England*, ii, p. 156); Vice-Admiral of Norfolk by 1626 (*C.S.P. Dom.*, p. 410). One of this name matriculated from Trin. Coll., Camb., Michaelmas 1609. T. S. married first Margaret or Margery Fuller, by whom he had four daughters, and afterwards Mary Eden, d. of — Eden, LL.D. (? Thomas Eden, LL.D. 1616, Master of Trinity Hall, 1626, to which College Herrick went in 1617). Blomefield does not give the dates of these marriages, of which the first took place on 27 March 1618 (Boyd's Marriage Index, Middlesex 1601–25, Society of Genealogists; and copy, ibid., of Register of St. Michael, Crooked Lane), and the second in 1637 (Boyd, Essex 1626–50, North Weald Basset). The first marriage was eventually unhappy. In May 1634 there is a reference in *C.S.P. Dom.* (p. 53) to articles against Sir Thomas for continuing to cohabit with Mary Eden, notwithstanding the order of the court. In June (ibid., p. 113) he was fined for non-payment of alimony to his wife. In June 1635 (ibid., p. 216, *Acts of the Court of High Commission*) the estate of Sir Thomas 'was disposed of for the maintenance and provision of his mother, wife and children'. In February 1635/6 (p. 487) the king took the matter up and Sir Thomas was charged with incest (with his wife's sister), adultery, and blasphemy. No further proceedings are recorded in *C.S.P.* It must have been about this time that the first Lady Southwell died. Sir Thomas himself died before 16 Dec. 1642, when the administration of his estate (he is now described as of Hangleton, Sussex) was granted to his widow Mary (Prerog. Court of Canterbury, Wills and Administrations). The administration was soon after passed to Sir Matthew Mennes, principal creditor (brother of Herrick's friend, Sir John M.), Mary S. having died without having fully administered the estate (ibid., 20 Jan. 1642/3). The administration of the estate, or what was left of it, came (ibid., May 1654) to John Benbow, son of Sir Thomas's daughter Frances. Herrick's poem was doubtless written for Sir Thomas's first marriage.

53. 2. In this and in the Crewe Nuptiall Song (112. 3) Herrick seems to have been indebted, directly or indirectly, to Renaissance authorities on Roman marriage customs and symbols, but his knowledge also of Latin poetry often makes it difficult to see exactly whence he derives his ideas. Some of his details and phrases point to an immediate reliance on Jonson's *Hymenaei* and the notes thereto, these largely obtained from the accounts of Roman weddings given by Giraldi, Scaliger, Brisson, &c. (see D. J. Gordon, 'Hymenaei: Ben Jonson's Masque of Union', *Journal of the Warburg and Courtauld Institute*, vol. viii, 1945, pp. 107–45). Jonson's own Epithalamion, included in *Hymenaei* (ll. 445–564), was undoubtedly part of Herrick's inspiration, giving the model for the metre in the Southwell piece, except that Herrick's stanza has ten lines instead of eight. Herrick, moreover, was interested enough in rites and ceremonies of all kinds to read the Renaissance antiquarians with zest. Yet what he could learn from them may well have attracted him less than the works of the Roman poets themselves, and it is probable that such lyrical or descriptive poetry as Catullus, lxi, lxii, and lxiv, or Lucan, ii. 355 sqq., was also very much in Herrick's mind while he wrote these pieces. The connexion with Catullus is examined by J. A. S. McPeek in *Catullus in Strange and Distant Britain*, pp. 221–31.

Herrick's lore is not all classical in origin. See, for some of the customs he refers to, Brand's *Observations on Popular Antiquities*, enlarged by W. C. Hazlitt, 1870, vol. ii; also note to 124. 3. heading. Herrick thinks of the ceremonies as taking place at the bridegroom's house; Roman marriages were celebrated at the home of the bride.

54, l. 42. *Domiduca.* See *Hymenaei*, l. 293:

And Domiduca home her steppes doth stay.

Domiduca is one of eight masquers each of whom has a name representing a function of Juno. This is in the tradition from Martianus Capella, *De Nuptiis*, which came to Jonson at least in part through Giraldi. See Gordon, loc. cit., p. 149, on Jonson's note, *Works*, vii, p. 220.

54, l. 43. *Genius.* See *Hymenaei*, ll. 537–40. Jonson's note, following Giraldi, begins '*Deus Naturae, siue gignendi.* And is the same in the male, as *Iuno* in the female.' (For the immediate sources of this and following notes by Jonson see Gordon, loc. cit.)

54, ll. 51–54. *Hymenaei*, ll. 361–2:

The longing *bridegroome*, in the porch,
Shewes you againe, the bated torch;

with note: 'It was a custome for the *man* to stand there, expecting the approach of his *Bride*.'

55, l. 55. *Hymenaei*, ll. 43–44: 'fiue Pages . . . bearing fiue tapers of virgin waxe'. Jonson's note (p. 210) says: 'Those were the *Quinque Cerei*, which *Plutarch* in his *Quaest. Roman.* mentions to be vsed in *nuptialls.*' Jonson explains the number five in *Hymenaei*, ll. 196–211, with reference to Plutarch and Martianus Capella. Five cannot be severed into equal parts:

one will euer
Remaine as common; so we see
The binding force of *Vnitie*.

55, ll. 71–74. *Hymenaei*, l. 50: [Hymen] 'a yellow veile of silke on his left arme'. Also note by Jonson: 'the *rite* was to ioyne the marryed payre with bands of silke'. Ibid., l. 180: 'The blushing veyle shewes shamefastnesse.'

55, ll. 84–90. *Hymenaei*, note to l. 289: '. . . a fashion with the *Romanes*, that before the new-married *Brides* entred the houses of their *Husbands*, they adorned the postes of the gates with wollen tawdries, or fillets, and anointed them with oyles, or the fat of wolues, and bores; being superstitiously possest, that such oyntments had the vertue of expelling euills from the familie.' Also a note to l. 482 (the bride to lift her feet high over the threshold) suggests that this was for 'the auoyding of *Sorcerous* drugs, vs'd by Witches to be bury'd vnder that place, to the destroying of *marriage*-Amitie, or the Power of generation'.

55, l. 89. *deads.* See note to 40. 2. 3.

56, l. 96. *Close kisses.* Martial, vi. 34. 1: 'Basia . . . pressa.'

56, l. 112. *ripe for men.* Virg. *Aen.* vii. 53: 'Jam matura viro.'

56, l. 117. *reaks.* Pranks, games.

56, l. 118. *Barly-breaks.* See 33. 3 and note.

56, l. 120. Cf. Sidney, *Astrophel and Stella*, Fourth Song, st. 5, l. 4: 'Yong folkes [fooles *1591*], take time while you may.' See also 84. 1 and notes.

56, l. 122. *to gather Nuts.* See, e.g., Catullus, lxi. 127–30.

57, ll. 125–6. *Hymenaei,* ll. 176–9:

Like are the *fire*, and *water*, set;
That, eu'n as *moisture*, mixt with heat,
Helpes euerie naturall birth, to life;
So, for their *Race*, ioyne *man* and *wife*.

57, l. 130. *Diadem.* Prov. xvii. 6: 'Children's children are the crown of old men.'

57, ll. 145–6. Cf. Jonson, *The Entertainment at Highgate*, *Works*, vii, p. 140, ll. 120–1 (from Claudian):

If, thereto, added all the gummes,
And spice, that from PANCHAIA comes . . .

57, l. 159. *luckie Birds.* Cf. Catullus, lxi. 19–20: 'cum bona . . . alite'.

58, l. 162. *whitest wooll.* Cf. 86, l. 14; also Jonson, *Und.* li. 15–16 (*Works*, viii, p. 225), and *Love's Welcome at Bolsover* (1634), ll. 166–7 (*Works*, vii, p. 813).

58, l. 170. Job v. 26: 'Thou shalt come to thy grave in a full age, like as a shock of corn cometh in in his season.'

58. 1. 1–2. *mute . . . fish.* Hor. *Carm.* iv. 3. 19: 'mutis . . . piscibus'.

58. 3. 1–2. Cf. Jonson, *Volpone*, III. vii. 221–4:

Whil'st we, in changed shapes, act OVIDS tales . . .

59, l. 12. Ibid., l. 225:

And weary'd all the fables of the gods.

59. 1. From Hor. *Ep.* i. 18. 111–12.

59. 2. *heading. Protestation.* Cf. 108. 2. 2 ('Protestant') and note to that poem.

59. 3. 7–8. *transfer . . . from her.* Pass, give off, from herself. See 9. 2. 9–12 and note.

59. 3. 9–10. See note to 157. 2. 8.

60. 2. 4. Ovid, *Met.* i. 523 (cf. *Her.* v. 149): 'nullis amor est medicabilis herbis.' Cited by Burton, 3. 2. 4 (p. 537).

60. 2. 5–6. Burton, 3. 2. 4 (p. 539) quotes Ovid, *Met.* x. 377 ('nec modus aut requies, nisi mors, reperitur amoris'), and adds 'Death is the common *Catastrophe* to such persons.' Burton then cites Anacreon 51 [48], translating

Would I were dead, for nought God knowes
But death can rid me of these woes.

(Bergk, *Anth. Lyr.*, p. 225.)

60. 3. Seneca, *De Const. Sap.* x. 4: 'haec non nego sentire sapientem'. Cf. id., *Ep.* lxxxv. 29.

60. 4. Based on Theocritus, xxiii. 19–49, but, as Delattre (p. 404) suggests, possibly influenced by the version in *Carminum Iani Baifii Liber I*, 1577, ff. 10–11, where, as in Herrick's poem, the boy of Theocritus appears as a girl:

O fera cruda puella, ferocis alumna leaenae,
Saxea, quam fugit omnis amor . . .

It is not unlikely that 'And' in l. 1 is a misreading of 'Ah!' See 74. 3. 1 and 312. 3. 5; on the other hand, see 48. 3. 1 and 301. 1. 1.

60. 4. 3. Cf. Beaumont and Fletcher, *The Maid's Tragedy*, II. i. 119: 'I'll trouble you no more'.

60. 4. 6. Cf. Beaumont and Fletcher, *Philaster*, III. ii. 160–1:

whilst I
Go seek out some forgotten place to die.

61. 2. 1–2. Rev. xxii. 2.

61. 2. 3–4. John v. 4.

63. 1. Cf. Hor. *Carm.* iv. 10.

63. 1. 1–7. Cf. Anacreontea, 7. 1–5.

63. 1. 7. See 271. 2. 5 and note.

63. 2. 2. *washt.* See 45. 1. 36 and note.

63. 3. 8. *Prince D'Amour.* A name for the Mock King at early French court entertainments, applied to the Lord of Misrule at the Inns of Court. Cf. Davenant's masque of 1635/6, *The Triumphs of the Prince D'Amour.* But Herrick may be using the term in its less restricted sense.

64. 1. *heading. green.* Pale. See *O.E.D.* s.v. A. I. 3.

64. 2. *heading.* Joseph Hall, 1574–1656, Bishop of Exeter 1627–41 and of Norwich 1641–7. See *D.N.B.*

64. 2. Cf. Martial, iv. 86.

64. 2. 3. *blood-guiltinesse.* Shame indicated by blushing (a meaning not recorded in *O.E.D.*). Cf. 'Blush-guiltinesse', 274. 1. 6.

64. 2. 10. *Bishop't.* Confirmed.

64. 3. *heading.* Lucy, daughter of Henry Percy, ninth Earl of Northumberland, lived from 1599 to 1660. She married James Hay, first earl of Carlisle, in 1617. She was famous for her beauty and wit, and was much involved in the political events of her time. See *D.N.B.* (Lucy Hay). De Fonblanque, *Annals of the House of Percy*, p. 399, observes that 'her "chamber", as it was called, was unlike any other reception-room in England at that time, and seems to have partaken rather of the character of the *salons* of brilliant Frenchwomen a century later'. With this poem cf. Waller's on 'The Countess of Carlisle in Mourning' (*Poems*, ed. G. Thorn Drury, i, p. 22).

64. 3. 6. Cf. Jonson, *Catiline*, I. 12–13:

As a dire vapor, that had cleft the ground,
T'ingender with the night, and blast the day . . .

64. 3. 9. *I fancie none!* The original reading, 'I fancie more!', is almost certainly an error, but Grosart's emendation, 'One fancie more!', adopted by Moorman, is no more convincing. Such a self-conscious reflection would be extremely uncharacteristic of Herrick and 'One fancie more!' is awkwardly followed by 'but'. 'I fancie none!' fits the context and agrees with Herrick's claims or pretences elsewhere to wholeness of heart (e.g. 12. 4 and 17. 1). Elizabethan and seventeenth-century printers often confused 'n' with 'm' and 'r'. A modern instance of 'none' misprinted as 'more' occurs in K. McEuen's *Classical Influence upon the Tribe of Ben*, p. 136: 'let more wanting be'.

64. 3. 10. *Freedome in Captivity*. Cf. 198. 1. 30: 'freedome . . . fetter'.

64. 12. *Chains of Darknesse*. Cf. 2 Pet. ii. 4.

65. 1. Cf. Anacreontea, 8. 1–10.

65. 1. 6. Hor. *Carm.* iv. 7. 17–18.

66. 1. 2. *long-black-Thumb-nail*. Cf. Joseph Hall, *Satires*, vi. 1. 1–2 (*Poems*, ed. A. Davenport, p. 87):

> *Labeo* reserues a long nayle for the nonce
> To wound my Margent through ten leaues at once.

66. 2. From Martial, viii. 69, with a different development.

66. 3. 2–3. Cf. 28. 1.

67, l. 8. *expansion*. See note on 82. 2. 4–5.

67, l. 19. *That Leading Cloud*. Exod. xiii. 22.

67. 2. 4. *Heare . . . speak*. Cf. Joseph Hall, *Meditations* (1616), iii. 63: 'the best is to entertain all, and trust few'. See 333. 5. 2 and note; also *O.D.E. Prov.*, 'Hear and see . . .', 'Hear much . . .'; and cf. *Hamlet*, I. iii. 68.

67. 3. See the section on 'May Day Customs' in Brand's *Popular Antiquities* (ed. W. C. Hazlitt, 1870, i, pp. 120–8), and cf. the poem 'Sister, awake! close not your eyes' in Bateson's *First Set of English Madrigals* (Bullen, *Lyrics from the Song-Books of the Elizabethan Age*, 1889, p. 198).

67. 3. 2. *god unshorne*. Cf. 299. 1. 13 and Hor. *Carm.* i. 21. 2: 'intonsum . . . Cynthium'.

67. 3. 5. *sweet-Slug-a-bed*. Cf. Chaucer, *Cant. Tales*, A. 1042:

> For May wole have no slogardrie a nyght.

68, ll. 32–35. Cf. Lev. xxiii. 40–43; Ovid, *Fasti*, iii. 528:

> Sunt quibus e ramis frondea facta casa est.

68, ll. 35–36. *white-thorn, &c.* Cf. Jonson, *Hymenaei*, ll. 53–54 (*Works*, vii, p. 211): 'a *youth* . . . bearing another light, of *white thorne* . . .'; and ll. 172–3 (p. 215).

69, ll. 43 sqq. Cf. Ovid, loc. cit. 525–6.

69, l. 51. Cf. Burton, 3. 2. 3. 4 (p. 484): 'willing to embrace, to take a greene gowne, with that Shepardesse in *Theocritus Eidyl.* 27. [l. 53] to let their Coates, &c.' See *O.E.D.* s.v. 'green', *a.* and *sb.*, A. 1. 1. *g.*

69, l. 56. *Locks pickt*. Cf. Shakespeare, *Venus and Adonis*, ll. 575–6:

> Were beauty under twenty locks kept fast,
> Yet love breaks through and picks them all at last.

Cited by Burton, 3. 2. 3. 2 (p. 454).

69, ll. 57–70. The sentiment of these famous lines had been so frequently anticipated in classical and later literature that it is difficult to specify influences. Herrick, however, is clearly indebted not only to Latin poetry but to the Bible (where the thought of 'carpe diem' is introduced in order to be deprecated). It is further worth noting that some major elements in his amalgam, largely compounded from Wisd. of Sol. ii. 1–8, Prov. vii. 18, Catullus v, and Ovid, *Fasti*, vi. 771, were collected also by Burton into a single passage, 3. 4. 2. 1 (p. 684), with which Herrick's lines probably have some direct connexion: '*Our life is short and tedious, and in the death of a man there is no recovery, neither was any man knowne that hath returned from the grave, for we are borne at all adventure, and we shall bee hereafter as though wee had never beene; for the breath is as smoke in our nostrils,* &c. *and the spirit vanisheth as the soft aire. Come let us enjoy the pleasures that are present, let us chearfully use the creatures as in youth, let us fill our selves with costly wine and ointments, let not the flower of our life passe by us, let us crowne our selves with rose buds before they are withered,* &c. *Vivamus mea Lesbia et amemus,* &c. *Come let us take our fill of love, and pleasure in dalliance, for this is our portion, this is our lot.*

Tempora labuntur tacitisq; senescimus annis.'

See 84. 1, 228. 2 and 3, 238. 3 and notes. To passages there cited add Tibullus, i. 1. 69; Propertius, ii. 15. 23–24; Persius, v. 151–3; Anacreontea, 8. 7–10; also id. 44.

69, l. 58. *harmlesse follie.* Cf. Hor. *Carm.* iv. 12. 27–28.

69, ll. 61–62. See 84. 1. 5–8.

69, ll. 65–66. See 111. 5. 5–6; also 133, ll. 29–30 and note.

69, l. 66. *fable.* Ps. xc. 9: 'we bring our years to an end, as it were a tale that is told'.

69. 1. 4. Cf. Jonson, *Und.* lxxxiii. 69: 'circumfused light'.

69. 2. 3. *harder Fates.* Cf. Hor. *Carm.* ii. 6. 9: 'Parcae . . . iniquae.'

70. 1. *heading. Horace. Carm.* iii. 9. *Robert Ramsey.* Organist of Trinity Coll. Camb. His setting of Herrick's 'The Curse' (49. 2) is in Add. MS. 15227, f. 3 and MS. Don. c. 57, f. 11. 'fl. 1609–39' (*D.N.B.*, q.v.).

70. 1. 1. Jonson's version, *Und.* lxxxvii, has the same initial line with 'Whilst' for 'While'. (*Works*, viii, p. 293.)

71. 1. 2–8. Cf. Burton, 3. 2. 3. 2 (p. 459): 'A corall lip . . . a sweet smelling flowre, from which Bees may gather hony, *Mellilegae volucres quid adhuc cava thyma rosasq, &c.*' [Joh. Secundus, *Bas.* xix.]

72. 2. *heading. Endymion Porter.* See note to 41. 2. *his Brothers death.* It has been suggested that this refers to the death of Porter's brother, but the drift of the poem makes it seem almost certain that Herrick's own brother is meant; this was probably the William Herrick in the title of the next poem (73. 1), doubtless the brother born in 1593, as William, the eldest child of Nicholas Herrick, born in 1585, appears to have died in infancy. (See Introduction, p. xii.)

72. 2. 1. Cf. Burton, 2. 3. 3 (p. 330): '*Nondum omnium dierum Soles occiderunt*, as *Philippus* said, All the Sunnes are not yet set, a day may come to make amends for all.' (Livy, 39. 26.)

72. 2. 5–7. Cf. Catullus, v. 4: 'soles occidere et redire possunt'.

72. 2. 14. *the old stock.* Cf. 17, l. 23.

73. 1. *heading. William Herrick.* See note to 72. 2. Mentioned in Julian Herrick's will (Grosart, i, p. lxxxvi), from which it also appears that he had two children. He had died by June 1632, if, as is likely, he is identical with the William Herrick of the parish of St. Margaret's

Westminster, in respect of whom an administration was then granted to his creditor, Humphrey Fox, with the consent of the widow, named Elizabeth. (P.C.C. Administrations, 1632.) See note to 145. 2.

73. 2. *The Olive Branch.* One of Herrick's poems which may have been influenced by George Herbert. See also 346. 4, 357. 4, 368. 1, and 369. 3.

75. 1. This poem is referred to by Herrick in 'His age . . .', p. 135, ll. 97–98. Cf. Martial, viii. 68. 5–8: 'condita perspicua &c.'; and Montaigne, iii. 5 (*Tudor Trans.*, p. 108): 'The verses of these two Poets, handling lasciviousnesse so sparingly and so discreetly, as they do, in my conceit seeme to discover, and display it nearer; ladies cover their bosome with networke; priests many sacred things with a vaile, and painters shadow their workes, to give them the more luster, and to adde more grace unto them.' Cf. also Jonson, *Discoveries*, ll. 314–17: 'It is an Art . . . to apparell a Lye well, to give it a good dressing; that though the nakednesse would shew deform'd and odious, the suiting of it might draw their Readers.' See an article by H. V. S. Ogden, 'Variety and Contrast in 17th Century Aesthetics' (*Journ. Hist. of Ideas*, x. 2, April 1949, pp. 159–82). See 34. 1 and note; also 158. 1, 164. 1, 271. 2. 9–16, and 294. 4. 3–6.

75. 1. 5. Cf. Jonson, *Ode ἐνθουσιαστική*, ll. 11–12 (in *Loues Martyr*, 1601; *Works*, viii, p. 365):

Cleare as a naked vestall
Closde in an orbe of Christall.

76, ll. 41–56. Cf. the advice given by Ovid, *Ars Am.* ii. 609 sqq., and see Montaigne, ii. 15 (*Tudor Trans.*, p. 344): 'Beauty with all her might, hath not wherewith to give a taste of her selfe without these interpositions . . .'

76. 2. Cf. 102. 3.

76. 2. 8. *Sceanes.* See 247. 4. 7 and note.

77, ll. 9–12. See Phineas Fletcher, 'On Womens Lightness', st. 4: 'False is their flattering colour &c.'

77. 1. *heading.* Cf. Publilius Syrus, 189: 'Excelsis multo facilius casus nocet.'

77. 1. 2. *The fattest Oxe, &c.* Cf. Joseph Hall, *Meditations*, ii. 30: 'Who sees an ox, grazing in a fat and rank pasture, and thinks not that he is near to the slaughter?' and Jonson, *Volpone*, v. xii. 150–1.

77. 2. 3. See *O.D.E. Prov.*, 'Like loves like', citing Taverner, 'Symylytude . . . is mother of loue.' See also Tilley, *Prov. Eng.*, L294, 'Likeness causes liking (love).'

77. 2. 11. *Osiris.* Cf. Spenser, *Faerie Queene*, v. vii. 4: 'Like as Osyris signifies the Sun.'

77. 2. 18. See Homer, *Od.* i. 58; Ovid, *Ex Ponto*, i. 3. 33–34; Hor. *Sat.* ii. 5. 4.

77. 2. 19, 24 sqq. Cf. Jonson, *Catiline*, I. 102–4: 'Wherefore frownes my sweet? &c.'

77. 2. 30. Cf. Tibullus, i. 5. 11: 'lustravi sulpure puro'.

78, l. 58. See Num. xi. 5.

78, ll. 61–64. The reference is to C. Cassius Longinus, one of Caesar's murderers. Cf. Seneca, *Ep.* lxxxiii. 12: 'Cassius tota vita aquam bibit.' See also Hor. *Carm.* iii. 21. 11–12; quoted by Montaigne, ii. 2 (*Tudor Trans.*, p. 17).

78, l. 68. See Ovid, *Her.* ix. 51–52.

79, l. 85. *Circumstants.* Bystanders.

79, l. 88. It is easier to understand the association with beer of 'Tap' and 'Toast' than of 'Turf'. But 'Turf' may mean the commoner sort of people. Cf. 'clod'. See the punning on 'Turfe' and 'Clay' in Jonson, *Tale of a Tub*, I. v. 5–7; and note on 398. 3. 12 below.

79. 1. *heading. Impossibilities.* See 59. 2; 244. 4; and 339. 3 (with note).

79. 2. 3. Seneca, *Thyestes*, 596–7: 'dolor ac voluptas Invicem cedunt'.

80. 2. *heading, and* 81, l. 45. Cf. Burton, 2. 3. 7 (p. 356): '*Live merrily as thou canst*'; and Ovid, *Am.* iii. 9. 39: 'Carminibus confide bonis.'

80. 2. 4, 5. Ovid, *Am.* iii. 2. 44: 'aurea pompa venit'.

80. 2. 10. *Arabian Dew.* Ovid, *Her.* xv (Sappho to Phaon). 76: 'Arabo . . . rore.'

80. 2. 23–24. The wine has an aroma (l. 26) so rich that Ovidius Naso, sensing it, would think he was using everyone's nose. Cf. Jonson, *Cynthias Reuells*, v. iv. 309–11: 'pure *beniamin*, the only spirited sent. . . . You would wish your selfe all nose, for the loue ont.'

81, l. 32. *bite the Bayes.* See 39. 3. 8 and note.

81, l. 33. Cf. Jonson, *Volpone*, III. vii. 218–19: 'vntill my roofe whirle round With the *vertigo*'. See Juvenal, vi. 304–5.

81, ll. 41–44. Ovid, *Am.* iii. 9. 39–40:

iacet, ecce, Tibullus:
Vix manet e toto parva quod urna capit.

81, ll. 46–48. Cf. Ovid, loc cit. 28:

Diffugiunt avidos carmina sola rogos.

See motto on title-page of *Hesperides* and note; also Jonson's translation of Ovid, *Am.* i. xv. 41–42 in *Poetaster*, I. i. 83–84:

Then, when this bodie fals in funerall fire,
My name shall liue, and my best part aspire.

81, ll. 51–52. Cf. Martial, x. 2. 12:

solaque non norunt haec monumenta mori.

82. 1. 1–2. Cf. Catullus, lv. 20: 'verbosa gaudet Venus loquella'.

82. 2. 4–5. *expansion . . . Firmament.* See Gen. i. 6: 'firmament' (marg. 'expansion').

83. 3. 1–4. Cf. 323. 4. 1–4.

84. 1. *To the Virgins, to make much of Time.* See 69, ll. 57–70 and note. Here again Burton had collected much of the traditional thought and used some of the phrasing which Herrick shapes into a poem. See

Burton, 3. 2. 5. 5 (pp. 576–7): 'such aboue the rest as haue daughters to bestow, should be very carefull and provident to marry them in due time. . . . For if they tarry longer to say truth, they are past date, and no body will respect them. . . . A Virgin, as the Poet holds, *lasciva & petulans puella virgo*, is like a flowre, a Rose withered on a sudden.

Quam modò nascentem rutilus conspexit Eous
Hanc rediens sero vespere vidit anum. [Ausonius, *Idyl.* 14.]
She that was erst a maid as fresh as May,
Is now an old Crone, time so steales away.

Let them take time then while they may, make advantage of youth, and as he prescribes,

Collige virgo rosas dum flos novus & nova pubes,
Et memor esto aevum sic properare tuum;
Faire maids goe gather Roses in the prime,
And think that as a flowre so goes on time.

Let's all love, *dum vires anniq; sinunt*, whiles we are in the flower of years, fit for love matters, and while time serves.' Burton then quotes Catullus, v. 4–6, with Jonson's translation:

Sunnes that set may rise againe,
But if once we loose this light,
'Tis with us perpetuall night.

adding '*Volat irrevocabile tempus*, time past cannot be recal'd.' See also *O.D.E. Prov.*, 'Marry your daughters betimes . . .'

Perhaps the nearest anticipation provided by a single work is that of Philostratus in his *Letters*, No. 17 (Loeb, *Alciphron &c.*): *Ἔστιν ἔαρ καὶ κάλλους καὶ ῥόδου, ὁ δε μὴ χρησάμενος τοῖς παροῦσιν ἀνόητος ἐν οὐ μέλλουσι μέλλων καὶ βραδύνων ἐπ' ἀπιοῦσι· φθονερὸς γὰρ ὁ χρόνος καὶ τὴν ἄνθους ὥραν ἀφανίζει καὶ τὴν κάλλους ἀκμὴν ἀπάγει. μηδὲν μέλλε, ὦ φθεγγόμενον ῥόδον, ἀλλ' ἕως ἔξεστι καὶ ζῇς, μετάδος ἡμῖν ὧν ἔχεις.* Cf. Letter 55: . . . *ἐχθρὸς γὰρ ὁ θεὸς καὶ τῇ κάλλους ὀπώρᾳ καὶ τῇ ῥόδων ἐπιδημίᾳ . . . εἰ δὲ μελλήσαις, ἀπελήλυθε. μαραίνεται καὶ γυνὴ μετὰ ῥόδων, ἂν βραδύνῃ. . .*

84. I. I. Cf. Spenser, *F.Q.* II. xii. 75. 6–9:

Gather therefore the Rose, whilest yet is time . . .

also Fairfax, *Tasso*, xvi. 15. Col. C. H. Wilkinson draws my attention to a citation of Herrick's line in J. Phillips's *A Satyr Against Hypocrites*, 1655, p. 20:

Do not the wicked Heathen speak and say,
Gather your Flowers and Rose-buds while you may?

84. I. 3–4. Cf. Catullus, lxii. 39–48: 'ut flos &c.'

84. I. 5. 'Heau'ns glorious lampe' appears in Fairfax, *Tasso*, vii. 116. I.

84. I. 9–12. Cf. Ovid, *Ars Am.* iii. 65–66:

Utendum est aetate. Cito pede labitur aetas,
Nec bona tam sequitur, quam bona prima fuit.

Cf. Tibullus, i. 8. 47–48; Propertius, iv. 5. 59–60; Publilius Syrus, 119. Seneca enlarges on this theme in *Ep.* cviii. 24 sqq. He refers to Virgil, *Georg.* iii. 67, 284, and *Aen.* vi. 275. Lodge translates one of Seneca's observations, 'the better days fly away, the worse succeed'. See also Seneca, *Hippol.* 773–6:

> res est forma fugax; quis sapiens bono
> confidat fragili? dum licet, utere.
> tempus te tacitum subruit, horaque
> semper praeterita deterior subit.

Jonson, *Epig.* lxx. 6:

> Each best day of our life escapes vs, first.

and *Epicoene*, IV. iii. 40–42: 'Besides, ladies should be mindfull of the approach of age, and let no time want his due vse. The best of our daies passe first.'

84. 1. 13–14. *use your time &c.* Cf. Seneca, *Hippol.* 446–51: 'Aetate fruere &c.'; and Burton, loc. cit. (p. 588): 'Marry whil'st thou maist, *donec viventi canities abest morosa*, whilest thou art yet able, yet lusty.' See also 56, l. 120 and note.

84. 2. 7–8. See *O.D.E. Prov.*, 'Lies upon the ground . . .'. The Latin sentence by Alain de Lille, 'Qui jacet in terra non habet unde cadat', is quoted by Burton, 2. 3. 3 (p. 328). Cf. Seneca, *Ep.* xx. 8: 'redige te ad parva, ex quibus cadere non possis'; and Publilius Syrus, 267.

84. 3. See 131. 2 and 132. 1; and cf. Catullus, lxviii. 13 sqq.

84. 3. 2. Ps. cxxxvii. 2 ('willows' A.V., 'trees' B.C.P.).

85. 1. Cf. Hor. *Carm.* iii. 30. 1–2: 'Exegi monumentum &c.' and other tags quoted by Burton, 1. 2. 3. 14 (p. 123).

85. 1. 9–16. Burton, ibid. (pp. 123–4): 'Of so many myriades of Poets, Rhetoricians, Philosophers . . . scarce one of a thousands workes remaines, . . .' Cf. also Montaigne, ii. 16, 'Of Glory', *Tudor Trans.*, p. 360. For Herrick's acquaintance with this passage see note to 412, ll. 103–4.

85. 2. Seneca, *Ep.* iv. 7: 'momento mare evertitur. eodem die ubi luserunt navigia, sorbentur'.

85. 3. *heading. birth of Prince Charles.* 29 May 1630. *Nic: Laniere.* 1588–1666. Master of the King's Music, 1625. See *D.N.B.*

86, l. 14. *whitest Wool.* See 58, l. 162 and note.

86, ll. 20–22. Cf. Dryden, *Astraea Redux*, 288–9: 'The star, that at your birth shone out so bright . . .' and Claudian, *De Quarto Cons. Honorii*, 184 sqq.:

> visa etiam medio populis mirantibus audax
> stella die . . .

86, l. 35. Cf. 119. 1. 12. Montaigne, iii. 9 cites Plautus, *Stichus*, v. iv. 10, in the form 'Non ampliter sed munditer convivium', which Florio (*Tudor Trans.*, p. 235) translates 'Not a great but a neat feast'.

86, l. 38. See 365. 1. 10.

87, l. 46. *quickly give, The swiftest Grace &c. Greek Anth.* x. 30. Cf. *O.D.E. Prov.*, 'Gives twice &c.'

87. 2. 9. *Ball of Wild-fire.* A fairly common expression, as in Fletcher, *Philaster*, II. iv. 191.

88, ll. 19–21. Cf. *Greek Anth.* v. 74 (Rufinus).

88. 2. 1–2. Acts iii. 6.

89. 1. *heading. Lord, Bernard Stuart.* ?1623–45. Sixth son of Esmé Stuart, third Duke of Lennox. Killed at Chester. See also 170. 2 and note.

89. 1. 1. See 91, ll. 41–43 and note.

89. 1. 16. Cf. 168. 1. 5 and 199. 3. 2; Ovid, *Met.* xv. 158: 'morte carent animae'; and Tacitus, *Agric.* 46: 'non cum corpore extinguuntur magnae animae'.

89. 1. 19. *chosen seed.* Deut. iv. 37.

89. 3. *heading.* See *O.D.E. Prov.*, 'Great boast and small roast.'

89. 3. 4. *sow's cleft eare.* Persius, vi. 70: 'fissa fumosum sinciput aure'.

90. 2. *heading. The Fairie Temple.* The dating of this and the other fairy-poems, 119. 1, 165. 1, and 223. 3, is hard to determine. They *may* have preceded Sir Simeon Steward's *A Description of the King of Faeries Clothes* (1626) and Drayton's *Nymphidia* (1627). See Drayton, *Works*, ed. Hebel: vol. v, ed. K. Tillotson and B. H. Newdigate, pp. 202 (note) and 222–3; and M. W. Latham, *The Elizabethan Fairies*, 1930, pp. 208–11. The John Merrifield to whom 'The Fairie Temple' is dedicated was probably son of John Merrifield of Crewkerne, Somerset. Admitted to Inner Temple in 1611; raised to the bench in 1638.

90. 3. 9. *Rimmon.* 2 Kings v. 18.

91, l. 28. 'Tit' and 'Nit' occur in Drayton's *Nymphidia*, l. 167; also 'Trip' (l. 32) in *Nymphidia*, l. 162.

91, ll. 41–43. All these classical tags occur in Jonson, *Sejanus*, v. 171–7. See also Jonson's notes.

91, l. 52. *Mood . . . Tense.* See *O.E.D.* s.v. 'Mood', *sb.*^{2} 2. *b.*

91, ll. 54–56. Herrick alludes to controversies about the shape and material of altars. Cf. C. Harvey, *The Synagogue*, 'The Communion Table', st. 4, l. 4: 'Square, oval, many-angled, long, or round'.

91, l. 59. *Cockall.* Knuckle-bone. Used in the game of cockal or dibs. See *O.E.D.*

92, l. 68. *fetuous.* Featous; well-formed, elegant.

92, l. 70. In Prayer-Book of 1549, the Priest at the beginning of the Communion service is to stand '*afore the middes of the Altar*'.

92, l. 73. *watched.* Watchet; blue or green.

92, l. 85. *board.* Cf. the expression 'God's Board' applied to the Communion Table in the Prayer Book of 1549. See *O.E.D.* s.v. 'Board', *sb.* 6.

93, l. 117. *Fasting-Spittle.* Saliva of a person fasting. See *O.E.D.* s.v. 'Fasting', and cf. Jonson, *Volpone*, II. vi. 20: 'A little capons grease, and fasting spittle'.

93, ll. 120–1. Tobit vi. 17, &c.

93, l. 125. *Chanters side.* Cantoris, not Decani.

93, l. 131. *Lady of the Lobster. O.E.D.* s.v. 'Lady', 1. 10: 'The calcareous structure in the stomach of a lobster, serving for the trituration of its food; fancifully supposed to resemble the outline of a seated female figure.' The expression occurs in Dorothy Osborne's *Letters* (ed. Moore Smith, p. 42). *O.E.D.* has no example earlier than 1704. Herrick's context suggests 'Our Lady' and perhaps also Phil. iii. 19: 'whose God is their belly'.

93, l. 142. *Feast that's now provided.* See 119. 1.

94. 1. *heading.* 'Katheren Bradshawe d. of John. Christened 30 Nov. 1614' is an entry in the Registers of St. Margaret's, Westminster. See A. M. Burke, *Memorials of St. Margaret's Church.*

94. 1. 10. *crowne of life.* Cf. Rev. ii. 10.

94. 2. *heading.* Cf. Cicero, *De Sen.* xix. 70: 'neque sapientibus usque ad "plaudite" veniendum est'.

94. 2. 2, 6. See 334. 5 and note.

94. 2. 10. See on heading; also 123. 4. 2 and note.

94. 3. 9. *Oile.* See 41. 2. 6.

94. 3. 10. Cf. Tilley, *Prov. Eng.*, C589, 'Confession of a fault is half amends.' Also Seneca, De *Beneficiis*, i. 1. 3, transl. Lodge: 'the mind sufficeth, though the meanes be deficient: For he restoreth a benefit that willingly oweth the same.'

95. 1. 5–6. Ps. xli. 3.

95. 1. 14–15. Hor. *Sat.* i. 5. 73–74.

96. 1. Anacreontea, 6.

96. 2. 2. *circummortall.* Herrick, who was fond of compounds beginning with 'circum', probably coined this one, meaning beyond or above mortal (see *O.E.D.* s.v. 'Circum-'). Cf. 168. 1. 3.

96. 2. 4. *Via Lactea.* Cf. 405, l. 55 and Burton, 3. 2. 2. 2 (p. 459): 'that *via lactea*'.

96. 3. Cf. Simonides, 69. 10–13; in Bergk, *Anth. Lyr.*, p. 250.

96. 3. 2–6. See Persius, v. 151–3, and note to 69, ll. 57–70.

96. 3. 4. *black Death.* See Hor. *Carm.* i. 28. 13.

96. 4. 1–2. Prov. ii. 2; Job. xxxvi. 10.

97, ll. 13–14. Cf. Hor. *Epod.* viii. 3–4:

et rugis vetus
frontem senectus exaret

and Ovid, *Ars Am.* ii. 118; also Massinger, *The City Madam,* I. i (Mermaid, I, p. 404): 'Time hath not ploughed One furrow in your face.'

97. 1. Cf. Burton, 3. 3. 4. 1 (p. 619): 'A dishonest woman cannot be kept . . . It is in vaine to locke her up . . .'; and Ovid, *Am.* iii. 14. 48.

97. 2. 1–2. Ovid, *Ars Am.* iii. 105:

Cura dabit faciem; facies neglecta peribit.

97. 3. 1. *Mop-ey'd.* Short-sighted. See *O.E.D.* s.v.

97. 3. 5–6. *Marriage . . . mend.* Cf. Burton, 2. 2. 2 (p. 239): 'but as

Platerus addes, *si nubant sanantur*, they rave single, and pine away, much discontent, but marriage mends all'.

97. 4. 4. Luke iv. 23: '. . . this proverb, Physician, heal thyself.'

98. 1. 1. See Martial, vi. 93. 1–2, and Smith, *Dict. Antiq.*, s.v. 'Fullo'.

98. 2. 1–2. Cf. Martial, vii. 89: 'I, felix rosa &c.'

98. 3. Cf. Martial, vii. 39.

98. 5. Cf. Donne, *Epig.* 'Phryne' (ed. Grierson, i, p. 77):

Thy flattering picture, *Phryne*, is like thee,
Onely in this, that you both painted be.

99. 2. *Draw Gloves.* 'An old parlour game . . . which consisted apparently in a race at drawing off gloves at the utterance of certain words.' (*O.E.D.*)

99. 3. Apparently related to the song in Fletcher's *Valentinian*, v. ii. 13–22: 'Care-charming Sleep &c.'

99. 3. 1. Cf. Hor. *Epod.* v. 45–46:

quae sidera excantata voce Thessala
lunamque caelo deripit.

See also 334, ll. 16–17 and note.

99. 3. 6. *civil Wildernesse.* See 28. 1. 12 and note.

101. 1. *heading. Westmorland.* See note to 40. 1.

101. 1. There is some general resemblance to Tibullus, ii. 1.

101. 1. 21. *crosse the Fill-horse.* Bestride the shaft-horse. The earliest instance of 'cross' in this sense given in *O.E.D.* is of 1760.

102, l. 40. *Fanes.* Obsolete form of fans.

102, ll. 49–50. Cf. 127, ll. 45–46. A Roman, not an English, custom. See Ovid, *Fasti*, 1. 665:

Rusticus emeritum palo suspendat aratrum.

Cf. Tibullus, ii. i. 6.

102. 3. Cf. 76. 2.

103, l. 16. Ovid, *Rem. Am.* 344: 'pars minima est ipsa puella sui'. Often quoted, e.g. by Montaigne, ii. 12, and Burton, 3. 2. 2. 3 (p. 471).

103. 1. 1. *Care-charming.* See note to 99. 3.

103. 3. Cf. Catullus, iii: 'Lugete, o Veneres Cupidinesque . . .'.

104, ll. 11–12. *Lesbia . . . Sparrow.* Catullus, iii. 3 sqq.

105. 2. Partly based on Hor. *Carm.* ii. 9.

105. 2. 2. See 188. 2, 293. 1, and notes.

106. 1. *Upon Groynes.* Jonson's Epig. cxvii is 'On Groyne'.

106. 3. *heading.* See note to 46. 2.

107. 2. 3. *This Sacred Grove.* Perhaps referring to the Garden of the Hesperides. See note to title-page.

108. 1. *heading. Duke of York.* Afterwards James II. Born 14 October 1633.

108. 1. 8. *Chick of Jove.* Cf. Burton, 1. 2. 3. 10 (p. 108): 'Some few amongst the rest, or perhaps one of a thousand, may be *Pullus Iovis*, in the worlds esteeme . . .'; also id. 1. 2. 4. 6 (p. 154). See Forcellini s.v. 'Pullus': 'Docet enim Festus puerum quem quis amabat, pullum vocari solitum. Hinc Q. Fabium . . . pullum Jovis appellatum esse.'

108. 1. 13–16. See Butler, *Hudibras*, II. i. 571–2 (ed. Gilfillan, i, p. 129):

Where'er you tread, your foot shall set
The primrose and the violet.

108. 2. *To Anthea.* Herrick may, consciously or not, have been influenced by a passage in Burton, 3. 2. 3. 1 (pp. 519–22), under heading 'Symptomes of Love': 'They are commonly slaves, captives, voluntary servants, *amator amicae mancipium*, as *Castilio* tearmes him, his mistris servant, her drudge, prisoner, bond-man, what not? . . . *All his cares, actions, all his thoughts, are subordinate to her will and commandement*; her most devote, obsequious, affectionate servant and vassall. . . . Heare some of their own confessions, protestations . . . *Thraso* the souldier was so submisse to *Thais* that he was resolved to doe whatsoever she enjoyned. *Ego me Thaidi dedam, & faciam quod jubet*, I am at her service. *Philostratus* in an Epistle to his mistris, *I am ready to dye sweet-heart if it be thy will. . . . Command me what you will, I will doe it, bid me goe to Sea, I am gone in an instant, take so many stripes, I am ready, runne through the fire, and lay downe my life and soule at thy feet, 'tis done.*' The letter of Philostratus is No. 23 (Loeb).

109. 1. Suetonius Paulinus in Tacitus, *Hist.* ii. 25: 'satis cito incipi victoriam ratus, ubi provisum foret, ne vincerentur'.

109. 2. Tacitus, *Ann.* vi. 8: 'tibi summum rerum iudicium di dedere, nobis obsequii gloria relicta est'.

109. 3. Ovid, *Am.* iii. 4. 9–10:

Cui peccare licet, peccat minus. ipsa potestas
Semina nequitiae languidiora facit.

Cf. Burton, 3. 3. 4. 1 (p. 619): '*they will . . . offend least when they have free liberty to trespasse*'. Also Martial, i. 73.

109. 4. Cf. *Greek Anth.* vii. 182 (Meleager).

110. 3. 17–18. Cf. Massinger, *The Picture*, III. iv (ed. Gifford, iii, p. 175): 'If you spend this way too much of your royal stock . . .' See also 289. 2. 17–19.

110. 4. 2. Cf. Ovid, *Met.* vi. 574–5:

Grande doloris
Ingenium est, miserisque venit sollertia rebus.

Also Tilley, *Prov. Eng.*, C840, 'Crosses are ladders that do lead to heaven.'

111. 2. *heading.* Laugh and lie (or lay) down was a card-game.

111. 3. 3–4. Cf. 29. 1. 11–12.

112. 2. 3–4. Cf. Plautus, *Mostellaria*, I. iii. 117: 'mulier recte olet ubi nihil olet'.

112. 3. *heading.* 'Sir Clipsby Crewe, son and heir of Sir Ranulphe Crewe [q.v., *D.N.B.*] . . . born 4 Sep. 1599, and knighted . . . 1620. He married, at St. Margaret's, Westminster, 7 July 1625, Jane, second d. of Sir John Pulteney, of Misterton, co. Leicester. . . . She died 2 Dec.

1639, in her thirtieth year. . . . In his will, dated 13 April, 1647, . . . he desired to be buried near his wife, "in the Abbey Church of Westminster".' (Chester, *Registers of Westminster Abbey: Burials*, pp. 142–3.) Matriculated Fellow Commoner from St. John's Coll., Easter 1616; adm. Lincoln's Inn 1619. Member of Parliament 1623–6. Died June 1648. (*Alumni Cant.*) See Evelyn, *Diary*, ed. Wheatley, i, p. 297: 28 Feb. 1647/8, 'we din'd with Sir Clepesby Crew . . . . [He] has some fine Indian hangings, and a very good chimney-piece of water-colours by Breughel, which I bought for him.'

112. 3. 1–11. Cf. Jonson, *Hymenaei*, ll. 83–91 (Hymen's speech, beginning 'What more then vsuall light').

112. 3. 18. Cf. Gen. xxvii. 27: 'the smell of a field which the Lord hath blessed'; and Martial, iii. 65. 7.

113, ll. 31–33. See Catullus, lxi. 6–15 and cf. Jonson, *Hymenaei*, ll. 48–51: 'Hymen . . . his head crowned with *Roses*, and *Marioram*, in his right hand a *torch* of *pine tree*.' See also note to 261. 4. 3.

113, l. 31. *sacred ground.* See note to 366. 1. 4.

113, l. 34. See 54, ll. 51–54 and note.

113, l. 48. See *O.D.E. Prov.*, 'Bride the sun shines on . . .'.

115, l. 108. *light their Tapers &c.* Cf. Jonson, *Und.* xix. 1–2, and *Hymenaei*, ll. 737–8. Also *Cynthias Reuells*, v. iv. 441.

115, ll. 116–17. *fold The Armes.* Embrace. Cf. Jonson, *Sejanus*, ii. 44–45.

115, l. 123. *misterie.* Art (see *O.E.D.* s.v. 'Mystery²'), here with a suggestion of symbolism.

115, ll. 136–40. Cf. Crashaw, 'In Memory of the Vertuous and Learned Lady Madre de Teresa . . .' (*Poems*, ed. Martin, p. 134), ll. 100–4:

> Of a death in which who dyes
> Loves his death, and dyes againe,
> And would for ever so be slaine!
> And lives and dyes, and knowes not why
> To live, but that he still may dy.

116, l. 158. *two Nations.* Gen. xxv. 23.

116. 2. See Terence, *Eun.* I. ii. 25: 'plenus rimarum sum . . .'.

117. 1. 1–2. Ovid, *Her.* i. 12:

> Res est solliciti plena timoris amor.

117. 2. 2. Burton, 2. 3. 7 (p. 355) quotes Ausonius, *Epig.* viii. 7: 'Fortunam reverenter habe.' Cf. Jonson, *Volpone*, III. vii. 88–89.

117. 3. Martial, viii. 24. 5–6:

> qui fingit sacros auro vel marmore vultus,
> non facit ille deos: qui rogat, ille facit.

118. 1. Tacitus, *Germania*, 43: 'nam primi in omnibus proeliis oculi vincuntur'.

118. 2. 1–2. Cf. Hor. *Carm.* ii. 12. 26–27.

118. 2. 5–8. See 224. 3 and note.

118. 2. 8. Cf. Juvenal, i. 79: 'si natura negat . . .'.

118. 3. 6. Catullus, xii and xxv; and Martial, xii. 29.

119. 1. 1. *Shapcot.* See 168. 1. heading. Probably Thomas S. of Shapcott, bapt. 16 Feb. 1586–7 at Knowstone; md. Urith, d. of Henry Sotherin of Cheshire; died 3 Feb. 1669–70. (*Visitations of the County of Devon,* 1531, 1564, 1620, with add. by J. L. Vivian, p. 677.) Presumably it was his son who was admitted to the Inner Temple in 1632 as the son and heir of Thomas Shapcott of Exeter.

119. 1. 8. *set on bread.* See Gen. xliii. 31.

119. 1. 12. See 86, l. 35 and note.

119. 1. 37 sqq. There may be some reminiscence of the 'ingredients' mentioned by Corvino in *Volpone,* II. vi. 18–20. See note to 93, l. 117.

120, ll. 46–47. *broke-heart, &c.* An allusion, probably, to stories of contests between a nightingale and a lute-player, as in Famianus Strada's Latin *Prolusiones,* 1617. See the enlarged version of this by Crashaw (*Poems,* ed. Martin, p. 149) and the paraphrase by Ford in *The Lover's Melancholy* (pub. 1629), I. i (Mermaid, pp. 11–12). This contains the expression 'And brake her heart', which is a departure from the exact sense of the Latin original.

120. 4. 2. *times of old.* Ps. xliv. 1.

121. 1. 2. Martial x. 23. 7–8, quoted by Montaigne, iii. 5 (*Tudor Trans.,* p. 63). Cf. 35, l. 10; 233. 1. 34–35; 321. 5; and 328. 1. 9–10. See also *O.D.E. Prov.,* 'Lives long that lives well' and 'Well done is twice done'.

121. 4. *heading.* For Master Edward Norgate see *D.N.B.* He is mentioned in *C.S.P. Dom., 1625–6,* p. 209, no exact date, as Clerk 'in reversion' and ibid. *1629–31,* p. 532, *1631,* 10 March, as 'one of the Clerks of the Signet Extraordinary'.

122. 1. *heading. Prudence Baldwin.* See also 151. 3 and 262. 1. She outlived Herrick, being buried at Dean Prior on 6 January 1678 (Parish Register).

122. 1. 3 and 5–6. Cf. Jonson, *Epig.* xiii. 2: 'they gaue a cock to ÆSCVLAPE'.

122. 2. 4. *Each way.* Everywhere. Cf. 45, l. 14; 195. 1. 4; 204. 4. 10.

122. 3. 6. Jonson introduces 'Hercules Bowle' in *Pleasure Reconciled to Virtue,* l. 10. Simpson refers to Macrobius, *Saturnalia,* v. xxi. 16, and points out that in Plutarch's *Life of Alexander,* σκύφον Ἡρακλέους ἐκπιεῖν means to drink a huge draught.

122. 4. 4. *the Kings Commandement.* Referring to the annual proclamation enjoining 'restraint of killing and eating of Flesh this next Lent'. See, e.g., Rymer, *Foedera,* xvii, pp. 131–3.

123. 2. Cf. Hor. *Ep.* i. 4. 14: 'grata superveniet &c.'

123. 4. 1. See also 150. 3. 1; 236. 2. 1; 252. 2. 1 and note; 317. 1. 2.

123. 4. 2. See *O.D.E. Prov.,* 'End crowns all (*or,* the work)'. Cf. 293. 4. 2.

124. 2. 1–2. Cf. Jonson, *Epig.* ci. 7–8:

> It is the faire acceptance, Sir, creates
> The entertaynment perfect: not the cates.

124. 2. 4–8. Prov. xv. 17; xvii. 1.

124. 3. *heading.* Henry Northleigh, son of Robert, of Alphington, Devon, matriculated from Exeter Coll. Oxford, 2 Dec. 1631, aged 18 (*Alumni Oxon.*). Admitted to Middle Temple 27 May 1633, as son and heir of Robert, of Matford, Devon (*Registers of M.T.*). From *Visitations of the County of Devon*, 1531, 1564, 1620, with add. by J. L. Vivian (p. 584), it appears that he married Lettice, d. of Henry Yard, in 1639 at Walborough (marriage recorded in Parish Register at Dean Prior, 5 Sept. 1639). In *Visitation of Devon* for 1620, as published by the Harl. Soc., 1872, she is described as d. of Edward Yard (ob. 1612) and as being eleven years old in 1620. The 'Porch' seems to be that of the bridegroom's house, as in 54, l. 53 and 113, l. 34, not that of the church, as Brand suggests (op. cit. ii, p. 83).

124. 3. 7. *Do all things sweetly, &c.* Perhaps a reminiscence of 1 Cor. xiv. 40.

124. 3. 14. *one death.* 'on' was a variant form of 'one', but is doubtless a misprint here. Cf. 38, l. 144 and 281. 3. 5.

125, l. 8. Cf. Hor. *Carm.* i. 4. 19–20.

125. 1. 4–6. Publilius Syrus, 373: 'Male secum agit aeger medicum qui heredem facit.' Cf. Jonson, *Volpone*, I. iv. 22–24:

I often haue
Heard him protest, that your physitian
Should neuer be his heire.

126. 3. *heading. Sir Simeon Steward.* See *D.N.B.*; also note to 90. 2, and p. 454. He was probably known to Herrick at Trinity Hall, Cambridge, where he lived 'for many years'.

126. 3. 1. Rumours of this kind were rife in 1623. See Walter Yonge, *Diary at Colyton and Axminster* (1604–28), Camden Soc., 1848, p. 71: 26 October 1623 '. . . rumours lately have been given out for firing the navy and house of munition, on which are set a double guard.' Cf. Webster, *The Devils Law-Case* (1623), III. ii. 13–14:

Betray a Towne to'th Turke, or make a Bonefire
A'th Christian Navy . . .

and Jonson, *The Staple of News* (?1625), III. ii. 54–55: 'A burning *Glasse* . . . To fire any *Fleet* that's out at *Sea*'.

126. 3. 2. *Tittyries.* See Yonge, op. cit., p. 70: 'The beginning of December, 1623, there was a great number in London, haunting taverns and other debauched places, who swore themselves in a brotherhood, and named themselves *Tytere tues* [Virgil, *Ecl.* i. 1] . . . There were divers knights, some young noblemen, and gentlemen of this brotherhood, and they were to know one the other by a black bugle which they wore, and their followers to be known by a blue ribbond. There are discovered of them about 80 or 100 persons, and have been examined by the Privy Council, but nothing discovered of any intent they had . . .' See also *C.S.P. Dom.*, 6 Dec. 1623, 21 (p. 125), Chamberlain to

[Carleton]; and cf. Jonson, *Fortunate Isles* (1624), ll. 306–8 (*Works*, vii, pp. 717–18): '*Domine Skelton . . . Tityre tu* of those times.'

126. 3. 4. Parliament was summoned in January 1623/4 for 12 February. (Yonge, op. cit. p. 71.)

126. 3. 10. Cf. Propertius, iv. 1. 61–62: 'Ennius hirsuta cingat sua dicta corona &c.'

126. 3. 13 sqq. Cf. 231, ll. 56–59.

126. 3. 14. *That's*. Misprinted 'That'. See 231, l. 57, where the mistake is not made. *Fox-i'th'hole*. See *O.E.D.* s.v. 'Fox', *sb.* 16. *d.*

127, l. 19. Cf. Burton, 3. 2. 3 (p. 536): 'Choosing Lords, Ladies, Kings, Queenes, and Valentines.' See also 317. 2.

127, l. 20. *Hey, for our town green*. See note to 229, l. 51, and cf. Beaumont & Fletcher, *Knight of the Burning Pestle*, IV. v:

> With scarfs and garters as you please, and 'Hey for our town!' cried.

127, ll. 23–24. See Tibullus, ii. 5. 81–82:

> et succensa sacris crepitet bene laurea flammis,
> omine quo felix et sacer [? satur] annus erit.

See also 7. 3. 5.

127, l. 32. *ninth*. See Hor. *Carm.* iii. 19. 11–15.

127, l. 38. *Decembers*. Years; as in Hor. *Ep.* i. 20. 27.

127, l. 41. Cf. Anacreontea, 8. 7–8; Wisd. of Sol. ii. 8. See note to 69, ll. 57–70; also 133, l. 33.

127, ll. 45–46. See 102, ll. 49–50 and note.

127. 1. 3. Cf. 303. 2. 6.

127. 1. 3–4. Cf. Tibullus, ii. 1. 13–14:

> casta placent superis: pura cum veste venite
> et manibus puris sumite fontis aquam;

also Jonson, *Sejanus*, v. 174–5: '*pure hands, pure vestments*, and *pure minds* . . .'. See Jonson's note. Cf. 91, l. 42.

128, l. 7. Cf. Rev. v. 8: 'golden vials full of odours'.

128. 1. 1. Theocritus, xvii. 1; Virg. *Ecl.* iii. 60 ('Ab Jove principium'); *Greek Anth.* xii. 1 (Strato).

128. 1. 3. Cf. Hor. *Carm.* iii. 6. 6.

128. 2. 12. Cf. Tibullus, i. 2. 66: 'nec te posse carere velim'.

128. 3. 3–6. Cf. Hor. *Carm.* iii. 1. 25–32.

128. 3. 10. Ps. xci. 5–6.

129, l. 11. Cf. Seneca, *De Const. Sap.* x. 4, transl. Lodge: 'a wise man receiueth some strokes, but he rebateth them, he healeth them . . .'; and Jonson, *Und.* xv. 184 (of Fortune):

> But what she gives, thou dar'st give her againe.

129. 1. 4. Cf. 131. 3.

129. 2. 2. Ovid, *Met.* i. 331: 'rector pelagi'. Cf. ibid. xi. 207.

129. 3. 6. Cf. Jonson, 'To . . . Robert, Earle of Somerset', l. 23 (Ungathered Verse, *Works*, viii, p. 384):

> And when your yeares rise more, then would be told . . .

129. 4. 2. Cf. 9. 1. 6 and Propertius, ii. 13. 29:

osculaque in gelidis pones suprema labellis.

130. 1. Seneca, *Ep.* cxv. 14: 'an dives, omnes quaerimus, nemo, an bonus'; quoted by Burton, 1. 2. 4. 6 (p. 161). Cf. Juvenal, iii. 140–4 and Plautus, *Menaechmi*, IV. ii. 6.

131. 1. *heading.* William Soame was adm. at Corpus Christi Coll. Camb. in 1597. 'Doubtless s. of Sir Stephen, knt., of Betley, Norfolk, and of London (Lord Mayor in 1598) . . . Knighted, Nov. 21, 1614' (*Alumni Cant.*). His mother was Ann, d. of William Stone of London (see *Visitations of London*, 1633–5, p. 251, and note to 176. 1), and sister of Julian Herrick, Robert's mother. Sir William Soame was of Great Thurlow, Suffolk.

131. 1. 4. Cf. Massinger, *The Maid of Honour*, I. ii (Mermaid ed. i, p. 319): 'but all these [sc. gifts] bound up Together in one volume!'

131. 1. 8. *Rain-bow in perfumes goes out.* Cf. W. Browne, *Britannia's Pastorals*, i. 2. 333–7.

131. 1. 10. *Benjamin.* 'Corruption of benjoin, earlier form of benzoin.' (*O.E.D.*)

132. 2. Tacitus, *Ann.* xiii. 27: 'paucorum culpam ipsis exitiosam esse debere, nihil universorum iuri derogandum; quippe late fusum id corpus'.

132. 3. *heading. John Wickes.* Or Weeks. B.A., St. John's Coll. Camb., 1612/13; Fellow, 1613; of Devon. MA. 1616; B.D. 1623. Incorp. at Oxford, 1617. Created D.D. (Oxford) 1643. With Herrick ordained deacon (Peterborough) 24 Apr., and priest 25 Apr., 1623. Rector of Shirwell, Devon, 1627; there in 1634. Prebendary of Bristol, 1633. Vicar of Banwell, Somerset, 1640. Dean of St. Burian, Cornwall. Chaplain to Archbishop Laud. (*Alumni Cant.*; see also *Alumni Oxon.*) Described by Wood (*Fasti*, ed. Bliss, ii, col. 68) as 'a jocular person'. There are several references to him in *C.S.P. Dom.* between 1629 and 1634, e.g. 5 July 1629, p. 5: 'John Weekes to Endymion Porter. Begs to be mentioned to the King for Deptford, Dr. Peterson being now Dean of Exeter. . . . If the writer's prayer be not sufficient for Porter, it is no great journey for the writer's little B. to go down on her knees, and to join with him in the versicle of the Litany, "We beseech", etc.' Cf. letter to Endymion Porter, 3 Oct. 1633, p. 230, ending 'your epicene chaplain, both he and she, John Weekes and little b.' See also ibid., p. 316 and 1633–4, p. 445.

132. 3. 1–4. See Hor. *Carm.* ii. 14. 1–4.

132. 3. 8. Hor. *Carm.* i. 28. 20: 'saeva . . . Proserpina'.

132. 9–12. Hor. *Carm.* ii. 14. 21–24.

133, ll. 19–20. Hor. *Carm.* iv. 7. 13–14.

133, l. 26. *Anchus . . . Tullus.* Hor. *Carm.* iv. 7. 15 ('Tullus et Ancus', the order in Herrick MSS. See p. 482).

133, l. 30. Hor. loc. cit. 16: 'pulvis et umbra'.

133, l. 33. See 127, l. 41 and note.

133, l. 40. *white . . . stone.* As in Martial, x. 38. 4–5.

133, l. 48. The reference is to Vedius Pollio, who in anger ordered a slave to be flung into a pond to be eaten by lampreys. See Seneca, *De Ira*, iii. 40.

133, *after l. 48, second of two additional stanzas* (p. 483), l. 7. *what she gives not, &c.* Cf. Seneca, *Ep.* lix. 18: 'quod non dedit fortuna, non eripit'.

133, l. 50. *Salt-seller.* Hor. *Carm.* ii. 16. 14.

133, l. 54. *baudery.* Material dirt. See *O.E.D.* Cf. Jonson, *The Alchemist*, v. v. 41: 'The seeling fill'd with *poesies* of the candle.'

134, l. 68. *circular.* Complete, perfect; at one. Cf. Hor. *Sat.* ii. 7. 86: 'totus, teres, atque rotundus.'

135, l. 112. Cf. Fletcher, commendatory poem to Beaumont's *Poems* (1640):

The matchless lust of a fair Poesy.

135, l. 118. *my Iülus.* My son. See Virgil, *Aen.* i. 277–8.

135, l. 120. Ps. xxv. 6.

135, l. 122. *wild Apple.* Sc. (log of) wild apple-tree.

136, ll. 131–2 *as in MSS.* (*see p.* 484). *Hind.* Probably Richard Hinde, who matriculated from St. John's Coll., Camb., in 1611. B.A. 1614/15. M.A. 1618. Vicar of Higham, Kent. (*Alumni Cant.*)

Goderiske or *Godderick.* Possibly Henry Goodrick, who matriculated from Clare Coll. in 1614. B.A. 1617/18; or John Goodrick, who matriculated from Magdalene Coll. in 1612 (op. cit.).

Smith. Presumably James Smith, 1605–67, divine and poet. See *D.N.B.* Collaborated with Sir John Mennes (see 194. 2) in editing *Witt's Recreations*, &c.

Nansagge or *Nansogg.* Martin Nansogg. B.A. from Trinity Hall, Camb., 1613; M.A. 1617. Fellow 1616–28. Incorporated at Oxford 1615 and 1622. Nominated to archdeaconry of Cornwall but never installed. Vicar of Cornwood, Devon, 1628 (but there was another incumbent in 1629). See *Alumni Cant.* and *Alumni Oxon.* Also *C.S.P. Dom. 1629–31*, p. 253, 8 May 1630: 'Bishop Hall to Bishop Laud, in reply to a complaint against him of his late Chaplain, Mr. Nansog. The writer, prevailed upon by Nansog's importunity, made a void appointment in his favour of the Archdeaconry of Cornwall. It was contested, and in consequence of some foul miscarriages of Mr. Nansog's tongue against the writer and his family, he became a stranger to Nansog, and withdrew his appointment. If a favour really meant cannot be forfeited by unworthiness, the writer is cast, else he hopes he is free.' A further letter from Bishop Hall on this subject is cited ibid., p. 258 (14 May 1630).

136, l. 148. *Sphering.* Turning. See *O.E.D.* s.v. 'Sphere', *v.* 4.

137. 3. *heading and* 1–3. Herrick means Anne Villiers, Buckingham's niece, not Mary, his daughter. Anne was the daughter of Sir Edward Villiers, Buckingham's half-brother. She married Robert Douglas,

Lord Dalkeith, who succeeded his father as Earl of Morton in 1649, but died the same year. See *Complete Peerage*, art. 'Morton'. Princess Henrietta Anne (q.v. *D.N.B.*), fifth d. of Charles I, was born in 1644 at Exeter, where, Clarendon says, the King found her 'under the care and government of the lady Dalkith, (shortly after Countess of Mourton, by the death of her husband's father,) who had been long before designed by both their majesties to that charge'.

138. 1. 3. *Black.* Burton, 3. 2. 3. 2 (p. 462), observes that 'Of all eyes . . . black are most amiable, entising, and fairest.' *rowling.* See note to 254. 2.

138. 1. 4. *Double chinn'd.* Herrick presumably means dimpled. See 405, l. 33. *forehead high.* See 404. 1. 5.

138. 1. 6. Cf. 7. 4. 9–10.

138. 3. A version of Martial, i. 38.

138. 5. 4. Ovid, *Ars Am.* iii. 475–6: 'neque te facilem &c.'

139. 1. 2. *Sciography.* This passage is cited in *O.E.D.* s.v. 'Sciagraphy', 2. *a*: 'a sciagraphic [see meaning 1] delineation or picture'. But Herrick's context suggests rather meaning 3: 'an outline, draught, rough sketch' as opposed to the completed work or 'incarnation'. Cf. Cudworth, *Intell. Syst.* 146 (1678) (as quoted in *O.E.D.* for this sense): 'The first sciography and rude delineation of atheism.'

139. 6. 1. Cf. Eccles. i. 9, 10; Juvenal, i. 147–9.

139. 7. 1–6. Cf. Gen. ix. 13, 14. See also 237. 2.

140. 1. *heading.* Bridget Lowman was the second d. of Philip Lowman and of Anne or Agnes, d. of Jo. Giles of Bowden Esq. (*Visitation of Devon*, 1620, Harl. Soc., 1872.) See 419. 1 and note. Anne Lowman, Bridget's mother, was a sister of Sir Edward Giles.

140. 2. 6. Cf. Jonson, *Kings Entertainment*, ll. 272–3 (*Works*, vii, p. 91):

What all the minutes, houres, weeks, months and yeares,
That hang in file vpon these siluer haires . . .

141. 1. *heading.* See *O.D.E. Prov.*, 'Long and lazy'; also 'Fair and sluttish &c.'

141. 3. *heading.* See art. Philip Herbert (1584–1650) in *D.N.B.* He succeeded his brother, William, third Earl of Pembroke, in 1630.

141. 3. 2. Cf. the final line of Dryden's *Astraea Redux*:

The world a Monarch, and that Monarch you!

141. 3. 12. *regard, reward.* Cf. Jonson, *Fortunate Isles*, ll. 292–4 (*Works*, vii, p. 717):

& he was paid for it,
Regarded, and rewarded: which few *Poets*
Are now adaies.

142. 3. 4. *shoulders . . . eares.* Grosart suggests the meaning that Paske 'does not ask for a debt overdue, but sends a shoulder-tapper to arrest the debtor'.

142. 5. 2. Cf. Ps. lxxxiv. 11 (A.V.): 'the Lord will give grace and glory'.

143. 1. 1. Cf. Hor. *Carm.* iii. 30. 6: 'non omnis moriar'.

144, ll. 5–6. Cf. Job xxix. 6 and Mic. vi. 7.

144. 1. *heading. turn'd to mourning.* Cf. 2 Sam. xix. 2 and Lam. v. 15.

144. 1. 13–18. Cf. Job xxx. 31 and Ps. cxxxvii. 1.

145. 1. *heading.* Anne, d. of Sir Thomas Soame (see 176. 1, 131. 1 and notes), was the second wife of Sir Thomas Abdy, created baronet in 1641. She died at 57 in 1679. (O. Manning, *Hist. and Antiqs. of Surrey*, iii, p. 203.) The phrase 'now Lady Abdie' may have been added to the title some time after the poem was written.

145. 1. Cf. Martial, xi. 8; iii. 65; and v. 37.

145. 2. *heading. Elizabeth Herrick.* Canon Charles Smyth kindly refers me to A. M. Burke, *Memorials of St. Margaret's Westminster*, pp. 100 and 555, showing that Elizabeth Herrick, d. of William, was christened 31 March 1619 and buried 26 May 1630. See Introduction, pp. xii and xv, and note to 73. 1.

146. 1. *heading. Sir Lewis Pemberton.* 'Robert Pemberton, gentleman usher to Queen Elizabeth for thirty years, died 1609, was succeeded by his son, Sir Lewis Pemberton, who was Sheriff of Northamptonshire in 1621.' (*Victoria Hist. of Northamptonshire*, iv, p. 45, Rushden.) From *Alumni Cant.* (q.v. for further details) it appears that L. P. matriculated from Christ's 1592–3, was knighted in 1617, married Alice Bowles, of Wallington, Herts., and died in 1640. See also Shaw, *Knights of England*, ii, p. 165.

With this poem cf. Martial, iii. 58; Jonson, 'To Penshurst' (*Forest*, ii); and Carew, 'To Saxham' (*Poems*, ed. Dunlop, pp. 27–29).

146. 1. 5. *worn Threshold.* Cf. Martial, x. 10. 2: 'limina . . . teras'. See also 350, ll. 13–14 and note.

146. 1. 22. Cf. Ruth ii. 14: 'dip thy morsel in the vinegar'.

146. 25. Plautus, *Miles Gloriosus*, III. i. 146–7:

nam hospes nullus tam in amici hospitium deuorti potest
quin, ubi triduum continuom fuerit, iam odiosus siet.

146, l. 37. *Brest unhid.* Open heart.

146, l. 38. Hor. *Epod.* 2. 2: 'prisca gens mortalium'.

147, l. 47. Seneca, *De Const. Sap.* xiv. 2, transl. Lodge: 'if a Porter be ouer currish'.

147, l. 58. *Trebius.* See Juvenal, v. 19; and Joseph Hall, *Satires*, v. 2. 112–16, &c.

147, l. 65. Cf. Jonson, *Epig.* ci. 18–20: 'partrich . . . raile, and ruffe'.

147, l. 71. Martial, ix. 93. 1: 'immortale Falernum'.

148, l. 87. *of distemper.* To intoxication (see *O.E.D.* s.v. 'Distemper', *sb.*[1] 4. *d*); or ? intemperately.

148, l. 99. *Goodnes and Greatnes.* See *O.D.E. Prov.*, 'Goodness is not tied to greatness.'

148, l. 100. *marbles.* Cf. Martial, viii. 3. 6 and x. 2. 9. See also 85. 1. 21–24 above.

148, ll. 112–14. Cf. Hor. *Ep.* i. 1. 51: 'sine pulvere palmae'; Ovid, *Ars Am.* ii. 537: 'nulla, nisi ardua, virtus'; Seneca, *Ep.* xxxi. 7: 'non est viri timere sudorem'; id. *De Prov.* ii. 4: 'marcet sine adversario virtus'; and Milton, *Areopagitica*, ed. Hale, p. 18: 'I cannot praise a fugitive and cloister'd vertue . . . where that immortal garland is to be run for not without dust and heat.'

148, ll. 115–18. Cf. Jonson, 'To Penshurst', ll. 45–47.

149, l. 128. *Star-chamber.* Heaven; divine judgement. See *O.E.D.* s.v., 2. *b.*

150. 1. Probably influenced by Plautus' epitaph on himself (Gellius, i. 24), beginning 'Postquam est mortem aptus Plautus, comoedia luget'.

150. 1. 9. *Holy-Rage.* Cf. Jonson, *Und.* lxx. 80: 'Possest with holy rage.'

150. 1. 11. *praises-proofe.* ? signs of admiration.

150. 1. 13. Ovid, *Ars Am.* i. 106: 'scaena sine arte fuit'.

150. 1. 15–16. *hist . . . the Alchymist.* There appears to be no other record of this occurrence.

150. 3. *his Nephew.* Not identified. It is not known that Herrick was related, through his mother, Julian Stone, to the painter Henry Stone ('Old Stone'), who died in 1653 (see *D.N.B.*). He was a successful follower of Van Dyck (see l. 6). Herrick had a 'niece' named Mary Stone (see 257. 1 and note).

150. 3. 3. *Coxie.* Flemish painter, 1499–1592.

151. 2. 3–4. Cf. Hor. *Carm.* ii. 7. 10.

151. 3. *heading. Prew.* See note to 122. 1, title.

151. 3. 1–4. Cf. Massinger, *The Maid of Honour*, III. i. (Mermaid, p. 347):

O summer-friendship,
Whose flattering leaves, that shadowed us in our
Prosperity, with the least gust drop off
In the autumn of adversity.

152. 1. Cf. Hor. *Carm.* iii. 3. 1–5.

152. 4. *heading. Sir Edward Fish. Calendar of Wills, P.C.C. 1655–60*, p. 143; 1658: 'Fish, Sir Edward, Bart., widr., Chertsey, Surrey.'

153. 1. Cf. Jonson, *Discoveries* (*Works*, viii, p. 639, ll. 2492 sqq.): '*Art* must bee added, to make all these perfect. . . .'

153. 5. Cf. Martial, xi. 66.

153. 6. 4–6. *fire brand* &c. A reference to the story of Meleager.

154. 3. Martial, xi. 104. 7–8. See also 75. 1 above and note. Contrast 202. 3, 'Art above Nature'.

154. 5. Cf. (?) Cornelius Gallus, *Frag.* i. 1–2:

Occurris quum mane mihi, ni purior ipsa
Luce nova exoreris, lux mea, dispeream.

155. 1. 1–2. Cf. Catullus, xcv. 8: 'et laxas scombris saepe dabunt tunicas'; see also Hor. *Ep.* ii. 1. 269–70, Persius, i. 41–43, Martial, iii. 2. 4–5; iv. 86. 8, &c.

155. 1. 6. The reference is to 'King Edward the Fourth and a

Tanner of Tamworth'. (Child, *Popular Ballads*, 1898, v. pp. 75–77.) An edition of this ballad was entered in Stat. Reg. on 9 Dec. 1615, for John Trundle, the publisher referred to in l. 12. (Arber, iii. 579.)

155. 1. 7. See 'Fryar and Boye' in *Percy*'s *Folio MS.*, ed. Hales and Furnivall, iii, Appendix, pp. 9–28.

155. 1. 8. *Robin Rush. Alias* Friar Rush. See H. Morley, *Early Prose Romances*, 1889. An edition of the story was published in 1620.

155. 1. 9–11. *Tom Chipperfeild.* Perhaps the person referred to in *The Life and Death of Griffin Flood Informer . . . Wherein is also declared the murther of Iohn Chipperford Vintner . . . London . . .* 1623. '*Chipperford*' appears as '*Chipperfield*' in the text, C2ᵛ. There may have been a ballad. The other references in these lines have not been traced. A similar attitude to ballads appears in 412, ll. 89–91, presumably written about 1623. See Introd., p. xxxvii.

155. 1. 12. *Tim-Trundell.* See note to l. 6. John Trundle is referred to in Jonson's *Every Man in his Humour*, I. iii. 63.

155. 1. 15–18. Likely to have been added during the Civil War.

155. 1. 17–18. Seneca, *Thyestes*, 884–5:

vitae est avidus quisquis non vult
mundo secum pereunte mori.

See 25. 1. 3–4 and note.

155. 3. 3–6. Cf. Burton, 3. 2. 5. 1 (p. 541): ''Tis in vaine to set upon those that are busie . . . *Cedit amor rebus, res age tutus eris* [Ovid, *Rem. Am.* 144].' See 53, ll. 10–14 and note.

155. 4. 1–2. (?) Maximinianus (sometimes attributed to Cornelius Gallus):

Sed mihi dulce magis resoluto vivere collo.

Quoted by Montaigne, iii. 5 (*Tudor Trans.*, p. 75).

156. 4. 4. Cf. *A Midsummer-Night's Dream*, III. ii. 443:

Bedabbled with the dew and torn with briers;

also 247. 4. heading and ll. 1–2.

157. 2. 8. *Juno . . . perfum'd.* See Homer, *Iliad*, xiv. 170–4. Cf. 59. 3. 9–10.

157. 3. 1–2. Hor. *Carm.* iii. 25. 1–2: 'Quo me, Bacche, rapis tui Plenum?' Quoted Burton, 3. 2. 2. 1 (p. 447).

158. 1. 4. See 75. 1 and notes.

158. 4. Martial, i. 19; viii. 57. Cf. Kendal, *Flowers of Epigrammes*, 1577, p. 4ᵛ (Spenser Soc., 1874, p. 24).

158. 5. 1. Cf. Song of Sol. ii. 5; v. 8.

159. 1. Probably referring, like 26. 1, to the separation of Charles I and the Queen during the Civil War.

159. 1. 3. *feast.* Perhaps a misprint for 'feasts'.

159. 1. 19. *divinely redolent.* Cf. R. Brathwait, *A Spiritual Spicerie*, 1638, p. 226: 'A reply to a rigid Precisian, objecting, that flowers from Romish Authors extracted, became lesse wholesome and divinely redolent.'

160. 2. Cf. Hall, *Satires*, iv. 5. 59–60:

The ding-thrift heire, his shift-got summe mispent,
Comes drouping like a pennylesse penitent.

161. 1. Abbreviated from (?) Martial ('Epigrams ascribed to Martial', Loeb, ii, p. 520, 2), 'In Varum'.

161. 1. 4. *give me else.* The Latin is 'aut appone dapes, Vare, vel aufer opes'.

161. 3. *heading. Clipseby Crew.* See note on 112. 3. heading.

161. 3. 1–10. Cf. Ps. lv. 12–14.

162. 1. 3. *in print.* In proper style.

162. 2. 2. Proverbial. See *O.D.E. Prov.*, 'Hold that will away.'

162. 3. Borrowed, like many other 'observations', chiefly in *Noble Numbers*, from *Notes and Observations vpon some Passages of Scripture. By I.G.* [John Gregory, orientalist, 1607–46, q.v., *D.N.B.*] *Master of Arts of Christ-Church Oxon. . . . Oxford . . . 1646.* This distich renders a passage in Gregory's ch. xix, p. 92: 'whosoever say the Doctours in *Beracoth* shall set his Bed *North* and *South* shall beget male children. *Ps.* 17. 14 *&c.* Therefore the Iewes hold this Rite of *Collocation* . . . to this day.' The continuation of this passage is versified by Herrick in 386. 3. See note thereto.

162. 4. 2. *As Salust saith.* Herrick apparently refers to 'Ad Caesarem . . . Oratio', iii. 2: 'Equidem ego cuncta imperia crudelia . . . metu agites'; but Sallust is there deprecating rule through fear.

162. 5. *Greek Anth.* x. 28 (Lucianus). In Farnaby's *Florilegium epig.*, 1629, pp. 14 and 15.

163. 2. Herrick is probably translating, but does not make his author's meaning very clear.

163. 3. Cf. Martial, viii. 35.

163. 5. Cf. Gregory, op. cit. (on 162. 3), ch. xix, p. 91: 'The *Iewes Kitchin* . . . is divided as their *Synagogues* where the Women pray by themselves in another Roome. They are indeed of the Congregation, but not of the Company'; also Bacon, 'Of Friendship': 'a crowd is not company'.

163. 6. See 11. 1. 3 and note.

164. 1. See 75. 1 and note.

165, l. 12. *too.* The same spelling at the end of a line occurs on p. 377, l. 23.

165. 1. Cf. Drayton, *The Muses Elizium*, Nymphal 8, and see Drayton, *Works*, ed. Hebel and Tillotson, v, pp. 222–3, for some parallels (not very close) with Herrick's phrasing.

165. 1. 1. *Shapcot.* See note to 119. 1. 1.

165. 1. 2. *Fairie Court.* Jonson gives this name to Drayton's *Nymphidia* in l. 79 of the verses prefixed to *The Battaile of Agincourt* and other poems by Drayton published in 1627. (Jonson, *Works*, viii, p. 398.)

165. 1. 9. *Bee with Thyme.* Cf. Virgil, *Ecl.* v. 77: 'Dumque thymo pascentur apes.'

165. 1. 13. *Lust ha's no eares.* Cf. Propertius, ii. 16. 36: 'Turpis amor surdis auribus esse solet', and Tilley, *Prov. Eng.*, B286.

165. 1. 14. *Hay in's horne.* Hor. *Sat.* i. 4. 34: 'faenum habet in cornu'. Hay was bound as a warning round the horns of an ox supposed to be dangerous. See *O.D.E. Prov.*, 'Hay in one's horns'.

165. 1. 18. From Accius (*Trag. Rel.*, ed. Ribbeck, p. 136). Quoted, e.g., by Suetonius, *Caligula*, 30: 'Tragicum illud subinde iactabat: "Oderint, dum metuant".'

165. 1. 26. *redeem.* Gain, reach. See *O.E.D.* s.v., 12 (this instance only is given).

165. 1. 28. *Lemster Ore.* A very fine kind of wool associated with Leominster. The meaning of 'ore' is uncertain. See *O.E.D.* s.v. 'Ore[7]'.

166, ll. 70–71. It is suggested in *N. and Q.*, 9th S. ix, 1902, p. 178, that this refers to the use of a worn silver coin (with a sharp edge) to cut the ligament in the mouth of a tongue-tied infant.

167, l. 98. *comply.* Enfold.

168. 1. *heading.* See 119. 1. 1 and note.

168. 1. 3. *Circum-mortall.* See note on 96. 2. 2.

168. 1. 5. See 89. 1. 16 and note.

168. 3. 2. *one.* It has been suggested that this means 'won', but as Herrick seems to be referring to his own heart it may be that 'one' is the past participle of 'owe', to possess, and the meaning of the line 'when I had owned a heart'.

169. 1. 2. Tibullus, iii. 2. 6: 'frangit fortia corda dolor'.

169. 2. Cf. Bacon, *Colours of Good and Evil*, 3 (ed. Wright, 1863, p. 250): 'fame may be onely *causa impulsiva*, and not *causa constituens*, or *efficiens*'. Cf. Burton, 'Democritus to the Reader, p. 6: '*Bewitched with this desire of fame* . . . To be counted writers, *scriptores ut salutentur*. . . .'

169. 3. 24. *Iphis.* See Ovid, *Met.* xiv. 698–764.

170. 2. *heading.* Herrick was mistaken about the name of the then Duke of Lennox. He was James Stuart, who succeeded to the title in 1624, his uncle Ludovick, second Duke, and his father, third Duke, brother to Ludovick, having both died in 1624. James himself died in 1655. His three brothers killed in the war were George, in 1642, John, in 1644, and Bernard, in 1645 (see 89. 1). There was another brother, named Ludovick, who became seigneur of Aubigny, was educated for the Church, and was made a canon of Notre-Dame; but he could not have been the Ludovick whom Herrick addresses. See *D.N.B.* art. 'James Stuart, fourth Duke of Lennox'.

171. 1. Martial, vii. 47. 11–12.

171. 2. 3. Cf. Seneca, *Ep.* lxxxiii. 24: 'quae gloria est capere multum &c.'

171. 2. 4. The Heidelberg tun was famous. Cf. Jonson, *Und.* lii ('My Answer'), 6: 'But yet the Tun at *Heidelberg* had houpes.'

171. 4. 1. An echo, probably, of Jonson's 'Ode to himselfe' published with *The New Inne* in 1631, 'Come leaue the lothed stage &c.'

172, l. 8. *Topick*. Place. See *O.E.D.* s.v., B. II. 5.

172. I. I. Cf. Seneca, *Herc. Furens*, 178 sqq.: 'Dum fata sinunt &c.'; also Tibullus, i. I. 69; and Propertius, ii. 15. 23–24. See notes to 69, ll. 57–70 and 84. I. 13–14.

172. 3. 3–4. Mildmay Fane's *Otia Sacra* was published in 1648.

172. 3. 8. *Bælus eye*. Cf. Pliny, *Hist. Nat.* xxxvii. 55, transl. Holland, 1601, ii, p. 625: 'The stone called Belus eye is white, and hath within it a black apple, the mids whereof a man shall see to glitter like gold: this stone for the singular beautie that it hath, is dedicated to *Belus* the most sacred god of the Assyrians.'

173, ll. 13–14. Hor. *Carm.* iv. 9. 29–30.

173. I. 3–6. See I Kings xvii. 12–13.

173. 4. Martial, viii. 19.

174. I. Cf. Sir John Harington, *Epig.* iv. 45 (1618), cited Burton, 2. 2. 6. 4 (p. 300): 'Moll, once in pleasant company, &c.'

174. I. 18. *Feature*. Beauty.

174. I. 19–20. Cf. Burton, 3. I. I. I (p. 406): 'Omnia munda mundis, a naked man to a modest woman is no otherwise then a picture . . .'

174. I. 23 sqq. Cf. Massinger, *The Picture*, II. ii (ed. Gifford, iii, p. 162):

> Such is my full-sail'd confidence in her virtue,
> Though in my absence she were now besieged
> By a strong army of lascivious wooers,
> And every one more expert in his art,
> Than those that tempted chaste Penelope;
> Though they raised batteries by prodigal gifts,
> By amorous letters, vows made for her service,
> With all the engines wanton appetite
> Could mount to shake the fortress of her honour,
> Here, here is my assurance she holds out,
> And is impregnable.

175, ll. 45–46. Cf. Seneca, *Ep.* iii. 3: 'quidam fallere docuerunt, dum timent falli, et illi jus peccandi suspicando fecerunt', quoted by Montaigne, iii. 9 (*Tudor Trans.*, p. 194); Webster, *The White Divel*, I. ii. 91–92: 'women are more willinglie & more gloriouslie chast, when they are least restrayned of their libertie'; and Burton, 3. 3. 4. I (p. 619): 'For when she perceives her husband observes her and suspects, liberiùs peccat . . . and will therefore offend, because shee is unjustly suspected.'

175, ll. 53–57. Cf. Tilley, *Prov. Eng.*, S475, 'Compelled sins are no sins.'

175, l. 58. *Cyane . . . Medullina*. Plutarch, *Parallels*, 19 (*Morals*, transl. Holland, 1603, pp. 911–12). Their fathers had offended Bacchus and were therefore made drunk by him so that they unwittingly committed incest: '*Cyanippus* a Siracusian . . . deflowred forcibly his owne daughter, named *Cyane*. . . . *Aruntius* . . . forced his owne daughter *Medullina*.'

175, ll. 61–64. Cf. Publilius Syrus, 710: 'Voluntas impudicum non corpus facit.' Seneca, *Hippol.*, 735: 'mens impudicam facere, non casus solet'. See also 359. 1, 370. 3, 389. 8, and 392. 2. 31–32.

175, ll. 69–72. *compression, &c.* The manuscript readings (see p. 488) suggest that 'compression' means a signet or signet-ring, supposed to have magical properties. See Child, *Popular Ballads*, 1898, i, Introduction to 'Hind Horn', and the ballad itself (p. 205, form G):

And whan that ring turns pale and wan,
Ye may ken that your love loves anither man.

176. 1. *heading. Sir Tho. Soame.* Brother of William Soame (see 131. 1 and note) and father of Anne (note to 145. 1). See *Visitations of London*, 1633–5, p. 251. Thomas Soame, 'alderman of London', was knighted on 3 Dec. 1641, at Hampton Court. (Shaw, *Knights of England*, ii, p. 211.)

176. 1. 6. Patres conscripti.

176. 1. 8. Cf. Cicero, *Pro Plancio*, 30. 72: 'coronam . . . civicam'.

176. 2. 3. *Your date is not so past.* Cf. Burton, 3. 2. 5. 5 (p. 576): 'For if they tarry longer to say truth, they are past date, and no body will respect them.' See note to 84. 1.

177. 2. See 36, l. 62 and 148, l. 114 and notes; cf. Joseph Hall, *Meditations*, i. 26: 'There was never good thing easily come by. The heathen man could say, "God sells knowledge for sweat".' See also *O.D.E. Prov.*, 'Nothing for nothing.'

177. 6. 2. *Citie . . . Field.* Gen. xxxiv. 28.

177. 6. 4–6. *by day . . . night.* Cf. Ps. xci. 5.

179, l. 23. *Mowes.* Stacks or heaps.

180. 1. 6. Cf. Jos. Hall, *Meditations*, i. 54: 'no tree bears fruit in Autumn unless it blossom in the Spring.' Also Seneca, *Hippol.* 455–7.

180. 4. 1. Peter in *2 Henry VI*, I. iii. 193 swears 'By these ten bones'.

181. 1. *heading. Tho. Falconbirge.* Referred to in *C.S.P. Dom.* between 1640 and 1644. Appointed auditor of accounts of the Commissioners of Excise (1641–3, p. 485, 11 Sept. 1643). 'Tho. Fauconbridge, the Receiver General at Westminster' (1644, p. 151, 8 May).

181. 1. 14. See Hor. *Carm.* ii. 10. 9–12, and Ovid, *Rem. Am.* 370.

181. 1. 15–16. Cf. (?) Seneca, *Octavia*, 896–9, and Seneca, *Hippol.* 1133–4.

181. 4. 2. Seneca, *Ep.* iv. 8: 'quisquis vitam suam contempsit, tuae dominus est'. Transl. Lodge: 'whosoeuer contemneth his life is Lord of thine'. See 240. 3. 2.

182. 2. 1. Seneca, *Hippol.* 430: 'malus est minister regii imperii pudor'.

182. 2. 2. See 330. 1. 1, 331. 3, and notes. Cf. Seneca, *Oedipus*, 703–4:

Odia qui nimium timet
regnare nescit; regna custodit metus.

Also Jonson, *Sejanus*, ii. 178–81 (from Lucan, viii. 484–95; transl. separately by Jonson; see 'Ungathered Verse', l, *Works*, viii, p. 422).

182. 3. 7–8. Cf. Martial, xi. 6. 12–13.

182. 4. 1. Cf. Beaumont and Fletcher, *The Maid's Tragedy*, II. i. 87–92:

> I could never have the power
> To love one above an hour.

183, ll. 17–18. Cf. 233. 1. 17–18.

184, l. 25. Cf. Ovid, *Met.* xv. 583: 'rumpe moras'.

184. 1. 1–4. Cf. Burton, 3. 2. 3. 1 (p. 508): 'As a tulipant to the Sunne (which our Herbalists call *Narcissus*) when it shines, is . . . a glorious flowre exposing it selfe, but when the sunne sets, or a tempest comes, it hides it selfe, pines away, and hath no pleasure left. . . .'

185. 2. 5–8. Cf. Jonson, *Forest*, ix. 3–4:

> Or leaue a kisse but in the cup,
> And Ile not looke for wine.

185. 3. *heading. Sir Richard Stone.* A first cousin of Herrick, whose grandfather on his mother's side was William Stone, of London and Segenhoe. Each of William Stone's sons, Richard and John (who both went to Cambridge), had a son Richard, as shown in the following table:

William Stone

Richard, matric. from Caius Coll., 1575.	John, matric. from King's Coll., 1584.
Richard, matric. from St. John's, 1614; adm. Inner Temple 1614 (of Segenhoe, Ridgmont, Beds.). Apparently not knighted.	*Richard*, adm. Inner Temple 1612–13 (of Stukeley, Hunts.). Knighted 1641.

See *Alumni Cant.*; *Inner Temple Register*; *Visitation of London*, 1633–5 (Harl. Soc., p. 265); *Visitation of Bedford*, 1566, 1582, and 1634 (Harl. Soc., p. 143); and Shaw, *Knights of England*, ii, p. 212.

185. 3. 1. *white Temple.* Ovid, *Fasti*, i. 70: 'candida templa'.

185. 4. Cf. 269. 4. Martial, vi. 15; iv. 32; iv. 59.

186, ll. 9–10. See Virgil, *Culex*, 397–410.

186. 3. *heading.* Dorothy Parsons was daughter of John Parsons, organist of Westminster Abbey, who died in 1623. See *D.N.B.*

187. 1. 4. Martial, i. 18. 5: 'scelus est iugulare Falernum'.

187. 2. 2. *liv'd, or lasted.* See 328. i. 10 and note.

187. 4. 2. Plutarch, *Solon*, 2 (North, in *Tudor Trans.* i, p. 208): 'being nowe olde, he commonly used to saye this verse: I growe olde, learning still'. See also Erasmus, *Adagia*, s.v. 'Diligentia'.

187. 5, *heading.* Sir Edward Sackville, fourth Earl of Dorset (1591–1652), was son of Robert, second Earl (1561–1609). Succeeded his brother Richard, third Earl (1590–1624). See *D.N.B.*

187. 5. 1–4. Cf. Burton, 'Democritus to the Reader', p. 3: 'though I live still a Collegiat student, as *Democritus* in his garden, and lead a monastique life, *ipse mihi theatrum* [Seneca quoting Epicurus in *Ep.* vii.

11], . . . I hear what is done abroad, how others run, ride, turmoile, and macerate themselves in court and countrey. . . .'

188, 1. 1. Isa. xxxviii. 12: 'Mine age is departed, and is removed from me as a shepherd's tent.'

188. 2. *heading*. See *O.D.E. Prov.*, 'Hope (well) and haue (well).'

188. 2. See 72. 2. 5–7, 293. 1, and notes. Cf. Hor. *Carm.* ii. 10. 17–18, &c.

188. 2. 2. *contracted brow*. Hor. *Sat.* ii. 2. 125: 'contractae . . . frontis'.

188. 2. 4–5. *Repurgation &c.* Ovid, *Met.* v. 286:

Fusca repurgato fugiebant nubila caelo.

188. 2. 5–6. Ovid, *Trist.* ii. 142:

Nube solet pulsa candidus ire dies.

Tibullus, iii. 6. 32:

Venit post multas una serena dies.

188. 4. *heading*. See note on 46. 2, heading. Perhaps a daughter or sister-in-law of Elizabeth Wheeler.

189. 1. 6. Ovid, *Her.* xvi (Paris to Helen). 288:

Lis est cum forma magna pudicitiae.

Quoted by Burton, 3. 3. 1. 2 (p. 601).

189. 2. Seneca, *Ep.* lxxv. 3: 'aliter homines amicam, aliter liberos osculantur'.

189. 3. *heading*. See *O.D.E. Prov.*, 'Cross and (or) pile.'

189. 4. *heading*. See 112. 3, 304. 3, and notes.

189. 4. 8. *spring*. Cf. 361. 1. 8.

190, l. 15. Cf. Seneca, *Ep.* lxxviii. 11: 'desideria ipsa moriuntur'.

190, ll. 19–22. Job. iii. 17–19.

190, l. 29. The allusion is to the Court of Requests, instituted for the hearing of 'poor men's suits'.

190, l. 43. *Testaments ingrost*. Wills written out in form.

190, l. 47. *Platonick yeere*. The period of *c.* 30,000 years (see 265. 1. 5–6) during which the heavenly bodies were supposed to go through all their possible movements and return to their original positions. See *O.E.D.* s.v. 'Platonic'; also 443. 2. 7–8 and note.

191. 1. *heading and* l. 4. *Mary Willand*. ? Sister or daughter of Leonard Willan. See 298. 6 and note.

191. 1. 2. *expansive firmament*. See 67, l. 8, 82. 2. 4–5 and notes.

191. 2. 2. Ovid, *Rem. Am.* 462:

Successore novo vincitur omnis amor.

191. 4. Cf. Anacreontea, 40.

191. 4. 4, 5, and 8. Cf. Anacreontea, 8. 7–10.

191. 5. 1–2. See 351. 3. 4 and note; and cf. Montaigne, iii. 9: '*Nunquam simpliciter fortuna indulget*'; *Tudor Trans.*, p. 238: 'Fortune never favours fully without exception.' Burton, 2. 3. 1. 1 (p. 305) quotes '*Fortuna nunquam perpetuò est bona*' and also translates Dionys. Halic. (viii. 27): '*It never yet happened to any man . . . nor ever will, to have all things according to his desire, or to whom fortune was never opposite & adverse.*'

192. 1. See an article by R. S. Forsythe on '"The passionate shepherd" and English poetry', *P.M.L.A.*, xl, pp. 692–742, 1925.

192. 1. 13. *Paste of Filberts.* Cf. 269. 5. 5.

193. 1. *heading. Susanna Herrick.* Probably Suzan, daughter of Herrick's brother Nicholas and of his wife Susanna (see 304. 2). (*Visitation of London*, 1633–5, Harl. Soc. i, p. 377.) There was, however, another Susanna Herrick, daughter of John Herrick, the poet's uncle; she married John Nurse at Leicester in 1630. (*Leic. Marriage Bonds*, p. 303.)

193. 2. *heading. Susanna Southwell.* Perhaps a sister of Sir Thomas Southwell (see 53. 2 and note), none of whose four daughters bore this name. See Blomefield and Parkin, *Hist. Norfolk*, p. 275.

194. 1. Cf. Suckling, 'A Ballad upon a Wedding', st. 8.

194. 2. *heading. Sir John Mynts.* See *D.N.B.*, art. 'Mennes' (1599–1671). Knighted, 1642. Appointed commander of the king's navy, 1645. Friend of James Smith. See note on 136, ll. 131–2.

194. 3. 1–4. Anacreontea, 51.

194. 3. 5–8. Cf. Lyly, *Euphues*, Epist. Ded.: 'We commonly see that a blacke ground doth best beseeme a white counterfaite, and Venus according to the iudgement of Mars, was then most amiable when she sate close by Vulcan.'

194. 4. Cf. Burton, 2. 3. 7 (p. 351): 'and as *Ammianus* [Lib. xviii. 1. 4] well hath it, *Quis erit innocens si clam vel palam accusasse sufficiat?* if it be sufficient to accuse a man openly or in privat who shall be free?' This quotation appears for the first time in the fourth edition of the *Anatomy* (1632).

194. 5. 1–2. Cf. Hor. *Carm.* iii. 30. 14–16.

195. 4. As shown by the Dean Prior Parish Register there was a local family with the name of Dundrige.

195. 5. 12. *yet.* So far.

196. 2. *Preposterous &c.* Erasmus, *Adagia*, s.v. 'Absurda &c.': '*Praepostere.* Quum sentiemus rem praepostere geri, veluti quum populus imperat principibus &c.' Cf. (?) Seneca, *Octavia*, 579: 'Male imperatur, cum regit vulgus duces.'

196. 3. Cf. *A Winter's Tale*, IV. iii. 122–5.

196. 5. *heading.* See Ovid, *Fasti*, vi. 226: 'coniunx sancta Dialis'.

196. 5. 3. *Inarculum.* Herrick's note is translated from Paulus ex Festus in *Glossaria Latina*; ed. Lindsay, iv, p. 237): 'virgula erat ex malo Punico incurvata, quam regina sacrificans in capite gestabat'.

197, l. 11. Num. xvi. 46 (and 45 for 'consume').

197, l. 13. See ibid. 46: 'Take a censer &c.'

197. 1. Cf. 191. 4 and Anacreontea, 7, 8, and 40.

197. 2. See Plutarch, *Symposiacs*, vii. Translated Holland (1603), p. 742: '. . . a pleasant conceited man . . . who when he had supped alone at any time, was wont thus to say: Eaten I have this day, but not supped; shewing thereby, that meales would never be without mirth and good companie, to season the same, and to give a pleasant taste unto the viands.'

197. 3. 1. Cf. Sallust, *Catiline*, viii. 1: 'profecto fortuna in omni re dominatur'. Quoted by Montaigne, ii. 16 (*Tudor Trans.*, p. 352).

198. 1. 3. *eternal fires.* Martial, x. 47. 4: 'focus perennis'; cf. Jonson, *Leges Conviviales*, after no. 24: 'Focus Perennis Esto' (*Works*, viii, p. 656).

198. 1. 13. *Horace to be read.* Cf. Jonson, *Epig.* ci. 21–22; also Cornelius Nepos, *Atticus*, 14. 1: 'neque umquam sine aliqua lectione apud eum cenatum est . . .'

199. 1. *heading. Mr. Stephen Soame.* Probably either (*a*) the son and heir of Sir William Soame (131. 1), who went to St. John's Coll., Camb., in 1633 (*Alumni Cant.*); or (*b*) the second son of Sir William's brother, Sir Thomas (176. 1) (*Visitations of London*, 1633–5, Harl. Soc. No. 17, p. 251). These two Stephens would be kinsmen of Herrick (second cousins) because they were grandsons of Sir Stephen Soame who married Ann Stone, sister of Julian, Herrick's mother.

199. 1. 3. *Lip.* Gen. xi. 1 (Wyclif: 'the erthe was of oo lip'). *Leven.* Batch, quality.

199. 2. 3. See 218. 4, 335 (final line), and notes.

199. 3. See 89. 1. 16 and note.

200. 2. 1–3. Cf. Martial, x. 96. 5–6.

200. 2. 6. *content makes sweet.* Ecclus. xl. 18.

200. 4. 1–2. Cf. Hor. *Carm.* iii. 30. 6–7; see also 81, ll. 46–48 above, and note.

201. 3. *heading. John Weare.* See 'Counsellor John Were of Silverton, and the Siege of Exeter, 1645–6', by J. Heald Ward (*Devonshire Association*, xlii, 1910, pp. 383–90). Probably identical with the person of that name who matriculated from Oriel College, Oxford, in 1611 (*Alumni Oxon.*). Died 1676.

201. 3. 10. Cf. Cicero, *De Legibus*, I. vi. 19: 'eamque rem illi Graeco putant nomine [*Νόμος*] a suum cuique tribuendo appellatam.' Also *Titus Andronicus*, I. 1. 280: 'Suum cuique is our Roman justice.' See note to 394. 4.

202, l. 25. *Forked-Fee.* Cf. Jonson, *Epig.* xxxvii. 2: 'on both sides he takes fees'.

202, l. 27. See *O.D.E. Prov.*, 'Shave an egg . . .'

202. 3. *heading.* Contrast 154. 3, 'Clothes do but cheat and cousen us.'

202. 3. 14. *wild civility.* See 28. 1. 12 and note.

202. 3. 18. Cf. Burton, 3. 2. 3. 3 (p. 465): 'It is a question much controverted . . . Whether naturall or artificiall objects be more powerfull? . . . for my part I am of opinion, that though beauty it selfe be a great motive . . . artificiall is of more force, and much to be preferred . . . *Iohn Lerius* the *Burgundian cap.* 8. *hist. navigat. in Brasil* is altogether on my side . . . *I dare boldly affirme* (saith he) *that those glittering attires, counterfeit colors, headgears, curled haires, plaited coates . . . costly stomachers, guarded and loose garments, & all those other coutrements . . . cause more* *inconvenience in this kinde* [sc. are more tempting], *then that Barbarian homelinesse* . . . His country-man *Mountagne* in his *Essayes* [iii. 5], is of the same opinion . . . that Beauty is more beholding to Art then Nature.'

203. 2. *heading. Bridget Herrick.* Probably the poet's niece, daughter of his brother Nicholas, and sister of Suzan. See note to 193. 1.

203. 3. Cf. Dyer's sonnet '*Prometheus* when first from heaven hie', especially the concluding couplet:

The difference is, the Satires lippes, my hart,
He for a while I evermore have smart.

(In Sidney's *Certaine Sonets*, publ. with *Arcadia*, ed. of 1598.) The story of the satyr, without the application, occurs in Plutarch, *De capienda ex inimicis utilitate*, 2 (B. E. Perry, *Aesopica*, 1952, No. 467, p. 506); for other references in Elizabethan literature see the note on Dyer's poem by H. E. Rollins in his edition of *England's Helicon*, ii, p. 192. Lyly's *Campaspe*, 1584 (*Works*, ed. Bond, ii, p. 341) provides one example.

204. 4. 15–16. See *O.D.E. Prov.*, 'Every block will not make a Mercury.'

205. 5. Delattre (p. 425) compares the concluding lines of Secundus, *Basia*, 2.

205. 5. 1–20. Cf. Tibullus, i. 3. 57–66.

205. 5. 1. Cf. Ps. lxviii. 13: 'a dove that is covered with silver wings'.

206, ll. 25–26. Cf. Marlowe, *Hero and Leander*, i. 52: 'Whose tragedy divine Musaeus sung.'

206, l. 41. *Ivorie wrists.* Cf. Chapman, *Odyssey*, vi. 141: 'Nausicaa, with the wrists of ivory.'

206, l. 45. *Snakie.* Probably meaning venomous.

206, l. 50. Cf. Beaumont and Fletcher, *The Maid's Tragedy*, II. i. 108:

With flattering ivy clasp my coffin round.

206, l. 53. *Evadne.* In *The Maid's Tragedy.*

207, l. 57. *now is.* The reading of 1640 'shall be' suggests that the poem as then published was written before Jonson's death in 1637.

207, l. 61. The original reading 'he one chiefe' has been generally accepted and conveys a meaning; but it is awkward both in itself and in its context. 'one' and 'our' are confused elsewhere in the text of 1648 (60. 2. 5; possibly also 197, l. 7 and 315. 3. 2); the reading adopted, which also allows for possible confusion of 'h' and 'b', 'be our chiefe', links up grammatically with l. 59. Jonson uses the expression 'our chief' in *Epig.* lvi, 'On Poet-Ape' (*Works*, viii, p. 44): 'Poor POET-APE, that would be thought our chiefe.' Mrs. C. Rickert tells me that there is an instance of 'our' misprinted as 'one' in J. Kimedoncius, *Of the Redemption of Mankind* (1598), and corrected in the errata-list.

207. 2. Martial, i. 98. Cf. Jonson, *The Magnetic Lady*, III. iv. 38–41:

You cannot but with trouble put your hand
Into your pocket, to discharge a reckoning.
And this we sonnes of Physick doe call *chiragra*,
A kind of Crampe, or *Hand-Gout*.

207. 3. 2. Cf. Beaumont and Fletcher, *Philaster*, v. iii. 145–6: 'and their silks only to be worn before sore eyes'.

207. 4. See 11. 1 and notes. Cf. Burton, 3. 2. 3 (p. 517): 'count all her vices, vertues, her imperfections, infirmities, absolute and perfect . . . if dwarfish and little pretty, if tall, proper and manly, our brave Brittish *Bunduica* . . .'; p. 519: 'every action, site, habit, gesture, he admires, whether shee play, sing, or dance, in what tyres soever she goeth, how excellent it was, how well it became her, never the like seen or heard.' Herrick (and Burton) may have been remembering Ovid, *Amores*, ii. 4, apart from the quotation in l. 8.

207. 4. 8. Ovid, loc. cit., l. 44: 'Omnibus historiis se meus aptat amor.'

208. 1. Burns knew this poem, though he did not know that Herrick was the author. See *Letters of Burns*, ed. Ferguson, ii. 209; also Critical Notes, p. 489 above. It seems likely that Burns took the poem from *L53* or *P59*, or some later issue of either; not, as R. G. Howarth suggests in *N. and Q.* clxxv, p. 153, 1938, from Carew's *Poems*. Herrick himself refers to the poem in 'His age . . .', p. 135, l. 99.

208. 1. 6. Propertius, i. 12. 16: 'non nihil aspersis gaudet Amor lacrimis'.

208. 3. 3. *Cecubum*. Cf. Hor. *Carm.* iii. 28. 2–3, &c.

208. 4. 2–3. Seneca, *Thyestes*, 613–14; quoted by Marlowe, *Edward II*, IV. vi. 53–54; transl. by Jonson, *Sejanus*, v. 902–3:

For, whom the morning saw so great, and high,
Thus low, and little, 'fore the 'euen doth lie.

209. 3. 1–2. Ovid, *Ars Am.* i. 249–50:

Nocte latent mendae, vitioque ignoscitur omni,
    Horaque formosam quam libet illa facit.

209. 3. 1. *thefts*. Amorous intrigues. Cf. Catullus, lxviii. 140: 'furta Iovis'.

209. 3. 2–6. Proverbial. See *O.D.E. Prov.*, 'Joan is as good &c.'

209. 3. 8. Jer. vi. 30: 'Reprobate silver.'

210. 1. *heading*. *free*. Forward, familiar.

210. 3. *heading*. *Master John Wingfield*. Married Herrick's sister, Mercy, at Little Thurlow, Suffolk, in 1611. See note to 269. 5. Adm. Gray's Inn, 3 Feb. 1607–8, as 'of Brantham, Suffolk, gent.' Matriculated from Christ's Coll., Camb., Easter 1608; B.A. 1611–12; M.A. 1615. (*Alumni Cant.*) The poem was no doubt written before Wingfield was knighted. This was in 1619 (Shaw, *Knights of England*, ii, p. 171).

210. 5. Cf. Ovid, *Am.* i. 15. 33–34; Martial, viii. 3 and x. 2.

211. 2. 1–2. *Pushes*. Pimples or boils. *Tucker*. Fuller; cloth-finisher. *burle*. Remove lumps from.

211. 3. 2. *Box*. Martial, ii. 41. 7: 'dentes . . . buxei'.

211. 5. Cf. Seneca, *De Clementia*, i. 3. 3: 'pestifera vis est, valere ad nocendum'.

212. 3. *heading. Little and loud.* This instance alone in *O.D.E. Prov.* Not in Tilley, *Prov. Eng.*

212. 4. Ovid, *Ex Ponto*, ii. 7. 8:

tranquillas etiam naufragus horret aquas.

212. 5. 1–2. See *O.D.E. Prov.*, 'Great pain and little gain will make a man soon weary.' Also 253. 3 and note.

212. 6. 2. See 66. 1. 2 and note.

212. 6. 4. Cf. Jonson, *Epig.* i:

Pray thee, take care, that tak'st my booke in hand,
To read it well: that is, to vnderstand.

213. 1. Cf. Seneca, *De Providentia*, 6. 2; transl. Lodge: '*Democrates* cast away riches, supposing them to be the burthen of a good minde.'

213. 2. 1. Cf. 33. 2. 4 and 213. 3.

213. 3. 2. Cf. Hor. *Ep.* i. 10. 41:

serviet aeternum, quia parvo nesciet uti.

214. 1. 5–6. See 85. 3.

214. 2. 12. *Tyrian Dewes.* Tibullus, iii. 4. 28:

stillabat Tyrio (*or* Syrio) myrtea rore coma.

214. 2. 14. Hor. *Carm.* i. 1. 36:

sublimi feriam sidera vertice.

Cf. Jonson, *Sejanus*, v. 8–9: 'I feele my aduanced head Knocke out a starre in heau'n.'

214. 4. *heading.* See 255. 2 and note.

214. 4. Cf. Claudian, *De Quarto Consulatu Honorii*, 296–302:

in commune iubes si quid censesque tenendum,
primus iussa subi. . . .
componitur orbis
regis ad exemplum . . . .
mobile mutatur semper cum principe vulgus.

215. 1. 1–3. Hor. *Carm.* iii. 3. 1, 3–4: 'Justum et tenacem . . .'.

215. 2. 15–16. See 58. 3. 1–2; 59, l. 12; and notes.

215. 2. 17–18. The references are to Antiope, Leda, Europa, and Alcmena.

216. 2. *heading. Elizabeth Lee.* Daughter of Sir Francis Leigh, of Addington, Surrey; married (? *c.* 1630) Sir Humphrey Tracy, third Bt. See Manning and Bray, *Hist of Surrey*, ii, p. 560; iii, p. 248; also *Complete Baronetage*, *Cal. Committee for Compounding*, pp. 952–3, and *Lords' Journals*, viii, p. 79. I am indebted to Mr. R. S. Lea for this information. Research at P.R.O. has not revealed the date of the marriage. Another Elizabeth Lee (of Stoneleigh, Warwickshire) married the grandson of the first Lord Tracy, but apparently too late to be identifiable with the person addressed by Herrick.

216. 2. 5, 15. Cf. Ovid, *Ars Am.* ii. 727–8:

Ad metam properate simul. tum plena voluptas
Cum pariter victi femina virque iacent.

217. 1. Metre as in Jonson, *Gypsies Metamorphos'd*, ll. 262–6 sqq. (*Works*, vii, p. 573): 'The faery beame vppon you &c.'

217. 1. 20. Cf. Fletcher, *The Loyal Subject*, IV. i. 43: 'And pour'd his soul into thee, won thee.'

218. 2. 2. Cf. Donne, *LXXX Sermons*, 1640, Serm. xli, p. 403 c: 'and the Son receives none, but by love, and this cement and glue, of a zealous and a reverentiall love, a holy kisse . . .'.

218. 3. Martial, i. 1. 3–6; i. 25. 8; v. 10. 11–12. See also 314. 2.

218. 4. 2. Cf. Ovid, *Trist.* ii. 353:

Crede mihi, distant mores a carmine nostro.

and Martial, i. 4. 8:

Lasciva est nobis pagina, vita proba est.

Burton quoting and translating this, 3. 1. 1. 1 (p. 406), alliterates as Herrick does: 'Howsoever my lines erre, my life is honest.' See also 335 (final couplet) and note.

218. 5. Cf. Ovid, *Am.* i. 15. 39–40:

pascitur in vivis Livor; post fata quiescit,
cum suus ex merito quemque tuetur honos.

Marlowe, *Ovid's Elegies*, translates l. 39: 'The living, not the dead, can envy bite.' Jonson also translates in *Poetaster*, I. i. 81–2.

218. 6. 11. *Westmorland.* See note to 40. 1.

218. 6. 12. *Newark.* Either Robert Pierrepoint (1584–1643), created Viscount Newark in 1627 and Earl of Kingston-upon-Hull in 1628, or his eldest son Henry (1606–80), second Earl of Kingston and first Marquis of Dorchester (see 301. 1). Robert tried to remain neutral at the outset of the Civil War, joined the King in 1643, and was killed that year. Henry sat in the Parliament of 1628–9 as Viscount Newark. He was created Marquis of Dorchester in 1645. See *D.N.B.* for both these persons.

219. 1. See 9. 1 and note.

219. 1. 3. *Cut off thy haires.* A custom at Greek funerals, referred to in *Odyssey*, iv. 264–5 (Chapman):

It is the only rite that wretched men
Can do dead friends, to cut hair, and complain.

See 271. 1. 3 and 360, l. 38. Cf. Jer. vii. 29: 'Cut off thine hair, O *Jerusalem*'; also Job i. 20.

219. 2. 11–12. See 17. 1. 5–6 and note.

220. 1. 1–2. Cf. Joseph Hall, *Meditations*, iii. 78: 'We think ten in the hundred extreme and biting usury.'

220. 3. 18–19. See *O.D.E. Prov.*, 'Leave (off) with an appetite.'

220. 3. 25. *Vertue, &c.* Cf. Hor. *Ep.* i. 18. 9: 'virtus est medium &c.' and see Tilley, *Prov. Eng.*, V80, 'Virtue is found in the middle.'

221, ll. 46–47. Cf. Erasmus, *Adagia*, s.v. 'Frugalitas': 'Parsimonia summum vectigal.'

221, ll. 48–49. See *O.D.E. Prov.*, 'Haste makes waste.'

221, l. 50. See ibid., 'Every extremity is a fault.'

221, l. 51. See ibid., 'Soft fire makes sweet malt.'

221, l. 52. Cf. Tilley, *Prov., Eng.*, M1295, 'Who too much grips, &c.'

221, l. 58 *Aprill*. See 23. 2. 1–2 and note.

222, l. 61. Ovid, *Ars Am.* ii. 152:

Dulcibus est verbis mollis alendus amor.

223. 3. 11. *Huckson*. The underside of the thigh. (*O.E.D.* s.v. 'Hockshin'.)

224. 1. 4. Seneca, *Hercules Furens*, 182: 'nec sua retro fila revolvunt'.

224. 3. 1–2. Cf. Burton, 3. 2. 3. 3 (p. 470): 'But why is all this labour, all this cost . . .? *Because forsooth they would be faire and fine, and where nature is defective, supply it by art.*

Sanguine quae vero non rubet, arte rubet (Ovid) [*Ars Am.* iii. 200] and to that purpose they annoint and paint *their faces*, to make *Helen* of *Hecuba* . . .' See also 118. 2. 8 and note.

224. 4. 1–2. Cf. Hor. *Carm.* iv. 7. 1.

224. 4. 5. Cf. Virgil, *Georg.* ii. 335:

Sed trudit gemmas, et frondes explicat omnes.

and Ovid, *Fasti*, i. 152:

Et nova de gravido palmite gemma tumet.

224. 4. 8. *Tyrrean*. At the hands of Tereus.

225, l. 14. *Oake, or Holme*. Cf. Hor. *Carm.* iii. 23. 10: 'quercus inter et ilices'.

225. 1. Metre as in Jonson, *Masque of Queenes*, ll. 75–78 sqq.: 'The Owle is abroad &c.' Cf. 239. 1; 247. 2; 256. 1; 317. 2.

225. 1. 18. *noone of Night*. Midnight (*meridies nocti*). See 333. 6. 11–12. The expression was perhaps first used in English by Jonson; see *Sejanus*, v. 325 and Jonson's note. It occurs also in *Gypsies Metamorphos'd*, l. 265.

226. 1. *heading*. Cf. Claudian, *Epig.*, ii, 'De sene Veronensi qui Suburbium numquam egressus est.'

226. 2. St. Bernard, *Sermones in Cantica*, Serm. xxx. 3 (*Opera*, Migne, ii, col. 935): 'Lacrymae poenitentium vinum eorum [sc. angelorum]'. Cf. Crashaw, 'The Weeper', st. 6 (*Works*, ed. Martin, p. 80).

226. 3. Cf. Donne, *LXXX Sermons*, 1640, Serm. xvii, p. 170 D: 'The Physitian comes in like an enemy, with a knife to launce, with fire to cauterize, but *opponit se morbo*, he is but an enemy to the disease, he means the patient no harm.' See also Seneca, *De Clem.* i. 17. 2.

226. 4. 3. Cf. Calpurnius, *Ecl.* ii. 64–65: 'Laribus consuevimus horti Mittere primitias.'

226. 5. 2. *sperrables*. The headless nails used by cobblers.

227. 1. Delattre (p. 427) compares this with Jean de Bonnefon, *Pancharis*, xviii:

Donec pressius incubo labellis
Et diduco avidus tuae, Puella,
Flosculos animae suaveolentes,
Unus tum videor mihi Deorum
Seu quid altius est beatiusve.

Mox ut te eripis, ecce ego repente
Unus qui Superum mihi videbar,
Seu quid altius est beatiusve,
Orci mihi videor relatus umbris
Seu quid inferiusve tristiusve.

227. 2. 8. *O.E.D.* s.v. 'Compartment' gives 'compartiment' as a variant form and suggests that '*Compartlement*' in this line is a misprint. *O.E.D.* also quotes Bailey s.v., 'Fine bindings of books are said to be in compartiment.' See also the quotation ibid. from Littré.

228. 1. *heading*. See *O.D.E. Prov.*, 'Long looked for . . .'.

228. 2. 2. Cf. Martial, i. 15. 12 and v. 58. 7–8.

228. 3. Cf. Seneca, *Herc. Fur.* 865–6:

nemo ad id sero venit, unde numquam
cum semel venit, potuit reverti.

229. 3. 2. *slippery*. Cf. Cicero, *Philipp.* v. xviii. 50: 'cupiditatem dominandi . . . lubricam'.

229. 4. *heading*. Endymion Porter (see note to 41. 2, heading) received in 1625 a pension of £500 a year as Groom of the Bedchamber, an office which he had held previously and now continued to hold. He is referred to in Walter Yonge's *Diary* (Camden Soc., 1848, p. 66), Jan. 1622/3, as 'Porter, of the Prince's bedchamber'.

229. 4. 2. Seneca, *De Brev. Vit.* ii. 4: '. . . suus nemo est'.

230, ll. 17–18. See *O.D.E. Prov.*, 'Content is more than a kingdom.'

230, ll. 23–24. Cf. 259. 1. 8 and see *O.D.E. Prov.*, 'Master's footsteps fatten the soil'; also George Herbert, *Outlandish Proverbs*, No. 486. (*Works*, ed. Hutchinson, p. 338.)

230, l. 28. Cf. quotation of 1601 in *O.E.D.*, art. 'Plough', *sb.*[1]: 'whosoever doth not maintain the Plough, destroys this Kingdom'.

230, ll. 46–61. See 126. 3. 13–20 and notes. Cf. Burton, 3. 2. 3 (p. 536): 'Instead of those acurate Emblems, curious Impreses, gaudy masques, Tilts, Turnaments, &c. They have their Wakes, Witson-ales, Shepheards feasts, meeting on holy daies, country dances, roundelaies . . . Choosing Lords, Ladies, Kings, Queenes, and Valentines.'

230, ll. 48–49 and 53: Cf. Burton, 3. 2. 3 (p. 532): 'Young lasses are never better pleased, then when as upon an Holiday after Evensong, they may meet their sweet-hearts, and dance about a May-pole, or in a towne greene under a shady Elme.'

231, ll. 70–71. Virgil, *Georg.* ii. 458.

231, l. 75. Martial, x. 47. 11.

231. 2. *heading*. *Arthur Bartly*. Perhaps the Mr. Arth: Berkley mentioned in Evelyn, *Diary and Correspondence*, ed. Wheatley, iv, pp. 123 and 126, as officially receiving letters addressed to the King, 2 Nov. and 4 Nov. 1641.

231. 2. 5. Cf. Seneca, *Ep.* xxi. 5: 'possum mecum duratura nomina educere.'

231. 2. 6. Ps. xiv. 5 (A.V.) or 9 (B.C.P.): 'in the generation of the righteous' (Vulg. 'in generatione justâ').

232. 1. Cf. the song in Jonson's *Poetaster*, II. ii. 162–88: 'If I freely may discouer, &c.'

232. 1. 6–8. See 28. 1 and notes. 'Sweet neglect' is in Jonson, *Epicoene*, I. i. 100, and *Cynthias Reuells*, III. iii. 38.

232. 1. 9–10. See 138. 1. 3; 254. 2 and note.

232. 1. 11–12. See 52. 3. 4 and note.

232. 1. 15–16. Martial, xi. 104. 21–22:

Lucretia toto
Sis licet usque die: Laida nocte volo.

Cited in a marginal note by Burton, 2. 2. 6. 4 (p. 300).

232. 1. 17–18. Martial, i. 57. 4:

Nec volo quod cruciat, nec volo quod satiat.

232. 3. Cf. Massinger, *The Old Law*, iv. 1 (ed. Gifford, 1813, iv, p. 533): 'the same rosemary that serves for the funeral, will serve for the wedding'.

232. 4. 3. See *D.N.B.* art. 'John Tradescant', 1608–62.

232. 4. 6. Deaf, as applied to nuts, meant empty, hollow. Cf. p. 486, note to 165. 1. 46–54 (l. 6 of quotation).

233. 1. *heading*. *John Wicks*. See note to 132. 3. heading.

233. 1. 11–12. Martial, x. 47. 5, 9–10.

233. 1. 13. Hor. *Carm.* ii. 14. 21–22: 'placens uxor'.

233. 1. 15 sqq. Martial, viii. 77. 3–8; ii. 59.

233. 1. 17–18. Cf. 183, ll. 17–18.

233. 1. 22–29. Ovid, *Ars Am.* iii. 61–66. Cf. 2 Esdras iv. 5. See also 69, ll. 57–70, 228. 2 and 3, and notes.

233. 1. 31, 33. See 328. 1. 3–6 and 9–10.

233. 1. 36–39. See 133, ll. 25–32 and notes.

234. 2. 2. Cf. (?) Seneca, *Octavia*, 457: 'Decet timeri Caesarem.' 'At plus diligi.' and Jonson, *Discoveries* (*Works*, viii, p. 600, l. 1191): 'the mercifull *Prince* is safe in love, not in feare'.

234. 3. *heading*. Denham's *Cooper's Hill* was published in 1642.

234. 3. 3. *Pean.* Probably, though not certainly, referring to Apollo (Paean).

234. 3. 11. *unloose.* Cf. Luke iii. 16.

235, l. 10. *North-down Ale.* See Nares, s.v. 'Cock-ale'. The meaning of 'North-down' is not clear. *O.E.D.* gives 'Some kind of liquor'.

235. 1. 2. *say no, to take it.* See 249. 4 and note. Cf. Ovid, *Ars Am.* i. 274. The English saying was proverbial, as in Shakespeare, *Richard III*, III. vii. 50, but always ending '*and* take it', not '*to* take it', as here. See *O.D.E. Prov.*, 'Maids say "Nay" and take.'

235. 2. 1. Ovid, *Rem. Am.* 746:

Divitiis alitur luxuriosus amor—

and *Ars Am.* ii. 278: 'auro conciliatur amor'. See also 258. 1. 3. Cf. *O.D.E. Prov.*, 'Love lasts as long as money endures.'

235. 3. 1–2. See 318. 1 and note.

235. 4. 2. Ovid, *Am.* i. 9. 46:

Qui nolet fieri desidiosus, amet.

236. 1. Tacitus, *Agric.* 45: 'Nero . . . subtraxit oculos suos iussitque scelera, non spectavit.'

236. 3. 5. *toucht.* Tested with a touchstone.

236. 4. 2. Tacitus, *Ann.* i. 47: 'maior e longinquo reverentia'. See 237, l. 10.

237, ll. 7–12. *if such glory, &c.* Cf. Burton, 3. 4. 1. 1 (p. 635): '*Moses* himselfe, *Exod.* 33. 18. When he desired to see God in his glory, was answered that hee might not endure it, no man could see his face and live . . . a strong object overcometh the sight . . . if thou canst not endure the Sunne beames, how canst thou endure that fulgor and brightnesse of him that made the Sun: The Sun it self and all that we can imagine are but shadowes of it.'

237. 1. 1, 6, 7. Acts ix. 37.

237. 2. 1–8. Gen. ix. 11–17.

237. 3. Cf. Joseph Hall, *Meditations*, iii. 81: 'Satan is ever more violent at the last . . . The first and second blow begin the battle; but the last only wins it'; and Montaigne, i. 41 (*Tudor Trans.*, p. 297).

238. 1. 2. Martial, xii. 10. 2: 'Fortuna multis dat nimis, satis nulli.' (In Lily's Grammars.)

238. 2. 3. *Tansie.* A pudding or omelet flavoured with tansy.

238. 3. See 228. 3, 233. 1. 22–39, and notes.

238. 3. 4. Ps. civ. 33.

238. 4. Cf. Martial, vii. 25, 1–4, and Jonson, *Barth. Fair,* I. i. 34–36.

238. 5. 1. *Post and Paire.* This game is referred to by Jonson in *The Alchemist*, I. i. 55. See *O.E.D.* s.v. 'Post' *sb.*[4] *b.* *Slam.* Also called ruff and honours. See *O.E.D.* s.v. 'Slam' *sb.*[2] 1.

239. 2. Cf. Martial, x. 13: 'Cum cathedralicios &c.'

239. 2. 5–7. *Mules . . . shod with silver.* Suetonius, *Nero*, 303: 'soleis mularum argenteis'.

239. 2. 8. *axeltree.* Probably, as Palgrave suggested (*Chrysomela*, p. 193), a funeral car; not in *O.E.D.*

239. 2. 10. *Persian Loomes.* Cf. Jonson, *Und.* lxxvii. 4.

239. 2. 11–12. Hor. *Ep.* i. 2. 47–48.

239. 3. Cf. Cicero, *De Amic.* xv. 54.

239. 4. 1. See *O.D.E. Prov.*, 'Poverty is no sin' (or 'disgrace').

239. 5. See 25. 1. 3–4 and note; cf. Seneca, *Ad Polyb. de Cons.* xii. 2: 'est autem hoc ipsum solacii loco, inter multos dolorem suum dividere'. Also Shakespeare, *Rape of Lucrece*, 790, and *King Lear*, III. vi. 116.

240. 3. 1. 1 Cor. i. 27.

240. 3. 2. Verbatim in 181. 4. 2. See note.

240. 6. 6–8. Pliny, *Hist. Nat.* ix. 58; cf. Jonson, *Volpone*, III. vii. 191–3:

> See, here, a rope of pearle; and each, more orient
> Then that the braue *Ægyptian* queene carrous'd:
> Dissolue, and drinke 'hem.

241. 1. Cf. Burton, 3. 2. 3 (p. 532): '*Constantine agricult. lib.* 11. *cap.* 18. makes *Cupid* himselfe to be a great dancer, by the same token as he was capering amongst the Gods, *he flung downe a boule of Nectar, which distilling upon the white Rose, ever since made it red.*'

241. 2. 2. *confirm'd.* Cf. *Coriolanus*, II. iii. 217.

241. 3. *Prepost'rous.* See 196. 2 and note.

241. 4. Phinn refers to *Life and Letters of Maria Edgeworth*, ed. Hare, 1894, ii, p. 280 (letter to Mrs. E., 16 Nov. 1840): 'You know the classic distich, which my father pointed out and translated for me, which was over the entrance door of the Cross Keys inn, near Beighterton:

> If you are told you will die to-morrow you smile:
> If you are told you will die a month hence you will sigh.'

Phinn also cites, without giving a reference, two Latin verses which Bishop Jebb (of Limerick) saw on an inn at Four Crosses, Staffordshire, in 1809:

> Fleres si scires unum tua tempora mensem.
> Rides, cum non sit forsitan una dies.

241. 5. Cicero, *De Invent.* II. lv. 166: 'Gloria est frequens de aliquo fama cum laude.'

241. 6. See 314. 3. 2 and note.

241. 7. *heading, &c.* Erasmus, *Adagia*, s.v. 'Impudicitia': 'Laxare fibulam. [Quotations from Martial and Juvenal.] Laxare itaque fibulam dicetur, quisquis perrupta pudoris lege, nullum libidini indomitae modum ponit.'

242. 1. 9. *O . . . Manners!* Cf. 29. 1. 9.

242. 1. 10. Cf. Rev. vii. 9.

242. 1. 11. *free-born Roman.* Acts xxii. 27–28.

242. 3. Cf. Burton, 2. 3. 3 (p. 315): '*οὐδὲν πενίας βαρύτερον ἐστὶ φορτίον*, no burden (saith *Menander*) so intolerable as povertie.' (Menander, *Monostichoi*, ed. Meineke, 450.)

243. 1. 14–15. Cf. Juvenal, vi. 48: 'auratam . . . caede iuvencam'; also Tibullus, iv. 1. 15.

244. 1. Cf. Tacitus, *Hist.* iv. 7: 'nullum maius boni imperii instrumentum quam bonos amicos esse'. Ibid. iv. 52: 'non legiones, non classis proinde firma imperii munimenta quam numerum liberorum'.

244. 2. Cf. Burton, 'Democritus to the Reader', p. 49: 'where there be many . . . lawes, many law-suits, many Lawyers, and many Physicians, it is a manifest signe of a distempered melancholy state, as Plato [*De legibus*] long since maintained.' Also Tacitus, *Ann*, iii. 27: 'corruptissima republica plurimae leges'; and Joseph Hall, *Satires*, ii. 3. 15: 'Wo to the weale where manie Lawiers bee.'

244. 3. Cf. Donne, Elegie viii, 1–6.

244. 3. 3. *Spike*. Lavender.

244. 4. See 79. 1. and note.

245. 1. Cf. Pliny, *Ep*. iv. 11. 15: 'Summam enim rerum nuntiat fama, non ordinem.' Herrick therefore means by 'Sum' (l. 2) the upshot, and by 'order' the processes or incidents leading to it.

245. 3. 4. *living water*. John iv. 10–11.

245. 3. 5. *strengthing bread*. Ps. civ. 15.

245. 3. 12. *pining sicknesses*. Isa. xxxviii. 12.

246. 2. 2, and 247, ll. 6–7. See Hor. *Carm*. ii. 10. 14, 17–18; ii. 9. 1–2.

247, ll. 9–10. See 343. 4. 3–4 and note.

247. 2. Cf. Ovid, *Ars Am*. i. 669–71. The title is that of a popular song, on which see Chappell, *Popular Music of the Olden Time*, i, p. 196.

247. 2. 3. Cf. Jonson, translating Petronius (*Poems*, 28 in Loeb ed.), *Und*. lxxxviii. 6–7 (*Works*, viii, p. 294):

But thus, thus, keeping endlesse Holy-day,
Let us together closely lie, and kisse.

247. 3. Martial, i. 19. 1–2.

247. 4. *heading and* 1–2. See 156. 4. 4 and note.

247. 4. 7. *Scene*. Curtain, veil. Cf. 76. 2. 8.

248. 1. Cf. 416. 1 and the lines in Fletcher's *The Mad Lover*, IV. i, beginning 'Charon O Charon'.

248. 2. 3. It is hard to find a meaning for 'gloves'; 'shores' would make better sense and in a seventeenth-century hand the two words might not always be easily distinguished.

249. 2. Cf. Hor. *Ep*. i. 7. 44: 'parvum parva decent'.

249. 4. 1–2. *they are shie*, &c. See 235. 1. 2 and note. The meaning here seems to be that they are shy about admitting their real desire to grant what they deny. Cf. Joseph Hall, *Satires*, iii. 3. 5–6:

For had I mayden'd it, as many vse,
Loath for to grant, but loather to refuse . . .

and *Two Gent. of Verona*, I. ii. 53–54.

250. 1. Cf. 22. 1, 22. 3, 22. 4.

250. 4. Eubulus in Athenaeus, xiii. 559. (Meineke, *Fragm. Comic. Graec.*, 1840, iii, pp. 260–1.) See also 283. 4 and note.

251, ll. 5–8. Possibly, as Delattre (p. 441) suggests, Herrick was here influenced by some memory of Jonson's *The Vision of Delight*, ll. 143 and 176–7. (*Works*, viii, pp. 468–9.)

251. 1. *Zenobias teeth*. Trebellius Pollio, whose description of Zenobia is referred to in Jonson, *Masque of Queenes*, ll. 616–30, says of her that there was 'tantus candor in dentibus, ut margaritas eam plerique putarent habere, non dentes'. (*Triginta Tyranni*.) *Scriptores Historiae Augustae* (Loeb, iii. 15, p. 138).

251. 2. Cf. Shakespeare, *Venus and Adonis*, 49–50.

251. 4. 1–2. *one*, &c. Fabius Cunctator.

251. 5. *heading*. *Sir John Berkley*. See *D.N.B.* He took Exeter in 1643 and kept it until 1646. He was thus in charge when Princess Henrietta Anne was born there. See 137. 3 and note.

252. 1. 1. *See O.D.E. Prov.*, 'Love begets love.'

252. 1. 3–6. Seneca, *De Benef.* i. 2. 5: 'Officia etiam ferae sentiunt &c.'

252. 2. 1. See 123. 4. 1 and note. Cf. Seneca, *Ep.* xx. 6: 'preme ergo quod coepisti &c.'

252. 4. Cf. Sallust, *Catiline*, i. 6: 'Nam et prius quam incipias, consulto, et ubi consulueris, mature facto opus est.' Also Prov. xxiv. 27 and Ecclus. xxxii. 19.

253. 1. Cf. 11. 1, 207. 4, and notes.

253. 1. 8–9. Burton, 3. 2. 3. 4 (p. 482), quotes Petronius, *Satyricon*, 126:

Tenta modò tangere corpus,
Iam tua mellifluo membra calore fluent.

253. 2. Cf. Catullus, xxii. 20–21:

Suus cuique attributus est error:
sed non videmus manticae quod in tergost.

and Seneca, *De Ira*, ii. 28. 8: 'aliena vitia in oculis habemus, a tergo nostra sunt'. Transl. Lodge: 'Other mens sins are before our eyes, our owne behind our backs.' See also *O.D.E. Prov.*, 'See not what is in the wallet behind.'

253. 3. *heading*. See *O.D.E. Prov.*, 'No pains no gains'; also 212. 5. 1–2 and note.

254. 1. *heading*, &c. Cf. Seneca, *Ep.* lxvii. 10: 'una virtus' (i.e. the highest virtue is a compound of all single virtues). Jos. Hall, *Meditations*, ii. 94: 'I care not how simple my heavenly affections are; which, the more free they are from composition, are the nearer to God: nor how compounded my earthly; which are easily subject to extremities.'

254. 2. Cf. Burton, 3. 2. 3. 3 (p. 466): 'For it is not the eye of it selfe that entiseth to lust, but an *adulterous eye*, as *Peter* termes it. 2. 2. 14. a wanton, a rolling, lascivious eye . . .' See 138. 1. 3 and 232. 1. 9–10.

254. 3. *heading*. This coming was on 29 Aug. 1645. See Clarendon, ed. Macray, ix. 81.

255. 1. Cf. Tacitus, *Ann.* iii. 30: 'an satias capit aut illos, cum omnia tribuerunt, aut hos, cum iam nihil reliquum est quod cupiant'.

255. 2. See *O.D.E. Prov.*, 'Like Prince, like people' (s.v. 'Prince'). Cf. Jonson, *Cynthias Reuells*, v. xi. 169–73.

255. 3. Cf. Burton, 1. 2. 4. 6 (p. 155): [Of the rich man] 'All the graces, Veneres, pleasures, elegances attend him.'

255. 4. 5. Ps. cxxii. 4: 'For thither the tribes go up.'

256. 1. 13. *at a dead lift*. In an extremity. Tilley, *Prov. Eng.*, L271, 'To help at a dead lift.'

256. 1. 15. *Roster*. Sc. roaster, 'a pig, or other article of food, fit for roasting' (*O.E.D.*, 'Roaster', 3.)

256. 1. 17–18. See *O.D.E. Prov.*, 'No Penny . . .'.

256. 2. *heading*. William Alabaster 1567–1640. See *D.N.B.*

256. 2. 7. Daniel v. 11, 14.

256. 2. 10. *to*. Before, at the hands of, in succession to. *Fillit*. Headband; here as a symbol of imperial power. Cf. Selden, *Titles of Honour*, I. viii. 2 (1672, p. 120): 'The Diadem . . . was no other than only a Fillet of silk, linnen, or some such thing.'

256. 2. 11–12. Daniel vii, viii (e.g. 8).

256. 2. 13. *times and seasons*. Acts i. 7; 1 Thess. v. 1.

256. 2. 15–16. Rev. x. 1–2; xx. 12.

257, l. 17. Herrick refers to Alabaster's *Ecce Sponsus venit. Tuba &c* . . . (1633) or his *Spiraculum tubarum* . . . (? 1633).

257, l. 19. *Aprill*. See 23. 2. 1–2 and note; also 221, l. 58 and 410, l. 34.

257. 1. *heading* and l. 4. *Mary Stone*. See 185. 3, heading and note. But this niece (see l. 10) has not been identified.

257. 2. Cf. Tacitus, *Hist.* i. 15: 'secundae res acrioribus stimulis animos explorant, quia miseriae tolerantur, felicitate corrumpimur.' Seneca, *Ep.* xciv. 74: 'melius in malis sapimus.' Bacon, 'Of Adversity', *s.f.*

257. 3. 1. Hor. *Ep.* i. 16. 79: 'mors ultima linea rerum est'. Seneca, *Consol. ad Marc.* xix. 5: 'mors dolorum . . . finis, ultra quem mala nostra non exeunt'.

257. 4. 1. *Tods of wooll*. Metaphor for white clouds.

258, l. 10. Hor. *Carm.* iii. 22. 4: 'diva triformis'.

258, ll. 17–18. Cf. Randolph, *Amyntas* (1638), III. i. 1–2: 'by thy-self—the sweetest oath That can be sworn'.

258. 1. 3. See 235. 2. 1 and note.

258. 1. 4. Cf. Terence, *Eun.* IV. v. 6 (732).

258. 3. 1–4. Cf. Tibullus, iv. 13. 9:

> sic ego secretis possum bene vivere silvis,
> qua nulla humano sit via trita pede.

259. 1. 1–2. Cf. Horace, *Ep.* i. 6. 48:

> hoc primus repetas opus, hoc postremus omittas.

259. 1. 7–8. See 230, ll. 23–24 and note.

259. 2. 5. *Brutus*. See 6. 2 and note.

259. 2. 6. *Cato the severe*. See 301. 1.

259. 2. 22. See *O.D.E. Prov.*, 'George-a-Green . . .'.

260. 2. Cf. Tacitus, *Agric.* 27: 'iniquissima haec bellorum condicio est: prospera omnes sibi vindicant, adversa uni imputantur.' Id. *Ann.* iii. 53: 'maius aliquid &c.'

260. 3. Cf. Seneca, *De Clem.* I. i. 3, transl. Lodge: 'The bloud of my meanest subiects is carefully spared by me.'

260. 4. Cf. Tacitus, *Ann.* iv. 34: 'spreta exolescunt: si irascare, agnita videntur'.

261. 1. 4. *Glory and worship*. Ps. 96. 6: 'Glory and worship are before him.'

261. 3. 2. See *O.D.E. Prov.*, 'Good shepherd must fleece . . .'

261. 4. 3. *Loves thornie Tapers.* See 113, ll. 31–33 and note. After the passage in *Hymenaei* there quoted, Jonson, still following his Renaissance authorities, continues: 'After him [sc. Hymen] a *youth* . . . bearing another light, of *white thorne*'; and in a note points out, with reference to Hymen's '*torch* of *pine tree*', that in l. 15 of Catullus, lxi, it is questionable whether 'pineam' or 'spineam' is the correct reading. Jonson also mentions the 'facem . . . ex spina alba' carried, according to Festus, by the youth in question, the Camillus.

261. 4. 6. See 54, l. 43 and note.

262. 1. See 122. 1. heading and note.

262. 2. 3. *lautitious.* sumptuous. *O.E.D.* records this instance alone.

262. 2. 8. *bastard.* Spurious. Cf. Browne, *Pseud. Epid.*, 1646, III. xii ('Of the Phenix'), p. 132: 'The Manucodiata or bird of Paradise, hath had the honour of this name.'

262. 2. 11. *larded.* ? Greased and polished.

264. 1. Cf. Martial, ix. 61. 15–16: 'atque oluere, &c.'

264. 2. Tacitus, *Ann.* iv. 4: 'quamquam arduum sit eodem loci potentiam et concordiam esse'.

264. 3. *heading.* See 181. 1 and note. 'Margarett Fauconberge d. of Thomas' appears in the Parish Register of St. Margaret's, Westminster as having been christened on 27 Aug. 1639. (A. M. Burke, *Memorials of St. Marg. Westm.*)

264. 5. 1. *Noble Numbers.* Probably in a wider sense than that of his 'pious pieces' (see p. 337). Cf. 19. 3. 7 and 217. 2. 5.

264. 6. Cf. 394. 1. 3–4 and 416. 1. 17–18.

264. 7. 2. Cf. St. Aug. *Enarratio in Ps. 83*, § 3: 'Desiderium eorum differtur, ut crescat.' (*Opera*, Migne, iv, col. 1057.) Also Ovid, *Rem. Am.* 405: 'sustentata venus gratissima'; and Tilley, *Prov. Eng.*, D213: 'Desires are nourished by delay.'

265. 1. 4. *Repullulation.* Cf. Donne, *LXXX Sermons*, 1640, Serm. xxix, p. 291C: 'and few of these [errors] have had any Resurrection, any repulullation . . .' and Serm. lxxiii, p. 746D: 'a disposition to a reviviscence, and a repullulation'. See quotation from Seneca in note to 292. 8.

265. 1. 5. *thirtieth thousand yeere.* See note to 190, l. 47.

267. 1. *heading.* *John Crofts.* Son of Sir John Crofts, of Saxham, Suffolk. The father died in 1628 and the son in 1664 (J. Gaye, *Hist. and Antiqs. of Suffolk*, 1838, p. 134). Lord Herbert of Cherbury, writing of his embassy to Paris of 1619, records that 'Mr. Crofts was one of my principal gentlemen, and afterwards made the King's Cup-bearer; and Thomas Carew, that excellent wit, the King's Carver.' (*Autobiography*, ed. Lee, 1906, p. 106.) It may have been in the following February that Carew wrote his verses to be spoken '*To the King at his entrance into* Saxham, *by Master* Io. Crofts.' (See Carew, *Poems*, ed. Dunlap, 1949, pp. xxxi–xxxii, 30–31, and 226.) The date of Crofts's appointment to be cup-bearer has not been discovered but he is referred to as holding that office in *C.S.P. Dom., 1638–9*, p. 611. The identity of the 'Mr. Crofts' mentioned in various places in *C.S.P.* between 1625 and 1640 is not always certain; but 'John Crofts Esq. Cup-bearer to his late Majesty' is given as the author of three Hymns set by Henry Lawes in *The Second Book of Ayres, and Dialogues*, 1655 (see p. xxvi above).

267. 3. Delattre (p. 394) suggests that Herrick was here influenced by the speech of Eyre in Dekker, *Shoemaker's Holiday*, III. v (Mermaid, p. 46): 'Hum, let's be merry, whiles we are young; old age, sack and sugar will steal upon us, ere we be aware.'

267. 3. 4. *evill dayes*. Eccles. xii. 1.

267. 4. Tacitus, *Ann.* xiii. 56: 'deesse nobis terra in vitam, in qua moriamur, non potest'. Quoted by Montaigne, ii. 3 (*Tudor Trans.*, p. 26): 'Well may we want ground to live upon, but never ground to die in.'

268. 2. Seneca, *Agam.* 243: 'quem paenitet peccasse paene est innocens.' Quoted by Burton, 3. 4. 2. 6 (p. 709).

268. 3. 2. Cf. Cicero, *De Fin.* II. xxix. 94–95: 'Nam ista vestra: "Si gravis, brevis; si longus, levis" dictata sunt'; *Tusc.* II. xix. 44; Seneca, *Ep.* xxiv. 14; Montaigne, i. 40 (*Tudor Trans.*, p. 281); and Burton, 2. 3. 1. 1 (p. 305): 'Si longa est, levis est, si gravis est, brevis est, If it be long, 'tis light, if grievous, it cannot last.'

268. 6. Tacitus, *Hist.* iii. 58: 'omnia inconsulti impetus coepta initiis valida spatio languescunt'. Ibid. iv. 67: 'Sabinus festinatum temere proelium pari formidine deseruit.'

269. 4. Cf. Martial, iv. 59. See also 185. 4 and note.

269. 5. *heading. Mercie Herrick.* See note to 210. 3, and Introd., p. xi. She married John Wingfield at Little Thurlow, Suffolk (see note to 131. 1) in 1611 (Boyd's Marriage Index, Soc. of Genealogists, where the name appears as 'Hicick'). This is therefore presumably one of Herrick's earliest extant poems.

269. 5. 4. Deut. xxviii. 5 (Genevan): 'Blessed shalbe thy basket and thy dough' (A.V. 'store', margin 'dough, or, kneading trough').

270. 1. 1. Cf. 2 Esdras ii. 45; 1 Cor. xv. 53.

270. 1. 5. *incorrupted light*. See Wisd. of Sol. xviii. 4.

270. 2. *heading*. Cf. Seneca, *Ep.* cvii. 9: 'optimum est pati, quod emendare non possis'.

270. 2. 2. Seneca, *De Prov.* iv. 12: 'numquam virtutis molle documentum est'. Transl. Lodge: 'Vertuous instructions are neuer delicate.'

270. 2. 4. Cf. Heb. xii. 6–7: 'whom the Lord loveth he chasteneth &c.'

270. 3. 7–8. Lucan, vii. 819: 'coelo tegitur, qui non habet urnam'. Quoted by Burton 2. 3. 5 (p. 338): 'The Canopie of heaven covers him that hath no tombe.' Cf. ibid., p. 320: 'poore *Lazarus* ... hath ... the heaven a tombe'.

271. 1. *heading*. Leicester was taken May 1645. See Clarendon, ed. Macray, ix. 33–34.

271. 2. 5. See 63. 1. 7. Cf. Jonson, *Epicoene*, I. i. 106–7: 'take often counsell of her glasse'.

271. 2. 9–16. See Martial, viii. 68, 5–8 and notes to 75. 1.

271. 3. Caesar, *De Bell. Civ.* i. 72, quoted by Montaigne, ii. 34 (*Tudor Trans.*, p. 480): 'He was wont to say, that he esteemed that victory much more which was conducted by advise, and managed by counsell, then by main strength and force.'

272. 1. 4. *Primates.* Leaders.

272. 1. 5. 1 Sam. ii. 13–17.

272. 2. *heading.* See Tilley, *Prov. Eng.*, T64: 'The greatest talkers are the least doers.'

272. 2. 2. Plutarch, *Life of Phocion*, 25 (North in *Tudor Trans.* v, p. 94): 'O Hercules, quoth he, how many Captaines doe I see, and howe few souldiers!'

272. 5. Cf. Ovid, *Trist.* iii. 7. 47–48:

Ingenio tamen ipse meo comitorque fruorque:
Caesar in hoc potuit iuris habere nihil.

See also 371. 1 and note.

273. 4. 1. *wheales.* Pimples.

273. 4. 2. *Pimpleides.* Referring to Pimpla, a place and fountain sacred to the Muses. The word Pimpleus could also be applied to something thus sacred. Catullus (cv) applies it to Mount Helicon. See also Hor. *Carm.* i. 26. 9, and *Greek Anth.* v. 206. 3.

273. 4. 3–4. Cf. Shakespeare, *Henry V*, III. vi. 111–12: 'his face is all bubukles, and whelks, and knobs, and flames o' fire', and *1 Henry IV*, III. iii. 47–50: 'Thou hast saved me a thousand marks in links and torches, walking with thee in the night. . . .'

273. 6. 8. *consuming fire.* Deut. iv. 24, ix. 3; Heb. xii. 29.

274. 1. *heading. Amie Potter.* Daughter of Barnaby Potter, 1577–1642, Herrick's predecessor at Dean Prior and thereafter Bishop of Carlisle. See *D.N.B.* He married the widow of Edward Yard (ob. 1612), Elizabeth Northcote or Norcott; and Amy Potter was thus half-sister of Lettice Yard. See note to 124. 3, heading.

274. 1. 2. Cf. Jonson, *Und.* xxviii. 4.

274. 1. 8. *tonguelesse as a Crocodile.* Cf. Pliny, *Hist. Nat.* viii. 37, transl. Holland, 1601, viii. 25, i, p. 208: 'This beast alone . . . hath no use of a tongue.' See also Herodotus, ii. 68.

274. 3. Cf. Burton, 3. 1. 1. 2 (p. 412): 'Love . . . *Circulus à bono in bonum*, a round circle still from good to good.' See 13. 2.

274. 4. Cf. Burton, 3. 1. 1. 2 (pp. 408–9): 'For as . . . Plato defines it, *Beauty is a liuely shining or glittering brightnesse, resulting from effused good . . . Beauty and Grace are like those beames and shinings that come from the glorious and divine Sunne.*' See 33. 4 and note.

274. 5. 1–2. See 60. 2. 4 and note.

275. 3. 2–8. See 155. 1. 1–2 and note.

275. 5. 2. See 24. 2. 2 and note.

276. 2. 1. *recompence.* See 322. 1.

276. 2. 2. Seneca, *Herc. Fur.* 656–7: 'quae fuit durum pati, meminisse dulce est.' Cf. Virgil, *Aen.* i. 203.

276. 3. 5–6. Cf. Martial, iv. 38.

276. 3. 9–10, 12. Joshua x. 12–13. Propertius, iii. 20. 11–14.

276. 4. 2 and 5. *Gotire . . . Wilson.* See note to 39. 3. 13.

276. 4. 4. *Laniere.* See note to 85. 3. heading.

277. 1. Cf. Anacreontea, 7. Herrick's ending is different.

277. 5. 4. Cf. Virgil, *Ecl.* viii. 65: 'mascula thura'; Ovid, *Med. Fac.* 94; and Jonson, *Kings Entertainment*, ll. 615–16 (*Works*, vii, p. 103): 'masculine gums . . . which shall for euer burne'. Note by Jonson begins: 'Somewhat a strange Epithite, in our tongue, but proper to the thing: for they were only *Masculine* odors, which were offered to the Altars.' Jonson refers to the Virgil passage, &c.

278. 1. Cf. Ovid, *Her.* xiv. 21–22:

> modo facta crepuscula terris
> ultima pars lucis primaque noctis erat.

See 319. 4. 2 and note.

278. 2. *heading. J. Jincks.* Unidentified.

278. 2. 3. *bastard Slips.* Wisd. of Sol. iv. 3.

278. 3. 4. *But while.* Until.

278. 4. Cf. Aristotle, *Politics*, iii. 7. Erasmus refers to Aristotle's distinction in *Adagia*, 'Vltio malefacti': 'quod hic suum ac priuatum commodum spectet, ille populi rebus consulit'.

279. 1. See 209. 3 and notes.

279. 2. Cf. beginning of verses by Francis Quarles prefixed to Phineas Fletcher's *The Purple Island*, 1633:

> Man's *body's* like a *house* . . .
> . . . his ribs are *laths*, daub'd o'er,
> Plaster'd with *flesh* and *blood.*

279. 4. 4–6. Cf. Featley, *Clavis Mystica*, 1636, p. 182: '*Let us water* our plants, but not drown them, as those *that mourne without hope.*'

280. 1. *heading. Sir Thomas Heale.* Or Hele. Son of Thomas Hele, of Flete, Devon. Created baronet 1627; D.C.L. 1642. M.P. A commander of the royal forces at the siege of Plymouth 1648. Died 1670. (*Alumni Oxon.*)

280. 1. 1. *my powerfull Rhymes.* Cf. Shakespeare, *Sonnets*, 55. 2: 'this powerful rime'.

280. 2. 3. *Old Religion.* Cf. Ovid, *Fasti*, iii. 264: 'antiqua religione'; and *Met.* x. 693: 'Religione . . . prisca'.

280. 3. 2. *Unshorn Apollo.* See 67. 3. 2 and note.

280. 4. Ovid, *Ars Am.* ii. 233–4:

> Militiae species amor est. discedite, segnes:
> Non sunt haec timidis signa tuenda viris.

281. 1. Cf. Ovid, *Rem. Am.* 79–80, 91, 731–2; and see Tilley, *Prov. Eng.*, S714, 'Of a little spark a great fire.'

281. 3. See 38, l. 144 and note.

281. 4. 7–8. See 52. 3. 4 and note.

282. 1. Cf. Tacitus, *De Orat.* 36: 'hinc procerum factiones et assidua senatus adversus plebem certamina'.

282. 2. 6. *wimbling*. Boring, hole-making.

282. 2. 7. *poking-sticks*. Used for stiffening the plaits of ruffs.

282. 5. See 52. 3. 4 and note.

283. 2. 9 and 12. *Bee . . . Snake*. See *O.D.E. Prov.*, 'Honey is sweet, but the bee stings' and 'Snake in the grass'.

283. 4. 1–6. See note on 250. 4. Herrick in these first six lines continues Eubulus, who, after mentioning Penelope, observes that the list of good women is complete.

283. 4. 1. Cf. Burton, 3. 2. 5. 5 (p. 585):

> Heare me O my countrymen, saith *Susarion*,
> Women are naught, yet no life without one. [Ex Stobeo]

283. 4. 7. *Lais*. There were, at different times, two courtesans of Corinth so named. The opposition to Lucretia is made by Jonson, *Catiline*, II. 283: 'Will LAIS turn a LUCRECE?'

284. 1. Cf. Martial, xii. 88; xiii. 2. See also 80. 2. 23–24 and note.

285. 1. 7. Cf. Browne, *Pseud. Epid.*, v. xxii. 16 (1646, p. 269): 'We shall not, I hope, disparage the Resurrection . . ., if we say the Sun doth not dance on Easter day.'

285. 1. 22. See Isa. xlii. 9; Rev. xxi. 4, &c.

286. 4. 1. *Fillitings*. See 256. 2. 10 and note.

287. 2. Cf. Ovid, *Ars Am.* i. 659:

> Et lacrimae prosunt. lacrimis adamanta movebis.

287. 3. Cf. Hor. *Ep.* i. 19. 48–49.

287. 4. Tacitus, *Ann.* ii. 39: 'veritas visu et mora, falsa festinatione et incertis valescunt.' See 287. 6 and note.

287. 6. Cf. Hor. *Ars Poet.* 180–2: 'segnius irritant &c.'; Seneca, *Ep.* vi. 5: 'homines amplius oculis quam auribus credunt'; and Plautus, *Truculentus*, II. vi. 8: 'pluris est oculatus testis unus quam auriti decem'. See 287. 4 and note. See also Tilley, *Prov. Eng.*, E274, 'One eyewitness is better than ten earwitnesses.'

288. 2. See note to title-page (motto).

288. 3. *heading*. *William Lawes*. Elder brother of Henry Lawes. Killed at Chester, 1645. See *D.N.B.*

288. 5. 3–4. Prov. xxv. 27, xxvii. 7. Cf. *Greek Anth.*, Planudean App., i. 16, and see Tilley, *Prov. Eng.*, H560, 'Too much honey . . .'.

289. 2. 5–6. For these inns see Sugden, *Topographical Dictionary*, s.v. On the Triple Tun see also T. A. Kirby, *M.L.N.*, lxii, March 1947.

289. 2. 17–19. See 110. 3. 17–18 and note.

290. 1. See 260. 2 and note.

290. 2. 7–8. Cf. Martial, i. 35. 11.

290. 4. Cf. Montaigne, ii. 34 (*Tudor Trans.*, p. 483): 'According to Cyrus . . . "It is not the multitude of men, but the number of good men that causeth an advantage." '

290. 5. Cf. Jonson, *Forest*, xi. 87–90: 'He that for loue of goodnesse hateth ill &c.', and Horace, *Ep.* i. 16. 52–53 (l. 53 an inserted line which is not in the *textus receptus*):

oderunt peccare boni virtutis amore:
oderunt peccare mali formidine poenae.

Translated by Thomas Becon in *The Demands of Holy Scripture*, 1563 (*Prayers*, &c., Parker Soc., 1844, p. 619):

Good men do well of a virtuous intent:
Evil men do well for fear of punishment.

290. 6. *heading*. *M. Kellam.* Not identified.

290. 6. 3. Cf. 1 John iii. 17.

291, l. 8. *Tearce.* Tierce; one-third of a pipe.

291. I. 21. See note to III. 2.

291. 2. From Plutarch, *Quaest. Rom.* 82; referred to by Jonson, *Kings Entertainment*, note on 'Fasces', l. 83 (*Works*, vii, p. 85).

291. 3. Cf. Burton, 'Democritus to the Reader', p. 49: '*They that are poore and bad . . . abhorre the present government*' (translating Sallust, *Catiline*, 37: 'quibus opes nullae sunt . . .').

292. 1. Cf. Virgil, *Georg.* i. 82–83, and Jonson, *Und.* xvii. 16–18:

All is not barren land, doth fallow lie.
Some grounds are made the richer, for the Rest;
And I will bring a Crop, if not the best.

292. 1. 4. Ovid, *Ars Am.* iii. 82: 'continua messe senescit ager'. Id. *Ex Ponto*, i. 4. 13–14.

292. 2. Tacitus, *Hist.* iv. 3: 'tanto proclivius est iniuriae quam beneficio vicem exsolvere, quia gratia oneri, ultio in quaestu habetur'.

292. 3. Tacitus, *Ann.* xii. 31: 'ille gnarus primis eventibus metum aut fiduciam gigni'.

292. 4. Cf. Jonson, *Sejanus*, i. 554–6: 'The first ascents to soueraigntie are hard &c.' Tacitus, *Ann.* iv. 7: 'primas dominandi spes in arduo: ubi sis ingressus, adesse studia et ministros'.

292. 6. Ovid, *Ars Am.* iii. 121–2:

Prisca iuvent alios, ego me nunc denique natum
Gratulor. haec aetas moribus apta meis.

292. 8. Seneca, *De Clementia*, i. 24 and i. 8: 'Ferina ista rabies est, sanguine gaudere et vulneribus' . . . 'Quemadmodum praecisae arbores plurimis ramis repullulant, et multa satorum genera, ut densiora surgant, reciduntur; ita regia crudelitas auget inimicorum numerum tollendo.' Cf. Jonson, *Discoveries*, ll. 1167–9. (*Works*, viii, p. 599.)

293. 1. Hor. *Carm.* i. 7. 15–18: 'albus ut obscuro &c.'

293. 3. Cf. Burton, 2. 3. 7 (p. 353): 'It is an ordinary thing so to be misused, *Regium est cum benè feceris malè audiri*, the chiefest men . . . are so vilified . . .' [Diog. Laert. VI. i. 3.]

293. 4. 2. Cf. 123. 4. 2 and see note.

293. 5. 6. Exod. xxi. 6.

293. 6. See 327. 7 and note.

294. 1. 1–2. Cf. Sidney, *Astrophel and Stella*, 82. 12–14.

294. 1. 2. Cf. Marlowe, *Hero and Leander*, i. 406–7: 'he often stray'd Beyond the bounds of shame'.

294. 1. 3. Cf. Pliny, *Hist. Nat.* vii. 40: 'nemo . . . omnibus horis sapit'. Tilley, *Prov. Eng.* M335, 'No man is wise at all times.'

294. 1. 3–4. See 8. 1. 8 and note.

294. 2. 5. Cf. *Greek Anth.* vii. 216. 5–6 (Antipater Thess.).

294. 3. 1–2. Martial, ii. 90. 9–10:

> sit mihi verna satur, sit non doctissima coniunx,
> sit nox cum somno, sit sine lite dies.

294. 3. 4. See 198. 1. 3 and note.

294. 4. Martial, iv. 22.

294. 4. 3. See 75. 1 and note.

295. 1. 1–2. Ovid, *Med. Fac.* 83–84:

> Quamvis tura deos irataque numina placent,
> Non tamen accensis omnia danda focis.

295. 2. 1. *Parchment*. Cf. Burton, 2. 3. 2 (p. 311): 'this parchment nobility'.

295. 2. 2–6. Cf. Burton, ibid.: 'wherin lies their worth and sufficiency? in a few coats of armes, eagles, lions, serpents, . . . bends, fesses, &c. & such like bables'.

295. 2. 7–8. Cf. Burton, ibid.: 'Without means gentry is naught worth.'

295. 3. Cf. Anacreontea, 33.

296. 3. 22–24. Exod. xxiii. 15: 'none shall appear before me empty'. Cf. Exod. xxxiv. 20, and Deut. xvi. 16.

297. 1. *heading*. *Mr. Charles Cotton*. Probably the father (d. 1658) of the more famous Charles Cotton, who was only eighteen in 1648. Clarendon (*Life*, 1827, i, p. 36) writes of the father with enthusiasm and in terms compatible with Herrick's eulogy.

297. 2. 1–2. Cf. Browne, *Religio Medici*, 1642, p. 86: 'I am not of *Paracelsus* minde, that boldly delivers a receipt to make a man without conjunction'; and Jonson, *Mercurie Vindicated*, ll. 125–72.

297. 2. 9–10. Phinn suggests that this may allude to the sacrifice of plate to raise forces for the King.

297. 3. 4. Cf. 327. 4.

298. 3. 1. Ecclus. xxii. 11: 'Weep for the dead, for he hath lost the light.'

298. 6. *heading*. *Leonard Willan*. Author of *Astraea, or, true love's myrrour. A pastoral*, 1651, and other writings. His name appears in *Alumni Cant.* as having matriculated fellow-commoner from Christ's College in 1623.

298. 6. 4. Cf. Ovid, *Ex Ponto*, iv. 8. 74:

> Quodque aliis opus est, hoc tibi lusus erit.

299. 1. *heading*. *John Hall*. 1627–56. 'Poet and pamphleteer' (*D.N.B.*, q.v.).

299. 1. 2. Cf. Martial, viii. 70. 2–3; and Jonson, *Epig.* lxxix. 3–4.

299. 3. *heading. Elizabeth Finch.* Not identified.

299. 4. 4. *lustie.* Strong, substantial.

300. 2. *heading.* The King removed to Hampton Court on 24 Aug. 1647 and escaped therefrom on 11 Nov. See Clarendon, ed. Macray, x. 109 and 127.

300. 2. 7. *Altars smoake.* Virgil, *Ecl.* i. 43.

300. 2. 7–14. Cf. J. Gregory, op. cit. (1646) in note to 162. 3; chap. vii, pp. 29–33 (on 'some unobserv'd *superstitions* of the *Ancients* in the *foundations* and *assurances* of their Cities, Forts, &c.): 'Twas a Rule . . . to undertake nothing . . . inauspicatò, . . . the first was the *propitiation* of the place by *reconciling* the *Genius* with a respective *Sacrifice.* This Tradition . . . includes . . . laying the foundation of their Metropolitan Cities under a *certaine Configuration* of the *Heavens* . . . to take knowledge of the *Sunne* and *Moones* place in the *Zodiacque* . . . but especially of the *Ascendent* . . . the next care taken was of . . . the *part of Fortune,* . . . this *Fortune* and Genius of the City . . .'

300. 2. 19–20. Cf. Tibullus, i. 6. 63–64; Propertius, iv. 11. 95; and Seneca, *De Brev. Vit.* viii. 4: 'dicere solent eis, quos valdissime diligunt, paratos se partem annorum suorum dare'.

301. 1. *heading.* See note to 218. 6. 12.

301. 1. 1–2. See 259. 2. 6. Cf. Martial, i. Pref. 20.

301. 2. 4. *blush to death.* See 366. 1. 13; also Beaumont and Fletcher, *A King and No King,* I. i. 163.

301. 4. The name 'Mudge' occurs fairly often in the Dean Prior Parish Register.

301. 5. *heading.* See note to frontispiece, and Introduction, p. xviii. Harmar (*c.* 1594–1670), for a time an Under-master at Westminster, also held a number of other posts, including the Professorship of Greek at Oxford, and was the author of various works listed by Wood in *Athenae Oxon.* (1691, ii. 349). Herrick is not alone in crediting him with medical knowledge; Thomas Philipott, *Poems,* 1646, p. 34, attributes to him a 'Libellum De Lue Venereâ', which has apparently been lost. See also *D.N.B.*

301. 5. 4. *expansion.* See note on 82. 2. 4–5.

301. 5. 11–14. Plutarch attributes to Cicero (*Life,* 24; *Tudor Trans.* v, p. 338) the saying that Jupiter would speak like Plato in the Dialogues. Cf. Jonson, *Discoveries* (*Works,* viii, p. 641, ll. 2549–51).

302. 2. 3–4. See 25. 1. 3–4 and note.

302. 3. 4. *carbage.* ? Padding. See 76. 2. 6 ('In-laid Garbage') and *O.E.D.* s.v. 'Cabbage' *sb.*[2]

302. 5. 2. Tacitus, *Ann.* xiii. 19: 'Nihil rerum mortalium tam instabile ac fluxum est quam fama potentiae non sua vi nixae.'

302. 6. 1. See 10. 3 and note.

303. 1. 2. Cf. Jonson, *Epig.* cxx. 11: 'three fill'd *Zodiackes*'.

303. 2. 7. *Rex sacrorum.* See Ovid, *Fasti,* i. 333.

303. 3. Martial, i. 97: 'Cum clamant omnes &c.'

304. 1. 6. *Candlemas.* A display of candles.

304. 2. *heading. Susanna Herrick.* Wife of Robert's brother, Nicholas. See note on 193. 1, heading.

304. 3. *heading. Lady Crew.* See note on 112. 3, heading.

304. 3. 5. *my many children.* One of these was Randolph Crew, artist (1631–57). See *D.N.B.*

304. 4. *heading. Tomasin Parsons.* Second daughter of John Parsons. See note to 186. 3, heading, and Introduction, p. xvi. She was christened on 24 Sept. 1618. (A. M. Burke, *Memorials of St. Margaret's Church, Westminster.*)

305. 1. Cf. 333. 5. 2 and note.

305. 2. Cf. Plautus, *Miles Glor.*, 750–62.

305. 3. *heading. Tho: Herrick.* Probably the eldest son of Nicholas Herrick, the poet's brother. See Nichols, *Leicestershire*, II. ii, p. 631.

306, ll. 28–29. Cf. Sir John Harington, *Epig.* iv. 45 (1618):

> Then of sweet sports let no occasion scape,
> But be as wanton, toying as an Ape.

Cited by Burton, 2. 2. 6. 4 (p. 300).

306. 2. Cf. Plutarch, *Quaest. Rom.* 20 (*Morals*, transl. Holland, 1603, p. 856): '. . . one *Flavius* [marg. 'Or Phaulius'] had a wife, who used secretly to drinke wine, and when she was surprised and taken by her husband, she was well beaten by him, which [sc. with] myrtle rods.' Lactantius, *De Fals. Rel.* i. 22 (*Opera*, Migne, i, col. 245), gives the name as Faunus, not Flavius.

307. 2. See *O.D.E. Prov.*, 'Keeping is harder than winning.' Cf. Jonson, *Eng. Grammar*, II. vii, *Works*, viii, p. 546, l. 35; and Ovid, *Ars Am.* ii. 12.

307. 5. *heading. Grace Potter.* See note to 274. 1, heading.

308. 1. 27, 30. Cf. Burton, 1. 3. 1. 2 (p. 185, under 'Inconstancy'): 'erected and dejected in an instant'.

308. 3. 2. Cf. Seneca, *Ep.* lxxvii. 3: 'plus superesset viatici quam viae.' Quoted by Montaigne, ii. 28 (*Tudor Trans.*, p. 440): 'I have more to beare my charges, then way to goe.' Cf. Cicero, *De Sen.* xviii. 66: 'Potest enim quicquam esse absurdius &c.' See also 411, l. 54.

309. 1. Cf. Anacreontea, 50.

309. 1. 5–6. Cf. Ovid, *Rem. Am.* 805.

309. 3. Cf. Seneca, *De Clementia*, i. 22. 1: 'Ipsos facilius emendabis minore poena.'

309. 4. See 333. 2 and note. Cf. Virgil, *Aen.* ii. 354: 'Una salus victis nullam sperare salutem.' Quoted by Burton, 3. 4. 2. 2 (p. 693). See also Seneca, *Medea*, 163: 'Qui nihil potest sperare, desperet nihil'; Montaigne, iii. 12 (*Tudor Trans.*, p. 312); and *O.D.E. Prov.*, 'Despair gives courage to a coward.'

309. 5. Hor. *Ars Poet.* 372–3:

> mediocribus esse poetis
> non homines, non di, non concessere columnae.

310. 1. *heading. Lord Hopton.* 1598–1652. Defeated the Parliamentarians in Cornwall and was created Baron Hopton in 1643. See *D.N.B.*, 'Ralph Hopton'.

310. 2. *heading. His Grange.* A squirrel's nest.

310. 3. 3. *thumblesse.* Clumsy, helpless. See *O.E.D.* s.v., where, for this sense, this passage alone is cited.

310. 3. 6. Cf. Ecclus. xvii. 16: 'he nourisheth with discipline'.

311. 3. 2. Terence, *Heaut.* iv. ii. 8: 'nil tam difficilest quin quaerendo investigari possiet'.

311. 4. Cf. 236. 2, 252. 2, &c.

311. 4. 2. Cf. Sallust, *Ad Caesarem . . . Oratio*, vi. 2: pacis causa bellum gerunt, sapientes laborem spe otii sustentant.' *held up.* Sustained, kept going.

311. 5. 1. *flowing.* Cf. 261. 2. 2, 407. 1. 28, &c.

311. 6. 2. *Levell-coyle.* Game, racket. See 397. 4. 2; cf. Jonson, *Tale of a Tub*, III. v. 30: 'Young Justice *Bramble* has kept levell coyle.'

312. 1. Tacitus, *Ann.* iii. 54: 'ne corporis quidem morbos veteres et diu auctos nisi per dura et aspera coerceas'.

312. 5. 6. See 322. 2. 2 and note.

313. 1. Partly suggested by Anacreontea, 1.

313. 3. 3–4. See 85. 1. 9–16 and note; also 411, ll. 35–46.

314. 2. Martial, v. 10. 11–12. See also 218. 3 and note.

314. 3. 2. Seneca, *Medea*, 196: 'Iniqua numquam regna perpetuo manent.' Cf. id. *Troades*, 258: 'violenta nemo &c.' Cf. 241. 6.

315. 2. 1–2. See *O.D.E. Prov.*, 'St. Distaff's Day neither work nor play.' Also called Rock day, q.v. *O.E.D.* s.v. 'Rock' *sb.*^{2} 3. *b.*

315. 3. 2. *one.* See note on 207, l. 61.

315. 4. 1. *supremest kiss.* See note on 129. 4. 2.

316, l. 15. *Golden-cheap-side.* Cf. Drayton, *Englands Heroicall Epp.*, 'Mistres Shore to King Edward IV', l. 12 (*Works*, ed. Hebel and Tillotson, ii, p. 254): 'Nor seene the golden Cheape.'

316. 1. Tacitus, *Ann.* xii. 19: 'bellorum egregios fines, quoties ignoscendo transigatur'.

316. 3. See Tilley, *Prov. Eng.*, L236, 'One lie calls for many'; also 329. 3 and note.

316. 4. Tacitus, *Ann.* I. 72: 'cuncta mortalium incerta, quantoque plus adeptus foret, tanto se magis in lubrico dictitans'.

316. 5. Tacitus, *Ann.* xi. 7: 'sublatis studiorum pretiis etiam studia peritura'. Cf. Juvenal, x. 141–2.

316. 5. 2. Cf. Jonson, *Catiline*, i. 233: 'And had price, and praise.' See also 173, l. 12.

317. 1. 1. *on with thine intent.* See 311. 4 and note.

317. 1. 2. Cf. Tacitus, *Ann.* iv. 35: 'punitis ingeniis gliscit auctoritas'; and Jonson, *Sejanus*, iii. 475–6: 'the punishment Of wit, doth make th'authoritie increase'.

318. 1. Burton, 2. 3. 3 (p. 329), quoting Hor. *Carm.* iii. 3. 7–8, 'Si fractus illabatur orbis &c.', adds 'Though heaven it selfe should fall on his head, he will not be offended.' Cf. 235. 3.

318. 2. 1. *Know when to speake.* Cf. Eccles. iii. 7 and *O.D.E. Prov.*, 'Time to speak . . .'; also Virgil, *Aen.* iv. 293–4: 'et quae mollissima fandi Tempora'.

318. 2. 2. Cf. Sallust, *Ad Caesarem Epist.* i. 1: 'Scio ego quam difficile atque asperum factu sit consilium dare regi aut imperatori.'

318. 5. See 25. 1. 1–2 and note.

319. 1. See *O.D.E. Prov.*, 'Like will to like.'

319. 3. See 25. 1. 3–4 and note.

319. 4. 2. Cf. Ovid, *Am.* i. 5. 6: 'aut ubi nox abiit, nec tamen orta dies'. See 278. 1 and note.

319. 6. Seneca, *Hippol.* 249: 'pars sanitatis velle sanari fuit'. Quoted by Burton, 2. 1. 4. 2 (p. 228).

319. 7. Cf. Burton, 2. 1. 4. 1 (p. 227): 'Many of them to get a fee, will give Physick to every one that comes . . . *Arnoldus* . . . expressely forbiddeth it. *A wise Physician will . . . first try medicinall diet, before hee proceede to medicinall cure.*'

319. 8. Ovid, *Her.* v. 7–8:

> leniter, ex merito quidquid patiare, ferendum est;
> quae venit indigno poena, dolenda venit.

Line 8 quoted by Montaigne, iii. 13 (*Tudor Trans.*, p. 361).

320. 2. 1–2. Cf. Terence, *Adelphi*, I. i. 18–19: 'et, quod fortunatum isti putant, uxorem nunquam habui'. Quoted by Burton, 3. 2. 5. 3 (p. 566).

320. 3. Hor. *Ep.* 1. 2. 54:

> sincerum est nisi vas, quodcumque infundis acescit.

321. 1. 3. *cross.* Coin. See *O.E.D.* s.v. 'Cross' *sb.* 20.

321. 5. 2. Cf. St. Aug. *De Disc. Christiana*, xii (13) (*Opera*, Migne, vi, col. 676): 'non potest male mori, qui bene vixerit'. See also Tilley, *Prov. Eng.*, L391, 'He that lives well shall die well.'

322. 1. 1. 1 Cor. ix. 7: 'Who planteth a vineyard, &c.'

322. 1. 2. Cf. 139. 5.

322. 2. 2. Cf. 312. 5. 6; 355. 3. 2. Seneca, *Medea*, 176: 'Fortuna opes auferre, non animum potest.' Quoted by Burton, 2. 3. 3 (p. 331), with translation, 'She can take away my meanes, but not my minde.'

322. 3. *heading. George Parrie.* Apparently to be identified with the son of Henry P., Bishop of Worcester. Matriculated from Merton Coll., Oxf., Mar. 1616/17; B.A. Feb. 1618/19. Adm. Inner Temple, 1616. Advocate 1628. Recorder of Exeter. One of same name LL.D. from Magdalene Coll., Camb. (probably incorporated from Oxford). *C.S.P Dom., 1629–31*, p. 426, 1630. 27, gives 'List of persons excommunicated by Dr. George Parry, Chancellor to the Bishop of Exeter, with other particulars, designed to show that he had abused the power of excommunication for the sake of the fees.' Knighted 1644 at Oxford. Died 1670 (*Alumni Oxon.* and *Cant.*; Shaw, *Knights of England*, ii, p. 217.)

323. 2. 1. Names from Hor. *Sat.* i. 2. 27:

Pastillos Rufillus olet, Gorgonius hircum.

323. 3. Seneca, *Phoen.* 659: 'qui vult amari, languida regnet manu'. Cf. Jonson, *Panegyre* (*Works*, vii, p. 116), ll. 121–3.

323. 4. *heading. Eliza: Wheeler.* See 46. 2. heading and note; also 106. 3.

324. 2. 2. *the place.* Adverbial, 'in the place'.

324. 3. 2. *State.* Council or Court.

325. 2. Cf. Erasmus, *Adagia*, s.v. 'Divitum Praerogativa': 'Non bene imperat, nisi qui paruerit imperio.' Also Seneca, *De Ira*, II. xv. 4: 'nemo autem regere potest nisi qui et regi.'

326. 2. *heading.* Grosart found that a Mrs. Mary Portman was buried at Putney Parish Church on 27 June 1671.

326. 2. 1–2. Cf. 2 Cor. xii. 2–4.

327. 2. 4. Cf. Jonson, *Volpone*, v. ii. 11:

The pleasure of all woman-kind's not like it.

327. 4. 2. Cf. Plautus, *Cistellaria*, I. 1. 69: 'amor et melle et felle est fecundissimus'.

327. 5. Jonson's Epig. cxviii is 'On Gut'.

327. 5. 1. *Science puffs up.* 1 Cor. viii. 1.

327. 7. Cf. Cicero, *De Sen.* xii. 41: 'neque omnino in voluptatis regno virtutem posse consistere'. See 37, ll. 90–92 and notes; also 293. 6.

328. 1. 5–6, 9–10. See 233. 1. 31, 33. Cf. Seneca, *De Brev. Vit.* vii. 10: 'non est itaque quod quemquam propter canos aut rugas putes diu vixisse: non ille diu vixit, sed diu fuit'. Id. *Ep.* lxxvii. 20, transl. Lodge: 'as with a Stage-play, it skilleth not how long, but how well it hath been acted'. Jonson, *Und.* lxx. 58–59: 'To shew thou hast beene long, Not liv'd.' Also *O.D.E. Prov.*, 'Lives long that lives well.'

328. 2. *heading. Laurence Swetnaham.* J. L. Chester, *Registers of Westminster Abbey*, *Burials*, p. 180: '1673. May 2. Larence Sweatnam; in the East Cloister.' Chester notes that 'the baptisms of children of Lawrence Swettenham occur in the parish register of St. Margaret's, Westminster, as early as 1629, and in an Act Book of the Dean and Chapter, under draft of 10 July 1639, Lawrence Swetnam, Gent., is mentioned as a churchwarden of St. Margaret's'. Evidently there were two of this name, for a 'Mr. Lawrence Swettenham' was buried at St. Margaret's 2 Aug. 1648. (A. M. Burke, *Memorials of St. Margaret's Church; The Parish Registers, 1539–1660*, p. 619).

328. 3. 1. Acts xxi. 13.

328. 4. 3–4. Joshua xxiii. 14: 'I am going the way of all the earth.'

328. 4. 7. Lucretius, ii. 79: 'et quasi cursores vitai lampada tradunt'.

329. 1. *heading. Michael Oulsworth.* 1591–?1654. Fellow of Magdalen Coll., Oxf. Secretary to the third and fourth earls of Pembroke. Parliamentarian. 'Much satirized by royalist pamphleteers' (*D.N.B.* 'Oldisworth', q.v.)

329. 1. 6. *In the next sheet.* This is the final line of p. 390 (Cc3v) in *1648.* The pillar of Fame (335. 2) comes on p. 398 (Cc7v).

329. 3. Cf. Erasmus, *Adagia*, s.v. 'Libertas, Veritas': '*Veritatis simplex oratio* [Seneca, *Ep.* xlix. 12, quoting Eurip. *Phoen.* 479] . . . vt simplex & nuda veritas esset luculentior quia satis ornata per se est . . . . Mendacium vero . . . vanescit ac defluit, nisi aliunde ornatu quaesito circumlitum fuerit ac politum.' See also Tilley, *Prov. Eng.*, T593, 'Truth's tale is simple.'

329. 4. 2. *chafe.* Make to burn.

330. 1. 1. Cf. Seneca, *Thyestes*, 388: 'rex est qui metuit nihil'. See also 182. 2. 2 and note.

330. 2. Cf. Anacreontea, 7.

330. 3. 2. *gay cloathes.* Jas. ii. 3: 'ye have respect to him that weareth the gay clothing'.

330. 3. 5–6. Aesop, ed. Chambry, No. 266: *Ὄνος βαστάζων ἄγαλμα.* Cf. Joseph Hall, *Meditations*, iii. 63: 'The rich man hath many friends; although, in truth, riches have them, and not the man: as the ass, that carried the Egyptian Goddess, had many bowed knees; yet not to the beast, but to the burthen.' Cf. also Webster, *Appius and Virginia*, IV. i. 283–5, and see Erasmus, *Adagia*, s.v. 'Dissimilitudinis': 'Asinus portans mysteria.'

330. 4. *heading. Nicolas Herrick.* The fifth child of Nicholas and Julian, born Apr. 1589. See Introd., p. xii, and note to 193. 1. heading. His family is given in *Visitation of London*, 1633 (Harl. Soc. i, p. 377).

330. 4. 16. *Inapostate.* A believer.

331. 3. Cf. Seneca, *Thyestes*, 214–15:

> Vbicumque tantum honesta dominanti licent,
> precario regnatur.

See also 182. 2. 2 and note.

331. 8. From (?) Martial ('Epigrams ascribed to Martial', Loeb, ii, p. 522, 4):

> Tacta places, audita places: si non videare,
> tota places: neutro, si videare, places.

331. 9. 1. *keepe the meane.* See 220. 3. 25 and note.

331. 9. 2. *Conclave.* Room, dwelling-place.

332. 2. Cf. Cicero, *De Nat. Deorum*, ii. 64: 'Sus . . . cui quidem, ne putesceret, animam ipsam pro sale datam dicit esse Chrysippus'; also id. *De Fin.* v. 13. 38, and Jonson, *The Devil is an Ass*, I. vi. 89–90: 'soule, In stead of salt, to keepe it [sc. flesh] sweete'.

332. 3. 1–4. Cf. 376. 1.

332. 6. Cf. Burton, 'Democritus to the Reader', p. 18: ''Tis the same which *Tully* maintains in the second [*read* third] of his *Tusculanes* [III. iv. 9], *omnium insipientium animi in morbo sunt, & perturbatorum* [quotation not exact], Fooles are sick, and all that are troubled in mind.' Cf. Cicero, *De Amic.* xv. 54, quoted by Burton, 2. 3. 2 (p. 314): '*Nothing so intolerable as a fortunate fool.*'

333. 2. See 309. 4 and note. Cf. Sallust, *Catiline*, 58. 19: 'necessitudo, quae etiam timidos fortes facit'; and Tilley, *Prov. Eng.*, N62: 'Necessity makes the coward grow courageous.'

333. 3. 2. Plautus, *Rudens*, II. iii. 71: 'animus aequus optimum est aerumnae condimentum'.

333. 4. 1–2. Cf. Ovid, *Met.* i. 468–71.

333. 4. 5. *Extreames are fatall.* Cf. Tilley, *Prov. Eng.*, E224, 'Every extremity is a vice.'

333. 5. 2. Cf. Mic. vii. 5; Ovid, *Ars Am.* i. 753. See 67. 2. 4 and note; also 305. 1.

333. 6. For the metre see note to 225. 1.

333. 6. 11–12. See 225. 1. 18 and note.

334, ll. 16–17. See 99. 3. 1 and note; also Beaumont and Fletcher, *The Prophetess*, II. iii. 4–6:

and the pale moon
Pluck'd in her silver horns, trembling for fear
That my strong spells should force her from her sphere.

334. 1. *heading*. Cf. Propertius, iii. i. 17: 'opus hoc de monte Sororum'.

334. 1. Cf. Propertius, loc. cit., ll. 19–22.

334. 1. 1. *take thine ease.* Luke xii. 19.

334. 1. 4–6. *Crowne . . . corruption.* 1 Cor. ix. 25.

334. 2. 1. Cf. Ovid, *Trist.* ii. 316 (and elsewhere in *Tristia*):

Poenitet ingenii iudiciique mei.

See also 339. 2 and note.

334. 4. Ovid, *Ars Am.* i. 771–2:

Pars superat coepti, pars est exhausta laboris.
Hic teneat nostras ancora iacta rates.

334. 5. Ovid, *Rem. Am.* 811–12:

Hoc opus exegi. Fessae date serta carinae.
Contigimus portus, quo mihi cursus erat.

Cf. 94. 2. 2.

335. 1. 1. *young men, and maidens.* Ps. cxlviii. 12.

335. 1. 1–3. Ovid, *Ars Am.* ii. 733–4:

Finis adest operi. palmam date, grata iuventus,
Sertaque odoratae myrtea ferte comae.

335. 1. 6. Cf. the epitaph on Naevius quoted by Jonson in *Discoveries*, ll. 2545–8. (*Works*, viii, p. 641.)

335. 2. Cf. Hor. *Carm.* iii. 30, and Ovid, *Met.* xv. 871 sqq.

335 (*final couplet*). See 218. 4. 2 and note; also 199. 2.

335 (*final couplet*). 2. Ovid, *Trist.* ii. 354:

Vita verecunda est, Musa iocosa mea.

NOBLE NUMBERS

337 (*title-page*). *Hesiod. Theogony*, ll. 27–28.

337 (*title-page*). The date, 1647. The title-page of *Hesperides* bears the date 1648 and it has sometimes been supposed from the discrepancy that Herrick intended either to publish the *Noble Numbers* separately or to let them precede *Hesperides* in the one volume. Apart from any other difficulty in the way of these suppositions, they appear to overlook the fact that the signatures in the *Noble Numbers* run Aa–Ee, not A–E. The major part of the book could have been printed in 1647 (possibly in two divisions), and the rest, with the main title-page, in 1648. Unfortunately Thomason did not record the date on which his copy (Brit. Mus. E. 1090) was bought.

339. 1. 5. Cf. Cicero, *De Amic.* xxi. 79: 'omnia praeclara, rara'.

339. 2. See 334. 2 and note; also Ovid, *Trist.* v. 1. 7–8, 20.

339. 3. 1–2. Cf. 2 Esdras iv. 5, 7; v. 36. Also 59. 2, 79. 1, and 244. 4 above.

340, l. 16. Ps. xviii. 10.

340. 1. St. Aug. *De Ordine*, ii. 16 (*Opera*, Migne, i, col. 1015): 'qui scitur melius nesciendo'. Cf. Montaigne, ii. 12 (*Tudor Trans.*, p. 203): 'God is better knowen by our not knowing him, saith S. Augustine.'

340. 2. 2. Cf. Burton, 3. 4. 1. 2 (p. 652): 'that of *Aristotle*, *Ens entium miserere mei*'.

340. 4. Cf. St. Aug. *De Civ. Dei*, ix. 5 (*Opera*, Migne, vii, col. 261): 'sicut ipse Deus . . . irascitur, nec tamen ulla passione turbatur.' Cf. 397. 5.

341. 1. Exod. xxix. 39–42; Num. xxviii. 3–10.

341. 2. See 343. 1 and note; also 394. 7.

341. 4. 2. Ps. lxxiii. 9; Prov. xvii. 27.

342. 2. 8. *saving health*. Ps. lxvii. 2.

342. 3. 1–2. Contrast Exod. xxxiii. 23.

342. 5. Heb. xii. 6; Tobit xiii. 2.

343. 1. Cf. Calvin, on John v. 14 (*Opera*, ed. Baum, xlvii, 1892, p. 110): 'Si nihil ferulis proficiat erga nos Deus . . . novam personam et quasi alienam induere cogitur. Flagella ergo ad domandum nostram ferociam arripit . . .' Cf. 341. 2 and 394. 7.

343. 2. Cf. St. Bernard, *De Consideratione*, v. 7 (*Opera*, Migne, i, col. 798): 'Tam simplex Deus, quam unus est. Est autem unus, et quo modo aliud nihil. Si dici possit, Unissimus est.' See note to 396. 1.

343. 4. 3–4. See 247, ll. 9–10; Rev. iv. 5 and xiv. 2.

344. 1. Ecclus. ii. 1. Cf. 372. 1.

344. 2. 10. Matt. viii. 8.

345. 2. *Lip-labour*. Prov. xiv. 23.

345. 2. 2. *calfe without meale*. See Levit. ix. 3–4, where a bullock and ram for peace-offerings are associated with a meat-offering (meat = cakes of fine flour; see Levit. ii. 4). Herrick may also have remembered Hosea xiv. 2, 'the calves of our lips'.

346. 3. Tacitus, *Ann.* xiv. 10: 'perfecto demum scelere magnitudo ejus intellecta est'. Cf. Juvenal, xiii. 237–9 and G. Herbert, *Outlandish Proverbs* (*Works*, ed. Hutchinson, p. 352), 942: 'Sinnes are not knowne till they bee acted.'

346. 4. Perhaps the manner of George Herbert is here consciously adopted. See also 73. 2, 357. 4, 368. 1, and 369. 3.

347. 1. 3–4. Isa. xxix. 13. Jonson, *Epig.* xii, inveighs against the use of the expression 'God pays' by 'Lieutenant Shift'. Cf. Brainworm, *Every Man in his Humour*, II. v. 70 (Folio ed.).

347. 2. 4. *hold.* Keep your promise. Cf. *Sir Iohn Old-castle* (1600), Malone Soc., 1908, 797: 'say no more, but say, and hold'.

347. 3. 13–20. Cf. Jonson, *Volpone*, I. iv. 20–28: 'He ha's no faith in physick, &c.'

348, l. 30. Cf. Jonson, ibid. I. v. 35–36: 'I still interpreted the nods, he made (Through weakenesse) for consent.'

348, l. 38. *sins of . . . youth.* Ps. xxv. 6. Cf. 135, l. 120.

348, ll. 45–46. See 256. 2. 15–16 and note.

349. 2. 4. Rom. viii. 28.

349. 3. Heb. xii. 11.

349. 5. 7–9. Cf. Jonson, *Forest*, xi. 7–8:

we must plant a guard
Of thoughts to watch, and ward.

350, ll. 13–14. Ecclus. vi. 36. See 374, ll. 18–19; also 146. 1. 5 and note.

350, l. 22. *unflead.* Unskinned, e.g. by mice.

351. 1. 2. Ps. xxiii. 4. As in 394. 6. 2, Herrick misinterprets 'rod'.

351. 1. 7. Ps. xxvi. 2.

351. 3. 4. Hor. *Carm.* ii. 16. 27–28: 'nihil est ab omni parte beatum'; and cf. Ovid, *Met.* vii. 453–4: 'nulla est sincera voluptas &c.' See also 191. 5 and note.

352. 1. 4. See 51. 2. 3 and note.

352. 1. 5–6. See 355. 5. 5–6.

352. 1. 10. See 77. 2. 18 and note.

352. 1. 11–14. See 290. 5 and note.

353. 1. 1–2. Cf. Joshua xxiv. 15; 1 Kings xviii. 21.

353. 1. 3–4. Cf. Rev. iii. 15–16.

353. 2. Cf. 368. 2. 11–12.

353. 3. 1–3. Cf. Ps. lxxvii. 2, 4.

353. 3. 6–8. Cf. Ps. cii. 9.

354. 3. 4. *Rose of Sharon.* Song of Sol. ii. 1.

354. 3. 16. *mellifluous lips.* Song of Sol. iv. 11.

355. 3. *heading.* 1 Kings xxi. 10, &c.; 1 Pet. ii. 17.

355. 3. 2. See 322. 2. 2 and note; also 312. 5. 6.

355. 4. Prov. i. 26.

355. 5. 5–6. See 352. 1. 5–6. With l. 6 cf. Massinger, *The Renegado*, v. iii (ed. Gifford, 1813, ii, p. 220): 'I would not run but fly.'

356. 1. 1–2. Isa. lv. 10.

356. 1. 4. *fragments.* John vi. 12–13.

356. 1. 8. Luke vi. 38.

356. 3. 3–4. Cf. G. Herbert, 'Antiphon', ll. 11–12 (*Works*, ed. Hutchinson, p. 53):

But above all, the heart
Must bear the longest part.

See also 365, ll. 27–28.

356. 4. Cf. Seneca, *De Prov.* v. 1.

356. 5. 1. *seek of.* Try to learn about.

356. 6. 3–4. Ovid, *Ex Ponto*, iii. 4. 79:

Ut desint vires, tamen est laudanda voluntas.

Cf. Propertius, ii. 10. 5–6.

357. 1. 5. *cloud.* Cf. Ovid, *Ars Am.* ii. 619: 'quiddam nubis opacae'; and Hor. *Ep.* i. 16. 62: 'fraudibus obice nubem'.

357. 1. 7–8. Job xxiv. 15: 'No eye shall see me.'

357. 1. 9. Deut. xvi. 19: 'neither take a gift: for a gift doth blind the eyes of the wise, and pervert the words of the righteous'. See Tilley, *Prov. Eng.*, G105: 'Gifts blind the eyes.'

358, ll. 9–10. Hor. *Ep.* i. 6. 45:

exilis domus est ubi non et multa supersunt.

358. 2. Herrick could have had two or three of Quarles's *Emblems* (1635) in mind when writing this: Book I. xiv, on Ps. xiii. 3, 'Lighten mine eyes, O Lord'; Book III. i, on Isa. xxvi. 9, 'My soul hath desired thee in the night'; and (for ll. 14–15) Book IV. viii, on Song of Sol. i. 3–4, 'Draw me; we will follow [*or* run] after thee by the favour of thy good Oyntments.'

358. 2. 9. Ps. xli. 3.

358. 2. 10–11. Ps. xiii. 3; xviii. 28.

358. 2. 12. Ps. cxliii. 8; v. 3.

359. 1. See 175, ll. 61–64 and note.

359. 3. 1. *Ere hence we goe.* Ps. xxxix. 15.

360, l. 30. Cf. Burton, 2. 2. 1. 2 (p. 237): '*excessit medicina malum*, the physick is more troublesome then the disease'.

360, l. 38. *Haires.* See 219. 1. 3 and note.

361, l. 76. *Male-Incense.* See 277. 5. 4 and note.

361. 1. 1. *Harp, and Violl.* Isa. v. 12.

361. 1. 2. Ps. cxxxvii. 2.

361. 1. 3–4. Job xvii. 13.

362. 1. 2. Tacitus, *Agric.* 3: 'invisa primo desidia postremo amatur'. Cf. Daniel, *Rosamond*, st. 65.

362. 2. Cf. Hor. *Carm.* iii. 2. 31–32: 'Raro antecedentem scelestum &c.' Quoted by Burton, 2. 3. 7 (p. 349). See *O.D.E. Prov.*, 'Punishment is lame, &c.'; also Wisd. of Sol. xiv. 31 (Vulg.): 'peccantium poena perambulat semper iniustorum praeuaricationem'.

362. 3. 3. Cf. Featley, *Clavis Mystica*, 1636, p. 750: 'whatsoever is in God is God: for he is a simple act, and his qualities or attributes are not *re ipsâ* distinct from his essence'; and Bishop John Davenant, *On Colossians* (ii. 3), 1639, p. 166: 'proprietates Divinitatis non sunt accidentia, sed ipsa Dei essentia'. See also 378. 6 and 382. 4.

362. 4. 2. 2 Cor. v. 7, 5; 2 Esdras i. 37.

362. 5. 4. Prov. iii. 34: 'he giveth grace unto the lowly'. Cf. 1 Pet. v. 5.

362. 6. 1. Perhaps a reminiscence of *Twelfth Night*, II. iii. 51: 'Present mirth hath present laughter.'

363. 1. Cf. Jonson, *Und.* 1. 2 (*Works*, viii, p. 129).

363. 1. 13. *Feare.* Frighten.

363. 2. 7–8. Cf. 361, ll. 71–72. In Isa. xlviii. 18 and lxvi. 12 peace is likened to a river.

365. 1. 10. See 86, l. 38.

366. 1. 1. See 91, l. 43 and note.

366. 1. 3. 1 Cor. v. 8.

366. 1. 4. *holy ground.* Exod. iii. 5; Acts vii. 33.

366. 1. 13. *blush to death.* See 301. 2. 4 and note.

367, ll. 27–30. Referring to the King (l. 26). He is to treble his present years before he dies, and then to be reincarnated in his son.

367. 3. See 383. 4 and note. St. Aug. *De Civ. Dei*, xi. 22 (*Opera*, Migne, vii, col. 335): 'cum omnino natura nulla sit malum, nomenque hoc non sit nisi privationis boni'.

368, l. 18. Luke ii. 21.

368, l. 23. *treble Honours.* The gifts of gold, frankincense, and myrrh.

368. 1. 2. Ovid, *Fasti*, iv. 731: 'virginea . . . ara'.

368. 2. 11–12. Cf. 353. 2.

368. 2. 13–18. *Greek Anth.* x. 108. Cf. 'Plato', *Alcibiades*, ii (Loeb, p. 244). Translated again in *Spectator*, 207.

369. 1. 1. Acts iii. 6.

369. 1. 2. See 356. 6. 3–4 and note.

369. 1. 3–4. Cf. Ovid, *Ex Ponto*, iii. 4. 81–82.

369. 2. 8. *long white stole.* Cf. 286. 4. 6 and Ovid, *Fasti*, vi, 654: 'stola longa'.

370. 1. The thought as a whole is derived from Seneca, *De Prov.* iii. 4: 'idem facit fortuna . . . Catone'. Transl. Lodge: 'The like doth fortune, she seeketh for the strongest to match her, some passeth she ouer with a scorne, she attempteth the most confident and couragious sort of men . . . she tryeth her fire vpon *Mutius*, pouertie in *Fabricius*, banishment in *Rutilus*, torments in *Regulus* [sc. Atilius], poyson in *Socrates*, death in *Cato*.' Herrick omits Rutilus and introduces Scaeva and Horatius Cocles. S. Daniel draws upon this of Seneca in 'To Henry Wriothesly', sts. iii and vii. Cf. 148, ll. 112–14.

370. 1. 1. *God . . . wantons.* Seneca, *De Prov.* i. 6: '[Deus] bonum virum in deliciis non habet.' Transl. Lodge: 'He maketh not a good man a wanton.'

370. 1. 2. Cf. Seneca, op cit. iv. 8: 'dux lectissimos mittit, &c.'

370. 1. 11. *bastard-slips.* See 278. 2. 3 and note. Cf. Heb. xii. 8.

370. 2. 2. Cf. Virgil, *Aen.* x. 887.

370. 3. See note to 175, ll. 61–64. Cf. St. Aug. *Confess.* vii. 3 (Loeb, i, p. 343).

371. 1. 1. See 272. 5 and note. Ovid, *Trist.* iii. 7. 46:

Raptaque sint, adimi quae potuere mihi.

371. 2. 5–6. Cf. Bacon, *Adv. of Learning*, II. i. 4: 'the sun, which passeth through pollutions and itself remains as pure as before'. *immortal Eye.* Cf. Plutarch, *Morals*, transl. Holland, 1603, p. 603: '*that great immortall eie* . . .'.

372. 1. See 370. 1 and note; also 344. 1 and note.

372. 2. 1. *soundlesse pit.* Jonson, *Und.* lxxxiv. 4. 11.

372. 3. 5. Isa. xliii. 19.

372. 4. 2 Cor. iv. 17.

372. 5. 2. Acts xvi. 33.

373. 1. 12. *without Thee.* Without Thy permission.

373. 2. *heading.* Acts ix. 36 sqq.

373. 2. 2. Ps. cxxxvii. 2.

374, ll. 18–19. See 350, ll. 13–14 and note.

374, l. 34. *Lordly dish.* Judges v. 25.

374, l. 41. *Reaming.* 'Stretching out in threads; ropy; forming masses of filaments' (*O.E.D.* art. 'Reaming', *ppl. a.*[1]).

374, l. 43. Acts ix. 39. See also ll. 82–83.

374, ll. 45–46. Prov. xxxi. 18: 'her candle goeth not out by night'.

375, ll. 54–56. Song of Sol. iv. 13–14. Quoted by Burton, 3. 4. 1. 1 (p. 635).

375, l. 74. Ps. xlv. 3; Prov. xxii. 11.

375, ll. 77–80. Song of Sol. vii. 2.

375, ll. 88–90. Luke xix. 40.

376. 1. 4–6. Cf. 332. 3 and Donne, *LXXX Sermons* (1640), Serm. xiii, p. 129*a*: '*Iob* . . . said grace when he had no meat.'

376. 3. 2. 1 Cor. vi. 2–3.

376. 4. 5–6. Luke iii. 11; Matt. x. 10.

376. 4. 7–8. The poor man is made to halve each loaf (or separate two loaves joined together), Herrick reserving the right to choose which he will keep.

376. 5. Metre as in Jonson, *Gypsies Metamorphos'd*, ll. 496–9 sqq. (*Works*, vii, pp. 581–2.)

377, ll. 20, 24. Jonson, op. cit., ll. 395, 398, rhymes 'attendinge' and 'endinge'.

377. 2. 4. *wave-offring.* Exod. xxix. 24, &c. Herrick makes 'wave' refer also to the movement of the boiling water. Cf. 397. 4.

378. 3. Cf. Calvin, *Comment. in Matt.* xvi. 28: 'Scimus quam vere dicatur vulgari proverbio, in desiderio celeritatem quoque moram esse'; and Sallust, *Jugurtha*, 64. 6: 'animo cupienti nihil satis festinatur.'

378. 4. St. Aug. *Enarr. in Ps. xxxi.* ii. 26 (*Opera*, Migne, iv, col. 274): 'Etiam Unicus sine peccato, non tamen sine flagello.' Quoted by Burton, 2. 3. 1. 1 (p. 307) with transl. 'God . . . hath one son without sin, none without correction.'

378. 5. 2. Cf. Collect for 12th Sunday after Trinity: '. . . and art wont to give more than either we desire, or deserve'.

378. 6. See 362. 3. 3 and note.

378. 8. 2. 'Saturitas' or fullness of bread, as in Ezek. xvi. 49.

379. 1. Rev. vii. 17, xxi. 4; Isa. xxv. 8.

379. 5. 3. Ps. lxxxii. 6: 'I have said, Ye are gods.'

379. 7. Cf. St. Aug. *Enarr. in Ps. cxxvii.* 10 (*Opera*, Migne, iv, col. 1683): 'Dulciores sunt lacrymae orantium, quam gaudia theatrorum.'

379. 8. Wisd. of Sol. xvi. 20–21.

380. 1. From Cassiodorus, *Expos. in Ps. xxxiv.* 30 (*Opera*, Migne, ii, col. 250): '*Reverentia* est enim Domini timor cum amore permixtus.'

380. 2. Pausanias, *Attica*, i. 17. 1, speaks of the altar to Mercy in the market-place at Athens.

380. 4. 1–2. St. Aug. *Epistolae*, ccv, 'Ad Consentium', 16 (*Opera*, Migne, ii, col. 947–8), quotes Jas. i. 13 and refers to 'tentatio probationis'. Cf. 389. 5 and 390. 1 and 2.

380. 6. 2. *Forum . . . Vineyard.* Matt. xx. 3–4 (Vulg.): 'in foro . . . in vineam'.

380. 7. *heading*, &c. Maldonatus, *Comm. in Matt. xxv* (1617, col. 285): 'Hieronymus & Hilarius moram sponsi poenitentiae tempus esse dicunt.'

380. 8. *Roaring.* Ps. xxxviii. 8; also xxxii. 3 in A.V.

380. 8. 1. *weeping part.* Act of weeping. See *O.E.D.* s.v. 'Part', *sb.* 11.

381. 3. St. Aug. *Enarr. in Ps. xxxix.* 6 (*Opera*, Migne, iv, col. 437): 'intelligimus montes, claros quosque et magnos Ecclesiae spirituales viros'. *Enarr. in Ps. cxxiv.* 4 (ibid., col. 1650): 'montes . . . sive Angeli, sive Apostoli, sive Prophetae'.

381. 4. 3. 1 Cor. xii. 31.

381. 5. 2. *sheeps dispersion.* Matt. xxvi. 31.

381. 7. Cf. St. John of Damascus, *De Fide Orthodoxa*, i. 9 (Basle, 1548, i. 12, p. 47): 'ueluti quoddam pelagus substantiae infinitum, & interminum'. (*Opera*, Migne, i, cols. 835–6.)

382. 1. *Clouds.* Acts i. 9; Rev. i. 7.

382. 3. Cf. Burton, 3. 4. 1. 1 (p. 634): '*Coelum pulchrum, sed pulchrior coeli fabricator*, if heaven be so faire, the sunne so faire, how much fairer shall he be, that made them faire?'

382. 4. See 362. 3. 3 and note; also 378. 6.

382. 6. 2. Cf. J. Gregory, op. cit. in note on 162. 3; ch. ii, p. 5: '*Our Saviour . . . in that great case of dereliction.*'

382. 7. See 343. 2 and note. Cf. Boethius, *De Trinitate*, 3 (*Opera*, Migne, ii, col. 1251): 'Ubi vero nulla est differentia, nulla est omnino pluralitas, quare nec numerus.'

382. 8. *heading.* Ezra ix. 7; Jer. vii. 19; Dan. ix. 7, 8.

382. 8 and 383. 1. Cf. Cassiodorus, *Expos. in Ps. xxxiii.* 5 (*Opera*, Migne, ii, col. 235): '*Vultus* autem . . . significat praesentiam, quae potest mutato colore confusionem pati, si ei coelestia munera subducantur . . . *Erubescere* . . . decepti est, qui ad sua desideria non valet pervenire.'

383. 1. *shame* . . . *face*. Ps. xliv. 16.

383. 2. 1. *Jacob* . . . *Beggar*. Gen. xxxii. 26.

383. 4. See 367. 3 and note. Cf. Aquinas, *Cont. Gent.* ii. 41. 6: 'malum . . . inquantum est malum, est non ens'.

383. 5. 1. Luke x. 41. St. Aug. *Serm.* ciii. 2 (*Opera*, Migne, v, col. 614): 'Repetitio nominis indicium est dilectionis.'

383. 8. Cf. J. Gregory, op. cit., p. 75: 'The Scholiast *Psellus* . . . *The Chaldaean Paradise* (saith he) *is a Quire of divine powers incircling the Father.*'

384. 1. Cf. Gregory, op. cit., f. *3v (To the Reader): 'The Jewes when they build a house are bound to leave some part of it unfinished in memory of the destruction of *Jerusalem*.'

384. 3. Gregory, op. cit., pp. 24–27 (chap. iv) under running-title '*Sitting and Silence*', explains Jewish mourning customs and the Jewish and Roman laws forbidding lamentation in capital causes. 'This is to tell the reason why the *Blessed Virgin* and the other Women which *stood* afarre off, (as the other Gospells) or neare . . . were not to make any solemne, usuall shew of Lamentation. The Mother of Jesus must needs be reduced to the Extreamest state of sadnesse and contristation. . . . But *She* stood up still in a resolute and allmost impossible complyance with the Law. . . . 'Twas necessary. And they might not sit downe in that case . . . They were to stand, as by the wrong posture to free the Company from any suspicion of Mourning for a Malefactour.

'Tis true indeed that we read of *Mary Magdalen*, and the other *Mary*, sitting over against the Sepulchre, and they *sate* there to mourne over the dead, . . . but this was after leave obtained of the Governour to bury the body. This leave vouchsafed . . ., the two *Maries* might *sit* downe and weepe over the Sepulcher in the open and usuall manner.'

384. 3. 7–8. Mark xv. 47; Matt. xxvii. 61.

384. 4. Cf. Gregory, op. cit., p. 111 (chap. xxii) under running-title 'Light' and with reference to white apparel: 'The funerall Tapers . . . are of the same harmlesse Import . . . to shew, that the departed soules are not quite put out, but having walked here as the children of the *Light*, are now gone to walke before God in the *Light* of the *Living*.'

384. 4. 4–5. Rev. iii. 4.

385. 1. 3–4. Cf. 167, ll. 106–7.

385. 2. Cf. Gregory, op. cit., p. 135 (chap. xxxi, 'Isay. 57. 15'): 'All things are full of God. He is therefore called . . . *Hammakom, the Place*. Or that Fulnesse which filleth *All* in *All*.' See also 394. 2.

385. 2. 2. Eph. i. 23.

385. 3. Cf. Gregory, loc. cit., pp. 137–8: 'Thus God is said to be nearer to this man then to that, more in one place then in another. Thus he is said to depart from some and come to others, to leave this place & to abide in that, not by Essential application of himselfe, (much lesse by locall motion) but by Impression of Effect.' See also 387. 1, 388. 4, and 394. 2.

385. 4. Cf. Gregory, loc. cit., p. 138: 'As he is to all & in all places, he is called in the Holy Tongue, *Jehovah*, *He* that is, or Essence.'

385. 5. Cf. Gregory, loc. cit, p. 138: 'With just men, saith he [sc. St. Bernard], God is present, *in veritate*, In deed, but with the wicked, dissemblingly, ('tis the Fathers expression) *in dissimulatione*.'

385. 6. Cf. Gregory, loc. cit., p. 138: '*He is said to dwell there* (saith *Maimon*) *where he putteth the markes or evidences of his Majesty and presence*. And he doth this by his *Grace* and *Holy Spirit*.'

385. 7. Cf. Gregory, op. cit., p. 86 (chap. xviii) under running-title 'Oriens Nomen ejus': 'So Saint *Ephrem* upon those words of *Jacob*, this is the house of God and this is the Gate of Heaven. *This saying* (saith he) *is to be meant of the Virgin Mary, who became as it were another Heaven, truly to be call'd the House of God, as wherein the Son of God that immortall word inhabited; and as truely the Gate of Heaven, for the Lord of Heaven and Earth entered thereat; and it shall not be set open the second time, according to that of* Ezekiel *the Prophet*. And I saw (saith he) *a Gate in the East. the glorious Lord entered thereat, thenceforth that Gate was shut, and is not any more againe to be opened. Caten*: *Arab*: C: 58.'

386. 2. Luke vii. 44; John xx. 16. Cf. St. Ambrose, *Expos. in Lucam*, x. 161 sqq. (*Opera*, Migne, i, cols. 1938–9 (on Luke xxiv. 1–4).

386. 3. See note to 162. 3. The passage from Gregory there quoted continues: 'And yet all this . . . is none of the right reason why the Iewes place their Beds North and South. They are bound to place their *Beth Haccisse*, or house of office, in the very same situation . . . the reason of the last is the reason of the first . . . *That the uncomely Necessities of Nature . . . might not fall into the Walke and Wayes of God, whose Shecina or dwelling presence lyeth West and East, &c.*'

386. 4. 2 *and* 4. Cf. St. Aug. *Serm.* ccclxiii. 27 (*Opera*, Migne, v, col. 1631): 'Sabbatum erit perpetuum, quod a Judaeis celebratur temporaliter, a nobis autem in aeternum intelligitur.'

386. 4. 3. Cf. id., *Serm.* cclxx. 5 (Migne, v, col. 1242): 'ille vere observat sabbatum, qui non peccat'.

386. 5. Cf. Gregory, op. cit., p. 28 (chap. vi, 'Noah's *Lent*'): '*Noah* and his Sonnes (so I finde it in the Easterne Traditions) *kept a Solemne Fast, taking meat but once a day, . . . And* Noah *was the first who made the* 40 *dayes Holy*, (or instituted the *Quadragesimall* Fast) *in the Arke, Caten. Arabica. Cap.* 24.'

386. 6. Gen. l. 20.

387. 1. See 385. 3 and note.

387. 2. 2 Esdras viii. 1; Matt. xx. 16, &c.

387. 5. Cf. Burton, 2. 3. 3 (p. 316): '*Dantur quidem bonis*, saith *Austin*, *ne quis mala aestimet, malis autem ne quis nimis bona*, good men have wealth that we should not think it evill; and bad men that they should not rely on or hold it so good.' Cf. Seneca, *De Prov.* v. 1.

387. 6. Cf. St. Basil, *Homil. in Ps. xxviii* (*Opera*, Paris, 1618, i, p. 176): 'duo sunt in igne potissima, vstiua vis & illustratoria . . .' (*Opera*, Migne, i, cols. 297–8.)

387. 7. Cf. Gregory, op. cit., p. 118 (chap. xxv, 'Heb. 12. 24'): 'But did the bloud of *Abel* speake saith *Theophylact*? Yes. It cryed unto God for vengeance, as that of sprinckling for Propitiation, and Mercy.'

388. 1. Cf. Gregory, loc. cit., p. 118: 'And the Bloud of *Abel* was so Holy and Reverend a thing, in the sence and Reputation of the old World . . . that the men of that time used to sweare by it.'

388. 2. Cf. Gregory, op. cit., p. 134 (chap. xxx, 'Luke 15. 10'): 'The words have a reflexe upon that old position in the Hebrew Divinity . . . *That a Repenting man is of greater esteeme in the sight of God, then one that never fell away.*'

388. 3. Cf. Gregory, loc. cit., p. 135: 'The Doctours in the *Talmud* say . . . *That one day spent here in true Repentance, is more worth then Eternity it selfe, or all the dayes of Heaven in the other world.*'

388. 4. See 385. 2 and 385. 3 and notes; and cf. Gregory, loc. cit., pp. 135–6: 'He is there where Nothing else is, and Nothing else is there where He is not . . . *God* . . . by his *presence*, *power*, and *Essence*, immutably existeth in every *Nature* and *Being*, . . . He is otherwise and more excellently present with Saints and Holy Men, by his *Grace* and *Holy Spirit*. But most of all and most excellently present by *Union Hypostaticall*, in the second person in whom the *Fulnesse of the Godhead dwelleth bodily*, *&c.*'

388. 5. Cf. Gregory, op. cit., pp. 128–9 (chap. xxvii, '1 *Cor.* 15. 36'), transl. from 'Mathaeus Blastares *Hieromonach*[*us*] *Gr. MS. in Arch. Baroccian. Bib. Bod.*'; 'And how should all these stalkes grow up from one graine *of corne, and that as good as dead? The wonder of this is farre above that of the Resurrection of our bodies, for then the Earth giveth up her dead but one for one, but in the case of the Corne she giveth up many living ones for one dead one.*'

389. 3. Cf. G. Fletcher, *Christ's Victory and Triumph*, iii, st. 26:

> Ah me! how dearly God his servant buys!
> For God His man at His own blood doth hold,
> And man his God for thirty pence hath sold.

389. 5. Cf. 380 4. 1–2 and note.

389. 8. See 175, ll. 61–64 and note. Cf. St. Aug. *De Vera Relig.*, i. 14 (*Opera*, Migne, iii, col. 133): 'Usque adeo peccatum voluntarium est malum, ut nullo modo sit peccatum, si non sit voluntarium.'

390. 1 *and* 2. See 380. 4. 1–2 and note; also 389. 5.

390. 6. The four keys are traditional and originate in Rabbinical literature. See, for example, footnote to an article by E. Tew in *N. and Q.*, 5th S., 1877, viii, p. 130. The accounts vary, though 'rain' (Deut. xi. 17), 'grave' or 'tomb' (1 Sam. ii. 6), and 'womb' (Gen. xxx. 22) seem fairly constant. For Herrick the keys of Hell, womb, and tomb would of course have Christian associations as well, supplied, e.g., by Rev. i. 18: 'I am alive for evermore, Amen; and have the keys of hell and of death.'

391. 3. Cf. Isa. lviii. 3–7.

391. 3. 20. Acts vii. 51; Rom. ii. 29.

391. 3. 21. Joel ii. 13.

391. 3. 22. Cf. G. Herbert, 'Lent', ll. 43–44 (*Works*, ed. Hutchinson, p. 87):

Yet Lord instruct us to improve our fast
By starving sinne . . .

392. 2. 11–20. Cf. Hor. *Ep.* i. 4. 13:

omnem crede diem tibi diluxisse supremum.

392. 2. 16–20. Cf. Browne, *Rel. Med.*, 1642, p. 182:

Sleepe is a death, O make me try,
By sleeping what it is to die.
And downe as gently lay my head
On my Grave, as now my bed.

392. 2. 31–32. See 175, ll. 61–64 and note.

393. 1. 1. Isa. xxiii. 18: 'durable clothing'; Luke xii. 33.

393. 1. 3–4. Luke, ibid.; Matt. vi. 19.

393. 2. 5. *Mountaine.* Exod. xix. 18.

393. 5. Ezra ix. 13.

394. 1. 3–4. Cf. Burton, 1. 2. 3. 10 (p. 109): 'Even in the midst of all our mirth, jollity, and laughter, is sorrow and griefe.' See 264. 6 and 416. 1. 17–18.

394. 4. Cf. Gregory, op. cit., p. 59 (chap. xiv, '*Mat*: 6. 1'): 'The poore indeed in Scripture are called *Domini bonorum nostrorum. Prov.* 3. 27. *Withhold not good from them to whom it is due* . . . And therefore to give to the poore is but *suum cuique tribuere. Aristotles Justice.*' Donne, *LXXX Sermons*, 1640, Serm. ix, p. 94 B: 'S. *Bernard* sayes truly, in the . . . person of the poore, to wastfull men . . . you are prodigall of that which is not your own, but ours.'

394. 6. 3. Incorrect interpretation of 'rod' in Ps. xxiii. 4. Cf. 351. 2. 2 and 398. 1. 4.

394. 7. See 343. 1 and note; also 341. 2.

395. 1. St. Aug. *Enarr. in Ps. xxix*, ii. 19 (*Opera*, Migne, iv, col. 225): 'Confessio gemina est, aut peccati, aut laudis.'

395. 2. St. Aug. *De Civ. Dei*, xvi. 5 (*Opera*, Migne, vii, col. 483): 'descendere dicitur, cum aliquid facit in terra, quod praeter usitatum naturae cursum mirabiliter factum, praesentiam quodammodo ejus ostendat.'

395. 3. 1. *Good and great God!* So Jonson begins *Forest*, xv.

395. 3. 4. *plead my cause.* Ps. xxxv. 1.

395. 5. St. Aug. *Enarr. in Ps. ci (cii)*, ii. 7 (*Opera*, Migne, iv, col. 1308): 'Non enim laus fidei Christianorum est, quia credunt mortuum

Christum; sed quia credunt resurrexisse Christum. Nam mortuum et paganus credit.' Cf. *Enarr. in Ps. cxx* (cxxi), 6 (ibid., col. 1609); and Donne, *LXXX Sermons*, 1640, Serm. xviii, p. 180 C.

396. 1. Cf. Caryl, *Comm. on Job*, iii. 6, 'let it not be joined &c.' (1676, i, col. 193, but the Comm. on chapters 1–3 was published in 1643): 'The *Rabbins* have a conceit, why after the work of the second day was finished, God (beholding what he had done) did not add any approbation to it . . . by saying it was good; The reason . . . was this, because then was the first disunion . . . that ever was, *All before was one, (sub unissimo Deo) under the one-most God*; I shall leave this fancy to the *Rabbins*. But there is somewhat in the notion it self, namely, that division and disunion are the evils of the creature.'

396. 2. A. Willet, *Synopsis Papismi*, 1614, p. 858, quotes the short treatise formerly attributed to St. Augustine, *De predestinatione et gratia*, 4: '*Indurare Deus dicitur, quem mollire noluerit*: God is said to harden, whom he will not mollifie.' (St. Aug., *Opera*, Migne, x, col. 1668.)

396. 3. St. Basil, *Hexaemeron*, v, 'De germinatione terrae', 45 (*Opera*, Migne, i, col. 106): 'Verum rosa tunc spinis carebat . . .' St. Ambrose, *Hexaemeron*, iii. 11, 'De ortu arborum' (*Opera*, Migne, i. col. 188): 'Surrexerat ante floribus immista terrenis sine spinis rosa . . .'

396. 4. 4. Virgil, *Aen.* i. 199: 'dabit deus his quoque finem'.

396. 5. 2. 1 Pet. iii. 21. Cf. Donne, *LXXX Sermons*, 1640, Serm. xxxi, pp. 309 E to 310 A (with reference to St. Augustine): 'In Baptisme . . . our corrupt affections, and our inordinate love of this world is that, that is to be drowned in us . . .'

396. 6. Cf. St. Ambrose, *Expos. in Lucam*, Lib. ii. 44 (*Opera*, Migne, i, col. 1650): 'Aurum regi, thus Deo.'

397. 2. Herrick's interpretation of Lev. xi. 3–7 differs from that which A. Willet, in *Synopsis Papismi* (1614, B2^{v}), quotes from St. Aug.: 'He diuideth the hoofe, that diuideth and discerneth what is good, and what euill: and they chaw the cud, that do meditate of that, which they heare out of the word.' Cf. Hall, *Meditations*, ii. 51: 'He, that says well and doth well, is without exception commendable: but, if one of these must be severed from the other, I like him well that doth well, and saith nothing.'

397. 4. 2. *Levell-Coyle*. Game. See 311. 6. 2 and note.

397. 4. 3. *Wave*. See 377. 2. 4 and note.

397. 4. 4. *Heave-offering*. Num. xv. 20; xviii. 11. Herrick, as Pollard suggested, thinks of the pot being lifted off the fire.

397. 5. Cf. 340. 4. Montaigne, ii. 12, cites Cicero, *De Nat. Deor.* i. 17: 'Neque gratia, neque ira teneri potest' (*Tudor Trans.*, p. 204).

398. 1. 6. Rom. v. 20.

398. 3. 1. *Robe of Purple*. Mark xv. 20.

398. 3. 3. *houre is come*. John xiii. 1.

398. 3. 5–6. Cf. Burton, 3. 4. 1. 2 (p. 651): 'a rude, inconstant multitude'.

398. 3. 12. *Skurfe and Bran.* The common people. See note on 79, l. 88 and Jonson, *Tale of a Tub*, III. ix. 14: 'Then *Turfe*, or *Scurfe*, high, or low Constable.'

400. 1. 1–2. Lam. i. 12.

400. 1. 11. Rev. xvi. 19.

400. 2. 7–9. Isa. li. 17; Jer. xxv. 15.

402. 1. 3. Exod. iii. 5; Joshua v. 15.

403. 1. 1. John xx. 15.

403 (*final couplet*). Rev. i. 8, xxii. 13.

ADDITIONAL POEMS

404. 1. This poem, also attributed to 'R: W' (see Critical Notes, p. 493), is possibly a development from Jonson's 'Charis', 5 (*Und.* ii).

404. 1. 5. Cf. Burton, 3. 2. 2. 2 (p. 459): 'An high brow like unto the bright heavens.' But much of the description is conventional.

404. 1. 8. *flattring vine.* See 120, l. 48.

404. 1. 27. *Whose . . . perfume.* See 102. 1. 4.

404. 1. 29. *tongue . . . small.* Jas. iii. 5.

405, l. 33. Cf. 138. 1. 4, and Burton, loc. cit.: 'dimple in the chinne'.

405, ll. 41–42. Cf. Aemil. Magn. Arborius, *Ad Nympham Nimis Cultam*, 24: 'Quum teretes digiti dent pretium lapidi.' (*Poetae Lat. Min.*, ed. Lemaire, ii.)

405, l. 55. *the milky vally.* Cf. Burton, ibid.: 'and make a pleasant valley *lacteum sinum*, between two chaulkie hills'.

405, l. 57. *sleeded or sleued.* Sleaved silk was silk separated into its filaments (floss-silk). The ppl. 'sleyd' is recorded. See *O.E.D.*, s.vv. Sleave, *sb.* and *v.*

405, l. 58. See 74. 2. 7–9.

405, l. 60. *Riphean snowe.* Virgil, *Georg.* iv. 518.

405, l. 66. *prominent.* Substantive, in the obsolete sense of eminence, protrusion.

405, l. 67. *milky high waye.* Cf. Burton, loc. cit. (of the neck): 'that *via lactea*'.

405, l. 70. Cf. Marlowe, *Hero and Leander*, ii. 298.

406, l. 79. See 139. 2. 2.

406, l. 87. *silver tride.* Ps. lxvi. 9.

406, l. 94. See 113, l. 24: 'pounded Cynamon'.

406, ll. 105–8. Cf. Carew, 'Epitaph on the Lady S.', ll. 1–3. For the doctrine see e.g. Cicero, *De Re Publica*, ii. 42. 69.

407. 1. In MS. Harvard Eng. 626 F (see Critical Notes) this poem occurs between 'His age' (132. 3) and 'The parting Verse' (174. 1).

407. 1. 1–2. Ps. xxxix. 15.

407. 1. 10–11. See 129, ll. 11–12.

407. 1. 13–14. See 200. 2. 7–8.

407. 1. 16. *Prophetique Bayes.* See 79, l. 92: 'Prophetique Daphne.'

407. 1. 30–31. See 173, l. 11.

408, l. 44. *bedd of spice*. Cf. 274. 2. 1 and 361, l. 61.

408, ll. 50–51. See 165. 1. 10: 'Cherry harvest'; and 419. 2. 8.

408, l. 54. See 416. 1. 7–8 and note.

408, ll. 54–55. Ps. lv. 22.

408, l. 59. *White*. The reading 'With' might be a misreading of the form 'Whith'.

408, l. 59. *handes as smooth*. See 380. 5. 1.

408, l. 64. Cf. Milton, *Samson*, 270–1. See 64. 3. 9–12.

409, l. 95. *Wise=Distrust*. See 67. 2. 2. *shey*. Shy.

410. 1. See Introduction, p. xxxvii.

410. 1. 17. *Bell-man of the Night*. See 207, l. 62, and 349. 1. 1.

410. 1. 18. *Noone of night*. See 225. 1. 18 and note.

410. 1. 21–22. *ode* (= *odd*) *Number*. Cf. Jonson, *Pleasure Reconcil'd*, l. 32 (*Works*, viii, p. 480):

> & emptier of cups, be they euen, or od—

and Plutarch, *Symposiacs*, iii. 9 (Holland, 1603, p. 695): 'What is the meaning of the common proverbe: Drinke either five, or three, but not fower?' *Nyne*. See note to 127, l. 32. *full with God*. Cf. Featley, *Clavis Mystica*, p. 544: 'the soule that is full of God, and full with God'; and Hor. *Carm*. ii. 19. 6: 'plenoque Bacchi pectore'.

410. 1. 27. *Crownd with Rose Budds*. See 127, l. 41 and note.

411, ll. 35–46. See 85. 1. 9–16 and note; also 210. 5. 1–2 and 313. 3. 3–4.

411, l. 43. *Holde . . . fiers*. See 198. 1. 3.

411, l. 54. See 308. 3. 2 and note.

411, ll. 55–56. See 35, ll. 19–20 and notes.

411, l. 56. *In Conceipt bee ritch*. Cf. Burton, 2. 3. 3 (p. 324): 'I have a little wealth . . . sed quas animus magnas facit, a kingdome in conceit.' See also Seneca, *Ep*. i. 5 and elsewhere.

411, l. 59. *Guesse*. Guest (see *O.E.D.*). W. C. Hazlitt's emendation to 'Kisse', approved by other editors, is not necessary.

411, l. 66. See 233. 1. 39, &c.

411, l. 71. *the Grecian Oratour*. Cf. Plutarch, *Demosthenes*, 26 (*Tudor Trans*. v, p. 307): 'oftentimes he would cast his eyes towards the contrie of Attica, and weepe bitterly'.

412, l. 75. *Tullye*. Plutarch, *Cicero* (loc. cit., p. 347): '. . . but cast his eyes still towardes Italy.'

412, l. 84. *Hoofy*. Referring to Pegasus. Cf. Jos. Hall, *Satires*, i. 2. 29: 'the hors-hoofed well'.

412, l. 90. *Base Ballad=mongers*. Cf. 155. 1. 5–12.

412, l. 100. *Hand-mayde*. Cf. Featley, *Clavis Mystica*, p. 149: 'The Arts are holy in their use onely, which is to attend upon sacred knowledge . . . humane arts and sciences . . . to be *hand-maids* to the sacred and saving science of *Divinity*.'

412, ll. 103–4. Cf. Montaigne, ii. 16 (*Tudor Trans*., p. 360: 'The reward of well doing, is the doing &c.' (from Seneca, *Ep*. lxxxi. 19). See also Burton, 2. 3. 7 (pp. 351–2).

413. 1. See 52. 2. heading and note. Apparently written when Williams was released.

413. 1. 2. *fled December*. See 127, l. 38 and note.

413. 1. 13–14. Cf. Burton, 2. 3. 3 (p. 331): 'A wise mans minde as *Seneca* holds, *is like the state of the world above the moone, ever serene*,' and Marcellus Palingenius, *Zodiacus Vitae*, viii. 249 and ix. 180–1:

Supra autem lunam, lucis sunt omnia plena . . .
Omne quod est supra lunam, aeternumque bonumque
Esse scias, nec triste aliquid coelestia tangit.

413. 1. 20. See 25. 2. 1.

414. 2. 8. *coole it with a teare*. See 50. 2. 10 and 269. 1. 6.

414. 2. 9. *Since . . . retire*. See 324, l. 22; and cf. Drayton, *Idea*, 61: 'Since there's no help, &c.'

415. 1. 1. Cf. Ovid, *Rem. Am.* 705: 'Phoebus adest. sonuere lyrae.'

415. 1. 2. See 80. 2. 5 and note.

415. 1. 6. See 45. 1. 36 and note.

415. 1. 9–10. See 76, ll. 50–51, and 287. 2.

415. 1. 11. *Evadne*. See 206, l. 53 and note.

416. 1. *heading*. *Lord Hastings*. Son of the sixth Earl of Huntingdon. He died 24 June 1649, aged 19, just before he was to have married Elizabeth, daughter of Sir Theodore Turquet de Mayerne, physician. She afterwards married Pierre de Caumont, Marquis de Cugnac, but died herself in 1653 at the age of 20. See *Letters of Dorothy Osborne*, ed. G. C. Moore Smith, p. 67. For the form of this poem see 248. 1 and note.

416. 1. 7–8. Cf. 408, ll. 54–55; also Propertius, iv. 7. 60.

416. 1. 17–18. See 264. 6 and 394. 1. 3–4.

417, l. 29. Cf. Virgil, *Aen.* vi. 665.

417, l. 36. Cf. Fairfax, *Tasso*, xviii. 48. 3 (1624, p. 325): 'And from that floud which nine times compast hell.'

417. 1. *heading*. *Jemmonia Walgrave*. Appears in *Visitation of Essex* for 1612 (Harl. Soc. i, p. 309), as 'Jeminath unmar.' d. of 'Edward Waldegrave of Lawforde in com. Essex Esquier'. She married John Crew at Lawford in 1622 (Boyd's Marriage Index, Soc. of Genealogists). Her husband was a cousin of Herrick's friend Clipseby Crew, and afterwards first Baron Crew of Stene. See John Crew and his father, Sir Thomas Crew, in *D.N.B.*, where Jemmonia or Jeminath appears as Jemimah. Boyd gives the form 'Jemima'. One of her six sons was Nathaniel Crew, Bishop of Durham 1674 (q.v., *D.N.B.*); the elder of her two daughters, Jemimah, married Sir Edward Montagu or Mountagu, afterwards first Earl of Sandwich (q.v., *D.N.B.*).

418, l. 43. *Pickaxe . . . spade*. Cf. *Hamlet*, v. i. 100. It is possible that Herrick wrote 'With the Pickaxe and the spade', which would make better sense.

418, ll. 57–58. *this Gorgon . . . stone*. Cf. Burton, 3. 2. 2. 2 (p. 458): '*and Medusa like turne thee to a stone*'.

419. 1. *heading*. *Sir Edward Giles*. Son and heir of John Giles, of

Bowden, Devon. Baptized at Totnes, 21 July 1566. Matric. from Exeter Coll., Oxf., 1 Feb. 1582/3. Student of Middle Temple 1584. Knighted 1603. M.P. for Totnes 1597–8. Married Mary, d. of Edmond Drewe of Hayne, Devon. Died *s.p.* 28 Dec. 1637 at Dean Prior. (*Alumni Oxon.* and J. L. Vivian, *Visitations of Devon* 1531, &c., p. 409.) See 140. 1. heading and note. The verses are quoted and attributed to Herrick by John Prince, *Danmonii Orientales Illustres*, 1701, p. 334. Herrick is there said to have been 'very Aged' when he wrote the verses.

419. 1. 1–2. *No trust . . . Men.* See 81. 1. 7–8 and 148, ll. 100–1. For the phrase 'as Men' see also 81, l. 47, and 146, l. 12.

419. 1. 4. *eternal Monument.* See 30. 2. 10.

419. 1. 5. 'Pay' may be connected with 'Spent' in l. 3, but this is doubtful and with 'Pay' the transition to 'But' in l. 6 is awkward. It seems likely that the engraver read 'Pay' for 'Say', the reading adopted here. Cf. 289. 1. 5. 'What more . . . But' then means 'What more . . . except'. 'these' presumably refers to 'Times, Titles, Trophies' in l. 3.

419. 2. Cf. 51. 3.

419. 2. 8. *Cherry harvest.* See 165. 1. 10 and 408, ll. 50–51.

419. 2. 10–14. See 20, ll. 5–8 and 57, l. 148.

419. 2. 14. *all the yeare.* See 20, l. 8; 138. 2. 4; 269. 5. 8; 366, l. 21; additional stanzas after l. 48 of 'His age' (see p. 482): 'Clusters all the yeare'.

420. 2. See note to 49. 2 and cf. 87. 2.

421. 1. 4. *blended dust.* See 133, ll. 26–27 ('pulvis et umbra'); 233. 1. 38.

421. 1. 5. *signe.* See 288. 2. 2.

421. 1. 6. *no neat distinction.* See 140. 1. 5: 'this neat distinction'.

421. 1. 9. *pride forme colour.* See 49. 2. 4.

421. 2. For similar elegiac dialogues see 248. 1 and 416. 1.

421. 2. 13. *infernall Jove.* See 133, l. 28.

421. 2. 14. See 224. 1. 4 and note.

422, l. 24. See 265. 5. 2.

422. 1. *heading.* Parkinson has not been identified[1] but 'm^r Pallauicine' is probably Toby or Tobit or Tobias Palavicino, 3rd son of Sir Horatio P., q.v. in *D.N.B.* Both this son and the second son, Henry, matriculated from Clare Coll., Camb., at Michaelmas, 1606. Both married daughters of Sir Oliver Cromwell. Henry became a merchant and a political agent. He was knighted in Feb. 1610/11. When he died in 1615 his bother succeeded to the estate at Babraham which is referred to in l. 5 of this poem. Toby purchased much of Great and Little Shelford, but squandered his wealth and was imprisoned for debt (*Alumni Cant.*). In 1626 he claimed £14,000 from the City of London, which had long before become bound for a large sum lent by his father to Queen Elizabeth. (*C.S.P. Dom. 1625–6*, p. 459. See also *C.S.P. Dom. 1625–49*, p. 256, and *1640*, p. 620.)

[1] In Harvard MS. Eng. 626 F, f. 78^v the name (without initial) is attached to one of Jonson's poems, 'My Picture left in Scotland' (*Und.* ix).

422. 1. 4. *A harmles Ghost*. See 73. 1. 17 and 289. 4. 1.

422. 1. 12. *peaceful vrne*. See 278. 3. 6.

422. 1. 14. *silken sleepe*. See 35, l. 38.

422. 1. 15–16. *loue . . . Auncestry*. See 278. 3. 6–8.

424, l. 6. *putt . . . Hebritian*. Discredit thee as a Hebrew scholar.

424, l. 8. *prick. Hebrew*. Referring to the points or dots in Hebrew script, signifying the vowels, &c.

424. 1. 1. *sounds*. Implies, means.

424. 2. 11. *Kitt*. St. Christopher's was a tobacco. Dr. J. T. McCullen refers me to John Chamberlayne, *The natural history of coffee &c.*, 1682 (*Harl. Misc.*, 1, p. 521*b*).

424. 2. 18. *Verinahs*. Verinas or Varinas. 'A superior quality of roll tobacco' (*O.E.D.*), named after Varinas in Venezuela.

425, l. 56. *Collyrium*. Usually either an eye-salve or a suppository. Here generalized to an antidote.

426. 1. 16. *sciopedes*. Or Sciapodes. A fabulous Indian race mentioned by Pliny, *Hist. Nat.* vii. 2. 23, who used their feet as they lay on the ground to provide a shade in hot weather.

431, l. 15. *night=reale*. If this is the correct reading it appears to be a variant form of night-rail, meaning night-robe.

431, ll. 47–48. *time . . . furrow*. Cf. 97, ll. 13–14.

437. 1. 3. *our*. Probably a mistake for 'your'.

437. 1. 7–8. *before &c*. Cf. 447. v. 1–2.

437. 1. 11–12. *black . . . opposite*. See 194. 3. 5–9, 406, ll. 105–8, and notes.

437. 1. 24. *Carcanett*. The word occurs seven times in Herrick's published poems.

438. 1. 3. *this, & this*. Cf. 247. 2. 2–3.

438. 1. 5–6. *one*. For 'on', as frequently in this manuscript.

439, ll. 27–28. *You . . . violett*. Perhaps the most Herrickian of the lines attributed to 'R. H.' Cf. 108. 1. 13–16 and 456, ll. 61–62.

439. l. 30. *lip . . . Corall . . . ruby*. Cf. 12. 1. 3–7.

439. 1. 15–16. *sect . . . dialect*. People who converse by kissing. For 'bussing' see 189. 2.

440. 1. This poem is clearly related to 203. 2.

440. 2. 1–2. *eyes . . . light*. See 443. 1. 6.

440. 2. 9. *due . . . Excellence*. See 76, l. 38: 'their proper excellence'.

440. 2. 10–11. *Lilly . . . lawne*. See 75. 1. 1–4.

440. 2. 12. *more . . . sight*. Verbatim in 75. 1. 18.

441. 1. 11. *gentle ayre*. See 408, l. 54 and 416. 1. 7.

441. 1. 15–16. *weepe . . . keepe*. See 158. 5. 5–6.

441. 1. 21. *stroaking sunne*. See 408, ll. 57–58; also 440. 2. 12 and note.

441. 1. 22. *vailing*. See 440. 2. 1.

441. 1. 23. *Ecclipse*. See 440. 2. 13.

441. 1. 25–26. *sweet . . . westerne winde*. See 103. 2. 1.

441. 1. 27. *spire*. See 55, l. 67.

442, ll. 35–36. *scope . . . hope*. See 211. 4. 2–3.

442. 1. 1. *Ile dote noe more*. See 209. 2. 7–8.

442. 1. 5–14. Cf. stanza additional to 74. 3 on p. 469 (ll. 5–8).

442. 1. 6–7. *her haire to fetter mee*. See 232. 1. 11–12, and 293. 5. 1–4.

442. 1. 8. *Trophy I can reare*. See 85. 1. 17–18, and 419. 1. 3–4.

442. 1. 9. *rest*. Tranquillity.

442. 1. 11–12. *Just . . . heate*. See 236. 5. 2.

442. 1. 14. *looker on*. See 232. 1. 13. *Live free*. See 12. 4. 12; 53, l. 11; and 183, l. 17.

442. 2. 1. Cf. Burton, 2. 3. 7 (p. 355): '*embrace opportunity, loose no time*.' 'Gather ye rosebuds' (84. 1) is headed 'Loose No time' in MS. Harl. 3991, f. 145v.

442. 2. 7. *winter comes*. See 443. 1. 9.

442. 2. 8. *ripe for men*. See 56, l. 112. Cf. Jonson, 'To Penshurst' (*Forest*, ii), l. 54.

443. 1. 2. *Ould time*. See 84. 1. 2.

443. 1. 9. *winter comes*. See 442. 2. 7.

443. 1. 11. *too Late*, &c. See 63. 1. 12–15.

443. 2. 1–2. *like vnto a Dewe Of pearle*. See 125. 2. 19 ('To Daffadills'): 'as the pearles of Mornings dew'.

443. 2. 7–8. *that great yeare . . . spheare*. See note to 190, l. 47, and cf. 265. 1. 5–6.

443. 2. 10. *that great Aprill*. See 257, l. 19 and note.

443. 2. 15. The word that baffled the copyist may have been 'benjamin' (= benzoin); see 131. 1. 10.

443. 2. 21–22. *my teare And my late Primrose*. The reference seems to be to 43. 1 ('The Teare sent to her from Stanes') and to 208. 1 ('The Primrose'). Herrick mentions 'The Primrose' also in 135, l. 99.

443, l. 25. *reames*. Foam. See 374, l. 41 and note.

443, l. 26. *pibbly*. Cf. 'peebly', 35, l. 43.

443, ll. 35–37. *hirs . . . Building*. See Plutarch, *Quaest. Rom.* 61 (*Morals*, transl. Holland, 1603, p. 870): 'How commeth it to passe, that it is expresly forbidden at Rome, either to name or to demand ought as touching the Tutelar god, who hath in particular recommendation and patronage, the safetie and preservation of the citie of Rome: nor so much as to enquire whether the said deitie be male or female?'

443, l. 38. *fallne Palladium*. The image of Pallas called Palladium was said to have fallen from heaven.

443, ll. 48–49. *a frost Dissolu'd*. Cf. 233. 1. 27.

443, l. 49. *n'ere to bee found againe*. Verbatim in 125. 2. 20 ('To Daffadills'). Cf. also 69, l. 64.

LETTERS

445. i, ll. 1–2. *my Brothers occasions*. See note to 34. 3, heading.

446. iii, ll. 2–3. *Qui timide rogat*, &c. See note to 8. 3. 2.

446. iii, l. 6. *Tempora &c.* See Tilley, *Prov. Eng.*, T343, 'Times change &c.'

446. iii, l. 13. *Homo homini Deus.* Caecilius, *Com.* 257 (Loeb): 'Homo homini deus est, si suum officium sciat.'

446. iii, ll. 15–16. *Arcisilaus*, &c. See Plutarch, *How to tell a flatterer from a friend*, 22 (*Morals*, transl. Holland, 1603, p. 102).

447. iii, l. 19. *which modesty would conceale.* See 24. 2. 2 and note.

447. iii, l. 24. *Time hath deuoured.* Ovid, *Met.* xv. 234: 'Tempus edax rerum.'

447. iii, l. 26. *florida aetas.* Cf. Catullus, lxviii. 16: 'iucundum cum aetas florida ver ageret'; and Prov. xvii. 22 (Vulg.): 'animus gaudens aetatem floridam facit'.

448. v, ll. 12–13. *vsquequo . . . Domine.* Ps. xiii (xii Vulg.). 1: 'Usque-quo, Domine, oblivisceris me . . . .'

449. vii. l. 11. *sed votis puerilibus opto.* Ovid, *Trist.* v. 8. 11, quoted by Montaigne, iii. 13.

ADDENDA

A. *To footnotes:* 14. 2. 1 Pearls,] Pearls *48* 71. 2. 3 *Prig's*] *Prigs's 48* 133, l. 17 3.] *om. 48* 166, l. 42 mosse like *MSS. except F* (moslike): mosse-like *48* 166, l. 56 enchequered *MSS.*: enchequered. *48* 348, l. 45 12.] 11. *48* (*repeated*) 375, l. 81 9.] *om. 48* 392 (*heading*) Death.] Death *48* 394. 3. 1 That] Tthat *48* 405. 38 kisse. *WR*: kisse *MSS.* 408. 39 theis,] theis *MSS.*

B. *To Critical Notes:* **36,** l. 46 enameled] bediapurd *Ash* **36,** l. 51 While] whilst *HM* **45.** 12 shine] shrine *F* **49.** 2 Fol. 1. 27 has heading: To a periurd Lover Fol. 1. 8 has heading: A Reply to the same: (sc. to 420. 2) **77.** 2. 11 thy] y^e *F* **77.** 2. 12 mid-day] Middayes *F* 17 salutes . . . of] Which he salutes w^{th} *F* **78,** l. 62 thy] the *A19 A30 H S17* **78,** l. 65 that brave] that *F* **79,** l. 79 Fill each part] Till each part's *F* **133,** l. 48 Lampries] Lampry *HM* **134,** l. 82 those] theys *HM* **145.** 2 In Stow's *Survey*, 1633, p. 812, from a memorial tablet in St. Margaret's, Westminster (see *T.L.S.*, 13 May 1955, p. 253), headed: In Memory of the late deceased Virgin Mistris Elizabeth Hereicke 2] The Grave-verse up in mournfull Jet *Inscription* 3 mournfull] dapl'd *Inscr.* 5 wonted] weeping *Inscr.* **158.** 5. 6 that] whilst *Ac71* **166,** l. 59 off] *om. F* **174.** 1. 6 me] thee *Ash* **175,** l. 55 passage] passing *R* **420.** 2 and **443.** 1 are also in MS. Folger 1. 8, ff. 8^v and 7^v; **420.** 2 has heading: Vpon his periur'd Mistris: **443.** 1 has heading: Sonnet: Otherwise there are no readings in either not found elsewhere.

INDEX OF TITLES

INDEX OF FIRST LINES

INDEX OF FIRST LINES

INDEX OF FIRST LINES

INDEX OF FIRST LINES

INDEX OF FIRST LINES

INDEX OF FIRST LINES

INDEX OF FIRST LINES

INDEX OF FIRST LINES

INDEX OF FIRST LINES

INDEX OF FIRST LINES

INDEX OF FIRST LINES

PRINTED IN GREAT BRITAIN
AT THE UNIVERSITY PRESS, OXFORD
BY CHARLES BATEY, PRINTER TO THE UNIVERSITY

· BLACKWATER SPIRITS ·

PREVIOUS GLYNIS TRYON MYSTERIES BY MIRIAM GRACE MONFREDO

North Star Conspiracy

Seneca Falls Inheritance

· BLACKWATER SPIRITS ·

MIRIAM GRACE MONFREDO

A THOMAS DUNNE BOOK

ST. MARTIN'S PRESS · NEW YORK

 For information, address St. Martin's Press, 175 Fifth Avenue, New York, N.Y. 10010.

Design by Sara Stemen

Library of Congress Cataloging-in-Publication Data

Monfredo, Miriam Grace.
Blackwater spirits / Miriam Grace Monfredo.
p. cm.
"A Thomas Dunne book."
ISBN 0-312-11754-X
1. New York (State)—History—1775–1865—Fiction.
2. Seneca Falls (N.Y.)—History—Fiction. I. Title.
PS3563.05234B58 1995
813′.54—dc20 94-40980
CIP

First edition: February 1995
10 9 8 7 6 5 4 3 2 1

• ACKNOWLEDGMENTS •

Those who have engaged in historical research will know how much an author owes to others: to reference librarians, town and county historians, and additional informative and helpful people. I am fortunate to have access to numerous fine libraries in western New York: the Rare Book Division of the Rush Rhees Library, University of Rochester; the Rochester Public Library, Rundel Memorial Building; The Strong Museum Library; the Seneca Falls Historical Society, and particularly the Rochester Museum and Science Center, with its material on the Iroquois.

I am especially grateful for the Edward G. Miner Medical Library's History of Medicine division at the University of Rochester, and I wish to thank librarian Christopher Hoolihan, head of special and technical services.

I am also indebted to those individuals who have made unique contributions: Betty Auten, Seneca County Historian; Ellen Brown, former owner of The Shoestring Gallery of Art; Francis Caraccilo, Seneca Falls village planner and director of Seneca Falls Urban Park, and Gail Caraccilo, planning assistant; Gene Holcutt, refuge manager of the Montezuma Wildlife Refuge; G. Peter Jemison, Seneca artist and historic site manager of Ganondagan State Historic Site; Dan Hill, a Seneca/Cayuga, for his introduction to evocative Native American flute music; David Minor of Eagles Byte; and Nancy Woodhull and Bill Watson for loaning Glynis Tryon their historic (1840) Cayuga Street residence in Seneca Falls, New York.

Special thanks to my husband, first reader Frank Monfredo, for his invaluable assistance with legal history and trial development and for after-dinner strategy sessions; and to my daughter, Rachel J. Monfredo, of the Museum of Fine Arts, Boston, Department of American Decorative Arts and Sculpture, for everything from dulcimers to

women artists, soup to nuts and then some, including gourmet meals. Also to my father, Horst J. Heinicke, M.D., for medical information. And abiding gratitude to my editor, Ruth Cavin.

And to my friend and companion of seventeen years, my little West Highland lassie, Shaduff Balman Lyrae: Rest In Peace.

• AUTHOR'S NOTE •

The major characters in *Blackwater Spirits* are fictitious, but actual historic figures do appear from time to time. The interested reader will find them annotated in the Historical Notes at the end of the novel.

For reasons now obscured by time, there are two bodies of water named Black Brook in Seneca County, New York. The Black Brook referred to in *Blackwater Spirits* has its source near the village of Waterloo and flows east to the village of Seneca Falls, then north to an area known today as the Montezuma National Wildlife Refuge. These entities are factual, as is Black Brook Road. Black Brook Reservation is entirely fictitious, however; there is no Native American reservation in Seneca County.

An explanation is in order concerning the two different spellings of what has been variously translated as "people who build an extended home," or "people of the longhouse." The present-day Iroquois spelling of this is *Haudenosaunee.* Lewis Henry Morgan's work *League of the Ho-de-no-sau-nee, or Iroquois,* published in 1851, used a phonetic spelling that resulted from Morgan's desire to appeal to the primarily Anglo-American reading audience of the mid-nineteenth century.

In memory of my grandmother,
Grace Tryon Warren
1882–1974

• PROLOGUE •

WINTER 1847

T*he ice. O-we'-za. The ice could crack.*

But the trail had ended. He *must* cross the river. The young half-blooded Iroquois ignored the warning murmur of spirits beneath the frozen surface of Black Brook, and urged his horse over the ice to the trail beyond as fast as he dared. Halfway across, the ice cracked.

The youth heard a sharp report at the instant his horse drew its hindquarters into a crouch, struggling for purchase on the river's shifting skin. Repercussions like musket shots split the cold air. Instinctively the youth loosened his grip on the reins; here the horse knew better than he. The animal faltered before it recovered its footing and lunged forward, snorting in fear as it scrambled up the bank of the river. With a roar the ice behind gave way.

But once more on the hard-packed dirt of a trail, the horse unexpectedly shied. Only then did the youth acknowledge that he had been shadowed. And while *tah-yoh-ne,* the gray timber wolf, followed closely now, it would not attempt to cross the broken ice-capped span of water; the wolf could sense danger where the human could not.

The youth twisted in his saddle to look back, and he called to the shadow. On the river's far side, the wolf would not show itself, but glided as unseen as a ghost through snow-dappled underbrush. The youth again urged his horse forward. The trail eventually curved south while the river beside it narrowed to a stream, and then faintly, from somewhere beyond, came the anguished screams of women. Reining in, the rider quickly dismounted. The horse hung its head wearily, steam rising from its nostrils.

Crouched at the far edge of the streambed, the wolf raised its muzzle to search the air as if to confirm the scent of only the one human.

Then it cleared the stream in a single leap. The young Iroquois sensed the wolf closing the distance between them, and he turned the horse to give its rump a sharp slap. As the horse cantered off, the youth again called to the wolf, before he began to run.

He moved with the litheness and strength of his Iroquois forebears. And as swiftly as if he bore wings. His moccasins barely grazed the snow, a silent drum of *my brother, my brother, my brother,* steadily beating the rhythm of strides. Measuring every footfall.

Beside him, wind-stripped branches swept the stream's frozen surface, and where the ice was thin or broken, water glittered like black glass. Now and then the runner eyed the water warily, but his attention centered on the path ahead. And what he would find at his destination. He remained only marginally aware of the gray shadow now at his heels; but when the trees began to thicken, to become dense forest, the youth slowed and glanced back. The eyes of the wolf, outlined with black markings, had become luminous golden ovals. It raised its muzzle to howl.

The runner checked his stride to watch as his protector veered up a small hill, its outline stark against the milky winter sky. With a flick of tail the wolf vanished. The runner picked up his pace and entered the domain of Ga'-oh, spirit of the winds.

Towering hemlock now loomed over the footpath, their snow-weighted boughs curving like claws toward the forest floor. Amid the hemlock rose sacred white pine of the Iroquois. The pine thrust their branches upward as if to ward off the taller trees' threat; as if to guard the runner on the path below. High above the earth-bound creatures, an eagle shrieked its warning.

The youth's acute sense of hearing, like that of his kindred spirit, the wolf, now caught again the sound of women's anguish, long before they could be seen. Quickening his pace still more, he raced over the footpath, his way guarded to either side by the white pine. By Ga'-oh, whispering through their branches. Ahead of him, cries of grieving rent the near-twilight to rise on the air like his own frosted breath. *My brother, my brother.*

The forest suddenly thinned. The runner slowed, then paused at the edge of a clearing, his eyes on a solitary oak ahead, and on the two women under it on their knees. Above them, a body dangled from a rope noose. The youth took this in even as his peripheral vision

scanned the clearing for signs of the lynching party. There remained only churned snow. Bootprints and hoofprints.

The two women, one young, one aging, got to their feet and pulled their graceful, shawl-like blankets around themselves while the youth went toward them across the roiled snow. Despite the tears on her weathered cheeks, he saw in the eyes of the older woman a hard light. And when she spoke, hers was a voice that rang with the harshness of knife against stone: "You come too late, Walks At Sundown. Too late for your brother."

The young, sweet voice of the other woman came to him now, raw with pain. "They took him. They did . . . *that* . . . and then they hanged him! But their law says—you *told* us—that first there must be a trial."

"Trial!" The older woman spat the word, and brushed her eyes with the back of a leathery hand. "White man's law! Law that you, Walks At Sundown, think we should honor. What should we honor, when this law lets white men drag your brother from the longhouse? Take his manhood. Ask *him*"—she pointed to the man at the end of the rope—"ask what *he* thinks of this law! But he will not answer . . ." The woman's voice broke, and she sank to her knees, gazing up at the body of her elder son.

Walks At Sundown raised his own eyes to see above him the cruelly battered face and, below the belt of his brother's tunic, a dark stain spreading over the buckskin leggings. Blood still dripped from between his legs, one slow drop at a time, into the snow.

For a long moment, Walks At Sundown remained with gaze fixed on the body swinging slowly above him; then he moved toward his mother. On her knees, she bowed in grief. Walks At Sundown stood over her, stared down at her hunched shoulders, and wiped his palms over and over again on his leggings.

At last his mother straightened and looked up at him, saying, "You, Walks At Sundown of the Wolf Clan, are bound by the code of your ancestors. You, who were born Haudenosaunee, People of the Longhouse, know what it is you are required to do."

Their eyes met, mother and son, and between them a fresh antagonism surfaced. But Walks At Sundown said nothing; there was nothing his mother would hear. He took several quick steps backward and then, with a running leap, grabbed a low branch of the oak to swing himself up into the tree.

He drew his knife from its quillwork sheath. Sharpened on whetstone, honed razor-keen, the knife severed the hemp rope with a single slash. Still grasping the length of hemp, Walks At Sundown lowered his brother's body into the arms of the women below.

When they had lain the dead man on the ground, his mother went to the edge of the stream, where she lifted her face to the Great Spirit. Walks At Sundown and the younger woman waited. The snow-bleached sun dropped behind the pines.

While the three figures stood as motionless as a tableau sculpted in ice, neither Walks At Sundown nor the women turned their heads toward a faint sound beyond the clearing. There, cowering behind a tree, a white-skinned girl choked on the tears that coursed down her face. But before she might be approached, she rose to flee through the forest.

She ran until her lungs failed, then hurled herself against the nearest tree, grinding her forehead into its rough gray bark until the snow under her feet reddened. Long strands of fine yellow hair whipped back and forth in her frenzy before they snagged on the bark, wrapping themselves around the tree trunk. The girl moaned softly as she tore the captive strands from her scalp.

At last, when the spirits of darkness began to gather, she threw herself into the snow. If she lay there long enough, she could die. She *would* die. Like the hanged man in his mother's arms. Just as cold.

Some time later, a horse emerged from the trees. Its rider reined in, stared down at the still form dusted with snow, then dismounted to look more closely. A thread of vapor issued from between the girl's lips.

Wolves howled in the forest. Dark water murmured beneath the frozen surface of the stream, and the wind spirit Ga'-oh sighed through the pines. But He'-no the Thunderer, spirit of vengeance, remained silent.

For now.

• 1 •

As our territorial history recedes from us, each passing year both deepens the obscurity upon the Indian's footsteps, and diminishes the power of the imagination to recall the stupendous forest scenery by which he was surrounded.

—Lewis Henry Morgan, *League of the Ho-de-no-sau-nee, or Iroquois,* 1851

AUTUMN 1857

The low-pitched toot of a boat horn sent Glynis Tryon's gaze to the tall windows that faced the canal. She was seated at her desk in the Seneca Falls Library, and thus could see only the crowns of aspen that grew along the towpath below, their autumn-gold leaves shimmering in a breeze off the water. Beyond the trees, the sky shone with the blue brilliance of stained glass. A perfect September day.

Glynis pushed back her chair, rose, and went to stand at a mullioned window. On the canal below, one of two flat-bottomed boats, both loaded with grain and riding low in the water, was in the process of passing the other. This meant several minutes of intricate maneuvering, as teams of mules and their drivers were some two hundred fifty feet ahead of the boats and connected by long tow lines. Tangled lines could halt canal traffic for almost interminable periods. But on this occasion, as on most, the procedure was accomplished cleanly. And a good thing, too, Glynis thought, as more boats began to appear from the locks upriver; the harvest was a busy season in western New York.

Coming east from the village factories, the boats carried large crates of parts, which were labeled COWING FIRE ENGINES and GOULD PUMPS. The canal boats would head northeast to join the Erie Canal system, then either travel west or continue east to New York City and

the ocean beyond. It gave Glynis acute pleasure that these goods manufactured in Seneca Falls were shipped all over the world. For might not someone, necessarily a very small someone, hide herself inside one of the crates and find herself in, say, England or even Peru?

Glynis smiled at this whimsy and remembered how, when she'd been younger, the thought of seeing Europe could set her daydreaming for hours. And yet she had not done much traveling in the years—fifteen it was now—since she'd graduated from Oberlin College and settled in Seneca Falls. And though she'd had times of regret, difficult times, most often she felt fairly satisfied with her choice of education and career rather than marriage and children.

Behind her, a low murmur of male voices ceased abruptly. She turned from the window to see her assistant, Jonathan Quant, bending over an open book that was held by Jeremiah Merrycoyf. Glynis suddenly recalled an illustration from Dickens's *Pickwick Papers,* prompted by Jonathan's earnest young face under a thatch of unruly hair, his rumpled sack coat and carelessly knotted neckcloth and, beside him, lawyer Merrycoyf's short, rotund shape straining the buttons of a frock coat, the stem of his unlit pipe jabbing at the page before them.

"Exactly what I wanted," Merrycoyf said at last. "Thank you, my boy, for locating it with such dispatch."

Jonathan nodded happily, prodding with his index finger the thick-lensed spectacles that had slid down his narrow, well-shaped nose. He returned to his tidy desk on the far side of the open room while Merrycoyf snapped the book shut, placed it under his arm, and lumbered toward Glynis.

Watching him cross the wood-pegged floor, Glynis thought, No, not Dickens but Clement Moore. She never saw the lawyer but that she wasn't reminded of Saint Nicholas. Short white beard, round cheeks that barely supported the wire-rimmed spectacles perched on them—his nose being far too small for this—Merrycoyf customarily looked content with his world. "You found it, then, Jeremiah?"

"Indeed yes, Miss Tryon. The efficient Mr. Quant has once again come to my aid. Now if you would be so kind as to sign this out . . . But tell me, my dear, do you get much call for Morgan's work on the Iroquois?"

"Not much." Glynis smiled in reply as she bent over her desk to

sign the card. "But at least it's here when we do." She nudged aside the usual clutter on her desktop to find a small Seth Thomas clock, and straightened. "If you're leaving now, Jeremiah, I'll walk out with you. I have a small task to perform for Abraham Levy. A welcome task," she added in response to Merrycoyf's raised eyebrows. "I'm to meet the afternoon train that's bringing the new doctor."

"Ah, yes." Merrycoyf's brows lowered. "A young cousin of Abraham's, isn't it?"

Glynis nodded, and plucked her broad-brimmed straw hat from the hall stand beside the door; settling the straw carefully over her topknot, she gave its brim a rakish tilt. But then, after catching a glimpse of Merrycoyf's amused expression, she rearranged the brim to a more modest angle. While tucking in stray wisps of reddish hair, she called over her shoulder, "I'll be back in a bit, Jonathan."

Merrycoyf swung open the door. He stood aside while Glynis gathered in her long, full skirt and petticoats to accommodate the opening, then followed her out. In the far distance a train whistle sounded as they climbed several shallow steps to the wide dirt road that was Fall Street.

When Glynis hurried off in the direction of the station, Merrycoyf stood watching a black Morgan horse, with Constable Cullen Stuart astride, turn into the road behind her. The constable dismounted, caught up with Glynis, then walked along beside her.

Merrycoyf shook his head and could be heard to mutter under his breath, "That man's been waiting for years now—wonder if she'll ever make up her mind to marry him."

Her forehead creased in a frown, Neva Cardoza reluctantly turned her attention back to the train window. Although the people inside the passenger car had proved more interesting than the monotonous landscape outside, she supposed they were entitled to some privacy—the right not to be inspected by a disapproving stranger. But since her recent graduation from the Female Medical College of Pennsylvania, she had seen practically no one other than the diseased and dying, and now found she rather resented these travelers, who looked so robustly healthy. This somewhat disturbed her. Had she become more comfortable with the ill than with the well?

Neva's frown deepened as she watched yet more acres of dense forest stream past her window. Wasn't there anything other than *trees* in western New York? An hour after the train had pulled out of New York City, she had seen trees enough to last a lifetime. Mile after mile of the things. There were no majestic stone buildings, no crowded, bustling streets, no tidy parks. No omnibuses or elegant carriages, concert halls or museums. No Fulton steamboats, or wharves swarming with dockworkers whose muscled, sunburned backs, glistening with sweat, always unsettled her, made her turn away lest they notice her watching.

All she had seen from the train since it left the Hudson River valley was one other river—with the odd Indian name of Mohawk—hundreds of streams, a few small towns, scattered farmhouses, and many thousands of cows. And trees!

How had she gotten herself into this? She had never before set foot outside cities, those of New York and Philadelphia, yet here she was: an educated, reasonably intelligent, young Jewish woman headed full-steam toward the outer reaches of civilization. But of course she knew very well how she had gotten into this. Papa. Papa and Jacob Espinosa. Papa and Jacob Espinosa and a dowry. A dowry discussed before she, Neva, had even been consulted!

"Why do you want to disgrace me?" Papa had shouted. "Why do you think you can be a doctor? How did this happen—that my *daughter* wants to be a doctor? You should want to be a wife. And a mother. A respectable woman, as you have been taught by your own mama. Didn't you teach her this, Sheva?"

"I taught her," Sheva Cardoza said, gazing with annoyance at Neva. "She didn't listen. She never listens."

"But *you* are the one"—Papa now accused Mama, which Neva thought to be only fair—"the one who let your cousin Ernestine send her to that deceitful school. A school that would teach girls they can do just the same as boys. What were you thinking, Sheva?"

"I was thinking," Mama retorted, "that after Neva saw what it was about, she might give up this foolishness of doctoring."

"But, Papa," Neva began, mostly to interrupt their incessant arguing about who was to blame, not that it would do any good, "Papa, you don't understand. You won't even *try* to understand."

"What is to understand?" In high drama, Papa flung his hands in

the air, then brought them back to clutch at his chest. This, Neva knew, was to inspire guilt when, because of her, he finally succumbed to heart failure. But at the moment, he somehow managed to go on, "Jacob Espinosa, a fine, fine boy from a prosperous family, wants to marry you. But no! No, you would rather disgrace me. That I understand!"

And so it went. Day after day. While they waited, all of them, for her to come to her senses: Papa, Mama, her two older brothers—who both had decided long ago that she was unbalanced—and her younger sister Esthera. Beautiful Esthera, all the while crying her eyes out because Papa said she couldn't marry until Neva did, and nice boys wouldn't wait for her, Esthera, *forever,* and why did Neva *always* have to ruin *everything?*

During all of this, Jacob Espinosa hovered at the core of Neva's misery, wringing his hands solicitously. Jacob, with his sickly-looking white skin and his small, nearsighted eyes. His musty odor of old wool. His unbearable *niceness*! Besides which, Jacob Espinosa had to be, without doubt, the dullest person Neva had ever known. The thought of having to listen to his tedious monologues for the remainder of her days, and the image of his perpetually perspiring hands, his long, clammy fingers crawling over her body . . . Neva shuddered.

No! She would learn to *like* trees!

Her head came up with a jerk. The engine wheels were shrieking like banshees, which meant the train was about to stop again. It had stopped, so far as Neva could tell, at every village and hamlet in western New York. But this stop should be hers: Seneca Falls. She looked through the window at a squat brick station house coming into view, while a few brown chickens ran squawking from the track, feathers swirling in their wake.

She hoped this Abraham Levy who was supposed to meet her had received the last wire, the one that said she would be taking an earlier train. Abraham Levy was a fourth cousin—on her father's side. So Neva had been told. She'd never met him. She didn't want to meet him now, since to have voluntarily left New York City he must be a lunatic.

Still, Neva reassured herself, even in the middle of nowhere people got sick. And Dr. Blackwell had said—she'd *promised*—that if Neva worked in Seneca Falls for a few months' time, she, Elizabeth Black-

well, would guarantee her a position in the Infirmary when she returned: the New York Infirmary for Women and Children which had opened just a few months before. Begun by Elizabeth and Emily Blackwell and Marie Zakrzewska, it was the first hospital ever to be run entirely by women doctors. Neva wanted desperately to be *there.* But Elizabeth had insisted that the recent graduate needed still more education, more exposure to "the lessons of life"—whatever *that* meant! But how she could learn anything in Seneca Falls, New York, which didn't even have a hospital, Neva couldn't fathom.

And this Dr. Quentin Ives she was supposed to train with—what if he turned out to be one of those condescending know-it-alls who hated the very idea of female physicians? Not that Neva wasn't accustomed to them. Well, Dr. Ives would soon find out she wasn't a simpleton or a servant—a glorified nursemaid fit only to empty chamber pots.

When she descended to the station platform, Neva saw no one who appeared to be looking for her. So where might Abraham Levy be? She would wait only a few minutes. Why should she have to depend on some man who, from the looks of it, couldn't even tell time? Surely the Ives house wasn't very far; the town didn't look big enough for anything in it to be far.

As Neva glanced around, she experienced an unfamiliar anxiety. A sense of insignificance. This was a town that didn't even show up on some maps! Who would know if she lived or died? Who would even care? Maybe Papa had been right. Maybe she *was* a bad-tempered, stubborn girl who deserved to be alone, and who certainly didn't deserve someone as nice as Jacob Espinosa. But if she gave up now and went back to New York, without training and without a job, she'd almost have to marry Jacob. Even if she didn't deserve him!

She fought back an unexpected rush of tears. No, she would *not* cry. She would pick up her two valises and walk into town. Casting about for the baggage cart, she saw two people coming around the station house: a woman, and a man holding the reins of a black horse. They both looked her way and then started toward her. The woman, who smiled warmly at Neva, had an intelligent face, expressive, with large, alert gray eyes and lovely pale skin; high cheekbones were surrounded by strands of reddish hair escaped from under her broad-

brimmed straw hat. Probably in her late thirties, she was not what one would call exactly pretty, this woman, but arresting. Someone who would be noticed in a crowd.

The man walking beside her reminded Neva of the rugged-looking Texas Rangers she'd seen in magazine illustrations: rangy and strong-featured, with thick sand-colored hair and mustache. As good-looking a man as Neva had seen in the flesh anywhere.

As they neared her, Neva stood waiting with a nervousness that she tried to conceal with an impatient frown.

When Abraham Levy had asked Glynis Tryon to meet his cousin, he'd sounded apologetic. But surely Neva Cardoza would understand, Glynis had said, that Levy's Hardware store couldn't close in midafternoon during the harvesting season. Glynis would explain this and bring Neva back with her. Besides, she was eager to meet the young woman physician. The town desperately needed another doctor.

When Cullen had joined her on Fall Street, they'd gone on to the station together. "I think that must be Dr. Cardoza now," Glynis told him as they'd rounded the station house. "Standing next to the baggage cart."

"Let's hope it's *not* her," Cullen said. "She looks mad. You sure she's the one?"

But the young woman fit the description Abraham had given: slender and small, not much over five feet; dark brown crimped hair, pulled back severely into a knot; and widely spaced dark eyes. And Cullen was right. She looked angry.

"Neva Cardoza? Are you Dr. Cardoza?" Glynis asked. When the young woman nodded, Glynis extended her hand, introducing herself and Cullen. "Abraham Levy has a sick employee, and he can't leave his store untended. So he asked if I'd meet you."

"How *very* considerate of him!" Neva responded with a toss of her head.

Glynis sensed Cullen's immediate irritation, and felt a little of her own. But she then realized that the young woman would have no knowledge of life in a farming community.

And Neva Cardoza immediately apologized. "I'm sorry—I'm tired and out of sorts from the train ride," she explained. "And I do appreciate your coming. It's certainly not your fault that Mr. Levy is so—"

"Busy," Cullen interjected, so smoothly that Glynis glanced at him, expecting sarcasm to follow. But he went on, "Harvest time's busy for Abe—and he works hard." Cullen pointed at the two bulging valises. "Those yours?"

"Yes," Neva answered, her voice sounding considerably less peevish. "Yes, and they're very heavy, I'm afraid."

But Cullen had already lifted the valises and begun walking with them toward a farm wagon. "John," he called to the wagon's driver. "Could you drop these off at . . ." Cullen turned back to Neva. "You staying with the Iveses?"

"Yes, for now I am."

Cullen nodded, swinging the valises into the wagon as if they were feather pillows. Glynis thought Neva Cardoza looked impressed. That wasn't unusual; most women found Cullen impressive. But Glynis suddenly wondered what this young woman from New York City had expected to find here. Nothing but country bumpkins? No, that was unfair; Dr. Cardoza probably had no such preconception, no idea of what she'd find. And she must be overwhelmed, so far from home. Who wouldn't be anxious and uncertain?

"On the way, we can stop at Levy's Hardware so you can meet Abraham," Glynis told her as they began to walk. "It's just around the corner from the Ives house."

"That's not necessary," Neva replied swiftly. "I'm in no hurry to meet him."

Glynis didn't look at Cullen beside her. She didn't have to look; she could feel his disapproval of Neva Cardoza. But Glynis thought the young woman, despite their explanations, probably didn't understand Abraham's absence and felt hurt by his seeming lack of interest. Glynis thought she herself might feel that way, coming into a strange town to be met by strangers. And she wasn't ready to pass judgment yet on this badly needed doctor.

They reached the wide dirt road that ran through the center of Seneca Falls; Fall Street, and the Seneca River, which ran parallel to it, divided the town north and south.

"That's my library over there," Glynis said, gesturing to the small

fieldstone building at the far corner of Fall and Cayuga streets. "It's just above the walled canal section of the river. Most of our mills and factories are on the other side, across the bridge there."

She paused, noticing that the woman was studying her intently.

"*Your* library?" Neva asked. "Then you're a librarian?"

When Glynis nodded, Neva said, "I think, now, that I've heard about you from my cousin Ernestine—Ernestine Rose?"

When Glynis nodded again, Neva went on, "Yes, and you write a newspaper column, and you're involved in women's rights. Miss *Tryon,* of course! I didn't recognize your name at first." And with that, Neva Cardoza smiled at last, a wide and generous smile that transformed her rather plain face into one that was extremely appealing.

Glynis didn't believe that Cullen had caught this transformation; he looked distracted, undoubtedly thinking that just exactly what the town needed was one more suffragist!

They walked west on Fall Street, moving around horses and farm wagons and elegant buggies, pony carts and lightweight runabouts and phaetons. Glynis pointed out to Neva the newly constructed hotel; a watchmaking and jewelry store; Erastus Partridge's Bank of Seneca Falls, with its new plate-glass windows and brass tellers' cages; Cuddeback's grocery; the drugstore, the bakery, the tailor's; Jeremiah Merrycoyf's law office; Hoskins's Dry Goods on one side of the road and Lathrop's Dry Goods on the other; and the Wayne County Mutual Fire Insurance Company.

Neva stepped onto a wood plank sidewalk to peer into the windows of the Widow Coddington's millinery shop. "I've never liked hats much," she said, her eyes going to Glynis's straw. "But I'll need one here—no buildings to blot out the sun!" The attractive smile flashed again.

Glynis started to comment, but was interrupted by a shout. "Constable! Constable Stuart—wait!" An obviously agitated, heavyset man hurried across the road toward them.

"What's the matter, Jack?" Cullen said when the man reached them.

"Where you been, Constable? I need to talk to you—right now!" the man panted, winded by his sprint across the street. He ignored the women if he even saw them, as his eyes were locked fast on Cullen.

"This is Jack Turner," Glynis said to Neva. "He has a farm north of town," she explained, attempting to introduce him.

Turner's attention was elsewhere. "Constable, you got to do something," he panted. "You got to!"

"Slow down, Turner," Cullen said. "What's the trouble?"

"Somebody means to kill me, Constable, that's the trouble. And you got to stop it!"

"It? What're you talking about, Turner?"

The man looked furtively up and down the street. "Constable Stuart," he said anxiously, "can't we go to the lockup—your office, I mean." He jerked his head toward Glynis and Neva. "I mean *alone*?"

Glynis couldn't imagine what Neva Cardoza might be thinking, but she herself wondered if Jack Turner had lost his mind—or, more likely, had lifted a few too many pints in the Red Mills Tavern.

Cullen, possibly wondering the same thing, just nodded good-naturedly. "O.K., Jack. C'mon to the lockup." He turned to Neva. "Welcome to our quiet little town, Miss . . . that is, Dr. Cardoza. Nice to meet you." And he gave Glynis a wry, glad-to-get-out-of-*here* grin, before starting up the street with Jack Turner.

Glynis realized that all this time the young woman beside her hadn't said a word. Although faintly uneasy herself about Turner's agitation, she smiled at Neva. "I'm sure it's nothing serious," she offered. "Jack Turner likes his beer too much, that's probably all it is."

Neva looked skeptical, but nodded. Although they began walking again, after a few steps Neva put her hand on Glynis's arm. "Miss Tryon, up ahead there . . ." She pointed to a shop set back from the street with a sign that read LEVY'S HARDWARE.

The space in front of the shop was filled with farm implements: threshers, harvesters from the new Auburn plant, John Deere plows, and Pennock seed-planting drills. Recently the hardware store had expanded to include the cooper's shop next door, where barrels of every size had been piled, open ends outward, to form a gigantic honeycomb.

Several tall, woven splint baskets placed beside the shop entrance caught Glynis's attention; she hadn't seen them there before. In front of the splint baskets were stacked a number of smaller baskets woven from corn husks. They looked like the ones made by Iroquois women that she'd seen at the Seneca County Agricultural Fairs.

"That's Abraham's hardware store," Glynis said now to Neva. "Are you sure you don't—"

"No! If you could just show me the way to Dr. Ives's house."

"Oh, I'll go with you," Glynis offered, and to reassure the young woman, she added, "I think you'll like both Katherine and Quentin Ives."

She waited while Neva skirted first chickens, then a lean brown goat occupying the middle of the road; it was eating something unidentifiable, and was eyed by Neva from New York City with great distaste. She had just given it wide berth when she pulled up short to stare at a sturdy, ruddy-cheeked man emerging from the hardware store. He headed toward the women with a vigorous stride.

Glynis braced herself, not having any idea what Neva's response would be. "That's Abraham," she said quietly. "I really don't think we can avoid him now."

They couldn't, and as Abraham Levy approached them, his mouth, above a short, curly black beard, curved in an engaging grin.

"Afternoon, Miss Tryon," he said. Then, "And since you look just like your father—*you* must be the little Neva Cardoza."

For a moment, a pregnant silence swelled. Then, finally, "Yes, I'm *Doctor* Cardoza," she said acidly.

"Well, you can't expect me to call you *that,* can you?" Abraham laughed. "You're hardly more than a girl—"

"Frankly, Mr. Levy," Neva broke in, "I'd rather you didn't call me anything. And I suppose it's because I'm 'hardly more than a girl' that you wouldn't trouble yourself to meet my train."

Abraham's smile withdrew. "I couldn't get away," he said shortly.

"Obviously not!" Neva shook some dust from the hem of her skirt with a snapping sound. "Well, don't let this *girl* keep you from your important business."

With dismay, Glynis watched the two strangers glare at each other, the space between them crackling.

She bit down on her lip and sighed quietly to herself.

Later that afternoon, Glynis made her way home to 33 Cayuga Street through a shower of bright yellow leaves, the first of the season to fall. Her landlady's boardinghouse, a two-storied Federal structure

with a gable roof, sat across from the village park. When Harriet Peartree's other boarder had left town several years before, to join his daughter's family in Syracuse, Glynis and her landlady had moved to this smaller house from a Gothic cottage one block away. Both places had been left to Harriet by one of her three deceased husbands.

In the kitchen, over a supper of beef and kidney pie and stewed tomatoes, Glynis told Harriet of the encounter between Abraham Levy and Seneca Falls's new doctor.

"And it was embarrassing," Glynis concluded. "At least it was for me, though I doubt if either one of them noticed—they were too busy shooting angry looks at each other. And it's really too bad, Harriet. After all, the young woman doesn't know anyone, and I'd rather hoped Abraham would be able to show her around. Now there's obviously no hope of that! But Katherine Ives took to Neva right away."

"Katherine Ives takes to everybody," Harriet pronounced, spearing one of her own translucent watermelon pickles. "Young woman would have to be a witch for Katherine not to like her. Is she?"

"A witch?" Glynis smiled. "No, although some of our town's menfolk might like to think so. She's just a bit . . . well, I guess *outspoken* could be the word. But it's possible that what I saw of Dr. Cardoza today came as the result of fatigue. And her uneasiness at being in a strange place."

"I don't know about that." Her landlady grinned as she got up from the table and went to the stove. "Young lady sounds like she might have been born difficult!" Harriet's hazel eyes twinkled as she returned with a plate of baked apples smelling of caramelized sugar and cinnamon. "S'pect Quentin Ives will have his hands full."

"You know, Harriet, something odd happened on the way to the Iveses'. Jack Turner came running up to Cullen on Fall Street, insisting someone meant to kill him."

"Can't say as I'm surprised," Harriet stated. "He's a bully, that man Turner is." She passed Glynis the cream pitcher.

"Really? Why do you say that?"

"I know his wife, Sara. Poor little thing always has one bruise or another, sometimes more than one. She tires to cover up, explain it away by saying she's clumsy, that she's fallen or bumped into something. And the Turner youngsters—they always look frightened. It's a

shame!" Harriet pushed silvery blond hair from her face as she shook her head.

"I didn't know that about Jack Turner," Glynis said slowly. "But surely he wasn't suggesting his wife would retaliate."

"No. No, of course not," Harriet agreed. "I just meant that maybe for once Turner took out his bad temper on somebody his own size. Somebody who could have threatened him."

"I suppose so. Well, I certainly expect it to come to nothing. By the way, Harriet," she said, wanting to leave the sad and not uncommon plight of the Turner family, "where did you get this?" From the table she had picked up a small, narrow-necked bottle made of some tightly woven material. "And what is it?"

Harriet smiled. "It's a salt bottle. Made from corn husks."

"A salt bottle . . . doesn't it leak?" Glynis shook it slightly. "No, I guess it doesn't." She pulled out the stopper, a section of corn cob, from the bottle's neck to pour a small quantity of salt into her open palm. "Doesn't it have a liner of some sort?"

"No, no liner. It's woven so tightly they say it can even hold water. But mostly it's for salt. The outer husks absorb moisture so the salt inside stays dry."

Glynis ran her fingertips over the bottle's dense surface. "Did you by chance get this at Levy's Hardware? I saw some baskets there today."

Nodding, Harriet motioned toward the heavy oak sideboard against the wall opposite the kitchen window; on its top sat a shallow woven basket mounded with waxy Northern Spy apples. "Got that, too. I was there when a young Iroquois woman from Black Brook Reservation came in with them. And Abraham told her she could bring more items for him to sell."

"Those women make beautiful things," Glynis said. "I've seen them at the county fairs—maybe they'll bring in some of their silver jewelry. And those quill-worked bags. But who was it brought the baskets? I know one or two of the reservation women."

"She called herself Sunlight Weaver," Harriet answered. "Told me that when she was first born, her mother—a weaver herself—put her into a basket she'd made. Sunlight coming through the splints wove a pattern on the baby's face."

Glynis smiled; this Iroquois method of naming an infant had always seemed to her both poetic and logical, infinitely preferable to accommodating a wealthy great-aunt by saddling an innocent with the lifelong burden of Sophonisba or Tryphenia. And the Iroquois birth name could be changed later in life. Thus a skillful corn grower might become Plentiful Harvest; a fast runner might be Wind Chaser; a silent and reclusive man—Walks At Sundown.

"I think it's so hard," Harriet said, "the way some of those women go off by themselves—into the woods usually—to give birth alone. I couldn't imagine doing that myself."

Glynis couldn't imagine it either. But it was their custom, and had been for centuries. Many of the Iroquois held on to their ancient ways. Or were trying to.

She got up from the table and went to stand by the kitchen door while Harriet heated water for the dishes. Gazing out into the back garden, Glynis thought she saw, from the corner of her eye, a flash of white beside the chrysanthemum bed. No, it wasn't Duncan, she told herself sadly; the little white terrier, with her for years, had died last spring. But she still imagined she saw a trace of him now and again, as if a phantom Duncan still roamed the house and yard. His gravestone, though, lay undisturbed beneath the lilac bush.

As she turned back to the kitchen, Glynis brushed at her eyes. She missed him.

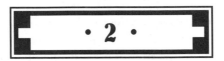

• 2 •

Higher education for women produces monstrous brains and puny bodies, abnormally active cerebration and abnormally weak digestion, flowing thought and constipated bowels.

—Dr. E. H. Clarke, c. 1850

On the following afternoon, Glynis, having at last completed a lengthy acquisition order, shut the top drawer of her desk, turned the wick of her new engraved-glass, oil-fueled study lamp—a present from Cullen—and prepared to close the library. As she'd told her assistant, "There's no point in staying open any longer, Jonathan. No one will come in after four—not until harvesting is over."

Jonathan Quant, his curly, snarled hair just visible over the spine of a book, nodded absently. He'd been buried in this same book all day, and Glynis crossed the room to his desk to see what had so captured him.

"Mary Jane Holmes's new novel!" she said. "That's what has absorbed you?"

Jonathan's smile was sheepish as he put down *Meadow Brook* to gaze up at Glynis with myopic blue eyes made huge by his spectacles. "I thought I should take a look at it. And it's a good thing we've got two copies—everyone's reading it."

Perhaps not everyone, but half the women in Seneca Falls couldn't seem to get enough of Mrs. Holmes's sentimental novels. Or those of any of the other romantic female authors, now that the prejudice against women's writing had begun to diminish somewhat. That Mrs. Holmes lived in Brockport, New York, just west of Rochester, only added to her astonishing appeal. And this while Hawthorne and Mel-

ville sat on the library shelves gathering dust. Indeed, Hawthorne himself recently lamented that America had been "wholly given over to a d——d mob of scribbling women."

"So, how is it—the novel?" Glynis asked.

"Not too bad, actually," Jonathan said. "You haven't read it yet?"

"No, and I probably won't. There are too many other things I need to—" She broke off as the library door swung open. Zephaniah Waters, who was Cullen Stuart's young deputy, burst into the room. "Well, Zeph—hello. What is it?"

"Miss Tryon," Zeph panted, sweat beading his somber, square black face and crisp, nappy hair. "Constable Stuart wants to see you right away. Didn't you hear the commotion up the street just now?" He tugged at the cuffs on his sleeves, which were too short, always, for the long adolescent arms inside them.

"No, I didn't hear." Glynis shook her head. "What's happened?"

"It's Jack Turner," Zeph answered, his bright jet eyes alive with excitement. He rocked back on his heels. "His wife found him just a while ago—found him dead. Dead as a doornail."

"What?"

Zeph's expression, as usual, indicated impatience. "I said that Jack Turner is—"

"Yes, I heard you say that, Zeph," she interrupted. "I just meant—well, how? How did he die?"

"Don't know yet. They took him—that is, took his *body*—to Doc Ives's office. And Constable Stuart wants you to meet him there. Right now!" he again urged her.

By the time they got to Ives's, a crowd had begun to gather. Glynis left Zeph and weaved her way from the street to the house through a score of onlookers. Once inside, she located Katherine Ives just emerging from the examining room, a room that had once been the Iveses' front parlor. "Katherine? Is Cullen here?"

"He's in there." Katherine pointed to the closed door. "Go on in, Glynis. If you need me, I'll be in the kitchen with Sara Turner."

When she opened the examining room door, Glynis's head jerked back from a smell like that of rotting cheese. She gritted her teeth and forced herself into the room, where she found not only Cullen, but

Quentin Ives and Neva Cardoza, all three of them bent over the body stretched out on a long table. Glynis noticed that Neva's face had a pallor not there the day before. The young woman looked up to give Glynis a brief nod.

Cullen straightened and moved from the table. "Glynis, I need you to talk to Sara Turner. She's been like somebody struck dumb since she got here, and there are things we need to know."

"But, Cullen, what happened? How did Jack Turner die?"

"That's what we're trying to find out," Quentin Ives answered. He opened a cupboard to pull from it two jean-cloth aprons, one of which he handed to Neva. "Turner obviously vomited before he died," Ives continued. "The front of his shirt's covered with it. We've got to learn what he ate today, and possibly his wife would know."

"Dr. Ives?" Neva said hesitantly. Although she looked pale, her voice sounded steady enough, Glynis thought. There was also an unexpected note of deference in the voice. "Dr. Ives," Neva said again, "the vomited matter looks rather peculiar. Almost black."

Quentin Ives nodded. "Yes. And notice the dark blue particles—they look a little like soot. What might that indicate to you?"

Having tied the bibbed apron around her waist, Neva bent again over Turner's body, while Glynis swallowed hard and turned away to edge toward the door. Cullen followed her out into the hall.

" 'What might that *indicate* to you?' " Cullen mimicked. "Sounds like a classroom in there."

"Well," Glynis offered, "Neva is supposed to be training with Quentin."

"Good! And when they get done admiring the colors of the 'matter' on Turner's shirt, then maybe they can consider what the hell happened to him."

"I think that's what they *are* doing, Cullen. And in light of what Jack Turner said to you yesterday . . . By the way, did Neva tell Quentin Ives about that?"

"I don't know. Until just a minute ago, she'd been speechless, which was certainly a relief."

"Cullen! Don't be so hard on her. She's only just arrived here, remember." But Glynis knew Cullen's annoyance stemmed from frustration, or even perhaps some sense of accountability for whatever had happened to Jack Turner.

Cullen shrugged and motioned toward the kitchen. "Try to find out what Turner's wife knows, will you? Katherine Ives doesn't want to pester her with questions, but I assume you can be more hard-hearted about it."

Glynis did not find this assessment of herself a particularly attractive one, and it crossed her mind that just a few years before she would have taken issue over it with Cullen. At the moment, however, it seemed relatively unimportant.

She headed for the kitchen.

Sara Turner, small and gray-looking, sat slumped in a straight-backed wooden chair, staring at her hands, clasped around a small Bible. She didn't look up when Glynis entered. Katherine Ives, standing just inside the door, shook her head in sympathy.

"Poor little thing hasn't said a word since she got here," Katherine whispered to Glynis. "She's clearly in shock. What a dreadful thing this is—and Sara's not in any shape to face Cullen Stuart's questioning."

Glynis decided she'd better talk to Sara alone. Cullen had been right—Katherine would be too softhearted to press the woman. "Would you mind, Katherine, leaving me with Mrs. Turner for a few minutes?"

Katherine's eyebrows lifted, but she nodded and left the kitchen as Glynis went to sit beside Sara Turner.

"I'm Glynis Tryon, Mrs. Turner. I think we've met before." This brought no response. In fact, the woman seemed to shrink further into herself, and Glynis had the feeling that Sara Turner might before long disappear entirely.

"Mrs. Turner," she tried again. "This must be very painful for you, and I wish I didn't have to ask, but we need to know what Mr. Turner might have eaten today. I'm sure you want Dr. Ives to find out why your husband died."

With this, the woman finally raised her eyes to Glynis. "I don't care," she said thickly.

Glynis hoped her face didn't reveal her shock. Not only at Sara Turner's words, which were shocking enough, but at the discovery—now that Glynis could clearly see her face—that the woman was hardly older than herself. Sara's whole demeanor had suggested advanced age and infirmity. But Glynis saw that the slack jaw, the

round-shouldered slump, and the lackluster eyes were those of a woman perhaps forty years old whose life must be exceedingly harsh. Indeed, Glynis wondered if Sara Turner had the strength to care about anything. She wished desperately that she could leave the poor woman alone, but proximity to death rarely allowed for that. Especially sudden, unidentified death.

"Mrs. Turner, I'm really sorry to intrude—but if you could just answer a few questions?"

Sara Turner sighed heavily and gave Glynis the briefest of nods before her gaze went back to the Bible she fingered.

Glynis bent toward the woman. "Were you with your husband when . . . when he became ill?"

"No. I just come home—found him a-lyin' there. With no breath. I knew he was dead."

"Ah, where had you just come home from?"

"Been to Waterloo, most all the day. Margaret—that's my sister—she's expectin', you know?"

Glynis nodded encouragingly. "What time do you think that was?"

"Don't rightly know—somewheres around three, maybe."

"So when you got home, Mrs. Turner, what did you do first?"

"Stabled the horse. I sees that Jack's in from the fields, 'cause his horse is there, and I was hurryin' so's he won't get mad 'bout his dinner not bein' hot—you understand?" She gave Glynis a searching look.

"Yes, I understand." Perhaps more than the woman realized. By this time, Glynis had seen the bruises on Sara's jaw, the broken blood vessels in her hollowed cheeks, and the hand that hung from a wrist no longer sound.

"So you went straight to the kitchen then, Mrs. Turner?"

"Found him there on the floor. Covered with puke—he'd been sick on himself, see . . ."

"Was he sick often?" Glynis inserted.

"Never. Never got sick. Not a day, even after he'd been drinkin' all night."

"You said, a minute ago, that you knew he was dead right away. What did you do then?"

"Went down the road for help. Neighbors, they brung him"—her head bobbed toward the hall—"and me into town here."

"Was there anyone else at your farm? Any hired hands, for instance, or your children?"

"No. The kids're hired out, apprenticed in the next county. We don't need 'em at home no more, he says."

"Your husband said that?"

Sara Turner nodded. For the first time Glynis saw tears forming. "He says they got to work, so he sends 'em off. Says the farm's been doin' poorly of late, and we got no money for kids. Or hired hands."

Glynis did not want to think about this. About laws that gave fathers the absolute right to apprentice their children away, disown them, send them off—anything—without mothers having any say at all. And she had long ago become convinced that women stayed with abusive husbands because, without exception, men received custody of children in the few divorce proceedings that did take place.

She tried to disregard these thoughts, and said, "Mrs. Turner, do you know what your husband might have eaten today? For example, when you got home, was there anything in the kitchen that you yourself hadn't prepared?"

The woman started to shake her head, then seemed to hesitate.

"Yes?" Glynis prodded.

The hesitancy gave way to, "No, nothin'."

Glynis frowned, wondering whether to pursue this possible evasion. But she couldn't, the woman looked so fragile. So pathetic. "Just one last thing, Mrs. Turner. Yesterday, Mr. Turner told Constable Stuart that he believed someone meant to kill him . . ." Glynis stopped as Sara Turner's head jerked toward her.

"He said that?" The woman's mouth twisted. For a split second, Glynis even wondered if Sara Turner might be about to smile! But instead her mouth reset itself firmly, and she looked straight into Glynis's eyes. "I shouldn't be surprised," she said flatly.

Glynis felt her stomach tighten. "You aren't surprised at what your husband said?"

"Ain't surprised somebody wanted to kill him. That's been true for . . . for quite a few years back."

Glynis urged Sara to give her more explanation, but the woman refused to elaborate. She gripped her Bible and sank back into her enigmatic silence, relieved only by a sigh now and then.

At last Glynis leaned forward to clasp the woman's undamaged hand. "Thank you, Sara. I won't trouble you any more." It hardly seemed appropriate to offer further condolence for Jack Turner's death.

As Glynis left the kitchen, Sara Turner's head bent again over the Bible in her lap. Cullen, pacing outside the examining room's closed door, looked up as she came down the hall, then gestured toward the Iveses' back door. "Let's go out on the porch and talk," he said. "They're doing the autopsy in there."

Glynis heard from behind the door a sudden clatter of metal, as if an instrument had been dropped. Wincing, she walked quickly toward the back porch, wondering how Neva Cardoza was holding up.

As she and Cullen settled into the cushions of the wide porch swing, there came the murmur of voices from the street.

"Still a bunch of people there," Cullen said. "Folks never seem to get enough of calamity—long as it's somebody else's." His boots pushed against the porch floor, and the ropes holding the swing creaked softly.

Glynis felt her tension begin to lessen as the swing moved gently back and forth. "I don't think Sara Turner knows exactly what happened, Cullen," she said. She related her conversation with the woman.

When she'd finished, Cullen grunted. "That's all she says—she came home and found him dead?"

Glynis turned to look at him. "Yes. Why, don't you believe her? And if not, why not?"

Cullen shook his head. "I'm not saying I don't believe her. But Jack Turner had a strong appetite for drink. He could get real unpleasant, and rumor has it he beat his wife and kids. Maybe Mrs. Turner came home and found him drunk, and—"

"And what, Cullen? She's a very small, frail woman—what could she have done?"

He shook his head again. "I don't know," he shrugged. "I'd think Turner died of something like heart failure, except for yesterday—what he said."

"What *did* he say, after you left us?"

"Same thing you heard. He kept repeating that somebody meant to

kill him. He seemed positive of it, Glynis. I must have asked him a hundred times *why* he thought that. He wouldn't—or couldn't—say. I finally decided beer had pickled his brain. Sent him off. And now . . ."

"Cullen, you can't blame yourself for what's happened. If he wouldn't tell you anything—"

She broke off because he suddenly sat forward, stopping the swing's motion with a sideways lurch. "Turner did say one thing, come to think of it," Cullen said thoughtfully. "He muttered something like if he got killed, it'd be because . . . because of the brook. Then he clammed up. Acted like he was sorry he'd said anything."

"The brook? What brook? That doesn't make sense. Unless he meant some legal issue—but it still doesn't make any sense."

"No. No, of course it doesn't, and I told him so. And he lit out right after that."

"Well," Glynis sighed, "maybe the autopsy will provide some explanation. It did seem bizarre, though, Sara Turner so calmly announcing that she wasn't surprised somebody wanted to kill her husband."

They heard Quentin Ives call, and when they got back inside, the physician stood in the hall outside the examining room, removing a blood-spattered apron. Neva appeared just behind him; she looked even paler than she had earlier.

"So?" Cullen said. "You find anything?"

"Oh, yes," Quentin answered quickly. "We certainly did find something."

Neva stepped forward and took several shaky breaths. "Could we go outside? I really need some fresh air."

Glynis didn't doubt it.

They trooped back out onto the porch, passing the kitchen where Sara Turner still sat, still staring at her lap.

Quentin Ives leaned against the porch railing. "Turner had no heart problems that I knew of, but I looked for that kind of thing first." He shook his head. "Nothing there that could have caused his death. Heart looked good."

Cullen made an inarticulate sound, and Glynis knew he didn't want to hear all the things that *couldn't* have caused Turner's death. Quentin must have gathered this also, because he said, "All right, Cullen, I guess you want an answer."

"Right. What *did* you find?"

"Found inflammation of the stomach, small intestines, and colon. Badly inflamed, stomach full of grumous fluid and blood. But most telling were the particles adhering to the stomach lining."

With that, Glynis had a grim premonition of what might be coming, and Cullen repeated, "Particles?"

"Particles of arsenic."

Glynis sagged against the porch railing to catch her breath. At the same time, Neva Cardoza gazed at Quentin Ives with what only could be described as admiration.

". . . and you're telling me," Cullen was saying, "that Jack Turner died from poison."

"Little question about it," Quentin said firmly. "It would take about three grains of arsenic to kill someone Turner's size. Even considering the fact that he'd vomited, we found the equivalent of that. Would you agree, Dr. Cardoza?"

Neva seemed startled, and flushed slightly. "Oh, yes. Yes, I would agree!" But her voice sounded tense.

It must have been hard for her, Glynis sympathized, to have this occur on only her second day in town. But she certainly appeared impressed with Quentin.

Cullen gripped the porch railing and stared off at the sky. But Glynis, recalling her questions of Sara Turner, asked, "What time do you think he died?"

"Hard to tell," Quentin said. "Arsenic retards decomposition, so it could have been any time in . . . well, say the last twelve hours."

"So we have to find out," Cullen said, turning back to the porch, "what he's eaten since this morning."

"Or drunk," Neva spoke up unexpectedly. "Arsenic can be masked by any number of things."

"Such as?" Cullen said to her.

"Well . . ." Neva hesitated, turning to Quentin.

"Go ahead," Quentin told her. "You seem to know a great deal about poison."

Neva flushed again, but said to Cullen, "Just about anything that's bitter can mask the taste of arsenic. Like chocolate or rhubarb, lemon flavoring—or wine or beer."

"Oh, great!" Cullen slapped his hand palm down on the railing. "That's just great. Jack Turner made his own wine."

"But," Glynis said, "he also bottled it. If the arsenic *was* in the wine, couldn't we find sediment traces in the bottle?"

"And then what?"

"Well, we could . . . I don't know," she floundered. "But surely it would be useful to know if arsenic *was* in the wine or not. And in the wine he made."

"True," Cullen said, "or his wife could have baked him a nice chocolate cake full of poison before she so conveniently left town. That so, Quentin?"

Quentin Ives frowned. "Didn't find any evidence of chocolate. Any food at all, as a matter of fact."

Glynis followed this with, "I don't see why you're so anxious to blame Sara, anyway, Cullen. Isn't it likely that Jack Turner, when you asked him about it yesterday, would have mentioned that it was his *wife* who intended to kill him?"

Cullen shrugged. "Not if he thought she was sick and tired of getting beaten—don't think he'd have mentioned that. At any rate, we're not going anywhere with speculation—I'd better take a ride out to Turner's. See what I can find."

He went down the porch steps, leaving the others to stare at one another in silence.

Neva watched Constable Stuart stride off around the corner, as Glynis and Quentin Ives went back inside. Still feeling shaky, she remained on the porch. She found she was also wretchedly tired. Just one day in this "quiet little town," as the constable had phrased it, and already a murder—even if nobody had actually called it that. Maybe it wouldn't be quite as boring here as she'd feared. But the most agreeable aspect of Seneca Falls so far was Dr. Quentin Ives.

He seemed nothing like the self-important doctors at the medical school. After she'd unpacked last night, they had sat, she and Dr. Ives, on this same back porch while he'd asked questions about her education, about what she wanted to do with it, and even listened to her answers. As if they were important. He'd discussed—*discussed,* not

preached—areas of medical controversy: the current dispute about which was the better anesthesia, ether or chloroform; whether dentistry should be a profession separate from medicine and surgery. Things like that. Quentin Ives had talked with her as though she were entitled to have an opinion.

He had broader knowledge than did most of the physicians by whom she'd been taught in Philadelphia. She guessed this came from not only having a good mind, but being a country doctor who had to know something about everything. Quentin Ives couldn't afford to concentrate in just one or two areas of medicine, as many physicians were now beginning to do. And he didn't have many professional colleagues to assist in diagnosis; he was the only surgeon in Seneca Falls.

Neva's thoughts were interrupted by Dr. Ives and Glynis Tryon coming back out on the porch, then greeting someone who had just rounded the house. Neva looked over the porch railing to see Abraham Levy coming toward them.

"Had some trouble this afternoon, I heard," Abraham said, standing below the porch steps. The coarse blue cotton of his work shirt strained over his shoulders, and where the top button was undone at his neck, a few curly black hairs glistened with sweat.

Neva quickly looked away, listening, however, to the others explain the "trouble." She herself didn't intend to say anything to Abraham Levy. The minute she'd laid eyes on him the day before, she could tell—even if she hadn't known beforehand—that he was related, no matter how distantly, to her father. He had the same arrogance, the inflated sense of himself, the dogmatic I-am-right-about-everything attitude. She didn't like it in her father. She liked it even less in this man.

After all, he wouldn't even bother to meet her train—probably felt it beneath him.

Neva suddenly realized all of them were staring at her. "I'm sorry," she said to Glynis Tryon and Dr. Ives. "I wasn't paying attention. Did you say something?"

"Yes," Abraham Levy answered, as if she had addressed *him*. "I asked how you were doing?"

"I am doing *just fine*! Why shouldn't I be?" She pretended not to see Quentin Ives's eyebrows rise, or the look he gave Miss Tryon.

“No reason,” Abraham Levy said, his mouth tightening. “Just thought our fresh air might have made you more agreeable. Guess I was mistaken.”

As Neva sucked in her breath, Abraham pivoted on his heel and began to stride toward the road. But he turned to say to Quentin Ives, “Your grass here’s getting tall. Better bring your scythe in for sharpening.”

Neva missed Dr. Ives’s reply; turning her back on the insufferable Levy, she had shoved open the porch door. Her cheeks burned, and she pressed them hard with her clenched fists, before entering the house and escaping the sound of his voice. Behind her, the door slammed noisily.

• 3 •

The only religious sect in the world, unless we except the Quakers, that has recognized the equality of woman, is the Spiritualists. They have always assumed that woman may be a medium of communication from heaven to earth. . . . The Spiritualists in our country are not an organized body, but they are more or less numerous in every State and Territory from ocean to ocean.

—*History of Woman Suffrage*,
edited by Elizabeth Cady Stanton, Susan B. Anthony, and Matilda Jocelyn Gage

It's good of you to come with me," Neva Cardoza said to Glynis while they waited on Fall Street, outside Boone's Livery. "I either walked or took the omnibuses at home—in Philadelphia, too. I doubt I'll ever learn to drive one of those contraptions." She gestured toward the small, two-seater, four-wheeled phaeton to which a bay horse was being harnessed by one of Boone's young stable boys.

"You'll learn," Glynis said, and smiled. "We've all had to, those of us women who need to get places on our own—and who don't have the means to hire drivers. Why don't I give you a lesson today?"

Neva looked dubious, Glynis thought, but the young woman agreed readily enough. She had now been in town for little less than a month, and Quentin Ives had decided she should be seeing more of his patients. Dr. Cardoza was certainly qualified, he'd said, to handle the more routine things a rural physician encountered.

Neva had come by the library the day previous for some books on western New York's history. "I guess if I'm going to be here awhile, I should know something about the area," she'd said.

Glynis applauded this interest and, while locating materials, had

noted that the young woman had lost her sallow complexion. Neva's cheeks glowed with a becoming ruddiness.

Glynis extracted two heavy books from the shelves beside her desk. "This first one, *The Jesuit Relations,*" she explained, handing it to Neva, "is a collection of reports—letters and journals mainly—sent back to Quebec and France during the seventeenth century by Jesuit missionaries. It's thought that missionaries were the first whites to have contact with American Indians. At least they were the first to chronicle the contact."

Neva made a small face. "Jesuit missionaries? You mean Catholic priests?"

Glynis nodded. "And you should keep that in mind when the Indians are described as heathens and barbarians, because, of course, the Jesuits came to convert these people to Christianity. But the Iroquois—the only Indians I'm familiar with—already possessed a rich, spirit-based religion.

"The other book," she went on, "*League of the Ho-de-no-sau-nee, or Iroquois,* was written by Lewis Henry Morgan, a Rochester lawyer; Morgan did his research assisted by Ely S. Parker, a Seneca Iroquois."

"*Seneca* Iroquois?" Neva echoed. "I thought the Indians around here were *all* Iroquois—"

"It's a Confederacy," Glynis interjected. "If we can find some time in the next few days, I'll try to explain what I know of it."

"I have to make some calls with Dr. Ives today," Neva told her, "and tomorrow morning I'm supposed to go to the . . . the Grimm farm, I think it was. Do you know how far that might be?" she asked, her expression one of misgiving, "Because I'll probably have to walk—I don't know how to handle a carriage."

"It's too far to walk, but I'll go with you, if you like," Glynis offered. "Young Pippa Grimm has been sick, and I should take her some more books."

"Pippa—she's the one I'm supposed to see," Neva said. "Quentin—that is, Dr. Ives—" she corrected herself, flushing slightly, "said she'd had scarlet fever. The last time he saw her was several weeks ago, and he wants to be sure she's recovered without complications. To tell the truth, I rather hoped you'd offer to come with me."

Her smile had been a grateful one.

Now, on Saturday morning, Glynis flicked the reins of the carriage

horse, and they wheeled across Fall Street to turn north onto another, narrower, dirt road.

"This becomes Black Brook Road," Glynis said, "and to the right over there is Black Brook itself. Notice how the water looks stained or dusky? That's because of tannin in the leaves and wood from the trees along its banks."

"Is that where the word *tanning* comes from?" Neva asked.

Glynis nodded. "There are a lot of streams and brooks named 'Black' something or other, wherever there are oak woods. This particular Black Brook flows east to Seneca Falls village, then heads north, getting deeper and wider, until it empties into swampland called the Montezuma Marsh."

Despite the autumnal color of the leaves, a soft October wind seemed almost as warm as that of high summer, and it lifted the brim of Neva's new straw hat. She grabbed at the hat, retied its long green ribbons under her chin, then took a deep breath. "Well," she said, exhaling, "the air here certainly smells different from New York City's." She said this somewhat reluctantly, Glynis thought.

"Are you very homesick?" she asked Neva, the reins loosely held while the road remained flat. "I should think you might be, by this time."

Rearranging her small black leather satchel under her feet, Neva didn't answer immediately, and Glynis glanced sideways to see if she'd heard the question. But then Neva said, "No, oddly enough, I'm not." She spoke slowly. "I even had to think for a minute about what homesickness feels like. Guess I've been too busy to notice." Her face darkened abruptly. "Yesterday, that Mr. Levy asked me the same thing."

Glynis thought it probably best not to comment on "that Mr. Levy." But then, to her surprise, Neva asked, "How old is he, do you know?"

"Ah, well . . . let's see." Glynis found this question intriguing, coming as it did from someone who, by all accounts, appeared to loathe Abraham. "I think he must be around thirty-five or thirty-six."

"Has he ever been married?" Neva's voice was so faint, Glynis had to lean toward her to hear. Well, well—such singular curiosity about Abraham Levy!

"I heard that Abraham was betrothed when he lived in England—

that's where he grew up," Glynis said. "But his intended died. I'm afraid that's all I know about it. I did hear that his mother was Spanish."

"Oh, yes," Neva broke in. "I know that! Not that I really care anything about it," she added emphatically. "I shouldn't have asked, Miss Tryon . . . I really don't know why I did."

Didn't she now, Glynis thought, swallowing a smile. Then, mostly to reassure Neva that she herself hadn't given the questions a second thought, she said, "Why don't you take the reins for a time? Here."

Neva reached for the reins without hesitation; the next minutes were devoted to driving technique. Their horse was an unfamiliar one to Glynis, possibly new to Boone's Livery, and while this made her a shade uneasy, the animal seemed complacent enough about the various tuggings and the inexpert poking with the whip. "Very lightly," Glynis instructed, "only enough to make him aware that you want a change of gait or direction. For example, just ahead where we want to bear right alongside Black Brook."

Neva negotiated the curve and smiled broadly, like a child mastering a difficult task. "Is that it ahead—the Grimm farm?" She pointed left with the whip.

"No, that's the Turner place."

Neva's smile disappeared. "Oh," was all she said.

They drew parallel with the Turner farmhouse; its roof and porch sagged badly, and sections of the fence fronting the road were missing altogether. Several sheep, their summer fleece matted and grimy, grazed on what appeared to be merely stubble. Small wonder that Sara Turner indicated the farm had been doing poorly.

"We should stop on the way back," Glynis said, "to see how Sara's getting on."

Neva murmured agreement.

She handled the horse with increasing confidence, so Glynis relaxed and sat back to watch. When they were a quarter of a mile past the Turner farm, they came abreast of several dilapidated structures to the right of the road. The blackened wooden skeletons of a farmhouse and barns were barely visible under a wrapping of wild grapevine and ivy. Several lilac bushes flourished beside the ruins of the house.

"What happened there?" Neva asked. "Fire?"

"A terrible fire," Glynis confirmed. "Four or five years ago. I remember that night, and seeing from my bedroom window what looked to be the whole northern sky ablaze. It was a real tragedy—Cole Flannery, the farmer who owned the land, and his hired hand, Dick Davis, both died in that fire. Fortunately, Cole's wife, Mary, and their children were away, visiting family in Syracuse when it happened, or they all might have perished."

Glynis shook her head; she still found the memory of that night disturbing.

The carriage now clattered up a moderate rise where the roadbed narrowed to become not much more than axle width. "The Grimm place is about half a mile up the road, on the other side of this hill," Glynis told Neva. "You're doing very well—why don't you take us all the way there?"

"The road's gotten so cramped, though," Neva said, peering ahead. "What happens if we meet another—"

Interrupting her, and making her concern all too real, came the sound of pounding hooves on the far side of the hill. Glynis sat bolt upright as a horse and carriage appeared at the top of the rise, racing directly toward them.

Neva gasped, and gripped the reins tightly. "Flex on the right rein," Glynis directed, "to pull his head around. Right rein! The other carriage will pass to the left."

"But there's no room!" Neva said between clenched teeth. She jerked her head to the right; the bank beside the road rioted with waist-high goldenrod.

"Neva," Glynis said anxiously, "slow the horse! Flex the reins with both hands: pull and release, pull and release. One, two, one, two . . . Never mind!" she said suddenly, glancing ahead at the rapidly approaching carriage. "Just haul back on both reins to make him stop. Use the hand brake!"

But the left rein slithered from Neva's grasp. The horse surged forward, while the oncoming carriage barreled toward them, clearly not about to give an inch.

"Neva!" Glynis shouted over the sound of rattling wheels. "Neva, use your whip—tap his left—*left*—hindquarters. *Left hindquarters! And use the brake!"*

Neva fumbled for the hand brake, nearly losing her seat. Glynis

sucked in her breath as Neva brought the whip down, at the same time hauling on the right rein. Abruptly the horse swerved right. The carriage gave a great bounce, nearly throwing out both women as the horse scrambled directly up the shallow bank. The vehicle tilted precariously, jolting from one side to the other. Glynis grabbed at its low side and winced as her head repeatedly struck the canopy. They jounced ahead, plowing through goldenrod, pollen spewing into the air and blossom heads flying. At last the drag of the carriage proved too much for the horse. He came to a quivering halt.

Glynis's fingers ached from gripping the side panel of the phaeton. She rubbed them while watching the carriage on the road below pass swiftly. And although its driver must have seen their predicament, it did not even slow. Glynis managed to catch a glimpse of a woman's face, flushed and angry-looking, gazing straight ahead while she repeatedly whipped her horse. The woman looked vaguely familiar.

Neva sat very still, her face white and moist with perspiration. But Glynis had learned about her something that was extremely telling—the young woman hadn't thrown up her hands helplessly in panic, as many would have done. While she climbed down from the carriage to retrieve the lost left rein, she glanced with sudden affection at the silent Neva. Glynis struggled through the weeds in her long skirts; the horse's head swung toward her, his muzzle sprinkled with golden specks. He acted as if nothing unusual had taken place. "As if," she said when she returned with the rein, "he just stopped along the way for some sweets."

Neva gave her a shaky look and tried to refuse the rein Glynis handed up to her. "I don't think I should drive," she said unsteadily. "I almost got us killed."

"It wasn't your fault," Glynis said with firmness. "As a matter of fact, you kept your head and did very well."

"How can you say that?" Neva argued. "The horse would have done fine if I hadn't confused him!"

"Perhaps," Glynis said doubtfully. "But you can't depend on the reasoning power of a horse. Horses are none too bright. Beautiful, yes—but not bright. Though they're not as stupid as some people." She gestured toward the dust just settling behind the other carriage, now vanished.

"Did you see the driver?" Neva's voice had an edge.

"Barely. She reminded me of—that is, she looked like someone I should know." Glynis shook her head, frowning. "Can't remember where I've seen her."

"Perhaps a lunatic asylum?" Neva offered.

Glynis smiled ruefully and nodded. "Perhaps. Now, are you ready? I'll guide the horse back to the road. But then you should drive," she insisted.

Once again on the road, the carriage jerked briefly while its wheels unburdened themselves of goldenrod debris. Glynis glanced sideways at Neva, startled to hear the young woman begin to laugh softly.

"I was just thinking," she answered Glynis's unspoken question, "how shocked my family would be if they could see me now. I'm afraid I'm not too tolerant of people who get themselves into dangerous situations. It always seems to involve just plain stupidity on their part. But look at what I did!"

Neva's voice, not sounding particularly chastened, trailed off as the southern edge of the Grimm farm came into sight. Sturdy fences enclosed grazing flocks, reminding Glynis of a landscape scene by the artist Susan Catherine Moore Waters, whose favorite subject was sheep. Grass grew lushly green. Black Brook meandered to the right of the road, then curved to flow under a wooden bridge that vibrated noisily beneath the carriage wheels.

"Before we reach the farm," Glynis said, "I should tell you a little about the Grimms. They're . . . well, let's say they're a somewhat unusual family." Neva's raised eyebrows had made Glynis decide on *unusual* rather than *peculiar.*

"Unusual? Why?"

"For one thing, they're very reclusive. Hardly ever come into town, any of them but Molly. She brings Pippa with her to the library occasionally."

Neva nodded. "Pippa, the one I'm to see?"

"Yes, Molly's daughter. When Molly was widowed—I'm told her husband died shortly after their marriage—she returned to her home and the Grimm family name. Obadiah Grimm, Molly's father, is the patriarch of the family; everyone thinks of him that way, I guess, because he resembles the Moses of Michelangelo: shoulder-length white hair and flowing beard, strong, rugged features—an impressive-looking man. And quite an intimidating one."

Neva was frowning, and now said, "All those old biblical males were intimidating! That's one reason I renounced religion—like my cousin Ernestine Rose, although she's had more success in renouncing her *family* than I have." She glanced at Glynis with an inquiring expression.

Glynis wondered if Neva thought she'd be shocked. "Well, yes, I know about your cousin," she said, smiling with what she hoped would convey understanding.

But Neva's frown remained. And when she didn't say more, Glynis continued with the Grimms. "There's also Almira. She's Obadiah's wife and Molly's mother, but you should draw your own conclusions about *her*. And then," Glynis went on, "there is Molly's brother, Lazarus."

"Lazarus?" Neva's frown deepened. "Strange name."

"According to the New Testament, Jesus was supposed to have raised him from the dead. Lazarus Grimm, however, is rather"—Glynis strained for charity—"let's just say he has the reputation of a rascal."

"A rascal? You mean a ne'er-do-well, et cetera?"

"Et cetera. Yes, you might say that. In any event, Lazarus Grimm left town several years ago, and hasn't been seen since, although it's been rumored that he joined some spiritualist community—I myself can scarce believe that, it would be so out of character for him. But the rumor simply adds a touch more mystery to the family's reputation, which comes, as I said, mostly from their reclusiveness, and from the fact that they're not well known in Seneca Falls. But I do know Molly, at least a bit better than the others, and I quite like her." Glynis smiled. "Perhaps I like her because she uses my library now and then."

The carriage was passing flocks of mottled gray sheep, and Neva gestured with the whip. "Those are merino sheep, aren't they?"

"Yes, they are," Glynis said with some surprise. "But how—"

"They originated in Spain, that's how I know. My father—he's Spanish—said they're the oldest breed of sheep. That's the kind of thing my father would find satisfying. The oldest, the strongest, the richest, the 'est' of anything, he'd boast about." Neva gave Glynis a brief, unreadable look. "That's my father!"

Glynis didn't have the leisure to consider this, as the Grimm farm-

house appeared to the right of the carriage. “Turn into that drive,” she directed Neva.

The dirt drive took them past a large but otherwise ordinary-looking gray farmhouse to its far side and an open area ringed with birch clumps. Some distance beyond was a gray barn, in front of which post-and-rail fencing formed numerous pens. Neva pulled the horse to a stop under autumn-yellow birch leaves rustling in the warm breeze.

“There’s Billy Wicken,” Glynis said, and motioned toward the Grimms’ hired hand, who, apparently unaware of their arrival, was shuffling toward an isolated sheep pen. But shuffling wasn’t the right word for Billy Wicken’s gait; he dragged his left leg behind him as if it were an afterthought. Even from a distance the man reminded Glynis of an elfin creature—Shakespeare’s Puck, perhaps. The tips of Billy’s large ears protruded through a tousled mop of straw-colored hair, his sharp nose and chin pointing the way ahead of him. Glynis involuntarily glanced at the clear sky; Billy’s eyes would reflect its color exactly, eerily changing from one day’s blue to another’s dark gray. And in winter those mirror eyes became almost ice-white.

Neva, too, was watching Billy. “Has he always been like that?” she asked.

“You mean his limp? Yes, ever since I’ve known him. And he’s worked here at least as long as I’ve been in Seneca Falls—that’s almost sixteen years.”

Neva nodded. “Does the paralysis affect his brain? Is he feebleminded?”

“Some say so,” Glynis answered. “I’m more inclined to believe he’s just slow. He has, after all, learned to do a great many things on this farm. But he is childlike.”

“Still,” Neva said, continuing to watch him, “there are varying degrees of feeblemindedness. How old is he?”

Glynis smiled. “He could be any age. The first time I saw him I thought he was somewhere around thirteen—and he still looks the same way.”

Billy had paused, his hand on the gate of the pen; although the hand looked withered, the arm seemed normal enough. He gazed off, jerked suddenly as if he’d just recalled something, then limped along the fence, peering over the top rail. Despite his affliction, Billy

Wicken could move surprisingly fast. He was also quite strong, Glynis recalled.

Glynis climbed from the carriage to follow Neva, who, carrying her black satchel, was already moving toward the man and sheep pen. The pen was occupied. A gray woolly back heaved up and down, accompanied by loud panting, and when Glynis reached Neva's side, it became clear that the merino ewe inside the pen was in labor.

Billy, at the pen's far side, looked across the fence at the two women. "Long time," he said finally, scratching his blond head. His forehead furrowed with obvious concern.

Neva moved toward him and pointed down at the ewe. "You mean she's been like that for . . . for *how* long?" she asked.

"Long time," Billy said again, after pausing to study Neva.

Glynis glanced around for some sign of the Grimm family. "Where is everybody, Billy?"

Shifting his gaze to her, he grinned in apparent recognition, then gestured with his right hand in the direction of Black Brook. "Gone."

Glynis wondered how the whole family could have disappeared. But then she remembered that Billy tended to ignore everyone but Molly Grimm and her daughter, Pippa. So Obadiah and his wife, Almira, could be inside the house. But where was Mead Miller, the hired hand who took care of the sheep?

Neva spoke softly. "I don't think Billy's particularly feebleminded. He's childlike all right, but he answered our questions appropriately enough. I wonder if he had a severe head injury—that is, rather than having been born that way." She now said more loudly, pointing to the gasping ewe, "Billy, has she been like that since early morning?"

Billy Wicken seemed to consider this. "Early morning?" he repeated, then bobbed his head. "Sunup."

At that moment the ewe went down on her knees, then rolled over on her side. Neva headed for the gate, lifted the latch, and yanked it open. Going directly to the suffering animal, she knelt beside it, opened her satchel, and pulled from it a small, trumpetlike wooden stethoscope.

Neva bent over the ewe's swollen belly, listening. Finally, she removed the instrument from her ears and straightened to say, "I think there are two lambs. Is that common?" She addressed this question to Billy Wicken.

Billy, staring at Neva's stethoscope, turned to Glynis with a worried expression. "Why is the lady poking a stick at—"

"No, Billy," Glynis interrupted him. "That's a tool to hear heartbeats." Billy did not look enlightened. Answering Neva, she said, "Yes, two lambs are common enough."

"But aren't lambs usually born in the spring?"

"Your father didn't tell you?" Glynis smiled. "Merinos are one breed that can lamb anytime of year."

"Fertil*est*," Neva said with a twitch of her lips. She rocked back on her heels. "Where's the one who takes care of these animals? Billy, do you know? Because this ewe's in trouble."

"Gone." Billy looked around, then repeated, "He's gone!"

Neva sighed heavily. Then, to Glynis's surprise, she unbuttoned the wristbands of her cotton blouse and began to roll up her sleeves. Billy watched for a moment, then took off toward the barn.

"Neva," Glynis began, "are you sure—"

"Yes. In medical school we students once delivered a lamb. It was a training exercise—and rightly so—before we were allowed to deliver human infants. Sheep are usually pretty docile, especially merinos. I don't think this one will give me much trouble. Problem is, I think the first lamb in the birth canal is positioned wrong."

"Wrong? Then what—"

"Have to find out," Neva said, with more confidence than Glynis felt. "It's supposed to be positioned with its head crouched between its forelegs. I might have to turn it . . ."

Neva broke off as Billy limped back across the yard with a plaid blanket under his arm, the handle of a water bucket in his undamaged hand. "Oh, good, Billy! Thank you."

Billy spread the blanket just behind the ewe. Still kneeling, Neva moved onto it before she plunged her right arm into the bucket, then drew it out dripping and began to insert her hand into the panting ewe.

Glynis quickly turned away. "I'll leave you now, if that's all right," she called over her shoulder. There was no reply as she walked toward the house.

By the time she reached the porch, a dog had begun barking somewhere behind the house. Following the sound, she walked toward the

rear yard, to be met by a black-and-white collie bounding across the grass, his tail wagging enthusiastically.

As Glynis reached down to stroke the dog's head, she heard a muffled cackle, silence, then another cackle. Searching for its source, she saw a curtain swing across a first-floor windowpane. That cackle could belong only to Almira, so Glynis waved at the invisible woman and started back around the house, the dog beside her.

"Miss Tryon?" Her name floated from the direction of Black Brook. "Miss Tryon . . . here!"

Glynis turned to see Pippa running toward her, hair the color of corn tassels floating behind like a long pale streamer. On the bank of the brook, Molly Grimm appeared, arms laden with wildflowers, and began to follow her daughter across the grass.

"Miss Tryon," Pippa gasped as she reached Glynis, "what are you doing here? Oh, I know—you've come to pick up your books."

"No, I came mostly to see you, Pippa. And you certainly seem to be feeling better than a few weeks ago. Dr. Ives will be glad to hear that." As she spoke, Glynis found herself, as always, drawn to the girl's sweet nature and her uncommon prettiness. Despite the pale hair, Pippa's eyes shone a deep chocolate and her skin, now flushed with exertion, had the color of ripe peaches. Glynis smiled at her choice of description and added, "You look good enough to eat."

Pippa smiled shyly and turned as her mother approached. In dappled sunlight filtering through the birch leaves, Molly Grimm's hair spun a gold much darker than her daughter's. The armful of coarse stems she carried bore flat white flower clusters, and watching Molly approach with her long, rose-colored skirt swinging gracefully, Glynis had the impression of a Flemish oil painting suddenly come to life.

"Molly, hello," Glynis said. "What have you been gathering? It looks like boneset."

Pippa answered, "It's Indian sage. That's what the Indian lady said, and it's—"

"Pippa," her mother interrupted, "Miss Tryon's right. It's called boneset or teasel."

"Or feverwort, isn't that also a name for it?" Glynis asked.

Pippa again started to answer, "Yes, that's why we got it. For tea. The Indian lady told us to—"

"Please, Pippa," Molly Grimm broke in with a patient smile, "take

these to the kitchen for me. They're scratchy, remember, so be careful." She reached forward to unload the herbs into Pippa's arms, but fumbled and dropped most of them. Awkwardness was so uncharacteristic of Molly that Glynis had a sudden sense of something strangely amiss. After Pippa had retrieved the fallen stems, Molly watched her daughter run with them toward the house. The dog barked joyfully at her heels.

Molly's soft blue eyes were as full of love as ever for the girl, Glynis observed, but the woman's expression also had a strained look. A tenseness not part of her usual composed appearance. Something *was* wrong.

"Pippa looks wonderful," Glynis said, wondering if Molly's tension could be caused by lingering concern over her daughter's illness. "Hardly as if she'd been sick at all."

"Yes," Molly agreed, "she does seem to be recovered."

But Glynis felt that the woman's eyes held more worry than she was admitting.

"Molly, I've brought a young physician with me. She's going to be in Seneca Falls for the next few months, training with Quentin Ives, and she'd like to examine Pippa."

"*She?* A woman doctor?" Molly gave Glynis an uncertain look. "I don't know if . . . but I suppose a woman would be all right now that Pippa's recovered."

Glynis decided not to comment. This certainly wouldn't be the first time Neva Cardoza had run into doubts about her competence. And Molly Grimm was known to be ferociously protective of her daughter. Well, let her see for herself.

As they began to stroll toward the house, Glynis remarked, "By the way, Molly, Dr. Cardoza and I had a rather unpleasant experience on the drive here. I wonder if you had an earlier visitor today? By any chance a woman?"

Molly's face stiffened. "Why do you ask?"

"Because she ran us off the road," Glynis explained. "She seemed to be in a great hurry. Odd thing is, her face looked familiar to me."

Molly abruptly stopped walking. "Oh, she was familiar to you, all right. It was Lily Braun."

"Lily Braun?" Glynis echoed. "No wonder I didn't recognize her. I haven't seen her in years. Not since she left Seneca Falls after . . ." Her

voice trailed away as she recalled the disturbing circumstances of Lily Braun's departure.

"Yes!" was all Molly Grimm said. But Glynis heard anger in that single word, and she was about to ask more when Pippa burst out of the house.

"Mummy, there's lambs down there"—she pointed toward the far side of the house—"I saw them out the window." And she took off in a run toward the sheep pens.

The two women followed. Glynis made a mental note to inquire further about Lily Braun, but then quickly forgot about her.

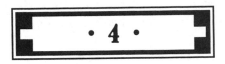

• 4 •

Take incense and pigeon's dung and wheat flour, a pinch of each, and temper with the white of an egg; and whereso the head acheth, bind it, and it shall vanish anon.

—A Leechbook or Collection of Medical Recipes of the Fifteenth Century

When Glynis and Molly Grimm reached the sheep pen, Pippa was hanging over the fence, watching Neva and Billy Wicken attempt to introduce a small gray lamb to its mother. They were meeting with no visible success, as the ewe repeatedly butted the lamb away, concentrating instead on her other, larger offspring.

"Why doesn't she like the little one?" Pippa asked anxiously.

From her kneeling position, Neva rocked back on her heels to answer the girl. "The bigger one came first, after I'd turned it and helped it out. The mother began licking it clean, and when the other one came, a few minutes later, the ewe ignored it. I don't know how common that sort of thing is with sheep."

"It happens occasionally," Molly Grimm volunteered. "Then usually Mead Miller takes the rejected lamb to another ewe, one that's lost her own. But right now there aren't any other ewes that have lambed recently. And, incidentally," she asked Billy Wicken, "where *is* Mead?"

Billy slowly shook his head. "Gone. Mead's gone."

"We can see that. Where's he gone to?" Molly said to him.

Billy's face flushed, and he looked away.

"Billy, where is Mead?" Molly persisted.

His face flushed darker, and not looking at Molly, Billy shook his head again.

Just then Neva, still trying to induce the ewe to nurse the smaller lamb, jumped back as the ewe nipped not only at her offspring but at Neva as well. "We obviously have an impasse here," she said unhappily. "Perhaps I did the wrong thing when I wiped this one dry"—she gestured to the rejected lamb—"because the mother might not recognize its smell."

They watched as the lamb tottered again toward its mother; this time the ewe's head shot forward, nipping it hard. The lamb let out a plaintive bleat and crumpled to the grass as its unsteady legs gave way.

"Please do something," Pippa said softly, her eyes bright with tears. "The poor little thing."

Neva looked from the unfortunate lamb to the girl. "You must be Pippa," she said, getting up from the grass. "I'm Dr. Cardoza."

Glynis saw that Neva's green skirt had bloodstains on it, but the young woman didn't seem to notice as she brushed off grass and twigs. "I suggest," Neva said to no one in particular, "that we try to find this Mead Miller. If he's the one in charge of these sheep, he certainly isn't doing his job." She gazed at the lamb, now pitiably trying to suck a corner of the blanket.

"We have to get some nourishment into it," she said to Molly Grimm. "Is there anything we might use as a feeding bottle—and make some sort of nipple arrangement?"

Molly nodded. "Yes, up at the house we can probably find something."

"I need some water to wash up," Neva added, "and then I'll take a look at you, young lady." This was directed at Pippa with a smile.

"Come along to the house," Molly told her. "And I'll ask Father if he knows where Mead Miller could be."

Glynis stayed behind, watching an obviously reluctant Pippa follow her mother and Neva toward the house; the girl glanced over her shoulder again and again at the forsaken lamb. Billy Wicken, on the other hand, had not taken his eyes off Molly and Pippa, and now gazed after them with a troubled expression.

"Billy," Glynis said to him, "I think you know where Mead Miller is, don't you?"

Billy pulled his gaze from the departing women to stare at the toe of his boot stubbing the grass. And he didn't answer.

"You know that lamb won't live long," Glynis insisted, "if we don't do something for it. We have to find Mead. Did he ask you not to tell where he'd gone?"

Billy finally looked up at her to nod unwillingly. "Said he'd come back soon. Not to tell. He'll come back."

"When did Mead say he'd be back?"

"Soon."

Glynis sighed, shook her head at Billy, and followed the others to the house.

While Pippa and her mother and Neva were upstairs, Glynis sat for what seemed hours over a cup of cold tea at the kitchen table, while Almira Grimm darted in and out of the adjoining pantry. The thin little woman didn't remain in one spot for long, and Glynis's head began to throb as she watched Almira hover, flutter like a hummingbird, then shoot off in another direction. Almira's hair also brought to mind small birds: a few graying brown strands were caught back in a bun, but the rest stood out from her head like the bent twigs of a poorly constructed nest.

Suddenly the outside door swung open, and Mead Miller strode into the room. "Billy says you all been looking for me." He scowled at Glynis. "Don't see why."

"One of the ewes lambed—" Glynis started.

"Yes, yes, and she's dandy," the man interrupted. "So why the dustup?" Broad-shouldered and muscular, Mead Miller stood with arms crossed over his chest, feet apart, straddling the kitchen floor like Colossus. Glynis just stared at him, not sure where to begin. He hadn't so much as glanced at Almira, who now fluttered beside Glynis, wringing her hands.

"They're mad at you, Mead Miller," Almira whined. "You best be careful now—you know what happens when *he* gets mad!"

Glynis assumed "he" must mean Obadiah Grimm, and she wondered what *did* happen when Almira's husband got mad. Mead Miller, however, ignored Almira as well as her implied threat, and said to Glynis, "So who's this here lady doctor? And why's she delivering *my* lambs?"

A door behind Glynis swung open with Neva's announcement,

"I'm Dr. Cardoza, and if you're so concerned about *your* lambs, why weren't you here to deliver them yourself?"

Mead Miller's mouth opened and closed rapidly as if he were attempting speech. Glynis pressed her lips together so she wouldn't smile, and decided she really did like Neva Cardoza. The young woman moved on into the room just as the outside door opened.

Obadiah Grimm stopped just inside the sill to glare at Neva. "Who are you, and what are you doing in my house? And *who* do you think you are talking to?" he thundered, his heavy-browed eyes flashing ominously.

For a moment it seemed as if no one even breathed, and Glynis stole a quick glance at Neva, who, her small jaw thrust forward, was moving resolutely around the end of the table until she stood within a few feet of Obadiah Grimm.

"If you're addressing me, my name is Dr. Neva Cardoza." Her chin lifted. "What I am doing here is checking on your granddaughter—that is, of course, if you are Mr. Grimm."

Obadiah Grimm's long, lean body and face, crowned with abundant white hair and beard, stiffened. He spoke harshly, "It is said in Proverbs that 'a foolish woman is noisy; she is wanton and knows no shame.' You are not welcome in my house, woman. Not you or your witchcraft. The girl is fine—we don't need you interfering. I expect you to be gone when I return!" With that, Obadiah brushed Neva aside and went through the inner door. Moments later, his boots could be heard stomping up the stairs.

During his speech, Glynis had watched Neva's hands clench at her sides, and was relieved when she said nothing more. "I imagine we should be on our way now," Glynis suggested. "Have you finished with Pippa?"

"Yes," Neva said. She glanced at the closed door through which Obadiah had passed. "She's recovered very nicely, and there don't seem to be any lasting effects that—"

Her voice broke off as from the upstairs came a series of sharp exclamations in what sounded like Molly Grimm's voice. Although the words were indistinguishable, there was no mistaking the anger in her tone. Glynis felt something unpleasant streak down her spine; coupled with Molly's odd reaction to her own earlier inquiry about Lily

Braun, she wondered what recently had occurred to so agitate the woman.

However, a few minutes later, as Glynis and Neva walked back to the sheep pen, Molly came after them. Her face looked composed, if somewhat pale. "I'm sorry about my father's rudeness, Dr. Cardoza," she said a little breathlessly. "It's just that he doesn't like strangers. But we're grateful, Pippa and I, that you came out."

Neva nodded. "Pippa looks very healthy. There's no vision problem and no hearing loss, which can sometimes occur with scarlet fever—she apparently came through it well. But I'm curious as to what Pippa told me about the medicine woman from the reservation." Neva pointed north. "Black Brook, is it?"

"Oh, that was nothing," Molly said quickly. "Just some herbs for tea she brought Pippa."

"I didn't know there *was* a medicine woman at Black Brook," Glynis said.

Molly hesitated, and her response seemed overlong in coming. "Well . . . she isn't always at Black Brook. She travels back and forth from the Cattaraugus reservation, near Buffalo."

"Who is she?" Glynis asked.

Again Molly hesitated. Finally she said, "Bitter Root—her name's Bitter Root."

"That's an appropriate name, I'd say," Neva commented. "Pippa sounded very fond of the woman. I think I'd like to meet her myself. Some of the old herbal remedies seem to work as well if not better than patent medicines. Of course," she added, "there are male physicians who think these things are dangerous, and others believe they're some kind of witchcraft." She looked pointedly toward the house.

Molly went a shade paler and began to reply, but she stopped as they'd reached the sheep pen. Pippa sat cross-legged on the grass, holding the orphaned lamb in her lap. Billy Wicken was feeding it from a glass jar of fluid, topped with what looked to Glynis like the thumb of a leather glove. The lamb tugged at the improvised nipple with surprising strength.

"Sugar water," Billy answered in reply to her question. "That's what Mead Miller said to give it. He said maybe the mother will feed it later." He grinned down at the lamb in Pippa's lap.

Glynis and Neva took their leave and began to walk with Molly toward their carriage. "Do you remember my brother Lazarus?" Molly asked Glynis.

"Yes. Yes, of course I do," Glynis answered, wondering what sort of mischief Lazarus had been up to now.

"He's coming home," Molly told her, "in the next few days. He wrote that he's had a spiritual awakening, and wants to share it with us."

Glynis couldn't deduce from the woman's enigmatic expression whether she accepted her brother's words at face value, or suspected some shenanigans. She herself simply smiled noncommittally at Molly, and nodded.

Under the first of the birch clumps, Neva and Molly stood talking, while Glynis went on for the carriage and horse, and suddenly stopped cold in her tracks. An eerie howl drifted from the woods north of the Grimm property. A wolf howling—at this time of day? The hair on the back of her neck rising, Glynis walked forward a few paces before drawing in her breath. There, some distance ahead at the edge of the woods, stood a large black and white paint horse. It was as motionless as the man astride.

It couldn't be! Glynis shut her eyes tightly, then snapped them open, assuming the ghostly vision would be gone. But it remained, the man and horse. And some inner sense convinced her of their substance.

"Jacques." Glynis barely breathed his name. "Jacques Sundown."

She took a few quick steps forward, then picked up her skirts and began to run toward the horse and rider. But the horse wheeled abruptly, and galloped into the woods.

Glynis ran a few more yards, then stopped. Might it have been someone else? No, it was Jacques Sundown; she had felt his presence as surely as if he had been standing directly before her. But he had been gone from Seneca Falls for three years. Why had he returned now?

Glynis directed the bay horse onto the dirt road, and they headed away from the Grimm farm. Several times she glanced to the north, but no black and white horse and rider reappeared.

She could feel Neva's eyes on her, and after a moment or two, the young doctor said, "Just before we left, I heard a very strange sound coming from those woods."

Glynis nodded. "Yes, it was a wolf."

"A wolf?" Glynis turned to see Neva's shocked look. "There are still wolves around here?"

"Not many. For a long time there's been a bounty on wolves. Most of them have been killed."

"You sound as if you're sorry!" Neva's voice held incredulity.

"I *am* sorry. They're beautiful and intelligent animals, and it doesn't seem right to exterminate them. There's never been any evidence of them attacking humans. Wolves are very shy, and they try to avoid people. The farmers hate them and insist that they kill their livestock. But they only go after old or sick animals. And the wolves were here first . . ." Glynis's voice trailed off as she realized how absurd this must sound to someone from New York City.

Neva began, "But they look dangerous—"

"So do the men with guns who kill them!" Glynis bit down on her lower lip, startled by her own anger. "Forgive me, Neva, I have a bit of a headache—and I'd rather not talk about it," she murmured, hoping this wouldn't hurt the other woman's feelings. But she still felt unsettled about seeing Jacques Sundown. *It had been so long.* So long without hearing anything from him, as though he'd vanished from the face of the earth. She'd never allowed herself to consider that he might have died, so she hadn't realized, until she saw him, how afraid she'd been that he had.

Neva remained silent, and Glynis gradually felt the initial jolt ebb, receding into a less complicated, and more manageable, puzzlement. How long had Jacques been here? Did Cullen know—and if so, why hadn't he told her? And, finally, why—why had Jacques Sundown come back to Seneca Falls?

Neva, at last, made a great show of clearing her throat. "Are you better—I mean your headache?" she ventured.

Glynis felt foolish for having tried to deceive a doctor. "Oh, that." She made herself smile. "I'm sorry, I hope I didn't offend you."

"No, no—not at all," Neva protested. "It was just unexpected, because you always seem so composed, so self-possessed."

“Me?” Glynis laughed. “If you only knew how hard I fight shyness! All the time.”

Neva gave her an unmistakably skeptical look. Then she shrugged lightly and said, “Well, if you feel up to it, I’d like to know something about the Iroquois—the Seneca Iroquois.”

Glynis shot her a quick glance. Surely Neva hadn’t seen Jacques Sundown. But even if she had, she couldn’t have known, not from a distance, that Jacques was Seneca. *Half-Seneca,* Glynis corrected herself.

“I’ll try,” she began, her eyes on the road ahead, “at least to give you a brief background so those books you borrowed will make some sense. I guess no one knows the exact origin of the Indian tribes that lived here for centuries—‘here’ being the territory that lies more or less between the Hudson and the Niagara Rivers. But according to Lewis Morgan’s research—he’s the author of one of those books—the tribes were at war continually with one another. Sometime during the sixteenth century, the five largest tribes created a confederacy. And by the way, today they prefer to be called *nations* rather than *tribes.* In any event, they called this confederacy the League of the Iroquois, or Haudenosaunee, meaning People of the Longhouse. A symbolic longhouse in this case.”

“Longhouse—what they lived in?” Neva asked.

Glynis nodded. “The nation farthest west in the original five-nation league was the Senecas. In the 1700s, a sixth nation joined the League—the Tuscaroras, living in what’s now Ohio—but the Senecas continued to control all of New York from west of Cayuga Lake to the state’s western border; they were the guardians or Keepers of the Western Door of the Longhouse. East of the Senecas were the Cayugas. And then the Onondagas, the Oneidas, and finally, the Mohawks, Keepers of the Eastern Door.

“Individually these nations were not strong enough to avoid the warfare I mentioned earlier, but once united under the one symbolic roof, they constituted a near invulnerable force. That’s why western New York had so few white settlers until well after the Revolutionary War.”

“So what happened?” Neva asked. “How did the Confederacy lose its power?”

“It’s a long, tortuous story, but the final death blow came when five

of the six Iroquois nations sided with the British during the war. So the colonial army made a sweep from Pennsylvania up through western New York and virtually destroyed the Iroquois farms and villages. The descendants of those Indians who survived are now either in Canada or on reservations in this country."

For a time Neva stared off, apparently deep in thought, at the ancient passing landscape. "How many Iroquois were there before they were driven out?" she asked.

"Morgan places the number at somewhere around twenty-five thousand or more; today there are far fewer than half that many, and not all of them, as I said, are in this country. But some *are* still here, at the Black Brook Reservation, for example. They're mostly Cayugas and Senecas; the Cayugas ended up with no land at all, and so are considered guests, so to speak, on the Seneca reservations."

"The spoils of war," Neva said.

"No, not exactly," Glynis shook her head. "It's more an issue of treaties disregarded. But that's a more complicated story." And a sad one, she thought, reminded of what was happening to the wolves.

She slowed the horse now as a lightweight buckboard, coming in the opposite direction, turned in front of them and rattled off down a rutted path to the west of Black Brook. Peering after the buckboard in a futile attempt to identify its driver, she explained to Neva, "That road goes to Jake Braun's farm. And Jake Braun happens to be the uncle of the woman who earlier ran us off this road."

"I thought you said you didn't recognize her."

"I didn't at first," Glynis said, "but Molly Grimm told me it was Lily Braun. Lily's a woman with a . . . well, to put it politely, a somewhat checkered past."

Neva immediately sat up straighter. "You mean you actually have those here in Seneca Falls—checkered pasts, I mean?"

"Oh, we have them, all right. Doesn't every place?"

Some distance after they again passed the burned remains of the Flannery farm, they turned into a drive, overrun with weeds, that led to Turner's. As they drew closer to the farmhouse, Glynis could hear hammering. This proved to be an adolescent boy nailing up braces to support the sagging roof of the front porch; he glanced sullenly at the two women when they climbed from the carriage.

"Is Sara Turner about?" Glynis asked him.

"What d'you want with 'er?" The boy's wary eyes didn't meet hers, but focused on a spot somewhere over her left shoulder. His speech slurred due to the nails he held between his lips. "Who'r'you?"

"My name's Glynis Tryon, and I just want to see how Sara's doing."

"She's doin' fine."

"Oh, well, good. Ah, may I have your name?" Glynis waited while the boy took the nails from his mouth; he stood looking at the women as if deliberating whether or not he should yield this information.

Finally he said, "Name's Jed Turner, if it makes a difference. And I dunno where she is—"

"Mrs. Turner's not home?" Neva interrupted brusquely. "That is, if you don't find that too demanding a question."

Glynis restrained a smile, but the boy's sullen expression didn't change, and he gave no answer.

"Then I guess," Glynis said, "we should probably be on our way if she isn't here. Would you tell her that Dr. Cardoza and I stopped . . ."

"Doctor? You're a *doctor*?" the boy blurted; his eyes widened, and he blinked at Neva. To Glynis's surprise, his expression became even more guarded, as if he was frightened. And at that moment the front door opened, and Sara Turner stepped out onto the porch.

"It's all right, Jed. I know 'em. G'day, Miss Tryon."

Glynis nodded, too startled at Sara's changed appearance to say anything. The woman looked very nearly healthy. And taller somehow. Glynis glanced at Neva from the corner of her eye to see her reaction. Neva looked as surprised as she.

Sara came down the porch steps. "Guess you met my boy here."

"Your son?" Glynis asked. But hadn't Sara said her children were sent away by their father?

"My son!" Sara repeated, the gladness in her voice unmistakable. "Got him and his brothers back yesterday."

"Sara, that's wonderful," Glynis declared, while Neva simply nodded. "You must be very happy about it."

"Guess I am, truth to tell," Sara said, but despite the circumstances, her expression had, for some reason, become as guarded as her son's. Surely Cullen's suspicions about Sara having a hand in her husband's death were not warranted. So why did she appear so uneasy?

Neva, her eyebrows raised, might have been thinking along the same lines because she threw Glynis an odd look, and turned toward the carriage. "Guess Mrs. Turner is doing fine," she muttered.

"We are *all* doin' fine," Sara said, the wary look still in place. "Don't you fret none about us. "But," she added, "it was real nice of you to stop by. And you be sure 'n' give my regards to that Dr. Ives." Glynis could have sworn Sara laughed softly under her breath.

By this time, Neva had climbed back into the carriage. Glynis, still standing in the drive, attempted to delay their departure by grasping the harness of the horse and turning him as slowly as possible toward the road. She knew Sara and Jed Turner were watching her, but she had no idea why she herself felt so uneasy. It was silly! The feeling that something was wrong here must be just her imagination. She shook it off with a shrug and began to climb into the carriage.

Without warning, Sara Turner called out, "It's not nearly the end of it, y'know, Miss Tryon," she said with a scowl. "Not nearly the end."

"End?" Glynis felt a chill. "Not the end of what, Sara?"

"Death. It ain't done yet."

"What do you mean?" As Glynis stepped toward her, Sara Turner moved several paces away. Then she whirled abruptly and started for the house. Both she and the boy climbed the porch stairs quickly, but before she went inside, Sara turned to say, "Mark my words—there'll be more death. You'll see."

"Sara, wait!" Glynis, trying frantically to form questions, had followed both Turners to the stairs. As she put her foot on the first step, Sara Turner went through the door, slamming it shut.

Glynis heard the latch drop firmly into place.

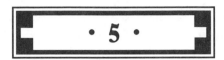

• 5 •

. . . and no such [liquor] license shall be granted except on the petition of not less than twenty respectable freeholders of this state, residing in the election district where such inn, tavern or hotel is proposed to be kept. . . .

—Chapter 628, section six, of the Laws of 1857,
enacted by the Eightieth Session of the New York Legislature

Although the day had been fair, later that evening a brief but violent storm whipped through the village. Water now chopped angrily against the walled canal section of the Seneca River, while a half moon riding the chill October wind barely lit the towpath behind Serenity's Tavern. Those hurrying along the road that fronted the tavern cursed the unpredictable weather; pulling their collars around their ears, they rushed through the oaken door when it swung open to admit them. Inside, the aroma of whiskey and tobacco, the crackling flames in the great stone fireplace, and the heat of closely packed bodies drove the cold from their bones.

On the first floor of the tavern, scores of lanterns hung over the long mahogany bar and gaming tables, while smoke rose in hazy blue strands toward the beamed ceiling. The small rooms above on the second floor held fewer lanterns, as what transpired there required little or no illumination. The tavern was also a brothel.

Serenity Hathaway, her starched petticoats and taffeta skirt rustling crisply, wound her way among tables as she crossed the sawdusted floor to the bar. She slipped onto a stool beside a black-haired young man who greeted her with very blue and very besotted eyes. Before Serenity propped her elbows on the bar, she tossed abundant hennaed hair over her bare shoulders, then, fingers arched under her

chin, offered the young man a view of creamy breasts spilling over the scant bodice of her gown. Brendan O'Reilly sighed.

"Brendan, my lad," Serenity began, her smile not quite reaching her sharp, kohl-lined eyes, "in case you haven't noticed, we are running out of time. How many more signatures do we need on that petition?"

Brendan O'Reilly sighed more fulsomely; whether this was a consequence of Serenity's question or of her bare proximity was unclear. "Three. We need three," he answered glumly. "And maybe two more are possible, but . . ." He shrugged.

Serenity's smile faded. "I depend on you, Brendan my lad. In fact, I more than depend. I pay you generously, wouldn't you agree?"

Brendan wiped beads of sweat from his forehead. "Serenity, I've tried to tell you—"

"No!" she interrupted. "No more excuses. That bloody damn law passed in April, more than six months ago. Constable Stuart's been in here every week since. And he's not come to gamble! Until we have those twenty signatures, he's got the right to close me down."

"Serenity," Brendan began again, "Stuart doesn't want to close you down. If he did, he'd have done it by now!"

"Wrong!" Serenity's tone reflected more than a little impatience with her handsome admirer. "That temperance female from Rochester—the oh, so virtuous Miss Susan Anthony—has been here rabble-rousing again, and now Stuart's got every self-righteous crackpot in town on his back. So far he's kept them at bay, but that can't last forever."

Her eyes narrowed. "Now, Brendan, you hear me well—*I want those signatures!* I don't care how you get them. I've already spent a fortune on payoffs, but those we can't get that way, we have to get another. And get them fast, laddie, or no more job. And no more Serenity either."

Brendan's tragic expression almost made Serenity retract her threat, but a sudden lowering of the tavern's noise turned her attention from the bar. Utter silence settled over the room.

One glance told Serenity why: Cullen Stuart had entered to stand just inside the door. He gave a cursory look around, but once he spotted Serenity, he nodded briefly at the men seated at the gaming tables, and started toward the bar. The noise gradually resumed.

"Evening, Constable," Serenity greeted Cullen when he reached her. She tapped the stool beside her, saying, "Sit a spell."

Cullen swung himself onto the stool. "Whiskey," he said to the bartender.

Serenity slipped off her stool to move behind the bar. "I'll take care of the constable," she told the bartender, and reached for a bottle of Alleman's finest. "On the house," she said to Cullen when she handed him the shot.

Cullen grinned. "Serenity, I'll take your whiskey, and I'll thank you for it, but that doesn't mean—"

"Naturally not," Serenity smiled, "I know you better than that by this time, Cullen Stuart. Never hurts to try, though."

"So how's the petition coming?"

"Don't waste words, do you, Constable? Well, my young friend here"—she gestured to Brendan O'Reilly, who had been scowling since Cullen sat down—"he tells me we're almost there. Just a couple more days'll do it. Right, Brendan, my lad?"

Still scowling, Brendan muttered, "Yeah, right." His knuckles whitened around the tankard he lifted and drained.

Serenity ignored him, and instead studied Cullen Stuart's face. Her tavern's prosperity, she often told herself, was due in no small part to her success in reading men; that she hadn't yet discovered this particular man's weakness annoyed her no end.

She leaned over the bar toward Cullen. "What's it take, my good man, to get you to overlook a few signatures? Tell me! I'll be happy, more than happy, to oblige." The smile was her most persuasive.

Cullen Stuart didn't seem to notice. "It's not up to me, Serenity. I've treated yours like any other business in town. But there's folks around here think liquor's a bad influence. And maybe it is, not that I think any law is going to fix it. But it *is* the law. So get your license. End of problem."

"Maybe," Serenity acknowledged reluctantly. "Now, these temperance troublemakers you're talking about—besides the meddling Miss Anthony, do you by any chance know a woman doctor—*Witch* doctor is more like it—name of Cardoza?"

Cullen grinned and nodded. "What's she done now?"

"She's been in here—"

"Here? In the tavern?" Cullen broke in. "She's been in *here*?"

"Here. Twice. Ranting about women and children. As if it's my fault that men drink too much and go home and beat up their wives and kids. This Cardoza's feisty as hell, like a little bantam rooster. Last time, I had Brendan here escort her to the door. Told her I'd have her arrested for disturbing my peace."

Cullen laughed. "Yours isn't the only peace she's disturbed since she got to town. What with her and Lily Braun . . . and by the way, have you seen *her* recently?"

"No!" Serenity snapped. "Lily comes in here, she'll get tossed out. Told her that years ago, when I fired her. But I heard she's all of a sudden got respectable; found herself a nice little deal when Dooley Keegan's widow sold her house. Lily moved into it a couple days ago. You know about that?"

"Just that I heard it, too. But I can't believe Lily Braun's become respectable—not by a long shot—so who's the man paying for it?"

Serenity shrugged, a gesture that dropped her bodice several inches. She didn't move to pull it up, but leaned farther over the bar toward Cullen, fixing him with a smile. "I'll be happy to find out for you, though, Constable. In return for—"

"For ignoring the petition, right? No thanks, Serenity. You just bustle out and get your signatures like a good, law-abiding citizen—"

He was interrupted by an explosive shout from across the room. More shouting followed, and chairs scraped the barroom floor as cardplayers jumped to their feet, backing away from the poker tables. A big man, his back to the wall, stood brandishing a knife.

"You goddamn cheating bastards!" the man yelled. He lunged forward with the knife, slicing the air in fast, choppy strokes.

"Brendan!" Serenity's voice got lost in the shouting, but Brendan O'Reilly had already leaped from the bar stool and was sprinting across the room. Grabbing a nearby chair, he hoisted it in front of him, then moved in on the knife-wielding cardplayer. Parrying with the chair to avoid the other's knife thrusts, Brendan managed to pin the man against the wall, while onlookers rushed to disarm him. The man then sank to the floor.

Brendan yanked the man up, twisted his arms behind his back, and wrestled him toward the back door. Cullen, who had started to draw his pistol, now shoved it back in its holster; shaking his head, he asked Serenity, "Mead Miller ever do anything like that before?"

Serenity frowned up at him. "Nothing like *that*! But he's been acting strange for weeks now."

"Strange? What do you mean, strange?"

"Edgy, like he's all the time looking over his shoulder. And he takes offense real easy. Miller's been in here a lot lately, and he's drinking more than he used to. But he won't get in again for a while!"

She watched Brendan saunter back from the door. "S'cuse me now, Constable," Serenity said with a grin. "Got to go reward my hero." She blew Cullen a kiss and sashayed up the length of the bar.

When Cullen left the tavern a few minutes later, he looked for Mead Miller. Wind-whipped leaves flurried in the road, but the man was nowhere in sight.

The next morning, seated on a straight-backed Shaker chair beside Cullen's desk, Glynis protested, "But why didn't you tell me Jacques Sundown had come back?"

She could hear her voice scaling upward and glanced self-consciously toward the open door of Cullen's office in the rear of the firehouse. To her relief, she saw no passersby. After she'd gotten up to close the door, and then reseated herself, she began again. "I don't understand, Cullen, since you say you knew, why you didn't tell me about Jacques. Why?"

Cullen sighed heavily, banged shut the wooden file drawer, and slid into his desk chair. "Guess I didn't think you'd care one way or the other. You and Jacques—well, you two didn't always get on so well."

Glynis caught her lower lip between her teeth. To some degree, Cullen was right. In the beginning, she and Jacques had had some difficulty, rather a lot of difficulty. But then he'd left Seneca Falls for—what?—six years? When he'd come back, the two of them had made adjustments, and had begun to arrive at some sort of understanding. But then Jacques had left again, saying only that he was going to a reservation somewhere, to see his mother. She hadn't even known he *had* a mother.

"Glynis?"

Cullen's voice startled her. When she looked up, he was staring at her with an odd expression. "What is it, Cullen?"

"I asked why you're so interested in Sundown's arrival."

"Because I . . ." Glynis paused, not entirely able to explain this. Finally she said, "Well, why wouldn't I be?"

Cullen shrugged, and began pushing some papers around on his desk. Without looking at her, he said, "To tell the truth, I'm a little sore at Sundown. He gets back maybe three, four weeks ago—doesn't even bother to let me know. He was my *deputy*. You'd think after three years he'd at least come by to say hello."

At that, Glynis smiled. "I can't imagine Jacques saying hello. Perhaps something like 'O.K.' Or, 'Good hunting weather,' but not hello."

"No, guess not." Cullen, too, smiled. "Anyway, I checked around some. Seems he's settled in at Black Brook Reservation. Built himself a log cabin. Looks like he's decided he's Indian after all, and doesn't want anything to do with us white folk."

Glynis rose and went to stand by the open window. She glanced out before she said, "But his father was a white man. A French trapper, he told you. And I just thought of something. Is his father still alive?"

"No. Died in Canada some years ago—that's why Jacques went to Montreal after he left town the first time. At least that's what he said. You saw him yesterday?"

"When I went out to the Grimm farm. He was riding along the edge of those woods, the ones between Grimms' and Black Brook Reservation. I thought he saw me, but then he just rode off."

"Sounds like Jacques. He never was what you'd call sociable."

"No. No, he wasn't." Although what Cullen said was certainly true, Glynis still felt hurt by Jacques's apparent indifference. But she pushed the emotion aside and said, "I also saw Sara Turner yesterday. She seems to have recovered from her husband's death very well. In fact, I'd say remarkably well."

"That so?" Cullen looked interested.

"Yes. She's gotten her children back from wherever Jack Turner apprenticed them, and one boy has already begun fixing up the place."

"Yeah? Glynis, consider this—remember Jack's reputation for being tight-fisted? Well, apparently he left a fair amount of money. Sara Turner said she found it under a mattress, if you can believe that.

All in all, I'd say the widow Turner has had a streak of good luck recently."

"Cullen! You don't still think Sara had something to do with his death? Or do you?"

"Not something I can prove. Never did find whatever the arsenic was in. Searched the place pretty well, but no wine bottle. Nothing, that is, except a small sack of arsenic in the barn."

"You didn't tell me that," Glynis said, surprised.

"Because Sara Turner swore it was for rats. And there's no evidence she's lying, at least none that any prosecutor would accept. No, either she's gotten away with murder, or . . ."

Still standing by the window, Glynis motioned him quiet. She'd just heard the rustle of an approaching skirt, and now she glanced out to say, "Here's Neva Cardoza."

Cullen's low groan was unmistakable.

Neva, her face flushed a dark pink, came hurriedly through the door. She gave Glynis a quick nod, then stepped to place a sheaf of paper on Cullen's desk.

"You told me to get a copy of the new temperance law, Constable—well, there it is! *Now* will you do something about those taverns?"

Cullen, who had gotten to his feet when Neva entered, sighed and sank back into his chair as she went on, "I've read this thing all the way through, several times. It states very clearly that it's designed to curb intemperance and to regulate the sale of alcoholic spirits. If tavern owners don't have liquor licenses, and there's still some that don't, then according to Section sixteen, you, the constable, are supposed to shut them down." She picked up one of the sheets of paper to wave in front of his face. "Says so right here!"

"Dr. Cardoza," Cullen said, again rising from his chair, "the legislature just passed this law in April. No other state's got anything like it, so the tavern owners have been taken by surprise. They need time to comply."

"Why?" Neva interrupted, glaring at him.

"Why what?" Cullen's voice sounded strained.

"Why should they have *any* time? The law takes effect immediately, says so in Section thirty-four. Constable Stuart, if you'd

bother to look at the misery that alcohol's inflicted on this town, you wouldn't wait a minute longer."

"Dr. Cardoza, I know that—"

"No! No, you don't! You know nothing about what happens when a husband and father comes home drunk every night. When he uses the money his family depends on, for their food and a roof over their heads, to buy liquor. But I *do* know." Her face flushing still more, Neva rushed on as Cullen tried to interrupt, "I've seen these wives and children. Malnourished. Beaten, and covered with bruises and sores. It's criminal. And you want to give tavern owners more *time*?"

"The law *also* states," Cullen said evenly, belying the color that had risen in his own face, "that to grant liquor licenses, commissioners of excise first have to be appointed by a county judge. Now that's been done, but just recently. So the tavern owners need the time—"

"The time for what?" Neva jumped in. "To buy off the commissioners? And don't look so shocked, Glynis, it happens all the time."

"Seneca Falls is not New York City." Cullen stressed each word. "And if you're going to slander these . . ."

"I'm not slandering—"

". . . folks, then you're also slandering me. And I don't take kindly to that, *Dr.* Cardoza!"

Neva continued to glare at Cullen. He, on the other hand, merely looked at her with irritation.

"I'm holding you personally responsible, Constable Stuart, for every woman and child that's harmed as a result of alcoholic excess. It's on your conscience!"

Glynis heard a sob catch in Neva's throat as the young woman whirled around and stormed from the office. Cullen stared after her with obvious exasperation. He shook his head, saying to Glynis, "Now, where were we? Before the cyclone swept through?"

"You know," Glynis said, "Neva does have a point."

"Now don't *you* start in on me."

"But since she's been here, Neva's spent much of her time with the poorer families in town. She knows what she's talking about."

"That's not the issue."

"It isn't? Then what *is*? That business owners, mostly men, are

more important to Seneca Falls than the welfare of women and children. That—"

"Glynis, spare me, please. I'm not getting into this men-versus-women thing again with you. And I mean it."

Glynis quickly got to her feet and went to the door. After she went through it, she closed it behind her very quietly.

She flexed the reins to slow the pace of the small, dapple-gray mare, her personal favorite from Boone's Livery, and gritted her teeth as the lightweight buggy jounced over Black Brook Road's rutted surface.

After the previous night's cold snap had brought the season's first frost, the air had again turned balmy. Altogether it had been a lovely, unusually warm fall, Glynis reflected; perhaps there could be hope the coming winter would not be as fierce as that of the year before. But this was something for which western New Yorkers hoped every year.

On this particular afternoon, however, the slant of the late-October sun turned everything it touched a pale gold; there would be too few more of these days before snow fell, and the unexpectedly mild weather seemed to Glynis a reprieve of sorts. A gift of which one should take advantage.

Although Black Brook ran to the right of the road, the graceful willows, scarlet sumac, and cattails on its banks concealed the stream itself. As the buggy rounded a slight curve, Glynis could see a white horse standing in the high weeds, only its upper body and switching tail visible, and she guessed someone must be fishing along the streambed.

She flicked the reins over the mare's back, quickening their journey past the Grimm farm. But there appeared to be no activity there—which, this being a Sunday, did not seem particularly odd. No doubt the Grimms were all indoors for noonday dinner. Glynis was just as glad none were around to question her; she wasn't sure how she would explain this trip of hers to Black Brook Reservation.

And surely there was little to be gained, she thought uneasily, by questioning herself too vigorously as to the reasons that impelled her to seek out Jacques Sundown. Simple curiosity should be reason

enough. And Cullen's remarks of that morning were not sufficient to satisfy her.

After another quarter-mile, she urged the mare up a long rise. At its crest she pulled back on the reins, and when they'd stopped, Glynis gazed down at the southern boundary of Black Brook Reservation.

The brook itself wound north through the heart of the reserve; some distance from the streambed, and on either side of it stood clusters of small log houses. Behind them lay fields dotted with orange pumpkins and hilled squash vines. Desiccated brown stalks rustled in the breeze. Outside each house, ears of corn hung by braided husks from drying posts in long festoons of gold and white, orange-red, and dark purple. Glynis had forgotten how many varieties of corn the Iroquois cultivated.

Gone were the great hickory and oak bark longhouses with their barrel-shaped roofs. Often as large as a hundred and thirty feet in length by some sixteen feet wide, a longhouse once sheltered several generations under its one roof. These generations consisted of maternal families: mothers and their husbands, their daughters and daughters' husbands, and their daughters' children. The families had lived side by side behind a central row of circular hearths.

Also gone now was the central position held by Iroquois women of centuries past. Glynis had first heard the creation legend of Ata-en-sic, the Sky Woman, from a young Seneca woman who, for a number of years, had sold woven baskets, and moccasins and garments elaborately embroidered with beadwork, at the Seneca County Agricultural Fair. As this artisan related the legend, many ages past a wizard, jealous of women's power to create life, caused the pregnant Ata-en-sic to fall from the sky into a great, watery void. Sky Woman's fate would have been to fall forever but for the water birds that caught and carried her in their widespread wings. They held her until the muskrat deposited dirt on the back of Hah-nu-nah the turtle, the Earth Bearer. The waterbirds then placed Sky Woman on his back. When the wizard had pushed her into the void, Ata-en-sic was clutching in her hands many seeds, which she now planted in the earth. She subsequently died, giving birth to twin brothers, the spirits of Good and Evil. Each brother claimed the Earth to be his dominion, and so began the endless struggle between strife and peace.

The Seneca woman had assured Glynis that, while the legend in its retelling had taken on variations over time, its essence had remained faithful to the lifegiving power of women.

It was for this same Seneca woman that Glynis now intended to look. It had been several years since she'd seen her, and Glynis couldn't be sure she'd recognize what now would be an older face, but her voice still must be unmistakable, rich and melodious, like the song of a wood thrush. Her name had been Small Brown Bird.

Glynis flicked the reins and the gray mare took off at a trot down the short hill to Black Brook Reservation.

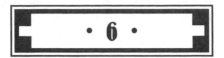

• 6 •

The Iroquois tribe . . . was not a group of families; neither was it made up of the descendants of a common father, as the father and his child were never of the same tribe. . . . Descent followed in all cases, the female line.

—Lewis Henry Morgan, *League of the Ho-de-no-sau-nee, or Iroquois*

After Glynis tethered the mare to the branch of a willow growing beside the stream, she walked toward the first of the log houses clustered along Black Brook's west bank. An old woman sat alone on a sagging wooden stoop. Her gray hair, caught in the single long braid designating a married female, fell over the shoulder of a bead-trimmed deerskin tunic, and on her hollow chest shone a circular silver brooch with scalloped edges. She wielded in her gnarled fingers a wooden pestle, crushing sunflower seeds—for their oil, Glynis supposed—in a mortar held between her knees.

When she greeted the woman, she received a brief nod. "I wonder," Glynis said, taking a step toward her and smiling hopefully, "if you might tell me where I can find someone called Small Brown Bird?"

The woman's lips parted in a gap-toothed smile. She pointed the pestle toward a dirt path leading into a stand of shagbark hickory. Glynis thanked her and followed the path, shadowed by overhanging branches, until the trees began to thin, and she heard the chattering trill of women's voices.

Ahead of her lay a grassy clearing, beyond which a cornfield stretched into the distance. Small Brown Bird was easily recognizable; she looked almost as she had years before, as she sat with a number of other women on tree stumps beside a six-legged corncrib. Behind

them soared a virtual mountain of unhusked corn. Stripped ears tied in neat bundles lay next to the crib, while the women braided together husks of others.

As Glynis approached, Small Brown Bird looked up from her lapful of corncobs. Her shiny black hair fell in two long switches indicating her unmarried status, and her dark oval eyes widened at the appearance of Glynis. She deposited the braided corn in a basket before gracefully rising to her feet.

"I don't know if you remember me," Glynis began. "We met several times at the County Fair. Although it has been some while."

But the woman had been smiling in obvious recognition. "Yes, Miss Tryon, I remember." Her flutelike voice was as beautiful as Glynis recalled. "You liked the beadwork I did. And you bought some moccasins."

Glynis nodded. "For my nieces, yes, and they loved them."

Small Brown Bird laughed shyly. The other women paused in their work to regard Glynis with pleasant if inquisitive expressions.

She stood there, feeling bulky and overdressed in long-sleeved, high-necked gray linen, tight-waisted over several petticoats that barely cleared the grass. The Indian women wore what she had heard called pantalettes, or leggings; most were of red broadcloth with a border of beadwork around the lower edges. The leggings hung straight to their moccasins. Over these, the women wore short tunics of brightly colored muslin or calico, gathered loosely at the waist. The garments looked comfortable and practical, reminding Glynis of the short-lived, long-lamented Bloomer costume that the suffragists had enjoyed before male ridicule had forced them back into their cumbersome dresses.

Small Brown Bird seemed to be waiting for Glynis to say something, her slender form bending forward like the willow at the edge of the stream. Glynis cleared her throat somewhat nervously. She was uncertain as to how she should begin, especially in front of the other women, and when she glanced toward them, found they were all watching her expectantly. She again cleared her throat. But shyness and the awareness of being an outsider made her tongue-tied.

Small Brown Bird gave her a gentle smile. "Every autumn after *onä'o',* the corn, is harvested," she explained, clearly to ease Glynis's embarrassment, "the women prepare it for storing. We are here"—

she extended her arm to include the others—"for *wadinowi'yă'ke'*, a husking bee. It is said that if there had been no corn, there would be no Haudenosaunee. But do you remember the story of Sky Woman I once told you?"

Feeling somewhat more at ease, Glynis smiled. "Yes, I thought of it, in fact, on my way out here."

Small Brown Bird nodded. "The Seneca legend says that corn, and also beans and squash, sprang from the breasts of Sky Woman when she gave birth to Good and Evil. And so, even after her death, she provided her children with food."

Small Brown Bird inclined her head to the other women before she moved away, indicating that Glynis should follow. They walked toward Black Brook until Small Brown Bird stopped in front of a small log house. She lowered herself to the stoop, gesturing for Glynis to do the same, then asked, "I think perhaps you wanted to talk alone with me?"

"Yes," Glynis said gratefully, "but I don't quite know how to put this." She hesitated, searching for words. "I believe there's someone here—a man, that is—whom I used to know."

But it was as if a curtain now descended over the other woman's face. Small Brown Bird abruptly looked away and gazed silently out over the stream. Although bewildered by the woman's reaction. Glynis thought she had no choice but to continue. "I saw—that is, I *thought* I saw—him several days ago. Of course I might have been mistaken."

Small Brown Bird's eyes swung back to her. The woman's voice was almost a whisper when she leaned toward Glynis to say, "Is it Walks At Sundown you look for?"

"Yes. Yes, it is." Glynis felt increasingly uneasy, but it was too late now to disguise the purpose of her visit. "I knew him as Jacques Sundown. Can you tell me if he's here?"

Small Brown Bird rose from the stoop. "Please, Miss Tryon, it's better that you don't look for him."

"But why?" Glynis, also getting to her feet, tried to ignore the voice inside her head: *Leave this alone. There's something wrong here. Just leave.*

But at that moment she heard a peculiar sound from the far side of Black Brook. A soft growling sound. Her skin prickled, and she sensed that if she turned to look, somehow a die would be cast. Some course

determined. But despite the premonition, she was incapable of *not* looking.

She turned. On the opposite bank of the stream stood Jacques Sundown, light through the trees glinting off the coppery skin and glossy black hair, the fine, high cheekbones of his face.

His expressionless gaze from across the ribbon of water made Glynis inhale sharply. Seeing him again brought the disturbing awareness that she had sorely missed him. She hoped this was not laid bare on her face. But he probably knew anyway. And he must have known exactly when she arrived there at Black Brook; he had always known, by some arcane process, where she was or would be. She found it still startled her.

Behind her, a door creaked open, then slammed shut. Accompanied by hurried footsteps, a woman's harsh voice demanded, "What do you want here?"

Glynis broke from Jacques's gaze and whirled around. An aging woman now stood not three feet away from her, repeating, "What do you want?"

Glynis stared dumbly at the woman. The tall, wiry figure's leathery face held a mysterious but unmistakable malevolence. Glynis's immediate reaction was to step back. But she discovered that she was nailed to the spot by her boot heels, sunk into the marshy bank of the stream. She fought the urge to free herself by tugging at them, with the possibility of a headlong plunge into Black Brook, and instead concentrated on somehow mollifying this forbidding woman.

"Please. Please excuse me," she said, her voice as conciliatory as she could make it, "but I'm afraid I don't understand."

"You need to leave!" the woman commanded, her eyes, black and hard, fixed with implacable fury on Glynis.

What could be the reason for this? The hatred in those hard eyes *must* have some reason. And yet . . . and yet it looked to Glynis as if the deep lines around the woman's eyes had been formed by timeless grief, much as ever-flowing water wears through rock.

Small Brown Bird, who had remained strangely silent, now spoke rapidly to the other woman. While Glynis was thankful for the temporary reprieve, she couldn't understand the words, which must have been in the Seneca tongue. Small Brown Bird seemed to be repeating

herself, her voice rising and falling in intervals that sounded like musical recitative. During this, the other continued to glower at Glynis, who lowered her eyes to the woman's doeskin tunic and spectacular necklace. Suspended by a strand of small silver and glass beads, the flat, oval-shaped, seashell inlaid with silver lay in the cleft between the woman's breasts.

At the sound of Jacques's voice, Glynis raised her eyes with caution. And although the woman had been glowering still, she turned when Jacques, having crossed the stream by way of a narrow footbridge, approached them.

As he strode forward, he called sharply to the older woman in Seneca. This, in itself, surprised Glynis; she had never heard Jacques raise his voice, not in all the time she'd known him. And, in addition, instead of his jean-cloth trousers and the collarless, yoked cotton shirts Glynis had been accustomed to seeing, Jacques now wore leather leggings and a loose overshirt of soft pale doeskin fringed at the hem. He had always worn moccasins.

When he reached the older woman, his dusky brown eyes held their usual flat expression. He spoke a short sentence to her, and the woman responded in the same intonation as that used by Small Brown Bird, but higher. Glynis desperately tried to concentrate on the speech pattern rather than on her own anxiety. Failing this, she began as unobtrusively as possible to work her boots out of the damp earth. She would leave with as much composure as she could muster. Plainly it had been a mistake to come here.

But Jacques turned to her and said quietly, "Cross the brook. Cross over and wait for me."

Glynis caught his signal to Small Brown Bird, who, motioning for Glynis to follow her, started briskly for the footbridge. Behind them the other woman's voice again rose harshly.

Glynis felt shaken enough to keep her silence until they reached the far side of Black Brook. As they passed the last of the log houses and headed into a stand of gray birch, Small Brown Bird said to her, "I hope you will forgive my sister. She is very troubled by your coming here."

"I gathered that!" Glynis replied with some warmth, although she was startled to hear Small Brown Bird refer to the woman as her sis-

ter. But perhaps theirs was a clan relationship only, and not blood kinship. "Why should she be troubled?" Glynis asked. "She doesn't even know me."

"You are a white woman. For her that is enough to know."

Small Brown Bird led Glynis over a rough trail and on into a clearing some distance beyond the reservation. Just ahead, and barely visible over tall grasses, stood a small log cabin. Glynis saw that the isolated cabin had been so situated that the forest rose directly behind it, boughs of hemlock even brushing its bark roof. Irregular-shaped cones lay scattered over a carpet of needles, and the air was fragrant with the scent of fir.

"That belongs to Walks At Sundown." Small Brown Bird pointed to the cabin.

Glynis found she wasn't particularly surprised at the secluded location. Even when Jacques had been assistant constable of Seneca Falls, he'd stayed resolutely beyond the boundary of white society, and apparently he chose to remain in a no-man's-land here as well.

Since they had stopped walking, and since she was not satisfied with Small Brown Bird's earlier answer, Glynis now said, "Please tell me what exactly went on back there?" She motioned in the direction of the reservation. "Why did that woman, your sister, object so violently to my being here?"

Small Brown Bird looked off into the forest, and Glynis wondered if her question might have been considered discourteous. But finally, still not meeting Glynis's eyes, Small Brown Bird said, "You must not think it is only *you* she objects to. She would object to any white woman."

"But why?" Glynis repeated. "And who *is* she that Jacques—that Walks At Sundown even responds to her. I've never seen him give much notice to *anyone*—especially to someone who obviously opposes him."

Small Brown Bird's smile came swift. "That is true of him most of the time. But this woman is his mother."

"His *mother*?" That being the case, Glynis decided she had probably said enough. It still didn't explain the woman's behavior, but perhaps Seneca mothers simply didn't like white women anywhere near their sons. "Since you called her 'sister,' " she said to Small Brown Bird, "does that mean you're Jacques's aunt?"

"Your people would call me that, yes. But to Senecas, the word *mother* has a wider meaning. It means not only the birth mother but also all her sisters. Since Walks At Sundown's birth mother and I are of the same clan—the Wolf Clan—I also may be called his mother."

Small Brown Bird smiled and, apparently seeing Glynis's confusion, added, "Or you might say a mother-aunt, because I *am* the blood sister of Bitter Root."

"That was Bitter Root? Jacques's mother is Bitter Root?" Glynis asked incredulously. "Isn't she a medicine woman?"

"She is."

"But then I'm afraid I really don't understand," Glynis persisted. There must be more here than she was being told. "I know, for instance, that Bitter Root brought herbs to the Grimm farm recently, when young Pippa Grimm was ill. Not only that, but Pippa implied this was not the first time she'd seen Bitter Root. And Pippa and her mother, Molly, are white."

For a moment, Small Brown Bird didn't respond. Then she asked, "Are you certain Bitter Root did that in recent time—went to the Grimm farm?"

"Yes," Glynis said, now more puzzled than ever. "Pippa herself told me."

A slight frown appeared on Small Brown Bird's face. Again she hesitated before she said, "Bitter Root is not concerned about Pippa Grimm in the way that she is troubled by you."

"Troubled?" Glynis felt as if she were flailing around in the dark. What could she possibly have done, in the short time she'd been at the reservation, that could trouble Jacques Sundown's mother?

Small Brown Bird sighed, as if about to undertake something unpleasant. "You must not know," she said, now looking closely at Glynis, "of Bitter Root's firstborn son?"

"Jacques has a brother?"

"He was Walks At Sundown's half brother." Small Brown Bird's voice began to falter. "Many Horned Stag. He is dead now, some years. He . . . he was killed. By white men."

Glynis stared, stunned, at the woman, hoping she might have heard incorrectly. Her next thought was that Jacques's brother must have committed some crime. But what if . . . what if he had died as the result of so-called "frontier justice"? Such things were done to Indians

by angry mobs who took the law into their own hands and ... No! But then she recalled that Jacques always had refused to talk of his family or his past.

Needing to know, Glynis steeled herself. "Why was Jacques's brother killed?"

Small Brown Bird studied Glynis's face with a look of concern, clearly weighing a reply; but then she turned, her eyes scanning the clearing behind them. And moments later Jacques appeared, wading through the grass and holding the reins of the dapple-gray mare. The buggy jounced behind. From the closed expression now on Small Brown Bird's face, Glynis knew no account of Many Horned Stag's death would be given. At least not this day.

When Jacques reached them, he said something in Seneca to Small Brown Bird. In response, she inclined her head to frown at him momentarily, before she turned to Glynis. "I will say good-bye to you now, Miss Tryon."

Before Glynis could reply, Small Brown Bird quickly walked off across the clearing. The tall grass waved in her wake.

Alone with Jacques, Glynis found herself inexplicably stricken with sudden shyness, and to avoid looking at him, she watched Small Brown Bird disappear into the far stand of gray birch. But then, from behind the cabin, came a peculiar sound much like a muffled bark. When she turned to look for its source, a large timber wolf suddenly materialized, loping from the forest. Its coat was dense, mostly gray, flecked with black and white guard hairs, and white markings on its muzzle and chest; black markings, as if drawn with a fine pencil, outlined its almond-shaped eyes, emphasizing an alert, intelligent expression. It came straight toward them.

"Jacques," Glynis whispered. "Behind you!"

Jacques registered no surprise. Indeed, with an unnerving display of nonchalance, he only muttered something under his breath. The wolf stopped in its tracks. Its ears pricked forward and and its muzzle lifted, searching the air, before its remarkable eyes came to rest on Glynis: fathomless, molten-gold eyes. It came to her with some surprise that she felt no fear. What she did feel was the presence of something benevolent. Something magical.

The wolf abruptly broke its gaze and turned to lope back into the

trees. Then it vanished. It was there one moment, gone the next, leaving not even the shallowest impression in the pine needles to indicate it had been anything more than illusion.

Glynis let out her breath and looked with question at Jacques. His face held what might have been amusement. In fact, he looked as close to smiling as Glynis had ever seen him.

"He's a spirit," Jacques said. "Just a spirit."

"A spirit of your Wolf Clan?" Glynis asked. "But why was he here now?"

As soon as she'd said it, she realized how absurd it sounded—as though she believed Jacques's definition. He was once again making fun of her. And as if to confirm this, his face lost its subtle expression. It smoothed to a flat stare. The years fell away, and it might have been only yesterday when she'd last seen that maddening, enigmatic look.

However, she was older now. She would try to maintain some dignity, although this had never been particularly successful with him before. "Jacques, please don't let's start this again."

"Start what?" His flat stare swept her face; then it altered, just slightly, to look again as if he might smile.

Glynis felt heat flood her cheeks. Here she'd come all the way out to this place, simply to be ridiculed.

She took several deep breaths. What was the matter with her? Why did Jacques always provoke such exaggerated impulses on her part—always, ever since she'd first known him? She thought she'd convinced herself long ago that the tension between them resulted from the difference in their backgrounds, that he didn't intend, really, to embarrass her.

Armed with this, she would try again. "Jacques, let's at least make an attempt to understand each other."

"What do you want to understand?"

"Well, to begin with, why you didn't let anyone know you were back. Back in Seneca Falls."

"I'm not in Seneca Falls."

"But you're not on the reservation, either—not really. You've isolated yourself in these woods and . . ." Her voice had begun to rise, and she paused, unwilling to sound like his mother. She took a breath and went on, "Why didn't you come into town?"

"Why should I come into town?"

"Well, to say hello—or something! I suspect it hurt Cullen's feelings that you didn't. And I know it surely hurt mine!"

Glynis pressed her lips together; she hadn't meant to say that exactly, or with such emphasis.

Jacques's expression changed. The near-smile returned, and something moved in his eyes, like light rearranging itself. The cool, flat brown warmed to gold. He took several long, almost involuntary strides forward, but then stopped a few feet short of her, his hands clenched at his sides.

A sudden, vivid memory of another such encounter with him swept over her. At that time, the intimacy of the moment had confused her. Now it aroused something far more disturbing than confusion.

The sound of a twig snapping, and a harsh voice coming toward them, created in Glynis a rush of panic. She averted her eyes from Jacques's gaze, and hastened forward to climb into the buggy. Somehow she found the reins in her grasp—did Jacques hand them up to her?—and she flicked them harder than she intended over the mare's flanks.

The buggy jerked forward, and Glynis clamped her teeth together as its wheels rolled over the uneven forest path. She did not look back. She wanted to, and how she kept herself from doing so, she didn't know. But she riveted her attention completely on guiding the mare through the trees. All the way to Black Brook Road.

Her breathing had slowed, her heart no longer slamming against her ribs, by the time she saw the Grimm farm ahead. She needed to get back to town. To where she knew what to expect. She was *thirty-nine years old;* she had thought she knew everything about herself there was to know.

Apparently not.

She and Jacques Sundown came from wildly dissimilar circumstances. And she was at least ten years older than he. She felt embarrassed by her response to him, and disingenuous as well. She was not a young girl. In point of fact, she might be old enough to enter her change of life.

Perhaps that was the explanation. But did it mean she would now

be capable of the startling things she had seen a few women do in this condition?

Like Moira O'Shaughnessy. Married in the Catholic church at seventeen, an exemplary wife and mother, Moira O'Shaughnessy at age forty-six had suddenly upped and and run away to Utica with an itinerant scissors-grinder. Or spinster Sally Monroe, who, after fifty-two years of irreproachable—indeed saintly—conduct, had been seen one evening, dancing down Fall Street in her diaphanous nightdress. And a year later married a handsome young schoolteacher.

Glynis began now to laugh, remembering that at the time she had felt shamefully envious of such free spirits, unchained at last from the terror of unwanted pregnancy.

By the time she was half a mile farther down the road, she thought she was recovering some innate good sense. There could be no point in blaming herself for inappropriate feelings toward Jacques Sundown; those were entirely beyond her control, as she had learned, or should have, years before. She could, however, hold herself responsible for what she *did.*

And what she would do—oh, how remarkably simple it was—would be to never see Jacques Sundown again.

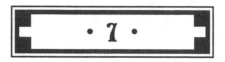

• 7 •

I have sent books and music there, and all
Those instruments with which high Spirits call
The future from its cradle, and the past
Out of its grave. . . .
—Percy Bysshe Shelley, "Epipsychidion"

The little gray mare, heading for home and feed, took the buggy briskly past the first fences of the Grimm farm. Glynis held the reins loosely in one hand; the lowering sun shone directly into her eyes, and she needed a free hand to shade them. Granted, the days were shorter now, but how had it gotten so late without her realizing? It must be close to six o'clock. And the air had begun to turn cool.

She was reaching for the shawl on the seat beside her when the mare suddenly shied, then reared, fighting for her head. The reins jerked from Glynis's hand. The mare surged forward. Glynis was thrown backward against the buggy seat just as she saw a small, dark shape slip under the front wheels, immediately followed by a child's high scream.

Glynis grabbed for the reins only to have them whip away from her outstretched fingers. She lunged forward several times before she retrieved them and managed to pull the frightened mare to a stop. Then she looked back. Pippa Grimm was running along the roadside, and Glynis could hear the girl's panicky sobs.

Oh, dear Lord, not the lamb. She was clambering down from the buggy when Pippa screamed again. Glynis whirled in the direction of the girl, snagging her skirt on the buggy's hand brake. She yanked it loose, disregarding the sound of ripping linen, and hurried to Pippa.

The girl knelt in the road, the lamb's small body clutched to her chest, her face buried in its nappy gray wool. Glynis stood rigid with guilt. The thought crossed her mind that the wages of sin were now being extracted from her, and that she would rather burn for eternity than be forced to witness this; this heartbroken child cradling her dead lamb.

She never should have searched out Jacques. If only she'd left the reservation a half hour earlier . . . maybe just a few minutes earlier . . .

"Miss Tryon! Miss Tryon, look!"

Pippa's eyes gleamed up at her like ripe chestnuts. "Don't cry, Miss Tryon—he's all right. See? He's not hurt at all."

Glynis looked. And indeed, the lamb had begun struggling to escape Pippa's viselike grip, wagging its absurd, stumpy tail with vigor. It paused in its struggle briefly, however, to regard Glynis with what she could have sworn was reproach.

"Pippa, what happened?" Glynis choked out the words, guilt still grinding her between its teeth. "I didn't even see the lamb."

"I took him out of the pen—he hasn't been out in ages 'cause Mead Miller's been gone somewhere—and he just got away from me," Pippa explained, her voice high with joy. "He ran out into the road before I could catch him. But I guess the wheels didn't go over him."

"That's right, Miss Tryon," came a pleasant masculine voice from behind Glynis. "It's not your fault. Not at all!"

Glynis turned to look into the sympathetic eyes of Lazarus Grimm. Despite her distress, she couldn't help thinking, *And so the prodigal son returns. Offering absolution, no less.*

The lamb suddenly leaped from Pippa's arms and bounded off. The girl followed, laughing, as it dodged to elude her again.

Glynis sighed with relief. Now all she wanted was to get home, and she turned with some impatience to the man beside her. But as her guilty shock receded, she suddenly noticed how gaunt he looked. How different!

In the past, Lazarus had always appeared slightly bloated—some had termed it debauched—and the change in him was startling. For the first time, Glynis could see a square, clean-shaven chin, hollowed-out cheekbones, and a slender, patrician nose. Dark brown locks of hair curled over his forehead. There was about the hair, she decided,

an artfully contrived negligence, although, truthfully, she didn't recall what his hair had looked like before. But his skin she did recall. Now pale, almost translucent, in the past it had been mottled as if he were constantly feverish. At the moment, Lazarus didn't look at all feverish. He looked, in fact, much like the marble bust in her library of a youthful Shelley: *The Poet kept mute conference with his still soul.*

Whence had gone the profligate Lazarus Grimm? The man standing before her looked positively aesthetic.

"Miss Tryon?" he said in the pleasant voice. "I'm Lazarus Grimm—perhaps you don't remember me."

Remember him? She couldn't imagine there were too many in Seneca Falls who would not. She hoped she hadn't been gaping at him, but the transformation was astonishing. Perhaps he had been ill.

"Of course I remember you, Lazarus. Your sister said you were coming back." Molly hadn't mentioned any illness. Maybe she hadn't known.

"Yes, I'm back home at last." Lazarus smiled. "Home to stay."

His wandering step, obedient to high thoughts, has visited the awful ruins of the days of old.

Forget Shelley, Glynis told herself. What stood before her was no aesthete. Lazarus Grimm had swindled aging widows out of money, hardworking men out of property, and persuaded a congregation in Buffalo to purchase from him, sight unseen, what proved to be a fourth of Montezuma Marsh for their new church.

And Lazarus didn't even own Montezuma Marsh. This was definitely a man to treat with caution. Glynis nodded politely to him and began walking along the roadside toward the buggy, where the mare stood placidly chewing clover. To her discomfort, Lazarus fell into step beside her.

"Are you still a librarian, Miss Tryon?" he asked. Glynis glanced at him from the corner of her eye. He looked sincere. This was undoubtedly when he was most dangerous.

"Yes," she said carefully. She probably also should mention that librarians did not make much money. But they both turned as a voice floated from the direction of the Grimm house. Molly was coming toward them.

"Glynis!" Molly's serene face looked apologetic. "I just heard what happened. Pippa's been told and told not to let that lamb out,

but . . ." Molly gave Glynis the smile of a resigned, forgiving mother. Pippa was fortunate.

"Oh, and your skirt's torn, too," Molly sighed. "I hope you aren't very upset."

"I'm all right now, Molly."

Molly turned to Lazarus. "Did you ask Glynis? About the theater?"

The theater? Oh, no, Glynis thought. Surely he hadn't dreamed up some scheme involving The Usher Playhouse. The love of Vanessa Usher's life—after Vanessa herself, it was.

"It's getting quite late," she said, gazing significantly toward the sinking sun. "I'm afraid I'll have to hurry to get home before dark."

But the sun was not sinking nearly fast enough, because Lazarus said to her, "I wonder if you would be so kind as to give me an introduction to your neighbor Miss Usher. I'd like to propose something to her about—"

"Perhaps we might speak of this another day," Glynis broke in. "I really do have to leave now."

Lazarus smiled graciously. "Of course, Miss Tryon. I have plenty of time. Plenty of time for the Lord."

Glynis assumed she hadn't heard correctly. Something about being bored?

"You see, Miss Tryon," Lazarus continued, "I have had a spiritual experience. A true awakening. I have renounced my former ways and stand before you a man reborn. I have seen the Lord's purpose for me. However, that you might find this hard to believe, I can imagine."

He couldn't begin to imagine. Glynis threw Molly a questioning look, thinking she would confirm that her brother had been ill. *Was* ill. But Molly stood smiling up at Lazarus with a sister's blind, adoring eyes.

". . . find faith," Lazarus was saying, "and then we can communicate with them."

"Excuse me?" Glynis asked, hoping fervently that what she'd heard was not what he'd said. "Communicate with whom?"

"Our dear departed ones," Lazarus said. Said with reverence. "So you can understand the compelling need, Miss Tryon, to find a place for believers to gather. And I would like to convince Miss Usher that her theater could be that place."

Glynis looked to the sky. The sun, finally, sat as round as a ball on

the horizon. *Thank you, Lord.* "I'm afraid I *must* leave," she said, pointing to the west.

As she started toward the buggy, Molly caught her arm. "Oh, Glynis, I meant to ask you"—her forehead wrinkled slightly—"have you seen Mead Miller today? In town?"

"No, I haven't. Why?"

Molly's frown deepened. "We haven't seen him either, not since early last night. Oh, well," she sighed, her forehead smoothing, "it's probably nothing to worry about. Mead does this occasionally. He doesn't have family hereabouts, so I can't imagine what he does on his Saturday nights."

Glynis wondered if Molly really couldn't figure out where a man like Miller might spend his free time. Or was this euphemistic language for her brother's benefit? In which case, given Lazarus's colorful history, it was surely wasted effort.

Before they could further detain her, she walked determinedly to the buggy. As she climbed in, and flicked the reins over the mare's flanks, she hazarded a glance backward.

Lazarus and Molly stood arm in arm, smiling beneficently at her. Lazarus lifted his hand in a wave. Or a blessing, perhaps? "I'll be into town to see you soon," he called to her. Molly beamed up at him appreciatively.

And here all this time, Glynis had believed Molly to be the one sane adult in the Grimm family.

She waved briefly, then turned her gaze firmly back to the road.

When she passed the abandoned Flannery farm, the blackened ruins of house and barns stood starkly etched under clouds streaked by sunset to fiery crimson; the memory this evoked was not a pleasant one. But by the time she drove the game little mare past the Turners' place, the sky had begun to soften toward mauve. She should have left the Grimm's sooner. Yes indeed, *much* sooner! She smiled bleakly to herself. What a long and peculiar day it had been.

Later she would remember thinking this; it was just before she heard the high, piercing whinny of a terrified horse. Startled, she turned to look toward Black Brook. It was the white horse she had seen earlier, on her way out to the reservation.

The animal was rearing, again and again, and it continued to call in a high-pitched whinny. Glynis slowed the mare. Over the tall weeds, she couldn't see much more than the horse's head and its front legs pawing the air, but it was clearly in distress. Must have snagged its reins on something. She sighed, looking again at the sky. It would be dark soon. But the horse could lame or strangle itself before someone else came along, or its owner, some farmer no doubt, missed it. Much as she wanted to, she couldn't leave it. She'd already experienced guilt enough this day.

Reluctantly she pulled the mare to a stop and climbed wearily from the buggy to begin a trek through the weeds. She bunched up her torn skirt and held it as high as she could. Minutes later, her cotton stockings shredded and covered with burdock, she emerged from the weeds and stepped to the bank of the stream. Cattails rose from the water's edge like brown velvet pipe cleaners.

The horse shied away from her, but couldn't loose its reins tangled around a rotting tree stump. Glynis talked to it quietly, trying to soothe it, while watching her feet on the marshy ground. Suddenly she heard something sinister. A faint buzzing. She froze, peered cautiously ahead, then jumped back. The reason for the horse's terror became clear. Near its front hooves lay the broken, coiled body of a rattlesnake; it must have been seven feet long, as big around as a man's wrist. Its tail was still twitching spasmodically.

Glynis turned to bolt back to the road. But the rattler was dead. It couldn't hurt her if it was dead. And it was. She looked over her shoulder. Yes, without doubt. Dead. She turned back and, moving gingerly, her eyes half shut, she made herself step over the snake, while talking to the horse. She reached for the reins, and paused. Something smelled very odd. The dead snake? When she'd grasped the reins, she kicked the rattler a few feet away and had just begun untangling the horse when it abruptly reared. Its reins jerked her off balance. She had taken a large unintentional stride forward to right herself, when her shoe hit something soft. She regained her balance and then glanced down. An icy shock was followed by numbness that said what she saw was not there. *It couldn't be.*

Pressing her fists against her mouth, she turned away, instinct urging her to scream. And to keep screaming until someone came. So she wouldn't be alone with a dead man.

But she *was* alone. She took a deep breath, then another, before slowly turning back to look again. The man's upper body lay face-down in Black Brook, water lapping gently around his broad shoulders. Most of him lay concealed in marsh grass—the reason she hadn't seen him earlier. His boots were mud-caked, but the mud had dried. From the odor, she knew he had been there awhile.

The snake . . . the snake must have bitten him. But how could that be? He could have gotten help; snakebite took hours, sometimes several days, to kill.

She thought she heard something, and spun around. There *was* something, a whispering like someone moving through tall grass. Not the horse—he was standing quietly, his ears pricked forward toward the sound. She stood absolutely still, not daring to breathe.

"Leave." The voice came from directly behind her. "Leave now."

Heart leaping to her throat, Glynis whipped around.

Jacques Sundown reached out to grab the horse's reins before he looked down at her, no expression on his face, eyes level and dark. "You need to leave this. Get back to town."

In the wake of her fear, any resolve not to see him again vanished. And the alarm ringing in her head was silenced by relief. Her mouth, though, felt so dry she could barely talk.

"Jacques, thank God you're here. Look . . ." She pointed toward the body of the man in the stream. He's dead," she gasped inanely, as if Jacques couldn't see that. "But I don't think it was the snake." She pointed now at the crushed rattler.

Jacques didn't even look toward the body. He stood staring at her with those flat eyes. What was wrong with him? Just an hour or two ago they'd been together . . . now he was looking at her as if she were a stranger. Did he think she was somehow responsible for the man lying there? Of course not . . . any more than she thought *him* responsible. But what *was* he thinking? He acted as if . . . She took a step backward. Jacques acted as if he already knew about the dead man. But how could he?

"Jacques," she said, her voice quavering. "What are you doing here? *When* did you get here?"

He didn't respond, but went forward until he stood at the water's edge beside the dead man. He didn't look at Glynis but at the body when he said, "You know him? Know who this is?"

"No. Well, maybe . . . I mean . . . how could I?" she stammered, gesturing toward the man's head, facedown in the stream.

Jacques thrust his foot under the man's right shoulder, then lifted until the body rolled over. Glynis gasped, closed her eyes, and turned away.

"You know him now?" Jacques's voice bore an unfamiliar edge. Glynis told herself that he couldn't be angry at her, that this must be the way Jacques sounded when he was upset. She couldn't remember his ever being upset before.

"Look at him," Jacques said again. "See if you know him."

Glynis shook her head. "I can't look. And yes, I know him. It's Mead Miller."

"Yeah. Guess it is."

"But how could he have died? Do you think he fell, leaning forward to get water from the stream? Maybe he was drunk . . . and hit his head on a rock. Knocked himself unconscious and drowned!" She was gathering strength from the logic of the words. Yes, that must have been what happened.

"You see any rocks here?"

She looked into the stream, at its edge, on the bank. Carefully she looked again. "No. No, there aren't any rocks here."

"See any wound on his head?" Jacques's voice, she noticed, had lost some of its harshness; instead he sounded tired. "Any sign of injury?"

"Well, no. But maybe there's a bruise on the back of his head."

"He fell forward. Facedown."

"Oh. Yes. Jacques, I don't know *how* he died. That's what I was asking you."

"You think I know?"

Glynis bit down on her lower lip. He still hadn't told her why he was here. It didn't make sense.

"You get back to town now. Get Cullen Stuart out here. Before it gets darker."

"What are you going to do?"

"Go back to the reservation. Nothing to do here."

"But, Jacques, should I tell Cullen that you . . ." Her voice trailed off. It had been dawning on her that it looked rather strange, Jacques appearing when he had. Unless he'd followed her to make sure she

reached town safely. He'd done that before, years before. Once it had saved her life.

But could she explain that to Cullen? "What should I do, Jacques?"

Jacques shifted his weight, and reached for the reins of the white horse. "Do what you want."

He turned the horse in the direction of the road and gave its rump a hard slap. The horse cantered off. And Jacques himself began to walk away.

"Jacques! Wait..." Glynis felt dismayed, and irritated, at her fear of abandonment. "I mean, would you wait until I get to my buggy?"

"Planned to." He gave her a long look. "You should know that by now."

And he disappeared into the weeds. Like a scout or a guide, she realized.

Glynis stumbled after him up the slight grade. She could hear the sound of the white horse ahead of her as it plowed through the weeds, and she followed the path it opened to the road. Darkness was closing in fast. Finally she felt hard dirt under her feet and heard the little mare nicker. Her shoes were soaked, squashing with every step, and her teeth chattered wildly. She dragged herself up into the buggy. Drawing the shawl around her shoulders, she flicked the reins over the mare's flanks, and felt Jacques Sundown watching her.

Glynis, what in hell were you doing on Black Brook Road anyway?" Cullen's voice was sharp as he untied the reins of his black Morgan. "You had no business being out there alone after dark."

He swung himself up into the saddle.

Even though she knew it to be concern he expressed, it sounded as if Cullen were scolding a naughty child. But she didn't have the strength to point this out. "I'd been . . . I'd been at Grimms' farm, and it got late faster than I realized. Then I saw the horse and . . ." Glynis sank to the railing of the Iveses' porch. She'd found Cullen there, talking with Quentin and Katherine.

"Quentin, I'll round up Zeph and some other men," Cullen said, turning the Morgan toward Fall Street. "Be back as soon as we find Miller's body. From what Glynis said, I think I know where along that

stretch of Black Brook he is. Sounds to me like Miller drowned, but I'll need you to verify it."

"I'll be here when you get back," Quentin Ives said. "Dr. Cardoza, too. Most likely we should do the autopsy tonight, rather than wait for morning. Apparently he's been in the water there a while."

He looked at Glynis for confirmation. She nodded, and nearly fell from her railing perch.

"Glynis, sit in a chair," Katherine ordered, taking her arm and leading her to one. "You're exhausted. And it must have been terrifying to find Mead Miller, and you all alone like that."

Glynis hesitated before she answered. Cullen was about to leave; now was the time to tell him about Jacques. "Yes," she said finally. "Yes, it was terrifying."

It was all she said.

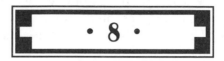

• 8 •

When Fate hath taunted last
And thrown Her furthest stone—
The Maimed may pause, and breathe,
And glance securely round . . .
—Emily Dickinson

Lily Braun leaned forward to instruct her carriage driver on the route she desired to take. After the driver nodded, touching his gloved fingers to the brim of his tall hat, Lily sank back against the soft leather cushions and smiled in satisfaction. She just hoped it wasn't too early in the day to be seen. Seen by everyone in Seneca Falls. *Look at me! Look at me, you smug little town with your smug little rules. Take a good look!*

She had defied the rules, and what had happened? Did anyone see her spirit broken? Impoverished and pleading for charity?

No, indeed!

Lily peeked around the ostrich feathers drooping over the brim of her white silk leghorn hat. There they were—bankers and lawyers and businessmen of Seneca Falls on their way to work. A few were her former customers. Good! They could hardly avoid seeing her. And women were out sweeping their porches, chasing their brats off to school, gossiping over their backyard fences. They'd really have something to gossip about *this* morning. Lily Braun. Lily Braun and her new, six-hundred-and-fifty-dollar, silk-fringed surrey with oil lamps, velvet carpet, and brass trim.

Lily ran her hand in its white kid glove over the rich leather seat, constructed by H. & C. Studebaker, one of the finest firms in the Car-

riage Builders National Association. The surrey had arrived in Seneca Falls by train from Indiana just three days past. It had been paid for, in advance, by a check drawn on the First Bank of Syracuse, New York, and signed by the bank president himself, John H. Stanhope.

Dear, sweet Johnny. She must find a particularly nice way to thank him for such a conspicuous drive through Seneca Falls. It was an event she'd anticipated for many months—anticipated, in fact, since the moment she had so fortuitously met John H. Stanhope. And, finally, here she was: the stylish lady of leisure taking the morning air.

She hadn't been up this early in years. The bright, clear light of morning had not always been agreeable to yesterday's Lily Braun. But that was then. Today's Lily welcomed the illumination.

Opening her beaded velvet reticule, Lily extracted a small looking glass; the sun's rays struck her reflection, and she indulged again in a smile. Soft curlicues of pale blond hair covered her forehead. On her ears sparkled clear, flawless emeralds—Johnny had exquisite taste—emeralds as hard and green as the kohl-lined eyes that beheld them. Eyes that could not be softened even by a satisfied smile. Who could mistake her now for an innocent? None could suspect that those shrewd eyes were formed not by her nature but by innocence savaged, after she had learned that love was kin to death.

It was thus with surprise that Lily saw in the looking glass a sudden glitter of tears. As if she were gazing at someone else. Someone who long ago had died.

Lily thrust the glass back into her reticule.

There, just ahead on the towpath, stood the tavern. Lily ordered the driver to slow the surrey. As ever, there were girls perched on the balcony railing and leaning out the open windows, brushing their hair in the sunshine and laughing about the previous night's customers. It was disappointing to Lily that her former employer, Serenity Hathaway, would undoubtedly still be lying abed. But Serenity would hear—oh, she would definitely hear—about the magnificent carriage. About the woman with pale, elaborately coiffed hair, who, dressed in elegant silk and feathers, had passed.

And surely by now all in town must know about the house—the house Johnny had bought for her from Dooley Keegan's widow. Lily smiled again, this time broadly. It was so right, so absolutely *right,* that

she should have Dooley Keegan's house. For as long as she needed. As long as it took to accomplish what she had returned to do in this wretched little town.

Lily rearranged her skirts so that her lace-edged satin petticoats were visible, and sat back. There was just one thing about this morning that she truly regretted—that her father was not alive to see her now.

The bastard.

Glynis turned onto Fall Street just as Seneca Falls's church bells began tolling eight. She walked a little faster, and immediately felt tightness in the muscles of her legs. Small wonder, considering her activities of the previous day. But she didn't slow her pace, since she wanted to reach the Iveses' before Cullen came looking for her. She still didn't know why she hadn't mentioned Jacques Sundown to him the night before. She'd told herself it had been because of exhaustion, that she'd been so tired she couldn't think straight.

But that wasn't it.

Hearing a clatter behind her, Glynis moved closer to the side of the road. She glanced back at the approaching carriage, looked again, then slowed for a still better look. There were not many surreys in town, and none so ostentatious as this one.

It was with astonishment that she recognized Lily Braun. Glynis had not seen the woman since the day she'd run Neva Cardoza and her off Black Brook Road. Now, looking neither left nor right, Lily sat behind a liveried driver. Glynis watched as the carriage went by, noticing that others on the street stopped to do the same. If Lily wanted to create a sensation, she had succeeded.

Glynis had lived in Seneca Falls only a few years when she had seen Lily Braun for the first time. She remembered Lily as a quiet, forlorn-looking young woman, unremarkable except for the waist-length hair that swung around her like silk veiling. Lily had returned to town, so it was said, to attend her mother's funeral. This caused no end of speculation, since Lily had been conspicuously absent at her father's death a year or two earlier; no one seemed to know the reason why. She had stayed in town just long enough to bury her mother; two older brothers had moved west years before.

The next time Lily made an appearance, four or five years ago, had been more interesting, if poignant. She arrived as a member of a traveling circus. The town was more than a little taken aback by Lily's new persona, that of a fortune-telling, palm-reading Gypsy called Madame Mysteriosa. The pale hair had been dyed black, a red kerchief and hoop earrings added, but underneath remained a profoundly sad-eyed woman. Her tragic look, moreover, simply heightened the Gypsy mystique—almost as if Lily had been employed for that very reason.

The night before the circus left town, some sort of dispute had occurred that involved Madame Mysteriosa and a circusgoer's money clip; the next thing anyone knew about Lily Braun, she'd been released from the lockup, her bail posted by Serenity Hathaway. Cullen had been markedly reticent about the whole episode, and Glynis thought she'd detected some pity in his attitude toward Lily.

Lily Braun's employment at Serenity's Tavern proved to be short-lived. This time neither Cullen nor Serenity was sympathetic to a charge of blackmail against Lily by one of the tavern's frequenters; the town never discovered the identity of the blackmailed man, although, Glynis remembered, it certainly had tried.

And now, here again was Lily Braun. Plainly this time her circumstances were very different. But why on earth would she come back? Glynis mused, as she came abreast of Levy's Hardware. Why return to a town that had very nearly ridden her out on a rail? It seemed irrational.

The hardware store hadn't opened yet when Glynis passed; arriving at the Iveses', she saw why. Abraham Levy stood on the porch with Cullen. Between them rested a long pine coffin. Glynis paused before climbing the steps, as she found herself still reluctant to tell Cullen about Jacques. And it might be too late. Cullen would justifiably wonder why she hadn't said anything the night before.

"Glynis, glad you're here," Cullen said, leaning over the porch rail. "There's a few more things I need to ask you—about when you found Mead Miller's body."

"Oh?" Glynis said to him cautiously. "I told you last night what I saw."

"Yes, but we may need to go over it again. Your friend Dr. Cardoza

thinks she may have found something. She's inside now, finishing up the autopsy."

"She's found something?" Glynis asked.

Cullen shrugged. "Don't know yet—but come on up here." He motioned to her. "Don't need to let the whole town in on this."

Glynis mounted the steps, assuming the whole town did not include Abraham Levy, since Abraham already looked fairly grim, as though worried about what Neva might have discovered.

Could Neva be the reason Abraham was here? Glynis wished she felt more like smiling.

"Morning, Glynis," Abraham said soberly. "Must have been hard for you, finding Mead Miller like that."

Glynis just nodded. Here was her opportunity. And if she didn't tell Cullen right now, right this minute, about Jacques's appearance last night, she risked having him find out another way, although how she couldn't imagine. But if Cullen did find out, he would realize she'd lied to him. Well, not exactly lied—simply neglected to mention a thing or two. *Lied.* But there was nothing to suggest that Mead Miller hadn't died accidentally. He'd drowned, simply drowned. So why was she being so secretive?

Because there was something malignant that she'd sensed about Miller's death. She couldn't put a name to it. But she felt it.

"Constable Stuart?" Neva Cardoza had opened the door and now stepped to the porch. "Constable, I think I know what killed that man. And if so, his death was no accident."

Glynis stared at Neva. Cullen and Abraham were staring too.

"Oh, Glynis, hello," Neva said. "They told me you found the man's body."

Miserably, Glynis nodded. "Yes, why?"

"Did you happen to notice the red spot on his neck?" Neva asked.

"Spot?" Cullen repeated. "What spot?"

Quentin Ives appeared behind Neva. "It's small," he said, "so I wouldn't be surprised if Glynis didn't see it last night."

"See what?" Cullen said. *"What spot?"*

"Made by a puncture wound," Quentin Ives said.

"Puncture wound?" Cullen sounded exasperated. "You want to relieve the suspense and just tell us what Miller died of?"

In response, Neva scowled and clamped her lips shut. Quentin Ives

didn't seem to notice. "Actually, Dr. Cardoza should tell you," he said. "She's the expert in this area."

"What area is that?" Cullen asked.

"Poisons, Constable Stuart!" snapped Neva, as if she assumed Cullen couldn't believe she was an expert in anything. "In medical school I studied under an expert in the field, who had himself studied with Dr. Robert Christison." She gave Cullen an unpleasant smile, adding, "Dr. Christison wrote a definitive text entitled *Treatise on Poisons*."

Cullen's own smile looked equally if not more unpleasant than Neva's when he said, "I'm gratified to have your credentials, Dr. Cardoza! But all I want to know is what the hell Mead Miller died of."

"Very well, Constable. We found evidence of snake venom, but—"

"Snake venom?" Cullen interrupted. "You mean rattlesnake?"

"If rattlesnakes are what you've got around here," Neva retorted.

"There *was* a rattler near the body," Glynis said. "It's what frightened the horse. The horse had killed it, though, apparently just before I got there—the snake's tail was still twitching. But I didn't think snakebite could kill that fast. I mean to say, Mead Miller looked as if he had been dead for some time."

"So maybe," Cullen said, "the snake had bitten him hours before you got there. Maybe Miller . . . wait a minute! When I saw him Saturday night at the tavern, he was fairly drunk. Maybe, on the way back to the Grimms' farm, he stopped along the brook to get some water, passed out, and the snake got him then. Bit him, and Miller didn't even realize it. Died while he was passed out."

"No, I don't think so," Neva disagreed, though her voice wasn't quite so testy now.

"Why not?" Cullen asked.

"Because," she said, "Glynis is right. It ordinarily takes quite a while for snake venom to circulate. Unless the victim is in poor condition. But Mead Miller was essentially a very healthy man. Our autopsy showed that."

"Yes, that's right," Ives agreed. "I don't think venom alone would have killed him. Not that fast, it wouldn't."

"How long do you think he'd been dead when Glynis found him?" Cullen asked.

"It's impossible to know exactly, but I'd say somewhere between fifteen and twenty hours," Quentin Ives said. "So he could have died

shortly after you saw him—possibly on his way back to the Grimms' from the tavern. In any event, that's not what's behind our reasoning, Cullen. There's more to what we found."

Cullen sighed, and shot Glynis a long-suffering look. "Think you could just spit it out?" he said. "Sometime today?"

Quentin Ives smiled. Neva did not.

Abraham Levy, who as yet hadn't said a word, appeared to hide a grin behind his hand, and settled into the porch swing as if expecting to be there for some time.

Neva looked again at Quentin Ives. He motioned her to continue. "What we found first," she began, "was that Miller hadn't drowned as you, Glynis, guessed he might have. There was no water in his lungs, though he was lying facedown in the brook. We noticed the petechial hemorrhage." She paused, then explained, "The small red spot. But you couldn't have seen it if his head was in the water."

Glynis nodded. But what did that mean? It still sounded like snakebite.

"Significantly," Neva went on, "there was the puncture wound, with evidence of discoloration and swelling near the site. When we did an examination of the internal organs, we found evidence of kidney failure, swollen lymph nodes, and necrosis—dead tissue—"

"All of which," Cullen interrupted, "are signs of snakebite. Aren't they?"

"Then this was no ordinary snake," Quentin Ives said, "to have bitten a tall man like Mead Miller in the neck."

"But couldn't he have been bending over the brook for a drink at the time?" Glynis asked.

"Possible," Ives answered, "but not probable. His head and neck would have been over the water. If he'd accidentally kicked or knelt on a snake, the bite would most likely have been on his torso or legs. That's partly why we believe, Dr. Cardoza and I, that poison was introduced by something other than snake fangs. And Miller's apparently swift death indicates that there must have been more than venom present."

"What?" Both Glynis and Cullen spoke, while Abraham Levy sat completely still, his gaze fixed on Neva.

"But most telling," Neva said, "was that the puncture wound was

too large to have been made by a snake—I know because I've seen fang marks, and they're smaller than this was."

"So," Cullen said, "what *do* you think caused the wound?"

Neva looked at Quentin Ives as if for corroboration. Glynis felt unreasonable fear sweep through her, and decided she almost didn't want to hear the answer.

Quentin said quietly, "Dr. Cardoza believes—and I should add that I concur—that what killed Mead Miller was a combination of snake venom and some other highly toxic substance, given the damage we found in the internal organs."

"You want to explain that?" Cullen asked, looking as perplexed as Glynis felt.

Neva appeared uncomfortable. But Quentin nodded at her. "I remembered reading in medical school," she said carefully, as if she didn't expect them to believe her, "about American Indians who . . ." She paused, then added quickly, "I don't recall a specific tribe being mentioned, but they immersed their arrowheads in ground-up snake and venom. Or they would make a snake bite a rabbit liver, then steep the poisoned liver in toxic herbs before they used it for their arrows. That would be a pretty potent brew. Aconite was one of the most common herbs used because it's so toxic and so easily obtained from monkshood, which grows just about everywhere. And aconite by itself can kill rapidly, we know, if it's mistaken for wild parsley and ingested," she said.

"But surely," Glynis protested, "Mead Miller wouldn't have eaten it . . . oh . . . the puncture wound." She pressed her lips together before she could say more.

"Yes," Neva responded. "The poison *could* have been introduced by way of an arrow. It would have worked very fast if shot into a neck vein."

"No. Arrow point's way too big," Cullen immediately argued. "I would have seen that size wound in Miller's neck."

"It was dark, Cullen," reminded Abraham quietly.

Glynis remained silent.

"It didn't have to be an arrow," Quentin Ives said. "I agree that would probably have made a very noticeable wound. But it might

have been something smaller . . . like a dart. Yes, in fact, a dart would have been just about the right size."

Cullen frowned at Ives. "I found a lot of burdock and thistle on Miller's clothes, but I didn't find anything else. As Abraham said, though, it was dark." Cullen turned to Glynis. "You didn't see a dart when you found him, did you?"

Glynis shook her head. She wished Neva hadn't mentioned American Indians. She knew Jacques hadn't killed Mead Miller, she knew that—and besides, why would he?—but it could look very odd if she mentioned his sudden appearance to Cullen now. She needed to think this through. And in the meantime she wouldn't say anything. Not yet.

". . . and I don't like this," Cullen was saying to Quentin Ives. "If what you're theorizing is true, then someone wanted it to look as if Miller drowned, or was killed by snakebite. And that means we've had two murders in this town in just a short time."

"Yes, Cullen," Quentin agreed, "of course I thought of that too. Although Jack Turner didn't die the same way."

"He was poisoned, though," Cullen said. "Seems to me what *kind* of poison doesn't make a whole lot of difference—both he and Miller are dead."

"And you know, something else has been bothering me," Quentin said. "Remember when Dooley Keegan died? About four years ago?"

Glynis looked at Quentin with uneasiness. She remembered Dooley's death, all right. The whole town had been shocked. Dooley Keegan, never sick a day in his life, had just keeled over during a hunting trip. He'd been with several other men who verified this. "I remember," she said now to Quentin. "But why do you mention it?"

"Because, at his wife's insistence, I did an autopsy on Keegan. She just couldn't accept that he'd died so abruptly. Natural on her part, I suppose—she maintained he'd always been in good health. But it looked to me as though he'd died of sudden, massive kidney failure. No reason to think otherwise."

"He wasn't very old, though," Cullen said. "We all wondered about that at the time."

Neva Cardoza had been listening attentively to Quentin. "But was there anything about that man's death," she asked, "which would make you think it was not as it seemed?"

"No," Cullen answered her. "Not that *I* remember, except . . . My God, Quentin, didn't you say something about a red spot on his neck? It's been so long, I can't recall exactly."

"Yes, it looked like a small puncture wound," Ives said, his face troubled. "I just now looked it up in my files. Couldn't remember until this morning, but I thought I'd seen, sometime in the past, the exact kind of wound that Miller had." Ives looked upset when he added, "Dooley Keegan! But at the time I assumed his neck puncture was something that took place while he was hunting; he was hiking through the woods, after all. I must admit, though, it bothered me some; but none of the other men could recall anything out of the ordinary happening to Dooley. And there was no reason to suspect anything sinister. But now I wonder."

"Yes," Cullen said, "I wonder too. It's unlikely we'll ever know the answer—Keegan's death was a long time ago."

"I thought you told me," Neva Cardoza commented, "that this was a quiet town, Constable Stuart." She stared at Cullen as though affixing blame.

"It was," Abraham Levy interjected, "until you arrived."

"Abraham . . ." Quentin Ives seemed on the verge of rebuke, but then apparently caught Abraham's grin. Neva just glared.

"You know, young woman," Abraham said to Neva as he got to his feet, "somewhere along the way you'd best find a sense of humor."

"I don't believe there's anything humorous about murder," Neva lashed back.

Abraham appeared to ignore this; he went to the pine coffin and lifted its lid. "You want some help, Quentin, getting Miller's body into this?"

Quentin Ives looked as if he couldn't quite believe the exchange he'd just heard between his friend Abraham Levy and his trainee Neva Cardoza. But he nodded briefly at Abraham and they went into the house.

Neva continued to glare at Abraham's disappearing back, then turned to Glynis. "Are you going to tell Constable Stuart about what Sara Turner said?"

Glynis had been about to do just that. "Neva and I stopped to see Sara on the way back from the Grimms', Cullen," she explained. "She

was very odd—Sara Turner, I mean—and said something to the effect that her husband's death wasn't the end of it."

"End of what?" Cullen asked her, frowning.

"Death, was what she said. That there'd be more death."

"Seems she was right," Neva said, frowning herself.

"Didn't you ask what she meant?" Cullen said to Glynis.

"Yes, of course I tried, but she ran into the house before I could get her to say more. It was very strange."

Neva nodded in agreement. "And Sara Turner didn't look much like a grief-stricken widow," she offered. "Quite the opposite, I'd say."

"That your impression, Glynis?" Cullen asked.

"Yes, it was. But how could Sara know that Mead Miller, or anybody else, was going to be killed? Unless she knew the reason why. Which might mean she knows, or at least suspects, why her husband was murdered."

"Unless she's the one who did it," Cullen said.

"But would Sara Turner kill Mead Miller too? That makes no sense, Cullen." Glynis looked at Neva for possible suggestions.

Neva shook her head. "I agree with Glynis. It's one thing for Sara Turner to have killed a husband who was tormenting her and her children," she said. "At least that's understandable, some might say justifiable, but"—she hurried on as Cullen looked about to take strenuous exception—"for her to kill yet another man eliminates that motive. And anyway, I don't think Sara Turner killed either one of those men. She doesn't seem the type."

"Oh, there's a specific 'type' of person who kills?" Cullen said. "Tell me about this, Dr. Cardoza. It'll certainly make my job a whole lot easier!"

"I only meant," Neva snapped, "that someone like Sara, who has apparently endured years of mistreatment, doesn't suddenly transform from a victim into an aggressor. Not usually. At least I wouldn't think so."

"That's right, Cullen," Glynis said. "There are many women in Sara's situation, tragically, but they don't abruptly do away with their husbands."

"Or else," Neva added, "we'd have a whole lot more dead men."

Cullen's expression turned combative. Then, unexpectedly, he shook his head. "No, I'm not getting into another one of those point-

less arguments. No!" he said firmly as Neva tried to break in. "I've got two murders to investigate. Now, if either of you wants to add anything about *those,* I'll listen. Otherwise, I'm heading out to the Turners'. And the Grimms'—see if they know why anybody'd want to kill Mead Miller.

"Glynis, you think Jonathan Quant can handle the library this afternoon? I'd appreciate it if you'd come with me. You know the people involved better than I do. And—"

He broke off as his deputy came running around the corner of the house. Zeph raced to the foot of the porch steps to sputter breathlessly, "Constable . . . Constable Stuart, you need to come with me. Real fast! There's trouble. At Levy's Hardware."

• 9 •

The trails of our Indian predecessors, indeed, have been obliterated, and the face of nature has been transformed; but all recollection of the days of Indian supremacy cannot as easily pass away. They will ever have a share in our history.

—Lewis Henry Morgan, *League of the Ho-de-no-sau-nee, or Iroquois*

Cullen started down the porch stairs. "What kind of trouble, Zeph?" he asked the young deputy.

Abraham Levy had shot through the door and was down the stairs and running in the direction of his Fall Street store before Zeph could answer.

"It's the Indians," Zeph said. "They're at Mr. Levy's store, and a bunch of folks are trying to make them leave—I think you'd better hurry, Constable Stuart."

Cullen nodded and, with Zeph beside him, took off at a brisk stride. Glynis followed at a slower pace. Even before she rounded the corner onto Fall Street, she heard argumentative voices; once in sight of Abraham's store, she saw a small crowd gathered in the road around oxen yoked to a rough dray wagon. Beside the dray stood four Iroquois women.

Glynis recognized only Small Brown Bird and the wiry, stern-faced Bitter Root. All four women wore broadcloth pantalettes, flannel underskirts, and overdresses of bright calico, but these were more elaborate than the ones Glynis had seen at the reservation. The dresses were buttoned with silver brooches; narrow bands of glass and silver beads shimmered at the hems. From Glynis's vantage point, the sparkle of beading and the bright fabrics made the four women resemble colorful, exotic birds surrounded by a flock of sparrows.

Cullen and Abraham stood on the front steps of the hardware store, being harangued by a heavy-framed white woman who gestured toward the Iroquois and shook her head repeatedly. Glynis moved closer.

"... and we don't want those savages in our town!" the woman finished. Glynis identified the speaker as Tillie Tyler. Standing beside Tillie, her much smaller husband, Lemuel, nodded his agreement after being poked by his wife's elbow.

"There's no law says these folks can't be here, Tillie," Abraham said reasonably. "Why're you raising such a dustup about this?"

" 'Cause you got their stuff in your store, Abe Levy, that's why," Tillie pronounced, arms akimbo, hands on her thick hips. "You just want to make money and you don't care how you do it. It's downright unneighborly and ... un-Christian is what it is."

Abraham Levy's ruddy cheeks went darker. "I haven't noticed, Mrs. Tyler, that religion's ever stopped you from asking for credit in my store when you needed it."

Tillie started to reply, but her husband plucked at her arm in timid appeal, and wagged his head at her.

A tall, haggard man, a farmer whose last name Glynis recalled as Daniels, stepped forward. "Why're you dealing with these here people anyhow, Abe Levy?" Daniels gestured toward the four women standing quietly beside their dray wagon. "They're meant to stay put on their own land, not come on down here causing trouble."

"I don't see them causing any trouble," Abraham replied. "Seems like the only trouble is what you folks are making. These women have got quality goods for sale—"

"Yeah," interrupted bootmaker Sam Carson, "and they're competing with us white folks. They make their moccasins a lot cheaper than I can make boots."

"And they ain't gotta pay no overhead, neither," another voice chimed in.

Beside Abraham, Cullen stood with arms crossed over his chest, not saying a word. Glynis didn't think he would interfere as long as things remained relatively calm. Unless someone broke the law, Cullen generally didn't involve himself in disputes. Occasional squabbles were normal, he'd told Glynis more than once—some people just by nature were greedy and selfish and cantankerous. No constable was

going to make them otherwise. In the past, however, Glynis had observed that Cullen's badge alone often worked to dissuade troublemakers.

"What's going on here?" asked a voice at Glynis's shoulder.

Glynis turned to find Neva Cardoza frowning at the restless and growing crowd. "Some think the Iroquois should stay on their reservation," she answered. "And they're angry, too, because Abraham is carrying the women's goods."

"That's ridiculous!" Neva said, so emphatically that several people pivoted to look at her. Neva ignored them. "I hope the unpleasant Mr. Levy isn't going to back down," she added, but in a somewhat milder tone.

Glynis had to ask. "Neva, why do you still insist that Abraham is unpleasant?"

"Because he still reminds me of my father."

Glynis wasn't sure how Neva's comment answered her question, but clearly this was not the time to pursue it. Especially since a buggy wheeling up Fall Street had stopped at the fringes of the crowd, and Lazarus Grimm was now jumping from the driver's seat. His pale, aesthetic face looked markedly eager. Molly and Pippa also began descending to the road, but Lazarus called something over his shoulder, and both climbed back into their buggy seat. Pippa, however, continued to eye the crowd with obvious curiosity.

Glynis wondered if perhaps Mead Miller's disappearance had brought the reclusive Grimms here this day. They might well have come to see Cullen about Miller. Had they by this time learned of the man's death? Perhaps not; the farm was so very isolated. Glynis felt a tremor travel the length of her spine as she considered the bizarre murder. She couldn't shake the sense that Mead Miller's death had to be linked to that of Jack Turner.

But other than the fact that the two men had lived on the same road, what could they have had in common to provoke murder?

To Glynis's chagrin, Lazarus had apparently spotted her, and now came toward her at a trot. "Looks like there might be trouble here, Miss Tryon."

Again Glynis noted that Lazarus looked remarkably unperturbed, perhaps even cheered, by this prospect. She concluded she should say nothing about Mead Miller; after all, she and Cullen were supposed

to go to the Grimm farm later that day. She just nodded to him briefly. But Neva nudged her with insistence until Glynis introduced him.

"Ah, yes, the new doctor in town," Lazarus said. By all appearances, he seemed genuinely delighted to make Neva's acquaintance. "My niece told me of your visit to the farm."

He turned to gesture at the buggy. Mistaking this for acquiesence, Pippa again began to clamber down. Lazarus shook his head at her vigorously, and Pippa's face registered profound disappointment when her mother pulled her back up beside her on the buggy seat.

Whatever Lazarus said next was drowned in harsh shouts from those standing directly in front of the store. Glynis craned to see over their heads, and finally moved closer to the dray wagon. The shouts apparently had been prompted by Bitter Root, who'd begun toting baskets of moccasins to Levy's shop. The shop's two doors stood open and the space just inside was empty; presumably all the baskets previously there had been sold.

"Levy!" shouted Sam Carson. "You give those squaws space in your store, you can just forget about my trade!"

Abraham's face flushed a darker red, but he replied civilly, "If that's the way you want it, Sam."

"Or my business either, Levy," shouted farmer Daniels.

Neva, who had followed Glynis, said, "Isn't your Constable Stuart going to do something?"

"He probably won't unless it gets out of hand. So far, people are just shouting."

"So far," Neva said, looking skeptical.

"How come you let those squaws squat in your store?" another voice shouted. "They maybe giving you somethin' you can't get down at Serenity's?"

This was greeted with a few raucous laughs, which dwindled quickly to be replaced by stony silence. Most of the men there, irate as they might be, wouldn't condone that kind of talk in front of womenfolk. White womenfolk, at least.

Abraham spoke into the void. "These women aren't getting space free. They're paying me a commission to sell their goods. And as far as I'm concerned, they're entitled to be here so long as they do pay."

Mutters of surprise greeted this piece of news. To Glynis's relief, a substantial portion of the crowd appeared to shrug, if only figura-

tively, and began to saunter off. But Tillie Tyler wasn't satisfied. "Makes no never-mind, Abe Levy," she said belligerently, "no matter how much those Indians're paying you. They don't belong here, and that's the truth! Next thing you know, they'll be buying all kinds of liquor and shootin' up the town. You see if they don't!"

Abraham gazed down at Tillie Tyler with barely contained exasperation. "Tillie," he said wearily, "you are an ignorant woman—no, don't you interrupt me. I'm entitled to my say. You have never—I repeat, *never*—seen Iroquois women shooting up anything. Now, these folks have got the right to try and sell their goods here. You don't like it—don't buy it! But that's the way it is."

With that, Abraham Levy stepped down and lifted several baskets from the arms of Bitter Root, who was now on her second trip to the shop. Ignoring the crowd, which by then had diminished to a handful, Abraham deposited the baskets and moccasins, then headed back toward his store. Bitter Root started toward the wagon where the three other women had begun to unload more goods.

Glynis watched as the women made their way forward. Their woven baskets were filled with cornhusk dolls, salt bottles, carved pipes, and beaded bags and pincushions; black pottery of so fine a texture that it resembled stone, and earthen bowls, of which a few were faced with wolf heads. Various other animals had been carved on the handles of wooden paddles and ladles. Those townspeople who remained stood quietly, and their expressions showed curiosity more than hostility.

Glynis stole a quick glance at Neva, who was standing quietly beside her. She'd heard the quick intake of breath when Abraham began to speak, and now saw something unfamiliar on the young woman's face. Although Glynis couldn't identify it precisely, it might have been respect. She couldn't resist saying, "Well, I guess Abraham didn't back off."

"No. No, he didn't," Neva agreed surprisingly, her words coming slowly as if with some reluctance. "No, he stood his ground." She looked at Glynis with the merest hint of smile. "Aren't you going to say 'I told you so'?"

Glynis was about to say Yes, when Bitter Root, in front of the store and loaded down with baskets, suddenly began to cough. It was a painful sound. The baskets dropped when she wrapped her arms

around her chest and bent almost double as, swaying precariously back and forth, she continued to cough.

Cullen stepped to the road with a look of concern. He moved to put an arm around Bitter Root's shoulders, but the woman thrust herself upright and, still hacking, flung off Cullen's arm.

"Keep away from me!" she gasped. "Don't need anything from white lawman."

Cullen took a step back as Small Brown Bird rushed forward and took her sister's arm to lead her to the steps. Once Bitter Root had been seated, the cough began to subside.

"I'm sorry," Small Brown Bird said over her shoulder to Cullen. "My sister was in distress, and so she was unkind in her words."

Bitter Root started to say something, but Small Brown Bird motioned to her with frantic gestures. Bitter Root's lips closed, but she stared straight at Cullen. Even from a distance, Glynis could feel the woman's hatred.

Cullen strode off down Fall Street, his face unreadable even to Glynis. And most of those remaining, while muttering uneasily, began to amble off.

"I wonder what that was all about?" Neva ventured.

Glynis shook her head. "I can't imagine, and—" She was interrupted by a familiar voice behind her.

"Glynis, what in the world is going on?" The clear voice rang accusingly as Vanessa Usher swept into Glynis's vision. Lovely, maddening Vanessa. Exactly the person they did not need here. And Neva, who had already met Vanessa several times, at once stiffened and adopted a wary expression.

"I *said*, Glynis, what is happening here?" Vanessa demanded.

"Oh, nothing you need concern yourself with, Vanessa. Anyway, it's over now."

"What's over? And just what do those outlandishly dressed squaws think they are doing?"

"Those *women* are simply minding their own business," said Neva sharply.

"Oh . . . well, if that's all they're doing, I shouldn't have bothered to stop," Vanessa retorted. "I thought something that might interest me was taking place." She gave Neva an airy wave of dismissal, then turned to leave.

"Ah, Miss Tryon, if you please?"

Glynis had forgotten Lazarus Grimm, who now hovered directly behind her.

"My dear Miss Usher," Lazarus said, bowing to Vanessa with a flamboyant flourish. "Miss Usher, I should very much like to speak with you on a matter of mutual interest. If you would allow Miss Tryon to introduce me, I would be forever grateful." He fixed Vanessa with an utterly charming smile.

Glynis had to give him credit; Lazarus had done precisely that most destined to pique Vanessa's curiosity. Vanessa who believed unshakably that all western New York men lacked even the most rudimentary knowledge of good manners; had only very recently shed their bearskins and emerged from caves.

She returned Lazarus's smile with equal charm. "Glynis, dear, do introduce this gentleman immediately."

Neva uttered an indistinguishable sound; while faint, it was somewhat louder than Glynis's sigh, hence the glare that Neva now received from Vanessa. "Of course," Glynis said, commencing to do as she had been commanded. But, my dear Miss Usher, she thought, don't blame me.

The introductions having been made, Lazarus bent over Vanessa's hand in a showy gesture. Glynis turned aside, determined not to laugh. She caught Neva's eye and saw that she, too, struggled for the solemnity this clearly historic meeting required. They both quickly moved away.

Glynis pressed her palm over her mouth. And under her breath, Neva muttered, "From what you've said about Lazarus Grimm, I'd say those two deserve each other."

Small Brown Bird had just returned from the shop, and Glynis walked to the dray wagon, saying, "I'm truly ashamed of the earlier scene here. Please don't think that all of Seneca Falls feels as those few people do."

"I don't think that," Small Brown Bird smiled shyly, "or we would not have sold so many things."

The two other women were still inside the shop, but Bitter Root had climbed with startling nimbleness into the wagon, apparently recovered from her attack. Glynis noticed that Neva had been studying the older woman with interest.

"Excuse me," Neva said now to Bitter Root, "but have you had that cough very long?"

Bitter Root moved her head to stare straight before her. But Small Brown Bird quickly said something to her in Seneca, and the older woman turned back to regard Neva with narrowed eyes.

"I told my sister that you are a medicine woman," Small Brown Bird explained to Neva, leaving Glynis to wonder how this information had been acquired. Then, as she saw Pippa coming toward them, she remembered that both Iroquois women had had contact with the Grimms.

"I could listen to your chest," Neva was telling Bitter Root. "In fact, I think I should. That cough sounds like something you should attend to."

But Bitter Root had turned at the sound of Pippa's voice, and watched intently as the girl came toward her. Glynis observed a smile spreading across the woman's face; a smile that planed the cold, rough lines and brought to Bitter Root's cheeks a copper warmth. With a start, Glynis realized that Jacques's mother must be considerably younger than she'd originally guessed—probably no older than her early fifties. That would account for her surprising agility. The Seneca woman's eyes, however, looked as ancient as the hills. An Old Testament image came suddenly, and for no obvious reason, to Glynis—that of Rachel and her lost children. *A voice was heard in Ramah, lamentation and bitter weeping; Rachel weeping for her children. . . .*

Pippa had scrambled up onto the dray and thrown her arms around Bitter Root's neck, and received in response a warm chuckle and like embrace. Glynis watched this display of affection from the dour woman in astonishment. Then she heard Molly Grimm directly behind her.

"Pippa, come along now—we have to leave." Molly's voice held an urgent note. "Do get down from there!"

Pippa looked at her mother with a strangely poignant expression. She seemed about to protest, but when Bitter Root gave her a swift shake of the head and a soft nudge, Pippa descended from the dray dutifully but with obvious reluctance.

"Good morning, Glynis. And Dr. Cardoza," Molly said somewhat breathlessly, as though she'd run from the buggy. "I'm sorry to be in such a rush, but we don't have much time."

Time? Glynis thought. The woman had been waiting for the past ten or fifteen minutes without a murmur. But Molly seized Pippa's arm to pull her from the dray, while at the same time calling for Lazarus to hurry. Lazarus bent to pass his lips again over Vanessa's hand, then walked toward the buggy. Glynis's gaze returned to Bitter Root with curiosity; the woman was watching Pippa, her eyes glittering but relaying nothing specific in way of meaning. Glynis noticed that Small Brown Bird did much the same, before a sudden enigmatic look flashed between the two Iroquois women. It happened so rapidly that a moment later Glynis couldn't be positive she'd really seen it.

Voices coming toward the dray broke into her speculation. The two other Iroquois women had returned and now smiled tentatively at Glynis and Neva, while Small Brown Bird said, "These are my sisters. Or, in your custom, perhaps they would be called cousins. But we are all of the Wolf Clan."

She introduced Sunlight Weaver and a much younger woman, really just a girl, Glynis thought, called Silver Combs. Both smiled and nodded to Glynis and Neva, then climbed nimbly into the dray. Sunlight Weaver gave the reins of the oxen a quick shake; with her round face and flat nose, she looked so very different from the hollow-cheeked, sharp-featured Bitter Root, and from Small Brown Bird and Jacques, too, that Glynis marveled they could all be related, no matter how distantly.

The dray wagon creaked slowly forward.

As Glynis watched it turn onto Black Brook Road, she observed Bitter Root's long backward glance as well as a wistful look on the face of Silver Combs that touched Glynis with sadness. How much did Iroquois youngsters know of white culture, and if aware of how much was inaccessible to them, did they care? From Silver Combs's expression, Glynis thought the girl did care.

"Why do we see only the women in town and not the men?" Neva asked.

"From what I know," Glynis answered, her eyes still on the departing wagon, "I'd guess the men wouldn't participate in what they might consider women's work." She gave Neva a rueful smile. "That seems to be true anywhere."

"But from the books you loaned me," Neva said, "I gathered that Iroquois women had at least some small amount of power."

"Their lot has changed dramatically in the past five or six decades," Glynis explained, "mostly because of the Indians' confinement to reservations. In the past, women were in charge of the agriculture: planting and harvesting and storage and preparation. And they did have a certain stature within the tribes. Not, I think, as much as we've been led to believe by the European male chroniclers, who, no doubt, were flabbergasted at the idea of descent following the female line."

Neva nodded and grinned. "What a shock those first white men must have experienced! Can you imagine the authority they believed the women had?"

"Exactly," Glynis agreed. "But now the Iroquois men, having lost most of their hunting grounds, and no longer engaging in war, have begun to adopt whites' farming methods—very slowly, to be sure. Not that long ago, an Iroquois male wouldn't have been caught dead planting or harvesting; again, that was woman's work! Some of the men still refuse, especially when they might be seen. But the upshot is that the women, who once controlled use of the land, have been forced to give up that control.

"And believe it or not," Glynis went on, "Iroquois women at one time had more rights regarding divorce and inheritance, and most certainly their children's lives, than white women have today."

Neva gave Glynis a tight smile. "It's depressingly familiar. Those four we saw just now appear to be strong women—it must be hard for them, considering their history."

"Oh, I think it's hard for all the Iroquois, not only the women."

Neva seemed to consider this, then shook her head. "No, life's always harder for women; men don't bear children. And, speaking of that," she said, brightening somewhat, "are you or are you not going to join our women's march on the tavern?"

Glynis sighed. They'd been over this before. "No, Neva, I'm not joining."

She received a look of indignation.

Glynis sighed again, and said with frank regret, "Neva, I can't. Serenity and I have a past . . . ah, well, an association. Of sorts."

Neva's eyes narrowed. "You've been *associated* with Serenity Hathaway? Forgive me, Glynis, but that's a little hard to imagine."

"I know it must seem that way. But the woman has helped me out several times in the past."

"*What?* Glynis, is there something about you I should know?" Something sordid and shocking?" Neva's mouth twitched.

Shaking her head and smiling, too, Glynis said, "No, Serenity and I just happened to cross paths. It's a long story. But I can't participate in trying to close her tavern down. Not," she added quickly, "that I approve of her . . . business."

"Her *business*," Neva responded tartly, "is responsible for a staggering amount of misery. I don't understand how you can overlook that."

"I'm not overlooking it. I'm just not prepared to do something that seems . . . I don't know . . ." Glynis stopped. This was getting them nowhere.

But Neva pressed on. "That seems what? Disloyal? Ungrateful? Glynis, if the devil himself once inadvertently 'helped you out,' would you feel compelled to support *him*?"

"It's not the same, and I'm not supporting Serenity. I'm just loath to join in publicly embarrassing her. Now, please, Neva, let's just consider this a difference of opinion. And let it go at that."

Neva now looked unmistakably angry. So angry that Glynis worried this would threaten their friendship. "Neva," she said carefully, "don't you think it's possible for us to disagree with each other occasionally, and yet still consider the other to be a friend?"

This seemed to shock Neva, as if it were an audaciously novel idea, but at least she appeared to be thinking it over.

At the sound of carriage wheels, Glynis glanced over her shoulder to see, for the second time that morning, Lily Braun seated in her elegant surrey. Catching the light with a sudden flash were the brilliant gems at Lily's ears. The jewels were the same green as the forlorn eyes that Glynis recalled, but given the emeralds—they looked like emeralds—and the beautiful carriage, she supposed Lily might not be so unhappy anymore. She certainly was not in poverty.

"Oh, I suppose so," Neva said, interrupting her speculation, and looking closely at her as if she were in another world somewhere, and might not have heard. "That reasonable people can disagree, that is," Neva explained. "But I didn't think we'd disagree, you and I, on something like a brothel. It's so . . . so . . ." Evidentally at a loss for words, Neva shrugged.

But then she smiled, if very faintly. "You know what I think, Gly-

nis? I think that what with murderers and bigots and exasperating hardware store owners, and librarians that tolerate brothel proprietors—well, I think that for a small town, Seneca Falls has more than its fair share of characters!"

Lily Braun had instructed her driver to take the carriage for one last turn around the village, just in case someone might have missed her earlier. She'd heard a crowd gathering at Levy's Hardware on Fall Street, but it had begun to disperse when the carriage drew near. Lily was in time, however, to see a buggy carrying members of the Grimm family swerve rapidly onto Black Brook Road. Maybe the almighty Grimms had heard she was out and about, and were trying to avoid her. Never mind, she told herself; they couldn't go fast enough or far enough. Not this time.

Lily's driver now abruptly pulled to the right to avoid a dray wagon rumbling from the hardware store. Lily's breath stopped when she saw its occupants. What were *they* doing here? She caught only a glimpse of the older woman seated in the wagon. Her face had grown more than ever like a meat-ax, Lily decided, but Bitter Root could have no ax to grind with *her*. Nonetheless, Lily turned her own face aside to be concealed by her hat brim when the vehicles passed.

When Lily again turned to look out, she saw two women engaged in conversation—obviously engrossing conversation, since neither glanced her way. Of the two, Lily recognized only Glynis Tryon; she had hardly aged at all, Lily observed with some envy.

Suddenly Miss Tryon turned to look in her direction. Lily's hands went to her ears, and she flicked the earrings to catch the light. As one of the very few in Seneca Falls who had been unfailingly kind to her, Miss Tryon had a right to see how well Lily Braun had managed.

Lily's hands flew from the earrings to her eyes. She brushed hurriedly at her tears before they could fall and spot the costly silk dress.

Neva Cardoza watched Glynis walk away, heading toward her library. The surrey carrying the woman, Lily Braun, had just turned north off Fall Street, and Neva found herself alone; with the toe of her

shoe, she traced a circle in the dust, and glanced guardedly over her shoulder toward Levy's Hardware. She had absolutely no reason to be dawdling there, so why was she doing so?

She took a few steps toward the shop.

"Interested in some baskets?" asked an affable male voice from behind her.

Neva turned to see Abraham Levy just coming from his store, carrying a number of empty wooden crates. Setting them down a few yards away, he began to separate an assortment of hand tools, tossing various of them into the crates. His blue cotton workshirt pulled taut over his muscular shoulders when he swung several large feed bags out of his way.

"Time to put some of these aside for the winter," he said conversationally, nodding toward the tools he was sorting. "Won't need them now until spring."

He didn't say more, and proceeded to winnow out various implements, apparently indifferent to Neva's presence. Well, why wouldn't he be? she thought with unaccountable disappointment. She supposed she hadn't made herself very congenial in the past. Her cheeks began to burn as his silence continued, and discomfort formed a hard knot in her throat. She knew she should leave, that she was making a fool of herself by simply standing there and gawking at him. *What was the matter with her?*

Clearing her throat loudly, she turned to go. But after several steps she paused. Wasn't he going to say *anything*? "Ah, Mr. Levy," she began, not turning toward him and thus speaking to empty space, "I just wanted to tell you . . . well . . . I thought you handled the . . . the earlier situation here very well."

She waited for a response. When he said nothing, nothing at all, she felt a humiliation so intense it made her lightheaded. She took several shaky breaths and started to walk away. And jumped at his voice when it came from directly behind her. "I don't think I quite heard that," Abraham commented, standing so close she could feel his breath on the back of her neck. "What was it you said?"

Neva spun to face him. "I said I thought you handled the—"

She broke off as she saw the smile and, worse, saw it broaden. "I'm glad you find me so amusing, Mr. Levy. But please don't let me take up your valuable time."

“Woman,” sighed Abraham, reaching for her hand, “what is the matter with you?”

Neva swallowed hard as his fingers closed around hers, then tried to pull her hand away at the same time recalling that, not two minutes before, she’d asked herself the same question. She stopped resisting and stood very still. Abraham’s hand felt strong and warm and dry, and she had a sudden unwelcome memory of Jacob Espinosa’s limp, sweaty fingers.

“I don’t know what’s the matter,” she said softly, biting the inside of her cheek in acute embarrassment. “I don’t know.”

“Well,” Abraham said, with an expulsion of breath that ruffled her hair, “that, at least, is a start!” He gave her hand a gentle tug. “I suggest we go inside and try to figure this out.”

• 10 •

Such [liquor] licenses shall not be granted, unless the commissioners are satisfied the applicant is of good moral character . . . he will not suffer his place of business to be disorderly . . . he will not suffer to be sold, any strong or spiritous liquors to be drank in his shop, or house, or in any out-house. . . .

—Chapter 628, section twelve, of the Laws of 1857;
enacted by the Eightieth Session of the New York Legislature

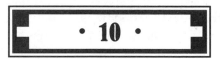

Serenity Hathaway lifted her voluminous skirts ever so modestly before mounting the steps to the law office. A brisk wind off the canal ruffled her gray wool cape and fluttered the demure ribbons of her bonnet. She wasn't taking any chances; she'd even restrained her flaming hair in a severe chignon. Her own mother wouldn't recognize her—if the poor old thing could see her and hadn't drunk herself to death years ago.

And Jeremiah Merrycoyf, upon opening the door, obviously did not recognize her either. Serenity bit back a smile as he adjusted wire-framed spectacles and harrumphed several times, peering at her closely. At last he stepped aside to usher her into his office with, "Have I had the pleasure of meeting you before, Madame?"

"Surely have, Mr. Merrycoyf—I'm Serenity Hathaway. And it's not Madame, it's *madam*."

She had to admire his self-control. He barely flinched. With a slight cough, genteelly contained behind a chubby hand, Merrycoyf gestured to a chair. Serenity lowered herself into it with utmost decorum, while thinking it a damn shame that this man had never set foot in her establishment. He was cute as a bug. She'd probably not noticed this before, because their only previous contact had been in a

courtroom. That kind of place did tend to put a damper on one's priorities.

"Miss Hathaway, madam; may I inquire as to why you're here today?"

Serenity grinned. Cute as a bug. "Mr. Merrycoyf, I need to hire your services."

"My services. I see." Merrycoyf had lumbered around his desk and settled himself in a large overstuffed chair. "I assume, Miss Hathaway, that you are speaking of legal services. Why are you in need of counsel?"

"To tell the truth, it's one hell of a thing, Jeremiah—I can call you Jeremiah?"

"Miss Hathaway, you are at liberty to call me whatever you wish. That does not, however, address my question. Your need for legal advice?"

"They want to shut me down. My tavern, that is."

"And who might 'they' be?"

"The self-righteous busybodies of this town, that's who."

"How do they propose to do this, Miss Hathaway?"

Serenity frowned, studying Merrycoyf at some length, before she said, "You'll pardon me for asking, Jeremiah, and I don't want to be crude, but—*don't you bloody well know the law?*"

He didn't miss a beat. "If you mean Chapter 628 of the New York State Code, which, as of the sixteenth of April this year, attempts to suppress intemperance and regulate the sale of intoxicating liquor—yes, I'm familiar with it."

Serenity exhaled with relief. "Had me worried there for a minute, Jeremiah. Anyway, these busybodies are pressuring the constable to shut me down. Because of that damn law."

"You didn't expect this to occur?"

"What—a mob of crazy women parading up and down in front of my tavern? No, sir, I did not! And that's what the scuttlebutt says is going to happen. Now, this kind of thing could be bad, real bad, for business. And I want to know how to stop them. I *can* stop them, can't I?"

Merrycoyf leaned forward. "Miss Hathaway, that is difficult to determine without more information. Happily, you are most fortunate in that, although I myself have pressing matters to attend in the com-

ing weeks, I possess the name of—please, Miss Hathaway, hear me out before you protest—the name of a young attorney whom I shall personally request to take your case."

Merrycoyf plucked a pen from its inkwell and began to write.

"Jeremiah, I don't want some kid lawyer still wet behind the ears."

Merrycoyf kept writing. Serenity cleared her throat to create an irresistibly silken voice. "I can, of course, pay you well . . . in fact, any kind of payment you'd like." She smiled her most generous smile.

He continued to write, very fast. "My dear Miss Hathaway, that is a most beneficent offer. But my schedule simply will not allow me to pursue your interests. And I assure you, Mr. Adam MacAlistair will be eager to assist. He has recently returned to Seneca Falls from the law school of Virginia's William and Mary College, where he acquitted himself most admirably. Fear not, my good lady, you will be in the best of hands."

Merrycoyf did not look up until he had signed the letter and sealed it in an envelope. Rising from his chair, he handed it across the desk to Serenity.

She couldn't remember ever having been so smoothly dispatched. She must be losing her touch. But she'd always known when to fold, and she did have to admire his style. "Make you a bargain, Jeremiah, darlin'. Just promise you'll watch over this Adam MacAlistair's shoulder, and I'll walk out of here nice and ladylike. Otherwise"—she smiled ominously—"there's no telling what I might do."

Merrycoyf adjusted his spectacles. "With that possibility in mind, my dear Miss Hathaway, let me assure you I have already," he gestured to the envelope, "apprised Mr. MacAlistair of that very thing."

Yes, indeed, she did have to admire his style.

You want to tell me what so riled that Indian woman this morning?" Cullen asked as he guided the carriage horse onto Black Brook Road. "She looked like she wanted to string me up on the nearest tree."

"I have no idea what was wrong," Glynis answered. "But it seemed very strange, I admit."

"Didn't think it was my imagination," Cullen said. "Guess the Indi-

ans hate all of us white men for what's happened to their land. Can't say as I really blame them."

Glynis glanced at Cullen on the seat beside her. And suddenly, for no apparent reason, the time he'd asked her to marry him came to mind. She'd refused, then immediately had second thoughts. But he'd said he wouldn't ask again. He hadn't.

That had been three years before. They had just gone on, the two of them, as always. Glynis had told herself over the years that if she were disposed to marry anyone, it would be Cullen. Which was undoubtedly the reason, she recognized abruptly, why she felt so uncomfortable about Jacques Sundown. She didn't even *know* Jacques Sundown—at least not in the way she knew Cullen.

"Glynis? You there?" Cullen had his you-aren't-listening expression.

"Sorry, I was just daydreaming. Can you remember an autumn ever being this fine? Almost November, and not even a really hard frost yet. It's still as warm as May."

Cullen now looked at her with his you-*weren't*-listening expression. "I asked if you knew anything about this march on Serenity's tavern?"

"Just that there's going to be one."

"When?"

"I don't know exactly. Soon, I expect—Neva is waiting to hear from Susan Anthony in Rochester."

"Those two are planning this together?" Cullen groaned. "What an unholy alliance that is! All the town needs, on top of two murders. The newspapers already are squawking about inadequate law enforcement. In other words, me."

Glynis tried not to smile. Though murder was not in the least humorous, Dr. Neva Cardoza and the temperance reformer Susan Anthony joining forces, on the streets of the same small town, could be a liaison Cullen might well lament.

He now eyed her suspiciously. "Are you taking part in this thing?" he asked in a wary voice.

"No, Cullen, I'm not."

"Thank God for that! Glynis, can't you talk Neva Cardoza out of this? It's just going to cause trouble."

"I don't have anything to do with it," Glynis again told him. "And I

want to keep it that way. But, frankly, I don't see myself why you don't close Serenity down. From what I've learned about the new law, she certainly seems to be in violation of it."

Cullen groaned again. "You know, I really wish the state legislature could find something to do with itself besides passing more damn laws."

Glynis didn't think this was an adequate answer, but it was apparently all Cullen intended to say. They were now passing the Turner farm, and she searched for a glimpse of Sara. The place looked deserted. Sara's words came back to her—*Death. It ain't done yet*—and Glynis experienced a sense of apprehension. "Cullen, I think we should stop."

"Why? It looks like nobody's home," he protested. "Wait. There's somebody out in that field." He pointed to a garden plot beyond the house.

Glynis squinted in the direction of his finger. With considerable relief, she spotted not one but several figures bending over what looked like rows of cabbage.

"Looks like everything's all right," Cullen said. "There's no need to stop and wrangle more with her."

Glynis agreed, if he would insist on wrangling.

A few minutes later they came in view of the old Flannery farm. "Seems a shame," Cullen said, gesturing toward the fields now overgrown with weeds. "The land's just lying fallow. It's a good piece of property, even if the brook does run narrow there."

A sudden thought came to her. "Cullen, do you remember that night the farm burned?"

"How could anybody forget it?"

"It was in the fall, five years ago, wasn't it?"

"I can still see the corncribs billowing smoke, and they were full, so it must have been the fall. Yes, fall of '52. Why?"

"The other day I was telling Neva about it, and later on I recalled something about the barn door. It had been bolted, I think, from the outside? It troubled you at the time."

"It troubled me, all right." Cullen looked thoughtful. "Only explanation that made sense was that the bolt had been thrown accidentally by one of the first people on the scene. Nobody could actually remember doing it, but what with all the confusion, who knows? And

nobody realized until later that Cole Flannery and Dick Davis were still inside. Found their bodies right next to the door. The bolted door. And you're right, it bothered me."

Glynis nodded. It bothered her, too, because while time had faded the memory, it now reappeared in stark relief.

"Glynis, why'd you ask about the fire?"

"On account of Jack Turner's death, and Mead Miller's. Isn't it a little strange that four men, four seemingly *healthy* men, have died in—"

"C'mon, Glynis," Cullen interrupted. "As far as Flannery and Davis are concerned, quite a few people in town besides them have died."

"That's exactly what I was thinking," Glynis said slowly. "Dooley Keegan, for instance. Another supposedly healthy man. How many others like him have died, do you suppose?"

Cullen gave her a wry smile. "People do die, you know. All the time. You sure you're not straining for some sinister connection?"

"There already *is* something sinister, Cullen. Two poison deaths in one month. Who's next?"

His expression indicated he had thought of this. "But I can't find any logical connection between Mead Miller and Jack Turner. Nothing to make me think there's going to be another."

"Sara Turner said there would be."

"Sara Turner might have had damn good reason to say that," he responded. "Throws suspicion someplace else, doesn't it? But I still think she's the one did in her husband. Though how I'm going to prove it . . ." Cullen's voice trailed off as ahead appeared the Grimm farm.

Sara Turner might have killed her husband, Glynis acknowledged, but Mead Miller? And Cullen didn't fool her for one minute. He was more concerned than he let on, but didn't want to upset her. Well, he hadn't succeeded; she was upset. Especially so, after recalling the Flannery fire. But if there was some connection between the deaths, it might be so obscure they'd never find it. Or there might be no connection at all, if a madman was loose in Seneca Falls.

But in that case, how did Sara Turner know?

* * *

The first person they saw, when they climbed from the carriage at the Grimm farm, was Billy Wicken, bending over the rail of a sheep pen. After he glanced up and saw them, he started in their direction. But, as if thinking better of it, he abruptly turned and limped toward the barn.

"Billy!" Cullen called. Billy seemed to hesitate, then kept right on going.

"Odd," Cullen said. "Wonder what's got into him?"

Shaking her head and also wondering, Glynis glanced around for Pippa; failing to see the girl, she looked for the lamb.

Pippa had a little lamb . . .

A door of the house opened, then slammed shut. Molly Grimm appeared and looked over the front porch railing in their direction. Her expression was clearly agitated. But when she recognized them, her face smoothed immediately, and she gave them a wave before descending the steps. As she walked toward them, Glynis caught, from the corner of her eye, a glimpse of something shadow-gray skittering into a nearby shed. When she looked again, it was gone.

Its fleece was . . . dark as coal.

"Glynis! Constable Stuart!" Molly exclaimed as she neared them. "I'm glad you're here."

Then why didn't she look it? Her face still reflected something Glynis would define as anxiety. Did she know yet about Mead Miller?

Her next words answered that. "We've only just found out about Mead Miller," Molly said tensely. "I can't believe it. I just can't believe it. He seemed perfectly fine when he left here."

"When?" Cullen asked her. "When did you last see him?"

Molly's reply came swiftly. "Saturday, late in the afternoon. He said he was going into town. That's all. That's all he said."

"How'd you hear about him?" Cullen asked.

Molly's face went blank. Almost as if she were loath to let emotion, any emotion at all, expose itself. Glynis watched her closely, while the woman shook her head slightly as if trying to remember something.

Cullen was waiting for Molly to respond to his not very profound question. She finally let out a brief sigh. "I think we're all so shocked

by Mead's death," she said. Not precisely an answer, but at least an explanation.

Cullen cleared his throat. "I guess I didn't hear you say who told you about Miller's—"

He was interrupted by a shrill shout from inside the house. Followed instantly by Almira Grimm bursting through the door to the porch.

For a moment, Molly stood frozen. Then, "Pippa! Where's Pippa?" she cried, and began to run toward the house. Glynis exchanged a puzzled glance with Cullen before they started after her.

"What the hell's going on?" Cullen muttered. "Why's she so worried about the girl?"

And everywhere that Pippa went . . .

"Cullen, wait!" Glynis stopped and looked toward the shed. "I think Pippa might be in there," she pointed, and began to walk to the low wooden structure. Cullen followed her. When they reached the shed, Glynis heard a male voice. She pulled open the shed door and, stepping inside, she smelled newly cut hay.

The lamb was sure to go.

On the dirt floor beside a wooden crate, the gray lamb lay sleeping. A shaft of amber light coming through a grimy window fell on Pippa; she stood on the crate, eyes closed, arms outstretched, the focus of a soft yellow radiance. Around her, dust motes flurried. Lazarus Grimm sat a few feet away on a three-legged stool. Gaunt face immobile, his gaze remained riveted on Pippa; Glynis didn't think he even heard them come in until Cullen said, "What's going on?"

Lazarus gave a start, sprang to his feet, and motioned frantically for them to be quiet. Glynis felt Cullen beside her tense, about to say something. Grabbing his arm, she shook her head. No, she mouthed at him, don't.

Cullen's eyebrows rose. But Glynis knew that if Pippa was sleepwalking, she shouldn't be suddenly wakened, and probably the same held true if the girl was in some sort of trance. And that was the way she looked.

Glynis glanced at Lazarus to confirm this, but he had turned back to watch Pippa, and his eyes were awash with tears. Anxiously, Glynis

stepped forward to touch his shoulder. "Lazarus?" she whispered. "What's happening to Pippa?"

"She has it." Lazarus, also whispering, answered, "The child has the gift."

"What gift? What're you talking about?" Cullen said. Although his voice was at normal volume, it seemed to thunder in the confined space.

Pippa made a plaintive sound, and trembled slightly. Her eyes blinked open and shut several times. She looked around for a moment, as if disoriented, but when she saw Glynis, she smiled and hopped down from the crate. "Miss Tryon—why are *you* here?"

Lazarus sprang forward to clasp Pippa by the shoulders. "Do you remember anything?" he asked the girl. "Do you remember what you said?"

Behind Glynis, the door creaked open. Molly Grimm rushed into the shed, silencing whatever Pippa might have been about to answer. "Pippa, what are you doing in here?" Molly swung to her brother with an accusing look. "Why is she here—you're not doing *that* again, are you?"

Lazarus opened his mouth to reply, but Molly didn't wait. She grasped Pippa's arm and began to pull the girl after her. Lazarus took several steps toward them before Molly whirled around to cry, "No!" and dashed from the shed with Pippa locked in her grip, stumbling behind.

As Glynis followed them out, she heard Cullen behind her saying, "I'd like to know what was going on, Lazarus—and I suggest you tell me."

Since Glynis had a pretty good idea what had gone on, she headed toward the house behind Molly and Pippa, who were just climbing the stairs to the porch, where Glynis could see Almira huddled in a rocking chair. A few feet farther, and she could hear the woman humming "Rock of Ages."

"Go into the house, Pippa," Molly directed, "and wash yourself. You smell like hay."

Pippa seemed about to protest, but sighed instead. Giving her mother a dejected look, she went inside.

"Mother," Molly said to Almira, "what on earth were you yelling about? You scared me half to death."

Why, Glynis wondered, remembering what had occurred, should Almira's yelling make Molly think something had happened to Pippa? After all, Almira's behavior was frequently inappropriate.

"Because he's gone," Almira said dreamily. "He's gone, just like all the rest. Gone away."

"Who's gone, Almira?" Glynis asked, climbing the steps quickly, and going to stand in front of the woman.

Molly answered, saying, "I expect she means Mead Miller. My mother always did have a soft spot for him, although why I can't imagine." She then made an awkward move, apparently designed to insert herself between Glynis and Almira.

But Glynis stood her ground, refusing to step back to accomodate Molly's rather obvious intent. Did she think she needed to guard her mother for some reason? Glynis leaned forward. "Yes, Almira, Mead Miller's gone," she said. "But what did you mean, 'just like all the rest'?"

"Glynis, really," Molly protested, laughing lightly. "You know Mother isn't always . . . well . . . clear-headed."

Almira abruptly cackled, "Not like you, Molly, my girl. Oh, no; not clear-headed like you."

"Mother! Mother, you've had a shock—why don't you come inside and lie down?" Molly bent forward to help Almira from the chair.

The woman shrank back. And her face, under the hair like a wild bird's nest, twisted as if she were about to cry. Glynis hesitated to interfere in what certainly was a family matter, but Almira seemed unusually frail. And not quite as deranged as she ordinarily did. Still, Molly's mother must be a trial for her.

"Mother," Molly insisted, again reaching for her, "why don't you—"

"Leave me be, girl!" Almira shouted, shattering the illusion of frailty. "Go find the poor young'un to torment."

Molly gasped, her face blanching as she backed against the porch wall. Glynis saw tears in her eyes, and felt an upwelling of sympathy for this woman who was attempting, however ineptly, to care for the aged child her mother had become. She also began to understand why Molly kept such a close watch on Pippa.

Lazarus and Cullen had appeared, coming across the yard toward the porch. Glynis wanted to question Almira further about her curi-

ous remark, but then heard on the inside stairs a heavy tread. Molly's crumpled face tightened and her shoulders straightened. The door opened, and Obadiah Grimm stepped to the porch.

He said nothing, but stood and waited for the two approaching men; after they'd climbed the stairs, Obadiah stared in turn at each person there. The mass of white hair above the granite features seemed to quiver in indignation as, finally, his stare came to rest on Cullen. "Constable, you here for some reason—some good reason?"

"That's right," Cullen answered evenly. Glynis wondered how he could appear so unaffected by Obadiah's intimidating presence. At least *she* found him intimidating.

"I need to find out," Cullen said, "what you people might know about Mead Miller's death. Since Lazarus here has already told me what he knows, why don't *you* start?" He trained his gaze on Obadiah.

Lazarus gave Glynis and Cullen a brief nod before he escaped into the house. The door closed behind him with a soft click.

"Don't know anything," Obadiah stated. "Why should any of us? Man's dead, that's all."

"No, that's not all," Cullen said. "Miller was killed—"

From her rocking chair, Almira erupted with a shrill wail. Obadiah spun to fix her with a glare. "Quiet, woman! Go inside if you can't be still."

Glynis felt blood rush to her cheeks, and bit her lip to keep from saying something that would cause Obadiah to order her off his property. But she furtively reached down and pressed Almira's shoulder.

Cullen, however, had continued, ". . . and I need to ask a few more questions. Sorry, Mr. Grimm, if it offends you, but frankly, that's too bad. I can always order you to my office in town, if you prefer. Your choice."

Obadiah Grimm's eyes narrowed to slashes as he studied Cullen. There was a long moment of silence, during which Glynis wondered if anyone else's mouth was dry.

Obadiah spoke at last. "Night before the Sabbath, Miller always went to that den of iniquity to partake of alcoholic spirits." His voice rose alarmingly. " 'For their wine comes from the vine of Sodom, and from the fields of Gomorrah . . . for the day of their calamity is at hand, and their doom comes quickly.' "

Cullen didn't move a muscle. "You referring," he said, "to all the patrons of Serenity's Tavern, Mr. Grimm—or just Mead Miller?"

" 'For the Lord will vindicate his people,' " Obadiah declared. "And now, Constable, in retribution for his sin, the man Miller has met his doom. That's all I need to know."

He turned on his heel, yanked the door open, and went back in the house. The door slammed shut.

Molly, still ghostly pale, stepped cautiously toward the door and said, "I don't know anything, either." Her voice carried a tremor. "Please, Constable Stuart, I'd like to go to my daughter."

Cullen scrutinized her briefly, then nodded. And Molly quietly followed her father into the house.

"Nobody left but us chickens," observed Almira cheerfully.

"Almira," Glynis said, "I'd like to ask you again what you meant when you said earlier that Mead Miller was 'gone, just like all the rest'?"

Cullen frowned, but left any comment unvoiced.

Almira ducked her head to give Glynis a hooded look. "The rest of what?" she said, so extravagantly innocent-sounding that Glynis concluded the woman knew very well what she'd asked. Moreover, Glynis had begun to wonder if Almira Grimm's demented behavior was a ruse. Some stratagem of escape. And if she herself had been forced to live with Obadiah Grimm, Glynis guessed she'd try to escape, too. One of the few ways a woman could: into insanity, or what passed for it.

Cullen made an impatient sound. Glynis turned to him and said, "Wait, please, Cullen. Let me try."

Cullen shrugged and went down the stairs.

"Almira," Glynis began again, "I think you understood what I asked you about Mead Miller's death. And it's very important. Now, what did you mean?"

"Don't know," Almira said. "Don't never know what I mean." Her face then took on a coy expression, and she leaned toward Glynis with a confiding gesture, as if she were about to impart some dark secret. "That girl of mine—she got herself trouble, you know. Big trouble." And with a knowing nod, Almira leaned back and folded her arms across her chest.

Dropping to a crouch beside the woman's chair, Glynis asked, "Your girl? Do you mean Molly or Pippa?"

Almira threw her head back and brayed. "The young'un? No, ma'am, she never told nobody *she* had a husband! No, ma'am, not her!" Almira pounded the arms of the rocker before she slid out of it and scurried into the house. After the door banged shut, Glynis heard a bolt being thrown.

Frowning in bewilderment, she rose and went down the stairs. "Cullen, did you hear what Almira just said?"

"I heard enough," Cullen responded. He started walking toward the carriage. "I say we get out of this madhouse."

But Glynis, much as she agreed with him, now started for the barn. "I still need to see Billy Wicken," she called over her shoulder.

She found Billy just inside the barn door, standing beside a stall. He turned his head away from her, but not fast enough; his eyes were red-rimmed, and it was plain that he'd been crying. He rubbed his good hand along the stall's top rail, then ran it through his tousled, straw-colored hair. The withered hand hung at his side.

"Billy, you and Mead Miller were friends, weren't you?" Glynis asked gently.

His head bobbed.

"I'm very sorry about his death, Billy. It's terrible to lose a friend, especially that way."

Billy's head swung toward her. His odd chameleon eyes mirrored the grayish wood of the barn, and he dashed a hand across them. "Who killed Mead, Miss Tryon?"

"We don't know that yet. But Constable Stuart is trying to find the person responsible. Do you know anything that might help him?" He looked confused, and Glynis realized her question had been too general. "Billy, did you see Mead Miller leave the farm last Saturday night?"

Billy nodded.

"Did he say where he was going?"

"Going into town, he said. He always did that, Saturday night."

Apparently, Glynis thought, the entire Grimm household was privy to Miller's activities on Saturday nights. "Did you see Mead again, Billy, say later that night? Or the next morning?"

"No. I didn't see him again. Not ever."

Glynis heard footsteps, and sensed Cullen coming up behind her. She motioned him to stay quiet. "Billy, remember the day last week I came out here? With the young woman?"

"The doctor?" he asked. When Glynis nodded, Billy said, "She helped the ewe. And Pippa's lamb." He began to smile.

"Yes, that's right. And the reason Dr. Cardoza had to help was that Mead Miller wasn't here, remember?" Glynis saw his smile waver, but she went on, "I know Mead asked you not to tell where he went, and you kept your promise to him, but now—I don't think Mead would mind if you told me now. It might be important."

The last trace of Billy's smile vanished. He dug the toe of his boot into the stall's hay. "You don't think he'd care?" he said at last.

"No, I really don't."

"And it's important?"

"Yes, Billy, it could be very important. Where did Mead go that day?" Glynis bent toward him, willing him to answer.

"Well, I guess it'd be O.K." Billy sighed softly. "He went to see Jake Braun."

"Jake Braun? Do you know why?" More important, she thought, was why Mead Miller had been so secretive. But she didn't want to remind Billy of that. "Do you know why he went to Braun's?" she repeated.

As Billy shook his head, Glynis felt Cullen's hand on her shoulder. He said quietly, "Miller used to work for Jake Braun. Up until just a few years ago."

Billy nodded vigorously.

"Well then, Billy," Glynis went on, "did Mead go to see Jake Braun often?"

"I don't know. But I don't think so. He never told me if he did."

Glynis nodded, and turned to Cullen. "Is there anything else we should ask?" She turned back to Billy to say, "You know Constable Stuart, don't you?"

Billy looked uncertain.

Cullen smiled. "Yes, we've met, Billy and I, haven't we?"

Billy gave Cullen a tentative smile and stared pointedly at his badge. "Are you going to find out what happened to Mead?" he asked.

"I'm going to try," Cullen said. "Billy, if you remember anything else—anything you think could help me—will you get in touch with me? Or with Miss Tryon?"

"How can he, Cullen?" Glynis said. "He can't get into town."

"Yes, I can!" Billy suddenly exclaimed. "I got a horse now. Molly gave me one. And I can ride, too."

"Good," Cullen said to him. "Then you'll let me know if you think of something?"

Billy's forehead wrinkled, in either a frown or in concentration, before he nodded. "I guess so."

Do you think he understood?" Cullen asked as he turned the carriage horse around.

Glynis, who had been watching a curtain draw back from an upstairs window of the house, returned her attention to Cullen. "Yes, I think so. Billy's speech is unsophisticated and a little slow, but I think he can understand. And Neva seemed to agree—she thought he might have had a head injury, which could account for it. That and the problem with the left side of his body."

She glanced back at the house as the curtain again moved across the window. "Cullen, please—let's leave here!"

"Can't be too soon for me," Cullen agreed, climbing into the carriage and flicking the reins. "Those are some mighty peculiar folks."

To Glynis's surprise, Cullen steered the horse away from the drive. Instead they went some yards south and onto a narrow lane. The carriage bounced, the wheels finding old ruts overgrown with weeds.

"What's this?" Glynis asked, gritting her teeth. "I didn't realize there was another way out of the Grimms'. Where does this go?"

"It's an old farm lane. And it's the back way to Jake Braun's."

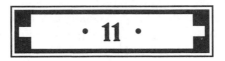

• 11 •

So from the world of spirits there descends
A bridge of light, connecting it with this,
O'er whose unsteady floor, that sways and bends,
Wander our thoughts above the dark abyss.
—Henry Wadsworth Longfellow, "Haunted Houses"

The farm lane eventually leveled out enough for Glynis to speak without severing her tongue. "What did Lazarus tell you," she asked Cullen, "about what he and Pippa were doing?"

"Lazarus told me what you expected him to," he answered.

When she stared at him incredulously, Cullen grinned. "C'mon, Glynis! You'd never have left that shed before you found out what was going on—unless you were pretty sure you already knew."

Glynis gave him a pained look. "I think Lazarus is training Pippa to be a medium . . . a trance-speaking medium. It's said that the best way to establish contact with the spirit world is through young female clairvoyants."

"So Lazarus told me. Claims the girl's a natural medium; she has the gift, he says, whatever that means. How can anybody believe that nonsense?"

"But a lot of people do. Cullen, you can't have missed all the furor about this. It's been in the newspapers for years."

"You know the newspapers will print anything. That doesn't mean I have to read it. And apparently I haven't missed much."

If he had ignored it completely, Glynis thought, he'd missed quite a bit. It had been ten years since the young Fox sisters had sworn up and down that they'd communicated with some dead peddler's spirit

in their house near Rochester. Although the notion had been around for some time, the Fox "visitation" was what had supposedly launched the spiritualist movement.

Glynis had thought at the time that it was something ready to happen anyway. There were too many people, and she admitted the majority of them were women, who felt the established churches had excluded them. The clergy of every major religious denomination had been, and still was, entirely male. And it was scarcely the first time in history that Americans had experienced what the preachers chose to call "a crisis of faith."

Cullen snorted in disgust. "This seance stuff..."

"Has mushroomed," Glynis interjected. "Yes, and now the Fox sisters are touring everywhere with lectures and demonstrations. Harriet saw them in Rochester. She said they were very impressive; they supposedly 'talk' with the dead by means of rapping sounds. They ask a question, and the answer comes by way of raps; so many raps for no, and for yes, and for an unknown . . . something like that. Although Harriet said they gave a spinetingling demonstration, she was skeptical. Thought it must be some sort of hoax."

"Good for Harriet!" Cullen retorted.

"But remember," Glynis said, "Harriet isn't very suggestible, and I doubt she wanted to hear from her dead husbands anyway."

Cullen laughed. "It's the most ridiculous thing I've ever heard of. Can you imagine anyone believing that?"

"It depends on how much someone wants to believe, I think. Horace Greeley does."

"I don't care if President Buchanan does."

"As a matter of fact, Cullen, I read somewhere that believers include some men in Congress."

"*That* doesn't surprise me!"

"Well, at this point," Glynis said, smiling, "there are not only thousands of mediums, but hundreds of spiritualist publications, including ten or twelve newspapers with large circulations."

In fact, the demand in town was so high, she had been forced to subscribe to several for the library. The most popular was *The Christian Spiritualist,* published by the Society for the Diffusion of Spiritual Knowledge. She hadn't trusted this name until she'd discovered it was one of the first such organizations; it had been formed about four

years before in New York City, and that probably wouldn't surprise Cullen, either.

"Folks in Seneca Falls aren't reading this stuff, are they?" Cullen said skeptically.

"Absolutely, they are." Glynis gave him a sideways glance. "Don't you have even the slightest curiosity about it? Just a little? After all, there are well-known, supposedly reputable people who swear they've witnessed communication with the dead. Who is to say it isn't possible?"

"*I* am to say. It's crazy. And to think Lazarus Grimm is planning to use that sweet little girl—I'm amazed you aren't outraged about that, Glynis."

"Oh, I will be if he really does it. But you just saw Molly Grimm. You can't think she's going to allow her daughter to be involved in that—no matter how much Molly adores her brother—if for no other reason than that she's so possessive of Pippa."

"The woman does realize her brother Lazarus is one of the world's greatest confidence men, doesn't she?"

"I don't think that even matters to her, Cullen . . . *Cullen*!"

The rifle blast sounded so loud and so close she couldn't believe they'd either one survived it. But in seconds, Cullen had shoved her out of the carriage and landed beside her in the tall weeds.

"Stay down! Just stay down," he said, his voice tense in her ear. "Don't move."

Flat on her stomach, Glynis had no intention of moving. But who could have shot at them? And for heavens' sake, why?

Crouching beside her, Cullen drew his Colt from its holster. At the same moment, another blast sent a bullet winging over their heads.

"Damn it!" Cullen yelled, cautiously starting to rise. "Stop shooting. We're not game, for chrissake—" Another roar, another bullet, dropped him back into the weeds.

"Someone's really trying to kill us," Glynis whispered. Her heart hammering, she tugged at Cullen's sleeve. "Please stay down!" she pleaded.

"And do what—just wait here until he runs out of ammunition? Or maybe gets lucky and hits us? Now listen, Glynis, you stay put. Right here! I'm going to try and get a look at him."

A whizzing sound this time, and a bullet thudded into the ground

to their left. Then another, directly behind them. Cullen flung himself over Glynis, as moments later another flew over them.

Then there was silence. "You all right?" Cullen whispered, rolling off her.

Glynis tried to answer, but found her breath cut off by the goldenrod pollen she'd inhaled. She choked, gasped, fought for air as another bullet passed over their heads.

Glynis finally managed a deep breath, while Cullen whispered in concern, "Are you all right?" He reached out to touch her cheek.

She nodded. "Cullen, what are we—"

"We're going to crawl toward the brook on our bellies, very slowly. And carefully, so the weeds don't move. It sounds like he's using a revolver now—which means he can get off six shots without reloading. Damn Colts, everybody in the country's got one. Every lunatic—"

The firing began again, and Glynis felt Cullen nudge her ahead of him. She wriggled forward, trying not to agitate the weeds around her. After what seemed like a mile but in truth probably was only a few yards, her skirts snagged on the undergrowth and she had to stop to untangle herself. When she glanced over her shoulder—Cullen was gone! He couldn't be; if she had to die, she wanted him there with her. She brushed particles of dirt from her dry eyes. She must be too frightened for tears.

More bullets zinged over her head. She ducked and, counting to six, lay with her face on her hands, biting her knuckles to keep from screaming. The urge to stand up and let herself be shot, just to get it over with, all but overwhelmed her.

Suddenly, except for blood pounding in her ears, there was no sound other than the drone of bees in the goldenrod. She had the terror-stricken thought that Cullen could have been hit. And if so, the killer might now be creeping up on her. If she raised her head, she would look directly into a barrel . . .

An angry shout. And another. She couldn't make out if it was Cullen's voice she heard.

A sudden rifle blast was followed immediately by another shout. It reached Glynis with breathtaking clarity. "Goddamn it, Jake—it's me! Cullen Stuart! Stop firing, you fool!"

Silence. Glynis pressed her face against her knuckles, hoping God could hear her. Then Cullen's voice again, "Glynis, c'mon! It's all right. C'mon out!"

She raised her head. What if it was a ploy? What if Cullen was being forced to call her?

"Glynis, it's O.K. But stay there if you want—I'll come get you."

He'd known what she feared. She rose slowly, pulling herself to a standing position only because Cullen kept talking to her, and because she could hear his voice getting closer. When he appeared through a cloud of pollen, apparently all in one piece, she stumbled forward to throw herself against him. He held her for much too short a time before he grasped her wrist and pulled her after him. When, moments later, they emerged from the weeds, a few yards away was a small, shingled farm house. And standing before it was Jake Braun. A Jennings rifle swung at his side.

She had seen the man a number of times. He'd always looked and sounded blustery, his stocky frame robust and his skin color that of a man who spent most of his time outdoors. But now Braun's face held a distinct pallor. His eyes looked bloodshot and red-rimmed, as if he'd not slept for days. Despite the man's evident loss of health, Glynis ardently wished she could swear as effectively as Cullen. That was the only appropriate response to Braun's sullen nod in her direction. But she was too frightened to say anything. So frightened she felt nauseated.

Cullen released her wrist and took several steps toward the man. "O.K., Braun, let's hear it again. You thought we were *who*?"

Braun's sullen expression didn't change. "Told you," he muttered.

"Tell me again!"

Braun's rheumy eyes shifted, then flew past Cullen's shoulder, and he jerked the rifle up into firing position. The gun wavered unnervingly. Braun's trembling had likely been the only thing, Glynis thought, that prevented him from killing both herself and Cullen.

"Put it down, Jake!" Cullen yelled. "There's nobody else here. Nobody!"

"Heard something," Braun said. He sounded genuinely terrified.

Cullen stepped forward and shoved the rifle barrel aside. Braun, caught off balance, staggered backward as Cullen wrestled the rifle

away from him and thrust it at Glynis. She reached for it reluctantly as Jake Braun started toward her.

"Hold it," Cullen said, "right there!" He unfastened steel manacles from his belt. "C'mon, Jake, I'm taking you in."

"No!" Braun took several more steps toward Glynis before stopping. His face registered desperation as she, her own hands shaking, disarmed the rifle. Braun's revolver apparently had been confiscated earlier, as the handle now protruded from one of Cullen's back pockets.

"You can't leave me without no weapon!" Braun shouted.

"What makes you think I'm leaving you?" Cullen answered. "You're coming into town, to the lockup. In case you didn't know, it's against the law to try to kill a lawman. To say nothing of an unarmed woman."

"You was on my property. You sneaked in the back way."

"Makes no difference," Cullen stated flatly. "You can't just start firing at anybody who happens by, Braun. You must know that, man! So what the hell *were* you doing?"

"Protecting myself."

"Sure you were, Jake. Miss Tryon and I were coming by to ambush you, is what you thought, right?"

"Couldn't see you in the weeds. Thought you was somebody else," Braun countered.

"And just who, Jake, did you think we were?"

"Them that wants to kill me."

Cullen's face expressed distrust. "Oh? And just who might that be?"

"I dunno know who it is. Why don'tcha ask Turner? Ask Mead Miller! 'Cept you can't, cause they're dead!" Then Jake Braun's mouth clamped shut, as if he'd said more than he wanted.

Glynis suddenly felt as if she were going to be violently ill. She moved quickly to the cabin steps, where she sat and bent forward, her head toward the ground.

After Cullen had paused to watch her, he continued talking to Jake Braun, but Glynis heard his voice as if from far away. The nausea, however, began to subside.

"You telling me, Jake," asked Cullen, "that Turner's and Miller's deaths involved you?"

"I ain't saying no more."

"Well, then, I guess you can't give me one good reason why I shouldn't take you in, right?"

"You can't take me, Constable. Somebody's gonna kill me."

"Then it sounds as if I should take you in for your own protection."

Hearing the edge in Cullen's voice, Glynis glanced up; he might not think Jake Braun was terrified, but she had begun to believe it. And how could Cullen discount the fact that two men had been very recently murdered? She straightened up tentatively. The nausea seemed to have receded, but her head throbbed.

Jake Braun's mouth opened and closed several times. Finally he managed to spit out, "You take me into town, Stuart, I'm gonna git killed fer sure."

"I guess we'll just have to chance it, since you won't talk."

"Can't," Braun insisted.

"Why not?"

Braun shook his head stubbornly.

Cullen looked over at Glynis. "You O.K. now?"

She nodded and started to rise, but then sat back down and said to Jake Braun, "How did you know about Mead Miller's death?"

Braun shook his head again.

"I can answer that," Cullen said to her. "Everybody in town knew by the time you and I left. And Lazarus Grimm told me Lily Braun was at the farm earlier this afternoon." He turned back to Jake Braun. "So I expect your niece Lily probably stopped by here and told you about Miller, didn't she?"

"No!" Braun yelled. "That filthy whore better not come here—"

"Watch it, Braun," Cullen growled. "Besides, I can remember a time when Lily was a nice girl. What was it changed her? How'd it happen she didn't even turn up for her own father's funeral?"

Jake Braun looked away. He kneaded his reddened eyes with his fists, then muttered as if to himself, "My brother . . ." He stopped.

"What about your brother?" Cullen's eyes narrowed as he watched the man, while Glynis struggled to recall something about Otto Braun besides his name.

"Nothing," Jake Braun said. "Nothing about him." Glynis thought he still looked frightened. And a man that scared might do anything. She hoped Cullen would say they could leave.

"I'll tell you what, Jake," Cullen said. "You come on into town and

tell me what the hell's going on around here—and I might be inclined to forget about charging you with attempted manslaughter."

"Can't do that. I'll git killed, I come into town."

Cullen looked exasperated. And angry. But Glynis decided he now at least half-believed Jake Braun's explanation. His problem remained, however, what to do with the man?

While her attention wandered, and with Cullen momentarily off guard, Jake Braun suddenly leaped to the steps. He grabbed Glynis, hauling her upright. Throwing a muscular arm around her neck, he spun her to stand in front of him. Cullen sprang forward, but not before Braun yanked a knife from his back pocket. He thrust the blade against her throat. She could feel the man's fear through his shaking hands even as her body went numb. Numb, and as cold as the steel blade poised at her jugular.

"Don't move, Stuart! You come one step closer, your woman's gonna git her throat slit. I mean it! Makes no never-mind to me if I kill 'er—'cause I'm a dead man anyway."

Glynis tried to hold her breath so she wouldn't move. As Braun's hands shook, the knife blade danced against her neck. She could feel small nicks being cut into the skin of her throat, but there was no pain. Her terror overrode everything.

She closed her eyes, knowing she had to regain her reason, telling herself that Jake Braun had nothing personal against her, that it was fear that drove him. So they had to lessen the fear!

Cullen stood absolutely still. Glynis could see the stark whiteness of his face, and prayed that he was thinking the same thing as she. *Lessen his fear!* Then the knife bit again.

"Mr. Braun," she gasped, "you're hurting me for no purpose. If you kill me, Cullen Stuart will shoot you in an instant."

Immediately, she knew she'd made a panicky error; Braun's grip tightened, and warm drops ran down her neck.

"Let her go," Cullen said, his voice cool and level. "You let her go, Jake," he said again, "and then we'll talk."

"No! No more talking. I got to git out of here—and she's gonna come with me. Go get me my horse, Stuart."

"Jake, you won't get far in your condition. Look at yourself, man! You need sleep."

Glynis gritted her teeth against the certainty that at any second the

knife would bite deeper into her throat. The irony was that she still didn't believe Braun really meant to kill her. And if he did, it would be accidental, because he was out of control. Because of his overwhelming fear. *So lessen it!*

"Mr. Braun, I don't think you want to hurt me. And I do believe you. I believe that someone tried to kill you."

Ever so slightly, the pressure against her neck let up. That was the key! He needed to be believed. She gazed toward Cullen, investing every ounce of energy she had left into making him hear her thoughts.

"Jake, listen to me," Cullen said. "Let's say I was wrong. Maybe somebody *is* trying to kill you. If you can't tell me the reason why, at least let me give you some protection. You have my word, Jake. My word that if you put down that knife, I'll give you the protection you need."

"How you gonna do that? You wanna put me in the lockup—somebody'll git me in there."

Glynis felt the knife blade move. It felt as if it had been turned, and now lay flat. She held her jaw rigid. *Please keep talking, Cullen.*

"No, nobody will get to you, Jake," Cullen answered. "I'll post my deputy on guard outside the lockup. I give you my word."

"Mr. Braun," Glynis said, trying not to move her chin against the blade, "if you let Cullen protect you, then you can at least get some sleep. How long is it since you've had any?"

"Dunno," Braun muttered. "Made two tries to git me already—I been watching for 'em . . . three, maybe four days."

"When'd you last eat, Jake?" Cullen asked, and Glynis saw him take several almost imperceptible steps forward. She held her breath, feeling her heart slam painfully against her ribs.

"Dunno. A while, it's been."

"Jake, I give you my word." Cullen's voice sounded so patient, Glynis thought. But perspiration ran into her eyes, and she couldn't even see him clearly.

"I swear nobody will get at you," Cullen said again, "if you come in with me. Think about it, Jake—you can't go anywhere in the shape you're in now. How much longer can you last without sleep?" Cullen edged a little closer.

"Hold it there, Stuart!" Glynis felt Braun's arm tighten around her.

She felt hope slipping away as despair raced to displace it. She was going to die. Any second now, Braun would rip the blade across her throat. She wouldn't be able to tell Cullen how much she cared for him. Even say good-bye.

But then Jake Braun's grip loosened somewhat. "You give me your word, Constable?" His voice had sounded increasingly groggy, and now his words slurred.

"My word! You've got it, Jake."

Glynis felt herself tipping backward, as if Braun was tottering. His hold on her slackened still more. She made herself concentrate only on what she should do, not on what could happen when she did. She had to do it fast.

Bringing her hands up to her chest, she slid them under his arm and flung it away from her, wrenching out of his grasp. Cullen leaped forward to grab her, and thrust her behind him.

Jake Braun took several slow steps backward. He swayed to and fro, as he might in a high wind. The knife dangled in his hand. Cullen reached out and snatched it, and tossed it into the weeds.

"You gave your word, Stuart," Braun said, now thoroughly glassy-eyed.

"Yes. Go get your horse, Jake, if you can manage it. We'll hitch it to the back of the carriage."

Braun looked at Cullen as if trying to focus, then shrugged and staggered toward the barn.

As Cullen now came toward her, Glynis had the sensation of black water rising swiftly around them both. It rose to her throat and she needed to warn Cullen, but she began to sink beneath the surface because she had no strength to swim . . . she should try to swim, she knew that . . . but she couldn't seem to move . . . it was so dark . . .

Suddenly she felt herself lifted into the air. And as Cullen carried her to the steps of the house, the water became the wetness of tears streaming down her face.

When, some time later, their carriage bumped down a short grade, Glynis winced in pain as she turned to glance over her shoulder. His horse hitched to the rear of the carriage, Jake Braun slumped in the

saddle, giving every appearance of a man asleep. She sincerely hoped this was the case.

Turning back, she flinched as fabric rubbed against her throat; Cullen had ripped her underskirt into strips with which he'd bandaged her neck. Glynis wasn't sure the amount of bleeding was worth the loss of a good petticoat, but she hadn't had the strength to argue.

Cullen now peered with concern at the bandage. His gaze moved to her eyes and he said gently, "Thank God you stayed calm back there, and didn't lose your head."

He was making some macabre joke, she thought for one shaky moment, but he apparently realized what he'd said, and grimaced convincingly. "Sorry! That's not what I meant."

"I hope not. I'm not ready to find anything about this humorous. I doubt if I will for quite a while."

Cullen reached to clasp her hand. And almost lost the reins as the lane dipped suddenly into a depression. Beyond was a small wooden bridge over Black Brook.

"What's this basin?" Glynis asked. "I've never noticed it before."

"You can't see it from the main road," Cullen answered. "It's the old dam site."

"Dam site? I didn't know Black Brook ever had a dam."

"It didn't. Almost did, though. Must have been before you came to Seneca Falls. A bunch of farmers got together—Jake Braun was one of them, in fact," Cullen said, glancing over his shoulder, "with the bright idea that they'd dam the brook to give themselves more water for irrigation. You know how the brook gets wider north of here?"

Glynis nodded. "Just before the Grimm farm."

"Right. And since it flows north past Black Brook Reservation and on into the Montezuma Marsh, these farmers decided all that water was just going to waste. So they started building a dam."

"Could they do that? Legally?"

"They tried. Even made a stab at talking Obadiah Grimm into letting them build it at the north edge of his property, so he'd get more water, too. Obadiah said he wasn't interested. His refusal caused some real hard feelings."

"Is that when he became such a recluse?"

"Maybe." Cullen thought a minute. "I don't remember what he was

like before that. But he did get called some interesting names. 'Indian lover' was about the only one I can repeat; some thought he refused because a dam would have cut off most all the water going into the reservation."

"Cullen, that would have been a catastrophe for those people there. Good for Obadiah! I wouldn't have thought it of him."

"I *didn't* think it of him. Because I don't believe that was the reason he refused to join the others. I think he was just too tight-fisted to spend money for the dam's construction. After all, he didn't really need it—it wouldn't have increased the brook's flow past his farm all that much."

"Since the dam didn't get built," Glynis said, "what happened to prevent it?"

"One of the young Seneca men went to Jeremiah."

"Mr. Merrycoyf got involved? That's a surprise. He doesn't like controversy, not at all."

"Remember, he was a lot younger then. And don't believe everything Jeremiah says about that, Glynis. He's always liked a good fight. Bet he still does, if he thinks he can win."

Glynis smiled, then winced and put a hand to her throat.

"It hurt?" Cullen asked.

"A little." She looked over her shoulder at the sleeping Jake Braun. "It would feel worse if I thought he really meant to kill me. But I don't. You know yourself, Cullen, people do bizarre things when they're frightened. And you *do* believe his story, don't you?"

Cullen shrugged. "I intend to find out if it's true. Maybe after Jake's had some rest, he'll talk sense."

The lane flattened out as it met Black Brook Road. Glynis turned to look north, then twisted on the seat. After some time, she turned back and asked, "So what did Jeremiah Merrycoyf do for the Indians?"

"Went to court. Stopped the dam's construction."

"Stopped it how?"

"English common law—law that goes back centuries—that protects people who own along a waterway. Who own *land,* that is, because nobody owns the water itself. It's known as riparian rights. The law says one riparian owner can't do anything that would perma-

nently interfere with the flow of water to another owner. That's oversimplified, of course, but it's the gist of it."

"And a dam to divert water for irrigating farms," Glynis said, "would certainly interfere with the flow of Black Brook."

"Right. That's what Merrycoyf argued, and the court agreed with him. Several courts, actually, because the farmers kept appealing the local judge's decision. They still lost in the end. Spent a lot of money doing it, too. But," Cullen added, "there was sure hell to pay for a while. Bad feelings against the Indians was the worst of it, even from folks who hadn't been involved in the dam project."

"Yes," Glynis sighed, "I can imagine. But who was the Seneca man with the good sense, to say nothing of the courage, to go to Merrycoyf in the first place?"

"It was so long ago I can't remember his name."

As they approached the village limits, Glynis put a hand to her throat. "Cullen, perhaps it would be better if . . ."

"Yes, I'll take you home first, then go the back way to the lockup with Jake. No sense letting the whole village know what went on."

"Harriet's going to have a fit when she sees me."

"She should. Better not tell her too much, though. Not while I've got Jake Braun in the lockup."

"No, of course not. He really might be in danger. But I hope you can get him to talk. The connection between . . ." Her voice trailed off.

"Glynis?"

"I just remembered something. Cullen, do you recall whether Cole Flannery was one of the men who tried to build that dam?"

"Well, yeah, come to think of it. He must have been—his farmland ran along Black Brook. Why?"

"I don't know precisely," she said. "But didn't Jack Turner say something to you about a brook—you know, the day before he died? We thought at the time it didn't make any sense. But maybe it did."

Cullen had shifted to stare at her. "Yes, I remember now—not Turner's exact words, though. What are you thinking?"

"I'm not sure," she told him. "Maybe nothing important."

Cullen had turned the carriage onto Cayuga Street, reminding her that she hadn't mentioned to him the black and white horse and its

rider she'd seen earlier, just as they'd left Jake Braun's path for Black Brook Road.

Glynis tried to ignore the pang of guilt. And the uncomfortable question of why—why *again* she hadn't told Cullen.

She would tell him tomorrow.

• 12 •

Whereas the retail and use of intoxicating drinks is an evil productive of more misery, crime and poverty than all other causes combined, and directly or indirectly a greater tax upon the inhabitants of this village than all other taxes . . .

—Minutes of the Board of Trustees
of the Village of Seneca Falls,
May 5, 1840

Mr. Merrycoyf, sir." Adam MacAlistair paused to clear his throat several times, and to rearrange his perfectly arranged neckcloth. "Ah, first of all, sir, please let me say how much I appreciate your referring Miss Hathaway to me. But I think I need to ask . . . that is, as you know, sir, I'm just starting out in the law." He cleared his throat again. "Well, is it possible that taking her case could . . . ah . . . hurt my reputation? Sir?"

From behind his desk, Jeremiah Merrycoyf studied the appealing young man standing before him. The lad's earnestness was no doubt sincere, and his concern under the circumstances quite appropriate. Still, he had to learn the practice of law somehow. And while encouraging Adam MacAlistair to represent Serenity Hathaway might resemble tossing a lamb into a lion's den, how the youngster acquitted himself—regardless of victory or defeat—could be significant. A rich experience for him, more important to his growth as a lawyer over the long haul than the flurry of public disapproval that would take place now.

Merrycoyf sighed and adjusted his spectacles. "My dear Mr. MacAlistair, I sympathize with your hesitancy. But—and it is a crucial *but*—the law must hold itself above and apart from mere person-

alities. Everyone is entitled to representation; surely they still teach that in law schools?"

"Oh, yes, sir, they do! And I quite agree with your premise, sir, Mr. Merrycoyf. It's just that this is . . ." The young man swallowed and ran a finger inside his starched white collar. "Sir, it's simply that this would be my first case, and Miss Hathaway my first client. I must question my worthiness to represent her with the competence she deserves."

Merrycoyf peered at Adam MacAlistair at length over his spectacles. After satisfying himself that no levity had been intended, he replied, "My dear fellow, while your humility is commendable, and your sentiment admirable . . ." Merrycoyf paused, recalling when he himself first began the practice of law. He'd all but forgotten how terrifying the responsibility appeared, how overwhelming his own inadequacy. And how failure loomed as fearsome as damnation.

While Adam MacAlistair stood fidgeting, Merrycoyf settled back in his chair and folded his hands over his stomach. "Let me put this bluntly, young man," Merrycoyf said. "You have to start somewhere! Now do sit down and stop squirming."

Adam MacAlistair sat.

"Now, then," Merrycoyf said, "I presume you have met Miss Hathaway, and that she has informed you of her difficulty?" The young man's sudden blush made answer to the first question unnecessary.

"Ah, yes, sir. Yes, I met with Miss Hathaway this very morning." His face reddened still more. "And she looks—that is, her case—very interesting."

"Indeed, yes," Merrycoyf agreed, concealing a smile. "And so, my young colleague, where do you intend to begin?"

"I believe I should make application for an injunction, sir. That the remedy for Miss Hathaway's distress is to stop those who wish to interrupt her business."

"Oh?" Merrycoyf steepled his fingers under his chin. "In other words, you wish to stop people from doing what they haven't yet done?"

"Well, yes," Adam MacAlistair frowned. "Because they are *going* to do it."

"And do you have sound reason for your application—that is, are those whom you wish to enjoin intending to do something illegal?"

Adam MacAlistair answered quickly, "I mean to find a reason for arguing that they will be."

Behind his spectacles, Merrycoyf's eyes twinkled. Yes, indeed, this bright young lawyer was on his way to a rich experience.

Hearing ten chimes of the brass Seth Thomas clock in the downstairs hall, Glynis stretched and yawned, and pushed back the lightweight cotton coverlet. She had slept round the clock. Sunlight streamed through her open bedroom window. Any other year, by this time windows would be shut fast against bitter wind if not snow. Like nearly everyone else in Seneca Falls, she had begun to feel uneasy about the remarkable weather—and about what it might augur. For what should they prepare: the mildest winter in memory—or the harshest in history? Would each day of sunshine be followed by another, or would the sun tomorrow disappear in exhaustion for months? The paradox here, she thought to herself, smiling, was that while western New Yorkers complained religiously about their cursed winter weather, its absence provided grounds for anxiety, a sense of being lulled into complacency. The calm before THE STORM, it was feared. On the other hand, what could they do about it? They might as well enjoy it.

She stretched again, and winced in discomfort. Her neck hurt. So did her ribs. And memory of the day before brought her upright in the bed—although, truthfully, the whole thing now seemed more like a nightmare than reality. Her hand cautiously explored her neck. No—it had been real.

The previous night, after her landlady had examined her and hit the roof, Harriet had swabbed the cuts with witch hazel that stung and comfrey ointment that also stung, then wrapped Glynis in long strips of muslin from ear to collarbone. This had left her feeling partially mummified. She couldn't possibly appear in public this way.

When she reached the downstairs, the ruffles of her high-necked blouse fluttering against her bandages, Harriet was just waving goodbye to someone out the kitchen door.

"Who was that?" Glynis asked, going quickly to the coffeepot on the stove.

Harriet shook her head and asked, "How are your wounds?"

"They're fine, Harriet."

"Good. Leave the bandages on until tonight, then I'll have a look." Harriet gestured to the table and the plate of graham muffins and glass jar of crabapple jelly.

After pouring her coffee, Glynis leaned over a pot of oatmeal porridge just to breathe in its familiar, comforting smell. "But who was just here?" she asked again on her way to the table.

"You sure you want to know?" Harriet's smile looked mischievous as she passed the jelly jar.

Glynis groaned. "That means it must have been Vanessa Usher. What was she doing here this early?"

"Early? It's near to noon."

"Then why was she here this late—except that Vanessa rarely gets up before noon."

"You'd better prepare yourself, Glynis. Because Vanessa came to invite us"—Harriet grinned—"to attend a seance! More than one, actually—she intends to hold them Saturday nights all winter."

"You're not serious." But on Harriet's face Glynis could clearly read that she was. "Well, I'm not attending, Harriet—don't even *try* to persuade me. I won't go."

"You know Vanessa will insist."

"Let her insist. I'm not the susceptible young thing she used to coerce so shamelessly. Not anymore. No."

"Aren't you even slightly curious about what Vanessa's up to?"

"No! Anyway, I can guess. In fact, I'll wager—whatever amount you'd like—that these seances involve Lazarus Grimm, don't they?" With some satisfaction, Glynis observed Harriet's surprise.

"How did you know?"

"I know Vanessa, that's how. Is she really in cahoots with him already? No, don't answer, I'm not interested. But tell me this—are they charging admission?"

"Well, as a matter of fact . . ."

"Aha!"

". . . there will be a donation requested."

"Aha, again! Where are they to be held—these spirited money-raisers?"

Harriet grinned and said, "I thought you weren't interested."

"I'm not. Are they going to use The Usher Playhouse?"

"For the first spiritualist meeting they will; the seances are to be at Vanessa's house. What do you suppose one wears to a seance?"

"A look of gullibility. How should I know, Harriet? In any event, I don't have to worry about what to wear because I'm—"

"Not attending. Yes, Glynis, I heard you the first time."

It was midafternoon before Glynis could leave the library and walk to the lockup. In the air hung the distinctive smell of burning leaves, and behind the church spires, huge white clouds billowed like sails before a shifting wind. Wind with a bite that announced the tardy autumn like a trumpet blast. The beautiful extended summer must be fleeing south.

When she rounded the firehouse and entered his office, Cullen was seated behind his desk. "Jake Braun hasn't said a word about this conspiracy to kill him," he grumbled. "In fact, sleep seems to have made him even more closemouthed."

Glynis shook her head. "I don't understand his reluctance. Or does he feel that he's still in danger?"

"He hasn't mentioned it. But he's been as stubborn as ever. And he wants to leave."

"Do you think it's safe, Cullen, to let him go?"

"Hard to say. But I can't hold him here much longer without charging him. So . . . are you willing to swear out a complaint against Braun?"

"Me? For what?"

"For *what*! How about shooting at you, for starters? Attempting to kidnap you. Holding you against your will. Threatening to kill you?"

"Cullen, Jake Braun didn't intend—"

"How do you know what he intended?"

"Well, why don't *you* make the complaint?" Glynis asked. "And then—"

At that moment a florid man burst through the office door, shouting, "Constable, there's gonna be a riot! You'd better come quick."

Cullen got to his feet. "What're you talking about, Charlie?"

"My wife, she just went cross the bridge to meet up with those other crazy women. I'm telling you, Constable, there's gonna be trouble."

"You want to calm down and be a little more specific?"

"The tavern! They're gonna try and close down Serenity's Tavern."

Cullen groaned. "Oh, hell! This"—he frowned at Glynis—"is your friend Dr. Cardoza's doing."

"Please don't look at me like that, Cullen. I'm not even a participant. But I don't see how you can fault Neva for walking peaceably in front of a public building."

"It's not a public building."

"The public uses it."

"You've spent way too much time with Jeremiah Merrycoyf, you know that?" muttered Cullen as he buckled his holster. "Right, let's go, Charlie. And Glynis, would you tell Zeph to get somebody to stay with Jake Braun? Then have him meet me at the tavern."

"Cullen, you're not going to involve that boy in this?"

"He's not a boy—he's my deputy. And yes, he's going to be involved. Maybe your friend should think of the consequences before she does something so damnably stupid!"

Before Glynis could reply, Cullen strode out the door.

In the adjoining room, she found Zeph Waters, his boots up on a desk, reading. Glynis bent down to see the title and could make out only the name of Henry Wadsworth Longfellow on the book's spine.

"Poetry, Zeph?" she smiled. "I thought you said you'd never be caught dead reading that."

Startled, Zeph swung his boots to the floor and clapped the book shut. "Just looking at *Hiawatha,*" he explained sheepishly.

"You needn't sound so embarrassed," Glynis said. "Longfellow's a master storyteller, and he's very popular."

Zeph shrugged, obviously still embarrassed, as he glanced over his shoulder toward the holding cell.

"You're to find someone to stay here with Jake Braun," she told him, "so you can meet Constable Stuart down by the tavern on the canal."

"What's doing there?" Zeph asked, expectation bright in his eyes. He surely suspected what was doing, Glynis thought; there had been plenty of rumors about the temperance march.

"Zeph, why don't you just go and get someone as Cullen asked?"

He walked toward the door, then stopped and turned to look back at the cell and at Glynis. "How can I? Can't leave the prisoner."

"It shouldn't take you long. I'll stay here with Jake Braun," Glynis offered.

"Miss Tryon, I don't think that's such a good idea."

"It's a fine idea." Glynis looked pointedly at the wall-hung gun rack. "If anything happens . . . well, you're the one who taught me how to shoot, remember, Zeph? Now go ahead."

He looked hesitant, but she nodded at him, and he finally left, reluctantly. Once outside, though, Glynis knew he'd dash so as not to miss any of the goings-on down at the tavern. For that matter, she didn't want to miss them, either. But she had something to do before Zeph returned.

Quickly she went back to the holding cell, where its sole occupant, Jake Braun, sprawled on a cot, staring at the ceiling. Beside the cot, a tray holding several empty tin plates sat on the floor. A pack of playing cards lay on the gray wool blanket rumpled at the man's feet.

"Good afternoon, Mr. Braun," Glynis said as she went to stand before the bars of the cell.

Braun turned his head to give Glynis a nod. Otherwise, he didn't budge from his reclining position.

"Constable Stuart said you didn't care to talk about what happened yesterday," she began. "I don't understand how you expect him to help if you won't tell him anything."

"Don't expect him to help me none. It's not his business."

"Well, yes, it is. People getting killed violates the law." Glynis kept her voice patient. "Two men have been murdered, and you said someone was trying to kill *you.* So it *is* the constable's business, Mr. Braun, whether you like it or not. But tell me, what is the connection between you and Jack Turner and Mead Miller? Because I'm certain there is one."

Braun turned his face to the wall.

Glynis searched for a way to jolt him out of his fatalism, if that's what was keeping him silent. "Mr. Braun, a few days ago, Sara Turner told me there would be more deaths." Braun rolled back to look at her. And Glynis now noticed beads of perspiration on his forehead. "How would Sara Turner know that?" she continued.

"She don't know nothin'," Braun mumbled.

"Oh, I think she does," Glynis disagreed.

Abruptly, Braun got to his feet. He looked at Glynis a moment, then walked to the cell window, where he stood staring out.

Why wouldn't he talk? She decided to try a stab in the dark. "How many of you farmers," she asked suddenly, "were involved some years ago in the attempt to dam up Black Brook?"

Braun whirled from the window. "Leave it alone—just leave it be!"

Although bewildered by the man's reaction, Glynis persisted, "Why should I leave it be? I think it may be a reason—"

"It ain't no reason, and you don't know what you're talkin' about! And you ain't never gonna know. Not from me, not from nobody, cause nobody else's left—"

He broke off at the sound of a door opening. Voices came down the short hall. As Zeph appeared with the young black man who worked at the livery, Glynis bit her lower lip in disappointment. Braun had been about to say something; she was sure of it.

Frustrated, she had no choice but to leave the lockup. When she headed down Fall Street for the bridge and Serenity's Tavern, Zeph caught up with her moments later. He sprinted past, anticipation spread thick as jam across his grinning face.

By the time Glynis crossed the bridge and started up Ovid Street, racing gray clouds had overtaken the white; a pale sun still managed to poke through now and then but a chill wind gusted from the northwest.

Glynis shivered and walked faster, pulling her shawl tightly around herself, while at the same time trying to keep her green merino wool skirt and her petticoats from blowing around too revealingly. After turning onto West Bayard Street she could see ahead to where a small crowd had formed. She walked on, then paused before turning down the short, well-worn dirt road that ran in front of the two-story clapboard tavern. The few oak trees on the shallow slope did not block her view of what was taking place below.

Wind ruffled the Seneca River beyond the tavern as it did the dark cloaks and shawls and the brightly colored bonnet ribbons of the

gathered women. Blowing skirts exposed white flounced petticoats. From where Glynis stood, she could pick out Neva Cardoza and the strong, familiar profile of Susan Anthony. She looked for, but couldn't find, Elizabeth Cady Stanton; the only possible reason for Elizabeth's absence would be that she was trapped at home with her brood of six children. And in fact, although Glynis recognized a number of others—including Vanessa Usher's sister Aurora—many of the women seemed to be either beyond childbearing years or very young. There were, nonetheless, several children grasping their mothers' hands. Glynis counted roughly thirty-five women, but the voices carried upward by the wind sounded like a vastly larger number. And they sounded angry.

While Zeph stood at the far edge of the crowd, Cullen had stationed himself on the tavern steps; Glynis couldn't help smiling at his annoyed expression. The heavy oak door behind him remained closed. Over his head, the gilt scrollwork letters that spelled SERENITY'S TAVERN gleamed brilliantly in the darkening afternoon.

Glynis started down the road, but had gone only a few feet before she stopped again upon hearing Susan Anthony's clear, emphatic voice. The woman sounded exactly like the schoolteacher she had been. "Ladies, please line up!" she directed over the lively babble. A relative quiet descended promptly. "Come now, let us move quickly! Please line up behind Dr. Cardoza and me. Step smartly now—let us not waste time."

Bustling like a mother hen among her chicks, Susan Anthony gestured and pointed until, after some minutes and a great deal of confusion, the women seemed positioned to her satisfaction. Glynis moved from the road, after catching Cullen's eyes on her, to stand in the shadow of a still fully-leafed oak. She didn't want to attract Susan and Neva's attention for fear of being commandeered to join; Glynis knew she wouldn't have the nerve to refuse, while at the same time her age-old shyness cringed at this spectacle in the making. Besides, she meant what she'd said to Neva; though she agreed the tavern should be closed, she felt indebted to Serenity for help in the past. What she hadn't told Neva or anyone else, and never would, was that, in spite of herself, she rather liked Serenity.

Susan Anthony had placed herself beside Neva at the head of two

wavering columns of women, and now motioned for them to follow her. Stumbling forward—and jostling into and over each other—the women began a ragged circular procession in front of the tavern.

Gradually the jostling eased as the participants found their pace. The random chattering ended. In its place came a silence that Glynis found moving in its simple dignity; she was also moved by the courage of the women below. Ordinary women, wives and mothers, risking their families' severe disapproval and, in a few cases, their very well-being. No, perhaps these women weren't so ordinary after all. Some of them wouldn't feel they had even the right to defend themselves, or their children, against husbands who came home, abusive and demanding, from the taverns. The law certainly didn't give them that right. And yet here they were.

The lines of women circled for some minutes without incident. Cullen moved from the front steps to stand beside Zeph at the far side of the building; this move quickly proved fortuitous, as a stream of foul-smelling refuse suddenly poured from an upstairs tavern window. The mood of the march and its dignified silence was broken, pierced by shocked screams of those spattered when the offal hit the ground.

Susan Anthony whirled in her tracks, gesturing to the women to back away. Neva's small face, what Glynis could see of it, had reddened with fury; she whipped her skirts aside and stalked to where a large placard, attached to a pole, leaned against a tree. Snatching the pole, Neva hoisted the placard into the air, and quickly rejoined the women. The procession had regrouped under Susan Anthony's resolute guidance, and again began to circle, now well away from the tavern windows.

Glynis could now read Neva's sign: SPIRITS OF MISERY AND CRIME BOUGHT AND SOLD HERE! appeared on one side. The other side read, CLOSE DOWN THIS UNLAWFUL ESTABLISHMENT!

While Glynis didn't find these sentiments particularly inflammatory, the door of the tavern suddenly burst open. And through it, in all her henna-haired glory, stepped Serenity Hathaway. For women who before now had never seen the tavern's proprietor—which, Glynis assumed, would be most of them—Serenity's appearance must have come as something of a shock. For this was no debauched and dissipated hag, the wages of sin writ clear on her forehead. Standing

before them was, without question, one of the most ravishing creatures ever to tread the soil of western New York. And the creature was plainly outraged.

With her hair tossing in the wind, Serenity swished the voluminous folds of her bustled taffeta gown around behind her. From where Glynis stood, the woman resembled nothing so much as the figurehead of a square-masted brigantine—chin high, breasts thrust forward, heading into a high gale—a pirate ship, primed for war.

For a long moment, a quiet held fast that only an act of God could have breached. Even the rouged and kohl-eyed women who now leaned out of every tavern window were apparently struck dumb. Serenity fixed her smoldering eyes on Neva Cardoza, who might very likely be, Glynis decided, the only female Serenity could recognize. Neva looked to be glaring just as fixedly back.

Glynis was reluctant to take her eyes from this standoff lest she miss something, but finally risked a quick glance at Cullen. He stood, feet apart, hands in his pockets, looking very much as though he were watching a performance at The Usher Playhouse.

Serenity's husky voice broke the silence. "Get off my property!" Turning to Cullen she ordered, "Constable Stuart, remove these persons!"

"Afraid I can't do that," Cullen said to her, not shifting his stance. Glynis observed that beside him, Zeph looked extremely uncomfortable. Well, it served him right, being so eager to get there!

"We have every intention of staying, *Madam* Hathaway," rang Neva's voice as clear as a ship's bell. "This is an illegal establishment, and we demand that it close. Furthermore, we intend to exercise our right to protest its illegality until it does close!"

Hoofbeats sounded on the road behind Glynis. She turned to see a chestnut mare with a good-looking young man astride, cantering briskly down the tavern road. Upon reaching the entrance, the young man dismounted, gave the assembled women an engaging and somewhat apologetic smile, and walked toward the steps. "Miss Hathaway, may we have a word?"

"About time you got here," Serenity said to him. "You going to get rid of these troublemakers?"

The young man, whose name, Glynis finally recalled, was Adam MacAlistair, shook his head briefly. He motioned to the near side of

the tavern, and took Serenity's elbow to guide her there. They disappeared around the corner of the building.

Susan Anthony executed a sweeping motion with her arm. The women resumed their moving circle. But they did so now accompanied by catcalls from those hanging out the tavern windows.

Glynis stepped away from the oak, and crossed the road to make her way unobtrusively down the slope. She told herself this was none of her business, but curiosity managed to dislodge her sensibility. And no one would notice what she was doing, given the crowd and the noise.

When she reached the corner of the tavern, she heard voices and went forward along the building's side wall; the voices, she decided, must be coming from the towpath behind the tavern. Cautiously she peered around the corner. Nearby on the path stood Serenity and Adam MacAlistair.

Glynis had hoped this might be the case, as she didn't think Serenity would chance her customers or employees overhearing the battle plan. More to the point, Glynis felt certain that Adam MacAlistair—from what she remembered of him before he left for law school—would never set foot in a brothel. At least not when he might be seen.

Glynis had just started to go forward to show herself when Serenity suddenly said, "Now listen here, Mr. Smart Young Lawyer." She placed her hands firmly on the curve of her hips. "I expect you to do something *now*! Not tomorrow or next week, but now!"

"Miss Hathaway, I've tried to explain to you—"

"I'm not interested in explanations," Serenity interrupted. "I'm interested in results. I want those damn women gone. Can you think, for one minute, that we're going to get customers while those self-righteous shrews are parading back and forth? Not on your sweet ass, we're not!"

Glynis pulled back into the shadow of the tavern. Adam MacAlistair seemed to be doing an unusual amount of swallowing, and his face had taken on a pink hue. He ran a finger inside his white collar. "Ah, yes, Miss Hathaway—yes, you could be right."

"*Could* be? I *am* right! Half my customers are married men, and those could be their wives out there. You think those men are going to just waltz past them big as life? *Do you?*"

"Well, no . . . that is . . . no, probably not." Adam shook his head vigorously.

Glynis backed up against the tavern wall, pressing her hands over her mouth. It shouldn't have been funny, none of it, and she was ashamed of herself for laughing—but this poor young lawyer was really out of his depth. Why on earth had he agreed to represent Serenity in the first place?

"And I'm going to seek an injunction to stop them," he was saying. "But I have to go to Waterloo, where the county court is, to request it."

"When?" Serenity snapped. "When is this going to happen?"

"Tomorrow, possibly. The very soonest I can get a hearing," he said earnestly. "But, Miss Hathaway, I must warn you, it won't be easy."

"That is *your* problem!" Serenity announced. "But I can tell you this much—you do whatever is necessary to get rid of those women. *Whatever!* Buy the judge, if you have to. I'll pay!"

Adam's face lost its pink color. All its color. "Oh, no! No, I don't think it would be wise to—"

"I'm not paying you to think! I'm paying you to look after my best interests," Serenity snapped again. "Now do it!"

She spun around and strode toward the tavern's rear entrance, her heels clicking angrily on the flagstones underfoot. Glynis waited while Adam MacAlistair followed her, wiping his pale forehead with a large handkerchief. He had one foot on the bottom step when he shook his head, stepped back down, and continued on around the far side of the building.

Glynis walked quickly back to the front entrance; she should be embarrassed, skulking like a common snoop.

She found the march coming to a straggling halt while the participants watched a small black buggy barrel down the dirt road. Surely not a customer! A second later she identified the driver of the buggy as Lazarus Grimm.

He reined in the horse close to the marchers, who stepped back hurriedly as he jumped from the carriage. "A doctor! I need a doctor!" Lazarus shouted. "Is Dr. Cardoza here?"

Glynis saw Neva start forward, then hesitate. Too late, as Lazarus

had spotted her and rushed toward her. "Dr. Cardoza, please come with me. It's my father—I think he may be dying."

The assembled women let out a collective gasp, followed by murmurs of disbelief. Glynis, also disbelieving that something like death could befall Obadiah Grimm without his permission, moved closer to hear.

"Mr. Grimm," Neva asked, "when did your father become ill?"

"He's not ill! He . . . he seems to have taken a bad fall. Please, Dr. Cardoza, I truly think he may die." His face was ashen; he looked not only terribly upset, but as if he might himself keel over. "I tried to get Dr. Ives," he explained breathlessly, "but his wife said he'd gone to Tyre for a birth. Dr. Cardoza, I implore you to come!"

Neva turned and said something to Susan Anthony. She then turned to take Lazarus's arm, as if she thought he needed support. "Very well, Mr. Grimm. Of course I'll come with you." But her expression appeared distressed as she glanced around the crowd. Glynis hurried to join her.

"Oh, Glynis, I thought I saw you earlier. Is there any possibility that you could . . . ?"

"Dr. Cardoza," Lazarus broke in, his voice shaky. "We have to go right now!"

"Yes, Neva," Glynis said quickly, "you go ahead with Lazarus. I'll get a carriage and follow you out there."

Lazarus grabbed Neva's arm, and together they rushed to the buggy.

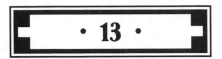

• 13 •

To know the life of a wounded man, whether he shall live or die. Take the juice of lettuce, and give the sick to drink with water; and if he cast it up anon, he shall die; and if he do not, he shall live. And the juice of mouse-ear will [do] the same. *Probatum est.*

—A Leechbook or Collection of Medical Remedies of the Fifteenth Century

Lazarus Grimm ground his teeth and continued to urge the horse forward at breakneck speed, while Neva gripped the side panel of the wildly swaying buggy. She felt inescapably that she would be thrown out, her skull fractured, and left for dead. Grimm might not even note her absence. And just where, she'd like to know, was this quiet little town to which Constable Stuart had referred when she first arrived in Seneca Falls? The place was a hotbed of lunacy.

Of this, Lazarus Grimm was a prime example; he had said practically nothing since they'd careened on two wheels onto Black Brook Road, driving hellbent for leather. As the road evened out some, Neva let go of the buggy's side momentarily to hug around her shoulders the shawl Glynis Tryon had tossed to her just before Grimm goaded the horse up the tavern drive. Although the earlier wind had died, the twilight held a frosty chill. Neva again grabbed the buggy's side as it struck a bump in the road, launching them into the air to land with a bone-jarring jolt. She gave Lazarus Grimm a sideways glare; did he have to risk her life as well as his own?

She had tried without success to make him slow the reckless pace, so she decided to try once more for information. "Mr. Grimm, what symptoms did your father exhibit after his fall? For example, did he appear to be unconscious?"

"No!" Lazarus slapped the reins harder against the horse's flanks.

"So he was conscious?" Bump. Jolt. "You don't know? Well, did he speak to you?"

"No."

"Did he move—for instance, try to sit up?"

"No."

"Mr. Grimm, your monosyllabic grunts are not at all useful," Neva snapped. "I'm simply trying to determine how serious your father's condition might be."

Lazarus turned his gaunt face to her; he looked suitably contrite. "I'm sorry," he said as the carriage took a great hop, then settled back on its undergear with a rattle like graveyard bones. Like *their* bones would sound if he didn't slow down.

"You do realize," Neva said to him, "that I can't help your father if I'm lying dead in a ditch. Please exercise some prudence, Mr. Grimm."

To her surprise, he flexed the reins and actually slowed the horse, again throwing her a contrite look. "I apologize, Dr. Cardoza, if I've frightened you. The truth is, I'm not sure my father will even be alive when we get there. Molly insisted I go for a doctor, but if she hadn't . . ." He shook his head at the futility of it.

"Mr. Grimm, I've met your father, and he struck me as an extremely hardy individual," Neva told him. "He may just have sustained a slight concussion. That wouldn't be enough to—"

"No! He's hurt more seriously than that," Lazarus broke in. "And I blame it all on that woman," he added tersely. "Father was so disturbed after she left that . . . Who knows . . . ?"

"What woman?" Neva asked, wondering who could have the wherewithal to disturb Obadiah Grimm.

"Lily Braun!" Lazarus ground his teeth and, to Neva's distress, urged the horse to a faster pace.

Lily Braun had been at the Grimm place again? But why should Lazarus believe she had anything to do with his father's accident? Neva lost her next thought as the carriage took another mighty bounce. Her spine vibrated and her tailbone ached; her coccyx, she corrected herself. She'd obviously forgotten anatomical terms and likely everything else she'd learned in medical school. No surprise

there. Since coming to Seneca Falls, she'd set exactly four fractures and assisted at six births—seven, including the Grimm's lambs. She had treated unsuccessfully a rash that had appeared mysteriously on the body of the mayor's wife and that, some days later, disappeared just as mysteriously. She had removed thorns from children's feet, a steel sliver from a man's earlobe, and several porcupine quills from the muzzle of a large, enraged dog. Also a shard of glass embedded in the snout of a six-hundred-pound sow who clearly hadn't wanted the glass removed.

On the other hand, in barely one month she'd assisted in two autopsies that had established death by means of poison. Some quiet little town!

But mostly her time had been occupied with the malnutrition of poverty, and bruises and swellings and cuts, nearly all attributable to intemperance. And for this Elizabeth Blackwell had exiled her from New York City? If it were the evils of drink Dr. Blackwell wanted her to experience, Neva thought she could have done this perfectly well in New York. And there, at least, she wouldn't have had her peace of mind disturbed by Abraham Levy. But this was no time to think of him!

As if pursued by demons, Lazarus now took the buggy into the Grimm drive. When he pulled to a stop in front of the barn, Neva felt so rattled that she was uncertain she could walk without assistance. She found this would not be necessary, however, as Lazarus seemed determined to drag her all the way to the barn. She eyed the sweating horse with resentment as they rushed past.

The twilight had shaded into dark blue, but when she stepped into the barn she still needed a minute for her eyes to adjust to the dimness. Gradually the shapes of farm tools, hung from hooks and leather loops, revealed themselves. It surprised Neva, even afforded her a perverse sort of pride, that as she walked past them, she could recognize objects she'd not known existed before she came to Seneca Falls: triangular spades, shovels and pitchfork, sheep shears, pruning chisels and saws, tree scrapers and long-handled, pronged gatherers for harvesting fruit without it bruising.

Stored on shelves next to the tools were powders, Epsom salts for purging, salt black, bottles of turpentine for delousing sheep, and sev-

eral bags whose labels said they contained arsenic; Neva wondered if this was a safe place to keep it. But it was probably for barn rats, she decided, and thought fleetingly of Sara Turner.

Lazarus had sprinted on ahead. Neva looked to the far end of the barn, where lanterns illuminated a small group standing silently around a prostrate figure. Overhead was a hayloft. She hurried forward, clutching her black bag; it was fortunate she'd come to consider it as an appendage and had had the bag with her at the tavern, because Lazarus Grimm never would have consented to stop for it at Dr. Ives's.

Even before she reached Obadiah Grimm, Neva could hear his labored, raspy breathing. Those who were standing moved aside to let her through. No one spoke. She quickly knelt beside him on wisps of sweet-scented clover hay, opening her bag to extract her stethoscope.

Obadiah's skin held a waxy pallor the white of his hair and beard; however, beneath a glaze of sweat, his expression appeared markedly tranquil, as if he were experiencing no pain. It was shock, Neva decided, after drawing back his eyelids and noting that the pupils had so dilated that little of the irises showed, and blood suffused what white was visible. She carefully pulled away the blanket that had been placed over Obadiah's body. The shirt covering his torso was saturated with blood; when she'd unbuttoned it, she realized it would be impossible to remove entirely without incurring more blood flow.

After she positioned the stethoscope, the heartbeat she found was rapid and weak, and the pulse in his wrist thready. After listening for several minutes, Neva removed the stethoscope to sit back on her heels. She looked up at the silent assembly: Molly Grimm and her mother, Almira; Billy Wicken; and, of course, Lazarus. Two other women were also there, standing apart from the others, beyond the light cast by the lanterns.

"Was someone here when he fell?" Neva asked. "Did anyone see what happened?"

No one answered. They simply stared at her.

"Doesn't *anyone* know what happened?" Neva asked again, this time directing the question specifically to Molly. The woman's face was tear-streaked and, Neva noticed absently, slightly swollen on one side.

Molly seemed startled to be singled out, and she clenched spas-

modically the torn lace trim that she'd been fingering on her collar. "We're not really sure . . ." she began, then paused to look with confusion at her brother.

"Can you just tell us how bad it is?" Lazarus asked.

"I'm afraid it's very bad," Neva answered quietly. She bent over Obadiah again and tried to locate the origin of the bleeding. When she probed the area directly over his heart the flow increased, and she found what felt like a small puncture wound.

She spoke to Lazarus. "I thought you said that he fell."

Lazarus nodded glumly. Neva looked over the heads of those standing around her. "Did he fall from up there—from that hayloft?" Not, she supposed, that it really mattered.

Gazing up at the loft, Lazarus again nodded. Neva scanned the others' faces. Billy Wicken's forehead wrinkled in apparent puzzlement; Almira, her face wooden, showed no response; and Molly indicated agreement with her brother.

Since she'd gotten there, Neva had run through her mind every medical procedure she could think of, but nothing would save this man now. Given his loss of blood, it almost defied belief that he had lasted this long. Frustrated by the sheer hopelessness of it, Neva bent forward to repeat her examination, and heard Obadiah's breathing stop. When it began again, it was faint and even more labored. And his heartbeat had slowed ominously.

"Could I have more light?" Neva asked.

Billy Wicken limped over to a lantern suspended from a beam. When he returned with it, Neva directed him to hold it above Obadiah's torso while she probed the wound and its surrounding area. She thought she'd found something, and had bent closer to see, when suddenly someone gave a harsh cough, and one of the two women Neva couldn't see stepped forward into the light. She now recognized her as the Seneca medicine woman, Bitter Root. Her companion was the sweet-voiced woman who had also been at Abraham's store.

Without even glancing down at the moribund figure, Bitter Root spoke directly to Neva. "Hole in his heart." The woman then pointed to Obadiah's chest.

"Yes," Neva agreed, somewhat surprised, "the heart's likely been punctured."

"Why don't you *do* something?" Lazarus's voice was frantic. "He's obviously dying. Do something!"

Before Neva could answer, Bitter Root replied, "Nothing to do. I told you before, he has heart hole. Nothing to do for that."

Molly moaned softly, "Oh, no—that can't be."

"I'm afraid it's true," Neva said as gently as she could. "We might try a pressure bandage, wrapping it around his chest, but I don't think he'll last long enough for us to do even that. I'm sorry." From the corner of her eye, she saw Bitter Root nod once in agreement. It occurred to Neva to wonder how the woman happened to be there.

"You have to try something!" Lazarus insisted.

Molly murmured a few words in a solicitous tone to Billy Wicken, who had been chewing on his lower lip and rubbing his withered hand against his side. He lowered the lantern he held, and gave Molly a searching look. While gazing up at Obadiah's family, Neva suddenly realized that his wife, the ordinarily voluble Almira, had remained completely mute. The woman's expression seemed almost dreamy; it was as if she were a thousand miles away. Neva chided herself for not recognizing sooner the possibility that Almira Grimm might be drugged. Opium addicted? Laudanum, most likely.

Suddenly, Obadiah gasped loudly. Those standing around him went rigid, then leaned forward, watching him warily as if they might miss his last moment. Neva was about to put her stethoscope to the man's chest when she realized his expression had altered. His face was contorting in a fierce grimace, his mouth opening and closing. His lips moved slightly as Neva bent over him.

The words came faintly, interrupted by the gasps and gurgling that indicated internal bleeding. Neva could barely hear him.

"Jere . . . Jeremiah . . ." the man sighed. His breathing abruptly stopped. It started again with a shallow wheezing like that of a perforated bellows.

"Mr. Grimm, can you say that again?" Neva asked.

Lazarus dropped to his knees and pushed Neva away with unnecessary force. He spoke agitatedly. "What is it, Father? What are you trying to say?"

The dying man's words were not quite loud enough for Neva to understand. She bent forward, despite a glare from Lazarus that made her wonder if there might be something he didn't want her to hear.

Obadiah sighed, "Jere . . . seven . . . tea he leaven . . ." This was followed by a rattle deep in his throat.

Lazarus frowned and shook his head. "What are you saying, Father—is it Jeremiah Merrycoyf you're asking for? Is there something you want us to tell him? Father?"

In reply, a small froth of blood bubbled from Obadiah's slack mouth, and his eyes stared unseeing at his son. Neva reached for the pulse in his neck. There was none.

As she got to her feet, Neva felt a sudden chill that had nothing to do with the dampness in the barn. Something seemed wrong with what she'd been told about Obadiah's fall; or rather, what she had not been told. She cast her eyes over the barn floor, at the same time nudging aside hay with the toe of her high-laced shoe.

Finally, though, the sense that she was intruding made her move away from the sounds of grief and from those who grieved. Glancing around, she saw with uneasiness that the Seneca medicine woman was staring at her intently. The sharp, dark eyes held Neva's own before they darted suddenly to the hayloft. Bitter Root gazed upward, then abruptly turned and went to stand beside her quiet companion.

Neva wondered if one of the family had summoned the women, or if, instead, they had been drawn there by some intuitive portent of death. Then, as if pulled by an invisible cord, she went to stand under the loft, and gazed upward.

Can't you make that horse move any faster?" Abraham Levy shouted to Cullen over the clatter of the carriage wheels.

Glynis, seated beside Cullen, thought the horse was moving quite fast enough. Obviously not, though, for Abraham, who, from the rear seat, had shouted the same thing several times since they'd left the Fall Street livery. He had arrived while she and Cullen waited for a horse to be harnessed; when he'd heard Neva was on her way to the Grimm farm, he'd insisted on going with them. Glynis wondered if he realized that his extra weight was what slowed their progress. If he did, he didn't seem to care.

Cullen didn't answer Abraham's question, but continued to peer intently ahead into the gathering darkness. The two small carriage lamps were not much help. Glynis herself had offered to take the

reins; she told Cullen that during the past week she'd made this trip so many times she didn't require light. She needn't have bothered. No man was going to let a woman drive, not while he could still draw breath.

When they turned off Black Brook Road into the Grimms', the house ahead appeared dark. But from under the barn door shone a wedge of light. The three of them climbed from the carriage, the men walking directly to the barn, while Glynis paused to study a rectangular shape some yards away, under a clump of white birch. As her eyes adjusted to the darkness, she gradually confirmed it to be a wagon. Tied behind it, and what had first caught her eye, stood the distinctive black and white paint horse. She couldn't imagine what Jacques Sundown might be doing there.

As she began to walk toward the horse, Glynis heard voices coming from the barn. When she turned, the door had swung open, silhouetting the two men. A third figure was there also, dressed in a full skirt; it looked like Neva Cardoza. Glynis stood indecisively; if she went to join them, Jacques might leave before she found out why he was there.

As she watched, two of the backlit figures in the door moved away from the barn. The other—from his height, Glynis determined it to be Cullen—went on inside. Glynis started toward the pair, but they hurried to stand under the low, spreading branches of an oak, remaining apart for only a moment before they merged into a single shape.

Although thoroughly astonished, Glynis smiled to herself and waited until the two separated before she went toward them. Neva, in a shaken voice, was saying, ". . . and I couldn't do anything for him . . . not anything!"

Abraham clearly intended to draw her close again; as she approached them, Glynis spoke loudly. "Neva, what's happened?"

The two jumped and hastily moved farther apart.

"Glynis, you frightened me," Neva said, her voice still unsteady. "Of course," she added belatedly, "I'm glad you're here."

Under the circumstances, Glynis did not find this convincing. "What's happened to Obadiah?" she asked again.

"He's dead," Abraham answered.

Glynis inhaled sharply at the abrupt announcement, and yet she

wasn't totally surprised. Either Neva's words had prepared her, or she had begun to anticipate death at every turn. "But surely he didn't die from a fall?" she asked incredulously.

"He fell from the hayloft," Neva said. "That's what they all claim, the family, that is, and Billy Wicken. Although . . ." She hesitated, then went on, "although Lazarus and Molly were the only ones doing any talking."

"What about Pippa?" Glynis asked. "Was she there?"

"No. No, she wasn't, come to think of it. I don't know where she is."

"One of us should find her," Glynis said, glancing around at the horse and wagon. "But Neva, what did you mean, 'that's what they all claim'?"

"I'm not sure. But I won't sign a death certificate without an autopsy, even if they are opposed to it."

"Why do you think they'll oppose it?" Glynis asked with some surprise.

"Because they already have," Abraham answered her. He turned to Neva. "You told Cullen Stuart that as constable he could order an autopsy performed—you sure that's true?"

"Yes, I think so," Neva said. "It was true in New York City, anyway, in the absence of a coroner."

"What exactly did the family tell you," Glynis asked, "about Obadiah's accident?"

"Not much. I never did find out if he was alone when he fell. And just before he died, he tried to say something—whether to me or to a family member, I don't know. It was very odd." Neva shrugged slightly, shaking her head.

"Did you hear him?" Glynis pressed her.

"Some of it," Neva frowned. "But nothing that made any sense. Something about Jeremiah Merrycoyf."

A high-pitched alarmed voice came from the house as Molly Grimm, calling for Pippa, hurried down the porch steps. When she reached them, Neva asked, "Isn't Pippa in the house?"

"I can't find her!" Molly's hair tumbled over her shoulders, and her dirt-smudged skirt trailed bits of straw. "I left her there inside, and now she's gone."

Glynis was struck by the intensity of the woman's anxiety.

Granted, Molly's father had just died; that certainly could account for it, except that the near-hysterical concern for Pippa had begun weeks ago.

"She's gone!" Molly cried again. "We have to find her!"

"The child certainly couldn't have gone very far," Abraham offered in an overly reasonable tone. "After all, we've been standing right here. She couldn't have gone past without one of us seeing her, even if it is dark. And what would she be doing out here in the dark, anyway? She could get hurt."

At this, Molly gasped, while Neva shot Abraham a black look. "That wasn't the most helpful thing to say," she muttered to him.

Abraham appeared to be genuinely baffled by this reproof.

"Was Pippa in the barn, Molly," asked Glynis, suddenly anxious herself about the girl, "when your father . . . when he fell? Could she have seen what happened?"

"No!" Molly's response was emphatic. "No, of course she wasn't there!" She turned toward the barn and said breathlessly, "But I'm afraid . . ." Her voice trailed off. She started back toward the house, followed by Neva and Abraham.

Glynis remained, determined to find out why Jacques Sundown was there, and why he didn't show himself.

A long, low whine made her whirl toward the paint horse and the wagon. Through the darkness gleamed two gold eyes, and the whine became short, imperative barks. A premonition of danger, not to herself but, unaccountably, to Pippa, made Glynis pick up her skirts and run toward the wolf.

But it had vanished when she reached the wagon. She stood in uncertainty and heard a faint noise some yards away. Even though her eyes had adjusted to the night, she narrowed them in nameless dread as she moved cautiously toward the sound. Then she sucked in her breath. Some distance ahead of her, a filmy white apparition appeared to hover just above the ground.

Glynis stood paralyzed while trying to reassure herself there were no such things as ghosts. Surely not.

Again a faint sound, now distinguishable as fabric rustling, made her take several cautious steps forward. The apparition took on corporeal identity, as Glynis could now see Pippa standing a few yards away, clad only in a white nightdress that fell to her calves. Below the

nightdress, Pippa's legs and feet were bare, creating the illusion that she floated. But she must be half-frozen.

Her eyes were squeezed shut. Glynis wondered if the girl might be in some sort of trance again, and so said nothing, but moved quietly toward her. She stopped short after a few steps. Looking ahead, she saw where it was that Pippa stood—teetering on the edge of a ravine, at the bottom of which lay Black Brook. And there the brook flowed over an outcropping of rock and boulders. If Pippa took just one step backward . . .

Glynis stood stock-still, afraid of making a sound that might startle the girl. How could she reach Pippa without alarming her? As she debated, out of the darkness loped the gray wolf. It went straight for the girl. Glynis clutched her fists against her mouth, shutting off a scream, as the wolf clasped the hem of Pippa's nightdress in its jaws, braced its front legs, and tugged gently. Pippa was forced to take a few small steps forward. Glynis started toward her. But a rock in the girl's path made her trip, and for a moment she tottered unsteadily. Her eyes flew open, and when she flailed her arms, Glynis heard fabric tearing. The nightgown ripped apart, sending the girl stumbling backward. Glynis lunged for her. Too far away to catch her, she instead fell helplessly to her knees, watching in mute horror as Pippa, her arms raised as if in supplication, disappeared over the edge into the ravine.

Glynis heard a heartrending cry, and scrambled to her feet. Before she could get to the place where Pippa went over, Jacques Sundown appeared, climbing from the slope with the girl in his arms. Glynis rushed forward, but Jacques shook his head at her and walked toward the wagon. He gently deposited Pippa, her eyes closed again, on the wooden seat, while Glynis, right behind him, whispered, "Jacques, is she all right?"

"She's all right."

"How did you manage to catch her?"

"Circled around. Went partway down the slope. Thought the wolf could keep her from going over until I got behind her."

Glynis glanced around, but there was no sign of the gray wolf. She hadn't really believed there would be. "Jacques, what was Pippa doing out here, anyway?" Glynis wanted to ask what *he* was doing out there, but didn't think she'd get an answer.

Pippa made a soft sound, something between a sigh and a moan,

and stirred a little on the seat. Her eyes opened sleepily, and she started to sit up, suddenly awake and seeming none the worse for her misadventure. But she began to tremble.

Her shaking increased, as if she were palsied. When Glynis hurried to her, the girl moaned and wrapped her arms around her knees, curling herself into a tight ball. She wrenched away from Glynis's hand on her shoulder, and cast her eyes about wildly.

Glynis climbed onto the seat and pulled Pippa to her, despite the girl's struggles to free herself. As Glynis spoke reassuringly to her, holding her close and stroking her hair, the struggles gradually ceased.

During this, Jacques had stood quietly by the wagon. Still holding Pippa, Glynis looked down at him to say, "Jacques, did you see how she got on the edge of the ravine? Was she sleepwalking?"

"Don't know what she was doing. Didn't see her until I heard the wolf."

"But how could she get from the house unseen by any of us?" Glynis asked him.

"Tunnel."

"Tunnel? What tunnel?" she said.

"Runs from the house to the barn. Grimm had it dug to use in winter when the snow got deep. Couple years back, he made it longer, so runaway slaves could get to the ravine and Black Brook. To head north without being seen."

"You mean this farm is a station on the Underground Railroad? I never knew that. So Pippa might have used the tunnel to . . ."

She stopped as Jacques's eyes suddenly shifted past her; a moment later, Cullen came striding out of the darkness. "Glynis, what're you doing out here? We've been looking all over the place for you. The girl's mother is beside herself, and Dr. Cardoza's trying to calm her . . . Sundown! I'll be damned. Where'd you come from?"

Given the fact that the two men hadn't seen each other in three years, Glynis thought Cullen's greeting a bit abrupt. He didn't smile, and she noticed that he made no move to shake his former deputy's hand. Probably he was still smarting from Jacques's indifference, but it wouldn't be like Cullen to hold a grudge.

"Jacques just kept Pippa from falling into the ravine, Cullen," she

explained, and saw his expression change. She went on, "Somehow she'd gotten herself onto the edge there, and went over."

"How'd she get there?"

Glynis looked at Jacques, waiting for him to tell Cullen about the tunnel. Jacques said nothing.

But in the meantime, Cullen had stepped forward and extended his hand. "It's been a while, Jacques."

"Yeah." Jacques took Cullen's hand briefly. "A while."

Pippa squirmed against Glynis and gave a soft moan.

"We better tell her mother the girl's all right," Cullen said. "Wait around, will you, Jacques? Want to talk to you—I may need an extra deputy, the way things are going around here."

He lifted an oddly submissive Pippa from the wagon seat, and carried her off toward the house. Glynis wondered if he realized that Jacques hadn't answered him.

She waited until he was out of earshot to ask, "Do you think you'll accept Cullen's offer, Jacques?"

"No." Said without the least hesitation.

He went to the back of the wagon to untie his paint horse. Glynis climbed down and went toward him. He'd swung himself into the saddle and was looking down at her, about to say something, she was sure, when two women appeared, coming from the direction of the barn. Glynis recognized Small Brown Bird, then Bitter Root. She felt herself stiffen. What were they doing there?

Small Brown Bird stopped in front of Glynis, but Bitter Root brushed past her without a word. Before the woman climbed into the wagon, however, Glynis saw a veiled look pass between mother and son, a look that carried something disturbing; something Glynis interpreted as antagonism, at least on Bitter Root's part.

"Miss Tryon," Small Brown Bird said. "I didn't know you were here."

"I didn't know *you* were here, either," said Glynis, annoyed with herself for reacting so negatively to Bitter Root's presence. The older woman's obvious dislike of her didn't mean she'd done something to deserve it.

"We have been with the old Mr. Grimm," Small Brown Bird explained.

"How did you happen to be here tonight?" Glynis asked.

"The girl came for us after her grandfather was hurt."

"Pippa? Pippa went to the reservation—by herself?" Glynis realized too late that her surprise might have sounded like mistrust.

Small Brown Bird seemed about to reply, but Bitter Root began to cough, and proceeded to choke out several unintelligible phrases. The younger woman quickly gave Glynis a shy smile before climbing into the wagon beside her sister. "Good night, Miss Tryon," was all Small Brown Bird said. She took the reins Bitter Root thrust at her, and flicked them over the horse's back.

Bitter Root looked over her shoulder at Jacques. She said a few short phrases to him, which were met with silence. With a jerk of her body, the woman turned from him to face front. And the wagon pulled away.

Jacques brought the paint to stand within a few feet of Glynis. Shivering now with cold she hadn't noticed before, she waited for him to say something. He gazed down at her; she raised her eyes to his and held them, until tension made her turn away. At last he said quietly, "You should stay away from here. Don't ask why."

Glynis swallowed her words; of course she'd been about to ask. Why *should* she stay away?

"At least tell me why you so flatly refuse Cullen's offer," she said.

"It's better you don't get mixed up in something you can't understand."

"That's not an answer, Jacques. Something strange—no, something diabolic—is happening in this town. I need to know if it in any way involves you; I feel that it does, even though I can't find a reason. But I never told Cullen how you appeared the night I found Mead Miller's body. Never told him I'd seen you at all. I—"

"Why?" he asked. "Why didn't you tell him?"

"I don't know. I don't even know why you *were* there. I don't know why you've come back to Seneca Falls, or why you won't take the deputy's job. Cullen needs you—there have been two murders, and maybe more." She could hear her voice rising, but couldn't stop herself. "I don't know why your mother's taken such a profound dislike to me—or why I even care about any of these things!"

But that wasn't true.

Jacques sat motionless, his eyes shadowed by darkness, and part of

her urgently wanted to believe she could become indifferent to him if she chose. He suddenly leaned forward in the saddle. She saw his eyes harden into cold, glittering glass. Even his voice was hard when he said, "You should stay away from the reservation. Stay away from *me.* I don't want you hurt."

He turned the paint horse and rode off. He didn't look back.

A half moon lit the road ahead of the carriage with pale light, and frost on tall dried thistles made them look to Glynis as if they'd been dusted with fine white flour.

Beside her Cullen flexed the reins and asked, "What d'you mean, Sundown said no to the job without any explanation?"

Teeth chattering, Glynis shook her head, then turned on the seat to look back at Abraham and Neva, following closely in a dray wagon that also carried Obadiah Grimm's body. Glynis pulled her share of the plaid carriage robe up to her chin, in a futile effort to keep from shaking with cold.

Cullen didn't press her further about Jacques, for which she was grateful. She couldn't talk about him. She didn't want to talk, period. It seemed like days since they'd driven out to the Grimms'. The final scene there, one that had ensued over the suggestion that a postmortem be performed on Obadiah, had left her, and, she assumed, everyone else drained.

She'd been surprised at Neva's dogged determination to take the body back to town that night. Molly and Lazarus had been equally opposed to it, he frowning and muttering about profanation and desecration and reincarnation. To Glynis's astonishment, Neva had replied, "If you had even the slightest knowledge of what you were talking about, you'd know that reincarnation means return of the soul in a *new* form. In which case, what happens to your father's present body is totally inconsequential."

In response to this, Molly had gasped, Cullen had scowled, Abraham sighed long and wearily, and Lazarus said simply, "Oh."

"In any event," Neva stated, "I'm not signing a death certificate until I satisfy myself as to what he died of."

Glynis, listening to Neva with mounting concern, had backed her without reservation. She felt she knew the young doctor well enough

to be certain Neva's demand was not made capriciously. She must believe something was amiss. "And, Cullen," Glynis argued, "we've had more than our share of suspicious deaths lately."

The discussion continued at length, growing more and more acrimonious as Molly and Lazarus dug in their heels. They absolutely refused, they said, to allow their father's body to be moved anywhere but into consecrated ground.

"I'm not sure this is worth it," Cullen said in an aside to Glynis. "Give me one good reason why we can't wait until tomorrow, when I can get a court order for an autopsy."

"Because by tomorrow," Glynis responded, "they may already have buried him. Then you'll have to get an order to exhume him. And by that time . . . well, who knows?"

But Almira Grimm, who until then had looked totally disinterested, suddenly stunned them all. "Take him," she said to Neva. "Take him—it makes no difference."

"Exactly," Neva had said, whirling to face Cullen and Abraham, and motioning them toward Obadiah's body. "Strike while the iron's hot," she had whispered under her breath to Glynis. "No telling what that lady's going to do next."

And so, Glynis mused, here they were at close to midnight—a two-cart procession into Seneca Falls with the remains of a man who had avoided the town most of his life. She had no idea what Neva thought she'd find. But even Cullen had seemed impressed by her tenacity.

"She doesn't expect to do an autopsy tonight, does she?" he now asked.

"I expect so," Glynis said. "And if she wants to, do you think you can stop her?"

"No." Cullen shook his head. "Not for a minute!"

• 14 •

[Educated] girls come to marriage tired, and unequal to its obligations . . . should pregnancy ensue, a big-headed child and a narrow pelvis imperil her life and that of her offspring.

—Dr. William Goodell, c. 1850

Rain mixing with snow confronted Glynis the following morning. She drew the hood of her black wool cape more tightly around her face and, watching her feet, stepped cautiously to avoid thin patches of ice all but hidden in the ruts of Fall Street. She'd nearly lost her footing several times, though the ice came as no surprise; by the time the short procession bearing Obadiah Grimm's body had arrived in town the night before, the temperature had plummeted to bone-chilling cold.

Receiving no response to her knocks on the Iveses' front door, Glynis pushed it open, called out, then followed a flow of warm air coming down the hall. Even before she reached the back kitchen, she heard Cullen saying, ". . . and how can you be sure?"

When Glynis approached the open doorway, she saw him standing with arms crossed, leaning against the opposite wall. He looked up and nodded to her distractedly. His gaze then returned to Neva Cardoza, huddled in a chair directly in front of the stove; black cast iron, the stove sat on four curved feet near the central chimney of the house into which it was vented.

Neva's hands were wrapped around a mug of steaming coffee, coffee so strong that Glynis could smell it clear across the room. She gave Glynis a brief half-smile before she turned back to Cullen. "How can I be sure of *what?*" Neva asked him. "If you mean how did I know

someone was lying, I suspected that even before I did the autopsy—suspected it after I first examined Obadiah Grimm."

"So why didn't you say something when I got there? Why wait until now?" Cullen's question was put to her in a tight voice.

"Because I wasn't certain what I was looking for. I only knew there was a problem of logic with the family's story of Obadiah's fall, because they neglected to mention that he'd fallen *on* something. And I knew he must have—he sustained a punctured heart. And I found more than one wound."

"Maybe they honestly didn't know," Glynis offered.

"That's what I first thought," Neva said. "But then I remembered that there was no sharp object near him when I got there. I checked the floor around him. Whatever he'd fallen on had been removed by the time I arrived—*if* he fell."

"I still don't see why you suspected something was wrong right away," Cullen said, frowning.

"The wounds were in Obadiah's *chest*," Neva answered. "When I arrived, he was lying on his *back*. Now, when he fell, he either landed on his back—in which case, why the chest wounds?—or he landed facedown, somehow impaling himself on something. Something that should have been there, unless it had been removed. By someone."

"How many chest wounds were there?" Glynis asked.

"When Dr. Ives and I did the autopsy, we found three evenly spaced punctures, deep ones, including the one that pierced his heart."

"Three . . . evenly spaced?" Cullen repeated. "You mean"—he paused—"you mean caused by something like a pitchfork?"

"Something *exactly* like a pitchfork," Neva responded.

Glynis cringed at the image this aroused. "But that would seem to indicate," she said slowly, "that if Obadiah fell from the hayloft and landed facedown, impaling himself on the fork, then someone subsequently rolled him over and pulled it out . . ."

"And deliberately didn't tell me," Neva finished. "I say it was deliberate because I certainly asked, a number of times, if anyone knew what happened. The impression they all gave was that Grimm had been alone when he fell."

"But obviously," Cullen said, "he couldn't have been, at least not for long. Not unless he pulled out the fork himself and then . . ."

"Then wiped it clean and hung it back up with the other tools," Neva said with a sardonic smile. "And the pitchfork hanging in the barn had no blood on it. I checked."

"A farm that size surely would have more than one," Glynis said, frowning. "Why couldn't that particular pitchfork have been removed from the barn altogether? And who first discovered Obadiah, do we know that?"

"Billy Wicken told me he did," Cullen said.

"Was he alone?" Glynis asked. "Did Billy say he was alone when he found Obadiah?"

"That's what he said." Cullen's expression implied doubt. He turned to Neva. "Maybe he was afraid to tell you he'd removed the pitchfork. Could have thought that by doing it he'd made Obadiah's situation worse, and didn't want to own up to it."

"That's possible," Glynis agreed. "And he might have been reluctant to say anything about that in front of the family members. Did either of you ask him later, when he was by himself?"

Both Cullen and Neva shook their heads.

Glynis thought for a moment; it just didn't feel right. "No," she said, finally, "I don't believe that's what happened. Because if Billy had removed the pitchfork, why on earth would he wipe the tines clean and hang it back up? Unless . . . unless he thought he needed to protect someone."

"Or needed to protect himself?" Neva added.

Glynis and Cullen stared at her. Cullen spoke first. "You mean you think Billy speared Grimm with that fork on purpose? Meant to kill him?"

Neva lifted her shoulders in a small shrug. "Could be."

Glynis shook her head. "No, wait a minute. We're all three of us assuming the fork was removed by someone living there at the farm. What if it was someone else entirely? Someone who left immediately afterward and—"

She broke off abruptly. Jacques Sundown had been at the Grimms'—and she didn't know when he'd arrived. But he could have come with his mother and aunt when Pippa fetched them. Meaning *after* Billy had found Obadiah. That would make sense. With night coming, Jacques wouldn't have let the women go alone to the farm, so he'd ridden along with their wagon. Then something else struck her.

Would Molly have let Pippa go for the medicine woman in the first place? Surely not. But if Pippa had used the underground tunnel to leave the house unseen, as she'd done later that night, Molly wouldn't have known.

"Glynis?" Cullen was frowning at her. "Glynis, I said, have you got any ideas about who might have had reason to kill Obadiah?"

Glynis said nothing, just shook her head. Something else was now bothering her, but she couldn't put her finger on it.

Cullen turned to Neva. "You?"

"No, I don't. But you do realize, Constable, that this is the third autopsy I've performed where the cause of death—"

"Yes!" Cullen's tone was harsh with annoyance. "Yes, of course I realize it. And, as the newspapers have trumpeted, I'm no closer to finding out who killed Jack Turner and Mead Miller than I was before this happened to Obadiah. Common sense tells me the first two deaths were connected in some way, but I'm damned if I can see how. If *you* can, I wish you'd say."

Apparently startled by Cullen's request, Neva's face lost its look of indignation. "Well, I can't, Constable. Arsenic in wine, snake venom delivered by dart, and pitchfork impalement—where could be the link?" she said, looking with question at Glynis. "Maybe there is no connection."

"I think there is," Glynis said. "Perhaps the very fact that the means of murder have been so dissimiliar, and also unusual, is a link in and of itself. Didn't you once tell me, Cullen, that in a series of murders committed by the same person, a pattern usually can be found?"

Cullen nodded. "Not that there's been all that many, at least not in this country."

"You mean that have been uncovered," Neva inserted. "After all, autopsies aren't performed that often, not without reasonable cause. And doctors haven't known how to identify most poisons, not absolutely, until this century—even this decade. So who knows how many there may have been?"

"Yes," Glynis agreed, "and that's why these are so fiendishly clever. If Jack Turner hadn't alerted you, Cullen, you wouldn't have looked for anything suspicious when he died. The same was true of Mead Miller. Now there's Obadiah . . . and Jake Braun, who says *he's* going

to be killed. But neither Jack Turner nor Jake would give you any explanation for their fear. Why? It seems fairly clear that if we could find the reason, we might find the murderer."

"Well, it's not me," announced Abraham Levy as he entered the kitchen. "I wouldn't know the first thing about poisoning someone."

"You have a point," Glynis said to him.

Neva rose from the chair. "I'll be ready to go in a minute," she told Abraham. She left the room, studiously ignoring Cullen's raised eyebrows.

"We'd best hurry. The train leaves in thirty minutes!" Abraham called after her.

Cullen's eyebrows went higher. "The train?" he repeated.

Abraham obviously struggled not to smile. "My monthly buying trip to Rochester," he said. "The good doctor wanted to come along and see the new hospital that's just opened. A former medical professor of hers wrote to say a doctor's there that Neva might want to meet. He's supposed to be an expert on poison."

"That's a piece of good luck," Glynis said, throwing Cullen a hopeful look. "And there's a hospital?" Her sister Gwen, in Rochester, had been complaining for years about the lack of such a facility. "Who's opened it?" she asked Abraham.

"Truthfully, I don't think it's much of a hospital," Abraham said. "A woman named Hieronymo O'Brien—she's a nun with the Catholic Sisters of Charity—has opened it. And I hear it's just a couple of old, abandoned sheds."

"I'm eager to meet this nun," Neva said, returning to the kitchen with a dark red wool cloak over her shoulders. "Mr. Levy says she's caring for fifty or sixty people there."

She and Abraham started for the door. But Neva looked back over her shoulder to say, "If you should need me, Constable Stuart, I'll be returning this evening. I just hope there's no occasion for another autopsy!"

She called good-bye to Glynis, who could then hear Neva's heels clicking lightly down the porch stairs, followed by the more substantial thump of Abraham's boots. Having detected in Neva's voice a certain unfamiliar lilt, Glynis glanced with a smile at Cullen, who stood staring after the departing pair with an expression of disbelief. He'd started to say something when the sound of boots running up

the stairs stopped him. Someone banged on the door several times before it flew open, and Zeph Waters rushed inside.

The young deputy's face looked stricken. "Constable . . . Constable Stuart, I'm really sorry."

"You know, you're getting to be a regular standard-bearer of bad tidings, aren't you, Zeph? What's the matter now?" Cullen asked him.

Zeph stared at the floor, then took a deep breath and gazed at Cullen with an expression of abject misery. "It's Jake Braun, Constable Stuart. He's escaped." Following Cullen's explosive expletive, Zeph swallowed hard several times. "It's my fault, sir, and I still don't know exactly what happened, but . . . he's gone!"

"What d'you mean, you don't know what happened?" Cullen said with unconcealed exasperation.

Zeph shook his head. On the left side of his face, Glynis now saw a large angry-looking bruise. "What about your face, Zeph?" she asked. "Did Jake Braun do that to you?"

The boy looked so ashamed, Glynis was sorry she'd asked.

"C'mon, Zeph," ordered Cullen, "spit it out. How did Braun get away?"

"He . . . that is, I took him out to the privy like he asked. He'd just started to go inside, when the door flew open and caught me on the side of my head. Next thing I knew, I was lying on the ground and . . . and the prisoner was gone."

Cullen sighed deeply. "All right, Zeph. Can't be helped now. Braun was just waiting for the opportunity, and besides, I couldn't have held him much longer anyway without charging him. But, Deputy," he said sternly, "I hope you learned something from this."

Zeph, his expression now unmistakably one of relief, nodded vigorously. "Yeah, let the prisoners shit in their trousers . . . Oh, I'm *sorry*, Miss Tryon!"

With difficulty, Glynis kept her face straight, while Cullen scowled darkly. "No, that's not what I meant, Zeph! Keep a safe distance from the prisoners at all times, that's what you should have learned. And clean up your language!"

Clearly chastened, Zeph nodded again.

"Well," Cullen said to Glynis, "I guess we'll just have to hope Jake Braun was wrong about somebody wanting to kill him."

"You're not going after him?"

"Can't go chasing after a man without a reasonable charge—and I didn't hear you offering to place one against Braun. So to hell with him—he's on his own!"

In the Waterloo courthouse, attorney Jeremiah Merrycoyf stood quietly before the bench of Seneca County judge Thaddeus Heath. While Judge Heath read over the legal papers Merrycoyf had presented him, the lawyer glanced at his client, who fidgeted beside him; Lazarus Grimm certainly hadn't wasted any time. His father had been dead a little less than twenty-four hours, and here he was, petitioning for appointment as administrator of Obadiah's estate.

"Mr. Merrycoyf," said Judge Heath, putting down the papers at last. "It is stated here that Obadiah Grimm, the petitioner's father, died intestate. Without a will. Is that true to the best of your knowledge, sir?"

"Yes, Your Honor," Merrycoyf replied. "The late Mr. Grimm had been my client, in matters involving real estate, for a number of years. Although I tried to persuade him otherwise, he repeatedly told me he saw no reason for a will."

No reason to spend his money drawing one up, was what the tight-fisted Obadiah really meant, Merrycoyf thought.

Judge Heath nodded. He picked up two sheets of paper and brandished them at Merrycoyf. "These waivers from the next of kin—the wife, Almira, and the daughter, Molly—were obtained without coercion on the part of the petitioner?"

"Oh, *no,* Your Honor!" Lazarus burst out. "I would never—"

"I'm not asking you, Mr. Grimm, I'm asking your lawyer," interrupted Judge Heath.

Ah, thought Merrycoyf, my client's reputation precedes him. But Molly Grimm and her mother had agreed to the waivers without a murmur. "No, Your Honor," Merrycoyf answered. "Both, to my knowledge, signed willingly."

"But why the rush here?" said the judge, scowling. "Obadiah Grimm hasn't even been buried yet, has he?"

"No, he hasn't. And this *is* an unusual circumstance," Merrycoyf agreed. "However, my understanding is that the Grimm family's crop of cabbage has been loaded onto a canal boat, and is now waiting to be

transported to market in New York City. Before the load can leave, the boatman is demanding an authorized signature. And the canal is due to be drained any day now for the winter, Your Honor."

The judge nodded, apparently satisfied with Merrycoyf's explanation, and now addressed Lazarus Grimm. "I suppose," Judge Heath said, "that since under the law the estate of your father is to be divided among his surviving spouse—that is, your mother—Almira and his two children—yourself and your sister—which one of you is appointed doesn't matter that much."

"Yes, Your Honor," Lazarus replied. "But I consider myself well qualified to be the administrator."

At this, Judge Heath peered down at him with a skeptical expression, while Merrycoyf found himself wishing his client would keep his mouth shut. He then realized the judge had transferred his gaze from Lazarus to him.

"Mr. Merrycoyf," asked Judge Heath, "is there an issue of other surviving heirs?"

"As submitted in the petition, Your Honor," Merrycoyf answered.

"Very well. The request of the petitioner, Lazarus Grimm, is granted."

"Thank you, Your Honor," Merrycoyf said. Beside him, Lazarus smiled broadly at Judge Heath and seemed determined to comment further, but Merrycoyf took firm hold of the man's arm and turned him around. As he then nudged Lazarus somewhat ungently toward the center aisle, a clerk brushed by them on his way forward to the judge's bench.

"Judge Heath, sir," panted the clerk, "there is a request for a restraining order from the young gentleman attorney in the back of the room. He is quite insistent on being heard, Your Honor."

Merrycoyf looked toward the rear of the courtroom, where, to his surprise, he saw Adam MacAlistair dashing up the aisle with several rolls of paper under his arm.

As he went by, Adam shot Merrycoyf a cryptic look. But he kept on going, straight to the front of the room, saying to Judge Heath, "If the Court please, Your Honor, my name is Adam MacAlistair and . . . and with your permission, sir, may I approach the bench? Sir?"

"This is very irregular, young man," Judge Heath growled. "I don't

believe you are listed on today's docket. In fact, I know you're not. Mr. Merrycoyf's was to be my last case."

"No, sir. That is, I mean, yes, sir—I'm not scheduled today. But if you will allow me to proceed, I think Your Honor will understand the reason for my . . . my irregular conduct, as it's a matter of some urgency. If you please, sir."

Merrycoyf had paused halfway down the aisle to observe Adam MacAlistair's less than refined approach. But his face carried such earnest appeal that Merrycoyf thought he himself would have found it difficult to deny the young lawyer a hearing. And Judge Heath, although ordinarily not noted for his charity, apparently was of like mind.

"Mr. MacAlistair, I trust this will not take long?"

"No, sir, not long at all."

"Very well. Proceed."

Merrycoyf suddenly remembered his client, and turned to find Lazarus Grimm standing directly behind him. "Mr. Grimm, I'd like to stay and listen to my young colleague present what will be his first case. If you don't mind." Merrycoyf avoided the possible objection from Lazarus by immediately seating himself.

He needn't have worried. He saw that Lazarus Grimm, too, had been watching the proceedings with curiosity and now slid into a chair readily enough beside Merrycoyf.

". . . and proceed forthwith, Mr. MacAlistair," Judge Heath was saying.

"Yes, sir," Adam said as he finished unrolling on a table what appeared to Merrycoyf to be plat maps and deeds and titles that he'd carried forward with him. Adam straightened and said to the judge, "Your Honor, sir, I am applying for a restraining order on behalf of my client—my client who is a business owner in the village of Seneca Falls."

Merrycoyf nodded approvingly. Smart lad—don't reveal your client's name yet, not if the judge doesn't ask. Serenity Hathaway's lively establishment was surely known here in Waterloo if not through all of western New York.

"Yes, yes, Mr. MacAlistair," Judge Heath said. "Do get on with it."

"Yes, sir. My client, sir, is seeking an order that would prohibit cer-

tain people from exploiting the land on which the business is located."

"On what grounds is this order sought, Mr. MacAlistair?"

"Unlawful trespass, Your Honor," answered Adam. This said confidently, Merrycoyf noted, without a moment's hesitation. At least the young man had stopped stammering; in fact, MacAlistair seemed to be warming to his task. Unfortunately, it was difficult to see how he could possibly argue unlawful trespass. On a public road!

"Where is your client's business situated?" Judge Heath asked.

"Between the Seneca–Cayuga Canal and West Bayard Street, Your Honor."

The judge pulled himself upright in his chair. "Between Bayard Street and the canal?" Judge Heath leaned over the bench to peer down at the young attorney. "Perhaps you'd better tell me, young man—just what is your client's business?"

"A tavern, Your Honor. My client is a tavern owner."

Judge Heath nodded, his eyes narrowing. "And this tavern's name?"

"Serenity's, sir, and I should like the court to—"

"Just a minute! Am I correct in assuming that there is but one tavern in Seneca Falls called Serenity's?"

"Yes, sir, you are correct."

"Well, young man, I know the place in question, and—" Seeming to realize what he'd just inferred, Judge Heath quickly rephrased. "That is, I know the tavern and its owner by reputation. What reason could there be for asking relief against unlawful trespass? That tavern is notorious, Mr. MacAlistair, for its unrestricted access to those who wish to partake of gambling and alcoholic spirits and depraved behavior."

"But, Your Honor," Adam said firmly, "gambling and alcohol are not illegal. And yet there are those who wish to inhibit what you so rightly referred to as the tavern's previously unrestricted access."

Merrycoyf hid his grin behind a pudgy hand. And now what would Judge Heath do? Step into a quagmire by describing the activities *other* than gambling that took place at Serenity's? Just how would the good judge know about them? Young MacAlistair, despite his inexperience, had thus far played his hand shrewdly.

Judge Heath again peered down at the lawyer, and abandoned his previous line of questioning. "And what exactly does this trespass consist of, to which the owner of the tavern is objecting?"

"A hostile and disruptive mob of women who are parading in offensive fashion in front of my client's place of business, Your Honor. My client wants her property protected by an order prohibiting this activity."

"Be more specific," Judge Heath demanded.

"Miss Hathaway's business is such that potential customers are being discouraged—no, inhibited—from entering the premises."

"Indeed. Are you telling me, Mr. MacAlistair, that these little women are actually preventing grown men—"

"They are intimidating customers, yes, that's correct, Your Honor."

Judge Heath studied the earnest face before him as if seeking a wolf beneath the young man's impeccably tailored wool suit. Apparently not succeeding, the judge said briskly, "And just what is this female mob parading *on,* Mr. MacAlistair—not thin air, surely, so it must be the street. And Bayard Street is a *public thoroughfare,* young man."

Merrycoyf shifted in his chair and sighed regretfully.

"Yes, sir, Your Honor," Adam said. "Yes, Bayard Street *is* a public thoroughfare. However, Bayard Street does not run directly in front of the tavern. And the small dirt access road that is off Bayard, and *does* front the tavern, is *not* a public right-of-way."

"Can you demonstrate that?" said Judge Heath, his cold blue eyes skeptical. But Merrycoyf straightened and leaned forward.

Adam turned quickly, gathered the maps and deeds from the table, and handed them up to the judge. "As you can see from that deed, Your Honor, the dirt road in question has been in use for only fifteen years—not for the twenty years that legally is required to designate it a public thoroughfare."

Merrycoyf smiled as Judge Heath examined the plat maps, and scrutinized what looked to be title to the land on which the tavern sat. In the meantime, Adam stepped back and sank into a chair in the front row. But not before he sent Merrycoyf a long look across the room. Merrycoyf could not precisely translate this look, but thought it might ask: How am I doing? In reply, Merrycoyf simply nodded.

Anything more not only would have been unseemly, but could encourage Mr. MacAlistair to let down his guard. And this wasn't over yet.

Adam MacAlistair sprang to his feet as Judge Heath put down the maps. "Young man," the judge said, "I must admit your exhibits are fairly persuasive. Therefore, if you want the public barred from using the tavern's dirt access road, I can grant that."

Almost, Merrycoyf could hear what must be Adam's silent groan, and he wondered if Judge Heath might be testing the young man's mettle. This judge was no recluse; he unquestionably knew of the recent law requiring taverns to be licensed, and so could likely guess why the women were demonstrating. And Heath also probably guessed that Adam's tactics were delaying ones.

Lazarus Grimm, who, with eyes closed, had appeared to be snoozing, made a small motion with his hand. "What's going on?" he asked Merrycoyf softly. Merrycoyf whispered a brief explanation, while Adam MacAlistair recovered himself.

"Sir," Adam said, after a period of searching the ceiling, possibly for divine guidance. "Sir, Miss Hathaway does not want to bar *all* the public from using that road, certainly not her good cash-paying customers."

"I see. And just how," Judge Heath interposed, "am I to decide whom to restrict? Not being a total fool, Mr. MacAlistair, I am aware that Miss Hathaway does not wish males prohibited from accessing her establishment, however, does she expect all those of the opposite sex to be denied access?" He paused a moment to study Adam. "And," Heath then went on, "considering the nature of Miss Hathaway's business and particularly the gender of those whom she employs, does restricting females seem a plausible solution to you, Mr. MacAlistair?"

"No, sir, it does not," Adam responded quickly. "But my client, Your Honor, has a legal right that is being violated, and she asks for an injunction to prohibit specifically the aforementioned protesters from using *her* road for their dubious activity. Therefore," he said, whipping a folded document from his coat pocket, "I have taken the liberty of preparing such an order for your approval. If I may?"

Judge Heath quickly stifled a startled reaction, and said, "Yes, yes, hand it up here."

Scanning for some time the document Adam gave him, the judge said, "You propose, by way of a permanent injunction, to expressly prohibit Miss Susan Brownell Anthony, as well as members of the Women's State Temperance Society *and* their associates, from entering upon the lands owned by Miss Serenity Hathaway. Well, well."

Judge Heath looked down at the upright, clean-shaven, sober face of the young attorney. "Mr. MacAlistair, since this is your first appearance before me, I assume you are new to the practice of law. I warn you, sir, do not again strain the patience of this court by appearing unannounced.

"However, while I deplore your choice of client, young man, you *have* demonstrated sufficient cause for me to grant your restraining order. But only a temporary one, as the women have the right to respond and be heard, if they so wish. In the meantime, two exact duplicates of this order are to be prepared: one to be served on Miss Anthony, and one to be delivered to the constable of Seneca Falls, forthwith."

Judge Heath stood abruptly and immediately exited the courtroom. Adam MacAlistair stood quietly for a moment, staring after him, then whipped around to face Merrycoyf. He looked, the older lawyer thought, as the young Alexander might have, following his first military victory. The jubilant glow was near-blinding. Merrycoyf closed his eyes, remembering his own first courtroom triumph, and he suddenly felt very tired. Very tired and very old.

Perhaps it was time to step aside.

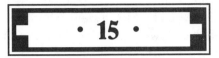

• 15 •

Intreat me not to leave thee, or to return from following after thee: for whither thou goest I will go; and where thou lodgest I will lodge; thy people shall be my people, and thy God my God.

—***The Book of Ruth,*** **1:16**

Although much of the view from the train window had been obscured by thick, rainy mist, Neva found the trip from Seneca Falls to Rochester an enlightening one. Abraham Levy had given her an unrequested but nonetheless engaging history of the Jewish community in the city on the Genesee River.

Of German and English extraction, the first Jews in Rochester arrived during the 1840s wave of westward migration. Come as transient peddlers from New England and New York City, they found Rochester a receptive town, and settled in to become clerks and grocers and jewelers or, more often, clothing merchants. And by now, Abraham told her, the Jewish community consisted of some nine thousand families. After years of holding their religious meetings in the third story of a rented hall, the Congregation Berith Kodesh had recently acquired its own synagogue.

Somewhere toward the end of Abraham's narrative, accompanied by the rocking motion of the train, Neva had dozed off. She jerked herself awake to discover him smiling down at her, apparently not in the least offended.

No, Abraham was not like her father. This man's warm, pleasant voice, his smell of wood shavings and pipe tobacco, his solid shoulder pressing against her own, made her feel what she could only describe as contented—inadequate as that description might be. But truly she

was lost for words, as it was an entirely unfamiliar sensation. And this made her question just how long she had been angry. Perhaps anger was not something bred in the Cardoza bones, as she had believed. Perhaps it was more like a fracture that refused to knit—one that required continuous nursing by each member of the family. No wonder they were all miserable—they were all exhausted! Since she'd never considered this before, to do so now felt somehow disloyal, even a shade dangerous. Because her father had taught that if one became too contented, too happy, one also might become complacent. And thus ripe for catastrophe. A Jew, he had said, must be forever vigilant.

"Watch out!" Abraham shouted now, just as Neva stepped off a Rochester sidewalk into a gutter filled with rainwater. His arm curled around her waist, lifted her effortlessly, then set her down on higher ground. He grinned, and raised the black umbrella again over their heads although the rain had become only a light sprinkle. His arm remained around her waist.

"Wet feet, I imagine," he said, looking down at her lightweight boots. "Have to keep your eyes open."

"Yes, I know," Neva agreed. And was immediately surprised at herself for not snapping that she *had* been looking. "I guess I've gotten used to having no real sidewalks at home." At *home*? Why on earth would she describe Seneca Falls as "home"?

Abraham gave her a sideways glance. "I'd have thought you'd be used to cities."

"Oh, I am, and Rochester is . . . well, it's not as big as New York, of course, but it has much the same feel, the same dirt and disorder, everybody and everything moving constantly."

"Have you missed that?" Abraham released his grip on her waist to take her arm, as they moved onto the bridge crossing the Erie Canal.

Neva found she couldn't answer him. If he meant did she miss the fleas and cockroaches and rats that were one with life in every big city, like the squalor and the clamor that never ceased—well, no, she didn't. If it meant did she miss her father's and brothers' endless shouting at her to be something, anything, other than what she was—she didn't miss that, either. She *did* miss her mother. And her cousin Ernestine Rose.

She felt a gentle tug on her arm, and looked up into Abraham's face. "Did you hear what I said?" he asked, his steps slowing.

"Yes, I heard. I just don't know how to answer."

He looked strangely relieved. "I thought maybe you were homesick—all the time."

Voices broke through the gray mist, and they saw a number of people hurrying toward them; always rushing somewhere, strangers were another ubiquitous element of big cities. Neva and Abraham moved to the railing of the bridge to let the others pass. Neva watched them, the anonymous people, then gazed down at the partially drained canal.

"No," she said to him then, "actually I'm not homesick. I thought I would be. And I admit I expected to hate Seneca Falls. I believed that, isolated as I was out here in the hinterland, all of life that was worthwhile would pass me by. But now," she said carefully, "I'm not so certain."

Abraham made a small sound, and looked down at her with a sort of shine in his eyes that made her flush and turn away. "How much farther is this hospital?" she asked, mainly to divert his gaze.

"Not much farther," he said, letting out a long breath that smelled like the peppermints he liked so much. "But I hope you won't be too disappointed in the place."

Disappointed was not the word, Neva thought, when they reached the corner of Genesee and Brown Street, and what optimistically proclaimed itself on a small sign to be St. Mary's Hospital. A dilapidated woodshed, its roof sagging precariously, connected two small stables. Rags and straw had been stuffed into several broken windows, and mud oozed against the foundation stones. Planks lay over the mud as far as the shed door, but this improvised walk had sunk nearly out of sight. From the corner of her eye, Neva caught something grayish brown skittering under the straw, and she recoiled against Abraham's chest.

He pulled her back, saying, "It looks worse than I'd expected. Why don't we just leave?"

"No," Neva protested. "I want to see how they can call this wretched place a hospital."

"Sure'n it's not what it's called that counts," came a voice from the doorway. "And who might you be?"

Neva and Abraham exchanged an embarrassed glance, then went forward as a small woman in black nun's habit stepped to the plank

walk. A white wimple covered her head to frame a round face and hide the ears that presumably supported the wires of her thick-lensed spectacles. Although the nun's face seemed pleasant enough, she appeared to be examining them rather closely.

Neva quickly introduced herself and Abraham. If the nun, who then identified herself as Sister Hieronymo O'Brien, was surprised to see two Jews at her establishment, she concealed it well.

"I'm a doctor," Neva explained, "from Seneca Falls." She started to correct herself and say New York City, but went on instead to explain further, "We don't have a hospital there, of course, and I'd like to look around. Would that be permissible?"

Sister Hieronymo, now smiling, said, "Oh, and I thank the good Lord it's not sick you are! We're full up. But sure'n you can look to your heart's content, my girl. And your gentleman friend, if he's of a mind, can wait in the kitchen."

The kitchen proved to be the ground floor of one of the stables, equipped with only one woodstove for both heat and cooking. Sister Hieronymo apparently saw Abraham studying with a puzzled expression the stove lids placed at intervals along the walls, because she sighed, "They're to keep out the rats, though the creatures come in just the same."

Neva and the nun left Abraham, and walked to the ground floor of the second stable, which housed the female patients; the loft over the kitchen of the other stable held the men, Sister Hieronymo explained. Neva counted perhaps twenty-five women on mattresses spread on the uneven wood floor. At the far end of the room, a man with stethoscope around his neck sat writing at a wobbly table. He eased his considerable bulk from a small wooden chair and stood, becoming perhaps the tallest man Neva had ever seen; he must be at least six and a half foot tall, she decided, and she put his weight at three hundred or more pounds. He didn't look obese, just big!

"Patrick Kelly at your service, Miss," he boomed, voice like a tympani. A few heads on the mattresses turned to look at Neva with dull-eyed apathy.

Sister Hieronymo laughed, a tinkle of sound that rang incongruously in the surroundings. "Not just 'Miss,' Patrick, but also 'doctor,' like yourself."

"Indeed. And where did you train, Miss Doctor?" He held out a huge paw of a hand.

Neva had to smile. That which might have sounded patronizing from another man had, from this one, a buoyant friendliness; he didn't intend to belittle her. And something suddenly shifted inside her, as if a long-carried burden had been eased. She gave Dr. Patrick Kelly her hand. When he gripped it, his hand completely enveloped hers.

"I trained in Philadelphia," she said, "at the—"

"Female Medical College, on Arch Street," Patrick Kelly said for her, smiling. "I know one of its founders, Joseph Longshore—he was a professor of mine."

"Yes, I know that," Neva responded. "And you also went to medical school there in Philadelphia. I've heard about you, you see."

A loud rap from directly below them sent Sister Hieronymo to the head of the rickety stairs. "I'll be leaving you, then," she called over her shoulder. "Young doctor wants to look 'round, Patrick—see to it, if you please."

At least an hour, maybe more, had passed, Neva realized, before she and Patrick Kelly descended to the kitchen. In front of the stove, feet up on a stool, Abraham sat reading Rochester's *Times-Union* newspaper. On the large table beside him lay a hammer and screwdriver and pliers, along with various items like a bucket handle that obviously had just been repaired. And Neva saw, too, that the room's broken windowpane had been replaced with new glass.

The outside door opened, and Sister Hieronymo bustled in, followed by a middle-aged nun, both of them with armloads of kindling.

"The kindness of people!" Sister Hieronymo remarked, putting down the wood. "Young carpenter left us this—and him not a Catholic, either." She smiled at Abraham as he got up to stack the kindling. The nun moved to the stove, reaching for a long-handled spoon with which to stir the soup simmering in a tin kettle. Whatever ingredients the kettle held smelled delicious, Neva noted with relief; Patrick Kelly had told her that when the hospital opened, several weeks before, the main food supply had been water thickened with flour.

"So what is it you think now, Dr. Cardoza?" asked Sister Hieronymo, stirring her soup with relish. "We're not quite so fancy as your New York hospital?"

Neva, helping the others stack the kindling beside the stove, didn't

know quite what to say. "I'm sure, Sister," she answered cautiously, "that when Rochester sees what you're doing here, you'll soon have a splendid hospital."

Patrick Kelly smiled. "Good lass—just the right thing to say. And it's true."

Abraham had returned to his chair at the table and, Neva sensed uneasily, was studying her. Had he begun to understand that she couldn't be what she feared he wanted? He had feelings for her, she knew that. But had those feelings begun to wane, seeing her here with sick and diseased people, in surroundings that were not what he thought a woman's should be? And, as if to confirm this, he now rose abruptly.

"We should be leaving," he said.

Sister Hieronymo turned from the stove, her eyes behind the spectacles shrewdly measuring him, and Neva wondered if the woman could be having the same thought she herself had just had. But the nun said nothing to Abraham beyond thanking him for the repairs. She then turned to ask Neva, "Will you be having a proper clinic in Seneca Falls one of these days?"

Neva lifted her shoulders in a shrug. "I'd be satisfied to begin with just a simple shelter for mistreated or abandoned women and their children."

"Ah, yes," Sister Hieronymo nodded. "Well, then, like us all, you'll be needing the Lord's help for that. I'll ask Him."

Neva smiled. "And it also takes money, but where to get it?"

"From those who most need to give it!" the nun said.

Neva had started to ask what she meant, when Abraham walked purposefully to the door. He had been more than patient, Neva recognized, and pulled her cloak around her. She said to Patrick Kelly, "When you write Dr. Thorndyke, you'll please ask him about what we talked of earlier—the snake venom?"

Abraham's eyes widened in question. "Snake venom?"

"Dr. Thorndyke studied under Robert Christison—the man I told you wrote that book on poisons," Neva said to him. "And Dr. Kelly here studied with Thorndyke."

Patrick Kelly nodded. "I'll ask him for certain. It sounds a bad lot you have there in Seneca Falls."

"You mean our quiet little town, where there's a murderer running loose?" Abraham said dryly. He opened the door.

Neva had refused to go to synagogue with Abraham. She had declined to meet Rochester's new rabbi, Isaac Mayer, or members of the Hebrew Benevolent Society to which Abraham belonged. Neither could she consider attending a dance and entertainment to be held later that evening, sponsored by the city's Jewish community. But he was most certainly free to go if he wished.

She now sat waiting for him at a table by the window of a small tearoom. It was several blocks from the former Tabernacle Baptist Church, where Congregation Berith Kodesh had newly located. The church had been purchased a year before, Abraham told her, despite Conservative opposition to the fact that there was no means in the former church for separation of the sexes. Women could not be properly segregated from men, it was argued, with simply an aisle between them.

"Oh, yes, that's right!" Neva said. "You men are so afraid you'll be contaminated by women."

"That's not the reason," Abraham replied. "Why are you so angry with your religion?"

"It's not *my* religion," Neva snapped. "I renounced it."

"You can't!" Abraham snapped back. "You were *born* a Jew. You can't just decide you're not Jewish."

"Can't I? Apparently you haven't been listening!"

They had argued all the way up Main Street. The earlier mood of closeness had been shattered by the time they climbed from the horse-drawn cab, and Abraham had stalked off to temple.

Neva fidgeted now in her chair and ordered another pot of tea. She would not recant her position. She had heard too often that her father, like other Jewish men, offered thanks every morning for having not been born a woman. She had listened to her cousin, Ernestine Rose, tick off on bejeweled fingers the inequities that existed, and would probably always exist, between Jewish men and their women. Neva wanted no part of it. Absolutely no part. No, not even a dance. It had been this last that sent Abraham steaming out of the tearoom into the rain. Well, let him steam!

She lifted something like her fifth cup of tea to her lips, determined to overcome the tears that threatened. If he didn't reappear soon, she would walk to the railroad station by herself. If something terrible happened to her—well, so be it. The high and mighty Mr. Abraham Levy could have that on his conscience!

But what if something had happened to him? She gripped the cup, then set it down, splashing tea into the saucer and onto the tablecloth. Hardly noticing it, she stared out at the wet street.

When, splashing through a downpour, he at last appeared outside the window, then came in the door, streaming water like a wet spaniel, she upset her cup of tea completely in her haste to get to him. Ignoring glances from the tearoom's other patrons, she drew him by the hand back to the table.

"Woman," he said wearily, just standing there, looking at her, "I don't know. I just don't know."

Neva pulled him down, still dripping, into the chair beside her. "I'm sorry," she said. "I'm truly sorry that I am such a trial to you, Abraham."

He brushed back curly wet hair from his eyes, gazing at her with such hope that her chest ached. "But," she said fiercely, "I cannot be what I am not. I cannot say I believe what I do not."

"You are a Jew," Abraham whispered, just as fiercely.

"All right! Have it your way. But I will never set foot again in a synagogue. I will never consider myself to be of a 'second sex,' inferior to men. Never, Abraham! Do you know how I had to fight to go to medical school? My brothers could go anywhere they liked, do what they liked. My father encouraged them, supported them, told them they were children he could be proud of. But me? No. Don't ask me to become a good Jewish girl, Abraham Levy—I can't!" Hot tears streaked down her face.

Abraham reached across the table and grasped her hand. He held it tightly when she tried to pull away.

"We must try to understand each other," he said, the patience in his voice so profound that Neva wanted to throw something at him.

"Why must we?" she choked. "We *can't* understand each other, so what is the use of trying? Why?"

"Because," he said, "I love you."

• 16 •

It is the custom of Indians when scouting, or on private expeditions, to step carefully and where no impression of their feet can be left—shunning wet or muddy ground.

—James Everett Seaver,
A Narrative of the Life of Mary Jemison: The White Woman of the Genesee

Jake Braun, slouched in the rocking chair, groaned fitfully. He twitched in nightmare, legs jerking in running motions, before he opened his eyes; with a start, he grabbed the Jennings rifle lying across his knees and leaped to the farmhouse window. An empty whiskey bottle rolled noisily across the floor and, as if he had left behind his ghost, the vacant chair continued to rock. At the window he peered out, then dropped to a crouch.

He positioned the rifle, his thumb ready on the hammer, and looked out into the gray dawn. Nothing stirred, not even the dry weeds. His glance went then to the door of the kitchen, latched and barricaded behind a chest of drawers. The door hadn't moved. He looked again through the window, then stood, and lowered the rifle slowly to his side.

"Damn it—damn it all to hell!" He rubbed his reddened eyes with a fist, then ran his fingers over the stubble on his chin.

"Gotta git outta here," he muttered to himself, and crossed to the opposite window, where a tin washbasin rested on the sill. He leaned over the basin to look out, then scowled when he saw that the narrow window was open several inches. Had he left it that way? He couldn't remember checking it the night before. "Can't think straight—gotta git outta here."

He squinted into the wavy glass hanging from a nail rusted into the window frame. "Gotta clean up, git out." He hoisted a bucket of water from the floor, scooped out a few floating insects, and emptied it into the basin. Stripping off a grimy shirt, he grabbed the cake of soap on the sill.

After rinsing his arms and chest, only a milky film of soap on his face remained, and he reached for the straight razor. But his hand paused in midair—had that been a sound outside? He jerked forward to see out, then raced across the room to the other window.

Nothing. No telltale grass waving, no strange noises, nothing. He was spooked, was all. Hearing things. Hell, why wouldn't he be? He shoulda went when Turner got it. No—shoulda sold out and went when Dooley Keegan got it. But the rest of 'em, they called it a freak accident. Yeah! And for chrissake, it was so damn many years ago!

He went back across the room, and again reached for the razor. And found his hand was shaking so hard he could hardly hold the damn thing. Spooked.

After cutting himself a third time, he threw down the razor and fumbled for a rag to wipe his face. But he dropped the rag, suddenly clutching at his throat, trying to swallow. He tried again, and choked on his spit. What the hell? *He couldn't swallow!*

His breath now came in short gasps. He labored for air, fear turning to terror when his legs began to twitch uncontrollably, and the room suddenly went dark. Clawing at his eyes, he collapsed to his knees. His rifle—had to git his rifle. He crawled blindly, in quivering jerks, toward the rocking chair where he'd left it.

His ghost rose from the chair to meet him.

Glynis unlocked the door of the library and looked up again at the leaden cloud cover. Although she was fairly early—and had for once beaten even Jonathan Quant there—the morning had a darkened cast that made it seem like late afternoon. Though not particularly cold, the air held a strange stillness that raised the hair on the back of her neck. No doubt a storm brewing.

She'd just removed her cloak and hung it in her back office, when she heard the outer door open. Jonathan, probably. But then a familiar

voice, which was not Jonathan's, called to her. She hurried out to the main room.

Elizabeth Cady Stanton, brown corkscrew curls clinging damply to her plump cheeks, stood by Glynis's desk. "Am I the first here?" she said breathlessly.

"Well, yes, you are. Why—who else is supposed to be here?"

"Susan is supposed to be. I got a note by messenger at the crack of dawn, saying to meet her here at eight-thirty." She glanced at the clock on Glynis's desk. "It's that now—and to think I practically undid myself getting here! I left Henry with the children, and he was not happy about it."

Henry Stanton was often unhappy about domestic matters, Glynis recalled. Curious that he didn't seem to understand why his wife complained of them.

The unmarried, childless Susan Anthony also complained. And her complaints stemmed from much the same source: too many babies! So many babies, in fact, that the National Woman's Rights Convention had not been held that year. There were too few available to organize it; women like Elizabeth Stanton, Lucretia Mott, Antoinette Brown Blackwell, and Lucy Stone, the pioneers of rights for women, had been either pregnant, or nursing mothers or, as Susan put it, were "awash in a rolling sea" of domestic obligations.

Just then the door flew open and Susan Anthony strode in, black wool scarf askew and cheeks flushed. She pulled off her gloves as she came toward them, saying, "Morning, Mrs. Stanton, Glynis. Is Neva Cardoza here yet?"

"Susan, what is going on?" Elizabeth said, a trifle testily. "Couldn't whatever it is have waited until a more civilized hour?"

"No! No, it could not. Because there is nothing the least bit civilized about what has happened."

Just then, Neva came through the door, looking, Glynis thought, remarkably cheerful for the hour. In fact, she very nearly glowed. Glynis observed her closely, and with some amusement, as Neva walked jauntily across the floor.

"Good morning, ladies. My, we are starting early—but such a lovely morning, isn't it?" Neva smiled expansively.

Glynis just stared at her, deciding that Neva was either on laudanum or in love.

Susan Anthony opened her purse and extracted from it a document that she handed to Elizabeth. "Read that," she said peremptorily.

"Susan, what—?"

"Just *read* it, Mrs. Stanton."

While Elizabeth scanned the document, Glynis pondered the oddity that though the women had known each other for years, Susan Anthony still called Elizabeth "Mrs. Stanton." At least in public, she did.

Now Elizabeth looked up at Susan with anger flashing back and forth across her face. "I can hardly believe this—it's an outrage!"

Glynis and Neva exchanged glances. "Do you suppose we might see that?" Glynis asked.

"Oh, yes, take it!" Elizabeth thrust the outrage at Glynis.

Neva moved to read it over her shoulder, and then exclaimed sharply, "But we have a right to freedom of speech! They can't do this. Can they?"

"They've done it!" Susan retorted. "They've actually given that *woman* a legal injunction that forbids us to set foot on a dirt road. And *she's* the one who's not complying with the law!"

"How can they do that?" Glynis asked. "None of you were in Waterloo at the hearing for this, I take it?"

"Certainly not!" Elizabeth snapped.

"Then how could the injunction be granted—if you weren't even there to plead your case?"

"How, indeed!" Susan said.

"And who is this Adam MacAlistair person who signed it?" Neva asked. "Is he the one who's representing that . . . that . . . that *woman*?"

Glynis noticed that the earlier glow in Neva's cheeks had begun to blaze. "He's a young lawyer from town here," she answered.

"A young whippersnapper is what he is!" Elizabeth said. "I know his family, and I just can't imagine what he is doing in league with Serenity Hathaway, of *all* people."

"What on earth do they teach these young men in law school?" Susan asked—rhetorically, Glynis decided as Susan answered it herself by saying, "And there, of course, is the obvious explanation—the only ones teaching and attending law schools *are* men!"

This sobering truth had the effect of silencing them all, until Susan said, "Well, does anyone have a suggestion about what we might do?"

The pragmatic Miss Anthony returns, Glynis thought, wondering just how she herself had managed to get caught up in this. She hadn't even marched. Nor had Elizabeth, for that matter, although she would have, had her domestic duties not interfered. And Glynis could not imagine Henry Stanton saying something like, "Oh, by all means, Elizabeth, go and close down a tavern or two. I'll be delighted to take care of things here at home until you return."

"Glynis!"

She realized they had all been staring at her. "Yes. Yes, I'm sorry, I didn't hear."

"I said," sighed Elizabeth, "could you talk to Jeremiah Merrycoyf about this? You know him better than we do."

"You mean, would Mr. Merrycoyf represent you?" Glynis asked.

Elizabeth nodded.

"Oh, I'm afraid not," Glynis said. "At least I don't think so. Mr. Merrycoyf was the one, you see, who several years ago recommended Adam MacAlistair for a scholarship to law school. Even contributed to it himself. Although," she said quickly, "I really shouldn't have mentioned that. No one was supposed to know. I don't think even Adam does."

They stared at her again.

"But who, then," Elizabeth said, "if not Jeremiah Merrycoyf?"

Glynis thought hard, discarding one alcohol-loving attorney after another. "Well, there's always Orrin Makepeace Polk, in Waterloo," she finally offered. "Mr. Merrycoyf doesn't like him personally, but says he's a fairly good lawyer. Mr. Polk might take your case because he's a Quaker."

"Good!" said Quaker Susan Anthony. "I'll talk to him this very day. Neva, could you come with me? Neva?"

But Neva didn't immediately respond. She apparently had been wool-gathering, staring with fixed gaze at the gray sky beyond the tall library windows. And when she did answer it was to announce, "Ladies, there might be another way." She smiled broadly. "Didn't Constable Stuart tell you, Glynis, that the Hathaway woman still needed one more signature on her license petition?"

Glynis nodded. "Yes, but—"

"Yes!" Neva said, her earlier mood clearly restored. "Then I may have an answer. Given me by a clever nun."

But before she could say any more, again the library door swung open, this time to admit Jonathan Quant, who rushed in, panting. "Sorry I'm late, Miss Tryon," he apologized, "but Constable Stuart stopped me on the way here. He said could you find Dr. Cardoza fast, and then meet him—"

Jonathan stopped and colored slightly. "Oh, Dr. Cardoza, I didn't see you."

"Why does he want *me*?" Neva asked, suspicion shadowing her face.

"I don't know," Jonathan answered, unbuttoning his pea jacket, "but whatever the reason, he'd like you to hurry. He said he'll be at Dr. Ives's."

In there," Cullen said, gesturing toward Quentin Ives's examining room when Glynis and Neva arrived. Glynis backed up against the wall for support. Though she didn't want to believe it, she had guessed why they'd been summoned. Her fear had been echoed by Neva, who moaned, "Oh, no, not another!" as together they dashed out of the library and hurried up Fall Street.

Neva shot Glynis a distressed look over her shoulder as she went on into the room, then closed the door behind her.

Still leaning against the wall, Glynis said, "Cullen, it's Jake Braun, isn't it?"

"Yes. Jake Braun."

"But how?"

"Don't know, not yet. He didn't have a mark on him, though. I looked for punctures, stab wounds, bullet holes, vomit from poison, you name it! Nothing. Nothing, that is, but a couple of nicks on his face from shaving—his razor was lying nearby."

"Who found him?"

"I did," Cullen said grimly. "Rode out to his place early this morning to check on him."

This didn't surprise her. When Cullen had said the day before that Jake Braun was on his own, she hadn't believed it. She knew he'd keep an eye on the man.

"Couldn't have been dead long when I got there—he was still warm. Dammit, I wish I'd gone last night."

"Cullen, I doubt it would have made any difference. Whoever's killing these men is too clever by far to make an attempt when anyone's around. They've all died when they were alone."

"No, not this time," Cullen said. "This time's different—that's assuming Jake *was* murdered, and I expect Quentin Ives will tell me he was. No, this time somebody else was there."

Cullen looked much more than upset, Glynis now realized; he looked almost as if he were in pain. And suddenly she was afraid. "Cullen, who was there?"

"You want to tell me," he said hoarsely, as if his throat had tightened, "why the hell my deputy would be skulking around Braun's place at the crack of dawn?"

"Your deputy! You mean—"

"My *former* deputy. Jacques Sundown."

"He was there at Braun's?" Glynis knew she was shaking her head, but couldn't seem to stop herself. Jacques couldn't have been there. Cullen must be mistaken.

"Yeah, he was there," Cullen said. "Just after I found Braun—he was lying on the kitchen floor—I heard something outside. When I ran out, that black and white paint of Sundown's was galloping away in the direction of the reservation, hellbent for leather."

Glynis bit down on her lip, plucking at her skirt and twisting the fabric between her fingers. Her previous deceit, in not mentioning Jacques's appearance after Mead Miller's death, now loomed so large she wondered how she ever could explain it to Cullen. "Did you go after Jacques?" she asked him, her stomach churning in apprehension.

"I yelled. Yelled my head off at him. Dammit, Glynis, I know he heard me! But I had to follow him on horseback half a mile before he stopped. Then he gives me some cock-and-bull story about how he was out exercising the horse."

"And you don't believe him?"

"No, I don't believe him! Not after your friend Dr. Cardoza told us about Indians and snake venom, and the dart business."

"But, Cullen, that doesn't mean *Jacques* had anything to do with Mead Miller's death."

"But you were the one who said the deaths had to be linked, remember?"

Glynis cringed and bit down again on her lower lip. Her con-

science jabbed her with painful urgency. She *had* to tell Cullen about Jacques, and tell him now. "Cullen, I—"

"And that's not all," he went on obliviously, but now scowling darkly. "I got to thinking about it, and you know the easiest way to deliver a dart?"

Glynis shook her head in mute fear.

"By air-gun," Cullen said. "A simple hollow tube. You stick an arrow, or a dart, inside the tube—the dart's got thistledown on it so it fits tight—and then you blow. In fact, we call them blow guns. And you know who invented this effective little weapon? Iroquois!"

"Cullen, aren't you jumping to a conclusion about this? About Jacques, I mean. There's no basis."

"No basis? Jacques and I used to hunt birds with air-guns. He's the one who taught me how to use the thing—and he was damn good at it. Don't know why I didn't remember it sooner. Maybe I didn't want to."

Cullen backed up to lean against the wall next to her. His face looked drawn and, completely uncharacteristic of him, his shoulders sagged. "Oh, hell, Glynis, you're probably right. I want to find the bastard who's killing all these people so bad, I'm grasping at straws in the wind."

Glynis started to agree, but Cullen went on as if he hadn't heard. "It's not that Sundown's incapable of killing—he's capable, all right. That night in the tavern, the night I first met him, backed up against the bar, I thought I was done for. Six drifters, mean-drunk, armed to the teeth—they were set to kill themselves a lawman that night. Didn't matter who—I just happened to be there. Sundown leaped over the bar from out of nowhere. I tell you, he appeared like one of Lazarus Grimm's spirits. He moved so *fast.* Before I knew what happened, he'd killed two of them in seconds with that knife of his. And as one of them went down, he grabbed the drifter's Colt and shot two more before they knew what hit them. The other two, well, they just threw up their hands."

Cullen stopped and bent over, his hands on his knees, staring at the floor. As if he were tired just thinking about it.

Although she'd heard some of this before, until now Glynis hadn't gotten the details. "What did Jacques do then, Cullen—when the two men gave up?"

Cullen straightened to look at her. "What did he do? Nothing. He just trained the Colt on them while I tied them up. Is that what you mean?"

"Yes. So he didn't keep firing, though he could have. He didn't kill them; he stopped shooting when the danger was over. Does that sound like a man who—"

"No," Cullen broke in, apparently seeing what she intended. "No, it doesn't sound like somebody who'd methodically kill off innocent men. But, Glynis, somebody's doing it!"

She moved away from the wall to face him. She had to do this, she *had* to. She and Cullen had never lied to each other. Never. What could she have been thinking that night?

"Cullen, I have to tell you something—no, please don't interrupt me. It's something about Jacques. And it's important!"

He'd started to speak, but he clamped his mouth shut and stared down at her. He must have believed it was serious, what she had to say, but she almost lost her nerve then. The way he just stared.

"When I found . . . right after I found Mead Miller's body," she began, with the knowledge that, in Cullen's eyes, she would be damning Jacques with every word, "well . . . Jacques appeared. He came riding up. No, not riding up, exactly, but he—that is, I don't know how long he'd been there, but it *couldn't* have been long."

"Glynis!" Cullen sounded astonished. He sounded astonished and he looked incredulous, and Glynis wanted desperately to take back the words. For Jacques's sake. For her own.

"Glynis, why didn't you tell me? *Why the hell didn't you tell me?*"

"I don't know. I really don't, Cullen, except that I was afraid you might think Jacques had—"

"You're right, I would have! I would have thought it was damn suspicious! I *do* think so." He looked down at her, shaking his head as if in confusion, then as if arguing with himself. Finally, "Glynis, what's going on with you and Sundown?"

"Going on? Nothing. Cullen, I don't know what—"

"Yes, you do know what I mean." The hurt in his voice was so acute, and was so painful to hear, that she took a step toward him, reaching out to touch his face. He brushed her hand away. The muscles in his jaw clenched, and there was a long pause until he said

more. "I know you went out to the reservation a few days ago, Glynis—and now I bet it was to see him, wasn't it? *Wasn't it?*"

She heard the very instant Cullen's hurt became anger. His voice began to pound at her. "You know, Glynis, the last time Sundown hit town, a couple of years ago, I thought I saw something—something between the two of you. But I convinced myself it was only him. Only him pining after a woman he couldn't have. Fact is, I figured you were the reason he left again."

"Cullen," she broke in, "you're wrong about this. And please, please don't say something you'll be sorry for—that we'll both be sorry for. You're wrong."

"No, I don't think so." His voice was cold.

Amid her distress for him, for both of them, and the terrible guilt she felt, Glynis pictured everyone in the Ives house listening to this. "Cullen, could we step outside? Please?"

But then the door to the examining room opened, and Neva came out, followed by Quentin Ives. Her dark eyes, brimming with anxiety, flew to Glynis. Yes, she'd heard them.

"Cullen, I'm afraid we haven't got much," Quentin said. Apparently he was going to ignore whatever he'd overheard.

Cullen continued to stare at her as if she were someone he didn't know. Had never known. Then, without another word to her, he turned away. "Sorry, Quentin, I missed that."

Ives cleared his throat. "We haven't found the cause of Braun's death. Can't find it, other than some signs of convulsions and respiratory failure. But what caused those, we don't know. We can't do anything but guess," he said, now glancing at Neva.

Cullen's eyes followed the glance. "Dr. Cardoza? What about those cuts on his face?"

Neva shook her head. "Those seem to have been from the razor, as you thought, Constable. I don't really disagree with Dr. Ives, except that . . ." Her voice trailed off. She seemed extremely uncomfortable, and avoided looking at Glynis.

"Except what?" Cullen said, more harshly than normal, Glynis thought, although she wasn't sure she'd followed the conversation. She just wanted to leave. Leave and try to think of a way to right things with Cullen. He was upset—with good reason—but he

couldn't really believe what he'd insinuated about Jacques and herself.

She suddenly realized no one was speaking. When she looked at the others' faces, she saw on Neva's something like agitation.

"Except *what*?" Cullen said to Neva again. "What don't you agree with?"

"Well," Neva said with uncertainty, "I'm not sure, of course, and I don't have anything firm to go on, but—it's his face. Braun's face. It's a strange color."

Quentin Ives added, "She thinks it could be the result of some kind of poison, Cullen. Something we can't identify."

Cullen turned and strode back into the examining room. Quentin Ives followed him.

"Glynis," Neva whispered, "are you all right? I heard."

"I'm sorry you did," Glynis said. "But there's nothing to do for it right now." She was determined to change the subject before she lost her fragile composure. "The color of Braun's face, you said. What color?"

Neva studied her a moment. Then she said, "Yellow. His face, the lower part of it, is yellow. It almost looks stained. Quentin thinks it's jaundice, and he's probably right, but somewhere, in the back of my mind, there's something I should remember. And I can't. Something to do with a poisonous substance that causes a peculiar yellowing of the skin. What confuses things is that any poison might cause jaundice if enough red blood cells are destroyed. So you can see," she said, frowning, "that if I weren't so sure we were dealing with a murder here, I wouldn't have thought about it twice. The color, I mean."

"And we need to know definitely whether it *was* poison," Glynis said. "Is there something, some book perhaps, that would jog your memory?"

"Not that I can readily think of. And on top of everything else, Dr. Ives is leaving for Albany this afternoon. He'll be gone several days, so if I find something . . . well, I'm on my own." She looked at Glynis doubtfully. "You do think I'm right to pursue this?"

"Yes, Neva, absolutely you are. And Quentin Ives, fine doctor though he is, can't know everything. You said yourself that postmortem identification of poison has been fairly crude until—"

"Wait—of course!" Neva said suddenly. "I know where I can get information. Dr. Kelly—Patrick Kelly. I just met him in Rochester."

"But he can't examine Jake Braun's body," Glynis said.

"He doesn't have to! All he might need is a tissue sample." Neva whirled and rushed into the examining room, calling to Quentin Ives.

Glynis didn't know whether to leave or stay, whether to try to reason with Cullen now, or wait until he'd had time to think about it. But *why* had Jacques been at Braun's? There must be a logical explanation.

The door of the examining room swung open and Cullen came out into the hall, a slender oblong package in his hands. He looked at her only for a moment, his eyes shadowed, then started to walk past her.

"Cullen?"

"Let's just leave it, Glynis. For now. I've got a lot on my mind." He went down the hall, not even glancing at her, and on out the front door.

She went after him. "Cullen, when can we talk about this?"

He took a few more steps, then stopped and turned. "I don't know." But he must have reconsidered, because he said, "I have to get this sample to Rochester. Then maybe . . . we'll see."

She watched him stride toward Fall Street. Light snow had begun to fall, the flakes brushing his head and shoulders. Then he turned the corner and was gone.

For some time, Glynis stood there alone, until she was veiled in soft, lacy white.

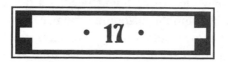

• 17 •

The walls of the palace were snowdrifts, and in them sharp winds had carved windows and doors. There were a hundred halls, all illumined by flares of the northern lights; they were huge and barren and cold. Vast and empty and cold was the Snow Queen's palace.

—Hans Christian Andersen, "The Snow Queen"

REIGN OF TERROR CONTINUES IN SENECA FALLS. So screamed the morning headline of the *Seneca County Courier.* Glynis winced at the newspaper's stark sensationalism, and glanced across the library at Jonathan Quant, who sat at his desk, hunched over the latest Mary Jane Holmes novel. Mrs. Holmes, Glynis thought, had nothing on the *Courier* in terms of lurid language. And it wasn't confined to the headline; the article under it began: "Seneca Falls remains gripped by the horror of two, and possibly three, unsolved murders. Citizens are said to be bolting their doors during daylight hours for the first time in village history."

Glynis tossed the paper onto her desk. The "possibly three" murders must mean those of Jack Turner, Mead Miller, and Obadiah Grimm. Since Jake Braun's body had been found by Cullen only that very morning, the newspaper's tally couldn't include him. Moreover, the newspapers had been told Obadiah's death might have been accidental; not that that would restrain the *Courier* beyond saying there had been *possibly* three murders.

She reached for the paper and continued to read.

> Seneca Falls Constable Cullen Stuart, in an interview conducted at his office in the No. 3 Firehouse, confirmed he has

> few if any suspects in the murder investigation, and no arrest is contemplated at this time. An unnamed source is reported as saying that town councilmen are highly displeased by the lack of progress in solving the unprecedented wave of homicides. One council member is said to have suggested that the investigation "may be beyond the resources of our town constable."

Glynis put down the paper. She had picked it up only because she couldn't concentrate on her work. But she had to concede that, even without the *Courier* whipping up hysteria, people were frightened with good reason. And again she felt the guilt, and the remorse, involving Cullen. He didn't deserve any of this. Even Harriet Peartree, ordinarily the most dauntless and understanding of women, had said last night as she bolted the doors, "Glynis, this is terrible—doesn't Cullen have *any* idea who's doing this? No? Well, why not?"

But now he apparently thought he did. Glynis shook her head and looked toward the windows, where clouds the sullen color of tarnished silver raced past. The flurry of snow had stopped by the time she'd arrived at the library from Ives', but a metallic smell in the air promised more. There was talk of a storm coming in over Lake Ontario; as she'd walked down Fall Street, shop owners had already begun rolling up their awnings and taking in displays from the plank sidewalks. November blizzards could be ferocious.

Storms from the Great Lakes didn't always track southeast and hit Seneca Falls head-on, but the New York Central rail line in and out of town often closed. Cullen might get caught in Rochester. Outside the library windows at that moment, however, there was no snow.

Glynis propped her elbows on her desk and stared at the beamed ceiling. The murders must somehow be connected. They had to be. She refused to believe they had been random killings, and besides, as she'd said earlier, the bizarre means of death linked them in one way.

She realized she had not even considered the possibility that Jacques Sundown might be the killer. Because he wasn't. There were some intuitive certainties that fell outside the tangible or the easily provable; Jacques's innocence was one of those. And intuition had served her well in the past; she couldn't disregard it now.

She did know that intuition carried no weight in a court of law. But

Cullen didn't have enough evidence to arrest Jacques. Being in proximity to a crime did not make one guilty. She smiled thinly, thinking of Cullen's comment that she'd spent too much time with Jeremiah Merrycoyf.

Too much time to ignore the compelling need to find some concrete answers.

Her chair scraped across the floor, as she pushed away from the desk and got to her feet. Jonathan started, and jerked his head toward her, sheepishly closing the novel.

"That's all right, Jonathan," Glynis said. "you might as well go ahead and read. With talk of a storm brewing, we won't get many more patrons in today. I'm leaving now to run an errand. If I'm not back by five, close up. But check the windows in case the storm comes tonight."

In her back office she retrieved her cloak and gloves. She had thought of something urgent, and it needed to be done before Cullen returned from Rochester.

As she guided the small gray mare onto Black Brook Road, the rear wheels of the carriage skidded on a patch of ice; the temperature had dropped several degrees since early morning. But still no sign of snow. Only the thick, fast-moving gray clouds that at this time of year habitually prowled the sky over western New York. Livery owner John Boone had repeated the rumors of bad weather to the north, but Glynis had told him not to fret, that she'd have his carriage back well ahead of any storm that might threaten.

But now, as she passed the Turner farm, she noticed uneasily that the metallic smell of the air had grown sharper. And the light wind, which had been blowing steadily from the northwest, suddenly gusted and shifted due north. Glynis drew on the reins, experiencing a moment of uncertainty; perhaps this was foolhardy, and she would do well to turn back. Still, she'd driven through snow before. She should have plenty of time to get to the reservation and back before it got too deep for carriage wheels.

Besides, if worse came to worst, she could always stop at the Grimms'. And while this prospect did not enthuse her, she felt that

what she needed to do would be worth the trouble. She shook the reins to urge the mare forward.

Just after she passed the abandoned Flannery farm, the wind abruptly picked up, its bite cold enough to pierce her sturdy hooded cloak; Glynis drew the hood around her face and now peered at the sky ahead with real misgiving. Layered like long rolls of fleece, dark clouds continued to scud swiftly southward. Then, as she watched with increasing alarm, the clouds began to tear apart, hurling themselves every which way like clumps of sodden wool. The entire sky suddenly appeared to be churning violently. When the wind began to rock the carriage, she knew she'd made a dangerous mistake. But now it was too late to turn back; she was far closer to the Grimms' than to town.

Overhead the clouds seethed like boiling stew. Turbulence created flashes of light as if a giant wick were being turned by a feverish hand. And the little mare had begun prancing skittishly and tossing her head, the wind blowing her mane parallel to the road.

The open carriage provided no protection. Glynis hunkered down to avoid being flattened against the seat, and the hair on her neck rose. The very air felt malevolent, and she cursed the stubbornness that had prevented her from turning back earlier. How much farther to the Grimms'? The mare kept slowing, shying from wind gusts and the dirt that whirled from the road, but Glynis urged her forward. Caught by the wind, a few flakes of snow spun haphazardly. Then, just ahead, stretched the long rise in Black Brook Road; the Grimm farm would be just a quarter-mile away. She might make it before the snow began in earnest.

The carriage started to climb the rise, and it was then, at the very moment her confidence returned, that Glynis heard the sound. A roar like a train, but louder. Her head came up into the wind, and her blood ran cold. Racing toward her was a wall of snow. It blotted out the sky and the road, the roar increasing until the ground trembled and the carriage shook. Even if she had known what to do, there was no time to act. She grabbed the side of the carriage as, with savage force, it struck. A great enraged beast howling out of its northern lair, it swept over the mare and the carriage as if they were trinkets. The carriage shuddered, and lifted off the road like a matchstick before it

dropped with a sickening lurch. The snow came so thick, Glynis could barely see the mare, and within seconds she was shrouded in white. And blind.

Now she couldn't find the horse. Or the road. There was nothing but snow. The carriage shook, tilting one way, then another. She had to get out before it toppled. Closing her eyes against the driving pellets of snow, she held the reins tightly in one hand, in desperate fear of losing them, and groped for the carriage step. The wind fought her every move, buffeting her against the wooden frame until, just as she felt the carriage begin to lift again, she jumped. Landing in a heap of petticoats, the reins lost, she heard behind her a shattering crash. She got to her hands and knees and, facing away from the wind, crawled back toward the carriage. It lay smashed, upended, wheels still spinning. To her left, she heard a high whinny of terror. Dear Lord, the mare.

Avoiding the wheels, she inched forward in a crouch along the splintered shaft until the horse's tail lashed her face. The little mare was down, thrashing and entangling herself still more in the traces.

Glynis found she could stand nearly upright. The howling wind had slightly diminished, although it still blew hard enough to send the snow in horizontal sheets. She saw that the mare was on her side, her back to Glynis. To unbuckle the traces, she'd have to remove her gloves; she peeled them off and thrust them under one arm. Her fingers already ached with cold. Her hands were numb by the time she'd unfastened the shaft and the collar, and the freed mare scrambled up, mercifully not lamed. But the gloves had flown. And by this time both Glynis and mare were blanketed with a thick layer of white; even in one piece, the carriage would have been worthless.

The driving snow made it impossible to see any distance. Disoriented, Glynis grasped the retrieved reins, trying to determine if they were still on the road and from which way the swirling snow came. She dreaded the idea of walking into the wind, but it came from the north. And north lay the Grimm farm. Now if she could only manage to stay on Black Brook Road. She plunged forward with the mare beside her, praying they were headed in the right direction.

The farm was at least a hope, if they could remain on the snow-covered road. If they wandered off . . . but she wouldn't think about that. She wouldn't think about past storms that had lasted for two or

three days, or that she could circle aimlessly until she dropped from exhaustion. It would be better if she didn't think at all. Just kept plodding, she and the mare. North.

Wind already had drifted the snow to above her ankles, and her lightweight boots were soaked through; clad only in cotton stockings, her feet throbbed painfully. Petticoats and her long wool dress dragged her backward, making each step forward exhausting. Her hair, loosed by the wind from its knot, whipped across her face, while the hood of her cloak billowed uselessly around her shoulders. The cold made even her bones hurt. And she thought she had never known such fear.

Isolated by the thick falling curtain of white, she prayed it would part, if only for a moment, so she could find a landmark—a fence, the brook, a bridge, *anything*. Several times, to see if she and the mare were still on the road, she went down on her knees to dig away the snow. But her knuckles were scraped raw, her hands so stiff and painful she had to give it up. She paused now and again to wipe her face with her skirt. At these times, fatigue so overwhelmed her that she almost convinced herself she could burrow down into the snow and rest. But that would be suicidal. At last she turned to the mare.

Not since she was a child had she ridden bareback. But surely it would be easier than walking. For several frustrating minutes she tried to pull herself up onto the mare's back. She couldn't do it, not with the weight of wet petticoats. She reached up under her skirt and yanked them off. Gripping one with her teeth, she tore it lengthwise into strips, and wrapped the fabric around her hands like bandages. The wind caught the remaining petticoats, tossing them away like scraps of paper.

She was so cold. But if, in this nightmare, she could find a single thing for which to be thankful, it was that this was November and not January, when the temperature might have been ten or twenty degrees below zero; that she couldn't have survived. But she wouldn't think about it.

Taking a deep breath, and with the muscles in her arms trembling, she managed to pull herself up onto the back of the mare. Flattening herself along its neck, she pressed her face against the coarse mane. The mare nickered softly. And they moved, very slowly, into the wind.

Glynis found she had no sense of time, no sense of how long they plodded forward. She wasn't even certain they still followed the road. They could have traveled a few yards or a few miles. The wind gradually lessened, but the snow continued to fall so heavily she couldn't see more than five or six feet ahead. It seemed as if they moved in place, not advancing or retreating, contained within a cocoon of white, spun by the fearsome Snow Queen.

The mare was tiring; Glynis felt it, and knew she should get off and let the animal rest. But while her thighs ached with the effort of gripping the horse, anything that meant relinquishing the warmth beneath her was unthinkable. Unwillingly, she gave the mare a poke with her heels. The horse took several quick steps forward—and balked. It happened so unexpectedly that Glynis had no time to ready herself. She pitched forward over the mare's head.

Landing hard, she heard a sharp crack, and felt herself breaking through a thin layer of ice. As she sank, water swirled up around her. Black Brook, she thought, frantically flailing her arms and trying to stand before the frigid water claimed her. Then her feet touched bottom. But the brook eddied around her, its current tugging at her with fiendish strength, determined to drag her under. She lunged forward, outstretched hands scrabbling for the bank. Her fingers found a tree root. Clutching it as best she could with numb hands, she used the root to heave herself out.

She crawled forward a few feet, then lay gasping in the snow. Her teeth chattered uncontrollably, and water streamed from her cloak and dress and hair, running down the bank to return to the brook. She had to get up. She *had* to. If she didn't, she would slide back into the water. It would not give her up again.

She managed to rise to her knees, calling to the horse for support. But the mare reared and shied away from her. Finally struggling to her feet, Glynis reached for the loose reins. She almost had them when the mare shied again, and the reins swung just beyond her fingers. She watched in frustration as the animal danced a few steps farther away. Whinnying once, a shrill, frightened cry, the mare took off in a whirl of white.

Glynis sank back into the snow. The horse couldn't leave her there alone. It couldn't. Again and again she called after the mare. But her only response was Black Brook; as if denied its rightful due, it slapped

The sound grew louder, more insistent. Glynis struggled to swim through wet mist, and tried to lift her hands to rub her eyes. Her arms were too heavy. She must be sheathed with ice, imprisoned by the Snow Queen; but she was mortal and would die.

Now she heard from a distance a soft sound—the sound of snow being brushed? Warmth touched her cheek. Something crouched beside her, stroking her face. She found she could raise her lids. Two golden eyes looked into hers.

Now it would be all right. The wolf could break even the most evil spell. She stretched out her arms, suddenly weightless, and the wolf moved into them. Its breath felt warm, its lips moving over her cheeks and mouth, and when it held her tightly to its chest, she could feel the strong thud of its heartbeat.

It lifted and carried her into the eye of the storm.

She moved against the wolf's fur, and felt herself cradled, her head tilted back while heat poured down her throat. She slipped down between dark layers of fur and felt them close around her.

It was a noise that woke her. A soft thump, then hissing. She smelled pine and dried corn and something sweet—maple sugar?—and when she opened her eyes, the shadow of flames danced beside her on a rough log wall. She thought she heard a door close.

When she tried to sit up, she slid back on silky fur. She was wrapped in some sort of pelt, and packed along either side of her were what felt like warm stones. Her hands slipped over the fur; when she breathed, it waved like short grass against her bare skin.

She struggled to sit up, lifting the fur to see what had become of her clothes. She still wore her cotton shift, although it felt unaccountably dry, but everything else was gone. Her eyes flew to a stone fireplace, beside which had been strung a line holding her bedraggled wool dress, long-sleeved muslin undergarment, and shredded cotton stockings.

Glynis felt her cheeks grow hot and thanked whatever good sense had made her wear the shift, however brief, instead of a boned corset.

angrily against the bank. A terrible fear, like the wicked Snow Queen she had somehow held at bay, now loosed itself. And she thought then, for the first time, that she would die.

She had no strength left, not even to scream—and who would hear her? Soaked to the skin, her clothes growing stiff, without even the horse for warmth . . . She hauled herself upright and lurched forward, determined to move, if only away from the malignant sound of the water. It belonged to the Snow Queen, the brook; it had been watching for her, waiting to pull her under. It waited still.

Floundering through drifts, collapsing every few feet, she fought panic and fatigue more than cold. And she feared for her sanity when white apparitions began to twirl around her like whirligigs.

Suddenly, directly in front of her, a huge shape rose out of the dark. It towered over her, swaying with menace. She threw up her arms to ward it off, and plunged headlong against it. Crying out, her mouth filled with snow; gasping for breath, she clawed mindlessly at the thing until, in a moment of grace, she felt under her nails the jagged roughness of bark. Tree bark. She laid her cheek against the thick trunk, standing quietly to catch her breath before dropping to her knees. Under the tree, she might be sheltered from the full brunt of the wind. She sank into snow that had drifted against the trunk, and closed her eyes.

She remembered then that she had something to do . . . something about Jacques Sundown. Perhaps she should call, and wait for him to come. It warmed her, the thought that he would find her. At least her body wouldn't be claimed by Black Brook. Not that it mattered very much . . .

A sudden gust of wind rocked her. She forced her eyes open. It didn't seem as cold. No, she told herself, that was death enticing her to sleep. She had to get up. Walk. Keep walking until Jacques came. She called to him, but the wind caught his name and threw it back to her.

Fatigue, like a massive weight, pressed her back into the snow. She would rest a little, then get up. She had to keep walking. Had to . . .

Something drifted into her consciousness. A faint, faraway sound—it might have been howling. Her eyelids strained to open, parted slightly, and fluttered closed again. It was only the wind, the wind howling through bare branches of the tree.

ment, two volumes proved to be Noah Webster's *American Dictionary of the English Language.* Furthermore, it was the 1841 revised edition, and had clearly been well thumbed. Jacques and a dictionary? It was as if she'd discovered Susan B. Anthony with a bottle of rum. Dickens, Hawthorne, Poe, and on across the shelves with authors Glynis herself would have recommended had he ever asked. The most startling, though, excepting the dictionary, were the Brontë sisters' *Jane Eyre* and *Wuthering Heights.* And all looked as if they'd been read, Glynis observed with a practiced eye, replacing the Brontës on the shelf.

She sank into the hard straight chair, her assessment of Jacques Sundown undergoing rapid revision. But where *was* he? The need to see him hadn't lessened, and in spite of the storm, she remembered what she'd originally intended. She glanced toward a cabin window, then got up, stiffly, to look out. The snow had stopped. And there was less of it than she would have imagined. Unless it had melted overnight. But then she realized she was seeing not the light of morning but the pale mauve dimness of a November afternoon. Late afternoon. But surely not—she had left Seneca Falls in early afternoon—it must be later than that. Or else . . . how long had she been here?

She had started back to the fire when a sound made her turn toward the door. Pushing loose hair from her face, she drew the fur robe more tightly around herself. The door opened and Jacques came in, brushing snow from his leggings and moccasins. He straightened, and Glynis saw him look toward the cot before he found her at the fireplace. His mouth curved slightly, and Glynis believed he might smile. Almost he did. "You all right—you look all right."

Not certain this was a question, Glynis nodded and asked, "How long have I been here?"

"A while." She must have looked confused, because he added, "Found you last night."

Last night?

Jacques came across the room, then stood looking down at her before he threw more logs on the fire. Glynis felt her face flush and, by way of pushing back her hair, pressed her hands against her cheeks. "I thought," she said with hesitancy, then with embarrassment as the memory gradually returned, "that the wolf found me."

Jacques seemed to be poking unnecessarily at the fire.

She let out a deep breath, and allowed herself to look around the one-room cabin.

A single chair, the cot she lay on, the stone fireplace with hooks holding cooking pots and a few utensils—and, surprisingly, next to it a bookcase of rough-hewn planks. The top shelf held a few earthen dishes, and wood carvings of what looked to be animals, an oddly curved pipe of black clay, and, positioned behind the rest, what must have been a javelin. Another shelf held a long, elaborately carved piece of wood ornamented with paint and feathers at one end, and what Glynis guessed was a piece of deer horn at the other; she shuddered involuntarily, as it was plainly an ancient war club and the horn would be honed razor sharp. The lower shelves held a goodly number of books. She squinted, but couldn't read the titles. Over the bookcase hung a rack holding a rifle and assorted knives. Ears of corn dangling from their braided husks were strung along another wall. Under these stood a pine chest, and hooks near the door held several deerskin garments, snowshoes, and what was her now tattered black cloak.

Beside her, a square pine table held a metal plate with three corn cakes, and a small pottery jug from which came the smell of maple syrup.

As she reached for the plate, she found her hands were shaking, but managed to stuff the cakes into her mouth in a paroxysm of hunger. Then, seized by sudden need, she climbed from between the layers of fur robe. Shaking out the heated stones, she wrapped the robe around herself, and stood in indecision. Should she go outside? She glanced quickly around, but couldn't see her boots. Then, with relief, she spotted in one corner a covered chamber pot, and hurried to use it before Jacques came back. She had little doubt that it was his cabin.

Still alone a few minutes later, she went to the neat pile of wood beside the fireplace and placed another log on the fire. The corn cakes had made her feel stronger, and she was warm, warmer than she'd hoped ever to be again. Besides sorely scraped and reddened hands, and wind-burned cheeks, she could find no other signs of her ordeal. But there did remain a grinding fatigue. She thought she could sleep for days. Meanwhile, where was Jacques?

She drew up the chair in front of the fire, but couldn't sit down until she'd looked at what the bookcase contained. To her astonish-

"Jacques, I said I thought," she repeated, "that the wolf—"

"Yeah."

"Yeah, *what?*"

"You thought the wolf found you." Jacques turned to stand with his back to the fire.

"Thank you," she said. "It's not adequate, of course, but thank you, Jacques. If you hadn't found—"

"What about the wolf?" And then, finally, he smiled.

"I don't know anymore," she said, smiling now herself, "whether the wolf is real or a figment of my imagination. Or is your spirit—your familiar, I think it's called. I don't know, and at the moment it's not as urgent to me as what we need to talk about." She added, "I was on my way here when the storm hit." But he probably knew that.

"O.K., what do you want to talk about?" he said, unexpectedly, as if he were initiating a normal conversation between them, which would be rare if not unprecedented.

"Why were you at Jake Braun's this—no, yesterday—morning? Cullen told me you were there when he found the body."

"Giving my horse a run."

"That's what you told Cullen. He didn't believe it. Neither do I, for that matter. Jacques, why were you there?"

"Stuart thinks I killed Braun, right?"

"That's not what I asked."

"O.K., you think I killed Braun."

"No! No, I don't. I know you didn't. But you're right, Cullen is suspicious. If you could just tell me what you—"

"No."

"Why not?" Glynis shrugged in irritation and felt the fur inch from her shoulders. She pulled it back up, and saw that Jacques watched her. She flushed again and looked away. They were alone here, isolated, and Glynis found to her distress that she was more flustered by her reaction to this truth than by Jacques himself. Which must mean it wasn't Jacques she worried about.

Going to the chair, she sat down firmly. She was determined to have this out, finish it, despite her inexplicable, unprincipled weakness for him. She supposed she should feel some relief at having finally confessed this—to herself, at least.

"Jacques," she said, thinking he must not realize how much danger he faced, "you surely know about the four deaths. And that Cullen has no real suspects."

"You said he suspected me," Jacques said, and she noticed his voice wasn't quite as flat as usual.

"You've shown up twice at a murder scene! Although Cullen didn't know you were there when I found Mead Miller—not until yesterday morning. I had to tell him, Jacques. I couldn't continue to deceive him."

"Why didn't you tell him before?"

"Because . . ." She stopped, then blurted, "Because I was afraid for you, why else!"

Glynis saw the subtle shift in his eyes. But there was none of the confusion with which she'd responded to this in the past. Getting up from the chair, she went to stand beside him at the fireplace. They hadn't finished this yet, and she was determined to disregard the man himself and concentrate on his situation.

"Jacques, I am truly afraid. If Cullen focuses his attention on you, he won't be searching for the real killer. And it could go on—the killing could go on and on."

"No," Jacques said. "It's over."

Stunned, Glynis suddenly recalled Jake Braun telling her in the lockup that "nobody else was left." Nobody except him, he'd meant. But, she now realized, he'd told her that *before Obadiah Grimm had died*!

"How can you say it's over?" she asked him. "Jacques, what do you know about this?"

"That it's over. There won't be more killing."

Glynis dashed at her eyes, at the tears that threatened. She wanted so much to believe him. "How do you know that?" she asked him again.

"You said you didn't think I did the killing. You mean that?"

"Yes! Yes, of course. But does it matter?" Even as she asked, she doubted he would answer.

"Yeah. It matters. I don't care much about anybody else."

She drew back slightly from the unfamiliar tension in his voice. But he reached for her and drew her closer, smoothing the fur at her shoulders, his fingers warm against her skin. Glynis tried to convince herself that no one would know what happened here. They were

alone, she and Jacques. No one could possibly know. Not anyone . . . and most of all, not Cullen.

No, Cullen wouldn't know . . . but she would. And she couldn't do this. At least not now . . .

She reached up, reluctantly, to catch Jacques's hands, and a muffled noise outside made them both start. Jacques shoved her behind him with one hand, while with the other he pulled a knife from his belt.

The door burst open.

There, framed by the soft light, Colt revolver leveled in his hand, stood Cullen Stuart.

• 18 •

Her officials within her
are roaring lions;
her judges are evening wolves
that leave nothing till the morning.
—Zephaniah, 3:3

There followed a silence so penetrating that Glynis barely registered the drip of snow melting from Cullen's boots. No matter how long she lived, she would not forget that silence, a charged, gravid stillness that stretched beyond her understanding of time itself, while Cullen stood there with his revolver aimed at Jacques Sundown.

At last, when it seemed they all three would turn to pillars of salt, Cullen said, "O.K. Sundown—lower the knife. Then don't move."

Jacques, the knife poised to throw, brought it down slowly. "Not going anywhere," he said evenly.

Glynis saw a muscle in Cullen's jaw move, then watched as his eyes raked the cabin. She didn't care to imagine what he must think—she and Jacques alone, his hand grasping her bare shoulder, her hair loose and tousled, her clothes hanging conspicuously on the line. And the rumpled cot.

In Cullen's single glance, Glynis felt years of her life, the years she had known him, plummet to where they could not be reached. And she could think of nothing to say or do that would bring them back. Or make it right.

"Drop the knife, Sundown. And let go of *her*."

Jacques released her shoulder in a slow, deliberate motion. The

knife remained in his hand. Glynis began to tremble; she hadn't realized how cold it was in the cabin.

Except for an occasional tremor in his jaw, Cullen's face seemed cast in stone. He didn't look at her. In fact, he didn't appear to see her at all. She felt invisible, as though for him she'd never existed. And how could she blame him?

"C'mon, drop the knife!" Cullen repeated.

"If I was going to use it, I would've. You know that." Jacques's voice was flat; it held nothing menacing.

Glynis let out a breath she had not known she'd been holding, and moved from behind Jacques. "Cullen, I—"

"It's better you don't say anything," Jacques startled her by interrupting. "He won't believe you anyway. Not now, he won't."

Glynis looked at Cullen. His cold expression confirmed Jacques's judgment.

"You know, Sundown," said Cullen, "it's probably better if *you* don't say any more. You're under arrest."

"Cullen, you can't believe Jacques killed those men," Glynis protested. "There's absolutely no evidence."

Cullen ignored her. He stepped forward, the hand without the gun pulling manacles from his jacket pocket. And Jacques raised the knife, not fast, but with calculation. Cullen stopped, and Glynis heard the revolver in his hand click as he drew back the hammer.

"Cullen, stop it," she cried. "You *can't* shoot him."

"Oh, I sure as hell can," Cullen said softly, not taking his eyes off Jacques.

Glynis stepped to Jacques's side. "Give me the knife, Jacques, please. Please. Cullen can't hold you with no evidence. You must know that anything he has is circumstantial."

Cullen's jaw tightened. This made her even more frightened for Jacques, but she repeated to him, "Please, just give me the knife. If Cullen is determined to take you in, let him. I'll go to Jeremiah Merrycoyf. He'll have you free in no time—and you know that, Cullen," she said, turning to him. "So why are you doing this?"

"Give her the knife, Sundown."

There was, again, a long silence. Glynis, in desperation spurred by

guilt, stepped forward to reach for the weapon. "Stay away from him!" Cullen ordered.

"Are you considering shooting me, Cullen?" Glynis heard herself say with an eerie composure; she was terrified one of them would be killed, if this absurd standoff didn't end. It would be unintentional if it happened, but someone would still be dead.

And Cullen—this just wasn't like him. With a resurgence of guilt, she surmised his vindictive attitude involved her. But it still wouldn't be like him. Cullen had never before let anger get in the way of his job. And Jacques had been his deputy—had saved his life, in fact. How could he believe Jacques had murdered all those men? And, dear Lord, for what reason?

Jacques, his eyes still on Cullen, said to her now, "This is dangerous. I don't want you hurt. Him either." He handed Glynis the knife.

Cullen moved fast, pushing Glynis out of his way to clamp the manacles on an unresisting Jacques. Glynis thought she had control of herself, so the fierceness in her voice surprised her when she said, "Why are you doing this, Cullen?"

"Because," he said harshly, not to her but to Jacques, "you're under arrest, Sundown, for the murder of that poor pathetic woman."

Glynis gaped at him, then whirled to Jacques. His head had snapped toward Cullen, while across his impassive features raced a fleeting expression. Glynis felt certain what she saw was surprise. But in the flick of an eye it was gone.

"Woman?" she asked in bewilderment. "Cullen, what on earth are you—"

"C'mon, Sundown," Cullen said, "let's go." He gave Jacques a shove toward the door, and said over his shoulder to Glynis, "I'd like to think you didn't know about this. So maybe you should take a look out back. By the woodpile. Take a good look. What you'll see is a dead woman—with Sundown's knife in her chest."

"No." Dazed, Glynis shook her head. "No, Cullen, you must be mistaken." Which sounded preposterous; he couldn't be mistaken about something like that. But he must be. "Who?" she whispered, still shaking her head, as if that might make it untrue. "Cullen, who is it?"

"Lily Braun."

Glynis swayed in disbelief, and to brace herself, she reached for

him. But Cullen shook off her hand. When he pushed Jacques ahead of him out the door, Glynis heard, from the woods behind the cabin, a chilling sound. Unearthly in its tone and intensity, the howl rose on the air, climbing higher and higher in pitch until it became a prolonged cry of mourning. As if the wolf foretold its own death.

And so as you can see, Jeremiah, Jacques Sundown's situation is very serious." Glynis moved to the edge of the chair and folded her hands on the lawyer's desk to study his reaction.

Seated behind the desk, Jeremiah Merrycoyf laced pudgy fingers over the rounded bulge of his waistcoat. His eyes glinted thoughtfully at her from behind the wire spectacles. "I daresay it sounds serious, Miss Tryon."

All these years, Glynis thought distractedly, and he still insisted, most of the time, on calling her "Miss Tryon." But until now he'd not said a word. Not once during her recital had he interrupted with so much as one question.

"Then I assume," she said to him, "you know why I'm here. I want you to represent Jacques. And I realize the bald facts look incriminating."

"Yes, they certainly do," Merrycoyf agreed. A little too readily, Glynis thought.

"There's a reasonable explanation, Jeremiah, I'm sure of it. Jacques Sundown did not kill that woman. Or anyone else. But why," she asked with some misgiving, "haven't you questioned me about what I've told you?"

"It's been my experience, Miss Tryon," Merrycoyf said, unlacing his fingers and sitting forward, "that you are a very reliable witness—so no, I don't question your account. Not of those things which you yourself have seen. But *someone* killed the woman Lily Braun. And someone has also been quite actively dispatching other citizens of our fair village. We won't speculate right now on whether this might be the *same* someone. But—"

"Remember, though," she interrupted, "that Jacques wasn't charged with the deaths of those men. Only with Lily Braun's."

"But," Merrycoyf continued, as if she hadn't spoken, "one can understand the inclination of Constable Stuart to arrest Mr. Sundown.

That inclination does not seem to me to be an unreasonable one. The body of Lily Braun was discovered, if I understand you correctly, behind Mr. Sundown's cabin. Beside Mr. Sundown's woodpile. In the victim's body was what the constable believed to be Mr. Sundown's knife. I will venture to say Constable Stuart had the right, indeed the obligation, to suspect that Mr. Sundown had dispatched the victim."

"I told you, Jeremiah, that Jacques Sundown is not a stupid man. Far from it. So why would he murder Lily Braun and then leave her body behind his own cabin?"

"Because he hadn't had time to remove it to less incriminating surroundings."

"But *I* was there—I could have stumbled onto it inadvertently."

Merrycoyf's eyes glinted. "Indeed. Perhaps Mr. Sundown had reason to believe you wouldn't be interested in stumbling around outside his cabin."

Glynis flushed furiously. "I told you very clearly *why* I was in Jacques's cabin."

Merrycoyf sighed. "Yes. Although I don't suppose you told me all of it. However," he went on as she tried to interrupt, "I can't take Mr. Sundown's case in any event."

"Why? Why not?"

"Because, my dear Miss Tryon, I am tired. I am an old man, ready to retreat to a quieter life. For the rest of my days, however short they may be."

"That's rubbish, Jeremiah! You're not one bit older than Harriet Peartree."

"Ah, the delightful Mrs. Peartree, yes. She, if I recall rightly, has buried three husbands. That alone might make one forget one's own years."

Despite her anxiety, Glynis had to smile. "What's happened to make you feel this way?"

"I've been observing the vigor of the young, the sharp wits of those newly launched in this profession—a profession that requires every ounce of vitality one can muster. But I, alas, no longer have that with which to muster."

Glynis sat back to think. What really had brought this on? Merrycoyf was normally the most equanimous of men. She wondered

if . . . "Was it you, by any chance, who inflicted Serenity Hathaway on poor Adam MacAlistair?"

Merrycoyf straightened with alacrity. "Mr. MacAlistair did a commendable job in a most unusual circumstance."

"Oh, he certainly did. And he now has a significant portion of the women in town outraged at him."

Merrycoyf smiled benignly.

Ordinarily she might find this as comical as Merrycoyf did, but not with Jacques's welfare at stake. He had been denied bail and now sat in the lockup, vulnerable to the town's mounting anger. She must somehow persuade Merrycoyf to defend him.

"Jeremiah, perhaps I have the answer to your despondency."

"I am not despondent, Miss Tryon, merely realistic."

"Very well. But I believe you owe young Mr. MacAlistair a debt of gratitude. He has undoubtedly, because of his association with Serenity Hathaway, lost a number of potential clients. Clients who will most certainly now turn to you. So you owe it to Adam to let him redeem himself in those clients' eyes by assisting you in an important trial. You were the one who encouraged him to go into law, and even contributed to his—"

"Miss Tryon! That is not public knowledge. You acquired that information in confidence."

"Yes, so I did. But consider this: I also have several debts owed me by you. You might say, in fact, that I am calling in my markers." She gave him a wintry smile. "Do I need remind you of the time, for instance, that I traipsed all over Henrico County, Virginia, for you? Or the time that I rescued your client, Mr.—"

"I think I have underestimated you," Merrycoyf broke in. "I had no idea you were educated in the parlance of gamblers, Miss Tryon. Calling in your markers, indeed."

He sounded very stern, and Glynis remembered a time when it would have intimidated her. Now she looked for, and found, the twinkle behind the glasses.

"Then you'll take Jacques's case?"

Merrycoyf's sigh was profound. "My dear, calling in your markers—as you so colorfully put it—will not produce a spirited or vigorous defense for your friend Mr. Sundown. Which, from what you've

told me, he requires in large measure. No, although I apologize most sincerely, I cannot do it."

Glynis bit her lower lip in distress. What more could she say? Oh . . . perhaps . . . yes, it was worth a try.

She rose from the chair and pulled on her gloves. "Very well, Jeremiah, if that is your last word. Needless to say, I am disappointed."

She started toward the door; then, as if it were an afterthought, she turned to say, "But I would imagine that the prosecutor assigned to Jacques's trial will be most gratified. He will, in a sense, finally have beaten you."

Merrycoyf's head came up sharply. "Who *is* the prosecutor?" he asked with more than casual interest.

Glynis waited for his interest to build.

"Miss Tryon, *who?*"

"Who else, for what promises to be a much publicized trial, than your old adversary, Orrin Makepeace Polk."

"Polk!" Merrycoyf half rose from his chair. "Why, he's older than I am! By several years, at least."

"At least," Glynis replied, and waited.

Merrycoyf sighed deeply. "For shame, Glynis." He stared at the ceiling, sighed again, then rose quickly from his chair; he'd managed to muster his frail resources remarkably well, she thought. "It appears that the first thing to do," he said, "is to remove my client from the charged atmosphere of the Seneca Falls lockup."

Glynis nodded, too troubled to savor her victory. "Yes, I agree," she said. "But would you tell me, Jeremiah, if you recently performed some service for Obadiah Grimm? Something for which he might have owed you money?"

Merrycoyf seemed taken aback by her question; behind his spectacles, his eyes blinked slowly. "No," he said, shaking his head. "No, I'd done nothing for Grimm in the past several years."

Something nudged at Glynis, but it remained just beyond her grasp. "Well, then," she asked, "can you tell me who was involved, some years ago, in an action brought by you for a Seneca man? It was to stop the building of a dam on Black Brook. The landowners, I believe, lived either on or near the brook. And Mr. Polk represented them."

Merrycoyf looked distinctly non-plussed. Then he sat back down to stare at her, comprehension gathering in his eyes. "There were eight men, eight *white* men, who were opposing my client," he said at last. "Yes, they all lived along Black Brook. And one of them was Otto Braun, Lily Braun's father."

"Jeremiah! Do you think—"

"What I think, Miss Tryon," he interrupted, "is if we travel down that particular path, we might well trip over Pandora's Box. Which, if opened, could prove quite dangerous."

Dangerous for whom, she wondered uneasily, Merrycoyf didn't say.

As Glynis walked up Fall Street between the two lawyers, it became obvious to her that, if need be, Adam MacAlistair possessed vigor enough for both men. He seemed exuberant over the summons from Merrycoyf, and Glynis was beginning to resent the excessive eagerness with which Adam anticipated Jacques's trial.

Merrycoyf was more taciturn. "We are not going to a church picnic, young man," he growled, "and I suggest you temper your enthusiasm until we know more. As of now, Miss Tryon may be the sole resident of Seneca Falls who believes our client innocent. And you can thank her for recommending your assistance."

Adam MacAlistair smiled at her warmly. She was certain he had not missed Merrycoyf's reference to "*our* client."

As they neared the turn to the firehouse, loud, aggressive voices reached them. Glynis walked more rapidly over the thawing road, sweeping her petticoats out of the mud's way. When she turned the corner, she stopped short. As did Adam and Merrycoyf behind her.

Cullen had positioned himself on one of the firehouse steps with a rifle in the crook of his arm. In the road just below him stood a group of men whose postures were clearly belligerent.

"What're you protecting him for, Stuart? He's killed off four good men—he don't deserve no protection."

Glynis strained to see the man who had asked the question. It was bootmaker Sam Carson, one of those who'd been in the agitated crowd at Levy's hardware.

"No-account red Indian!" shouted Lemuel Tyler, much more mouthy, Glynis noticed, in the absence of his wife, Tillie. "He's fixin' to kill all us white folk—I say hang 'im now."

Beside her, Adam had gone very quiet, but Glynis heard Merrycoyf's tongue cluck in disapproval. This seemed to her an inadequate response. "Jeremiah, don't you think this is a precarious situation?"

"No question about it, Miss Tryon. Precisely what we needed, in fact." Merrycoyf ambled forward, nodding pleasantly to the assembled men. He stopped and said something to Sam Carson, whose head then bobbed with apparent agreement.

"What's Merrycoyf doing?" Glynis whispered to Adam.

"I think he might be verifying a hostile atmosphere," Adam suggested.

"A hostile atmosphere appears unquestionable," Glynis retorted. She glanced around. More men were moving toward the firehouse; they appeared to be younger than those already there, and these new arrivals acted more truculent. It couldn't be a worse time of year, she thought anxiously; the hard work of the harvest was done, and these men not only had a craving to let loose, but the spare time for deviltry.

Cullen had now come down a step, and stood listening to Merrycoyf. When the lawyer turned to motion Glynis and Adam forward, the young man grasped her elbow to steer her through the men; although she heard some muttering, no one said anything directly to her or to Adam. As they went around the corner of the firehouse, she glanced back at Cullen, still on the step; when she'd passed him, she thought he'd looked in her direction, but if so, he had swung back to face the crowd again.

As she and Adam followed Merrycoyf into the lockup, Zeph Waters jumped to his feet. He nodded to her, then looked at the floor, scuffing his boots in obvious embarrassment. He *should* be embarrassed, Glynis thought. Jacques Sundown had once befriended Zeph when the boy sorely needed it. And now here he was, guarding the man in a cell. But in the next instant she forgave him and nodded in turn, sighing softly to herself; Zeph was only doing his job as Cullen directed. None of this had been his fault.

Jacques was in the back cell, seated on a cot—the same one Jake

Braun had occupied before his fatal escape. Zeph unlocked the cell door, then stood rocking from one foot to another.

"You may leave us now, young man," Merrycoyf said to him.

"Ah, sir, I don't know if I should."

"I can assure you that you should," Merrycoyf said, but not unkindly.

Zeph, looking miserable, shot Glynis a distraught glance.

"I think it's all right for you to leave us, Zeph," she told him. "But go and ask Cullen about it, if you'd rather. In the meantime, if it would make you feel better, you can lock the cell door."

He sent her a look of gratitude. Before he relocked the cell, Merrycoyf and Adam slipped in with Jacques, while Glynis remained outside the bars.

As Zeph hastened off in search of Cullen, Adam folded his arms across his chest and leaned back against the bars, while Merrycoyf walked to the cell window and stood peering out. Glynis took the opportunity to study Jacques. After two days in a cell, he looked the same. No better, no worse. He turned on the cot slightly and saw Glynis, apparently for the first time. His eyes flickered over her face, creating in her the now familiar tension, but his expression remained impassive. And he said nothing.

An hour later, he still had said nothing. Merrycoyf and Adam had certainly tried, Glynis thought with increasing despair. Both in turn had been persuasive, firm, sympathetic, annoyed, and, finally, had all but pleaded with Jacques to say *something.*

"Look here, man," Adam said, his tone exasperated, "how do you expect us to defend you if you won't defend yourself? If you won't answer a single question we put to you? We're not wizards."

Merrycoyf had turned back to the window, and was silent.

"Jacques," Glynis said, "Mr. MacAlistair is right. They can't help you without some cooperation."

Jacques turned to look at her. For a split second she saw a suggestion of something new in his eyes, a shadow of emotion, not fear certainly, not even discomfort; it seemed more like resignation.

And then, "I don't want help," he said flatly.

They were the first words he had uttered, and Merrycoyf spun away from the window to stand in front of his client.

"Mr. Sundown, because—and *only* because—Miss Tryon has in-

terceded persuasively in your behalf, we are committed to defending you. Whether you want our help or not. Now, if you wish us to spend the next weeks of trial preparation simply wandering around in the dark, so be it."

Jacques didn't look away from Merrycoyf, but his eyes betrayed nothing. And he remained silent.

"Jacques, please," Glynis urged him, "give these lawyers something to work with. You must see how dangerous your situation is—Lily Braun stabbed with *your* knife, in back of *your* cabin. Just tell us, at the very least, who could be trying to make it look as if you killed her."

For a bewildering moment, Glynis thought that Jacques might actually smile!

"Jacques," she said, despair raising her voice to a cry, "if you don't cooperate, you'll hang!"

He gave her a long, steady look, then got up from the cot and went to the window. She saw a barely discernible tautness in his shoulders, nothing more.

"Very well, Mr. Sundown," Merrycoyf sighed. "Constable Stuart has conceded that you need more protection than he can provide. You will be moved immediately, therefore, to the prison facility in Waterloo to await trial. I beg you to reconsider your position, and furnish us with that which we need for your defense. Otherwise, we will see you in court."

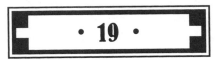

• 19 •

The wampum codes of De-ka-na-wi-da [founder of the League of the Haudenosaunee] and his helper, Hiawatha, furnished an almost ideal code for the ethnic culture with which it was designed to cope. By holding to their old laws the Iroquois became the dominant power east of the Mississippi. . . .

—Arthur C. Parker, *The Life of General Ely S. Parker*

Glynis stood at the top of the steps that led into the Seneca County Courthouse. She blew on fingers that were turning purple, and stiff with cold. Clenching her teeth to stop their chattering, she raised the ruffled hood of her dark green wool mantle, then drew up her hands inside its wide sleeves. She should go inside now. And she would, if she was able to ignore the conflict below on the Waterloo village square. Although apprehensive, she still believed a violent confrontation might be averted.

Snow mostly concealed the dry brown grass on the square in front of the courthouse; the ground underneath had frozen so hard it seemed inconceivable that, just weeks before, clumps of chrysanthemums and asters had bloomed there. Or that a few months from now, patches of snowdrops and fragrant violets would nestle against stone foundations of the two white-steepled Protestant churches facing the square. That they were dormant this day proved fortunate; flowers would not have fared well against the townsfolks' buttoned gaiters and boots, and the buckskin moccasins of the Iroquois.

The white men from Waterloo and surrounding towns looked to be some thirty or forty in number. And it first appeared to Glynis as if every male Seneca and Cayuga Iroquois from Black Brook Reservation also had gathered below on the green. But as she again scanned

the crowd, she saw that probably no more than twenty copper-skinned men stood silently before the taunts and threatening gestures of four or five Seneca County residents. Just how long their Iroquois stoicism could last was the question.

Glynis could hear snatches of the derision being leveled at the Iroquois. "Heathens! Murderers!" jeered one burly white man with his raised fist but a few feet from the flat stares of the silent men. Another sullen-faced white yelled something mercifully indistinct, then whooped in mockery while hopping from one foot to the other. Directly behind these, Glynis could see other white men, clustered in small groups, who seemed to be simply watching. Some were grinning.

Cullen Stuart and Zeph Waters had positioned themselves between the Iroquois and the troublemakers. From where she stood, Glynis could make out Zeph's young black face tightened in resolve. And she knew he would remain at Cullen's side, no matter what happened. Or however frightened Zeph might be.

Somewhat the same spectacle had taken place the day before, while inside the courthouse the jury was being selected. Cullen had managed to defuse that first confrontation. But overnight the mood had grown uglier, and Glynis saw Cullen's hand resting on his hip, next to the butt of the Colt revolver in its holster. She assumed everyone else could see this. If trouble erupted, nonetheless, how long could Cullen and Zeph maintain control? The afternoon before, Cullen had wired the U.S. marshal's office in Auburn for assistance; the return wire had indicated it could be some time until reinforcements could be spared.

Suddenly, on a narrow drive to the far side of the square, a horse and a small carriage appeared, clattered over the cobblestones, and drew up in front of the courthouse. Judge Thaddeus Heath stepped down. He walked a few feet, then stood scowling at the groups of men, while Glynis cautiously descended several steps to bring herself closer.

"What is going on here, Constable?" demanded Judge Heath brusquely of Cullen. His voice came as a surprise to Glynis; it was much larger than his slight stature would indicate.

"Nothing much, Your Honor," Cullen answered evenly. "Just a bunch of folks waiting on you. And now you're here, I'd guess they

can get on their way. Right?" Cullen spoke this last to the crowd, but stared directly at the handful of troublemakers.

"Constable, I want these men dispersed!" Judge Heath ordered. "This crowd could intimidate the jury. I want the area cleared now!"

Glynis clutched the hood of her mantle around her face as a sharp gust of wind carried away the responding mutters of the crowd. Not a one of them moved. Cullen's greatest concerns, he'd told Merrycoyf the day before, were that Senecas and Cayugas would begin pouring into Waterloo from the other Iroquois reservations in western New York, and that the town's troublemakers would grow even bolder. That this hadn't happened yet was encouraging, but then it might be a lengthy trial. And either verdict, innocent or guilty, would likely inflame one of the factions.

Judge Heath continued to scowl as Cullen gestured to the men. "All right, fellas, let's move," he said affably. "C'mon, my friends—move along!"

Zeph Waters stood rocking back and forth on his heels. Glynis saw the fingers of his right hand twitching above his holster, but they didn't touch the revolver. The youngster must be terrified. And for a long moment it looked as if none of the men were prepared to go anywhere. Glynis knew Cullen would not summarily order them to move unless Judge Heath forced his hand; without other lawmen to back him up, Cullen wouldn't risk a possible showdown. Moreover, he always preferred persuasion.

Glynis held her breath.

But then—whether it was simply Cullen's calmness, the diversion of the judge's arrival, or the severe figure of Judge Heath himself that broke the crowd's mood—with some grumbling the men began to disperse. Most of the whites ambled in the direction of Waterloo's main street; the Iroquois moved purposefully toward the courthouse.

Judge Heath himself came briskly up the steps toward Glynis. He started to go past her, then paused, his cold blue eyes giving her such brief but thorough scrutiny that she wondered what he knew about her—and possibly about her connection to Jacques. She stood there, flushed and uneasy, until Judge Heath, with a cursory nod, went on inside. His black morning coat swung from side to side with each assertive step.

After glancing down once more at the emptying square, Glynis

turned to follow the judge into the courthouse. She certainly could not blame the Iroquois for this volatile situation. And other than individual troublemakers, she could not really blame the townsfolk or even Cullen, who, she'd eventually been forced to concede, had only done his job. As he saw it, at least. No, the one to blame was the killer.

Gazing out through the courthouse windows an hour later, Glynis watched a red-tailed hawk circle. Some small unfortunate creature was about to die. Finding herself twirling a strand of hair around her fingers, Glynis tucked the strand back inside her topknot—but not before she had plucked from it one long gray hair. After jabbing a hairpin into place, she laced her fingers firmly in her lap.

She glanced up again at Judge Heath's bench, and the door behind it that led to his chambers. What could be taking so long? Glynis sighed heavily and watched snowflakes strike the windowpanes; windowpanes that only hours before had seen watery sunlight and blue sky. But, three days from the winter solstice, a cloak of white now swirled seasonably over a gray landscape. And brown bears finally had been observed shuffling irritably into their winter quarters.

The coal stove at the front of the courtroom now emitted a series of snaps and hisses, and Glynis became aware of the smell of damp wool and the heat of bodies tightly packed. But she remained chilled from the near hour-long sleigh ride from Seneca Falls; despite the carriage robes and oven-warmed bricks at her feet, only her hands tucked inside a beaver muff had been tolerably warm, and now she continued to clutch her mantle around herself. She let out her breath slowly. Then, after smoothing the green skirt of her winter walking dress, she tried to find comfort on the hard wooden chair. Failing this, she sighed again.

Across the center aisle, Cullen turned to give her a searching frown. Lines drawn by weather creased around his eyes and mouth; the lines seemed deeper than she remembered.

"Why do you suppose," she asked, addressing the aisle space between them, "this is taking so long?" Her voice sounded more curt than she had intended.

Under his frock coat, Cullen's shoulders lifted in a shrug, but he said nothing. Stretching his long legs into the aisle, he gave an im-

on of nonchalance. Glynis knew better. She glanced up at the dfather clock standing against the far wall. They had been in conference, the judge and two lawyers, for over half an hour. Meanwhile, the jury had been removed to one back room, the defendant to another. Almost as if Judge Heath had expected the prisoner would try to escape.

As if Jacques Sundown were the dangerous and brutal killer he was accused of being.

Glynis gradually became conscious of the low hum of restrained conversation. She didn't need to turn and look to know they were all there: those who had been subpoened; those who had reason to fear the trial's outcome, whatever it might be; those who hated Indians on general principles; and those Waterloo and Seneca Falls people who were merely observers, mixed among the others like seasonings in a stew. Therefore the courtroom was filled. Had been filled on the day previous, when jury selection took place—before and during which Jeremiah Merrycoyf argued that a panel composed entirely of white men could hardly be construed as the defendant's peers, and therefore did not qualify to sit in judgment.

Merrycoyf's arguments had been denied. Judge Heath had ruled, late the previous afternoon, that the trial would proceed with the jurors who had been impaneled.

Glynis now looked up as the door to his chambers opened and Judge Heath reappeared.

"Oyez! Oyez!" called the bailiff. "Let all who have business before the court come forward and you shall be heard. The trial of the People of the State of New York versus Jacques Sundown, also known as Walks At Sundown, is now in session. All rise!"

Chairs scraped against the floor as people scrambled to their feet. Judge Heath stepped to the bench and waited for the courtroom to reseat itself before saying, "This lengthy delay was necessary. There were several questions to be resolved, pertaining to expert witnesses whom the People and the defendant expect to call. We can now proceed, but I will repeat what I said yesterday. There will be no more outbursts of any kind in my courtroom. Those who do not abide by this admonition will be removed by the bailiff forthwith."

The judge straightened his black robe while directing a baleful eye over those seated below him. Because he had, the day before, ordered

several agitators removed, Glynis had small doubt that Judge H. meant what he said. But his statement did nothing to lessen the sir hostility vibrating throughout the courtroom. The presence of thre. remained barely suppressed.

"Bailiff," Judge Heath ordered, "bring in the jury."

Twelve men filed into the jury box. They were sober-faced, ordinary-looking citizens of Seneca County; Glynis hadn't yet observed one of them who could not be described as such. Whether this meant Jacques Sundown would receive justice at their hands remained to be seen. As they were seating themselves, Glynis turned to glance back at Neva Cardoza, who had chosen to sit next to the aisle in the last row.

Neva shot Glynis an angry look. Unquestionably, Neva believed that the witness whose expert qualifications the prosecutor had challenged was she. And that because she was female, she would be found wanting, no matter what her professional background. She might not be allowed to testify at all. Glynis bit down on her lower lip, and turned back to watch the two lawyers enter.

Orrin Makepeace Polk, prosecutor for the People of New York, stepped briskly to his table. But *stepped,* Glynis decided, would not be the most accurate word—*darted* better characterized Polk's entrance. His sharp features, like those of a ferret, and whip-thin body were fairly quivering with anticipation. And Glynis now fretted that Polk's personal antagonism toward Jeremiah Merrycoyf would heighten his usual combativeness.

Behind Orrin Polk, Merrycoyf entered and lumbered to his table. In contrast to the ferretlike prosecutor, Merrycoyf resembled one of the bears whose winter sleep was commencing. A pipestem protruded from the pocket of his black morning coat. He settled into his chair with a sharply expelled breath, then sat forward and straightened his wire-rimmed spectacles as Jacques Sundown was brought to the defense table by the bailiff.

Jacques's wrists were manacled. But he looked no more concerned than ever, and moved, even in these circumstances, with lithe, easy grace. His impassive eyes focused straight ahead. Glynis heard behind her soft exclamations of surprise from Waterloo's female spectators, those who had never before seen Jacques Sundown and were probably expecting, given the charges against him, someone more in com-

mon with the creature in Mary Shelley's *Frankenstein.* But it didn't matter; Jacques's striking looks could not save him. In fact, Glynis worried, his appearance might serve to convict him more readily with the all-male jury.

Judge Heath leaned over his bench to address Orrin Polk. "Mr. Prosecutor, we are ready for your opening statement."

As Polk gathered together his notes and rose to speak, Glynis glanced sideways at Cullen. His face, as he watched Polk go forward, bore a grim stillness that distressed her more than if he had scowled. He studiously avoided looking at her—did he still believe Jacques guilty as charged?

As Orrin Polk began what undoubtedly would be a lengthy oration, Glynis gazed again toward the snow-spattered windows.

And so, gentlemen of the jury," Polk said dramatically, coming at last to what sounded like his conclusion, "we will establish, without so much as a scintilla of doubt, that the defendant, Jacques Sundown, had the motive, the opportunity, and the means to commit the heinous crime of which he stands accused."

Glynis twisted with discomfort on the stiff wooden chair, and glanced to the rear of the courtroom. The Iroquois men stood ranged against the wall, shoulder to shoulder, arms crossed over their chests. Their dusky faces mirrored the impassive, stonelike stillness of Jacques, exhibiting no external reaction to Polk's words. Nonetheless, the tension created by their silent presence alone could be felt as a palpable force.

Before the prosecutor started back to his table, he nodded to the jury and Judge Heath, then bestowed on Merrycoyf a brief and self-satisfied smile.

The door of the heating stove clanked on its hinges when the bailiff pulled it open, and the fire inside hissed noisily as he shoveled in more coal. Glynis realized she suddenly felt hot. With a sigh, she untied the grosgrain ribbon of her mantle, and let the garment drop over the back of the chair; her wool dress was now more than warm enough.

Conventional wisdom said the stove must remain ablaze when it was too cold to open the windows, and yet everyone around her

looked uncomfortably overheated. Glynis sighed again, inhaling the smell of moist woolens, scent bags packed with dried lavender, pouches of pungent tobacco, and assorted other odors, not necessarily as agreeable, riding the close air.

From her seat on the aisle, two rows behind the defense table, she watched Merrycoyf get to his feet and nod when Judge Heath asked, "Does the defense wish to make an opening statement?"

Before he addressed the jury, Merrycoyf glanced toward the rear of the courtroom. Adam MacAlistair still hadn't returned. The young lawyer had shot out of the judge's chamber after the earlier conference; dashing by Glynis, and in answer to her raised eyebrows, he'd murmured, "Telegraph office." Glynis wondered, with a new surge of unease, what had prompted the sudden need to send a telegram.

"We surely do wish to make a statement, Your Honor," Merrycoyf now said as he shifted to face the jury. "Gentlemen, you have just heard the prosecutor describe the death of the woman Lily Braun as a heinous crime. While that is undoubtedly true, the crime was not committed by the defendant. Scientific evidence will clearly demonstrate that my client, Mr. Sundown, is innocent. And furthermore . . ."

Glynis guessed Merrycoyf's statement would, of necessity, be short. There wasn't much to say. In the past weeks, she and the two lawyers had learned nothing from Jacques Sundown that would shed light on the death of Lily Braun. They had learned some things from other sources, although by no means enough to ensure Jacques's acquittal. But they did know that the day on which Dr. Neva Cardoza first arrived in Seneca Falls, the same one on which Jack Turner voiced his premonition of death, had not been the beginning of this tragedy; that day, in retrospect, had marked only the beginning of the end. The true genesis of what they now confronted had been many years before.

Glynis glanced across the aisle at Cullen. She didn't know if he still believed what he thought he'd seen that day in Jacques's cabin. They had exchanged few words in the past weeks, and their encounters had been brief—as brief as a curt nod on Fall Street—as if the two of them were of remote acquaintance; as if they had experienced over the years simply a single, but unpleasant, encounter. Although one bitterly cold day she had tried to explain.

"Cullen, I'd like for us to talk."

"I'm working right now." This said with frosted breath as he watched skaters on the shallow frozen canal, plainly not wanting to look at her, and plainly not working at anything other than his own anger.

"But you need to hear what really happened that day," she'd persisted.

"Not now."

"When?"

"I don't know, Glynis."

But she had heard something catch in his voice, when he said her name, that made her grasp at hope. So she'd stood there shivering, rubbing her frigid hands together, waiting. He did condescend, finally, to look at her. But his face held such anger, and pain, that she flinched, hurrying away before tears could reveal her own unhappiness. She remained well aware that, while she hadn't done what Cullen tacitly accused her of doing, she'd been more than a little tempted. And this guilty knowledge kept her from yielding to anger of her own.

She'd been staring at her hands clenched in her lap, and now looked up to see Merrycoyf trudging back to the defense table, where Jacques sat silently, facing the judge's bench. The lawyer's opening had been short indeed.

Yet Merrycoyf had done all within his power to stall the opening week of the trial. In this he had succeeded, as it was now Friday. They would need the weekend recess, he'd said, to weigh the testimony of the prosecutor's opening witnesses; when Polk submitted the names of those he intended to call, Merrycoyf had expressed concern. Most jarring had been the prosecution's subpoena received by Dr. Quentin Ives. And now they must simply wait and see.

Because Jacques would not help them.

Glynis just had turned to rearrange her mantle when Adam MacAlistair came up the aisle. He went to the defense table and said something behind his hand to Merrycoyf before he seated himself to the other side of Jacques; Merrycoyf looked disturbed.

Judge Heath cleared his throat, poured from a carafe into a cup what looked to be tea, and said, "The prosecution may call its first witness."

Mr. Polk rose from his chair. "Yes, Your Honor. The prosecution calls Cullen Stuart."

Cullen moved into and up the center aisle without a glance at Glynis. The women in the courtroom sat a little straighter and watched from the corners of their eyes as he strode past them; several even gave their hair a quick pat. Cullen, however, looked neither right nor left. Nor did he look at Jacques after he'd reached the witness chair.

While he was being sworn, Glynis noticed dark smudges under his eyes, and again marked the deepening lines around his mouth. He also seemed pale. Since most of the time Cullen looked uncommonly healthy, the paleness worried her. But she knew she looked a little peaked herself, and a small spark of anger flared when she wondered if he, like her, had had trouble sleeping. She rather hoped so. And instantly felt ashamed.

Judge Heath leaned forward over the bench, his wintry eyes watching Cullen with interest. Glynis supposed the judge must know that Jacques had once been Cullen's deputy.

"State your name and your place of residence for the record, please," said the court clerk.

"Cullen Stuart, constable of the village of Seneca Falls, Seneca County, New York." He appeared at ease in the witness chair, and if he was at all troubled, he didn't display it. Orrin Polk stepped forward, not missing the opportunity for an ingratiating smile at the jury. "Constable Stuart, would you tell the court how long you have been a law-enforcement officer?"

"Sixteen years, more or less."

"Continuously?"

"Yes, except for several months in '54."

"And what did you do during those months, Constable?"

"I was employed by Pinkerton's Detective Agency."

"Ah, yes, Pinkerton's. In that case, I think we can safely assume that you are experienced in law enforcement. And what was your education?"

"Four years of college, and one year of law school."

Glynis caught Adam MacAlistair's surprised look. He wouldn't know that Cullen had hated law school, and had left mostly because he'd discovered he might be compelled to represent the guilty as well

as the innocent. He'd concluded that he preferred putting them in jail to getting them out.

Glynis stole a glance back at Neva Cardoza; Abraham Levy had arrived and now sat beside her, and Neva no longer looked quite as angry. Although that was probably subject to change, depending on what the judge had decided about her future testimony.

Polk restated at length Cullen's expertise in law enforcement—as if there were some question, Glynis thought in irritation.

"Constable Stuart," Polk at last began, "how long have you known the defendant, Jacques Sundown?" He pronounced it "Jacks Sundown," hissing the *s*'s like an irritated snake.

"Around ten years, on and off."

"On and off?"

"Jacques would leave town every so often—for extended periods."

"I see—yes, I see," Polk said as if giving this statement weighty consideration. "And what was your association with the defendant?"

"He was my deputy for some of that time."

"Your deputy. So he worked for you?"

"Yes."

"Constable Stuart, did you have any contact with the defendant other than your work affiliation? Did you, for instance, spend time together when you were both off duty?"

"In a small town, Mr. Polk, a constable is never off duty."

Glynis heard a few chuckles, and saw several members of the jury smile. But why was Polk going on about this at such length?

"So you had close contact with the defendant?"

Cullen seemed to be considering his answer overly long, before he said, "I don't know if I'd call it close. Jacques Sundown's not an easy man to know. He tends to avoid contact."

Glynis saw Adam glance at Merrycoyf, who shook his head slightly. She thought the young lawyer probably wanted to object to Polk's leading questions, but she didn't think Merrycoyf would, not without serious cause. A lot of niggling objections could provoke the jury, and Merrycoyf could safely assume, because he'd dealt with Polk before, that breaches of conduct would get even worse later on. She almost could see him sending Adam the message: Save the objections until they count.

"Tends to avoid contact," Polk echoed loudly. "I see. Would you, then, characterize the defendant as a taciturn man, Constable?"

"Yes."

"A solitary individual—a lone wolf, so to speak?"

"Yes."

"Please, Your Honor," Merrycoyf now said, "while I have great respect for Constable Stuart's judgment, he has already stated that he didn't socialize with Mr. Sundown. So why is he being asked to describe anything about my client other than his deputy's professional conduct?"

Judge Heath gave a brief nod. "Yes, Mr. Polk, I fail to see where your questions are leading. Please move along."

Polk snapped out his next question. "Constable Stuart, would you describe *your deputy* as an aggressive man?"

Adam MacAlistair twitched in his chair, staring pointedly at Merrycoyf. Again the older attorney shook his head.

"Aggressive? Yes, I'd say Sundown could be aggressive," Cullen agreed.

"Would you give us an example of this character trait?" Polk asked.

"Well," Cullen answered, "I've seen him attack in situations where most men would back off. Given the opportunity, Sundown would always put himself in an offensive position rather than a defensive one. But maybe," Cullen added unexpectedly, "that just means he has more courage than most men."

Jacques's shoulders stiffened imperceptibly; if Glynis hadn't been watching for his reaction, she never would have seen it. And Adam received a smile from Merrycoyf. Glynis imagined what he was thinking: You see, young man—give Mr. Prosecutor Polk enough rope and he'll hang himself.

As if to keep Cullen from further gratuitous speculation, Polk hurried on. "Do you recall, Constable, the defendant being present at the scene of several recent murders?"

"Objection!" Merrycoyf was on his feet. Adam MacAlistair wore a stunned expression, and was staring at Polk in disbelief.

"Your Honor," Merrycoyf said, "Your Honor, I object to the prosecutor's tactic most strenuously. He is attempting to inflame the jury. My client is not on trial for *several* murders!"

"Your Honor," Polk jumped in, before Judge Heath could speak, "I

am simply laying the groundwork here. I intend to connect these murders by means of motive."

"I object!" Merrycoyf stood, bending forward, the fingers of his hands pressing the table. "Your Honor, there is no foundation for the prosecutor to use the word *murder*. Cause of death has not been established, and my learned colleague knows it!"

"Yes, Mr. Polk," Judge Heath said, frowning. "Mr. Merrycoyf's objection to the word *murder* is well taken. I sustain his objection. But I will allow the prosecution some latitude if you intend to establish motive here."

"Your Honor—" Merrycoyf began, but the judge cut him off with, "Proceed, Mr. Polk."

Polk nodded and smiled appreciatively. "Constable Stuart, did you arrive at the scene of the . . . the untimely death of the man Jake Braun?"

"Yes, his body was still warm when I found him."

"Describe the scene, please."

"I got to Braun's house in the early morning. Inside, the victim was lying on the kitchen floor, not breathing. I found no heartbeat. I heard a horse out back, and when I went to the door, I saw Sundown riding off. Fast. I went after him on my own horse. Had to chase him—"

"Objection," Merrycoyf said. "The word *chase* is subjective and prejudicial. How does the witness know that my client was fleeing? He doesn't."

"Would you rephrase that, Constable Stuart?" the judge said.

Cullen looked vaguely annoyed, Glynis thought, before he said, "I *followed* Jacques Sundown to the edge of Black Brook Reservation before he pulled up."

"And did you ask him how he happened to be at the scene of a mur—of an untimely death?" Polk said.

Merrycoyf glared at him.

Cullen said, "I asked him. He said he was exercising his horse."

"And did you believe him?"

"No," Cullen said. "No, I didn't."

"Why is that?"

"Jake Braun's place is pretty remote. You have to know where it is to find it. And since it's not on the main road, or on the way to anywhere else, it's not easy to just stumble on it—exercising your horse,

for instance. Then there was Braun's attitude. He'd been sure he was being hunted. Insisted he was."

"Being hunted," Polk repeated unnecessarily. "You mean, Constable, that Mr. Braun knew he would be murdered—"

"Objection." Merrycoyf interrupted, adopting a we've-been-through-this-before expression.

"Mr. Polk," said Judge Heath, "I've admonished you about that once. Objection sustained."

"Yes, Your Honor," said Polk, not at all bothered, Glynis observed, since the damage, as far as the jury was concerned, had already been done.

"Constable Stuart," Polk went on, "did Jake Braun tell you *why* he felt endangered?"

"No. Wouldn't talk at all about why. He did make some comments to the effect that others had recently died. And he was genuinely terrified of something, I'll swear to that."

"Very good, Constable. I'm certain the court is quite willing to take your word for it. Now then, I'd like to ask you about another untimely death—that of one Mead Miller. Did you have the opportunity to locate Mr. Miller's body?"

"Yes. It was along Black Brook, about a mile out of town."

"Would you tell the court what you observed about Mead Miller prior to his demise?"

"On what turned out to be the night of his death, I saw Miller at a tavern, drunk and disorderly. He was obviously agitated, and he was thrown out of the tavern for fighting."

"Did you see him after that?"

"The next time I saw him, he was dead."

"And, Constable, did you become aware sometime later that the defendant had been at or near the vicinity of Miller's death?"

"Objection," Merrycoyf said. "Hearsay."

"Overruled," Judge Heath snapped. "The witness can certainly testify as to what he became aware of."

"Do you recall the question, Constable Stuart?"

"Yes. Jacques Sundown appeared at the time Miller's body was first discovered. Miss Glynis Tryon, who found the body, told me—"

"Objection!" Merrycoyf growled. "That is hearsay, Your Honor."

"Sustained." Judge Heath leaned over his bench. "Mr. Polk, that is rank hearsay."

"Yes, Your Honor," Polk said, sounding not in the least chastened, Glynis observed. She herself wanted to crawl under the chair. Both Polk and Cullen knew very well that Cullen couldn't testify to what someone had told him. To what were they leading?

"Constable, some days before the untimely death of Mead Miller, was there yet another untimely death in your village?"

"Objection!" Merrycoyf said firmly. "Immaterial and irrelevant."

"I will establish this as part of the pattern providing motive, Your Honor," said Polk.

"Objection overruled," said Judge Heath.

As the judge spoke, Glynis could see both Adam and Merrycoyf furiously making notes on their pads. Merrycoyf had said that the judicial rulings regarding testimony on previous deaths would be crucial. He had hoped against hope that the judge wouldn't allow them. An unavailing hope, it now seemed.

Polk cleared his throat dramatically. "Do you recall the question, Constable Stuart, regarding another death—*untimely,* of course?"

"Yes. Man's name was Jack Turner. His body was brought into town by his wife and some neighbors."

"And did you have some pertinent contact with the victim, Mr. Turner, before his death?"

Merrycoyf scowled but didn't object.

"The day before Jack Turner's death, he stopped me on Fall Street, insisting he was going to be killed."

"Did he say by whom?"

"No, he refused to say."

"I see. Now, then, would you please tell the court, Constable Stuart, if, some years ago, you were at the scene of a fatal fire at what was known as the Flannery farm?"

Glynis bit her lower lip. They were going to tie that fire in, she knew it. And she was the one who'd suggested to Cullen that there *was* a connection.

"Yes. I was there. Two men were killed in the fire—Cole Flannery and Dick Davis, a hired hand."

"When was the fire?"

"In '52."

"Did you observe anything at the scene that looked out of the ordinary, Constable Stuart?"

For a moment it appeared to Glynis that Merrycoyf would object. But he held his peace, although he seemed disturbed.

"The two men's bodies were found next to the barn door, as if they'd been trying to get out. But the door had been bolted from the outside."

"Did you inquire as to how this might have occurred?"

"Yes, but no one there, fighting the fire, came forward to say anything. I decided at the time that someone had done it by mistake during the initial confusion."

"And do you still think that was the case, Constable?"

"I don't know. I think it's possible that the fire was set, and the two men deliberately locked inside."

"Objection," Merrycoyf called. "That's pure conjecture on the witness's part."

"Yes, I'll sustain that objection," the judge said. "The jury is ordered to disregard the last statement."

"Tell me, Constable Stuart," Polk asked, "was there anyone else in the Flannery family at the farm that night?"

"No. Cole's wife had taken their children to visit relatives in Syracuse. Seems it was only the second time she'd ever been off the farm overnight without her husband."

"Your Honor," Merrycoyf complained, "I must object again to this immaterial and irrelevant line of questioning. We have gotten very far afield, here. Does the prosecutor really intend to question the constable about every death that's ever taken place in Seneca Falls?"

"If I have to—" Polk began. But he was interrupted by Judge Heath.

"Mr. Polk, I said I would allow you some latitude. But do you intend to connect this testimony to the matter at hand before this court?"

"Yes, Your Honor. As stated earlier, I intend to establish a pattern that will clearly demonstrate the motive for the crime of murder!"

Polk fairly shouted the word *murder.*

Adam sprang to his feet; he looked over Jacques's head at Merrycoyf and received a curt shake of the older lawyer's head.

Adam sat back down as Merrycoyf said sharply, "Your Honor, the prosecutor is clearly attempting to prejudice the jury with inflammatory assertions that have nothing to do with the case at hand. I cannot object strongly enough to this tactic. And I am shocked that the learned prosecutor would stoop to this chicanery."

"Your Honor," Polk protested, "I am merely establishing a foundation for the crime we are now prosecuting."

"Then I suggest you get on with it, Mr. Polk," Judge Heath said. He took a swallow from his teacup, and set it down with an emphatic *clunk*.

Polk walked to the witness chair to stand beside Cullen. "Constable Stuart, have you had occasion to go to the defendant's residence?"

"Yes."

"Describe where it is located, if you please."

"It's an isolated cabin on the southeastern edge of Black Brook Reservation. Backs up to the woods."

"Isolated, you say?"

"Yes."

"And is there a woodpile near the cabin?"

"Yes, a short distance behind it."

"Now, Constable, please tell the court for what purpose you went to the defendant's isolated cabin."

Cullen's jaw tightened, which Glynis recognized in him as proof positive of strain. Not that he looked as strained as she undoubtedly did. "The day after last month's severe storm," he began, "when I returned from a trip to Rochester, I was told by . . ."

Cullen paused, obviously anticipating Merrycoyf's objection, and quickly corrected himself by saying, "That is, I *became aware* that a horse, rented by Miss Glynis Tryon a few hours before the storm hit, had returned alone, and without a carriage, to the livery. Since no one, including her landlady, had seen Miss Tryon after that time, I assumed she'd been caught in the storm. I went in search of her."

Glynis had the distressing sense that every head in the courtroom was swiveling toward her, and again wished she could crawl under her chair. But she gripped her hands anxiously in her lap and stared straight ahead, praying for some semblance of dignity, and hoping she didn't look as flushed as she felt. Moreover, she had still worse to fear from Cullen's testimony.

She wondered, though, why in his search he would have headed north. Then she realized that the livery owner, John Boone, probably had seen her turn onto Black Brook Road. Going toward the reservation!

". . . and alongside the road," Cullen now was saying, "I found the carriage badly smashed. And some yards away I found a glove that I knew belonged to Miss Tryon."

Yes, he certainly would know it was hers; Cullen had given her those fur-lined gloves the previous Christmas.

"The carriage and glove," Cullen went on, "were about a quarter-mile from the Grimm farm. But when I stopped at the Grimms', no one there had seen her, so I went on north. I thought, if Miss Tryon was on foot, she might . . . she might have become disoriented in the storm. And ended up at the reservation."

Had Cullen *really* believed that? Or had he, right from the start, guessed she had gone to see Jacques? Glynis swallowed with difficulty; this was the part of his testimony she had been dreading the most. She had no way of knowing if Cullen, angry as he was with her, would try to protect her reputation. Whether he would actually testify that she'd been with Jacques. Unless Cullen had told Orrin Polk, no one else knew—no one but Merrycoyf. And she'd been told by Jeremiah that if he had to—to provide Jacques with an alibi—he'd compromise her in a second. But he'd vowed to avoid it if he could.

And so she just had to suffer the waiting.

But not for long, as Orrin Polk now asked, "To relieve our concern, Constable Stuart, did you locate the missing lady?"

Glynis wanted to duck her head, but before she could, Cullen's eyes found her. She forced herself to lift her chin and meet his gaze, and even hold it for an interminable moment.

Cullen's eyes swung back to Polk. "Yes," he said. "She'd found shelter, and she was . . . she was all right."

Glynis slowly let out her breath, and looked at Cullen with what she hoped conveyed gratitude. But his face had turned toward the jury.

"Well, splendid," Polk said, smiling. But then, in a flash, his expression transformed to something less pleasant. "Did you also then find the defendant's cabin?"

"Yes," Cullen said, now turning to look for the first time at Jacques.

"Tell the court what you found there."

Cullen's eyes narrowed, and he continued to stare at Jacques, while he said, "I saw some tracks—they looked as if they'd come out of the trees and led to the woodpile. When I went to check, back of the woodpile, I found the body of Lily Braun. It was partially covered with snow. There was a knife in her chest."

The courtroom had become very still. Though all must have been aware of what was to come, they waited with breathless attention.

"Constable Stuart, did you recognize the knife?"

"Yes. The blade was buried in the victim's chest, but the handle was visible. It was of bone, and distinctively carved."

"How?"

"With the head of a wolf."

"And had you seen this carved handle before?"

"Many times."

"And to whom did this vicious weapon belong, Constable?"

"To Jacques Sundown."

Polk waited until, after a collective intake of breath, the spectators had quieted before he said briskly, "Thank you, Constable Stuart. I have no further questions of this witness, Your Honor."

"Mr. Merrycoyf," Judge Heath said, "do you wish to cross-examine the witness?"

Glynis knew Merrycoyf would be assessing the damage. And would only question Cullen if he could be certain to blunt the previous testimony. Otherwise he would pass, not wanting to emphasize the harm already done.

"Yes, Your Honor," Merrycoyf said amiably, "I have just a few questions." Judge Heath motioned him to proceed. Merrycoyf remained seated while he said, "Constable Stuart, you mentioned some tracks behind Mr. Sundown's cabin. Did you follow those tracks to ascertain from where they came?"

"Couldn't follow them," Cullen said. "The snow had drifted over them by that time, and they were covered except for the few that went, as I said, to the woodpile."

"So those tracks might have originated anywhere, correct?"

Cullen shrugged. "I don't know where they came from, if that's what you mean, Jeremi—Mr. Merrycoyf."

"No, you couldn't know, my friend. Just one more question. My

learned colleague, Mr. Polk, has led you to describe Mr. Sundown's character as—"

"Your Honor," Polk interrupted, "if counsel for the defense had a complaint, he should have voiced his objection earlier."

Judge Heath peered down at Polk and said, "I don't hear counsel complaining now, Mr. Prosecutor. And let us please keep this sniping to a minimum, gentlemen. Proceed, Mr. Merrycoyf."

"Thank you, Your Honor. Constable Stuart, you described your deputy, the defendant, as aggressive. Had you ever seen Mr. Sundown behave aggressively toward a nonaggressive person? Someone not able to defend himself?"

Glynis recalled what Cullen had told her about the night he first met Jacques; she hoped Cullen remembered it. If he did, she knew he wouldn't lie about it. He didn't lie.

"No," Cullen said. "No, I never saw Sundown do that."

"Ever see him attack a woman?"

"Never."

"Thank you, Constable. No further questions."

"Your Honor," Orrin Polk said suddenly, "May I have leave to ask one last question on redirect?"

Judge Heath scowled, but said "Yes."

"Constable Stuart," Polk asked, "would you tell the court whether there have been any more untimely deaths, any at all, *since* the defendant has been incarcerated?"

"No."

"Thank you very much, Constable Stuart."

As Cullen left the witness chair, Judge Heath said, "Mr. Prosecutor, do you anticipate a lengthy examination of your next witness?"

"Oh, yes, sir, I do," Polk replied; the enthusiasm with which he said this, Glynis found alarming.

"In that case, we will recess one hour for mealtime. Court adjourned."

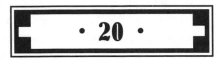

• 20 •

For ache of womb [stomach] of man or woman that hath eaten venom. Take green rue and wash it, and temper it with wine, and give to drink.

—A Leechbook or Collection of Medical Recipes of the Fifteenth Century

Glynis went down the courthouse stairs and into a small room off the entrance lobby. Merrycoyf and Adam MacAlistair had located chairs and seated themselves around a small table, as had Neva and Abraham Levy, and they'd begun eating whatever cold lunch they had brought from home. They did not present a cheerful picture.

The smell of coffee wafted in from somewhere. "I'll go find it," offered Adam, with what Glynis had begun to believe was inexhaustible vitality. Merrycoyf watched his young colleague bound out the door, and expelled a heavy sigh. He chewed slowly, not seeming to pay much attention to his food, which Glynis knew to be a very bad omen. Finally he turned to Neva, who'd been looking pointedly at him since Glynis arrived. And Merrycoyf sighed again.

"Does that sigh mean what I think it means?" Neva questioned him, anger poised in her tone.

"Yes, Dr. Cardoza, I'm afraid so. Judge Heath ruled that you cannot testify in the capacity of an expert witness."

"The wretched bastard!" Neva erupted, bringing a strangled sound from Abraham, and a long look over his spectacles from Merrycoyf. Adam had just come back through the door with several mugs of coffee, which, following Neva's outburst, sloshed alarmingly.

"I suppose I shouldn't bother to ask why," Neva added sharply, ignoring Adam's rueful inspection of a stained shirt cuff.

"No, probably not," Merrycoyf agreed.

"Well, *I* will," Glynis said, blotting the coffee on Adam's cuff with his handkerchief. "I take it Judge Heath has denied that Neva is a qualified doctor—because she's a woman?"

"Why else?" Neva snapped.

Merrycoyf sighed again. "We really don't have time to address the issue now," he said. "I intend to ponder it later, as this ruling could be to our advantage." Neva's head came up at this, as did Glynis's. "But frankly, young woman"—he peered at Neva—"it is not the most serious of our immediate troubles."

Neva's lips pressed tightly together, and Glynis expected to see steam pour from her ears. And she didn't blame Neva. But Jeremiah was right; there was no time now for this. She turned to Adam and asked, "Why did you go to the telegraph office earlier this morning—to send a wire to whom?"

Adam answered, "To Dr. Patrick Kelly in Rochester. Let's hope he can get here by Monday." He said to Merrycoyf, "Do you think he'll complete his case today? The ferret-face, I mean?"

Merrycoyf jerked erect in his chair. "Mr. MacAlistair!" he said sternly. "Please never let me hear you speak of a colleague in such a disparaging manner. Mr. Polk has had a notable career"—noted for what, Glynis observed, Jeremiah didn't say—"and he deserves respect whether you agree with his approach or not. Do I make myself clear?"

Adam nodded readily enough, but Glynis saw his mouth twitching, as was her own and Abraham's. Neva, however, still looked irate.

"Insofar as your question, young man," Merrycoyf went on, if somewhat less sternly, "it all depends. If things proceed as depressingly apace as they did this morning, I'd imagine Mr. Polk will rest his case today."

All of them were silent. There would be so little time to act.

Mr. Polk," Judge Heath directed, "call your next witness."

"The prosecution calls Dr. Quentin Ives."

As Ives came forward to be sworn, carrying a number of file folders, Glynis glanced back at Neva, who shook her head and mouthed, "No."

Glynis nodded with relief and turned to face the bench. Either Quentin Ives hadn't said anything to Neva, or hadn't yet discovered that his files had been rifled. Two nights before, after the subpoena had arrived, and while the Ives family had slept upstairs, she and Neva had crept with lighted candles into Quentin's small downstairs office. They worked as fast as they could by candlelight, not wanting to risk the brighter glow of lanterns. It took half the night to find the files for which they searched. They had had to go through patient records that went back ten years.

Not that their findings would do Jacques much good, but at least the defense would be spared the shock that this afternoon's testimony would undoubtedly bring. She and Neva hadn't told Merrycoyf how they had come by their ill-gotten information. And Merrycoyf, pragmatic soul that he was, hadn't asked. But Glynis suspected that he guessed and probably Adam did, too.

Quentin Ives was just now finishing his qualifications, and Merrycoyf had slumped in his chair as if asleep. Glynis knew better, but Adam, glancing over at him repeatedly, looked concerned.

"Dr. Ives," Polk began, "did you conduct an autopsy on the deceased Jack Turner?"

"Yes."

"Objection, Your Honor," Merrycoyf rumbled. Adam looked relieved. "Same objection of irrelevance and immateriality as previously made."

"Overruled, Mr. Merrycoyf," said Judge Heath. "Same ruling as previously made, subject to prosecutor's establishing motive. Continue, Mr. Polk."

"Dr. Ives, would you tell the court what you found?"

"We found Jack Turner's death to be a result of arsenic poisoning. By 'we,' " Quentin Ives turned to the jury, "I mean Dr. Neva Cardoza and myself."

Bless Quentin for that. Glynis imagined Neva was grateful, even though Judge Heath and Polk would ignore her participation. The physician now recited the medical findings on which they had based their conclusions about Turner's death.

"Did you also, Dr. Ives, conduct an autopsy on the deceased Mead Miller?" Polk asked.

"Yes, again with Dr. Cardoza. Our findings indicated that he had died as a result of poisoning." Ives again described their process of discovery, giving Neva credit for suggesting rattlesnake venom.

"Did you make any conclusion about how this poison was delivered to the victim?" Polk said.

"Not conclusively."

"Given your professional experience, have you an opinion, Dr. Ives?"

"Objection!" Merrycoyf said perfunctorily, as if expecting it to be overruled. It was.

"A hole in the victim's neck indicated that it had been pierced with a pointed object."

"Such as an arrow, Dr. Ives?" Polk asked loudly.

"Probably something smaller."

"For instance?" Polk prodded.

"Your Honor, I object," Merrycoyf said. "The good doctor has just testified that he found inconclusive evidence—"

"I'll restate the question," Ives jumped in. "Dr. Ives, could the poison have been delivered by means of a dart?"

Quentin Ives hesitated. Then, reluctantly, he said, "It could have."

"Are you familiar, doctor, with the Iroquois weapons known as air-guns, sometimes called blowguns, that use—"

"Objection!" This time, Merrycoyf sounded angry. "The witness has not been established as an expert in weaponry. And let the record show that I restate my previous and continuing objection—a strenuous objection—to the prosecutor's repeated inclusion in this proceeding of immaterial and irrelevant deaths. My client is not being tried for those deaths, Your Honor."

"Mr. Polk," Judge Heath said irritably, "I expect you to show a connection shortly with that of the victim Lily Braun, sir. And I will sustain the defense's objection to your last question of this witness."

But again, Glynis thought, the damage had been done. The jury might be ordered to disregard the prosecutor's question, but how could they? Their eyes had all swept to Jacques when Orrin Polk mentioned Iroquois air-guns. It would surely stick in their minds.

"Moving on, Dr. Ives," said Polk. "Did you conduct an autopsy on the body of Jake Braun?"

"Yes, again with Dr. Cardoza."

"Yes, yes, doctor. And what did you discover to be the cause of death?"

"Actually, I didn't discover the cause of death," Ives answered quickly.

Polk hesitated, then wheeled around and went to his notes on the table. The spectators in the courtroom stirred restlessly, as if waking from a monotonous dream, Glynis thought, wondering how Polk would handle this. She looked back at Neva, who sent her a smug smile.

"Ah, yes, Dr. Ives," Polk said, returning to stand by the witness chair. "I see now that a tissue sample of Braun's was sent to Rochester—to a Dr. Patrick Kelly. Why was that?"

"It was Dr. Cardoza's idea. She felt that Braun's death might be the result of nicotine poisoning, owing to the odd yellow tinge of his facial skin. It was somewhat different from the jaundiced color associated with liver failure, but we didn't have the expertise or equipment to determine that. Dr. Cardoza knew that Dr. Kelly was considered an expert in that area."

Polk stroked his clean-shaven chin momentarily, then seemed to make some kind of decision, as he said, "Dr. Ives, this Miss Cardoza—"

"*Dr.* Cardoza," Quentin Ives corrected him.

"Yes, well, she's just some sort of trainee under your supervision, isn't she?"

"No, Dr. Cardoza already has a medical degree, Mr. Polk. She's now simply fulfilling a residency requirement before being admitted to the staff of a New York City hospital."

Glynis didn't dare look around at Neva, who must be rubbing her hands with glee over the pompous Polk's blunder.

But Judge Heath suddenly said, "Mr. Prosecutor, shall we move along? This discussion hardly seems relevant to the case at hand."

"Yes, Your Honor," said Polk, in the relieved voice of one who had been tossed a rope as he sank in quicksand. "Yes, certainly. Tell us, Dr. Ives, did this Dr. Kelly in Rochester send you a report on his findings?"

"Yes. He verified that the postmortem tissue sent by Dr. Cardoza

indicated that Braun's corpse did indeed exhibit signs of nicotine poisoning. And this would be consistent with Dr. Cardoza's observation of the discoloration of the victim's face."

"Meaning what?" Polk said, looking dubious.

"Meaning that the poison was applied to Braun's face. Very likely it was put in something as innocent-looking as shaving lather or soap."

"And that could have caused his death?"

"Absolutely."

Polk seemed to have regained his bearings, as he now asked, "How soon would death have occurred after the application of the nicotine?"

"It could have been quickly."

"*How* quickly? Dr. Ives. Give us your best estimate."

Quentin Ives clearly recognized what Polk was driving at, because he sounded reluctant when he answered, "Death could have occurred anywhere from five minutes to four hours afterward."

"Five minutes? You did say *five minutes,* Doctor?"

"Well, that's the lowest estimate that—"

"Yes, of course," Polk cut him off. "Thank you very much," he said with obvious satisfaction. "Now, Dr. Ives, can you tell us the findings of your autopsy on the poor woman, Lily Braun?"

"No, I can't."

"I beg your pardon, Doctor?"

"I can't tell you what I found, because I didn't conduct the autopsy. I had been called out of town. So Dr. Cardoza did—"

"Thank you, Doctor. I have a few last questions." Polk went to his table and picked up a sheet of paper, then returned to stand by the witness chair. "Dr. Ives, have you brought those files requested by me and pursuant to this court's subpoena?"

"Yes." Ives indicated the files on his lap.

"Fine." Polk glanced at the paper in his hands. "Now, Dr. Ives, did you sign a death certificate for one Otto Braun on the sixteenth of April, 1848?"

Ives opened a folder and shuffled through several papers.

Glynis glanced back at Neva, who shrugged and shook her head slightly. In their nocturnal search, they'd left the physician's own du-

plicate death certificate on top of the other papers in the folder labeled BRAUN, OTTO, Glynis was sure of it. Still, she exhaled with relief when Ives stopped shuffling the papers, and nodded at Polk.

"Yes," he said, staring at what Glynis knew to be his duplicate of Otto Braun's death certificate. "Yes, here it is, and the date is as you stated—April '48," he told Polk.

"How old was Otto Braun at his death?"

"It says here that he was forty-two."

"And what did you list as the cause of death, Doctor?"

"Cardiac failure."

"At the time, did you have any reservations about your conclusion, Dr. Ives? I ask this because the victim was brought to you after having just been in a terrible wagon accident—or I should say *perhaps* it was an accident."

"I really don't remember, it was so long ago," Ives said.

"Were you aware at the time, Doctor, that wheels of Braun's wagon had unaccountably fallen off, going down a steep grade? Or that this wagon's hand brake was later found to be broken? Do you remember?"

"Objection!" Merrycoyf said angrily. "Not only is this testimony irrelevant and totally immaterial, but the event in question took place almost ten years ago. Does the prosecutor really expect the good doctor to remember every death he attends?"

"Overruled," said Judge Heath. "The witness is capable of stating whether or not he remembers."

"I don't remember," Ives now said.

"From your records, was there any indication before his deadly *accident* that the victim's heart was weak?"

"Objection!" Merrycoyf had lunged to his feet. "Your Honor—"

"Sustained," said the judge.

"I'll rephrase that for you, Dr. Ives. Did Otto Braun have any history of heart trouble?"

"No, but that doesn't mean that—"

"Thank you," Polk cut him off. "Dr. Ives, were you aware that the Otto Braun in question was the father of Lily Braun?"

Merrycoyf looked about to object, but instead sank back silently in his chair.

"Yes," Ives answered, "I seem to remember that."

"And that the Jake Braun mentioned earlier in your testimony was the brother of Otto Braun and the uncle of Lily Braun?"

"Perhaps I knew that. I'm not sure I made the connection," Quentin Ives said, looking puzzled.

Glynis felt so warm, she was experiencing lightheadedness. Or it could be from the intensity of the prosecutor's attack, she thought miserably. She watched Polk go to his table and retrieve more papers. This was proving worse than they had feared. But it was not, thanks to the midnight foray, completely unexpected.

"To continue," said Polk, "do your records, Dr. Ives, indicate that you signed a death certificate for one George Jackson in June of 1854?"

Again Ives shuffled. "Yes, apparently I did," he responded, grasping a document. "But I don't recall this at all."

"How old was George Jackson when he died?"

Ives scanned the duplicate certificate. "Thirty-four."

"The cause of George Jackson's death?"

"I have here that it was due to liver failure," answered Ives. He glanced through the file.

"Did Jackson have a history of liver problems?"

"Apparently not. I really don't recall this."

"Did you perform an autopsy, Dr. Ives?"

"No. An autopsy isn't usually done—"

"But why did you conclude that the cause of death was liver failure?"

"Probably because he was jaundiced."

"Jaundiced. You mean yellowish? Yellowish like Jake Braun?"

"Objection, Your Honor," Merrycoyf said, exasperation in his voice.

"Sustained," Judge Heath ruled. "Mr. Polk, would you please conclude whatever it is you are leading to? And I assume you *are* leading to something?"

"Yes, Your Honor. One last death certificate, Dr. Ives—that of a Dooley Keegan, signed by you in October of 1855. Do you recall Mr. Keegan's death?"

"Yes, I do."

"The cause of death was cardiac failure?"

"That's what I wrote here," said Ives, looking unhappily at the document in his hand.

"And Keegan's age?"

"He was thirty-one."

"Only *thirty-one*? And did he have a history of heart—"

"No," Ives broke in.

"You seem quite definite about that, Doctor. Did you have some question about your diagnosis at the time?"

Ives hesitated and stared down at the open folder he held. "Well, yes," he said finally. "Thirty-one is a young age for death from heart problems. But it's not unheard of, certainly."

"But you felt it was, perhaps, suspicious?"

"Objection!" said Merrycoyf. "Leading the witness."

"Overruled," said Judge Heath. "Answer the question, Dr. Ives."

"I thought it was unusual, yes. Especially since Dooley Keegan had no history of any illness at all that I was aware of."

"Dr. Ives, in retrospect, do you find the deaths of the three relatively young and healthy men just discussed to be, shall we say, questionable?"

"Objection! Irrelevant and immaterial!" Merrycoyf protested.

"Overruled. The witness is directed to answer."

"Well," Ives said slowly, "I suppose that in retrospect it might seem that way. But the deaths were separated by years. And young men occasionally do die suddenly. At the time, I had no reason to believe that the deaths involved anything other than natural causes."

"But now, Dr. Ives?"

"Your Honor," Merrycoyf said firmly, "Dr. Ives has already answered the prosecutor's question, several times. I object strongly to this harassment of a witness."

"He's not even your witness!" Polk snarled.

"Gentlemen!" Judge Heath admonished. "I believe, Mr. Polk, that the doctor has answered to the best of his ability. Objection sustained."

"Thank you, Dr. Ives," Polk said. "I have no further questions of this witness, Your Honor."

Glynis saw Adam lean behind Jacques to confer momentarily with Merrycoyf. Merrycoyf nodded and then stood.

Judge Heath said, "Do you wish to cross-examine Dr. Ives?"

"Yes, just briefly," Merrycoyf said, going toward the witness chair. "Please tell us, Dr. Ives," he directed, "if you recently signed a death certificate for one Obadiah Grimm?"

"Yes, I did."

"What did you list as the cause of death?"

"Death was due to a punctured heart," Ives stated emphatically.

"No question about it?"

"No question."

"Did his death look suspicious, Dr. Ives?" Merrycoyf turned to glower at Polk as if daring him to object.

Polk seemed to be considering it, but said nothing.

"Yes, it looked odd," Ives said. "Dr. Cardoza seemed to think—"

"Objection! Hearsay and conjecture," Polk said.

"Sustained."

"What did *you* think, Doctor?"

"I thought Mr. Grimm impaled himself on a sharp object that punctured his heart."

"An accident?"

Ives hesitated. "I don't know," he said finally.

Polk was on his feet, probably ready to call this irrelevant, Glynis guessed, because Obadiah Grimm didn't fit into the pattern he was trying to establish.

In any event, Merrycoyf quickly said, "No more questions, Dr. Ives. Thank you."

As Quentin Ives went back to his seat, Glynis turned to look at Neva, who gave a sideways bob of her head. Glynis followed her gaze and was startled to see the sweet-voiced Seneca woman, Small Brown Bird, seated in the last row by the door. The woman's head was down, staring at her hands folded in her lap. Glynis supposed she shouldn't be surprised; after all, she remembered, Small Brown Bird was Jacques Sundown's aunt.

She turned back as Judge Heath said, "Mr. Polk, call your next witness."

"The prosecution calls Mr. Theobald Fedmore."

A tall, lanky man with thinning hair made his way up the aisle; under his arm he carried a bulging file folder. Glynis thought she recalled seeing him in court earlier, but couldn't identify him. She was afraid, though, that she knew what he did and why he was there.

"Your name and your residence?" the court clerk asked after the witness had been sworn.

"Theobald Fedmore, and I live in Waterloo."

"Mr. Fedmore," Polk began, "what is your occupation, sir?"

"I'm the Seneca County clerk."

"And as such, Mr. Fedmore, do your duties include maintenance of the civil litigation records for the Supreme Court of Seneca County?"

"Yes."

"Very good. Mr. Fedmore, at my request, and pursuant to a subpoena issued by this court, have you brought with you documents concerning the case of Many Horned Stag versus the following: Jake Braun, Otto Braun, Dick Davis, Cole Flannery, George Jackson, Dooley Keegan, Mead Miller, and Jack Turner?"

"Yes, I have them here." Theobald Fedmore indicated the file folder on his lap.

Polk asked now, "And who was counsel of record for the parties named?"

Mr. Fedmore must have just reviewed the case, Glynis decided, as he didn't even open the folder before he answered, "Jeremiah Merrycoyf for the plaintiff, Many Horned Stag, and Orrin Makepeace Polk for all the defendants named."

Glynis looked at Merrycoyf, who again appeared to be drowsing, but now had a small smile on his lips.

"Mr. Fedmore," continued Polk, "are you acquainted with the pleadings?"

"Yes, I have reviewed them."

"Fine. And what was the nature of the claims?"

"Plaintiff Many Horned Stag, for the benefit and in the right of the Seneca Indian Nation, sought an injunction to prohibit the defendants from constructing a dam on Black Brook. This dam, the plaintiff claimed, would reduce the flow of water to the Black Brook Reservation, which is situated on the brook itself."

"And what," Polk asked, "was the position of the defendants regarding this worthwhile project?"

Glynis frowned at Polk's puffery, but saw that Merrycoyf's smile had broadened.

"The position of the defendants was that they all had farms situ-

ated on or near Black Brook," Fedmore answered, himself beginning to smile ever so slightly.

Mr. Polk now turned toward the window to ask in an uncharacteristically quiet voice, "What was the disposition of the case?"

Fedmore answered, "Plaintiff Many Horned Stag for the Seneca Nation was granted injunctive relief prohibiting the damming of water under the protection of riparian rights."

Adam MacAlistair's face bloomed into a wide grin, while Merrycoyf just continued to smile and doze.

"Mr. Fedmore, was a judgment of injunction issued and served upon each of the eight defendants?" Polk asked, rather peevishly.

"Yes."

"As of what date was this done?"

"The nineteenth of September, 1847."

"Thank you, Mr. Fedmore. No further questions."

"Cross-examine, Mr. Merrycoyf?" asked the judge.

Merrycoyf opened his eyes and sat forward. "How long have you been a clerk in Seneca County, Mr. Fedmore?"

"Fifteen years."

"And during that time, sir, were other injunctions rendered on any of those eight defendants in Seneca County Supreme Court cases?"

"Objection," Polk said, frowning. "That's totally irrelevant."

"It's not in the least irrelevant, my dear Mr. Polk," snapped Merrycoyf unexpectedly. "Not if you intend to try to somehow prove my client guilty by connection with this dam project you've burdened us with today."

The prosecutor howled "Objection!" again and again over the noise of laughter. Judge Heath was compelled to bring his gavel down a number of times before quiet finally was restored. Even Mr. Fedmore, Glynis noticed, had allowed himself a chuckle.

"Mr. Merrycoyf," said Judge Heath harshly, "I warn you against making any further such prejudicial statements during this trial. Do I make myself clear?"

"Yes, Your Honor," said Merrycoyf cheerfully. "But will the court direct the witness to answer?"

"I have objected," Polk said irritably.

"Mr. Polk, you brought up this issue in direct examination," Judge Heath said. "Objection overruled."

"I don't suppose you remember the question at this point, Mr. Fedmore?" said Merrycoyf.

"Actually I do, Mr. Merrycoyf. And yes, there were some other issues that involved a few of the defendants previously named—issues concerning fences and property lines and the like."

"I see," Merrycoyf said. "And can you tell me, Mr. Fedmore, to the best of your knowledge, did any of those injunctions result in someone's death?"

Polk's face was mottled red, and Glynis could see he longed to object if he could but find grounds. Before he did, Mr. Fedmore answered, "No. Not to my knowledge."

"Thank you," said Merrycoyf. "I have one last question. Did landowner Obadiah Grimm, whose farm also bordered Black Brook, take any part in the dam injunction case discussed here?"

"Obadiah Grimm?" Mr. Fedmore repeated. "No. No, sir, his name does not appear anywhere in that record."

"Thank you again, Mr. Fedmore. No further questions."

Merrycoyf returned to his seat beside Jacques at the table, while Judge Heath bent forward over the bench to ask Orrin Polk, "Mr. Prosecutor, do you intend a lengthy examination of your next witness?"

"I can't say, Your Honor. Perhaps."

"In that case," said the judge bringing down his gavel, "we will take a short recess. Court will reconvene in fifteen minutes."

"All rise," the bailiff called as the judge left for his chambers.

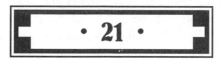

• 21 •

The present Iroquois, the descendants of that gifted race which formerly held under their jurisdiction the fairest portions of our Republic, now dwell within our limits as dependent nations, subject to the tutelage and supervision of the people who displaced their fathers.

—Lewis Henry Morgan, *League of the Ho-de-no-sau-nee, or Iroquois*

Glynis slipped into her mantle and made for the rear door. The courtroom had become oppressively hot, and even now the bailiff shoveled more coal into the stove. She inched past a clutch of people and headed for the stairs. When she reached the first-floor entrance, she saw a hand stretch over her shoulder to push open the door, and Adam MacAlistair's engaging grin followed her outside.

"Hot in there," Adam offered, his own overcoat unbuttoned.

"Like an oven," Glynis agreed. "This fresh air feels good—even if it's cold."

The snow-sprinkled square beyond the courthouse lay empty. Across it swept the long purple shadows of church spires as December's watery sun hung low in the southwestern sky. The darkest, dreariest month of the twelve, Glynis reflected, and she and everyone else should be at home, reading Dickens and preparing for Christmas.

"Do you think the jury sees yet what Polk is setting up?" Adam asked quietly.

"I don't know," Glynis answered. "It's hard to tell with juries—this one especially, because the men are all so unresponsive, or they seem to be. I'll admit I'm worried, though."

Adam nodded. "It doesn't look good." He had plainly lost his earlier exuberance.

"No, it doesn't," she conceded. "The worst thing is just sitting there, not able to do anything."

"Well, our client certainly hasn't helped. It's as if Sundown's been struck deaf, dumb, and blind. During the most damaging testimony, he didn't even blink."

"Just as he's been for the past weeks. And you know, Adam, we haven't any of us figured out why."

Adam frowned. "What is there to figure out? He won't talk."

"But *why* won't he?"

"I assume it's some Iroquois ritual of silence. After all, this whole week you've heard those Indians insisting Sundown shouldn't be in a white man's court to begin with. Lord help us if he's found guilty—"

"*If,* Adam!" Glynis broke in. "You haven't given up?"

He looked off at the gathering twilight. "I don't want to. But despite the fact that I dislike the prosecutor, he's doing a decent job, old ferret-face is."

He grinned, and Glynis forced a halfhearted smile. "But we still don't know the most crucial thing," she said. "If Jacques didn't kill Lily Braun, then who did?"

"Any ideas?"

Glynis sighed. "A few. And I keep thinking there's something obvious that we've missed, something right in front of us. Every so often, I feel a tug at my memory confirming it. Have you ever had that happen?"

"Yes, all the time during law school exams."

Glynis laughed. How young he was. And he did lift her spirits. *Spirits!* "You know, Adam, what we need is a seance."

Adam wrinkled his nose as if he'd smelled something unpleasant. "A seance?"

"Yes, we could raise Lily Braun's spirit and ask who killed her . . ." Glynis stopped. Her memory had again thrust something almost to the surface. But it slipped away. She shook her head in frustration.

Adam pulled a watch from his waistcoat. "Time to go in, I'd think." As they went through the door to the lobby, he asked her, "Have you ever been to a seance?"

"No. But my neighbor, Vanessa Usher, has become deeply involved with the spirit world. There's a seance held at her house every

week, I'm told, and these sessions include, unfortunately, Lazarus Grimm and young Pippa."

"I've met Lazarus Grimm," Adam said, "but who's Pippa?"

They began climbing the stairs with others heading toward the courtroom, and Glynis answered him over her shoulder. "Pippa is Molly Grimm's daughter."

"Molly Grimm?" Adam said, sounding puzzled.

"Yes, she's Lazarus's sister."

Adam paused on the top step. "But that's not possible," he said.

By the time Glynis and Adam hurried to their seats, Judge Heath was already seated on the bench, and Merrycoyf's annoyed gaze swept the room. He gave Adam MacAlistair a fierce scowl as the young man hurled himself into his chair.

Judge Heath glowered down at the defense table before he said, "Mr. Polk, call your next witness."

"The prosecution calls Sara Turner."

Glynis felt great sympathy for Sara Turner as she came slowly up the aisle, the poor woman—hadn't she had enough hardship without this? But Sara didn't look quite as frail as she had previously. She seemed to have gained some weight, and her face no longer looked cadaverous, nor did it have bruises. But she still held one wrist at an awkward angle. Her other arm cradled an old, dog-eared Bible.

As she sat down in the witness chair, Sara plucked at the seams of her flowered cotton dress; it was not what most women would have worn on a cold winter day. Not if they had the choice. Perhaps Jack Turner hadn't left much money after all.

This made her think of Cullen, and while Sara gave her name and address, Glynis took a quick look across the aisle to the row where he'd been seated. He wasn't there. Glynis found him standing under the windows, watching the Seneca and Cayuga men, although they didn't seem to have shifted since the trial began.

Her gaze returned to Sara Turner as Polk walked up to the woman and asked his first question. "Mrs. Turner, did you hear the testimony of Dr. Quentin Ives concerning your husband's unfortunate and untimely death?"

"Yes."

"And did you hear Mr. Fedmore, the Seneca County clerk, testify?"

"Yes."

"Now, I must ask you some questions, Mrs. Turner, but before I do so, I want to extend my sympathy to you for your untimely loss."

"Then why'd you make me come here?" Sara said softly.

"Because we must find the truth," Polk explained condescendingly, as if Sara were a child. "But I apologize for intruding on your grief."

"Weren't no grief," Sara Turner replied harshly.

Polk looked startled. "I beg your pardon, Mrs. Turner?"

A pin could have been heard to drop in the courtroom as Sara Turner repeated, "It weren't no grief."

"Ah, well . . . I see . . . I see," Polk stammered, looking very much as if he didn't. But he recovered admirably fast. "Well, in that case, Mrs. Turner, we'll just proceed forthwith. Yes. Now then, did you hear the names Mr. Fedmore gave during his testimony—the names of the defendants in the action involving the Black Brook dam?"

"I heard."

"Were the names familiar to you?"

"I knew 'em."

"You knew these men—they were your neighbors and friends, were they not?"

"Not mine, they wasn't. They was *his* friends."

"Your late husband's?"

"Yes."

"Now, Mrs. Turner, please think carefully. Do you know of any subsequent events—that is, any other things—that involved those eight men and the Indian man called Many Horned Stag."

Sara Turner appeared to shrink in the witness chair. It reminded Glynis of when she herself had questioned Sara in the Iveses' kitchen, and the woman had all but disappeared, as if she were but someone else's shadow.

"Yes. I know," she said in a whispered voice.

"Could the witness speak louder?" requested the court clerk.

"I know!" repeated Sara, without more prompting.

Polk took several steps backward. "Ah, yes. Mrs. Turner, would you tell the jury how you know of this subsequent event? For instance, did your husband tell you?"

"He told me nothin'. I followed them's how I know."

Glynis felt a chill shoot down her spine. She looked at Merrycoyf. He, and Adam too, sat perfectly still, attention riveted on Sara Turner. The jury, who couldn't know what was coming, looked mildly interested. And Jacques Sundown stared straight ahead.

"You say you followed them, Mrs. Turner. Can you tell us what happened to make you follow these men?"

Sara looked at Polk, then shook her head.

"Mrs. Turner," Judge Heath said in a surprisingly benevolent tone, "you must answer the prosecutor's question."

Sara's eyes darted around the courtroom. She was truly frightened, Glynis believed; no doubt she had lived with this fear for ten years.

"Mrs. Turner," Polk said, "do you remember telling Constable Stuart about this several weeks ago?"

Sara nodded slowly.

"Please tell the court what you told Constable Stuart."

Glynis looked back at Cullen. He was watching Sara Turner, and his face expressed real concern. He moved up the aisle toward the front of the room, nodding at the small woman in the witness chair.

Sara had obviously seen Cullen, because she nodded back at him and took a deep breath, then said, "I couldn't never talk about this before. Not while's he was alive, I couldn't."

"Your husband, Mrs. Turner?" said Polk.

"Yes."

"What made you follow the men?" Polk repeated.

"He comes to the door, that Otto Braun does, and tells him—"

"Tells your husband?"

"Yes, him—Otto Braun tells him to get his horse and come with them all. He says they're gonna get them that Indian. Because he raped his daughter . . . Braun's daughter."

"Who was 'them,' Mrs. Turner?" asked Polk.

"*Them!* The ones you named."

"All the men I named earlier, were they *all* there?"

Sara nodded.

"Let the record show," Polk said, "that the witness has identified the eight defendants in the Black Brook injunction proceeding, including her husband, Jack Turner."

Polk and Judge Heath both looked at Merrycoyf.

Not taking his eyes from Sara Turner, Merrycoyf said, "No objection."

"Where did the men go, Mrs. Turner?"

"They went to the reservation—must have done, 'cause I got a horse and rode up Black Brook Road after 'em, and then I seen 'em come across the brook with the Indian. I knowed somethin' bad was gonna happen. Just couldn't do nothin' to stop it."

Sara's hands had begun to shake; squirming on the chair, she tried to twist a handkerchief out of her dress pocket. Mr. Polk stepped forward and handed her a large white square from his own pocket. Sara took it and rubbed it across her eyes.

The courtroom was silent, motionless, as if all were framed in a daguerreotype. Glynis, too, couldn't take her eyes from Sara; she couldn't even begin to imagine what Jacques must be going through. And Small Brown Bird, she suddenly remembered. But she couldn't bring herself to look around.

Sara drew another deep breath. "Anyhows, they took that Indian into them woods . . . and they . . . and they strung him up."

It seemed to Glynis as if an eternity passed before Judge Heath brought down his gavel. It wasn't so much the noise—which was strangely muted—that needed attention, as the commotion of people moving in and out of the rear doors. When the rustling of skirts and clumping of boots ceased, Glynis turned around. The Iroquois hadn't moved. Neither had Small Brown Bird, who was still staring at her hands. Neva and Abraham, who, like Glynis, had known beforehand, hadn't left their seats. Otherwise, half the room had rearranged itself. A number of empty chairs had appeared. And there was a great deal of noise coming from outside the open door.

"Bailiff, make those people quiet down," Judge Heath ordered, "and close the door."

Glynis turned back to Sara Turner, aware of more rustling behind her as people apparently hurried back to their seats, while in the meantime, Sara hunched in the chair, clutching Polk's handkerchief over her face.

Glynis desperately wanted to go to Jacques, to say something to him—at the very least, to tell him how sorry she was. But of course she couldn't. How many in the courtroom, she wondered, knew that Many Horned Stag was Jacques's brother? Merrycoyf knew, but

hadn't until several days ago. It was Cullen who had told him—Cullen, who Merrycoyf said was more disturbed than he'd ever seen him before, and who related that for years there'd been rumors of a lynching near the reservation. But no body had been found, no proof offered, and no one had come forward with information.

Judge Heath now said shortly, "Continue, Mr. Polk."

"Mrs. Turner," said Polk, waiting until the handkerchief was lowered, "again I am sorry to have to ask you these questions. But there are just a few more. Did you actually see these men hang the Indian man?"

"No, not do it." Sara seemed to have composed herself; perhaps it was a relief to have it out after all these years.

Sara went on, "Man was already hangin' from a rope, time I got there. 'Cause I left the horse and went afoot till I found 'em. But I couldn't do nothin'. Nothin'."

"Then what did they do—the men, I mean?" Polk asked.

"They just goes ridin' off."

"Mrs. Turner, why haven't you come forward with this before?"

Sara Turner stared at Polk as if he were the stupidest man she'd ever laid eyes on. "You makin' a joke?" she asked.

"No, no, of course not," Polk assured her. "Were you afraid—afraid of your husband, for instance?"

"No 'for instance' about it! He said he'd kill me, I ever talked about what I seen. He'd a' done it, too. Sent my kids off, said they'd never come back if I talked about it. He sent 'em away!"

Sara, her hands trembling again, brought the handkerchief up to her face, her thin frame racked with silent anguish. How had Sara survived, married to a man like Jack Turner?

Glynis looked at Sara Turner, and thought of Jacques's mother, Bitter Root; it seemed as if women had forever grieved for their children. The Bible still tucked under Sara's arm made Glynis think again of the passage "Rachel weeping for her children." What Old Testament book was that from? A librarian should know; Obadiah Grimm would have known in an instant. Glynis drew in her breath and stared up at Sara Turner's Bible, and suddenly it came: Jeremiah. It was from the Book of Jeremiah.

Polk had cleared his throat, and now said, "Who else was at the scene of this . . . this hanging, Mrs. Turner?"

"There was a couple Indian squaws, and a boy." She jerked her head toward Jacques.

"Let the record show that the witness has identified—"

"Objection," Merrycoyf retorted. "The witness said 'a boy.' This dreadful event happened years ago—how could the witness know what that boy looks like now?"

"Sustained," Judge Heath said.

"Very well," said Polk with disturbing confidence. "Mrs. Turner, did your husband ever indicate that he feared for his life?"

"Yes. 'Specially after some of the others died."

"Ah, yes—after the others died. And did he say whom he was afraid of?"

"Well, he says more'n once, it must be that Sundown."

Glynis clenched her hands in her lap, thinking she might feel better if she could hate Sara Turner. But Sara was almost as much a victim in this as was Jacques.

"Just one more question, Mrs. Turner. Was there anyone else present at the scene of this tragedy? Other than those you've already mentioned?"

"Yes, there was. I seen her in the woods, watchin'."

"And who was that watching?"

"It was a girl. It was Lily Braun."

Glynis gasped in astonishment with the rest of the courtroom. Lily Braun? Why on earth had *she* been there? But then, abruptly, the memories that for days had eluded her rose to the surface of her mind. Glynis held them tightly. They might be the last hope for Jacques.

"Do you wish to cross-examine the witness?" Judge Heath asked Merrycoyf.

"No, Your Honor, no cross-examination."

Mr. Polk now approached the bench. "Your Honor, to save the inconvenience of subpoenaing the defendant's mother, who I understand is ill, I request the following: that I, as counsel for the People, and Mr. Merrycoyf, as counsel for the defense, do stipulate for the record that the Seneca man, Many Horned Stag, was the half brother of the defendant Jacques Sundown."

The courtroom reaction to this was as expected, and Glynis cringed as Judge Heath's gavel banged. But most of the jury members just leaned forward to look at Jacques: their expressions ranged from

surprised to indifferent to antagonistic, with one or two sympathetic glances. Glynis noted these last carefully.

Merrycoyf now answered Polk, "I so stipulate."

Judge Heath said to the clerk, "The stipulation is received and made part of the record. And now, Mr. Polk, do you have any idea how much more time you need to finish? It's late, and I would like to adjourn until Monday morning."

"Please, Your Honor. I have but one more witness, and the gentleman has traveled here under subpoena from Rochester. May we extend this session slightly so he won't need to return here?"

"Do you anticipate that your examination of this witness will be lengthy, Mr. Polk?"

"No sir, I do not."

"Very well, call your witness," directed Judge Heath, a trifle wearily, Glynis observed.

"The prosecution calls Mr. Lewis Henry Morgan."

Glynis twisted in her chair to watch Morgan stride briskly forward. She had met him several times in Rochester, and when he had traveled through Seneca Falls. As he passed her aisle chair, he nodded to her briefly before proceeding to the witness chair to be sworn.

Morgan did not appear to age; he must be close to forty, but an engaging boyish face, and a ready smile, made him look more like fourteen. Trained in corporate law, he'd made a fortune early in life by speculating in railroads and mining. Glynis knew enough about him to assume he did not want to be here. Not under these circumstances.

"Mr. Morgan, sir, we appreciate your taking time from your busy schedule to testify here," Polk said unctuously.

Morgan said nothing. Just sat there with his hands folded, studying Polk. Glynis noticed that Morgan already had taken a long look at Jacques.

"Mr. Morgan," Polk began, "you are the author, sir, of a work entitled *League of the Iroquois,* are you not?"

"Yes, but it's *League of the Ho-de-no-sau-nee, or Iroquois,*" Morgan gently corrected him. "The name Iroquois is a French invention, more or less."

"Yes, I see. Well, how long ago did you write this, Mr. Morgan?"

"Actually, I didn't write it alone. I collaborated with a Seneca man, Ely S. Parker, to whom the book is dedicated. And it was published six years ago, in '51."

"The book has been received with very great enthusiasm," Polk said, while Glynis watched Merrycoyf slouch in his chair and close his eyes, as if to disassociate himself from the prosecutor's obsequious behavior.

Polk spent no small amount of time extolling Morgan's professional and scholarly background, until at last even Judge Heath apparently had heard enough. He leaned over his bench to say, "Mr. Merrycoyf, would you be willing to stipulate that you accept Mr. Morgan's qualifications as an expert?"

"Oh, *yes,* Your Honor! Yes, indeed. Immediately."

A ripple went through the room, and Morgan himself grinned at Merrycoyf.

Polk shot Merrycoyf an annoyed look, then walked to his table, picked up Morgan's book, and opened it with a flourish to a bookmarked page. "Mr. Morgan, will you please identify the following passage for the court: 'To He'-no, he'—that is, the Great Spirit," Polk inserted, " '—committed the thunderbolt; at once the voice of admonition, and the instrument of vengeance.' " Polk stopped reading and waited for Morgan to answer.

"You want me to identify that, Mr. Polk?" Morgan smiled. "Well, I wrote it, if that's what you mean."

"That's what I mean," said Polk, looking unaccountably pleased with himself. "Now, sir, to what were you referring?"

Morgan stared at Polk for a moment. "That requires a fairly involved answer. How long do we have today?" He smiled again.

"Your Honor," said Merrycoyf, "while it is pleasant to hear the prosecutor's mellifluous voice, I am still waiting, as I'm sure everyone else is, to discover *why* the prosecution has called Mr. Morgan here."

"Are you placing an objection, Mr. Merrycoyf?" Judge Heath asked.

"Yes, I am. With no insult meant to Mr. Morgan, whose work I admire, this examination is irrelevant and immaterial."

Polk's response was passionate. "I intend to show motive for the defendant's murder of Lily Braun, Your Honor."

"Objection!" Merrycoyf spat.

"Yes, sustained," Judge Heath agreed. "Mr. Polk, it is late. Please come to the point."

Polk flipped rapidly to what Glynis could see was another bookmarked page. "And did you also write this, Mr. Morgan?" Polk paused dramatically before he read, " 'The greatest of all human crimes, murder, was punished with death. . . . Unless the family were appeased, the murderer, as with the ancient Greeks, was given up to their private vengeance. They could take his life whenever they found him, even after a lapse of years, without being held accountable.' "

The courtroom had become very quiet, and when Polk slapped the book shut, it sounded like a thunderclap. And so perhaps it was, Glynis thought with despair.

"Did you write that, Mr. Morgan?" Polk asked.

"Yes. But what must be understood is that—"

"Mr. Morgan," Polk cut him off, "did you write that this Iroquois code of vengeance is an obligation—not a choice, but an *obligation*—that a victim's kin must fulfill?"

"That's not the precise language, but . . . it's approximate. However—"

"Thank you, Mr. Morgan. No further questions."

Glynis realized full well what a blow had been struck. What could Merrycoyf do to soften it?

"Cross-examine, Mr. Merrycoyf?"

"Yes." Merrycoyf remained seated, saying to Morgan, "Is this vengeance obligation an absolute?"

"No, by no means," Morgan answered quickly. "For instance, if certain symbolic acts of contrition were performed, the victim's family could accept them as appeasement. The debt of revenge could be wiped out, so to speak."

"So the obligation is not unequivocal under every circumstance?"

"No. And, as you might suspect, the older Iroquois are much closer to the tribal ways than are the young," Morgan said, looking first at Jacques Sundown, and then turning to the jury.

"Thank you very much, Mr. Morgan," Merrycoyf said. "No further questions."

Polk grabbed Morgan's book and jumped to his feet. "I have one question on redirect, Your Honor."

"Just one question, Mr. Polk," responded Judge Heath.

"Mr. Morgan," Polk said, "in the Iroquois code of vengeance, if attempts at conciliation with the victim's family were not successful, then what happened?" But before Morgan could answer, Polk opened the book and read: " 'If the family, however, continued implacable . . . the question was left to be settled between the murderer and the kindred of his victim, according to the ancient usage.' Tell us, Mr. Morgan, did you write that passage, sir?"

Lewis Henry Morgan again looked at Polk for a long moment before he answered, "Yes."

Polk said, "No further questions, Your Honor. The prosecution rests."

"Then this court is adjourned," Judge Heath said, "until Monday."

"All rise," called the bailiff.

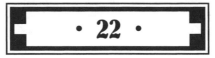

• 22 •

The Shapes we buried, dwell about,
Familiar in the Rooms—
Untarnished by the Sepulchre,
The Mouldering Playmate comes. . . .
—Emily Dickinson

The following evening, when Glynis walked into Vanessa Usher's parlor, her impression was that the familiar room had been redecorated by Edgar Allan Poe. Black velvet draperies had been hung from ceiling to floor, covering the four walls and the windows; the carpet beneath the heavy folds of fabric was a somber gray. All furniture had been removed, save a round table and eight chairs in the center of the room, and a black-lacquered, hinged screen positioned across one shadowed corner. Another deft touch of the bizarre was a pot of white lilies from the Ushers' conservatory, from which drifted a sickly sweet funereal odor.

Near the table a floor-standing, wrought-iron candelabra held two candles; this provided the sole illumination, barely enabling Glynis to see a handful of people standing about in the gloom. She took a wary step forward, concluding that this was very much like entering a sepulchre—unquestionably Vanessa Usher's desired effect.

The one vibrant note in the gloom was the carved rosewood frame of Vanessa's dulcimer. The lovely Vanessa herself, garbed in floor-length dove-gray velvet, sat as if suspended in thin air; closer inspection revealed a three-legged stool beneath her. She lightly struck the strings with the dulcimer hammers, producing a delicate resonance all but absorbed by the drapery. After listening a minute or two, how-

ever, Glynis recognized the melancholy refrain of an old Irish ballad.

She trusted that Neva had arrived earlier than the others, according to plan, and had concealed herself behind the screen. Vanessa had opposed their intrigue vehemently until they'd bribed her with a subscription to the new spiritualist newspaper *Banner of Light.* And told her that without their intervention, Pippa might be in danger. Still, Vanessa had consented only with extreme reluctance.

Those present included two women and a man unfamiliar to Glynis, in addition to Lazarus Grimm and Molly, and of course Pippa. The girl looked distressingly unwell.

"Miss Tryon, hello," Pippa said listlessly as Glynis went across the room to greet her, noting the girl's dull, red-rimmed eyes and slouched bearing, and she asked Pippa if she'd again been ill.

"Oh, she's just a little tired is all," answered Molly quickly, standing behind her daughter with her hands resting lightly on the girl's shoulders. "Isn't that so, Pippa?" she said softly, pressing her cheek against the girl's buttery-yellow hair.

"Yes, Mama."

Before Glynis had the opportunity to ask more, Vanessa set down her dulcimer and hammers, and rose to say, "Now that everyone's here, we should begin." She motioned them to the table, obviously an unnecessary gesture for all but Glynis, as the others already had begun seating themselves. Lazarus led Pippa quickly to a chair, then seated himself directly beside her.

"This is Miss Glynis Tryon, for those of you who don't know her," Vanessa announced. "Miss Tryon is a skeptic, but we can fervently hope for her enlightenment, and ask the spirits' indulgence. Do sit right here, Glynis, between Lazarus and me. No, no, Molly, let Sylvia sit next to Pippa—she never has before."

Molly looked concerned, and glanced protectively at Pippa before she went with obvious unwillingness to the only remaining chair. Glynis sat as directed, thankful that at least Vanessa had cooperated in the seating arrangement. On the other side of Vanessa sat one of the unfamiliar women, then the man, then Molly, the woman called Sylvia, and finally Pippa, beside Lazarus. Immediately upon settling themselves, the participants grasped the nearest hand of the person beside them. Before doing this herself, Vanessa reached out to snuff a

candle; the one remaining gave the room only the dimmest of light, like a match struck in a dark cave, Glynis thought with increased misgiving.

Seated beside Lazarus, she watched him closely from the corner of her eye. After the day she'd seen him in the shed with Pippa at the Grimm farm, she had gone to Neva, who'd guessed Pippa might have been in a deep trance, or mesmerized. Glynis then had collected for the two of them what little information she could find on the eighteenth-century physician Franz Mesmer. They found the answer, they thought, in the material on Mesmer's philosophical successor, Dr. James Braid; only a decade before, in the 1840s, Braid had coined the term *hypnotism.*

"I'll wager," Neva had declared, "that it's what these crazy spiritualists are doing—some kind of hypnotism."

"Which would mean that they aren't all charlatans," Glynis said. "At least some of them must truly believe they're in touch with the hereafter."

"They're deluding themselves," Neva retorted.

"Maybe so, but not intentionally."

"But Pippa is simply being used by Lazarus," Neva protested. "I'm told that the 'contributions' he requests at the spiritualist meetings are substantial."

Glynis frowned, then offered, "It's certainly true that Lazarus Grimm has a dubious reputation, but what if he really believes this otherworldly plane exists? If that's true, he could be unaware or ignorant of what he's doing when he hypnotizes Pippa. And it could be dangerous for her."

"Yes, in terms of what we've read about Mesmer," Neva readily agreed, "if Pippa is concealing from herself the memory of an event too overwhelming to recall."

The night before on the ride home from Waterloo, Glynis had insisted that she and Neva attend Vanessa Usher's weekly seance. That this might help Jacques as well as Pippa, she didn't mention at the time.

Vanessa now grasped Glynis's hand and that of the woman to her right, intoning dramatically, "Our spirit circle is closed." She looked expectantly at Lazarus.

Lazarus's tone contained a not-so-subtle reproach. "You all should

"Oh, dear Lord," Sylvia cried out suddenly, "it's my baby. It's my little girl."

Everyone's eyes shot open; they closed again quickly. Glynis was relieved that she saw no acknowledgment of the muffled snort that had just come from behind the screen.

Sylvia's face, though tear-streaked, had become radiant. In embarrassment, Glynis looked away; she felt unclean at being a party to this. Naturally Sylvia wanted to believe that what she heard was her beloved dead daughter; was there a grief more devastating than losing one's child? Undoubtedly this was the root of the spiritualist movement's appeal: people believed what they needed to believe. And while the spiritualists weren't the first to recognize the importance of promised immortality in easing death's anguish for survivors, they surely did offer better theater than had most of their predecessors.

Glynis shifted slightly in her chair so she could watch Pippa. The girl's eyes remained closed. But suddenly, in the midst of Sylvia's ecstatic sobs, a high-pitched voice said, "Grandfather, are you there? Is that you?"

With their eyes closed, the others wouldn't see that Pippa's lips hadn't moved. Glynis felt Vanessa's grip on her hand tighten, while Lazarus's hold on her other hand went oddly limp. As if he'd forgotten he was grasping it. But she couldn't concern herself with Lazarus just then. She kept her eyes fixed on Pippa, who as yet exhibited no reaction.

"Grandfather," came the voice again. "Grandfather, be careful. No! No, don't do that to my—"

Pippa's eyes flew open, just as Lazarus leapt to his feet. "Who's doing that?" he demanded. "Who said that?"

Pippa had begun to whimper. The whimpers rose to a keening wail. Glynis and Molly both sprang forward, but Lazarus prevented them from reaching the girl by wrapping his arms around her like a shield. "Keep away from her!" he ordered.

"Lazarus," pleaded Molly, "please let me—"

"No, keep away," Lazarus repeated. "Everyone must leave now. It's over. It's over for tonight."

With looks of confusion, and one of despair from Sylvia, the two women and the man moved toward the door, casting frightened backward glances at Pippa. The weeping girl had begun to writhe in Laza-

realize," he said pointedly, "that because we have a disbeliever present, the spirits may choose not to communicate."

Glynis was aware that all eyes swung her way. She was also aware that this was a common excuse of mediums: an unsympathetic presence would keep the spirits from revealing themselves. So far, researchers of psychic phenomena had found this circular argument to be invincible.

Lazarus continued, his voice growing ever more intense, "I must emphasize to you that if you have questions, they *must come through me* to the medium. This is imperative, otherwise she could become perilously confused. Do you all understand this?"

What Glynis understood was that Lazarus demanded to remain in control. And although she found his transformation from aesthete to commanding general nothing less than extraordinary, she nodded earnestly with the others.

He turned to Pippa. "Close your eyes. Go to sleep, Pippa. Sleep. Sleep . . . sleep . . . sleep . . ."

Pippa's eyes closed, and instantly she seemed to sink lower in her chair. Lazarus repeated the command until Glynis began to feel her own lids droop. She quietly took a deep breath, concentrating on the need to shut out Lazarus's voice and watch the others. Their eyes had closed. All but those of Lazarus. He didn't seem to notice Glynis's scrutiny as his attention focused steadily on the girl beside him.

He stopped talking. The room was still. Only the sound of soft breathing intruded.

"Sylvia," said Lazarus quietly, "you wish to talk to your daughter?"

"Yes. Oh, yes. Please ask Pippa to bring her here."

In response to this plea, Glynis felt a strong distaste. There was something of the indecent, even the obscene, in this summons to the dead. She tried to distract herself by wondering what Neva was thinking. But she probably didn't need to wonder. She half expected Neva at any minute to come flying out from behind the screen and denounce the entire business.

Gradually, though, Glynis became aware of an odd, repetitive sound, almost as if someone were humming. Someone *was* humming, though who it was among them she couldn't tell. Except that it sounded like a female voice.

fluence over his niece extended. Pippa pulled away from Neva and, wiping her eyes, said, "Yes, I want to go home. I'm sorry for what I did, Uncle Lazarus, but I'm all right now."

Lazarus smiled, and stroked the girl's wet cheeks. After a nod from him, Molly rushed with a faint cry to her daughter. Vanessa, who had been unexpectedly quiet all this time, now said cheerily, "Well, I suppose these things do happen—but we certainly can't let a little unpleasantness dissuade us from communicating with our loved ones on the other side."

While Glynis stood gaping at her, Vanessa escorted the Grimms to her door, chirping banalities at every step.

"Neva, do you think she'll be all right?" Glynis asked. "Pippa, I mean."

"I didn't think you meant the Witch of Endor, there," Neva said, watching Vanessa with a look of disgust. "And I don't know how the girl will be. When she gets back to the farm," she added, somewhat anxiously, "there'll be Almira. And Billy Wicken."

"Yes. I know that." It was all Glynis could bring herself to say.

"I suppose," Neva went on as if she hadn't heard, "there's nothing we can do about it. Lazarus was right. We can't keep Pippa here against his and her mother's will."

"But I think we *can* do something," Glynis said. "Not tonight, certainly, but I think you and I need to go out to the Grimm farm tomorrow."

Neva scowled. "They won't exactly welcome us, you know, none of them. I doubt we'll get anywhere near Pippa."

"I don't think that's necessarily true," Glynis protested. "Not if we can persuade the constable's deputy to come with us."

"How can we do that? And why do we want to?"

"We'll have to ask for Zeph, that's how. I think Cullen will listen to me about this, especially if it involves Pippa's welfare. But if he won't, we'll get Jeremiah Merrycoyf involved."

"Do we have to rely on one of those men? You and Cullen Stuart are barely speaking!"

"Yes, and I'd rather not involve him. But, Neva, we're *women,* and whether we like it or not, we don't have one jot of authority. Besides, at this point, I'll rely on whomever I have to."

rus's grasp, striking at him in a frenzy while she battered her head against his chest.

Molly stood frozen with fists pressed against her mouth, and Vanessa glared at Glynis, snarling, "I knew I shouldn't have let you come. You ruined it!"

Lazarus, his back to the screen, didn't see Neva when she emerged from behind it. "Pippa," she said, "listen to me—"

"Stay away from her!" Lazarus ordered Neva, his expression as forbidding as his voice. But he didn't register any surprise at finding her there, Glynis observed, so complete was his preoccupation with Pippa.

"No, I won't stay away from her. The girl needs help," Neva stated firmly. "Pippa, listen to me. There's no reason for you to be frightened. Nothing is going to happen to you! I promise."

Pippa's sobs, though they persisted, seemed to lessen in severity. Neva reached forward to grasp the girl's shoulder, and for a moment Glynis thought Lazarus would shove her aside. But Pippa managed to squirm from his grasp to hurl herself against the young doctor. Glynis glanced at Molly, who stood several feet away. The woman's face expressed such stark agony that Glynis wondered if Molly would ever forgive any of them for this, including her brother.

"Perhaps Pippa should stay at the Iveses' tonight," Neva suggested, speaking over the girl's head.

"No! Absolutely not," Lazarus objected. "She needs to be at home. With her mother, with her family."

"Her *family*," Neva retorted, "haven't done much to protect her, have they? I think—"

"Please," Molly broke in, her voice pleading, "please let us take her home."

"You don't need to beg," Lazarus said to his sister with a sudden gentleness, "she has no right to keep the girl here."

"No, but I strongly advise it," said Neva, still holding Pippa close.

"Pippa," Lazarus said, his eyes fastened on the girl, and his tone now one of concern, "don't you want to come home? You don't want to stay here, do you?"

Pippa's sobs had slowly diminished; she looked up at Lazarus as if seeking forgiveness. When Neva tried, unsuccessfully, to insert herself between the girl and her uncle, Glynis saw how far Lazarus's in-

"But why do we need to go to the Grimms'?" Neva insisted. "We already know that Pippa saw—"

Shaking her head, Glynis interrupted, "To prove Jacques Sundown didn't kill Lily Braun."

Neva caught her breath. "Do you know who did?"

"Yes, I think so," Glynis said slowly, "but I haven't put it all together yet. And we'll need more than my suppositions to keep Jacques from hanging."

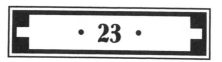

• 23 •

[Dr. Elizabeth Blackwell] has quite bewildered the learned faculty by her diploma, all in due form, authorizing her to dose and bleed and amputate with the best of them. Some of them think Miss Blackwell must be a socialist of the most rabid class, and that her undertaking is the entering wedge to a systematic attack on society by the whole sex.

—_New York Journal of Commerce,_ 1849

Glynis paused to look over her shoulder before she entered the Waterloo courthouse. The Monday morning sunlight came pale and hazy above the southeast horizon on this day of the winter solstice, and the weather had taken an erratic swing; the air felt as warm as April. Melting snow ran in rivulets and turned the roads into bogs, but the only ones truly grumbling about it were the liverymen. They'd had to put aside their cutters and retrieve the recently stored carriages.

On the square below Glynis, where scenes of the previous trial days had been played out, the mood had changed significantly. The townsmen were still there, but the rabble-rousers were fewer and were mostly, if not completely, ignored. The Iroquois stood just as silent, just as remote, and their bearing revealed little of the underlying tension as they waited to see what this white man's judge and jury would do to Jacques Sundown. History surely had given them grounds for distrust.

Word of Sara Turner's testimony the previous Friday had swept through Seneca County, and it was that, Glynis knew, which explained the subdued atmosphere below. Sara's account of the lynching had produced a firestorm of revulsion from Quakers and

abolitionists, most Christian pulpits, and, to their credit, the newspapers—although Neva insisted this was simply because it made good copy. Nonetheless, the confrontations had been minimal this Monday in Waterloo.

Cullen came briskly up the steps. "Quiet, down there," he said to Glynis, "and I hope it lasts. Until this is over at least. Then I expect we'll go back to the normal mutual dislike. But if Jacques is convicted . . ." He shrugged.

Glynis turned toward the door. She didn't want to think about it—about any of it. The more she learned concerning the events of ten years before, the more wretched she felt.

Behind her, Cullen said, "Glynis?" and reached for her shoulder. She stood in place, not walking away, not turning to face him. He released her shoulder and came around to stand in front of her. "Glynis, you want to tell me what happened that day? Day of the blizzard?"

Startled, all she could think to say was, "Why? Why now, Cullen?"

"I think maybe we should get this sorted out before . . ." He broke off as she frowned. And the silence wavered there between them until she said, "Before Jacques is convicted? Before he's hanged, you mean?"

"No, that's not what I mean."

"Cullen, you wouldn't talk to me about it before. Wouldn't talk to me at all, for weeks. And now . . . well, I don't want to talk."

"You think you have a right to be angry about this?"

"Oh, you're absolutely correct, Cullen! At this point I think I have every right to be angry. You haven't allowed me to explain, haven't allowed me a word in my own behalf for all these weeks. Even accused criminals are supposed to be assumed innocent until proven otherwise! But you've apparently had no doubt about what you *think* you saw that day. Well, go ahead and continue to think it—think whatever you like. I'm not going to explain myself at this late date regarding something I didn't do!"

She walked away, into the lobby and up the stairs, without looking back. And if she hadn't been angry before, she told herself, she was angry now.

Entering the courtroom with her heart beating rapidly, Glynis paused to calm herself. She then went directly to the defense table and stood waiting until Jacques was escorted in from the jail. Because

of the weekend's events, Merrycoyf had gone to the judge's chambers to revise his list of witnesses, and she realized she might not have another opportunity to speak with Jacques alone. Every time she'd visited him at the jail, there had been a guard present. Even now, after seating his prisoner, the bailiff stood just a few feet away. She moved in close to the table.

"It would have been so much easier, Jacques," she said softly, "if only you had told me."

Jacques looked at her with what might have been amusement. "You think you're a good spirit, a Ho-no-che-no'-keh? Think you can bargain with He'-no for my life?"

Glynis felt her face flush. "No, of course not. But if you had just explained it to me."

"No."

"You don't think I would have understood?" she asked him.

"You cannot understand."

"Yes, I think I can. What took place ten years ago created an afterlife of its own. As a result, and in addition to what is happening to you, three women's lives have been destroyed—one way or another. Perhaps a child's life as well."

"You know, then." And suddenly his eyes, no longer flat, held pain so graphic that Glynis had to look away.

When she turned back to him, she said only, "Yes, Jacques, I know. And while I've been torn in two directions about it, I told Jeremiah what I know; it's his decision now."

The door opened, and Merrycoyf emerged from the judge's chambers. He gave her a brief nod, then looked anxiously toward the rear door.

"Have you seen Mr. MacAlistair?" he asked Glynis.

"No, I haven't. Jeremiah. What if he doesn't get here with Dr. Kelly?"

"I do not care to consider that," Merrycoyf said.

While they'd been talking, Jacques's hands, lying together on the table, had clenched reflexively, and Glynis now pressed them quickly with her own. Hearing the bailiff behind her, she held Jacques's eyes momentarily, before she went back to the seat she'd had the previous week.

* * *

The defense may now present its case," said Judge Heath after completing the preliminaries. "Mr. Merrycoyf, call your first witness."

The men of the jury, Glynis noted, had been tight-lipped since they'd entered the courtroom; most tellingly, they did not look at Jacques. They undoubtedly felt that the defense presentation would be a waste of time, no more than a formal requirement of the legal system. Their faces indicated the trial had been all but over the previous Friday. Several of them even looked disgusted as Merrycoyf got to his feet.

"The defense calls Dr. Neva Cardoza."

Orrin Polk also rose. "Your Honor," he said querulously, "we discussed this witness in your chambers before the trial began. You made a ruling at that time; consequently there is no reason for defense counsel to try to present this woman as a doctor."

"Yes, Mr. Merrycoyf," Judge Heath said, scowling, "I have denied this woman the status of medical expert on the grounds that she lacks the proper qualifications."

Unlike everyone else in the courtroom, Glynis didn't turn to look at Neva. Both of them knew that the "proper qualifications" involved gender. But even Merrycoyf, although he was no staunch feminist, had been somewhat surprised when Judge Heath denied expert status to Neva solely because she was a woman. Glynis had not been surprised. Not with medical schools across the country rewriting their admissions policies to specifically prohibit women.

"Your Honor, with all due respect," Merrycoyf now said, "although this witness is denied the status of expert, she may surely testify. It is a basic tenet of law that any witness called is qualified to say what *she saw* and what *she did*, if relevant to the issues."

Judge Heath's scowl remained; he nodded, however, saying with a touch of testiness, "Very well, counsel. But Miss Cardoza may not give expert opinion as to the findings."

"Of course, Your Honor," said Merrycoyf as he turned and gestured to Neva.

Glynis was relieved to see, as Neva came forward, that her face did not reflect outrage; the young doctor walked up the aisle quickly,

looking straight ahead with no expression whatsoever. In fact, Glynis marveled, Neva did not appear in the least nervous.

Merrycoyf's first question, after Neva was sworn, concerned her educational background. Even this innocuous inquiry made Orrin Polk bristle. He half rose from his seat and, with his neck extended like a weasel about to strike, seemed prepared to remain in that position indefinitely.

"I attended the Female Medical College of Pennsylvania," Neva answered in a clear voice.

"And did you receive a medical degree, Dr. Cardoza?" Merrycoyf asked.

"Yes, last spring."

"And why did you come to Seneca Falls, Dr. Cardoza?"

"To train with and assist Dr. Quentin Ives, in preparation for a staff position in a New York City hospital."

"And have you, since coming here, been offered that position in New York?"

"Yes, one week ago. But I declined the offer, choosing instead to remain in Seneca Falls."

Although Glynis already knew this, she couldn't help turning around for a look at Abraham Levy. His smile warmed the entire courtroom. Possibly the entire county.

Judge Heath leaned forward to say, "Mr. Merrycoyf, please move along with the witness."

"Yes, Your Honor. Dr. Cardoza, shortly before his death occurred, were you called to the farm of Obadiah Grimm?"

"Yes."

"And were you present at the moment of Mr. Grimm's death?"

"Yes."

"Did Mr. Grimm say anything to you in the moments prior to his death?"

Before Neva could answer, Polk said, "Objection! That would be hearsay."

"No, Your Honor," Merrycoyf argued, "a dying declaration is an exception to the hearsay rule."

"That is correct, Mr. Merrycoyf," said the judge. "However"—he turned to Neva—"young woman, did Obadiah Grimm expire immediately following his words to you?"

"Yes, he did."

"Then the objection is overruled," Judge Heath said. "The witness may answer."

Polk sat down; he looked disconcerted, Glynis thought, but apparently not enough so to debate the judge about whether Neva, if she wasn't an expert, could recognize death when she saw it.

"What did Obadiah Grimm say, Dr. Cardoza?"

"He said, 'Jeremiah,' several times. That much was clear. He also said something that sounded, to me at least, like 'seven tea he leaven.' "

"Did that mean anything to you, Dr. Cardoza?"

"Not at the time, no. I thought perhaps it had to do with you, Mr. Merrycoyf."

"I will state for the record," Merrycoyf said, "that I had not seen or heard from Obadiah Grimm for several years."

"Do you object, Mr. Polk?" Judge Heath asked.

"No objection," said Polk, looking puzzled.

"Did you have occasion later to discuss these words with anyone other than the Grimm family, Dr. Cardoza?"

"Yes, I discussed them with Miss Glynis Tryon, who had known the family longer than I."

"Objection!" Polk yelped. "Hearsay."

"Mr. Polk," said Judge Heath, "we will never finish here unless some leeway is allowed. Now I can plainly see that Miss Tryon is here in court, and so defense counsel could call her for corroboration of this testimony should it be necessary. But if we can save time, let us by all means do it. Proceed, Miss Cardoza."

Neva answered, "I related to Miss Tryon what Mr. Grimm had said. We discussed this a number of times, but came to no conclusion about what he meant. Then, last Friday evening, she asked me to again repeat his words. She said she thought that Obadiah Grimm, given as he was to biblical quotations, might have been referring to a passage from the Old Testament Book of Jeremiah.

"Miss Tryon thought that 'seven tea' might be chapter seventeen—not seventy, because there is no seventieth chapter in Jeremiah—and that what I heard as 'leaven' could be verse eleven."

Neva stopped there, and looked at Merrycoyf.

"And subsequently," Merrycoyf said, "did you and Miss Tryon locate the passage in Jeremiah, chapter seventeen, verse eleven?"

"Yes, we did."

Merrycoyf walked back to the table, where he picked up a Bible. Opening it to a marked page, he now said to Neva, "Will you identify this as the passage to which you believe Obadiah Grimm referred?" Merrycoyf read: " 'As the partridge sitteth on eggs, but hatcheth them not; so is he that getteth riches but not by right . . .' Is that the one, Dr. Cardoza?"

"Yes," Neva said.

Merrycoyf closed the Bible and returned it to the table, before he said, "Thank you, Doctor. Now I would like to question you in regard to another death. Did you, Dr. Cardoza, perform an autopsy on the deceased Lily Braun?"

"Yes."

"Had you ever performed such an autopsy before?"

"Since I've been in Seneca Falls, I've assisted Dr. Ives in four of them."

Polk sprang to his feet, apparently to object, but when Judge Heath frowned forbiddingly at him, he clamped his mouth shut and sank back into his chair.

"And why did you not assist Dr. Ives on this occasion, Dr. Cardoza?"

"He had been called out of town. Constable Stuart brought the Braun woman's body to the Iveses' house and asked me to do the autopsy."

"Constable Stuart asked you to do it?"

"Yes."

"And as a result of your autopsy, Dr. Cardoza, what did you see—"

"Objection!" Polk protested. "The witness is not an expert. She cannot testify to anything medical in nature."

"Your Honor," Merrycoyf responded, "the witness can testify as to what she saw."

"Yes, yes, counsel," Judge Heath said. "Objection overruled. Please, Mr. Polk, exercise some discretion in your objections. Unless counsel asks this witness for a cause of death, I will allow her to answer his questions."

"Again, Dr. Cardoza," said Merrycoyf, "what did you *see*?"

Neva hesitated, presumably to choose her words with care. "What I *saw,*" she said, "was a knife in the deceased's chest. I saw no air in the surrounding tissue or chest wall or under the skin. Also, I saw no evidence whatever of external bleeding and also none of an internal nature, not even in the pleural cavity."

Judge Heath leaned over the bench. "Dr. Cardoza, was that unusual?" he frowned.

Clearly astonished to be addressed at all by this judge, not to mention his use of *Dr.* Cardoza, Neva blurted, "Unusual? It defied the laws of nature!"

Merrycoyf, observed Glynis, was having some difficulty restraining a smile. Orrin Polk, on the other hand, looked incendiary. Neither said a word, however. And Judge Heath continued frowning as he nodded at Merrycoyf to continue.

"What else did you see, or not see, Dr. Cardoza?" Merrycoyf asked.

Neva looked beyond him at Glynis, who nodded encouragement, and then went on with regained composure as she said, "Most important was the evidence that the deceased had eaten shortly before she died. The stomach contents contained a quantity of tea and biscuits. And there was acute inflammation of the stomach, as well as patches of bright scarlet on the mucous membrane."

"Was that, or anything else, *unusual,* Dr. Cardoza?" Merrycoyf asked, careful to emphasize Judge Heath's own word.

"Yes. And there was something else. Adhering to the stomach lining were small particles."

"Could you see what those particles consisted of?"

"Yes. They consisted of approximately three and a half grains of arsenic."

As the courtroom erupted in a bedlam of noise, Judge Heath, scowling furiously, pounded his gavel. The jury had long since stopped looking bored, and now for the most part wore expressions of total confusion. Orrin Polk was objecting, although he could barely be heard over the commotion. Glynis threw a quick glance to the rear of the courtroom; no one was leaving this time. And against the back wall, the Iroquois stood as still as death.

The gavel brought results only after Judge Heath further ordered the bailiff to remove those who would not comply with his order for silence. Gradually the noise abated.

"There will be no more such outbursts in my courtroom!" Judge Heath ordered. "In the event another occurs, the bailiff is instructed to immediately empty the room of spectators. I hope I have made myself clear."

With one more stroke of the gavel, he said, "Mr. Merrycoyf, do you have further questions of this witness?"

"No, Your Honor."

"Cross-examine, Mr. Polk?"

"Yes, indeed, Your Honor." Polk already was on his feet. "Would you tell the court, Miss Cardoza, whether, since coming to western New York, you have worked with anyone other than Dr. Quentin Ives?"

"Do you mean another doctor?"

"Yes, my dear, that's what I mean."

"Well, I worked several days with Dr. Witherspoon."

"Dr. Witherspoon the *dentist*?"

"Yes."

"And just how often does a dentist perform autopsies?"

"Objection!" Merrycoyf said.

"I withdraw the question." Polk smiled graciously. "Now tell us, did you usually discuss the autopsy findings with Dr. Ives, my dear?"

"I am not your 'dear,' Mr. Polk, and you will kindly refrain from addressing me as such. And yes, of course Dr. Ives and I discussed our findings."

"And did you discuss with Dr. Ives the findings to which you have testified today?"

"Yes."

"And did he correct any of your observations?"

"No, he did not."

"He didn't tell you what to say here?"

"No, he most certainly did not."

"Just answer the questions yes or no, Miss Cardoza. Didn't Dr. Ives suggest what you might say about the deceased's—"

"No, he did not!" Neva interrupted. "And for you to infer—"

"I have no further questions of the witness Cardoza," Polk said.

"In that case," said Judge Heath, "the defense will call its next witness. Thank you, Dr. Cardoza, and you may step down."

Before she left the witness chair, Neva favored Judge Heath with a very small smile.

At the rear of the courtroom, two men—one of them extremely tall—started up the aisle, inducing a prolonged sigh from Merrycoyf. He stood quickly to say, "The defense calls Dr. Patrick Kelly."

Glynis, too, sighed with relief. Adam MacAlistair's telegram had reached Kelly's housekeeper in Rochester, who had wired back that the doctor was spending his weekend at the fashionable Inn at Hemlock Falls. It was now obvious that Adam, having raced to Hemlock Falls by carriage, had succeeded in locating Kelly. Glynis imagined the young lawyer had probably enjoyed the escapade immensely, and Merrycoyf looked not only relieved, but distinctly impressed.

"Dr. Kelly, would you state your educational background for the court?" Merrycoyf now asked.

"I received my degree from Harvard Medical School. Before setting up practice in Rochester, New York, I studied in Philadelphia under Dr. Paul Mercutio, a specialist in toxicology, who himself studied under Dr. Robert Christison."

"Dr. Christison is the author of *Treatise on Poisons*, is he not?"

"Yes."

"Dr. Kelly, were you in the courtroom to hear Dr. Cardoza's testimony?"

"Yes, I was standing in the back."

"Based on her testimony, Dr. Kelly, can you formulate an opinion as to the cause of death of the woman Lily Braun?"

"Yes."

"What is your opinion?"

"As described by Dr. Cardoza, the appearance of the deceased's internal organs, specifically the stomach, indicates acute poisoning. It seems clear that prior to her death, the victim ingested arsenic, probably introduced in tea. And three and a half grains of it would be more than enough to kill an adult woman."

"Can you attribute the victim's death, then, to the arsenic?"

Kelly didn't hesitate. "I'll put it this way, Mr. Merrycoyf; her death was probably caused by arsenic poisoning, because it most certainly did not result from a knife wound."

"Can you explain that?"

"Yes, but Dr. Cardoza already has done so. She testified that she saw no blood."

"What would that mean?"

"It means that the woman was dead, again almost certainly of arsenic poisoning, *before* the knife ever entered her body."

"Objection!" snapped Polk.

"On what grounds are you objecting?" said Judge Heath.

"That it is conjecture on the part of the witness."

"The witness is a physician and an expert in toxicology," Merrycoyf retorted.

"Objection overruled. Continue, Mr. Merrycoyf."

"Thank you, Your Honor. Now, Dr. Kelly, can you draw a conclusion about the presence of a knife in the victim's body? Could that have been planted evidence to obscure the real cause of death?"

"Yes—"

"Objection!" Polk broke in shrilly. The man looked beside himself, and continued in a piercing tone, "That is an outrageously leading question on defense's part."

"Sustained," said Judge Heath. "The jury should ignore this conjecture of counsel for the defense."

Ah, yes, Glynis reflected, watching the jury hang on every word. Tit for tat, Mr. Polk.

"Thank you, Dr. Kelly." Merrycoyf smiled fulsomely. "No further questions."

"Do you wish to cross-examine, Mr. Polk?"

"I certainly do, Your Honor!" Polk jumped from his chair. "Isn't it true, Dr. Kelly, that you never met the woman Lily Braun—alive *or* dead?"

"Yes, that's true."

"And so you formulated your opinion about the cause of her death based solely on the testimony given by the witness Cardoza in response to questions by counsel for the defense?"

"There is little doubt that—"

"Please answer yes or no, Dr. Kelly?"

"Yes."

"And, Dr. Kelly, is that ordinarily the way you prepare to testify in court?"

"Now, just a minute—"

"No further questions of this witness, Your Honor."

"The witness may step down," Judge Heath said.

Patrick Kelly appeared very much, Glynis observed, as if he'd like to punch Orrin Polk in his sharp little nose. But Kelly settled for a withering look as he stepped from the witness chair.

Judge Heath stood up, saying, "At this time we will take a fifteen-minute recess."

"All rise!"

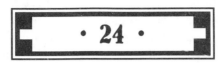

• 24 •

You will wait for me, my Gray Wolf,
For I soon shall come to join you.
O, my Gray Wolf, my Tah-yoh-ne,
Hear the voice of your Ah-weh-hah,
Only wait a few days longer
And I then will walk beside you.
—Mourning Song of Seneca woman Ah-weh-hah,
from Arthur Parker, *The Life of General Ely S. Parker*

Will you call your next witness, Mr. Merrycoyf?"

"Yes, Your Honor," Merrycoyf said. "The defense calls Small Brown Bird, member of the Seneca Nation."

Necks craning, the courtroom spectators turned to watch the woman come up the aisle. When she went past, Glynis gave her what she hoped would be interpreted as a sympathetic look; anything more than that, a smile for instance, would have been ludicrous given the ordeal Small Brown Bird now faced.

Immediately there followed a flurry of discussion, instigated by Polk, which involved himself, the judge, and the court clerk, concerning the prospective witness's mandatory oath before a Judeo-Christian God. Glynis scarcely could believe her ears—not when considering some of the thoroughly ungodly people in the past who, with nary a challenge put to them, had sworn and given testimony in this very courtroom.

Small Brown Bird stood quietly, exhibiting little emotion and a great deal of dignity. This day her pantalettes were not of bright calico but of deerskin, their elaborate border above her moccasins em-

ıdered with shell beads and porcupine quills, as was the hem of her ›erskin overdress, which was buttoned with silver brooches. She fingered a chain of silver beads that disappeared under the neckline of the dress. During a momentary pause in the deliberation swirling around her, she tilted her head slightly toward the men arguing, then pulled out the chain to reveal a large silver cross, saying in her musical voice, "I am a Christian."

Glynis swallowed a smile at the faces of the startled men, who stared dumbly at the Seneca woman, until the clerk scurried forward with the Bible. When presumably sworn to everyone's satisfaction, Small Brown Bird was permitted to sit in the witness chair.

"Will you give your name and place of residence to the court clerk," said Judge Heath, in an unusually subdued tone of voice.

"I am called Small Brown Bird. I live at the Black Brook Reservation."

Merrycoyf rose and went to stand next to the jury box—probably, Glynis determined, to verify that the jury could hear the delicate voice.

"How long have you lived there at the reservation?" Merrycoyf began.

"Many . . . fourteen years."

"And where did you live before that?"

"The Cattaraugus Reservation, near Buffalo."

"Are you related to the defendant?"

"I am sister to Walks At Sundown's mother."

"So you are his aunt?"

"As you say."

Merrycoyf shook his head at her slightly, and Small Brown Bird then said, "Yes."

"And so you were also aunt to the defendant's half brother, Many Horned Stag?"

"As you say. Yes."

"Miss—excuse me, Small Brown Bird—were you at the reservation on the day ten years ago that eight men came and took Many Horned Stag from his home?"

"Yes."

"Did you yourself witness this act?"

"I saw it. Yes."

Merrycoyf, apparently satisfied the jury could hear, and indeed the woman's voice carried well despite its lightness of tone, now moved back to the defense table and picked up a pad of paper. While he leafed through it, Glynis glanced at Orrin Polk. The prosecutor had perched at the edge of his chair and continually lifted from it, up and down, as if he sat on a hot griddle. He had risen several times, ostensibly to object, but lowered himself back down without speaking. He was uneasy about this witness for good reason: Polk didn't know, Glynis was fairly certain, why the Seneca woman had been called.

Merrycoyf now went to stand beside the witness box. "Were you in the courtroom last Friday?" he asked Small Brown Bird.

"Yes."

"Did you hear the testimony of the prosecution witness Sara Turner?"

"Yes."

"And did you hear Mrs. Turner connect the lynch-killing of your nephew, Many Horned Stag, with the Black Brook dam litigation—that is, the legal battle? And with the alleged rape of Otto Braun's daughter, Lily?"

"Yes, I heard."

"Do you share her view? Do you think that the Black Brook dam, and the fact that your nephew won the case, was the reason he was killed?"

"Revenge was not all of the reason."

"Or that he was said to have raped Lily Braun?"

"No. Many Horned Stag would not do that."

"Would you now describe the reason as you know it to be?"

Small Brown Bird sat quietly with her hands folded in her lap. Before she spoke, she looked down at her nephew. Jacques sat equally still; his face, from where Glynis sat, seemed without expression, but she couldn't see his eyes. Orrin Polk fidgeted in his chair, and looked ready to pounce for any reason he could find.

Small Brown Bird drew in her breath, and began, "Ten summers ago—when the dam trouble was happening—Many Horned Stag and the girl Lily, they knew each other—"

"Pardon me," Merrycoyf broke in, "but do you mean Lily Braun and Many Horned Stag met during the dam dispute? The dispute that her father and uncle were involved in?"

"Yes. That."

"Thank you. Please go on," Merrycoyf said.

"Many Horned Stag and the girl, they"—Small Brown Bird hesitated as if searching for the words—"they were in love. They wanted to marry, but her father, the girl's, would not allow it. All that autumn the girl asked her father to let them marry, but it was of no use. Then the girl told Many Horned Stag and me and his mother that—"

"Objection," Polk argued. "This is a recollection that is ten years old, and—"

"No, Mr. Polk," interrupted Judge Heath. "Your objection is overruled. We will hear the woman out. The fact that it *was* ten years ago that this lynching occurred, and that this is the first any of us have heard of it, means it is high time the truth was uncovered. I want to know what happened. Please continue . . . ah . . . Miss Brown Bird."

They had been so afraid; but Judge Heath *would* listen, Glynis thought with relief that nearly brought tears.

"What was it that the girl Lily Braun told Many Horned Stag?" Merrycoyf asked.

"She said that she was with child."

"His child—Many Horned Stag's?"

"Yes."

After a few outraged whispers, the courtroom again quieted. Remarkably quiet also was Orrin Polk, who had sat back in his chair after the judge's last ruling with an angry expression, but now looked almost as inquisitive as everyone else.

"Small Brown Bird, do you recall whether the defendant also knew of his brother's coming child?" Merrycoyf asked.

"He knew. He is the one who said they had better run away."

"Jacques Sundown—your nephew Walks At Sundown—told his brother and Lily Braun that they should leave?"

"He said it was dangerous for them to stay."

Merrycoyf nodded. "Yes. What happened next?"

"They planned to go the next day. The girl went to her parents' house to get things to take with them. She was coming back to the reservation the next morning."

"So she and Many Horned Stag could leave together?"

"Yes."

"What time of year was that?"

"The same time as now. Early in winter."

"Were the other men who lived on the reservation—other than Many Horned Stag and his brother Walks At Sundown—were they there at that time of early winter?"

"No. They were gone hunting, three or four days gone, all but the very old men."

"So the only able-bodied men on the reservation at that time were the defendant and his brother."

Small Brown Bird frowned in apparent confusion, before her forehead smoothed and she answered, "No. No, Walks At Sundown, he left in early morning of that day to go and get the other men hunting."

"Why did he do that?"

"He thought there would be trouble. But not so soon."

"You mean he thought that trouble would come sometime after the two lovers had gone?"

"Yes."

"After Walks At Sundown left that morning, what next occurred?"

"The girl did not come back. Many Horned Stag waited and waited until it was afternoon. Then he said that her father must have found out and stopped her. Many Horned Stag said he would go to her father's house and get the girl."

"And did he do that?"

"He was getting his horse ready. Then they came."

"They? You mean the men—the eight white men?"

"Yes."

Small Brown Bird's fingers knotted in her lap. Glynis could see her knuckles draw taut, and could see the glitter of tears that did not fall. She herself knew what was coming and wished she could leave the courtroom, but to do so would be to abandon Jacques. And Small Brown Bird.

Merrycoyf, his voice kind, now said to Small Brown Bird, "So eight men came into the reservation. I know this is difficult for you, but please tell us what happened then. Take as much time as you need."

The woman first gave Jacques a poignant look, then she turned and said to Merrycoyf, "The men took Many Horned Stag. They pulled him off his horse and tied a rope around his neck, and they dragged him into the woods. We tried to stop them, but they were too many.

We followed them. They dragged him to a clearing in the trees, and they . . ."

Small Brown Bird's voice broke, but she shook her head and went on, "The men, they looped the rope around Many Horned Stag's neck over a tree limb. Before they pulled the rope, they . . . they took his manhood."

Glynis was vaguely aware of rustling skirts and the rear door opening; she didn't have to turn to know people were leaving. Otherwise the room was quiet, until Merrycoyf said, "They took his manhood. I'm sorry to have to clarify this, but do you mean they castrated him?"

Small Brown Bird, now choking back tears, nodded and said, "Yes." It was all but lost in the scuffle that broke out in the back of the room.

Glynis turned to see Seneca and Cayuga men standing in front of the rear door, preventing those attempting to leave from doing so. Cullen stood talking quietly and obviously trying to reason with them. When women's cries of protestation reached Glynis, distracting her from her anxiety for Cullen, she turned to look at Judge Heath. Merrycoyf was also watching the judge, while members of the jury were, for the most part, staring either toward the back, or at Small Brown Bird.

Judge Heath's gavel struck loudly. "I want this courtroom quiet," he said. "It is understandable that some are upset by the testimony and wish to leave. But we need order here immediately."

Suddenly a Seneca man called out, "Everyone should sit down. There is a need for all to hear this." His voice sounded determined but controlled, not as reckless with fury as it might have been, Glynis recognized with relief.

In response, Judge Heath stood up and moved away from the bench. His black robes made him look like a monk—or an executioner. Glynis waited with anxiety like the rest of the courtroom, but her glance shifted back and forth between Cullen and Jacques, who had turned around for a quick glance, but now looked straight ahead at Small Brown Bird.

"Your Honor," Cullen said from the back of the room, "Your Honor, these men," he gestured to the Iroquois, "do have a point. They say that whatever happens here today will go beyond this courtroom in its consequences. And for that reason we should all lis-

ten. They have agreed, though, that the women wanting to leave can go. But everyone else, having been here for the prosecution's case, should stay to hear the defense. While it's an unusual approach, I don't think that under the circumstances it's entirely without merit, Your Honor."

"Constable Stuart, I don't like being dictated to in my own courtroom," Judge Heath said. "However, if these men will allow the ladies to leave, and if they themselves give you their solemn word that they will go peaceably back to the reservation at the conclusion of this trial—*no matter what the jury's verdict*—then we can proceed."

Glynis thought this posture of Judge Heath's to be either naive or sublimely arrogant. Didn't he understand that the Iroquois, and not he, were in control? That their goodwill would decide the outcome of this standoff? Cullen's approach had been far more conciliatory.

But when a male voice just behind Glynis said, "Well done, Judge Heath," he received for his effort a glare from the judge. Who perhaps did understand after all.

"Your Honor," Merrycoyf said loudly, "would you instruct the constable that no one who has been subpoenaed to testify should be allowed to leave?"

Glynis breathed more easily after she saw Cullen nod his agreement to Merrycoyf; she had worried about that. But perhaps the crucial person did not yet realize the implications of Small Brown Bird's testimony.

The rear door was then opened and many of the women, but not all, hurried out. Some men did also, as the Iroquois at this juncture didn't stop anyone. They had made their point, as Cullen had put it.

It was a few more minutes before order was entirely restored. While her sympathy centered on Jacques, Glynis felt most sorry just then for Small Brown Bird. The woman had composed herself admirably during the uproar, but her hands still lay knotted in her lap. She looked over at Glynis once, her expression one of sorrow. And Glynis herself felt again the smart of tears.

"May we proceed?" Merrycoyf asked Judge Heath. Glynis had earlier noticed Orrin Polk leaving quietly by way of the judge's door, but, after peering out to see that order had been accomplished, he now returned to the prosecution's table.

"Yes, Mr. Merrycoyf, proceed, if you please!" Judge Heath directed.

"I hope to finish soon," Merrycoyf said to Small Brown Bird. "After the eight men had hanged your nephew, what happened?"

"They left. They rode away. And then Walks At Sundown came. The wolf had found him . . ." She broke off at a gesture from Merrycoyf.

"Yes, please go on," he said to her quickly, obviously trying to avoid an explanation of his client's familiarity with wolves.

"Walks At Sundown first cut his brother loose, and we, after a little while, carried his body back to the reservation."

"When you say 'we,' " Merrycoyf asked, "do you mean you yourself, the young men's mother—Bitter Root—and Walks At Sundown?"

"Yes."

"But had there been anyone else in the woods while this despicable deed was taking place?"

"Yes, there was the girl Lily. She was hiding behind some trees, but we knew she was there."

"Did she go with you when you took Many Horned Stag back to the reservation?"

"No. We didn't see her again that day—Bitter Root and I didn't."

"Did you see Lily Braun sometime after that?"

"Yes. Walks At Sundown later found her lying in the woods. She had near frozen to death. He was afraid for her and for the child, so he took her on his horse to the nearest white people's house."

"Are you saying," Merrycoyf asked her, "that the defendant saved the life of the very woman whom he is now accused of killing? The woman who was the mother of his brother's child?"

"Walks At Sundown would not kill a woman," Small Brown Bird answered.

"No," Merrycoyf said. "No, I don't think so either. But to whose house did he take Lily Braun?"

"To Obadiah Grimm's house."

"And did Lily Braun stay at the Grimms'?"

"She stayed until the child was born, in the spring."

"Were you present at the birth of this child?"

"Yes, and my sister too. The Grimm family asked us to come to the farm to help because my sister, Bitter Root, she is a medicine woman."

"And was the child healthy at birth?"

"Yes, healthy." For the first time that day, Glynis saw Small Brown Bird's face relax slightly.

"What happened after the child was born?"

"Lily left the Grimms'."

"Had the Grimm family asked her to leave?"

"Yes, that is what she told us."

"And the baby?"

"Lily left the baby with the Grimms. Because she had no money, she said."

"Do you know," Merrycoyf asked, "if Lily Braun planned to leave the child there at Grimm's for long?"

"She said she would not come back—is that what you mean?"

"That's what I mean," agreed Merrycoyf. "Small Brown Bird, I know this has been very difficult for you. But your testimony has been important, and I thank you for coming. I have no more questions."

Judge Heath looked at Orrin Polk. "Do you plan to cross-examine this woman, Mr. Polk?"

Given the way the judge scowled when he said this, Glynis thought that even if Polk had planned to cross-examine, he might not now. And when he said, "No, Your Honor, no questions," the jury looked distinctly relieved.

As Small Brown Bird left the witness chair, she gave Jacques a forlorn, almost apologetic look before she started down the aisle.

"You have another witness, Mr. Merrycoyf?" Judge Heath asked.

"Yes, Your Honor. The defense calls Billy Wicken."

Toward the back of the room, a small commotion broke out and several people got to their feet. Glynis couldn't see exactly what was happening, but Cullen, in the meantime, had moved toward the source of the noise. He stood beside the last row of chairs, motioning with his hand. Glynis heard "No," several times, then a distinct "I don't want to!" But Cullen kept gesturing, and at last Billy Wicken moved with reluctance toward the center aisle. When he reached it, Cullen put his hand on Billy's shoulder, said something to him, then gave him a small push forward.

Despite herself, Glynis felt a rush of pity as Billy limped up the aisle. He looked so miserable, his expression so confused. Someone had made an effort to smooth his unruly hair; the result was an unfortunate cowlick that stood up like a rooster's comb, while his large, pointed ears still protruded through the mop of straw hair. Billy's chameleon eyes, now an indeterminate gray, darted from side to side as if looking for a means of escape.

There was some difficulty with his swearing in, and when he finally ended up in the witness chair, his voice sounded tremulous as he gave the clerk his name. Merrycoyf spoke briefly to Adam before he went forward; he seemed to take rather a long time before he asked his first question, but Glynis was aware that Merrycoyf needed to proceed with caution.

"Mr. Wicken, how long have you lived at the Grimm farm?"

"I . . . I don't know. A long time, maybe . . ." Billy shrugged.

"Would you think twelve years was about right?"

"Yeah, about right."

"Mr. Wicken—but would you mind if I call you Billy?"

"It's O.K., I don't mind."

"Good. Billy, where did you live before you went to work at the Grimms'?"

"Around. I lived around. No place, really."

"Were you hired as a handyman at the Grimms'?"

"Yeah. I did lots of things."

"What do you do now?"

"Not so much now. I take care of the sheep. I used to do it with Mead Miller until he . . . you know."

"Until Mead Miller was killed?"

"Yeah."

"Why don't you do as much now as you used to, Billy?"

Billy gave Merrycoyf a shaky grin, and held up his withered hand. "Why do you think?"

"Isn't your leg injured as well? How did that happen?"

Billy's eyes darted to the sides of the room.

"How did your injuries happen, Billy?" Merrycoyf repeated.

"Accident. I had a accident."

"What kind of accident?"

"Went down the stairs."

"You fell down some stairs?"

"Well—that's not right. I kind of was pushed."

"I see. Who pushed you?"

"It was a accident. He didn't mean to do it. He was just mad, is all."

"Who was just mad, Billy?"

Orrin Polk cleared his throat loudly before he said, "Objection, Your Honor. This line of questioning is totally irrelevant."

"I agree, Mr. Merrycoyf," Judge Heath responded.

"Your Honor," Merrycoyf said shortly, obviously annoyed at being interrupted just as he was gaining Billy's trust, "I need to establish a pattern here. Or, as my esteemed colleague would say, a motive for behavior."

"And I will allow you the same leeway, but only for a short time," Judge Heath growled. "Objection overruled."

"Billy," Merrycoyf immediately asked again, "who pushed you down the stairs?"

Billy shook his head. When Judge Heath leaned forward and ordered him to answer, he looked about to cry. But finally he said, "Mr. Grimm did—but he didn't mean to. He said so."

"Which Mr. Grimm was that, Billy?"

Billy looked surprised at the question. As if there couldn't be more than one, Glynis thought. "You know," he said to Merrycoyf, "*Mr.* Grimm."

"Do you mean Mr. Obadiah Grimm?"

Billy nodded. "Yeah."

"So as a result of being pushed down the stairs by Mr. Obadiah Grimm, you suffered paralysis in your hand and your leg—and a severe head injury, too, didn't you?"

"Your Honor!" Polk whined. "What in the name of heaven does defense think he is establishing?"

"Your Honor, I can recall Quentin Ives if necessary," said Merrycoyf, "to establish the extensive nature of Billy Wickens's injuries."

"The injuries appear to be self-evident," Judge Heath said. "If the prosecutor has an objection, it is overruled. Now get on with it, Mr. Merrycoyf!"

"Do you remember when the girl Pippa was born, Billy?"

"Yeah, I do."

"Did your accident happen before or after that?"

"After. It was after Pippa came."

"So, because of your injuries, did you spend a great deal of time with Pippa when she was small?"

"Yeah, I did. And Molly too, because they liked me."

"And Molly Grimm too. Very good. Would you say you took care of Pippa and Molly?"

Billy smiled broadly. "Yeah, I took care of them."

"Would you agree with me if I said that you wouldn't allow any harm to come to them—not if you could help it?"

"I wouldn't let anybody hurt them, you mean?"

"Yes, Billy, that's what I mean."

"You're right!"

"Good. Now tell me this, Billy—did there come a time, some months ago, when a woman named Lily Braun came to visit Pippa?"

Billy scowled, and nodded. "Yeah, she came. It wasn't good."

"Why wasn't it good?"

At that moment a sound from the back of the room made Glynis and everyone else turn to look. Lazarus Grimm was making for the door, gesturing to his sister behind him. Molly, however, sat with her eyes glued on Billy Wicken. Cullen stepped in front of the door, barring Lazarus's way, saying, "Back to your chair, Grimm. Nobody's leaving just now."

"Yes, take your seat back there!" Judge Heath ordered.

Lazarus shot the judge a frown, but Cullen took his shoulder and pushed him into a recently vacated chair on the aisle. Then he himself took a seat opposite, and nodded to Judge Heath.

During this, Billy had been moving his head and shoulders from side to side, and Glynis now saw why Merrycoyf appeared to pace in front of his witness. In fact, Merrycoyf had done this from the beginning of Billy's testimony, deliberately blocking his view to the rear of the courtroom.

Merrycoyf resumed his pacing now, and repeated, "Why wasn't it good when Lily Braun would visit the Grimms, Billy?"

"Molly got upset. Everybody got upset."

"Do you know why Lily Braun kept going to the Grimm farm?"

"No. Just that she wanted something."

"She wanted something. All right, Billy, now were you at the farm the day that Obadiah Grimm died?"

Billy frowned. " 'Course I was there."

"Did Lily Braun visit that day too?"

"Yeah, she did."

"And did people get upset again?"

Billy's head bobbed, trying to see past Merrycoyf's broad frame. Finally he said, "Yeah, real upset."

"And did you see what happened to Obadiah Grimm in the barn? Did you see him before he fell?"

Billy's face took on a stricken cast, and he weaved back and forth. Glynis assumed Judge Heath could observe from the bench what was going on. And Orrin Polk had begun to look worried.

"Billy, you have sworn on the Bible to tell the truth," Merrycoyf said, but very gently. "Now, what did you see in the barn that day?"

"A accident. It was a accident."

"Another accident, Billy? Like the one that happened between you and Obadiah Grimm?"

"Yeah, like that," Billy said readily.

"Tell us," Merrycoyf said in a sympathetic voice, while taking a few steps closer to Billy. "Tell us what happened to Obadiah Grimm."

"He was mad at Molly after she climbed up in the hayloft with him—to talk to him, I think."

"What was Obadiah Grimm doing in the hayloft?"

"Forking hay."

"Do you know why he was mad at Molly?"

Billy seemed to consider this, then said, "I think it was about Pippa. They were talking real loud, that's how I know."

"What happened while they were talking loudly?"

"He . . . he hit Molly!" Billy said excitedly. "He hit her hard in the face. She almost fell off the hayloft—just like I fell down the stairs."

"After Obadiah Grimm hit you?"

"Yeah. But Molly, she didn't fall. So he grabs her dress and he starts to shake her and she's crying . . ." Billy lifted from his seat now in a desperate effort to see the Grimms in the back of the room. But Merrycoyf again blocked his view.

"Did Molly grab his pitchfork to protect herself?" Merrycoyf asked kindly, reassuring Billy by saying, "It would be a natural thing to do."

Billy frowned and said, "Yeah, she got the pitchfork and old Obadiah he was so mad, he . . . he looked like he mighta run right into it."

"Yes. And then he fell backward off the hayloft."

"Yeah, he did."

"Billy, was Pippa there in the barn when this happened?"

"She *was* there, but then she was gone when me and Lazarus looked for her. I think she went in the secret passage."

"The passage from the house and barn, you mean?" Merrycoyf asked. "The one that takes you out to Black Brook?"

"That one."

"Why didn't you tell anyone what you saw, Billy? For instance, when Dr. Cardoza came and asked what happened?"

"I wouldn't tell. It was a secret, she said."

"She? Do you mean Molly Grimm?"

Billy's head bobbed. "And I wasn't sorry he got killed!"

"That's understandable, Billy. Now I want to ask you a few questions about the day of the blizzard. Do you remember the storm last month?"

Billy looked troubled, and didn't answer. He fidgeted in his chair, until Judge Heath bent toward him, saying, "Billy, you need to answer Mr. Merrycoyf's question." Like Merrycoyf, the judge spoke kindly.

Billy sighed loudly. "I remember the storm."

"Do you remember that Lily Braun came to the farm that day?"

Orrin Polk rose, beginning to object, although it seemed to Glynis that the prosecutor's heart wasn't in it.

Judge Heath interrupted him. "Let Mr. Merrycoyf finish this, Mr. Polk. I'm going to allow wide latitude with this witness." He said this quietly, as if not wanting to interfere with Billy's tenuous trust of Merrycoyf.

"Did Lily Braun come that day before the storm started?" Merrycoyf prodded gently.

Billy frowned and slowly nodded.

"What happened after she came?"

"She got mad."

"Lily Braun was mad at whom—at Molly?"

"No, Molly was being nice, real nice, to her. She got mad at Lazarus. So Molly told him to leave."

"Leave where?"

"The house." Billy looked as if he thought this should be obvious. Glynis wanted to turn and look behind her, but was afraid to do anything that might upset the delicate balancing act Merrycoyf was attempting. And the rest of the spectators, those that were left, seemed equally fixed in place.

"What did Lily Braun do then, Billy? After Lazarus left the house?"

"She got sick."

"Sick? How did she look?"

"She looked real sick. She was holding her stomach and making noises and then she fell off her chair onto the floor. I thought she was going to die. Then she did."

"She died? Lily Braun *died,* there in the Grimm house?"

"Yeah, she did."

While sounds of astonishment rippled softly through the room, Glynis had her eyes on Jacques. All she saw in the way of reaction was a shake of his shoulders, before he leaned back against his chair. And Orrin Polk just stared at Merrycoyf. But he said nothing.

Merrycoyf looked up at Judge Heath, who was glaring at the spectators, and received a nod. "Continue with your witness, Mr. Merrycoyf."

"Billy, after you saw that Lily Braun had died, what did you think?"

"I thought I should do something."

"Why?"

" 'Cause it was bad for her to be dead in the house. I knew that because Molly was crying. So I took the dead lady to the barn."

"Took Lily Braun's body—did you carry it?"

"Yeah, she wasn't very big. Not even as big as a sheep. I took her and put her on my horse. Molly gave me the horse, you know that?"

Merrycoyf nodded. "Go on."

"So I put the lady on the horse and I took her into the woods. It was snowing real hard."

Glynis started, and half-turned as a hoarse sound came from the back of the room. She didn't turn around; she didn't need to.

"Where in the woods did you take the lady's body?"

"To the end, by the reservation. There's a cabin right there. So I

left her and the horse by the woodpile, and I looked in the cabin's window 'cause I thought I could find a shovel and bury her. And nobody would know. But when I looked in the window, I saw some knives on a rack. Nobody was around, so I went in and got one. A big one, with a wolf. I thought it would be better than a shovel."

"And you put the knife in the lady's chest?" Merrycoyf asked.

"Yeah."

"Why did you do that?"

"So people would think she got killed by Indians."

"As indeed they did," Merrycoyf said. "What happened next? Did you leave then?"

"No, I was going to put the lady inside the cabin. But I heard something. Somebody was coming."

"Who was it, did you see?"

"Yeah, I hid behind the woodpile and I saw him." Billy pointed his finger at Jacques. "He was carrying Miss Tryon to the cabin, and she was covered with snow and looked like she was dead, too. And I got scared, 'cause I thought maybe he really had killed her—Miss Tryon. And I pulled my horse into the woods and then I went back to the farm."

"Thank you, Billy," Merrycoyf said. "You've done a fine job. And I have just one or two more questions. Tell me, when Lily Braun was in the Grimm house, was she drinking something just before she died? Something like tea, perhaps?"

Billy nodded. "Yeah, she was drinking tea."

"Who had made the tea for her?"

Billy smiled broadly. "Molly. She made it."

Glynis turned then, to look at Molly Grimm. The woman sat with her arms wrapped around herself, rocking back and forth, her sobs quiet but nonetheless heartrending. Cullen stood directly behind her. He responded to Molly's anguish by very gently placing his hands on her shoulders. And Glynis wondered how she ever could have felt anger toward this man.

Zeph was stationed by the door with Lazarus Grimm, who stared at his sister as if dumbfounded. Glynis questioned how much of this was an act. Was it possible he hadn't known? But if she had managed to figure it out, surely Lazarus could have. Granted that her initial guess was driven by the need to free Jacques; Lazarus might well have

been blinded by affection. Because he almost certainly knew that Molly had killed their father, if only accidentally. He had lied to Neva that night to protect his sister. And perhaps to protect his access to Pippa.

When Glynis first began to speculate about the Grimm siblings, she had suspected Lazarus, as the proximity of the farm to Jacques's cabin seemed all-important. And when she'd figured out Obadiah's dying quotation, it certainly seemed to implicate Lazarus: "... he that getteth riches but not by right ..."

But last Friday, Adam MacAlistair had said it was impossible for Pippa to be Molly's daughter. He told her that he'd reviewed the material submitted by Merrycoyf on Lazarus's petition for administration of his father's estate: Lazarus had sworn that Obadiah Grimm had no grandchildren. Then she recalled Almira Grimm saying, after a visit from Lily Braun, "that girl of mine got trouble—big trouble." When asked if she meant Pippa, Almira had laughed and said, "No, she never told nobody *she* had a husband." So Molly might not have been married—no one had ever actually seen a husband, just heard about one. Had Pippa been conceived out of wedlock? In that case, why did Lazarus swear there were no grandchildren? When Glynis asked Merrycoyf about this, he said he'd been told that Pippa was a foundling.

Obadiah's quotation from Jeremiah then took on an entirely different cast: "As the partridge sitteth on eggs, but hatcheth them not ..." It pointed a cruel finger at Molly.

Just as important was the indisputable fact that Molly became distraught whenever Lily Braun appeared—and why *had* Lily kept returning to the Grimms'? In retrospect it was clear: to get her daughter back. Had Obadiah threatened to give Pippa to her natural mother? That he was capable of it was borne out by his brutal dying words. They would probably never know if Molly used the pitchfork in self-defense or to deliberately kill him—Glynis believed the former—but they did know she had done it.

Given Pippa's behavior that night, Glynis had suspected that the girl might have witnessed something terrible; thus the reason she and Neva had contrived to have Neva interrupt the seance with "Pippa's" voice. Then, armed with the certainty, when she and Neva had gone to the Grimm farm with Zeph, they'd found a scrap of Molly's lace

collar caught in the flooring of the hayloft—the torn collar they all had seen the night Obadiah died. Almira had told them, among other things, exactly where to look.

Glynis now glanced again at Molly Grimm, who was being taken from the courtroom by Cullen; the eight men who murdered Jacques's brother had made this woman their victim as well. Molly had raised the child of Lily Braun and Many Horned Stag as her own; only to be threatened with having her beloved Pippa torn from her by a woman she viewed as abandoning her baby—and as a prostitute unfit to raise a child.

And yet it could be argued, Glynis now believed, that other than Many Horned Stag himself, Lily was the most tragic victim of that lynch mob.

Cullen had just returned to the courtroom as Merrycoyf, who had been talking to Judge Heath, stood back from the bench to say, "Your Honor, I move that the indictment charging the man Jacques Sundown with the murder of Lily Braun be dismissed."

Orrin Polk, staring toward the windows, merely said, "No objection." His shoulders drooped, and Glynis wished she could spare some sympathy for him. But Mr. Polk had taken a little too much relish in his job.

"Case dismissed," Judge Heath said. "The prisoner is free to go. But, Constable Stuart, I believe your investigation is not over yet—do you agree?"

"I agree, Your Honor," Cullen responded.

No, Glynis thought, with a bone-deep sadness; this was not yet over.

• EPILOGUE •

I will live in the Past, Present, and the Future. The Spirits of all Three shall strive within me.

—Charles Dickens, *A Christmas Carol*

When Cullen arrived unexpectedly the following morning, Glynis already had been up since dawn, dressed and brooding over coffee in the Peartree kitchen. She had not slept well.

"I figured you'd want to go out to the reservation today," he had said when she opened the door to him.

"I'd planned to, yes."

"I have a carriage out front."

"You want us to go out there . . . together?" Glynis asked, surprised and unable to disguise it.

"Yes, I believe we should," was all he said.

She could find no reason to refuse, and wrapped herself in her new, wine-colored merino wool cloak, no longer regretting the loss of the somber black one destroyed by the blizzard. They said little, but the silence between them did not feel as uncomfortable as Glynis had feared.

And, she now thought, this must be done today. The weather was changing again, and behaved more like the three days before Christmas that it was; a few snowflakes spun around them, and a watery sun appeared every so often. But once the winter snows began in earnest, everything north of town would be isolated for weeks at a time.

Passing the Grimm farm, Cullen broke the silence: "You probably haven't heard about Serenity's tavern license?"

Glynis, thinking of the ravaged Grimm family, was startled by this non sequitur, and murmured, "No, I haven't."

"You did know we're apparently going to have a Jewish wedding in Seneca Falls next spring?"

At that, she had to smile. "Yes, at least Abraham thinks so. But what does that have to do with Serenity Hathaway?"

"When I got back from Waterloo yesterday, Serenity and her sidekick, Brendan O'Reilly, came by to announce they'd finally gotten the last signature they needed on her petition."

"Oh?" Glynis said, simply to be polite, but not particularly interested one way or the other.

"The last petition signer was Lazarus Grimm."

"Who?"

"That's exactly what *I* said. But it seems that crafty little Neva Cardoza came up with a scheme some weeks ago. She went to Serenity—"

"Neva did?"

Cullen nodded. "She talked Serenity into making a generous contribution to Lazarus's spiritualist group, in return for Lazarus's signature on the petition, which he could give now that he's a landowner."

"I can't believe it. Neva didn't tell me. And besides, she wanted the tavern closed!"

"She didn't tell you," Cullen said, "because she knew you wouldn't approve."

"I don't."

"Well, there you are." Cullen nodded again.

"But *why*?"

Cullen's smile, the first she'd seen of it in some time, swept across his face. "Seems Neva then finagled Lazarus into giving *her* the money Serenity gave him."

"What . . . whatever for?"

"For a shelter. For abandoned wives and children of drunks. Neva suggested to Lazarus that it would be better for him to give the money to charity than to keep something, as she put it, 'so obviously tainted'!"

"No!"

"And, as you might guess, our Dr. Cardoza plans to run this shelter herself, now she's staying. But she told Lazarus he could hold his

spiritualist meetings there once a week, if he'd split the donations with her charity."

"Oh, Cullen!" Glynis felt laughter catch in her throat. She couldn't release it, not with what lay ahead, but it was good to know she was still able to feel it. And then she thought of Molly Grimm.

No one, including Cullen, had known what to do with the woman. Molly did not seem to comprehend, or even remember, what had happened. She could not grasp anything other than the certainty that she would lose Pippa. Jailing her, then putting her on trial for Lily's murder, struck everyone, even Judge Heath, as inhuman if she couldn't understand what it was she had done. Neva Cardoza had come up with an answer that, while unsatisfactory in some regards, seemed to most the reasonable course. Thus Neva and Abraham and Zeph were now on the train with Molly, taking her to the Rochester Asylum for the Insane. A terrible penalty, Glynis thought with sorrow, for a woman driven mad by desperation at the prospect of losing her child.

A few minutes later, as they started down the grade into Black Brook Reservation, Cullen said, "Glynis, I expect you know what I have to do?"

Apparently he'd come to the same conclusion she had some days before, and he didn't sound any more comfortable with it than she had been.

"I'd like to talk with her before you do anything, Cullen."

"I thought you would. All right, go ahead—there's certainly no hurry at this point."

But, ironically, the "hurry" was exactly what had triggered the answer. Why, she'd asked herself over and over, had the three remaining members of the eight-man lynching party been killed in a period of several weeks, when the first five had been spread over almost ten years? Because, for some reason, time was running out. Then, of course, there had been Jacques's uncompromising refusal to defend himself; at last she had come to realize that his was the silence of a protector. And finally, as she'd guessed early on, the methods of murder provided the key. Not one had been committed with a standard male weapon: a rifle or pistol or knife. None had involved physical proximity, as would have strangulation or suffocation. And none had required strength. Tenacity, daring, patience, and knowledge of poi-

sons, yes. Not strength. Even loosening wagon wheels could be done by a woman. And if Jacques had taught Cullen to use the Iroquois air-gun, then who might have likely taught Jacques?

Cullen now brought the carriage up next to the bridge, and tethered the horse to the same willow that Glynis had used weeks before. When he swung her down from the carriage, as he had so many times in the past, Glynis felt a sudden longing for what once had been between them—for what seemed unlikely to be again.

"I'll wait here, outside," he said to her. "You go ahead."

As she went toward the house, she saw Small Brown Bird standing in the open doorway. "How is she?" Glynis asked from the foot of the shallow steps.

"She is not good. It will be soon now."

Glynis nodded. "Yes, I thought as much. It's consumption, isn't it?"

Small Brown Bird tilted her head in acquiescence.

"I'd like to talk to her. Constable Stuart said he would wait."

"I was expecting him to come. You also, I hoped, would come. You helped Walks At Sundown. She knows that," Small Brown Bird said, inclining her head toward the house interior.

"But why didn't she help?" Glynis asked. "Her own son?"

"Ask her," Small Brown Bird said. "Only she can tell you."

As Glynis went up the steps, she saw Jacques come across the bridge. She didn't wait for him, but went on into the house.

Hovering inside was a faint turpentinelike odor, which suggested poultices of beth root and willow bark. Bitter Root lay on a narrow cot, covered with a thick woven shawl. She was coughing weakly when Glynis entered the room; the paroxysm lasted several minutes, during which Pippa, kneeling on the floor beside the cot, lifted the woman's head to wipe blood from her lips. Glynis was at first confused when she saw the girl there, before she recalled what the trial had revealed: that Bitter Root was, in fact, Pippa's grandmother.

And Bitter Root was dying; even Glynis could see that.

She went to stand by the cot, waiting for the coughing to subside. When it did, Bitter Root fell back against a blanket roll, plainly exhausted. She stared up at Glynis with eyes that, while dulled with pain, still held a flicker of hard light. She motioned with a feeble gesture for Pippa to go outside.

"I don't understand," Glynis said, after checking that Pippa was

safely beyond earshot. "Oh, not about those eight men—*that* I understand. It's not uniquely Iroquois, your code of vengeance. 'An eye for an eye' is probably as old as the human race. What I don't understand is how you could let your son stand trial without coming forward."

"I didn't kill the woman," Bitter Root said hoarsely. "You know that."

"But your son didn't either, and you knew *that.* You also must have known that the eight men you did kill would rise like ghosts to condemn him during the trial. They very nearly got him convicted of Lily Braun's murder, because he couldn't say a word in his own defense. Not without betraying you and your acts of retribution."

Bitter Root motioned to Small Brown Bird, who moved the blanket roll so the woman's head was slightly elevated. Bitter Root wheezed as she choked out, "Walks At Sundown was to perform the obligation to his brother. He would not. He tried to keep me from this duty."

"How?"

Bitter Root began to cough again. When Small Brown Bird tried to assist her, the woman waved her away.

"Miss Tryon," Small Brown Bird said, "my sister is weak. She is dying. This is very hard for her."

"Yes, it's been hard for everyone," Glynis said to her. "But then you tell me, if you know, how Walks At Sundown could keep this woman from doing whatever she wanted."

"He took her away, many times."

"Away?"

"After the first man, Lily Braun's father, had been . . . I think you would say *executed,* then Walks At Sundown took his mother to the Cattaraugus Reservation."

"So she wouldn't be suspected?"

"So she couldn't kill again. But as soon as he would leave, she always came back here."

"How many times did he do this?"

"Every time. Every time but this. He knew she was dying. He could not interfere."

"You mean that whenever she executed another man, Jacques would take her away? No wonder he kept leaving Seneca Falls with no explanation," Glynis said with astonishment. And no wonder he had turned up at the murder scenes, checking on the men that were

left—Mead Miller and Jake Braun. He had suspected that, even sick as she was, she would find them.

Small Brown Bird said, "It was difficult for her."

"For *her*! What about him—what about her son?"

Bitter Root raised her head slightly. "He was never whole Seneca—his father was a good man, but white. Walks At Sundown, he thinks like Seneca sometimes, thinks like the white man too many times. He believes in the white man's law. I say he should have his trial, he thinks the white man's law is so good!"

A shadow fell across the room as someone came through the doorway. Glynis turned to see Jacques. He walked to within several feet of her, then stood looking down at his mother. Glynis wondered how long he had been standing outside, and how much he had heard.

"There's no question," she said to Bitter Root, "that you succeeded—brilliantly, I would add—in avenging your son. Your other son. But keep in mind that the white man's law you despise so much did function. Walks At Sundown is free. From hanging. I suppose the question now is, will *you* free him?"

"He is free," Bitter Root said. "He has no more duty to his brother. I did this for him." She looked at her son then. There remained none of the antagonism that Glynis had witnessed before. In fact, a faint smile appeared on the woman's face.

She took several steps away from the cot to stand beside Small Brown Bird, who said softly, "She is content. She has finished the duty to her son, and she has her granddaughter here. It is enough."

Glynis nodded, and before leaving she gave Bitter Root a long last look. She received no concession from the woman. She hadn't thought that she would. When she turned to go, she saw Cullen standing in the doorway. He stepped aside to let her pass, and followed her out.

"Did you hear?" she said to him.

"Yes, I heard."

"What are you going to do . . . about her?"

Cullen sighed. "Glynis, what do you expect I'll do—haul a dying old woman into jail? Or have we gotten so far apart that you really don't know the answer?"

She did know. But he might not believe her if she told him that.

Not anymore. No more than Bitter Root would have believed that, had Glynis herself been a mother, and forced to watch done to her son what had been done to Many Horned Stag, her need for revenge undoubtedly would have been just as great. And she knew, as surely as did Bitter Root, that even if those eight men had been brought to trial, they almost certainly would never have been convicted.

Glynis turned to walk toward Black Brook and the carriage. But she stopped by the bridge, listening, with the sudden awareness that for some time she had not heard the wolf. Nor had she seen it. Not since the day, she now realized, when Cullen had arrested Jacques. Or in all the time he'd been in jail and on trial.

In Jacques's absence, had the wolf been killed by white men for a few dollars in bounty? Or pushed farther and farther north to die out like the rest of its kind? Glynis wiped at her eyes as a tide of tears threatened, more so than at any other moment in all the moments of recent time.

She became conscious of footsteps behind her, and heard Jacques say, "I need to talk to you."

She turned to face him, and to see Cullen standing at the foot of the house steps with Small Brown Bird. He kept glancing toward her and Jacques.

Jacques stood just looking at her. She felt again the involuntary attraction, and her cheeks began to burn.

"Thanks." His flat voice did not correspond to the expression in his eyes.

"It's not needed," Glynis said quickly. "I'm just so very sorry you had to go through so much. But, Jacques, you've saved me more than once. I'm not sure we're even yet."

"You sound like a white man. Or, maybe, He'-no."

"I certainly don't mean to!"

"Then don't talk about us being 'even'." His eyes warmed her despite the snow that now fell around them in cold, wet flakes, and Glynis remembered the moment in his cabin. The moment before Cullen arrived. But what would Jacques do now—go or stay? She was too afraid to ask.

Cullen had started walking, quickly, toward them. When he got to within a few yards, he said to Jacques, "Sundown, your mother is

dying. Obviously there's no point in . . ." He broke off, just shaking his head. "Look," he went on, "I can't apologize for arresting you. I'm sorry it all happened, sure sorry for you, but I was doing my job."

"Yeah, doing your job. I know."

A long look passed between them. Neither man held out a hand to the other. "Well," Cullen said, "probably after your mother goes, you'll be moving on, right?"

"Moving on."

"Yes, I'd guess you might not want to stay after—well, you know."

"No. I don't know."

Glynis stood watching them, holding her breath as she waited for Jacques to say he was leaving.

Then, "No, I don't think I'll leave," Jacques said. "Think I'll stay around for a while." He came very close to smiling.

Glynis let out her breath, giving in to her own smile.

Cullen looked narrowly at her, then back to Jacques. "So that's the way it's going to be?" Then he shook his head, and Glynis saw his jaw harden. "No, I don't give up that easily," he said to Jacques; he didn't sound particularly angry, simply determined. "So I guess we'll all three of us just wait. And we'll see."

Flushing, Glynis turned and hurried to the carriage.

It was as Cullen steered the horse out of the reservation that she heard it. The first notes. The howl soared up and over her as if riding currents of cold air. And then Glynis saw it. A flash of gray in the corner of her eye, it streaked past the carriage, heading up the long rise of Black Brook Road to disappear into the silvery winter sky.

• HISTORICAL NOTES •

AIR-GUNS, IROQUOIS Present-day usage of the term *air-gun* usually implies an actual gun that fires pellets propelled by compressed air or gas. And the term *blowgun* tends to be associated with Amazonian Indians. However, Lewis Henry Morgan, in his *League of the Ho-de-no-sau-nee, or Iroquois,* says the following: "The air-gun is claimed as an Indian invention. It is a simple tube or barrel, about six feet in length. It is made of alder, and also of other wood, which is bored by some artificial contrivance . . . a very slender arrow, about two feet in length, with a sharp point, is the missile. The arrow is discharged by blowing."

BANNER OF LIGHT The spiritualist publication *Banner of Light* was but one of many such nineteenth-century newspapers. The *Banner* began publishing in Boston in 1857, and professed to have subscribers in every state. The newspaper also held a free public "spirit circle" at its offices, and published the results each week. In addition, the *Banner* served as a conduit of communication between the various groups from which the Spiritualist movement drew its members. As Glynis Tryon pointed out, the majority of followers were women: those dissatisfied with the principal religious denominations; those already involved in social issues such as women's rights, abolition and temperance reform; and those who wanted radical changes in existing marriage laws.

BERITH KODESH The first Jewish congregation in Rochester, Berith Kodesh was founded in October of 1848; its earliest history has been recounted in the body of the novel. It is thought that the congregation was originally Orthodox, but became Reform around 1871. The spelling of Berith Kodesh was changed at the beginning of the twentieth century, and today the synagogue of B'rith Kodesh is situated in a beautiful parklike setting in the Rochester suburb of Brighton.

BLACK BROOK Until some seventy-five years ago, Black Brook was a flowing body of water of substantial size. Although parts of it today still can be

traveled by canoe, it has been ninety percent channelized for irrigation, so its flow is greatly diminished except in spring. The brook flows north from Seneca Falls into the Montezuma National Wildlife Refuge. Prior to the turn of this century, the Montezuma Marsh extended twelve miles north from Cayuga Lake and was, in some places, eight miles wide. The earliest human inhabitants of this area were Algonquins, followed by the Cayugas of the Iroquois nation; much of the Iroquois livelihood was supported by the marsh's plants and fish and birds. During construction of the New York State Barge Canal, which included a dam at the outlet of Cayuga Lake and subsequent alteration of nearby existing rivers, most of the marsh was drained. In 1937 the U.S. Fish and Wildlife Service purchased 6,432 acres of the former marsh. Since Montezuma lies in the middle of one of the most active flight lanes in the Atlantic Flyway, it is today an important refuge and feeding ground for migratory birds.

Blackwell, Emily (1826–1910) The older sister of Dr. Elizabeth Blackwell, America's first licensed female physician, Emily had been rejected by eleven medical schools before being accepted at Rush Medical School in Chicago in 1852. However, one year later the college yielded to pressure from the state medical society and revoked her admission. Not without a significant struggle did she manage, several years later, to complete her course work, with honors, at Western Reserve Medical College in Cleveland. In 1857 she was joined by her sister Elizabeth and the German-born Dr. Marie Zakrzewska (1829–1902) in founding the New York Infirmary for Women and Children (see below).

Dulcimer The hammered dulcimer dates from the tenth century, but the modern dulcimer, with its standard trapezoidal design, was developed during the sixteenth century. In the early to middle nineteenth century the dulcimer was a familiar instrument to American musicians. Easier to transport than its bulky cousin the piano, the dulcimer traveled west with the pioneers, and accompanied both folk dancers and singers, as well as religious services. Dulcimers were played at picnics, parties, contests, and clubs, or at any event at which rural and small-town peoples were gathered. Most pertinent to *Blackwater Spirits,* however, is the fact that, during the decade of the 1850s, the center of American dulcimer production was Chautauqua County, in western New York.

Female Medical College of Pennsylvania A group of Philadelphia doctors, thwarted in their attempts to place their private female students in regular medical schools, established the Female Medical College of Pennsylvania in 1850. (Its name was changed in 1867 to Woman's Medical Col-

lege of Pennsylvania, and in 1970 to Medical College of Pennsylvania.) The first regular medical college for women anywhere in the world, it began with a student body of forty, and a faculty of six. At its first commencement exercises, it has been recorded that fifty policemen stood guard against a threatened disruption by male medical students. On this occasion, one of the college's founders, Dr. Joseph Longstreet, said: "[The community] will expect as *much,* nay, *more,* than of your professional brethren. . . . Do not, because you are *women* regard yourselves as inferior."

FOX, MARGARET (1833?–1893) AND CATHERINE (1839?–1892) The nineteenth-century Spiritualist movement had its beginnings in 1848, with these two young girls, and what came to be known as the "Rochester rappings." The noises were attributed to spirits by the girls, and they began to attract sizable audiences for their demonstrations. Their older, married sister Ann Leah Fish began organizing regular public presentations of the girls' mediumistic abilities. Spiritualism took on a life of its own when Horace Greeley became convinced of the Fox sisters' authenticity, and endorsed them in his *New York Tribune.* Both girls' lives subsequently became tragic examples of unmitigated exploitation. Both underwent a severe slide into acute alcoholism from which they did not recover. Margaret eventually conceded that the whole thing had been a hoax, that her sister and she had produced the rappings by cracking their toe joints. But confirmed spiritualists at that point (1888) denounced this confession as a result of drunkenness. And Margaret soon retracted her confession and returned to spiritualism. Both sisters' later years were spent in poverty.

HOLMES, MARY JANE (1825–1907) Although born in Massachusetts, Mary Jane Holmes resided for most of her life in Brockport, New York. In close to fifty years, she wrote thirty-eight full-length novels and hundreds of magazine stories; these sentimental romances, uncompromisingly moralistic in tone, were immensely popular with women and girls, selling upwards of two million copies per book, many of them in paperbound editions. During her literary career, Holmes gave a substantial portion of her earnings to religious and charitable causes. A significant portion of her work may be found in the local history division of the Rochester Public Library's Rundel Memorial Building.

JEMISON, MARY (1742?–1833) Familiarly referred to by western New Yorkers as "The White Woman of the Genesee," Mary Jemison is best known through her own account, given at age eighty to James Seaver, M.D., and first published in narrative form in 1824. But most people initially meet Mary Jemison at her monument in Letchworth Park, New York. It was in

this area that Jemison lived for a good portion of her life, after she was taken prisoner at age twelve in Ohio by Shawnees. She was adopted as a sister by two Seneca women, later married and outlived two Seneca husbands, owned a substantial plot of land—now part of Letchworth Park—and refused to leave her adoptive people when given the opportunity to return to the white world. Her monument's bronze statue depicts Mary Jemison as a young mother who, in the season of early winter, walked hundreds of miles from Ohio to her future Seneca home in New York with her nine-month-old baby strapped to her back. In her own words, "Those only who have travelled on foot the distance of five or six hundred miles, through an almost pathless wilderness, can form an idea of the fatigue and suffering that I endured on that journey."

One of Jemison's descendants, the Seneca artist Peter Jemison, is today the historic site manager of the Ganondagan State Historic Site in Ontario County, New York, just outside of Rochester. Ganondagan was a seventeenth-century Seneca village; it is the only historic site in New York State dedicated to Native Americans that is operated by the New York State Office of Parks, Recreation and Historic Preservation.

A Leechbook or Collection of Medical Recipes of the Fifteenth Century Warren R. Dawson transcribed this manuscript, and he states in his introduction to the book that nothing is known of its history: "It has been in the library of the Medical Society [of London], founded in 1773, since its earliest days." Dawson made a complete transcript of the document in March 1932. The manuscript is a small quarto volume of ninety-eight folios of vellum; the leechbook occupies folios 1–95; the remainder of the manuscript is filled with the beginning of a botanical glossary in Latin. It contains therapeutic recipes including preparations of drinks, confections, salves, and other medicants. There are surgical directions, such as the use of an anaesthetic drink to render the patient unconscious before operating. An example of the original manuscript is: "ffor kestynge that comyth of cole. Ete myntis that be soden with flesshe." Translation by Dawson: For casting (vomiting) that cometh of cold. Eat mint that is sodden (boiled) with flesh."

Morgan, Lewis Henry (1818–1881) The pioneering ethnologist Lewis Henry Morgan has been called "the father of American Anthropology." His *League of the Ho-de-no-sau-nee, or Iroquois,* published in 1851, is considered the first scientific account of an Indian tribe; Morgan wanted to describe the Iroquois in their own terms, and while the work is flawed in this respect, as it contains many examples of white ethnocentrism, it remains a

classic of research for its time. Morgan also must be credited with being the first to propose the admission of women to the all-male student body of the University of Rochester. His will contained the following clause: "I desire to use my estate for the purpose of female education of high grade in the city of Rochester."

NEW YORK INFIRMARY FOR WOMEN AND CHILDREN Opening its doors at 64 Bleecker Street in New York City on May 1, 1857, the infirmary was begun by Drs. Elizabeth Blackwell, Emily Blackwell, and Marie Zakrzewska. It was the first hospital to be run entirely by women, its practice consisting of both medical and surgical services. Despite criticism from the male medical establishment, threatening mobs armed with pickaxes and shovels, and financial uncertainty, the infirmary quickly outgrew its original facilities and, by August 1859, moved to a new location on Second Avenue, with a dispensary as well as space for several female medical students. The infirmary received the sanction of a number of prominent male physicians who served as consultants.

O'BRIEN, SISTER HIERONYMO (1819–1898) A native of Washington, D.C., Sister Hieronymo came to Rochester, where she opened the city's first hospital, St. Mary's, in 1857. She presided over its growth from a stable to a building that, during the Civil War, housed as many as seven hundred soldiers. She later went on to establish a Home of Industry for young needy girls. The above is only a cursory sketch of this remarkable woman, who was the center of much controversy in Rochester, during and after the Civil War.

O.K. Readers of previous novels in the series have questioned the appearance of *"O.K.,"* frequently used by Cullen Stuart and Jacques Sundown, as perhaps anachronistic. But it is one of the oldest and most durable of Americanisms. A number of explanations surround its origin; the most favored, however, is that it began as an abbreviation of *oll korrect*—"all correct." In any event, *O.K.* originated early in the nineteenth century.

PARKER, ELY S. (1828–1895) Ely Parker, a Seneca Indian, was born on the Tonowanda Reservation in western New York, and he collaborated on Lewis Henry Morgan's study of the Iroquois. Well-educated, Parker was trained in the law and also became an accomplished civil engineer. He served as a military staff officer to General Ulysses S. Grant and, acting as Grant's secretary, copied the terms of surrender which ended the Civil War. In 1869, Parker was appointed Commissioner of Indian Affairs by

President Grant, becoming the first Native American to hold that position.

ROSE, ERNESTINE (1810–1892) The *Boston Examiner* said of Mrs. Ernestine L. Rose that she was "an excellent lecturer, liberal, eloquent, witty, and we must add, decidedly handsome." Rose had left Poland and her Jewish family soon after her mother died and her rabbi father remarried. Several accounts exist as to why she emigrated. Some contend that her father insisted she marry someone whom she despised—and that her refusal to do so came after a substantial dowry had been committed. Others insist that she was forced to leave following a dispute with her father over her rejection of Jewish teaching concerning the inferiority of women, and after her subsequent renunciation of the Jewish faith. (Readers can see in the above the inspiration for the character of Rose's fictional cousin, Neva Cardoza.) Before Rose left Poland, and as a gesture of her independence, she turned over a sizable inheritance to her father. She then moved to Berlin, where she supported herself by inventing and selling a household deodorant. After marriage, she and her husband lived in New York City, where she spent most of the remainder of her life working for abolition, temperance, and women's rights.

WATERLOO COURT HOUSE Also known as the Seneca County Court House at Waterloo, it was built in 1804 at a cost of fifteen hundred dollars. It stands today with the square in front, but the elms of yesterday are gone.

WATERS, SUSAN CATHERINE MOORE (1823–1900) Born in Binghamton, New York, Susan Catherine Moore began earning her tuition at a female seminary by still-life and animal drawings. After marrying William Moore, a Quaker, she became an itinerant portrait painter while traveling with her husband in southern New York State. Her greatest artistic interest was the depiction of sheep, and she kept her own models in a pen in her backyard. Indeed, possibly her best-known work is the oil painting *Sheep in a Landscape,* in the collection of the Newark Museum.

Items that appeared in the Historical Notes sections of *Seneca Falls Inheritance* and *North Star Conspiracy* have not, for the most part, been included in the above, although some notes in those volumes may also be pertinent to *Blackwater Spirits.* Since there is frequent historical overlap, this choice was made to avoid repetition and to prevent these sections from eventually becoming longer than the novels themselves.